CW00495906

The US Leaked Files, State Secrecy and Democratic Intelligence Oversight in Europe

The US Leaked Files, State Secrecy and Democratic Intelligence Oversight in Europe

Musa Khan Jalalzai

Vij Books

New Delhi (India)

Published by

Vij Books
(Publishers, Distributors & Importers)
4836/24, Ansari Road
Delhi – 110 002
Phone: 91-11-43596460
Mobile: 98110 94883
e-mail: contact@vijpublishing.com
www.vijbooks.in

ISBN: 978-81-19438-30-3 (Hardback)
ISBN: 978-81-19438-33-4 (Paperback)

Contents

Introduction   1

Chapter 1   The Wagner Rebellion, Spetsnaz, GRU, the Chechen
Militia, and the War in Ukraine   13

Chapter 2   Surveillance, Spyware-Pegasus, Secret Surveillance
in Poland and the European Union Intelligence Centre   33

Chapter 3   The US Leaked Documents, President Trump's Punch
on the Face of US Intelligence Management, Artificial
Intelligence Technologies, and The British Counter-
Extremism and Counter-Intelligence Capabilities   47

Chapter 4   Boris Johnson's Mismanagement of the State,
Cross border Mobility, Interoperability, Interactivity
and Interface of Different Policing and Intelligence
Agencies, Foreign Espionage, the MI5 and a Shift
from Silhouette to a More Public-Facing Role   66

Chapter 5   False Sense of Supremacy: Emerging Technologies,
the War in Ukraine, and the Risk of Nuclear Escalation   74

Marina Favaro and Heather Williams

Chapter 6   The Intelligence Dilemma: Proximity and Politicization–
Analysis of External Influences   97

Beth Eisenfeld

Chapter 7   The Social Ties that Bind: Unravelling the Role of
Trust in International Intelligence Cooperation   113

*Pepijn Tuinier, Thijs Brocades Zaalberg
and Sebastiaan Rietjens*

Chapter 8   The Construction of Secret Intelligence as a
Masculine Profession   134

Eleni Braat

Chapter 9   Assessing Intelligence Oversight: the Case of Sweden   151

Dan Hansén

Chapter 10   The Spy Power, Technological Innovations, and the
Human Dimensions of Intelligence: Recent
Presidential Abuse of America's Secret Agencies   172

Loch K. Johnson

Chapter 11   Cyber-Enabled Tradecraft and Contemporary
Espionage: Assessing the Implications of the
Tradecraft Paradox on Agent Recruitment in Russia
and China   190

Kyle S. Cunliffe

Chapter 12   The Ambiguity of Cyber Security Politics in the
Context of Multidimensional Uncertainty   214

Andreas Wenger and Myriam Dunn Cavelty

Chapter 13   Artificial Intelligence and EU Security: the False
Promise of Digital Sovereignty   245

Andrea Calderaro & Stella Blumfelde

Chapter 14   Towards Democratic Intelligence Oversight: Limits,
Practices, Struggle   267

*Ronja Kniep, Lina Ewert, Bernardino Léon Reyes,
Félix Tréguer, Emma Mc Cluskey and Claudia Aradau*

Chapter 15   Between a Rock and a Hard Place: The Precarious
State of a Double Agent during the Cold War   294

Eleni Braat & Ben de Jong

Chapter 16   Enemy image? A comparative analysis of the Russian
federation's role and position in the leading national
security documents of Estonia and the Czech Republic   316

Monika Gabriela Bartoszewicz & Michaela Prucková

Notes to Chapters   334

Index   447

Introduction

On 03 May 2023, two drones flared up and collapsed in Red Square as an assassination attempt on President Vladimir Putin. The US Secretary of State said that anything coming out of the Kremlin should be taken with "a very large salt shaker". Drones and modern military technologies have been used by both Ukraine and the Russian army. The danger correlated with military technology and crisis escalation is not a new phenomenon for the current age. As experts, Marina Favaro and Heather Williams (False Sense of Supremacy: Emerging Technologies, the War in Ukraine, and the Risk of Nuclear Escalation- 28 Jun 2023) elucidated conventional war and the use of nuclear weapons by the aggressor state: "In the course of conducting a conventional war, an aggressor could threaten attacks on nuclear forces, leading to inadvertent escalation by prompting a response. Lin describes inadvertent escalation as potentially occurring because of incomplete information, a lack of shared definitions, and communication breakdowns. Emerging technologies complicate this scenario because of their reshaping of what constitutes a "conventional" conflict and because of their integration with nuclear command and control.[1] Great Powers military and technological competitions have been a structural feature in South and Southeast Asia's politics. Moreover, a dominant territorial dispute in the South China Sea, the war in Ukraine and military confrontation in Taiwan prompted a rise of China into one of the major security issues in post-Cold War politics. Emerging technologies have mostly impacted the persisting escalation of civilians and military crisis. The war in Ukraine proved that Russian military technology was more sophisticated than the UK, US and European Union.

Discourse and war of words among intellectuals concerning the regulation of choice made by states in war to use disruptive military technologies has entered a crucial phase. New modern technologies, particularly artificial intelligence, are outstandingly transforming present-time war. The innovation of artificial intelligence technologies and their use in the battlefield has become an important topic of debate. 'Advances in communications technology, computers, information systems, and

1

surveillance and target acquisition systems have given rise to improved means of command and control to a commander. Systems integration engenders force multiplication and gives a high level of precision to the overall force, not just individual or massed fires. Advanced technological and human intelligence systems will continue to expand the commander's detection range, improve the quality of information and disseminate the data to required levels via near real-time digital transfer. The battlefield, therefore, is becoming more transparent while attempting to make it more opaque for the adversary' (Impact of Technology on Conduct of Warfare, By Vinod Anand. Strategic Analysis: A Monthly Journal of the IDSA). The Russian technological foresight hit the identification promising area of science aggrandizement. Recent research confirmed that Russia is struggling to better leverage technologies in military terms. Notwithstanding limitations, Moscow is pursuing an innovation strategy to closely monitor China and the UK technological developments. Moscow has invested heavily in developing hypersonic glide vehicles and cruise missiles, helping Russia secure its spot as one of the global leaders in this field.

The notion of disruption implies a pre-existing linear, temporal dimension that is meant to be disrupted. From the starting point, it must be cleared that the difference between the character of warfare and the nature of warfare existed. However, under the condition of informationized warfare, the requirement for effective and accurate decision-making and command and control has become more stringent because command and control systems have been playing an important role in and outside the battlefield. International security may face more challenges in the near future when Brain-Computer interfaces start an emerging dual-use technology. The last revolutionary military development that changed the nature and character of war was the onset of the nuclear age. Emerging and disruptive technologies have become a new field of military competition among Russia, US and China. Associate professor at the University of Sydney and associate Senior Fellow, SIPRI's China and Asia Security Programme, Dr Jingdong Yuan and Researcher with SIPRI's China and Asia Security Programme, Fei Su, in their research paper (Emerging and disruptive technologies, nuclear risk, and strategic stability) the role of disruptive technologies in war and peace:

"Chinese literature review December 2022) have highlighted different aspects of Disruptive military technologies: "Disruptive military technologies will not only change the mode of generating combat power but also trigger disruptive changes in combat theory and forms, alter the organizational structure of the military and military regulations, reshape the military system and lead to a new worldwide revolution in military affairs. A technological revolution can often spawn new military revolutions, while disruptive military technologies, with their unconventional development mode, can further improve capabilities for asymmetric warfare. Disruptive technologies continue to emerge and have become the driving force and powerful engine behind a new wave of military reforms. By seizing the opportunity for development brought about by disruptive technologies, not only will it pave the way for "curve overtaking" and "change-lane overtakes" to obtain critical core technologies, but it will also provide important support for innovative development in tactical theory".[2]

The European Union has been experiencing a complex nature of national security threats as the war in Ukraine has threatened their geographical and political existence. Neither diplomacy, nor engagement have prevented Europe's worst nightmare—the return of war on its soil. The EU is facing exponentially growing threats and challenges, ranging from conventional to transnational threats including hybrid threats, cyber-attacks and pervasive and persistent instability and conflict in its immediate vicinity and beyond. The future of Europe's security architecture will depend largely on how well it blends its dependence and deepening with NATO. China is a looming political and security challenge, but is also a key economic actor. Europe's relationship with the US under Donald Trump was more strained. While Europe's latest security misgivings were struck with an object on the war in Ukraine and the geopolitical bifurcation between the US and China, it also found itself grappling with diverse political opinions, energy security crises, the challenges of climate change and the need to accelerate green transition. There are compulsive arguments of an indivisible security between Europe and Asia that connect a lack of resistance against Russia to aggravating tensions over Taiwan amid worsening US–China relations. (Associate Fellow at the Manohar Parrikar Institute for Defense Studies New Delhi, Swasti Rao: Europe's Re-awakening: The Arduous Task of Re-linking Security Concerns-May 09, 2023)[3]

Nuclear power plants, research reactors and uranium enrichment plants in Ukraine may, at any time, come under potential attack from a state, terrorist and extremist groups. The possibility of a nuclear attack might be of several types-a commando type, missiles attack and mines explosions that might cause widespread dispersal of radioactivity, aircraft crash into an atomic reactor and cyber-attack. All would be disastrous. The problem of nuclear and biological terrorism deserves special attention from Russia, UK and Europe as the army of IS-K, Taliban and Central Asian terrorist groups are struggling to retrieve material of dirty bombs in which explosives can be

3

combined with a radioactive source like those commonly used in hospitals or extractive industries. The use of these weapons might have severe health effects, causing more disruption than destruction. The UK decision to produce more nuclear warheads and its militarization intentions means that the Johnson administration perceived nuclear war between Russia and Ukraine. China, the United States and Russia have already exhibited their military strength in South China and Black Sea, while these developments forced the UK to respond with strong action.

On 08 July 2023, TASS News Agency reported the US government's decision to supply cluster munitions to Ukraine out of despair, but the move won't affect Russia's determination to achieve the goals of its special military operation, Russian Ambassador to the United States Anatoly Antonov warned. "Cluster munitions are a desperate gesture. This measure tells the story that the US and its satellites have realized they are powerless. However, they do not want to admit their own failures and the failure of the attempts of Ukrainian forces to conduct an offensive against Russian regions. Hence this latest madness on their part," he said. The diplomat said he believed that by raising the stakes in the Ukrainian conflict, Washington is bringing humanity closer to a global conflict. "The current level of American provocations is indeed off the charts, bringing humanity closer to a new world war. The United States is so obsessed with the idea of defeating Russia that it does not realize the gravity of its actions. They are only increasing the number of victims and prolonging the agony of the Kiev regime," he warned. The ambassador stated that Washington turned a blind eye to civilian casualties, paid no regard to the concerns of UN Secretary-General Antonio Guterres, and shrugged off the objections from its allies. "The cruelty and cynicism with which Washington has approached the issue of transferring lethal weapons to Kiev is astounding. Cluster bombs can contain hundreds of sub munitions. When the bomb is detonated in the air, the submunitions are scattered over an area of tens of square meters. The UK was a particularly prolific user of cluster bombs in Kosovo, where they accounted for over half the bombs dropped by the Royal Air Force. British pilots fired 531 of the devices, each containing 147 bomblets with over 2,000 pieces of shrapnel. Up to 12 percent of the bomblets failed to detonate on impact, according to a report by parliament's defence committee. The cross-party group of MPs said: "That means the RAF left between 4,000 and 10,000 unexploded bomblets on the ground in Kosovo".

The EU and UK intelligence agencies have been fighting extremism, terrorism and radicalization, war in Iraq, Afghanistan and Libya, but facing domestic security challenges. After the Iraq, Syria and Afghan wars, relationships between policy makers and intelligence analysis evolved in multitudinous shapes. After the Paris terrorist attacks, the French Parliament designed legal strategies by overhauling the legal framework for intelligence surveillance mechanism. France maintains a strong and professional intelligence infrastructure that experienced and lived through different phases of world war-I and II, and the extensive Cold War period. Its share with different EU intelligence agencies on law enforcement level is considered indispensable and critical. The establishment of the National Commission (CNCTR) for the control of intelligence techniques in 2015 was the doorstep to the introduction of all around and wide-ranging security sector reform in France. States in Europe were forced to react quickly amidst rapidly changing geopolitical circumstances.

French politics is complex and indiscernible. In my book (The UK Big-3), I documented foreign intelligence interference in Denmark, Sweden, and Norway and Northern European states. The present riots in France abruptly became violent and the way they countered the police and law enforcement agencies, the way rioters demonstrated in a mysterious way of destruction, show that was not a protest only but the country was so badly punished by foreign intelligence agencies. We know French intelligence infrastructure is a professional and competent one, but representations of different cultures and political stakeholders within the law enforcement agencies make things worse. There are many holes that facilitate foreign spy networks infiltration into French society. France needs a competent and professional counterintelligence agency to check the operational mechanism of existing agencies. Ten days of rioting across France have once again exposed the country's acute social tensions at a time of growing political polarization. The latest protests demonstrate that France's impoverished, ethnically-mixed neighborhoods remain a powder keg, riven with a feeling of injustice, racial discrimination and abandonment by the state. The rioting is a reminder of the deep-seated social and economic problems in France's poorer districts and the long legacy of government neglect.

In July 2023, the French government authorized the police and law enforcement agencies to surreptitiously use mobile phones and other devices as their own surveillance tools. The provision, sanctioned on 05 July 2023, permitted police to remotely activate the cameras, microphones, and

GPS of suspects' phones, laptops, cars, and other connected devices. This move comes as part of a broader justice reform bill. The measure specifically targets individuals suspected of involvement in crimes, stipulating that only those implicated in crimes punishable by a minimum of five years in prison can be surveilled in this manner. The remote activation of devices is not only aimed at geolocation but can also be employed to capture audio and visual information pertaining to suspects allegedly engaged in terrorism, delinquency, or organized crime. On 01 June 2023, the European Parliament endorsed a report on countering foreign interference and information manipulation, calling for a whole-of-society approach to tackling the issue. The report advocates, in particular, for a move away from what it says is the "country-agnostic" approach to tackling foreign interference and information manipulation (FIMI) currently practiced by the Commission and the European External Action Service is the EU's diplomatic arm. For weeks, Terrorists and extremists were burning Police stations, libraries, schools, buildings and even targeted national critical infrastructure. A 2017 report found that young men in France perceived to be Arab or black was 20 times more likely to be stopped for an identity check. A parliamentary report on foreign interference in France, prepared upon demand of Marine Le Pen's far-right party highlighted China's growing interference, pointing to its methods that are becoming increasingly aggressive.

Expert and journalist, John Keiger highlighted the present civil war in the mirror of 2021 Islamic terrorism: "Go back two years to April 2021 and the wake of Islamic terrorism and 'gilets jaunes' riots. Twenty generals, a hundred mostly retired senior officers and a thousand military personnel signed a strident letter in the right-wing French weekly Valeurs actuelles addressed to the president, the government and parliamentarians. 'The hour is grave, France is in peril, and several mortal dangers threaten it.' It stated that members of the army would not stand idly by while French values were trampled by anti-racist doctrines, no-go areas and mob-rule. It appealed for 'honor to be restored to our rulers' and warned of 'disintegration' of French society as a result of government policy: 'there is no time for prevarication, if not, tomorrow civil war will put an end to the mounting chaos, and the deaths, whose responsibility will be yours, will be counted in their thousands'. (John Keiger, (The French riots threaten the state's very existence, The Spectator-02 July 2023).[2] The Yellow Vests Protests were also a series of extremists dance in France that began on 17 November 2018. At first the protestors advocated economic justice, later they called for institutional political reforms. On 29 November 2018, a list of 42 demands was made public and went viral on social media, becoming

6

a de facto structuring basis for the movement. The demands covered a wide range of eclectic topics, mostly related to democracy and social and fiscal justice.[4]

For countries in the former Soviet Union, these difficulties were felt especially acutely, given many countries' lasting ties to different great powers, including Russia and the European Union. Daniel Shapiro as a PhD student of Political Science at the University of Pennsylvania (Where do former Soviet countries stand: Euro-Atlantic Security Policy Brief. The European Leadership Network, June 2023) has argued that year two of the Russian invasion has inflicted huge fatalities on Ukraine: "There are a number of different trends that these data show. For one, looking at recent trends, nine of the ten measured countries voted less similarly to Russia in 2021 than in 2020. This could be seen as potentially important, as West-Russia relations had worsened from the time the UNGA met in 2020 to the analogous time in 2021, and the regional situation had changed as well (increased Western sanctions on Russia following the poisoning of Alexey Navalny, as well as an initial build-up of Russian troops on the Ukrainian border in April 2021, the 2020 44-Day War in Nagorno-Karabakh, etc.). However, in context, we can see that the relative uniformity of the trend observed from 2020 to 2021 can actually be seen in the two prior periods as well–2018 to 2019 and 2019 to 2020. From 2018-2019, with the small exception of Azerbaijan, countries moved further from Russia; from 2019-2020, with the small exception of Turkmenistan (and potentially Armenia), countries moved closer to Russia; and from 2020-2021, with a decent-sized exception of Turkmenistan, countries moved further from Russia again. At least based on these data, in which states with vastly differing relationships with Russia trended in the same direction, it would seem that other factors may have been at work in these years".[5]

The real issue of foreign espionage needed to be addressed within the European Union and France because without security sector reforms, countering foreign espionage are impossible. Secondly, in yesteryears, the EU member states spied on each other's institutions, intelligence agencies and politicians that resulted in mistrust and a new intelligence war between Britain and Germany. The three states that countered foreign espionage in a professional way were France, Germany and the Netherlands. These states intercepted foreign intelligence operatives who had planned to retrieve economic and military data and spy on the civilian population. The Netherlands, Norway, Sweden, Brussels and French intelligence agencies have lived through different phases of experiments, experiences and participation in the US and NATO war on terrorism in Afghanistan, and built professional infrastructures that protected the national security of their states. One thing, I want to elucidate here the causes of failure of intelligence agencies within the EU project is the lack of adequate intelligence information, trained manpower, flow of low-quality intelligence information purveyed by untrained, illiterate and ill-educated agents, failure to understand modern technology, and proper intelligence sharing with policy makers. The French and German intelligence agencies suffer from lack of check and balance and influence.

The Danish intelligence, Sweden, Norway and Finland intelligence infrastructure suffered huge failure when reports of Iranian and Chinese intelligence appeared in newspapers and social media. Iranian and Chinese intelligence agencies had established recruitment centers where educated people were being recruited to collect information of Iranian interests. China also spread its blanket to teach some lessons to its cronies. China and Iran were spying on EU embassies, the Defense Department and the intelligence infrastructure of Denmark, according to the Danish intelligence report (PET Report) uncovered espionage networks of Iran, China, and Russia in Denmark to recruit people from different segments of society. The PET report warned: "threat from foreign state intelligence activities targeting Denmark and Danish interests abroad presents our society with a number of significant political, security-related and economic challenges. In recent years, PET has uncovered several cases that illustrated how a number of foreign states were actively carrying out intelligence activities against Denmark. The authorities in other western countries had also uncovered cases of foreign espionage indicating the presence of a threat to their societies. PET assessed the threat from foreign state intelligence activities in Denmark was specific and persistent. The activities include espionage, influence operations, harassment, attempts to illegally procure products, technology and knowledge and, in exceptional cases, outright assassination attempts.

The double-dealing and sanctimoniousness has become starker while western military powers, notwithstanding their modern military technology-sent to Ukraine, were defeated and their all tanks, HIMARS, Leopards, Challenger and Air Defense Systems were severely destroyed by Russian army in June 2023. The wrecking of the dam was being called an act of "ecological terrorism" following the blowing up of the Nord Stream pipelines supplying Russian gas to Europe. Further, the dam was a significant obstacle to Ukrainian forces. Russia controlled the

8

Zaporizhzhia nuclear plant. When the Russian army controlled the nuclear plant in 2022, Ukrainian scientists warned that Russian forces had likely mined the compound. Expert, Lilia Rzheutska noted (Ukraine: What's the worst-case scenario for Zaporizhzhia?) that security of the nuclear site was under threat, and now as Russian army wants to leave and had security of the nuclear plant to Ukraine, the threat further exacerbated: Now, military staff in Ukraine have warned that Russian soldiers have supposedly also affixed "objects resembling explosives" to two blocks of the power plant. In late June, the International Atomic Energy Agency reported that it had found no indication of mines or other explosives at the power stations. IAEA Director General Rafael Mariano Grossi has announced that agency experts now require access to further parts of the power plant to conduct a more thorough inspection and rule out the presence of any explosives".[6]The use of nuclear weapons has been the Pentagon's hypocritical approach to the war. The NeoCons were firmly behind the Ukraine war. Mysteriously, why does the Biden government demand a $1.3 trillion nuclear weapons program? They sent modern military technology to Ukraine in order to accomplish the demand of black markets.

'For almost as long as the West supplies Ukraine with weapons to kill Russians, it is known that most of these weapons–billions of dollars and euros-worth of weapons, would never reach the front, but would instead be sold on the black-market. The West knew that from the very beginning. BBC and CNN were reporting on this calamity already in 2022. At one point BBC was reporting that up to 70 percent of the weapons supplied by the West would disappear on the black market' (Western Weapons to Ukraine: Black Market for Terrorists "On Command" Peter Koenig, Global Research, May 18, 2023). An independent geopolitical and military analyst, Drago Bosnic in his recent analysis (The Ukraine Counteroffensive has Stalled: Failures of Germany's 'Leopard-2' Battle Tanks, Global Research, June 16, 2023) of the Western worlds and European Union's modern military technology destroyed in Ukraine's war, and the killing of their soldiers and officers, the defeat of Neo-Nazi junta and NATO Alliance, has highlighted the war and its fatalities and noted that the entire world was seeing the debacle of NATO's much-touted heavy armour and other weapons recently:

"Despite decades of close cooperation between the former Ukrainian military and NATO, as well as close to a decade of much more intensive joint training between the belligerent alliance and the (then newly installed) Neo-Nazi junta that focused on interoperability and the implementation of NATO standards, the Kiev regime forces' performance against even the conscripted (although battle-hardened) Donbass militias within the Russian military has been embarrassingly poor. However, the political West is wholly unmoved by the deaths of tens of thousands of forcibly conscripted Ukrainians, as its only concern is "killing as many Russians as possible", per their own unrepentant admission. Still, the humiliating losses of such a large quantity of top of-the-line (on paper only, it would seem) NATO equipment and weapons has now exposed significant cracks within the political West, particularly the growing frustration and disdain Western Europeans have for the ever-hegemonic United States".[7]

Expert Jonathan Cook, author of three books on the Israeli-Palestinian conflict, and a winner of the Martha Gellhorn Special Prize for Journalism has highlighted the destruction of the Ukraine's dam and North-Stream Pipeline in his well-documented paper (Russia-Ukraine War: Another Act of Terror Met by Western Media Silence Coverage of the destruction of the Kakhovka dam and Nord Stream pipelines shows a western media willing to priorities anti-Russian propaganda over facts. Global Research, 18 June, 2023): "The western media has not only largely ignored these factors; it has also drawn a veil over its own recent reporting that might implicate Ukraine as the chief culprit in blowing up the dam. As the Washington Post reported back in December, the Ukrainian military had previously considered plans to destroy the Kakhovka–in other words, to carry out what is universally understood now as a major act of ecological terrorism. At the time, the plan barely raised an eyebrow in the West. The Biden administration also had a prime motive for blowing up Nord Stream: a desire to end Europe's energy dependence on Russia, especially when Washington wanted to line up Moscow and Beijing as the new targets in its permanent "war on terror". Not least, if true, it means that the Biden administration has blatantly lied for months in promoting a fiction: that Russia carried out the attack. The White House and European capitals knowingly misled the western media and publics".[8]

The Wagner militia was established by former GRU officer Dmitry Utkin and businessman Yevgeny Prigozhin in 2014. It came to prominence during the Donbas War in Ukraine, where it helped pro-Russian separatist forces from 2014 to 2015. The Night Wolves were also thought to be tacitly supported by the Russian government, and the Wagner militia commanders promoting the Night Wolves' brand of far-right rhetoric. The Western media have intimated that commander Prigozhin had contacted CIA: "It is evident that he tipped off US and British intelligence that he was about to pull Wagner fighters back from Ukraine into Russia. It was as if he wanted to know how the allies and Ukraine might react, and how it would change the war." This suggests that the Wagner chief has good contacts in the West—though there is no sign that Western nations helped him". Evening Standard (30 June 2023) noted. The Russian Government advised the MOD and FSB not to intervene militarily. Wagner troops splintered up, most of them were inclined to join Russia's regular Armed Forces. According to the US Treasury Department, Prigozhin uses Wagner mercenaries, along with his other multinational businesses, to operate a transnational criminal organization.[9]

On 06 July 2023, TASS News Agency reported the presence of Wagner commander Prigozhin in Moscow. President of Belarus, Alexander Lukashenko confirmed to the media that the Wagner Private Military Company (PMC) founder Yevgeny Prigozhin was not in Belarus, but rather was located in Russia. "As far as I've been informed, as of this morning, the fighters are at their permanent base camps where they have been located since withdrawing from the frontline for rest and recuperation. After Bakhmut (Artyomovsk in Russian-TASS), they withdrew to their camp. That's where they are located. As for Evgeny Prigozhin, he is in St. Petersburg. Maybe he went to Moscow, but he is not on Belarusian soil," he said at a meeting with representatives of foreign and Belarusian media outlets." Lukashenko also said that Prigozhin was not imprisoned. "We talked several times over the phone. I think, yesterday, we had a phone conversation in the afternoon. We discussed the PMC's further actions," he said, adding that the PMC chief told him that the Wagner fighters will "work toward Russia's well-being in the future and perform their duty until the end." The Belarusian leader stressed that he did not see any risk in deploying the PMC on Belarusian soil. "I do not think that Wagner would rebel somewhere and turn their weapons against the Belarusian leadership and government. I do not see such a situation today. I absolutely see no risks from deploying the Wagner PMC," the president noted. "If it becomes necessary to engage them, we will engage them immediately," he noted.[10]

President Zelenskiy is not a politician nor a technocrat. He is just a comedian who spent years making the audience happy. After the Russian military operation in Ukraine, he became a desperate man while managing affairs of the state desperately. Everything he is doing is on improvised bases. He was the west and NATO's darling and the EU desperate boy. He failed to defeat Russia and his counteroffensive also failed shamelessly. Expert and writer, Dr. Gordon M. Hahn in his recent paper (Dangerous Crossroads:

The Zaporozhiya Nuclear Plant, Zelenskiy's Next Simulacra? Impending "False-Flag". Global Research, July 05, 2023. Russian & Eurasian Politics 4 July 2023) has noted his failures on different fronts: "Russian forces have overpowering advantages in air, artillery, drone, heavy ground equipment (tanks, APCs) and are attracting Western supplied Abrams tanks and Bradley fighting vehicles rapidly. Ukrainian forces are now increasingly implementing their counteroffensive without air cover, tanks, and artillery, suffering massive casualties for minimal gains in territory, which are most often quickly lost again. In a recent Washington Post interview Zalyuzhniy recently berated the West for its unrealistic expectations regarding the counteroffensive, particularly in light of Western failure to supply Kiev with F-16s and sufficient numbers of tanks, APCs, artillery, and ammunition. He pointed out that NATO and Russian military doctrine stipulates one should possess air superiority before launching ground-based, in-depth offensive operations: "And Ukraine, moving to offensive operations, should follow which doctrine?"[11]

Research Fellow at the Manohar Parrikar Institute for Defense Studies and Analyses, New Delhi, Rajneesh Singh (Retd) in his research paper (The Wagner Group: A Tool of Hybrid Warfare-May 31, 2023) documented changing position of the Wagner Militia in Ukraine and Russia and noted that the militia helped promoting Russian Foreign policy across the globe. The militia was not a secret force, it was fighting in Libya, Mali and in Donbass region: "The Wagner has gained infamy for its role in the ongoing 'Special Military Operation' in Ukraine. There are, however, signs of growing schism between Wagner and the Russian Ministry of Defense. The Wagner group was founded around 2014 by Yevgeny Prigozhin, President Vladimir Putin's former caterer and confidant. The group is not formally recognized as it is illegal to serve as a mercenary in Russia. Despite its ambiguous existence, the group has operated around the globe, from Syria to the Central African Republic, Nigeria and elsewhere, furthering Russia's foreign policy objectives and the business interests of its elites. The group maintains close ties to the country's intelligence services and has undertaken a variety of security tasks, including training of local forces and VIP protection".[12]

Musa Khan Jalalzai
July 2023 London

Chapter 1

The Wagner Rebellion, Spetsnaz, GRU, the Chechen Militia, and the War in Ukraine

The war in Ukraine brought to pass modern intelligence tactics and technology that attracted all EU member states, the US, the UK and NATO alliance's intelligence infrastructures to make fit their intelligence agencies in the fight against Russia, by introducing new war strategies and intelligence reforms. President Putin has deployed private militias like Wagner and Spetsnaz commando forces to defeat NATO and Ukraine's technologically adorned forces. Wagner and Spetsnaz are private armies of mercenaries that have been fighting alongside the regular Russian army in Ukraine. The so-called mutiny, which saw Wagner fighters seized a major Russian city, was a response to government plans to take direct control of Wagner militias but it was not mutiny, it was a political plan or reorganization of Wagner militia infrastructure. It must be cleared that the Wagner Private Militia was established by Russian Military Intelligence (GRU) while the Spetsnaz Commando Force was established in 1949-as a military unit that supported the Russian army in Afghanistan, Syria and Libya. The strongest special unit carries out secret military operations behind enemy lines-capable of planting small nuclear weapons in the backyards of the enemies. Expert and writer, Stephen Bryen in his article (What didn't happen in Russia: There's been treachery but–so far–neither a general uprising nor an open fracturing of the security apparat-27 June 2023) noted that in Spetsnaz military commando force, and domestic intelligence agency FSB are the supporters of the Wagner Commander Prigozhen. (Russia's use of semi-state security forces: the case of the Wagner Group-Kimberly Martin, Post-Soviet Affairs, 27 February, 2019).[1]

On 27 June 2023, TASS News Agency reported President Putin's authenticating statement that the Russian government fully ensured the financing of the Wagner Private Military Company (PMC). "I want to note and I want everyone to know that the financing of the entire Wagner group was fully ensured by the state," he said. "We fully financed this group from the Defence Ministry, from the state budget," Putin added. From May 2022 to May 2023, the state alone allocated 86.2 bln rubles ($1 bln) to PMC Wagner in the form of salary to fighters and incentive rewards, the president noted. "Of that amount, remuneration equalled 70.38 bln [rubles], incentive rewards amounted to 15.87 bln [rubles], insurance payments totalled 110.17 bln [rubles]," he said. Meanwhile, Wagner's owner, the Concord Company, received 80 bln rubles ($940 mln) from the state in one year for supplying food and providing food services to the army, TASS News Agency reported.[2]

On 24 June 2023, Kommersant newspaper reported the criminal code of the Russian Federation about armed rebellion. On June 23, the National Anti-Terrorism Committee reported that after the statements of the founder of the PMC "Wagner" Yevgeny Prigozhin, a criminal case was initiated on incitement to an armed rebellion. According to the comments to the Criminal Code of the Russian Federation, an armed rebellion is understood as an organized action by a significant number of armed persons against the legitimate authorities. Article 279 "Armed rebellion" is used if the speech is prepared in advance, its participants are numerous and have serviceable weapons, and the organizers of the rebellion tried to overthrow the constitutional order or threatened the territorial integrity of Russia. The article applies both to the organizers and to those who actively supported them. According to the comments to the Criminal Code of the Russian Federation, liability begins at the age of sixteen. Kommersant newspaper noted.[3] However, President Putin addressed the nation and called the actions of the head of the private military company-Wagner, Yevgeny Prigozhin, a rebellion and an adventure. According to the President, those who rebelled betrayed Russia. He spoke about the difficult situation in Rostov-on-Don, but promised to take steps to stabilize it. According to him, the work of civil and military authorities is actually blocked in the city. "Resolute actions will be taken to stabilize the situation in Rostov-on-Don. It remains difficult," Mr. Putin said.[4]

Having confused and bewildered, American senators proposed to use nuclear weapons against Russia to save Ukraine, but they never realised that Russia is the world's strongest nuclear power that can wipe out the United State from the earth. Senator Lindsey and Senator Richard Blumenthat presented a resolution in the US senate and were signed by President Biden to attack Russia with nuclear weapons. The European Union doesn't want nuclear war in Europe while President Biden is acting like a mad man.

He suffers dementia and is imbalanced. The Russian Federation failed to completely defeat Ukrainian armed forces, and establish rule of law. On 24 February, the head of MI6 tweeted: "One year ago today, Russia illegally invaded Ukraine. But the Kremlin fatally underestimated both the courage and determination of the Ukrainian people, and the unity of their allies in the face of Russian aggression. MI6 stands proudly with Ukraine".[5]

However, leader of the Chechen militia in his interview said his forces were fighting U.S. and British intelligence services who wanted to split the country apart. Ramzan Kadyrov said he had seen the U.S. driving licence of a CIA operative who was killed in Ukraine. All strategies, tradecrafts, secret plans, military demonstrations and predictions of the US, UK and EU armies and secret services failed about the Ukrainian army's successes and failed to convince politicians that their political and military investment was reflective of their national interests, but their use and dissemination of intelligence on different levels also failed. The CIA and the Johnson administration were humiliated by the defeat of their militias in Ukraine. Russian missile attacks destroyed major part of their purveyed weapons. Predictions, propaganda and intelligence influence strategies of both Russia and NATO failed to exhibit a positive demonstration on a military level. Newspapers in the United States and Europe published fake stories of the actual fatalities of war, and misled policy makers. Experts and commentators, Huw Dylan and Thomas J. Maguire (Secret Intelligence and public diplomacy in the Ukraine War-Survival Global Politics and Strategy-02 August 2022) have spotlighted three main methods through which states use intelligence for influence and all ways have been in operation in Ukraine.[6]

Wagner Militia returned to Ukraine to fight the NATO forces, but CIA and the EU intelligence lost credibility due to their weak plans of tumbling the Putin regime. Both rivals, unfortunately, mixed intelligence with propaganda and political campaigns, and the way the UK, US, and NATO intelligence demonstrated in Ukraine caused humiliation and absurdity. 'Indeed, it is likely that one of the reasons for Russia's intelligence failings before and during its invasion was a tendency among intelligence officers to tell their chief customer precisely what he wanted to hear.'(Huw Dylan & Thomas J. Maguire (Secret Intelligence and public diplomacy in the Ukraine War-Survival Global Politics and Strategy-02 Aug 2022)[7]. In the United States, an intelligence leakage and the opening of Pandora box authenticated failure of the country's intelligence to retrieve support of African and Middle Eastern states against Russia. However, in the UK, publication of the report of Manchester terrorist attacks and acknowledgement of MI5 of its failure to intercept the terrorist before translating its anger into and a violent action communicated their weaknesses and tiredness.

The UK governments failed to introduce wide-ranging intelligence and security sector reforms in yesteryears. The whole intelligence infrastructure is out of fashion and outmoded and never brought home roasted Gallus-Gallus. Public perception about their operational mechanism is under whelming. Their control of communities by electronic intelligence surveillance failed to restore public confidence. In Norway, parliament singled out the accountability of transnational intelligence as an especially challenging problem in Europe. In yesteryears, foreign intelligence and espionage networks in the country caused torment because enhanced connectivity had facilitated free-form collaboration of all the elements involved, from the highest to the lowest, from the formal to informal-and most importantly from the local to the national and regional. Secrecy was often interpreted by political theorists as providing a discretionary space of action exempt from the rule of law and opaque to the cleansing effect of the democratic scrutiny. (Ambient Accountability: Intelligence Services in Europe and the Decline of State Secrecy. Professor Richard J. Aldrich and Daniela Richterova-PAIS, University of Warwick).[8]

Expert and senior researcher at the Institute of International Relations Prague, coordinator of its Centre for European Security, Dr Mark Galeotti (Russian intelligence is at (political) war-NATO Review 12 May 2017) in his commentary compared Russian foreign intelligence with CIA, Britain's Secret Intelligence Service (SIS)-MI6, and France's DGSE. Russia's Main Intelligence Directorate (GRU) is a military foreign intelligence service, again like so many NATO counterparts. The Federal Security Service (FSB) is a domestic security and counter-intelligence agency–while it is rather more carnivorous than the US Federal Bureau of Investigation (FBI), Germany's BfV or Italy's AISI, at a pinch one might think the analogy holds.[9] This excellent book circumscribes and encloses all aspects of intelligence studies, failures and successes in Europe and the United States, and documents failure of the US, EU and NATO intelligence operations in Ukraine, Iraq and Afghanistan. The best analysis of cyber security here painted the best picture of the causes of the politicization of secret agencies. The US and some EU agencies have been demonstrating as politicized actors within their states and abroad. The UK intelligence has been tied to the legs of Ministers who never studied intelligence and don't even know about the nature and operation of MI5 and MI6 infrastructures. As they are ignorant about the basic philosophy of intelligence, how can they make intelligence competent and professional?

The 21st century derived sociotechnical transformation and exponentially growing political power of cyber security and intelligence that established them as an important national security force. The information revolution of Edward Snowden in 2013 exposed the US, UK and EU intelligence surveillance and the use of facial recognition technologies by the police and domestic intelligence agencies against their citizens. Intelligence surveillance powers mean that journalists, lawyers and the general public are at risk of having their calls, text messages, internet history and other data collected and stored by the police and security services, regardless of whether they have done anything wrong. The intelligence war in Ukraine, and rising tensions between China and the United States over Taiwan, and the emergence of modern military technologies, shaped the war differently. Technological innovations in the world of intelligence resulted in a stronger shield to protect citizens against the many dangers that lurk across the continents. The UK Police shot through with Chinese camera technology, the Office Biometrics and Surveillance Camera Commissioner noted. Surveillance in the UK has often been criticised for violating the rights and freedom of the very people it's designed to protect.[10]

The Home Office Biometrics and Surveillance Camera Commissioner survey in the second half of 2022, asked all 43 police forces in England and Wales, as well as the British Transport Police, the Civil Nuclear Constabulary, the Ministry of Defence, and the National Crime Agency, about their use and governance of public surveillance camera systems including on drones and helicopters, body-worn video, ANPR and any other relevant systems.[11] Biometrics and Surveillance Camera Commissioner Fraser Sampson warned: "It is abundantly clear from this detailed analysis of the survey results that the police estate in the UK is shot through with Chinese surveillance cameras. It is also clear that the forces deploying this equipment are generally aware that there are security and ethical concerns about the companies that supply their kit. There has been a lot in the news in recent days about how concerned we should be about Chinese spy balloons 60,000 feet up in the sky. I do not understand why we are not at least as concerned about the Chinese cameras 6 feet above our head in the street and elsewhere". UK spy agencies sharing bulk personal data with foreign allies was legal, court noted. Domestic agency, MI5 still risks breaking the law on surveillance data through poor controls.[12]

Expert of Tech-journalist, VPN and Privacy Specialist, Mark Gill in his well-documented analysis, (What does the UK government know about you? Comparitech a pro-consumer website-20 May, 2021) has noted some aspects of the UK intelligence and surveillance accountability and actions of Privacy International: "The UK intelligence services are overseen by the Investigatory Power Tribunal. Any legal challenges against the security and intelligence agencies go through the Investigatory Powers Tribunal which, in its 15 years, has never found reason to oppose the agencies. However, as long as the UK is still a member of the European Union, it is still subject to EU policies and directives when it comes to surveillance. Many of the legal actions against GCHQ have been undertaken by Privacy International, a UK-based charity that fights for the right to privacy. While legal claims against the GCHQ have been limited in success, they were a factor in the creation of the Investigatory Powers Act 2016, which was written to improve the safeguards on the exercise of surveillance powers. Unfortunately, the Investigatory Powers Act also significantly expanded surveillance powers, reducing people's privacy in the process".[13]

Expert, Kyle S. Cunliffe (Cyber-Enabled Tradecraft and Contemporary Espionage: Assessing the Implications of the Tradecraft Paradox on Agent Recruitment in Russia and China) in his paper highlighted Russian invasion of Ukraine and US-China tension over Taiwan, technicality of intelligence as a key form of information collection. He also noted rising tension between the United States and China over Taiwan: "The invasion of Ukraine and rising tensions over Taiwan, echo the fact that the West has entered a new age of nation-state rivalry, one in which intelligence must be at the forefront of an effective defence. But while technical intelligence remains a key form of collection, when it comes to discerning Russia and China's most guarded secrets, including the plans and intentions of Putin and Xi, a clandestine human source–an agent, or spy–is required. The problem is that in seeking to recruit and handle those spies, intelligence officers must grapple with a new era of 'Moscow and Beijing Rules.'"[14] Intelligence agencies are playing an important role in public diplomacy in war and peace. In Ukraine's war, intelligence agencies of Europe and Russia have been demonstrating their plans and strategies and assessing the outcome of war. Some are operating inside the battlefield and some collect information about their citizens-fighting in Ukraine. Anyhow, intelligence is the best source of information and awareness. British thank-tanks established assessment and judgments of the war and predicted many things that turned around differently. The war and Brexit badly affected the UK intelligence community, their counter-offensives and financial resources. In my telepathic intelligence approach,

I view all EU agencies affected in many aspects because my brain waves are cruising across Europe and Ukraine and I receive updated information through my mind control knowledge. Expert Dylan, H.; Maguire, T.J in his paper, noted some aspects of secret intelligence and public diplomacy in the Ukraine War (Secret Intelligence and public diplomacy in the Ukraine War. Survival, 64(4), 33-74.Survival, 02 Aug 2022):

"The type of intelligence being disclosed can be categorised in another way. Intelligence that state disseminators consider to be accurate and reliable, and that is intended primarily for an internal audience, can be considered 'good faith' deployment. Intelligence that state disseminators have purposefully collected, collated and spun with the primary goal of influencing external audiences can be described as a 'strategic' deployment. Finally, intelligence that disseminators have purposefully fabricated to support an act of disinformation intended to confuse or deceive audiences is 'deceptive' deployment. In all three categories, the disseminating body is seeking to exploit the power and authority of 'intelligence' as something that is perceived to provide unique insights..... The Ukraine crisis may have rehabilitated the perceived ability of both the British and American intelligence communities to justify foreign interventions in the eyes of some sceptics. The Kremlin cares less about domestic reputational harm to its intelligence services. The risks of disseminating sensitive information to external audiences can be split into several categories. The first, adaptation costs, will be familiar to those who have, for example, observed the fallout from unauthorised leaks such as Edward Snowden's, with terrorist groups such as al-Qaeda and transnational organised-crime groups quickly upgrading their communications encryption.[15]

If we look into the pool of cyber security strategy (2022-2030), we can find controversies and misunderstandings, failure of government to professionally respond to the cyber-attacks of Russia, China and private information warriors. In the aftermath of the terrorist attacks in London, Manchester, Paris, Germany and Italy, all EU intelligence and policing agencies became subject to a hot-blooded assessment. The British, French and German intelligence agencies suffered from a lack of check and balance in the past. Their intelligence oversight on internal, legal and parliamentary levels to make sure intelligence is transparently purveyed to policymakers and law enforcement agencies have been weak and contradictory since 2015. Formal and informal intelligence multilateral relationships including Eye Five intelligence alliance, USAUK intelligence alliance, the Club de Berne between primarily the EU members states domestic intelligence agencies have so far been less effective. Maximator Intelligence Alliance (MIA) couldn't demonstrate professionally as their sharing process of intelligence has been underwhelming. Expert and analyst, Kyle S. Cunliffe in his paper (Cyber-Enabled Tradecraft and Contemporary Espionage: Assessing the Implications of the Tradecraft Paradox on Agent Recruitment in Russia and China) noted espionage and human intelligence practices:

"In the past, the perils of street surveillance, meaning the physical observation of foreign intelligence officers, led to new innovations in 'tradecraft', the methods used to recruit and handle spies. Tradecraft is often regarded as more of an art than a science, 'a combination of common sense and imagination'…..only a handful of agents, mainly volunteers such as Oleg Penkovsky and Adolf Tolkachev, were successfully operated within the confines of Moscow, while others, including Oleg Gordievsky, were merely kept 'on ice' (meaning operational acts were avoided) whenever they returned to the capital".[6]Democratic states use surveillance technologies to facilitate governance through social control. The official mechanisms of intelligence oversight and accountability in the United Kingdom are arguably disjointed and ineffective. Intelligence accountability is now a vast industry. Since the Snowden revelations in June 2013, many of which concerned the UK's Government Communications Headquarters (GCHQ), civil liberty campaigners and human rights organisations have become more interested in the issue of oversight and accountability. 'In some European countries, formal accountability only arrived quite recently and so there is often an assumption that its very presence is suggestive of progress. In the 1980s, only the Netherlands and Germany boasted parliamentary bodies tasked with intelligence accountability'. (Ambient Accountability: Intelligence Services in Europe and the Decline of State Secrecy Professor Richard J. Aldrich and Daniela Richterova-PAIS, University of Warwick).[16]

The war in Ukraine entered a crucial phase where NATO and the US have been defeated and their supplied weapons were destroyed. The UK government supplied Challenger Tanks but failed to secure its weapons and the state of Ukraine. Intelligence war is on the peak while all strategies of western intelligence failed and now hiding behind a shameless curtain. The west and its intelligence agencies demonstrated weakness and incompetency in the Ukraine war and lost credibility in Europe, and the United States. They also lost the arms market because their supplied weapons to Ukraine demonstrated unprofessionally. British intelligence recently confirmed that Russia was the UK's top security threat while failed to effectively respond to the networks of Russian intelligence in the country. Whilst the UK must have its own defensive and offensive capabilities, it must also be prepared to lead international action. In terms of attribution, it is apparent that not everyone is keen to adopt this new approach and to 'call out' Russia on malicious cyber activity. The Government must now leverage its diplomatic relationships to develop a common international approach when it comes to the attribution of malicious cyber activity by Russia and others. 'The UK is clearly a target for Russia's disinformation campaigns and political influence operations and must therefore equip itself to counter such efforts. The Russian elite have developed ties with a number of countries in recent years; it would appear that the UK has been viewed as a particularly favourable destination for Russian oligarchs and their money'. (Intelligence and Security Committee of Parliament-Russia-21 July 2020).[17]

The war in Ukraine disrupted the balance of power in Europe when Germany changed it foreign policy priorities by supporting Ukraine's army militarily. Prior to 2022, Germany was maintaining independent foreign policy by ways to avoid following US policies of global confrontational politics in Asia and Middle East. Politicians like Meiko Maas argued that Germany needed to counterbalance American EU policies and play a positive role and further strengthen the European Union. Alongside France, Berlin endeavoured to explore alternatives to NATO in line with this vision. Expert Sedat Laçine (The Effects of the Ukraine War on the European Balance of Power: From Dream World to Reality Modern Diplomacy, June 22, 2023) argued that the pre-Ukraine War era witnessed Germany's pursuit of an independent foreign policy and Germany sought to explore alternative approaches. Its pain of Second World War as the country was divided on East and West; the country's foreign policy was shaped by the United States while President Trump acted differently:

"President Trump swiftly shattered Germany's long-held assumptions about foreign policy. Adopting a transactional approach to international relations, Trump did not view Germany as a steadfast ally and indispensable friend forged over decades. Instead, he treated Germany as a debtor who had evaded settling its obligations for an extended period. Trump's viewpoint was evident in statements such as, "Germany owes vast sums of money to NATO & the United States must be paid more for the powerful, and very expensive, defence it provides to Germany. According to Trump, the United States had been fulfilling Germany's defence needs at an almost negligible cost, while the Germans were deemed to be exploiting American assistance. Trump consistently voiced his monetary demands and criticisms of Germany, seizing every opportunity to highlight them. Curiously, German elites and statesmen did not appear to take these criticisms with the gravity they deserved. Rather than carefully considering the critiques, they began discussing the belated pursuit of an independent German foreign and security policy, detached from the United States. According to this perspective, Germany should have severed its dependence on America years ago, making the criticisms all the more poignant".[18]

In 2018, Foreign Minister Maas categorically said that Germany must adopt an independent foreign policy. Mr. Mass spotlighted several areas of foreign policy and said the United States maintains a fragile alliance with its allies. Mr. Maas supported Germany's shift towards European integration. Germany and U.S contradicted each other on the EU project and the Paris climate agreement, nuclear talks with Iran and trade tariffs and Germany approached Russia to help the country in meeting the gas problems. The Nord Stream-2 and Nord Stream-1 pipeline construction strengthen the relationship between the two states. "The increase in German-Russian trade disturbed American presidents, especially Carter and Reagan, and they tried to slow down this trade. But the US policy of obstruction was doomed to be ineffective because the Americans did not offer the Germans an alternative to trade with Russia", expert Sedat Laçine noted.[19] The Ukraine War shifted priorities of the European Union member states. Russia invaded Ukraine and forced the United States to deploy nuclear and military weapons in Europe. According to expert and writer, Sedat Laçine, "Germany failed to recognize the insidious growth of Russian aggression in a timely manner, inadvertently creating a formidable adversary on its own doorstep. Had the Ukraine War not erupted in 2022, Germany's billions of euros would likely still be flowing into Russia today. However, can we solely blame Germany for this lack of foresight? The truth is that not only Germany but also the majority of the European Union committed similar miscalculations". Sedat noted.[20]

According to the Russian interference report (2020), 'several members of the Russian elite who were closely linked to Putin were identified as being involved with charitable and/or political organisations in the UK, having donated to political parties, with a public profile which positions them to assist Russian influence operations. It is notable that a number of Members of the House of Lords have business interests linked to Russia, or work directly for major Russian companies linked to the Russian state – these relationships should be carefully scrutinised, given the potential for the

22

Russian state to exploit them.[21] Senior Lecturer in Security and Strategic Studies in the Politics Department at the University of Exeter, UK, Catarina P Thomson in her paper (Foreign Policy Attitudes and National Alignments in Times of Chinese and Russian Threats: Public Opinion across Three NATO Members, The RUSI Journal, 29 Jun 2022) has argued that the Ukraine war has changed international system:

"Geopolitical considerations matter. China's development as a world power and Russia's territorial ambitions were considered critical threats, but not equally for citizens in the three sample countries. Before Russia invaded Ukraine, compared with publics in the UK and the US, it is hardly surprising to learn that citizens of a former Soviet state considered Russian expansionism as a more critical threat. Interestingly, citizens in the UK did not feel terribly threatened despite the UK military leadership's years-long messaging on the dangers of an assertive Russia. The strong commitment to multilateralism across all three samples suggests that joint action is likely to be supported across the board. This goes beyond recent shows of Western unity such as the current response to the war in Ukraine: it is the natural tendency of the majority of domestic audiences in the UK, US and Lithuania. This should prove encouraging news for NATO and international alliances more generally. Isolationist tendencies are low. This is particularly the case in the UK, which should reassure those who might have feared a post-Brexit UK taking a back seat from the world stage. Although one might contest the view that a referendum was the best way to decide whether the UK should remain in the EU, at one level voter were asked a rather straightforward question: would you prefer the UK to act on the world stage as part of a multilateral institution, or should it act unilaterally? The countries in this survey sample reserve the right to take unilateral action when needed – especially the more powerful ones."[22]

After the war in Ukraine, EU security became under threat from Russia, while NATO lost credibility to keep the organization united as some states don't want their military involvement in Ukraine. NATO has been defeated by Russia and now the project is under threat. The UK National Cyber Security Centre warned that Russia was behind the cyber-attack. "Russia has been behind a series of cyber-attacks since the start of the renewed invasion of Ukraine, it has been announced today by the UK and international allies. The NCSC noted.[23] The NCSC also assessed that the Russian Military Intelligence was almost certainly involved in the 13 January defacements of Ukrainian government websites and the deployment of Whisper gate destructive malware."[24] The National Cyber Security

Centre–a part of GCHQ–has issued advisory alongside agencies from the United States, Australia, Canada, France, Germany and New Zealand, to help organisations take action to reduce the likelihood and impact of future incidents. Experts, Óscar Fernández, Marie Vandendriessche, Angel Saz-Carranza,Núria Agell and Javier Franco in their research paper (The impact of Russia's 2022 invasion of Ukraine on public perceptions of EU security and defence integration: a big data analysis, Journal of European Integration. Volume 45, 2023-Issue 3: 02 May 2023) have argued that the 2022 Russian invasion of Ukraine sent shockwaves through Europe and led to rapid policy changes concomitant with variations in citizen perceptions.[25]

The EU courts of human rights once told Britain to put its security and intelligence services on the statute book in 1989 and 1994 respectively, expanding the regulatory framework. Expert, Melina J. Dobson (The Last Forum of Accountability: State Secrecy, Intelligence and Freedom of Information in the United Kingdom) has noted the structure of the UK intelligence oversight and its effectiveness: "One of the criticisms of the more formal elements of the oversight structure is that it concerns itself with efficiency and effectiveness, as well as lawfulness and civil liberties, issues that could be considered to stand in conflict with one another. Intelligence is a field of state secrecy par excellence, where secrecy reinforces the exclusion of outsiders by depriving them of knowledge about the reality of intelligence work. This secretive nature is at odds with demands for control of governmental conduct and publicity, rendering intelligence oversight a special oversight case. Moreover, the Intelligence and Security Committee has often been led by former cabinet Ministers who have previously worked closely with the secret services, including Tom King (Northern Ireland), Margaret Beckett (Foreign Office and Department of Trade and Industry) and Sir Malcolm Rifkind (Foreign Office). Parliament boasts a range of competing select committees that often conduct retrospective inquiries into major public issues or perceived problems related to intelligence. Furthermore, a range of bodies specialise in financial accounting including the Public Accounts Committee".[26] The Counter Terrorism Policing is a collaboration of UK police forces working with the UK intelligence community to help protect the public and our national security by preventing, deterring, and investigating terrorist activity. Police have a long history of working to prevent vulnerable people being drawn into criminal behaviour.

The government-led, multi-agency Prevent programme aims to stop individuals becoming terrorists and police play a key role. The 2018 contest has professionally outlined and elucidated the threat of terrorism and extremism in the UK. The Contest has warned that the UK has been facing different terrorist threats, while the rise of ISIS and Al Qaeda is an underwhelming development. "Daesh has been constrained militarily by the actions of a global coalition in which the UK is playing a leading role, which has eroded most of its territory and severely degraded its central propaganda apparatus. But Daesh's ability to direct, enable and inspire attacks still represents the most significant global terrorist threat, including to the UK and our people and interests overseas. Daesh's methods are already being copied by new and established terror groups". (Contest: The United Kingdom's Strategy for Countering Terrorism-Presented to Parliament by the Secretary of State for the Home Department-June 2018).[27] British counterterrorism and count extremism strategies, cyber technology developments, the backbreaking snooper surveillance and the use of facial recognition technologies authenticate perceptions that maintaining law and order and domestic stability needs technical approach not technological forces. Britain is facing precarious national security threats after Boris Johnson's mismanagement affairs of the state.

In March 2023, in its policy paper (Integrated Review Refresh 2023: Responding to a more contested and volatile world, Presented to Parliament by the Prime Minister by Command of His Majesty- March 2023) the UK government published the update of Integrated Review-setting out the next evolutionary step in delivering on its aims, against the backdrop of a more volatile and contested world. "As in 2021, it paves the way to greater integration across government in pursuit of the four campaign priorities that will guide national security strategy in this changing context. And it does so with further investment in national security".[28] On 2 March 2023 (Loch K. Johnson: Pegasus affair: the end of privacy and cybersecurity), 'the European Parliament's Panel for the Future of Science and Technology brought together experts on cybersecurity and data protection during a workshop entitled 'Pegasus affair: the end of privacy and cybersecurity?'[29] Newspapers in the EU brought to light intelligence operations-using the powerful Pegasus spyware. European Union governments and the European institutions set up their own investigations have been seeking ways to improve data protection in the EU. Since its creation, Russian cyber spies have regularly upgraded the Snake malware to avoid detection. Moreover, the Snake network can disrupt critical industrial control systems that manage our buildings, hospitals, energy systems, and water and wastewater systems.

The United Kingdom has claimed that its law enforcement agencies are struggling to stop people from being drawn into terrorism through the prevent strategy. Therefore, every state institution is bound to share data of every individual with the Prevent. By using and collecting data of the British citizens for Prevent, all state institutions don't know how their data might be used and processed. Several agencies are living in seclusion, often having no publicly available Prevent policy. Some critics developed a perception that the Prevent policies are also confused, failing to explain clearly how agencies that handle people's personal information could be relevant to Prevent. Human right campaigners and writers have been criticizing time and again for its discriminatory approach to minority communities. Rights and Security International in its recent report has critically documented some aspects and motive of the Prevent Strategy and its attitude towards minority communities (Secret, Confused and Illegal: How the UK Handles Personal Data under Prevent-2022):

"Under Article 8 of the ECHR, the UK government is obliged to uphold everyone's right to respect for their private and family life. This includes an obligation not to collect, store or otherwise process private information (generally including many types of personal data) about an individual except where this is specifically allowed by law and necessary to achieving a legitimate goal. Laws allowing the collection and handling of people's private information must be clear and accessible, and explain the circumstances in which the government or other institutions can process the personal data. We conclude that UK's current laws and practices violate this 'legality' requirement found in the ECHR, including because the existing laws and policies are not sufficiently clear or specific, while in many instances the relevant guidelines and policies are not even publicly available. The UK's handling of private information under Prevent will also violate this 'legality' element of Article 8 of the ECHR if it violates the country's own laws. In general, UK data protection laws provide that any gathering, storage or sharing of personal data will only be legal if the person has consented or if there is some other specific authorisation for the data collection and handling. If the person has consented, this consent must be free, voluntary and informed, meaning that the person must be capable of refusing and informed about how the data will be used, and cannot be forced to say yes. In the Prevent context, our research raises concerns about non-consensual data processing, with the government and public bodies frequently advising practitioners to avoid seeking consent before processing personal data".[30]

Expert and analyst, Director of the Surveillance Studies Centre, and professor of sociology at Queen's University, Kingston-Ontario and David Lyon (Security, Surveillance and Privacy, the Centre for International Governance Innovation (CIGI) in his paper has highlighted shift towards big data after the Snowden revelations: "By 2013, the Snowden disclosures indicated how the shift toward big data practices was happening with the National Security Agency (NSA) in the United States, but the shift was occurring simultaneously in Canada and elsewhere in the so-called Five Eyes countries. In Canada, the Communications Security Establishment (CSE) adopted a new analytic method from about 2012, which was described in "scientific revolution" terms. The switch was made from suspicion-led to data-driven approaches, heavily dependent on computing power and algorithmic analytics. Communications were to be monitored and analysed to discover patterns producing actionable intelligence (Thompson and Lyon, forthcoming 2019). ..Data breaches, surveillance overreach unfair outcomes in policing and security, and disturbingly protective secrecy have damaged citizens' trust in both corporate and governmental domains. Safeguards against erroneous and malicious use of data, and, importantly, transparency about government use of private surveillance companies to, for example, monitor dissent at pipeline sites are required. Turning to specific questions of the digital and to data in particular, how these are handled is of utmost significance. Although agencies such as the NSA and CSE develop their own methods, they frequently work in tandem with commercial providers and university research hubs to create new surveillance tools within a network of agencies that is far more than the sum of its parts.[31]

Director of US National Intelligence began releasing statistics relating to the use of critical national security authorities, including FISA, in the Annual Statistical Transparency Report. "In June 2015 by strengthening and uniting the US state and fulfilling right and ensuring effective discipline over monitoring act of 2015 freedom act amending FISA to formally require the government to publicly report many of the statistics already reported in the Annual Statistical Transparency Report. The USA Freedom Act also expanded the scope of the information included in the reports by requiring the DNI to report information concerning U.S. person search terms and queries of certain FISA-acquired information. See 50 U.S.C. and 1873(b). The FISA Amendments Reauthorization Act of 2017 further expanded the statistics required to be included", having quoted this report means to authenticate transparency in the US intelligence community.[32] On 24 May 2023, the EU Agency for Fundamental Rights releases a report (24 May 2023-Surveillance by intelligence services: Fundamental rights safeguards and remedies in the EU) in which it has been elucidated that "the report purveying partial update about the findings of the 2017 European Union Agency for Fundamental Rights (FRA) and Surveillance by intelligence services: Fundamental rights safeguards and remedies in the EU."[33]

The EU Agency for Fundamental Rights further elucidated that; 'the 2017 report spotlighted and argued that fundamental rights relating to the respect for private and family life (Article 7), the protection of personal data (Article 8) and an effective remedy and a fair trial (Article 47) of the Charter of Fundamental Rights of the European Union should be protected by setting up strong oversight systems and effective remedies open to individuals in the context of surveillance by intelligence services'.[34] After the Edwards Snowden-2013 revelations FRA gave importance to technical of intelligence collection and mass surveillance. The FRA report of 2017 spotlighted the right of family life and personal data. Legal frameworks on spyware were elucidated in the PEGA Committee report. In Germany, the 2021 surveillance reforms were a welcome development to control the BND and bring its international intelligence cooperation under democratic control. Finland also established an intelligence surveillance committee to monitor the country's intelligence system. Parliamentary oversight for monitoring activities of intelligence agencies is of great importance. In Austria, intelligence oversight is working effectively. In 2021, Austria reformed its oversight framework and established a new expert body.[35]

In Germany, the establishment of the Independent Supervisory Council in 2021 helped the government to bring intelligence surveillance into a legal framework. The Council, the FRA noted 'acted as a quasi-judicial oversight body tasked with the authorisation of surveillance measures. In the Netherlands, the Investigatory Power Commission is assessing the authorization to Ministers-ordering to be involved in surveillance operations. European Union Agency for Fundamental Rights-2023, an expert organization of intelligence and surveillance oversight in its recent report highlighted intelligence surveillance and oversight mechanisms in the European Union. This report is a partial update of the 2015 and 2017 European Union Agency for Fundamental Rights (FRA) reports entitled Surveillance by intelligence services: Fundamental rights safeguards and remedies in the EU:

"The oversight of intelligence services is organised differently across EU Member States, as highlighted in the 2017 FRA report and considering the recent developments in the frameworks of oversight bodies described in previous sections. The jurisprudence of the CJEU and the ECtHR has set minimum standards but leaves states with significant leeway to organise the oversight of the activities of their own intelligence services. This section specifically responds to the European Parliament's request for FRA to determine which oversight models were prevalent in the EU. FRA's research identified 18 different oversight frameworks in the EU. The following section describes five models covering most EU Member States, identified from the 18 oversight frameworks. When assessing the efficiency of an oversight framework, two key elements should be considered. First, the oversight framework should have oversight powers that correlate with the surveillance powers of the intelligence services, along with adequate resources and expertise to ensure effective oversight. Second, the oversight structure, including through the collaboration of different entities, should cover the full surveillance cycle, which the ECtHR refers to as "continuous control" (see FRA opinion 6 above). The models in this section focus on expert bodies exercising oversight over intelligence services during and after secret surveillance measures. In FRA's understanding, ex post oversight starts once the surveillance measure has been authorised by the bodies mentioned in the section 'Ex ante authorisation.'"[37]

The work of intelligence is reshaping due to the multifaceted security crisis and hostile environment where numerous stakeholders and secret units are operating with different espionage strategies. Every state wants to interfere in the internal affairs of another state in order to influence policy making and secure its national security interests. Digital transformation and innovation nanotechnologies and artificial intelligence are shifting the balance between secrecy and transparency in Europe. The EU and the UK are in deep crisis due to their mutual differences on intelligence cooperation and sharing. Britain's evolving relationship with the EC/EU and gradual emergence of European-level foreign and security policy cooperation has altered the means by which the country has articulated its interests. 'The end of the transition period in December 2020 severed Britain's access to the CFSP/CSDP and left the UK without a formal means of discerning the EU position and without an avenue for structured coordination with the EU27. Moreover, the UK government's refusal to implement the border checks required by the Northern Ireland Protocol soured political relations and undermined the willingness of either side to engage constructively in other areas'.(Withdrawal Symptoms: party factions, political change and

British foreign policy post-Brexit.Benjamin Martill, Journal of European Public Policy-2023).[38] Dr Miah Hammond-Errey, Director of the Emerging Technology Program at the United States Studies Centre at the University of Sydney-09 February 2023) has noted different aspects of intelligence characteristic and secrecy:

"The challenge of the engagement of policy makers with the inherent tensions between secrecy and transparency in intelligence has long existed. The inevitable advance of digital, data-driven technologies means tensions are becoming more public, making a realignment of secret intelligence capabilities with changing community expectations critical. The government has the opportunity, as part of its recent push for democratic resilience, to improve this system and increase trust in the intelligence apparatus and other institutions of government. We need to ensure the balance of secrecy and transparency is bipartisan and non-politicised as a lack of transparency tends to fuel authoritarianism. Governments need to preserve aspects of secrecy for national security, while also protecting democratic principles through accountability and transparency. In contrast, authoritarian governments are using the tools of intelligence for surveillance and oppression. The big data landscape has democratised intelligence capabilities that were once available only to nation-states and are now available to companies, data collectors and in technologies for sale. The increased politicisation of intelligence is visible in other democracies as well as instances where legal intelligence activity is seen as outside the norm of reasonable expectation".[39]

'Democratic states use surveillance technologies to facilitate governance through social control. Torin Monahan explains democratic surveillance as "intentionally harnessing the control functions of surveillance for social ends of fairness, justice, and equality...There are two types of video surveillance commonly used: stationary and aerial video surveillance cameras. The first type involves the use of stationary cameras mounted at key locations. The second type involves the use of aerial craft mounted with cameras, which can be manned or unmanned. (Surveillance Technology Challenges Political Culture of Democratic States. Inez Miyamoto)'.[40] 'The emerging claim to Digital Sovereignty has been coupled with vibrant discussions on the role of AI, including on data mining, algorithms accountability and leadership in the tech industry, which has become a prominent feature in European efforts to achieve strategic autonomy. The 2022 Strategic Compass sets out the EU's ambition to become a global leader in AI by reducing the dependency on external actors for emerging technologies, increasing the production of high-performance computer processors and the establishment of an independent data space'. (Artificial intelligence and EU security: the false promise of digital sovereignty. Andrea Calderaro & Stella Blumfelde).[41] The Internet has contributed to the growth of data sources for the advancement of technology intelligence, which gives organizations the ability to be aware of technology threats and opportunities. A UK based artificial intelligence firm in Yorkshire has been engaged in state surveillance to monitor social media. The firm signed deals with the Department for Culture, Media and Sport (DCMS) and Department of Health and Social Care to monitor threats to high-profile vaccine service individuals; The Telegraph newspaper reported.

In 2013, Edward Snowden's revelations were reported by the British newspaper-the Guardian, in which he elucidated that the US NSA was collecting phone records of millions of Verizon customers by the day. Snowden also uncovered the spying business of the UK electronic spy agency-GCHQ. Edward Snowden leaked and informed both domestic and international audiences on these novel actions of their own governments. News media had no existing discourse. In the US and UK violent surveillance systems were implemented and denied all types of citizens human rights to collect all types of information to make intelligence and law enforcement competent and fit to the fight against terrorism and extremism. But unfortunately, law enforcement agencies and intelligence failed to counter extremism, terrorism and foreign espionage before the London attacks. Modern technology enabled leaks that played a vital role in exposing the misuse of intelligence for political purposes. There are so many players and hackers who seek to enter the secrecy domain in Asia and Europe. Experts, Professor Richard J. Aldrich and Daniela Richterova in their paper (Ambient Accountability: Intelligence Services in Europe and the Decline of State Secrecy. Professor (PAIS, University of Warwick) have noted decline of secrecy and misuse of intelligence in Europe:

"Complex coalitions of actors-activists, victims, artists, journalists, judges, lawyers and politicians - have emerged on a national level demanding improved intelligence accountability. Most recently, in Slovakia such a coalition of citizens managed to reverse an almost 20-year-old amnesty verdict. This was put into place by the infamous Vladimír Mečiar, whose intelligence services kidnapped the son of the then Slovak President, Michal Kováč. The kidnapping caused an international outcry, but in order to prevent investigation Mečiar declared an amnesty on all actions connected to the event. In April 2017, pressure from this diverse coalition, fuelled by a recently-released fiction movie inspired by the kidnapping, prompted the Slovak parliament to overrule the amnesties. Here informal and formal accountability working together resuscitated an episode of unresolved Slovak intelligence history (Kern and Prušová: 2017). As controversial intelligence issues continue to emerge, we are likely to see more ambient accountability throughout the region. Attention is likely to focus on the alleged assistance of Central European countries in US mass surveillance".[42]

Chapter 2

Surveillance, Spyware-Pegasus, Secret Surveillance in Poland and the European Union Intelligence Centre

Close watch or surveillance over someone or something called monitoring surveillance. Surveillance is the monitoring of behaviour, many activities, or information for the purpose of information gathering, influencing, managing or directing. A general surveillance definition is the monitoring of individuals or observing something in order to gain information. Surveillance is used for a number of reasons and by numerous objectives. The surveillance meaning can be different depending on who is employing surveillance methods. Surveillance is used by citizens for protecting their neighbourhoods and by governments for intelligence gathering-including espionage, prevention of crime, the protection of a process, person, group or object, or the investigation of crime. It is also used by criminal organizations to plan and commit crimes, and by businesses to gather intelligence on criminals, their competitors, suppliers or customers. Religious organisations charged with detecting heresy and heterodoxy may also carry out surveillance. In his research paper, analyst and expert, Mateusz Kolaszyński (Secret Surveillance in Poland after Snowden Between Secrecy and Transparency) has highlighted Snowden's revelations and surveillance powers of Poland police and intelligence agencies. There has been no move towards transparency, while the construction of a modern intelligence agency was not completed in Poland.[1]

The role of Poland's constitutional tribunal in 2016 left a deep impact on the surveillance system in the country. All Polish governments supported reforms that tended to increase surveillance powers. "This practice is mostly influenced by the politicization of law enforcement and, first and foremost, intelligence services. Security services can push for beneficial solutions for themselves, such as unlimited access to information. The success of these policies also derives from the weakness of institutional arrangements, including limited possibilities of opposition, low public awareness, and a lack of real independent oversight. Overall, there is institutional support for broad surveillance powers and a lack of significant safeguards against such policies in Poland. Since Snowden's warnings about the extent and dangers of secret surveillance, Poland has had no radical rethinking with respect to secret surveillance practices. Since 1983, Polish law has used the term "preliminary investigation" (czynności operacyjno- rozpoznawcze) to refer to secret surveillance"[2]

The decision of the European Court of Human Rights raised questions as to how challenging is the oversight of international intelligence cooperation between secret agencies. However, the Court identified more doubts as to whether intelligence oversight was effective in Poland: "The protection of human rights guaranteed by the Convention, especially in Articles 2 and 3, requires not only an effective investigation of alleged human rights abuses but also appropriate safeguards-both in law and in practice–against intelligence services violating Convention rights, notably in the pursuit of their covert operations. The circumstances of the instant case may raise concerns as to whether the Polish legal order fulfils this requirement". In 1990, new intelligence surveillance law prompted some changes in regulations. The statutory regulation was expanded, and there were attempts to improve the rules in the ensuing years. Declassifying the mechanism of intelligence agencies during the democratic transformation generated some issues, like changing the statutory basis for secret surveillance; new intelligence and police services structure, increasing governmental control and external oversight. The Lower House of Parliament in Poland in 2016 passed laws that extended the reach of surveillance powers. Former project coordinator at the Helsinki Foundation for Human Rights in Warsaw, Poland, expert Barbara Grabowska-Moroz in her paper (The Polish surveillance regime before the ECHR-about:intel-Stiftung Neue Verantwortung) noted the power of secret services in Poland:

"As Polish law does not provide any specific control procedure regarding the conduct of the special services, it becomes a true challenge to assess which domestic remedies need to be exhausted to file a complaint to the European Court of Human Rights. Furthermore, it's almost impossible to provide evidence about secret methods used by police and the special services against a given person (due to the lack of notification), unless he or she eventually obtained access to it in their criminal trial. In order to overcome this procedural challenge, the applicants in Pietrzak v Poland and Bychawska-Siniarska v Poland lodged complaints to the chiefs of the special services, under Article 227 of the Code of Administrative Procedure. It is the general basis for lodging a complaint in any administrative proceeding in Poland. We filed complaints because we suspected them to be under surveillance—through the methods of access to metadata or even wiretapping — without having been informed. We emphasized that in light of the advocacy nature of our professional and public activities, there is a justified concern about the special services secretly collecting information about us, which could be used to intimidate us or hinder the progress of our legal cases. We argue that failure to inform the person who is subject to surveillance—combined with a lack of independent oversight over the conduct of these activities and the lack of justification for such activities—constitutes a breach of constitutional privacy rights".[3]

In late 2021, in his commentary on the use of spyware-Pegasus, editor of Notes from Poland (Critics of Polish government "systematically surveilled with spyware", finds EU report) noted that 'Pegasus had been used to hack the phones of figures critical of the Polish government, including a senator, a prosecutor opposed to the government's judicial overhaul, and a lawyer who represented senior opposition politicians. The findings were based on research by Citizen Lab, a cybersecurity watchdog based at the University of Toronto. Soon after, Poland's state auditor announced that it had evidence the government had bought Pegasus from Israel in 2017.'[4] Intelligence community of Poland is strong and complex due to the country's security situation. As a diversified intelligence, the Polish secret service is a very vigilant infrastructure. Expert and writer, Mateusz Kolaszyński in his research paper (Overseeing Surveillance powers-the Cases of Poland and Slovakia) has highlighted intelligence surveillance systems and legal limitations in Poland and Slovakia:

"Poland and Slovakia are very similar in terms of surveillance policy because a non-existent public debate on surveillance characterizes both countries. One exception to this rule is the incidental debates over the activities of intelligence services which are sparked off by the special status of these institutions in the political systems of both countries. Poland's and Slovakia's intelligence services have relatively broad powers in the surveillance field and at the same time are under the least control and oversight On one hand, in recent years, the intelligence services of these countries have expanded their surveillance powers On the other hand, Poland and Slovakia continue to have significant problems with intelligence accountability. In political life, we can observe very often that formal accountability mechanisms are failing. That is why, in recent years, constitutional courts and NGOs have played a crucial role in limiting surveillance powers. However, there are many examples of unaccountable and illegitimate functioning of Polish and Slovak security services. In both countries, these agencies are politicized-the politicization is connected with personnel and institutional alternations in these services".[5]

The Polish rule-of-law crisis has been a political conflict since 2015; where the Polish government was accused of failing to adhere to European constitutional law. The government of Poland continued to expand its hold on the judiciary resulting in the 2017 Supreme Court crisis, and the 2019 Polish judicial disciplinary panel law. The Polish legal system (Surveillance, Legal Restraints and Dismantling Democracy: Lessons from Poland Marcin Rojszczak-18 November 2020) was established 1989 while surveillance measures were applied by authorized bodies associated with so-called "procedural surveillance"....The scope of legal safeguards applied to operational and procedural surveillance was also shaped in a similar way. As a rule, interception of the content of communication required judicial authorization. Marcin Rojszczak noted.[6] Moreover, in a research paper (Surveillance, Legal Restraints and Dismantling Democracy: Lessons from Poland-Democracy and Security, Volume 17, 2021 - Issue 1, 18 November 2020), expert Marcin Rojszczak documented legal aspects of surveillance law in Poland:

"In the Polish legal system established after the political changes of 1989, the application of surveillance measures by authorized bodies was associated with so-called "procedural surveillance" (surveillance used as part of criminal proceedings) or "operational surveillance" (surveillance used as a means of detecting and preventing crime). As a rule, in both cases it was possible to use similar surveillance mechanisms–including those relating to the interception of the content of electronic communications, image and sound recording, and correspondence control. The scope of legal safeguards applied to operational and procedural surveillance was also shaped in a similar way. As a rule, interception of the content of communication required judicial authorization (ex-ante), materials from surveillance could not be freely used outside the proceedings in which they had been collected, and supervision of the surveillance activities of law enforcement authorities and security services was exercised by both courts and the prosecutor's office. However, this previous legal order has been significantly changed by the current parliamentary majority. As early as the first year of its rule, two controversial bills were presented and adopted that amended existing surveillance measures and introduced new ones. At the same time, a number of changes were introduced that weakened the effectiveness of the existing legal safeguards".[7]

Intelligence, global terrorism and cyber-attacks on financial institutions and banking sectors caused a complex and uncertain environment in Europe. The EU INTCEN is part of the European External Action Service (EEAS) under the authority of the EU's High Representative. The EU27 share broadly the same interests and are under the same threats, so they would be wise to merge their national intelligence agencies. This will allow for greater operational capability, less reluctance to share sensitive information between member states, and a more cost-effective force due to the principle of economies of scale. The EU Intelligence and Situation Centre is a civilian intelligence function of the European Union. Structurally, it is a directorate of the External Action Service and reports directly to the EU's High Representative for Foreign Affairs and Security Policy. Europe is raising its security profile and intends to be more sovereign in this area. Given the war in Ukraine or the new forms of great power competition, intelligence has a decisive role to play in building up Europe's security. France's National Intelligence and Counterterrorism Coordinator, Laurent Nuñez-Belda (May 16, 2022, How Intelligence Supports EU Security-Internationale Politik Quarterly), has briefly noted aspects of European Union Situation and Intelligence Centre:

"The main civilian gateway connecting the national intelligence communities to the European institutions is the European Union Situation and Intelligence Centre, or INTCEN, which is in charge of compiling and analysing the intelligence and the syntheses provided by the member states. INTCEN has managed to become the meeting point of the intelligence producers (national civilian services) and its users (European institutions). The relationship between the national services and INTCEN has steadily grown in recent years and INTCEN has become the natural partner of the member states on these issues. As far as military intelligence is concerned, the European Union Military Staff has a dedicated division, the EUMS-INT, which synthesizes the contributions provided by the member states' services. INTCEN and EUMS-INT join their efforts through the Single Intelligence Analysis Capacity (SIAC). Gathering internal, external, and military services, it is able to produce 360-degree analysis. The Threat Analysis, which laid the foundation of the Strategic Compass, has been drafted using SIAC".[8] Moreover, in their research paper, Professor Richard J. Aldrich and Daniela Richterova (Ambient Accountability: Intelligence Services in Europe and the Decline of State Secrecy-PAIS, University of Warwick) have noted the process of accountability through transparency:

"The more optimistic views of accountability through transparency suggest that in such a corrosive political climate, the media, whistle-blowers and civil society should step into the breach. However, the 13 region's traditional media-state and privately-owned newspapers, television and radio have a mixed record in this respect. According to media veterans, when they come across intelligence-related scandals, journalists are confronted with a dilemma: they must try to stay out of 'intelligence games' but at the same time must not keep important stories from their readers. Politicization also renders stories difficult to verify because of their instrumental use by political factions. This dilemma has resulted in three different approaches to intelligence scandals: the media have acted either as watchdogs, lap dogs, or have pretended to be asleep. The watchdogs have usually acted on anonymous leaks or built their stories around testimonies of insiders. For instance, under the 1990s semi-authoritarian regime of Slovak Prime Minister Vladimír Mečiar, some media joined forces with the political opposition and with what has become known as the 'parallel intelligence service".[9]

The issue of Russian interference in the UK has been a dominant factor in the country's political and intellectual discussion since the poisonous death of Alexander Litvinenko, a former officer of the Russian Federal Security Service (FSB) and KGB, in November 2006. On 4 March 2018, Sergei Skripal, a former Russian military officer and his daughter, Yulia Skripal, were poisoned in the city of Salisbury with a Novichok nerve agent. On 12 March 2018, the UK accused Russia of attempted murder and announced a series of measures against Russia, including the expulsion of diplomats. In March 2018, Sergei Skripal, a British citizen who used to work as a Russian intelligence officer, and his daughter, Yulia, nearly died after coming into contact with Novichok, a military-grade nerve agent originally developed by the former Soviet Union. Russian authorities immediately used the media and diplomatic forums to deny any involvement. In September 2018, British authorities charged in absentia two Russian military intelligence officers with conspiracy to murder, attempted murder and use of the Novichok nerve agent. By March 2018, more than 20 nations, including the United States, expelled 153 Russian diplomats and intelligence officers in support of the U.K. and in protest of the poisonings. In his analytical assessment of the INTCEN, expert Chris Jones (Analysis: Secrecy reigns at the EU's Intelligence Analysis Centre) has explained limitations of the INTCEN intelligence gathering and analysis:

"There are clear limitations to INTCEN's intelligence-gathering and analysis role. The intelligence and security services of all Member States are asked to provide information but, as Ashton said, "contributions depend on the availability of intelligence in the Member States' services and the willingness to share them." Member States are not obliged to provide INTCEN with information or intelligence, leaving INTCEN subject to the whims of various Member State agencies. Nevertheless, it is clear that the centre still views its work as being highly sensitive. Secret, confidential, and restricted In July, Statewatch requested a list of all documents produced by INTCEN during the first six months of 2012. Producing lists of documents upon request is accepted as common practice at the Council of the European Union, which has faced court cases and complaints to the European Ombudsman in the past over its failure to do so. It was therefore presumed INTCEN would provide such a list. The centre was not forthcoming. "There is no such document available," said the response. "You will easily understand that, in this particular case, information on the mere existence of a document produced by the EU INTCEN could prejudice the protection of the public interest as regards public security and/or international relations," explained EEAS Head of Division Cesare Onestini. However, "having regard to the spirit of transparency" a table was supplied outlining the number of documents produced and the topics they focused on".[10]

An open letter signed by 51 former intelligence officials (Press Release: Marco Rubio, Senate Intel Republicans Demand Answers from Intelligence Community on Biden Laptop Letter- 01 June 2023) concluding a New York Post article relating to then-candidate Joe Biden's son had "all the classic earmarks" of Russian disinformation. The US senate intelligence republicans demanded answer from intelligence community on Biden laptop letter. While intelligence is mentioned not by purpose, but by process, we can guess that something is being circulated which is not confined to state intelligence agencies. By articulating that this involves collecting, compiling, cataloguing, assessing, analysing and communicating data, it can be seen that this is strikingly similar to the intelligence cycle as outlined in the Intelligence Studies literature.[11] As writers Huw Dylan & Thomas J. Maguire (Secret Intelligence and public diplomacy in the Ukraine War- 2022) have described that the use of intelligence for influence during the Ukraine crisis demonstrated that none of these motives existed in isolation from the others, but rather can interact. In their research paper:

"Ahead of Russia's invasion of Ukraine, with the exception of verifiable satellite images and confidential briefings to trusted journalists, most 'intelligence releases' by London and Washington fell into the category of high-level, highly sanitised, intelligence-led communications. These were deployed in accessible formats from briefing lecterns and online, including on social media, through the likes of UK Defence Intelligence's daily 'intelligence update' on Russian military progress, with the intent of being widely disseminated and viewed. In the UK's case, updates were frequently but not always adorned with phrases such as 'we judge it to be highly likely', guided by a centralised intelligence-assessment 'probability yardstick' to regulate the communication of confidence and certainty. It used to be unusual to see such formal assessment language so widely used in public. Over the past five years, however, it has become increasingly commonplace. In the weeks since Russia's 2022 invasion of Ukraine, not only the UK and the US, but also NATO partners and Ukraine itself, have disclosed raw and finished intelligence on Russian actions. Examples include low-level signals-intelligence intercepts of communications between Russian troops and commanders by Ukraine and Germany to highlight poor morale and war crimes in occupied territory; Slovakian surveillance video of a Russian intelligence officer meeting an agent of influence recorded in 2021 as part of a wave of European expulsions of Russian intelligence officers; and British assessments of Russian disinformation methods".[12]

In a speech at St Andrews University in December 2018, Alex Younger, C of MI6, acknowledges: "We need to continue to tell them (the public) about the threat, explain the nature and extent of it, and be clear about what can be expected of us by the public. We need and rely on public cooperation and support for our work…. Informing the public increases their confidence that the authorities are addressing the problem and have the capability to respond appropriately to terrorist threats."[13] But public engagement of British intelligence raised some questions. In 2018, I personally tried to visit the MI5 officer in the London Borough of Hounslow; I was not allowed to go upstairs by the police. My purpose of that visit was to report my vulnerability and the threats I received from terrorist organizations. Now, on public engagement of intelligence, Mr. Alex Younger, C explained, no further explanation. In her PhD thesis, (The British Intelligence Services in the public domain: Thesis submitted in partial fulfilment of the requirements for the degree of PhD Department of International Politics Aberystwyth University 2019) Abigail Julia Blyth further elucidated the public engagement of British intelligence agencies:

"With the British Intelligence Services reluctant to engage directly with the public due to concerns surrounding secrecy, and that public engagement is viewed as a 'necessary evil', much of the engagement between the intelligence realm and the public occurs via key avenues of wider Government, academia, news journalism, and popular culture. In Britain, MI5, MI6 and GCHQ constitute Britain's Intelligence Services and, in this thesis, are referred to as the 'Big 3'. This is due to the fact that they all have a role in obtaining and monitoring intelligence, a theme which their websites and key pieces of legislation all determine. Indeed, their importance in gathering intelligence is not to be underestimated. In legislation which affects the 'Big 3' such as the Freedom of Information Act of 2000 (FoIA), the Justice and Security Act of 2013 (JSA) and the Single Intelligence Account, they are exempt from disclosing information on the grounds of national security".[14]

The UK intelligence surveillance faced several challenges. Privacy concerns began to collide with national security interests, and policy makers needed to prepare for a new intelligence war. Edward Snowden exposed communication surveillance that triggered political debate. There are countless private companies involved in intelligence surveillance in Britain, but their work and data is mostly contradictory and misleading. The use of electronic surveillance by MI5 and Policing agencies has been the main focus of intellectual forums for years. NASA and GCHQ cooperated on surveillance capabilities. The Regulation of Investigatory Power Act-2000 (RIPA) granted the power to public bodies to carry out electronic surveillance. RIPA and the Data Protection Act 1998 required a formal warrant before gathering private data by the government. Warrants authorizing interception of the content of electronic communications can only be issued by a democratically elected Member of Parliament, usually the Home Secretary, or another Secretary of State. On 25 July 2022, Human Rights Organization Liberty told the investigatory power tribunal that MI5 had breached surveillance laws since 2010, and provided false information to unlawfully obtain bulk surveillance warrants against the public. Despite knowing of data breaches since at least 2016 at the highest levels, MI5 failed to report to the Home Office or oversight bodies.

"Intelligence accountability is now a vast industry. European Court judgements prompted the United Kingdom (UK) to put its security and intelligence services on the statute book in 1989 and 1994 respectively, expanding the regulatory framework. Thereafter, the controversies over renditions and secret prisons attracted the attention of both the UK and

European courts". (The Last Forum of Accountability: State Secrecy, Intelligence and Freedom of Information in the United Kingdom. Melina J. Dobson).[15] The NSA, and BND came under severe criticism by mainstream society across EU and the US. There has been an intense debate in European electronic and print media about the underwhelming Achilles heel operational mechanism and tactics of their intelligence agencies. The involvement of EU agencies in power abuse, over-activation, politics, and corruption has made their performance absurd. Policy experts and intelligence analysts across Europe have recognized the motives of lone actors, and proposed wide-ranging security measures to counter emerging threats. Spain is in deep water. The country has not been exempted from lone-wolves attacks. In 2020, the UK government published a comprehensive report of Russian interference in the country, in which the main thing has been spotlighted was underestimation of the threat.

Professor Richard J. Aldrich and Daniela Richterova in their research paper (Ambient Accountability: Intelligence Services in Europe and the Decline of State Secrecy -PAIS, University of Warwick) have uncovered the influence of CIA and NSA on EU National accountability bodies and intelligence infrastructures: "National accountability bodies in Europe were vulnerable to pressure from the United States. In 2005 and 2006, State Department legal advisers toured Europe, urging America's allies not to inquire into these matters nationally and not to collaborate with pan-European inquiries, insisting that this would damage transatlantic intelligence cooperation in the war on terror. In Germany, they even offered the release of particular individuals held at Guantanamo in return for help in slowing any investigatory processes. The Americans were largely successful with national accountability bodies, but struggled with wider European bodies and also with some independent judiciaries Partnership and collaboration was important in probing these matters, for while whistle-blowers and journalists had sounded the alarm, it was more formal regional institutions who proved to be effective investigators, drawing their evidence from a bewildering range of sources, including amateur aircraft spotters logging serial numbers at the end of runways across Europe``.[16]

Modern and developed civilizations are characterized by a world culture of intelligence structured by political strategies, social and economic necessities that deploy surveillance to achieve political goals. European state such as Germany, Poland, Denmark, and France are never exempt from experiencing authoritarian drift. 'Surveillance can be understood as "the operations and experiences of gathering and analysing personal data for influence, entitlement, and management," mostly performed by states and corporations, but "may also be carried out by people in everyday life". Additionally, there exists a politically and economically "neutral watching or sensing," (Chapter 12: Why a militantly democratic lack of trust in state surveillance can enable better and more democratic security. Miguelángel Verde Garrido, Trust and Transparency in an Age of Surveillance Edited ByLora Anne Viola, Paweł Laidler-Taylor and Francis Group, 2021).[17] Revelations of Edwards Snowden in 2013 brought European and American intelligence infrastructure and their dances to different tangos to light. Germany and the UK were dancing to different American tangos, while other EU intelligence agencies were in an evolving and devolving process. Oversight surveillance and security sector reforms in these states were confronted by the old socialist stakeholders and infrastructures. Expert and writer, Miguelángel Verde Garrido in his paper (Chapter 12: Why a militantly democratic lack of trust in state surveillance can enable better and more democratic security. Miguelángel Verde Garrido, Trust and Transparency in an Age of Surveillance Edited ByLora Anne Viola, Paweł Laidler-Taylor and Francis Group, 2021) noted:

"Liberal democracies have formal institutions built upon a constructive lack of trust. Examples include the separation of powers, secret ballots, and whistleblowing. The separation of powers implies a lack of trust because it recognizes that dividing government into branches, separate and independent, is crucial to avoiding an unchecked concentration of power. Secret ballots, which exist in a number of voting systems, also imply a lack of trust in as much as they acknowledge that mechanisms to avoid excessive influences are required. Institutional whistleblowing implies a lack of trust since it accepts that wrongdoings within states—as well as corporations—may be intentionally obscured to avoid consequences. Therefore, protections are established to shield whistle-blowers from suffering retaliatory measures, and protocols are designed to investigate and right these wrongdoings. Civil societies can learn to constructively apply a lack of trust to oversight of security and intelligence functions, even if certain levels of secrecy are obligatory and limited transparency is the norm. Contrary to arguments that security and privacy are incompatible, efforts to simultaneously ensure privacy and security can be valuable in terms of "public policy" since addressing the intrusiveness of certain instances of security and surveillance can maximize "security benefits and privacy protections" (Ball et al. 2019, 14). "Good oversight is good security" because it "pushes governments to be as effective as possible in allocating their resources and selecting their targets".[18]

External oversight and intelligence accountability in Denmark has a long history, but recent incidents and misunderstanding have painted a dark picture of the Danish intelligence community. The intelligence infrastructure of the country has long been considered a vulnerable and an isolated organization that failed to effectively counter foreign espionage networks. As we all read cases of evolving intelligence oversight in Denmark but a wide-ranging intelligence and security sector reform programme has never been introduced. Intelligence interaction, cooperation and engagement with civil society have been weak in yesteryears. Though the PET agency tried to develop a good relationship with communities, results of these interactions have been murky. Experts and scholars, Sune J. Andersen, Martin Ejnar Hansen & Philip H. J. Davies have noted some important aspects of intelligence oversight in their paper (Oversight and governance of the Danish intelligence community, Intelligence and National Security-04 January 2022). They argued that the Danish intelligence is being controlled by Justice and the Defence departments:

"The Danish intelligence agencies fall under the jurisdiction of two different departments. PET has its administrative 'home' in the Justice department and the FE its 'home' in the Defence department. The Foreign Office also draws on the FE, although only indirectly through its work with the Defence department. Nonetheless, despite departmental affiliation, each agency's head answers directly to their respective Heads and Department and ministers. The Prime Minister's Office has been increasing its involvement in foreign and security policy since 1994. Although there is little publicly available information about the intelligence flow between the agencies and the Prime Minister's Office, the Prime Minister chairs the government security committee where both the Ministers for Justice and Defence are members alongside the Foreign Minister and the Finance Minister. As noted above, the Danish intelligence community consists of two main agencies, the Police Intelligence Service or PET, and the defence intelligence agency or FE. FE provides strategic and operational intelligence support to the defence staff and, less frequently, the armed services. It also serves as the national agency for SIGINT and foreign intelligence. Intelligence oversight in Denmark was confined to executive control for the first two decades after its post-war establishment, only reluctantly and gradually yielding to a limited degree of external scrutiny. Both FE and PET were placed on a statutory footing only in 2013. From inception, PET was responsible to the Justice Department and FE to the Defence Department, but since 1988 both agencies also fall under the authority of the Parliamentary Kontroludvalget

(Control Committee), established in 1988 with one representative for each of the five largest parties in the Danish Parliament".[19]

The pentagon leaked secret files containing data about Russia, and Egypt, but these files have authenticated that the US intelligence is now living in the past. The outdated, politicised and divided on ethnic and sectarian lines. The leak reveals how easy it was for a low-level employee on a US military base to obtain and then share highly sensitive US government information. By comparison, the contents of the documents on Ukraine leaked are far less explosive in nature. The files revealed that Egyptian President Sisi ordered his military industry the produce four thousands missiles for covert shipment to Russia. According to the Washington Post, Egypt has made this plan after a conversation with the US government. 'Supplying 40,000 rockets would really help the Russian military industrial complex, which, according to some estimates, produces about 20,000 large-calibre (152-mm and 122-mm) shells a month. However, since the Russian artillery uses from 20,000 to 60,000 shells per day during intense combat, 40,000 from Egypt is still a drop in the ocean'. (Pentagon leaks about Egypt, Russia suggest Cairo's ambivalence: Pro-Russian analysts did not rule out the possibility mentioned in the Pentagon document of Egypt armament of Russia, but lack of military exercises between the two nations suggests Cairo is playing it cautious.. Anton Mardasov. Al monitor April 22, 2023).[20]

State secrecy in the United States has a shameful history that every American security official and journalist wants to become worldwide popular by exposing the dirty business of the country's intelligence agencies. From Edwards Snowden to Texira and journalist Seymour Hersh, all American citizens are scared of his/her country's business of torture and killings in Iraq and Afghanistan. The Biden administration, CIA and Pentagon have now started a new business of destruction in Ukraine by supplying defective weapons to the Ukrainian army. Journalists and experts, Julian E. Barnes, Helene Cooper, Thomas Gibbons-Neff, Michael Schwirtz and Eric Schmitt in their joint analysis of leaked US documents (Leaked Documents Reveal Depth of U.S. Spy Efforts and Russia's Military Struggles: The information, exposed on social media sites, also shows that U.S. intelligence services are eavesdropping on important allies. New York Times, April 8, 2023) have critically elucidated the inability of US intelligence to secure classified files:

"The leak has the potential to do real damage to Ukraine's war effort by exposing which Russian agencies the United States knows the most about, giving Moscow a potential opportunity to cut off the sources of information. Current and former officials say it is too soon to know the extent of the damage, but if Russia is able to determine how the United States collects its information and cuts off that flow, it may have an effect on the battlefield in Ukraine. The leak has already complicated relations with allied countries and raised doubts about America's ability to keep its secrets. After reviewing the documents, a senior Western intelligence official said the release of the material was painful and suggested that it could curb intelligence sharing. For various agencies to provide material to each other, the official said, requires trust and assurances that certain sensitive information will be kept secret. The documents could also hurt diplomatic ties in other ways. The newly revealed intelligence documents also make plain that the United States is not spying just on Russia, but also on its allies. While that will hardly surprise officials of those countries, making such eavesdropping public always hampers relations with key partners, like South Korea, whose help is needed to supply Ukraine with weapons. One senior U.S. official called the leak "a massive intelligence breach," made worse because it lays out to Russia just how deep American intelligence operatives have managed to get into the Russian military apparatus".[21]

In June 2013, the story repeated itself. The Guardian and the Washington Post revealed a cache of 1.7 million documents collected by former CIA officer and then NSA contractor Edward Snowden. These files detailed large-scale electronic surveillance and interference by America's NSA in collaboration with European intelligence services such as GCHQ and the German BND. Formal accountability bodies such as the UK's Intelligence and Security Committee, composed of politicians, were remarkably quick to pronounce that nothing illegal had occurred and that all activities had been covered by ministerial warrants. On 21 July 2020, Intelligence and Security Committee published a Russian report and warned the government to take immediate action to effectively counter Russian espionage networks. Romania's new intelligence infrastructure and its stakeholders faced back-breaking and laborious resistance from its communist precursors' who wanted to push the reform convoy of democratic forces to the brink. The intelligence and security sector reforms received mixed messages from the international community. The persisting complications in Romanian intelligence are corruption, stakeholder's attitude, and the operational mood of former Securitate agents. Democratization of secret services and the policing forces in Romania has been a complicated issue since the dissolution of the Soviet Union when the old communist intelligence infrastructure refused to allow democratic reforms.

Chapter 3

The US Leaked Documents, President Trump's Punch on the Face of US Intelligence Management, Artificial Intelligence Technologies, and The British Counter-Extremism and Counter-Intelligence Capabilities

In the past ten years, I have put in writing more than seven books-spotlighting the operational mechanism of European and Asian intelligence agencies. These books also spotlight different technologies and practices being used in espionage to monitor the activities of civilians in offices, work places and houses. In yesteryears, states relied on tradecraft of dead drops or brush passes for covert information exchanges. Within the EU and Asian intelligence communities, techniques, methods and technologies are used in modern espionage. Agent handling is the management of espionage agents, principal agents, and agent networks by intelligence officers that are called tradecraft. Black bag operations are covert or clandestine entries into structures or locations to obtain information for human intelligence operations. Caltrop used by the US Office of Strategic Services. Concealment devices are used to hide things for the purpose of secrecy or security. Cryptography is the practice and study of techniques for secure communication. During my research and analysis in yesteryears,[1] I came across many new technologies and devices used in the operation of intelligence agencies in the EU. Though I had read about these technologies in research papers and books, the technologies used in intelligence surveillance and facial recognition operations were new.

Several EU and Asian states use different techniques to collect, process and analyse intelligence information, while technique tradecraft is quite different from that of developed states. What are the different types of intelligence tradecraft? GEOINT is one among several types of intelligence produced in support of national security, along with Human Intelligence (HUMINT), Signals Intelligence (SIGINT), Measurement and Signatures Intelligence (MASINT), and Open Source Intelligence (OSINT). When I entered into communication with different stakeholders of intelligence agencies in Pakistan, Afghanistan, India and EU member states,[2] I realised then that intelligence techniques and tactics used in the collection of information and handling of tradecraft are not the same. Their way of training, use of technologies and operational mechanisms are diverse. Some states are using techniques and tactics of World Wars-I-II and the Cold War, and continue to use these old methods, but their use of technologies changed. Intelligence Technologies crawls and monitors the whole Internet. The Centre for Technology Management has defined 'technology intelligence' as the capture and delivery of technological information as part of the process whereby an organisation develops an awareness of technological threats and opportunities.[3]

The Internet has contributed to the growth of data sources for technology intelligence, which is very important for advancing technology intelligence. Technology intelligence gives organisations the ability to be aware of technology threats and opportunities. A UK based artificial intelligence firm in Yorkshire has been engaged in state surveillance to monitor social media since years. The firm signed deals with the Department for Culture, Media and Sport (DCMS) and Department of Health and Social Care to monitor threats to high-profile vaccine service individuals. The Telegraph newspaper reported.[4] While logically asserts that it does not share evidence collected for the UK Government with Facebook, this partnership has ignited concerns among freedom of speech campaigners. Documents revealed that it produced regular Covid-19 disinformation Platform Terms of Service Reports" for the Counter-disinformation Unit–a secretive operation within the DCMS. Moreover, a secret unit has also been established to monitor lockdown critics. A clandestine UK Government unit dubbed the Counter-Disinformation Unit (CDU) has been implicated in a troubling endeavour to curb and control online discussions about the controversial Covid-19 lockdown policies. The covert operation allegedly involved the collaboration of social media companies in a strategic bid to quell supposed domestic "threats." The Telegraph reported.[5]

The applications of AI systems, including but not limited to machine learning, are diverse, ranging from understanding healthcare data to autonomous and adaptive robotic systems, to smart supply chains, video game design and content creation. 'The importance of artificial intelligence (AI) to UK industry (UK Research and Innovation) was recognised in the UK's Industrial Strategy White Paper: Building a Britain fit for the future, which identified AI and the data economy as one of the four Grand Challenges for current and future UK industrial leadership. The strength of this sector in the UK was also acknowledged in the government commissioned report Growing the AI Industry in the UK which stated that the UK has AI companies that are seen as some of the world's most innovative in an ecosystem that includes large corporate users of AI, providers large and small, business customers for AI services, and research experts'. Machine learning is the most common form of AI and largely relies on supervised learning, when computers are trained with labels decided by humans. Deep learning and adversarial learning involve training on unlabelled data to reveal underlying patterns.[6]

Artificial intelligence (Artificial Intelligence Technologies: Regulation Volume 732: debated on Wednesday, 3 May 2023, House of Common) 'plays a vital role in our economy and society, from helping doctors to identify cancers faster to powering smart devices and driverless cars. The explosion in AI potentially poses the same level of moral dilemma and is open to criminal use for Toggle showing the location of Column 100 fraud or impersonation and by malign players such as the Chinese Government. As leaders in AI, what should the UK be doing to balance safety with opportunity and innovation?"[7] Cyber-attacks, drones and satellites may have replaced tiny cameras and poisoned umbrella tips, but some of the old spying methods still come in handy. Intelligence gathering has two goals: accessing information and transmitting it safely for analysis - dead drops, ciphers, coded texts or any other encryption method might be used. Notwithstanding modern technologies used in intelligence operations and intelligence information collections, why do the majority of intelligence agencies fail to bring roasted Gallus-Gallus to their management?[8]

Most intelligence failures occur due to the lack of coordination, lack of funds, environment, corruption, and leaked cache of highly classified intelligence information. In France, Denmark, Norway, Germany, UK and the United States, there are numerous cases of intelligence failure. The Paris, Manchester and German terrorist attacks proved that spy agencies of these states needed reforms because at present capacity, they are unable to dance professionally. Their international involvement has broken their wings to fly. Their lack of reform, lack of public confidence, operational capabilities and lack of professional approach to domestic security and governance is an underwhelming story. They are not reconditioned and rely on weak and controversial illiterate sources. On 22 May 2017, twenty-two innocent people were murdered in Manchester at the end of a concert performed by the American artist, Ariana Grande. In addition, hundreds were injured. Many suffered life changing physical harm, many others psychological trauma.[9]

The head of the security agency "profoundly apologised" that he failed to thwart the suicide bombing in which killed 22 people. BBC (06 March 2023) reported the apology that followed the final report into the attack, which found failure of MI5 to stop the bomber. James Daly, Tory MP for Bury North, said there were "shocking failures" and "gross negligence" by the authorities. He told the House of Commons: "Too often in this place, an apology from an organisation seems to be enough when it's not." Addressing Home Secretary Suella Braverman, he asked: "Who is being held accountable? Who is going to be responsible? And will this information be passed on to the families?" Ms Braverman said that as the inquiry's report made clear, the responsibility for the attack "lies with the bomber and his brother". She added: "When it comes to whether lives could have been saved, the government is of course incredibly sorry and sorry is a weak word." BBC noted. The MI5 'profoundly apologized' for failings in run-up to Manchester Arena attack, Public inquiry found the 2017 bombing 'might have been prevented' if key piece of information had been acted on.[10]

On the evening of 22 May, a 22-year-old British-born Salman Abedi detonated an explosive charge in the foyer of the Manchester Arena, at the end of a concert attended by thousands of children. Abedi was killed in the explosion along with 22 innocent people, 10 of them aged under 20 and the youngest, Saffie Roussos, an eight years old girl. A further 116 people were hospitalized. (Attacks in London and Manchester, March 2017).[11] Independent assessment of MI5 and Police internal reviews unclassified, by David Anderson QC) the MI5 and the policing agencies failed to protect the concert. Unreformed agencies are always failed-bringing shame to the nation. Following the MI5 failure to intercept the London and Manchester attack, the CIA, FAISA and FBI also failed to protect their classified documents. In April 2023, the leaked documents exposed the sensitivity of the geopolitical situation, and how tension between Russia and Israel could escalate dramatically in the context of Russia's war in Ukraine. These leaked intelligence files were shared online in a gaming forum. Police arrested a 21-year-old U.S. Air Force National Guardsman named Jack Teixeira on suspicion of involvement in the leak. The National Security Council specifically declined to comment on the document detailing Israeli scenarios. The leak comes at a time when the conflict in Ukraine and ongoing tensions in the Middle East are becoming more closely linked. (A highly classified document explores how the Ukraine war could spill over into war with Iran. Ken Klippenstein, Murtaza Hussain, Intercept-April 13 2023)[12]

President Trump slapped the management of US intelligence agencies on the face and divided them on political bases. 'In his campaign to smother the notion that Russia hacked the U.S. election, he has thus far smeared the CIA and its sister agencies with accusations of politicizing intelligence, gross incompetence and even fabrication—to the horror of Republicans and Democrats in Congress, the foreign policy establishment and of course the intelligence community itself.' (How Trump's attacks on the intelligence community will come back to haunt him, Daniel Benjamin. January 12, 2017).[13] 'Current and former U.S. intelligence officers in unprecedented large numbers politicized intelligence in their opposition to the candidate and then President Donald Trump. The activists consistently refused, and still refuse, to accept responsibility for the politicization or the damage it caused to intelligence and broader national security. They declined to consider whether a well-established field of thought civil–military relations—contains insights about normatively appropriate behaviour by former senior intelligence officers, especially.' (Trump-Era Politicization: Code of Civil–Intelligence behaviour is needed. John A. Gentry, International Journal of Intelligence and Counter-Intelligence, 01 Sep 2021)[14]

President played an illegal role in dividing the US intelligence infrastructure on political bases. President Trump has publicly denigrated the value of the United States' intelligence community (IC), imperilling the morale and retention of intelligence officers. Unless he establishes a better working relationship with the IC, the White House not only risks hollowing out the IC but could also wind up politicising the intelligence process and misusing intelligence products. On 09 June 2023, former President Donald Trump was indicted on seven counts related to classified papers. TASS News Agency and Reuter reported the indictment of Donald by a federal grand jury for retaining classified government documents and obstruction of justice.[15] The indictment enmeshed the Justice Department in the most politically explosive prosecution in its long history.

The case adds to deepening legal jeopardy for Trump, who has already been indicted in New York and faces additional investigations in Washington and Atlanta that also could lead to criminal charges. Trump insisted that he was entitled to keep the classified documents when he left the White House and claimed without evidence that he had declassified them. The federal charges represented the biggest legal jeopardy so far for Trump, coming less than three months after he was charged in New York with 34 felony counts of falsifying business records. On 09 June 2023, Al Jazeera noted details of the charges: "Trump announced on Thursday night on his social media site Truth Social that justice department lawyers had informed his legal team that he had been indicted. Trump said he is due in court next week. According to two people familiar with the indictment, the former president has reportedly been charged with seven counts related to the mishandling of classified documents, but not authorised to speak publicly about it. The charges themselves are unclear and remain under seal, one person said. It was not immediately clear if anyone else would be charged in the case"[16].

Analyst and commentator Daniel Benjamin in his paper (How Trump's attacks on the intelligence community will come back to haunt him. Brookings, January 12, 2017) noted that disrespected intelligence spies cannot do their job properly: "Disrespected spies can't do their jobs. The charges Trump has levelled at the intelligence community (IC) are demoralizing. There may be no more effective way to undermine the CIA and other Intel agencies than charging them with politicization. The intelligence community lives and dies by its reputation for providing the unvarnished truth, and, though many may be surprised to hear it, the culture of these institutions is remarkably free of politics. I have been amazed, time and again, to hear from career intelligence people that they don't know the partisan leanings of people they work closely with; it is just not talked about. Trump's claim, after some of the first briefings he received last summer that he could tell by his CIA briefers' "body language" that they were dissatisfied because "our leaders did not follow what they were recommending" set off alarms on this count early on"[17].

While notoriously complex and highly dependent on specific contexts, in a more general sense, intelligence failures are commonly linked to the intrusion of power into the intelligence process. Intelligence, in this sense, rarely if ever works as a purely rational process in the way it ideally should. This process–including the key stages of collection, analysis, and dissemination–risks getting distorted as interests other than purely instrumental ones interfere. Power is, in this sense, almost exclusively seen as a problem in intelligence studies. The view of power as a problem and rationality as solution permeates much of the intelligence studies literature, not only that which directly concerns intelligence failures. As such it also offers a useful starting point for interrogating the subject of intelligence more broadly; by questioning a narrow yet dominant instrumentalist take on what intelligence is all about.[18]

On 01 June 2023, British General Sir James Richards Hockenhull admitted that he was directing Britain's Special Services in the war against Russia in Ukraine "I'm a career intelligence officer and certainly, for long periods of my career, it felt like I was responsible for making a jigsaw from the available information". There's a lot of confirmation and availability bias in some of the things that we've learned from Ukraine. Because of this, we should caveat those lessons slightly and make sure we're applying the right diagnostics and analysis to make sure that we're pulling through the correct lessons. This is open source for intelligence, but it's also open source and broader understanding which is supporting our intelligence making and decision making. If we can fully understand the availability of this information the impact will go beyond just thinking about intelligence or open source. Genera; James Richards noted. He also elucidated 'How we understand the posture of forces and the fusion of commercial imagery, tech data and social media analysis, provided significant insight into Russian deployments. This goes all the way back to spring 2021 through the autumn and winter of 21 into 22, showing us what was happening and where it was happening. That anticipatory intelligence is being used not just by sources inside the military but it's being projected for all to see and for all to interpret. James said he added that: "We had the ability to share information around Russian activity widely, whether it was in deployment, when fully deployed and postured for invasion, or indeed at point of invasion and beyond." Modern Diplomacy noted.[19]

In addition to these revelations, the US army and intelligence have been involved in the war in Ukraine against Russia. Analysts and commentators, Ken Klippenstein and Murtaza Hussain in their analysis (A highly classified document explores how the Ukraine war could spill over into war with Iran. Modern diplomacy on 01 June 2023, Intercept-April 13 2023), argued that the US secret documents sheds light on the growing risk of a U.S. conflict with Iran, as well as apparent Israeli efforts to directly involve the U.S. in operations targeting Iranian interests in the Middle East:

"A briefing document dated February 28, marked "Top Secret" and prepared by the Defense Intelligence Agency, details four scenarios it considers possible under which Israel could provide lethal aid to Ukraine—something Washington has sought but that Israel, which has ties to Russia, has refused to do. In one plausible scenario, the briefing says, "Russia continues to allow Iranian advanced conventional weapons through Syria, prompting Israel to request expanded U.S. support for Israeli counter-Iran activities in exchange for lethal aid to Ukraine." (Israel has accused Iran of transferring military equipment into Syrian territory that could be used against Israel in a future conflict.) The document also provides "background" to this scenario, which appears to refer to current circumstances that could set the stage for such a situation: "Israeli defined leaders are advocating for increased risk-taking to counter Iran, including proposing bilateral Israeli-U.S. operations." Both countries have been engaging in high-profile military drills as tensions in the region have risen. This January, the U.S. and Israel conducted their largest joint military exercise in history — an exercise that reportedly simulated airstrikes on Iranian nuclear sites. Another plausible scenario, according to the briefing, is that Russia "incurs casualties" from a periodic Israeli strike in Syria and directly targets Israeli aircraft with the help of Iran. The document also reports that Israel has "regularly requested" overflight support from the U.S. to carry out strikes against Iranian interests in Syria. The same document provides a laundry list of Israeli weapons that might be transferred to the Ukrainians in the quid pro quo that the U.S. is pushing for, such as Israeli-built surface-to-air missile and anti-tank systems. Such lethal aid might be transferred by Israel, the document notes, "under increased U.S. pressure or a perceived degradation in its ties to Russia."[20]

Analysts and commentators, Ken Klippenstein and Murtaza Hussain in their analysis noted that these documents appeared abruptly while the conflict in Ukraine and ongoing tensions in the Middle East are becoming more closely linked. "Since the start of the Ukraine conflict, Israel has been loath to become directly involved against Russia. It has sought to maintain communication channels with Russian forces in Syria as it carries out strikes against Iranian targets in that country, and has also generally welcomed the Russian presence there as a bulwark against Iranian influence. This understanding has come under increasing stress as Russian and Iranian ties have grown closer since the Ukraine war-something alluded to in the classified document``.[21] The United Kingdom left the European Union on 31 January 2020 but faced more trouble in dealing with the member states. The trade row with the European Union member states have put the Tory government in trouble, and its relationship with the EU remained complicated, while the vaccine war further conflagration their engagement. There was a transition period during which the UK remained part of the Single Market and Customs Union to allow for negotiations on the future relations. Tensions between the two sides also conflagration over Northern Ireland moved to extend temporary rule exemptions on trade across Irish Sea that forced Brussels to consider legal action against the British government. In March 2021, the British government published Integrated Review, in which a new picture of Global Britain has been painted to exhibit that the country has a bigger role to play in world politics. China and Russia have been illustrated as security threats, while the EU has been a reluctant friend. The UK and EU were still tightly bound by the complexities of vaccine supply chains. The United Kingdom departure from the EU on 31 January 2020 caused new security and foreign policy challenges. The EU helped the UK fighting domestic and international terrorism, espionage and serious organized crime. (Fight against Mass Surveillance, and Security Sector Reforms in Britain and the European Union).[22]

The issue of Russian interference in the UK has been a dominant factor in the country's political and intellectual discussion since the poisonous death of Alexander Litvinenko, a former officer of the Russian Federal Security Service (FSB) and KGB, in November 2006. On 4 March 2018, Sergei Skripal, a former Russian military officer and his daughter, Yulia Skripal, were poisoned in the city of Salisbury with a Novichok nerve agent.[23] On 12 March 2018, the UK accused Russia of attempted murder and announced a series of measures against Russia, including the expulsion of diplomats. The UK's official assessment of the incident was supported by 27 EU member countries including the US, Canada, and Australia. In August 2020, Russian opposition politician Alexei Navalny was poisoned with a Novichok nerve agent not by Russia, but his sickness vouched for Western sanction against important personalities in Russia.[24] (chapter-1 of Fight against Mass Surveillance, and Security Sector Reforms in Britain and the European Union).

In March 2023, in its policy paper (Integrated Review Refresh 2023: Responding to a more contested and volatile world. Responding to a more contested and volatile world, Presented to Parliament by the Prime Minister by Command of His Majesty- March 2023) the UK government published the update of Integrated Review-setting out the next evolutionary step in delivering on its aims, against the backdrop of a more volatile and contested world. "As in 2021, it paves the way to greater integration across government in pursuit of the four campaign priorities that will guide national security strategy in this changing context. And it does so with further investment in national security".[25] The Policy Paper noted that China was a greater threat to Britain. "We will work with our partners to engage with Beijing on issues such as climate change. But where there are attempts by the Chinese Communist Party to coerce or create dependencies, we will work closely with others to push back against them. And we are taking new action to protect ourselves, our democracy and our economy at home. Second, as threats and volatility increase, we recognise the growing importance of deterrence and defence to keep the British people safe and our alliances strong.[26] Our immediate and most urgent priority is supporting the self-defence and restoration of sovereignty and territorial integrity of Ukraine. This is not just about our values. We are acting because Ukraine's security is all of our security. Russia's invasion and continuing occupation of Georgia, invasion and occupation of Crimea, threats to the UK homeland and attempts to destroy Ukraine are assaults on European security. That is why we have committed at least £2.3 billion of support for Ukraine as it enters the second year of its war of national self-defence, just as we did in 2022".[27]

Overview of the review noted that "the 2021 Integrated Review, Global Britain in a Competitive Age (IR2021), set the UK's overarching national security and international strategy, bringing together defence, security, resilience, diplomacy, development and trade, as well as elements of economic, and science and technology policy. It is supported by a series of published sub-strategies, including the 2021 Defence Command Paper, the Defence and Security Industrial Strategy, the National Artificial Intelligence Strategy, the National Cyber Strategy, the National Space Strategy, the Strategy for International Development, the UK Export Strategy, the British Energy Security Strategy, the Net Zero Strategy, the Arctic Policy Framework and the UK Government Resilience Framework".[28] Moreover, in 2023, the Integrated Review strongly responded 'to Russia's illegal invasion of Ukraine. Putin's act of aggression has precipitated the largest military conflict, refugee and energy crisis in Europe since the end of the Second World War. It has brought large-scale, high intensity land warfare back to our home region, with implications for the UK and NATO's approach to deterrence and defence."[29]

In the UK, France, Germany, Netherlands, Italy, Greece and Brussels, the arrival of radicalized elements, and homegrown jihadists from Afghanistan, Iraq and Syria have challenged the authority of governments and law enforcement agencies. In the UK alone, the watch list of MI5 magnified 43,000 individuals' links with radicalized and extremist groups. British intelligence agencies supported the U.S.-led War on Terror, arresting civilians and handing them over to the CIA and U.S. military for interrogation. There was some degree of public condemnation over this partnership, but neither Parliament nor political parties were in any position to criticize security services. On 28 June 2018, the UK Parliamentary Intelligence and Security Committee's torture and rendition report was sharply criticized by human rights NGOs: "The report is bound to contain some revelations and criticism about the U.K.'s agencies, but even more worrying is what it won't contain," said Bellah Sankey, Deputy Director of Reprieve. "The committee only saw what the government allowed it to see, being denied access to individual intelligence agents and could only question senior officers who were not directly involved in alleged torture and rendition," Sankey continued.

Brexit was a serious challenge to all European states after 2021, but not the EU states alone, Britain faced serious challenges including exacerbation of terrorism and extremism. The UK intelligence agencies suffered deeply due to the bereavement of advanced intelligence information, collaboration and interoperability with the European intelligence agencies. The European Union struggled to reform institutions on state level, manage military crises and institutional innovation, but some states initiated security sector reforms, which was, later on opposed by their old communist intelligence and law enforcement agencies. The real issue that is still to be addressed was networks of foreign espionage within Europe, but without security sector reforms how can they counter foreign espionage? Secondly, in yesteryears, EU member states spied on each other's institutions, intelligence agencies and politicians that resulted in mistrust and a new intelligence war between Britain and Germany. The European Union as a security and intelligence actor from the perspective of counter-terrorism and counter radicalization needed Britain's intelligence cooperation. The EU intelligence has experienced a myriad of crises during the last ten years while terrorist organizations and home grown radicalised elements challenged authority of the state.

In Central and Western Europe, some states introduced major reforms in the field of law enforcement and intelligence, but the way their intelligence agencies were operating was not professional due to their consecutive failure to tackle national security threats in yesteryears. These reforms have had mixed results; sometimes states adopted a democratic model, and at times, it looked as though hardly anything had changed. The challenge of intelligence cooperation between the European Union and Britain is a complicated process. The lack of trust and attitude of both the British government and EU officials' irresponsible statements, further complicated the intelligence sharing process. The British intelligence infrastructure is so arrogant that its intelligence information is being collected by professional spies, so why should authenticated information be shared with the EU member state? The fact of the matter is their intelligence lacks public confidence, and professional security approach. All the UK intelligence agencies have accordingly failed to counter foreign intelligence networks. Intelligence agencies of South Asian states, Africa, China and Russia are openly dancing with impunity. Institutionally, intelligence cooperation relates to the intelligence interaction between the agencies respectively.

Failure of the US and UK Counterintelligence Strategies and the Manchester Terrorist Attacks

Intelligence agencies across Europe maintain a very poor record of professional approach when it comes to countering foreign espionage networks and illegal activities of foreign embassies. In 2020, the UK government published a comprehensive report of Russian interference in the country, in which the main thing has been spotlighted was an underestimation of the threat. On 21 July 2020, Intelligence and Security Committee published a Russian report and warned government to take immediate action to effectively counter Russian espionage networks.[31] Romania's new intelligence infrastructure and its stakeholders faced back-breaking and laborious resistance from its communist precursors' who wanted to push the reform convoy of democratic forces to the brink. The intelligence and security sector reforms received mixed messages from the international community. The persisting complications in Romanian intelligence are corruption, stakeholderism, and the operational mood of former Securitate agents. Democratization of secret services and the policing forces in Romania has been a complicated issue since the dissolution of the Soviet Union when the old communist intelligence infrastructure refused to allow democratic reforms.

In April 2023, two sets of classified documents of the United States painted a transmogrified face of the Biden administration. The documents were primarily related to the Russo-Ukrainian War, but also included foreign intelligence assessments concerning nations including North Korea, China, Iran, and the United Arab Emirates. 'A stunning leak of a cache of classified Pentagon documents appeared to be one of the most significant breaches of U.S. intelligence in decades, revealing national-security secrets

58

regarding Ukraine, Russia, Asia, and the Middle East, as well as details about U.S. espionage methods and spying on adversaries and allies. The Pentagon confirmed the leak's authenticity, while the documents were available online for months, U.S. officials weren't aware of the leak until April 6, 2023, the day it was reported by the New York Times. (What Secrets Are in the Leaked Pentagon Documents-and Who Leaked Them? Chas Danner).[32] The Associated Press reported that one document, March 9, 2023 reported that "In mid-January, FSB officials claimed UAE security service officials and Russia had agreed to work together against US and UK Intelligence agencies, according to newly acquired signals intelligence." The AP added. (Nikki Ikani and Christoph O.Meyer, the underlying causes of strategic surprise in EU foreign policy: a post-mortem investigation of the Arab uprisings and the Ukraine–Russia crisis of 2013/14, European security-2022)[33]

Politics in Britain has been unrolling into different outlooks and standpoints since the country's disconnection with the European Union and the well-built attacks of Covid-19. Terrorist attacks and several destabilizing attempts increased public's lack of confidence in law enforcement and intelligence agencies for a variety of reasons, including police failure to disrupt terrorist plots, deteriorating law and order situation, and media criticism of the government's lack of a strategic approach to security threats. Former Prime Minister Johnson's decision to centralise power after the COVID-19 attacks in 2019, to take all decision making processes into his own hands was criticized in newspapers. His government introduced a long-anticipated National Security & Investment Bill in January 2022 but never introduced reforms in state institutions. Former Prime Minister Gordon Brown warned in January 2021, that the UK could become a failed state without reform. "Unless the United Kingdom is fundamentally reformed, it could swiftly become a failed state because of rising concerns that the country is governed by a London-centric elite acting in its own interest". Brown warned. Moreover, Tim Ross expressed the same concern in his the New Statement (13 October 2021) article that multiple crises put under pressure the economy and state institutions of the country.[34]

All resources were diverted to counter-terrorism, and foreign intelligence surveillance through strategies, planes and mass surveillance under the umbrella of coronavirus. Infectious disease outbreaks clearly imposed terrible costs in terms of human suffering and mortality, as well as economic costs that threatened progress and stability in the United Kingdom, and that greatly out-distanced the costs of prevention and preparedness measures from privacy and private life to human rights. Every kind of human dignity has been signed-away to get data and watch lives of civilian population closely and remotely, those paying the price for the improvising designed national security strategies. The issues of Islamophobia, lack of reforms, and racism within the state institutions of the country have been widely discussed by experts and commentators in order to divert the attention of the government in power to the looming danger. These challenges have debilitated the voice of Britain on international forums, and incapacitated its enforcement capabilities to energetically respond to the waves of terrorism, foreign espionage, and extremism. External interference damages the state's fundamental institutions. Cyberterrorism, foreign espionage and intelligence operations, and targeted killings have badly damaged domestic governance. Politicians and parliamentarians have often asked a very unusual question about the future of the state. Some say "the UK is on the brink", the reason that the Scottish Independence Movement was getting stronger, while the security crisis in Northern Ireland has intensified. Within the two years (2020-2021) period, things shaped differently, while performance of union became controversial.

Now, due to the negligence of Boris Johnson, the state is now in a profound, political, social and financial crisis. Boris Johnso was furthering the agenda of Russia and the United States to cripple the British state. Security sector reforms halted while "Great Reset" continues to exacerbate the speed of unemployment, economic and financial crisis. Since the onset of Covid-19, we have entered a twilight world. As cases of COVID-19 rose across the globe, social and economic developments stopped. The implementation of restrictions in the UK forced the closure of non-essential retailers, arts, entertainment and recreation industry and the accommodation and food service activities industry had the highest percentages of businesses experiencing a decrease in turnover. Along with the tourism sector, Creative Industries were among the most affected by the Covid-19 crisis. Creative workers were already seeing devastating impacts on their income. Leaving behind the more fragile part of the sector could cause irreparable socio-economic damage.

The introduction of painful reforms accompanied by high inflation, bankruptcies and lack of public trust, resulted in a deep political crisis in Britain. The Johnson administration was investing in dying projects. The Tory party began to transform into a real oppositional force in the regions threatening China, Russia and the European Union member states by different means. In the 2020s, as a result of the coronavirus crisis, the Tory leadership became weak, frustrated and isolated due to its anti-state policies. The failure of the government to manage its population, ethnicities, racism and discrimination that prompted inequalities between regions, provinces, and areas where colours are confronting each other on social and political stratifications levels by the day. Racism is suddenly and at last everyone's business, and acting against it is everyone's responsibility.1 More so, at this time than ever, we now realise, since we cannot tackle covid-19 unless we tackle racism. Ethnic minority patients experienced differential outcomes in healthcare. Maternity and infant mortality were stark examples, but there was also evidence of differences relating to race in cancer survival, life expectancy, and diabetes care. Doctor, journalist, editor, and broadcaster, Kamran Abbasi (Covid-19: politicisation, "corruption," and suppression of science, BMJ, 13 November 2020) in his well-written comment on racism and politicization of health industry in the UK noted important points about the dynamic of social inequalities. He also raised a question about the secret function of the Scientific Advisory Group for Emergencies (SAGE) which was initially secret until a press leak forced transparency. Dr. Kamran also noted the leak that revealed inappropriate involvement of government advisers in SAGE, while exposing under-representation from public health, clinical care, women, and ethnic minorities:

"Science is being suppressed for political and financial gain. Covid-19 has unleashed state corruption on a grand scale, and it is harmful to public health. Politicians and industry are responsible for this opportunistic embezzlement. So too are scientists and health experts. The pandemic has revealed how the medical-political complex can be manipulated in an emergency—a time when it is even more important to safeguard science. The UK's pandemic response provides at least four examples of suppression of science or scientists. First, the membership, research, and deliberations of the Scientific Advisory Group for Emergencies (SAGE) were initially secret until a press leak forced transparency. The leak revealed inappropriate involvement of government advisers in SAGE, while exposing the under representation from public health, clinical care, women, and ethnic minorities. Indeed, the government was also recently ordered to release a 2016 report on deficiencies in pandemic preparedness, Operation Cygnus, following a verdict from the Information Commissioner's Office. The politicisation of science was enthusiastically deployed by some of history's worst autocrats and dictators, and it is now regrettably commonplace in democracies. The medical-political complex tends towards suppression of science to aggrandise and enrich those in power. And, as the powerful become more successful, richer, and further intoxicated with power, the inconvenient truths of science are suppressed. When good science is suppressed, people die"[35]

While state institutions failed by corruption, nepotism, racism, discrimination, and civil wars, world governments prepare strategies and plans of reinvention and reorganization to reestablish law and order there. In case of peace and stability, the process of reinvention becomes effective, while weaknesses and incompetencies of institutions are addressed. The British incompetent Prime Minister wanted to follow that streak to address diseases of state institutions. Privacy International (December, 2021) in its report noted strict surveillance measures of Britain and the EU to control pupation and maintain law and order, but this not a rational panacea. Surveillance and secretly watching the civilian population and violating privacy cannot help maintain security, and stability. Privacy International in its report noted different types of watchdogs, spy networks and intelligence agencies collecting information and data by illegal means. In 1999, the National Criminal Intelligence Service established the National Intelligence Model based upon the "collective wisdom and best practice" but counter-extremism and counter-intelligence capabilities of the British state have broken to control these illegal activities.[36]

If we look into the pool of cyber security strategy (2022-2030), we can find controversies and misunderstandings, failure of government to professionally respond to the cyber-attacks of Russia, China and private information warriors. In the aftermath of the terrorist attacks in London, Manchester, Paris, Germany and Italy, all EU intelligence and policing agencies became subject to a hot-blooded assessment. The British, French and German intelligence agencies suffered from a lack of check and balance in the past. Their intelligence oversight on internal, legal and parliamentary levels to make sure intelligence is transparently purveyed to policymakers and law enforcement agencies have been weak and contradictory since 2015. Formal and informal intelligence multilateral relationships including Eye Five intelligence alliance, USAUK intelligence alliance, the Club de Berne between primarily the EU members states domestic intelligence agencies have so for been less effective.[37]

Nuclear power plants, research reactors and uranium enrichment plants in Europe may, at any time, come under potential attack from terrorist and extremist groups as they have already established a strong network within the headquarters of the armed forces of some states. The possibility of a nuclear attack might be of several types-a commando type attack that might cause widespread dispersal of radioactivity, aircraft crash into an atomic reactor and cyber-attack. All would be disastrous. The problem of nuclear and biological terrorism deserves special attention from Russia, UK and Europe as the army of IS-K, Taliban and Central Asian terrorist groups are struggling to retrieve material of dirty bombs in which explosives can be combined with a radioactive source like those commonly used in hospitals or extractive industries. The use of these weapons might have severe health effects, causing more disruption than destruction. The UK decision to produce more nuclear warheads and its militarization intentions means that the Johnson administration perceived nuclear war between China and the United States in near future. China, the United States and Russia have already exhibited their military strength in South China and Black Sea, while these developments forced the UK to respond with strong action.

The Integrated Review elucidated the UK's intention to make more nuclear bombs. The Johnson administration abruptly reversed its disarmament policies and announced a significant increase in production of nuclear weapons up to no more than 260 warheads. Arms Control Association in its recent report noted the UK intention of producing more weapons in near future: "The UK currently has about 195 nuclear warheads, (Kingston Reif and Shannon Bugos- April 2021) of which 120 are operational, according to an estimate by researchers at the Federation of American Scientists. The UK deploys its entire nuclear arsenal aboard four Vanguard-class submarines, each of which is armed with Trident II D5 submarine-launched ballistic missiles. At least one submarine is always at sea on deterrence patrol. London maintains that a submarine on patrol would require several days' notice to launch a missile".[38]

Over the past 20 years, growing national security controversies mostly revolved around the failure of cooperation among the EU member states that resulted in mistrust and emergence of major spy networks in the region. If we look at the present cooperation mechanism, we can judge from the fact that intelligence interoperability and cooperation has failed to foster a strong and encouraging relationship with policy makers. When the UK left the EU in 31 January 2021, its relationship with the member states deteriorated, can categorically threaten that without UK intelligence cooperation, the EU will experience terrorist attacks and internal turmoil, but the EU is still strong and stable. Its trade row with the EU pushed the Tory misgovernment to the brink. There was a transition period during which the UK remained part of the single market and customs union to allow for negotiations on future cooperation, but the former UK Prime Minister Boris Johnson's extra-nationalistic and jingoistic approach to modern diplomacy vanished all hopes of good and friendly relationship with Europe. Tension between the two side conflagration over the border of Northern Ireland, and dynamics of the Johnson administration's domestic and foreign policy failed to address internal security crisis and international disinterestedness.[39]

However, British intelligence yelled on the interference of Russian intelligence agencies. The death of Alexander Litvinenko and Sergei Skripal authenticated the fear that FSB, MVD and GRU have been operating, interfering in domestic politics and killing their critics in Britain. The Tory government expelled Russian diplomats but never touched monographs of security sector reforms. The Teresa May government failed to introduce counterintelligence and counter terrorism reforms. The government's espionage strategy also failed shamelessly. They only published a 55-pages Russian interference report that couldn't purvey solid evidence of Russian intelligence interference in the internal affairs of the country. The 55-page report noted involvement of Russian intelligence in Britain. Moreover, in the majority of the EU member states, there are still in place intelligence cultures and infrastructures of World War-I, World War-II and Cold-War, and their intelligence agencies are still operating, collecting and processing intelligence information in militarized manners, and view each other with military glasses. The Nice, London and Munich attacks exposed the EU and UK national security approach, where political parties and civil society pointed to the incompetency of law enforcement and intelligence agencies. The issue of security sector reforms in France and Germany, and Eastern European States is often discussed in print and electronic media, but in reality, their zeal and resolve revolved around old mechanisms.

The lockdown and social distancing measures coupled with the direct effects of the virus on workers and firms disabled, patients, weak and poors, left a huge impact on the UK economy, industry, and law and order management. Debates started on whether the adverse health effects of a recession may be greater than the increased morbidity and mortality within the pandemic itself. The Covid-19 also prompted long-lasting structural changes in the UK economy, industries, travel and tourism, as well as hospitality. Strategies adopted to control the spread of coronavirus have failed, while corruption within the state institutions and within the government circle increased. The control measures have, therefore, had their own important consequences for people's ability to lead healthy lives, in addition to the direct impacts of the disease itself on health and wellbeing. The burden of disruptions to health care services disproportionately fell on those living in the most deprived areas and those with worse underlying health. The Covid-19 involved restriction, loss of income, patience and relatives, social isolation of a victim of domestic violence was a pre-existing key strategy for many abusers, something which many subjected to such abuses.[40]

Chapter 4

Boris Johnson's Mismanagement of the State, Cross border Mobility, Interoperability, Interactivity and Interface of Different Policing and Intelligence Agencies, Foreign Espionage, the MI5 and a Shift from Silhouette to a More Public-Facing Role

Boris Johnson' administration debilitated and incapacitated the British state and its institution by unwanted consecutive lockdowns, spending money and squandering financial resources with impunity. While he was deposed, the British state became in trouble and started sliding into the unholy-mess of Brexit. Its future was going to become gloomy outside Europe due to his government's economic and political confrontation with the EU market. The culture of racism, hatred, social and political discrimination intensified after the 2016-Brexit referendum. The Brexit crisis became a permanent headache for the government and civil society, which was going to damage the special relationship between the U.K. and the United States. The 2019 leak of a U.K. National Security Council meeting, in which cooperation on 5G infrastructure with Huawei—a Chinese technology company that was alleged to have close ties with the Chinese Communist Party's armed wing, the People's Liberation Army—was viewed by security experts as a matter of grave concern. If the company was permitted to operate with free-reign in the U.K., the country's relationship and intelligence cooperation with the U.S. would have deeply affected.[1]

Cross border mobility of people, interoperability, interactivity and interface of different policing and intelligence agencies couldn't restore confidence of military establishments, intelligence leaders and law enforcement stakeholders. That clefts and misconstruction still exist. Scientific collaboration, joint ventures and interoperability of police and intelligence infrastructures, and mismanagement of border altercations, further caused miscalculation and mistrust. The process of intelligence sharing among the EU member states had been extremely underwhelming after Brexit. UK security became vulnerable after its political and judicial separation from the EU project. Thus, Sweden, Finland, Estonia, Lithuania and Latvia jointly managed the flow of strategic and technical intelligence information and helped each other in fighting radicalization and extremism. Collaboration of Intelligence units, and operational police forces in the Baltic Sea and ground, as well as transnational collaboration associated with the rhetorical construction of fighters to defend their territorial integrity and national security, helped them in managing a better security infrastructure[2]

The EU and UK intelligence agencies were fighting extremism, terrorism and radicalization, war in Iraq, Afghanistan and Libya, but failed to address domestic security challenges since 2001. The UK intelligence agencies suffered deeply due to the bereavement of advanced intelligence information, collaboration and interoperability with the European intelligence agencies. Relationships between policy makers and intelligence analysis after the Iraq, Syria and Afghan wars evolved in multitudinous shapes. After the Paris terrorist attacks, the French Parliament designed legal strategies by overhauling the legal framework for intelligence surveillance mechanism. France maintains a strong and professional intelligence infrastructure that experienced and lived through different phases of world war-I and II, and the extensive Cold War period. Its share with different EU intelligence agencies on law enforcement level is considered indispensable and critical. The establishment of the National Commission (CNCTR) for the control of intelligence techniques in 2015 was the doorstep to the introduction of all around and wide-ranging security sector reform in France.

Intelligence reforms in Germany and France motivated their neighbours to make their law enforcement fit to the fight of terrorism and jihadism by introducing security sector reforms. The amendment of the legal framework for German intelligence by Parliament in March 2021 was a professional effort to bring intelligence under democratic control. Intelligence and security sector reform has been a critical element of bringing intelligence under democratic control. Intelligence agencies perform an important role in protecting national security, and national critical infrastructure.

The issue of foreign espionage once more appeared in newspapers when the British domestic intelligence agency (MI5) abruptly warned that Chinese intelligence agents were making things worse when they were introduced to parliamentarians. The MI5 said; "a female Chinese national was engaged in political interference activities on behalf of Beijing". But didn't explain why the agency didn't arrest her if she was a foreign agent. On 13 January 2022, Al Jazeera reported MI5's yell against the Chinese woman, and alleged: "she was working on behalf of the Chinese Communist party. MI5's own interference alert, which was circulated to parliamentarians, said anyone contacted by the woman should be "mindful of her affiliation" and its "remit to advance the CCP's agenda".[3] The Chief of the MI6 also warned that "China and Russia were racing to master artificial intelligence in a way that could revolutionise geopolitics over the next ten years. Richard Moore also argued that MI6 needed to adapt to new technology to survive". BBC correspondent, Frank Gardner (BBC-30 November 2021) reported Mr. Moore's public speech; "adaptation of artificial intelligence quantum computing and digital technology to completely transform the way human intelligence gathered by spies, presenting MI6 with major challenges in the digital age".[4]All policing agencies together with GP surgeries, As documented in my previous papers, foreign intelligence networks in Britain received underwhelming attention from Westminster. All institutions were dormant and never realised wolves behind their doors. They took this threat uncomplicated and painlessly and never thought of a professional approach to counter-espionage. Foreign and Commonwealth Office and Home Office never designed a competent strategy to counter Chinese, Russian and South Asian intelligence networks within the country. South Asian intelligence agencies under diplomatic cover are making things worse.

Edward Snowden exposed communication surveillance that triggered political debate. There are countless private companies involved in intelligence surveillance in Britain, but their works and data is mostly contradictory and misleading. On 25 July 2022, Human Rights Organization Liberty told the investigatory power tribunal that MI5 had breached surveillance laws since 2010, and provided false information to unlawfully obtain bulk surveillance warrants against the public. Despite knowing of data breaches since at least 2016 at the highest levels, MI5 failed to report to the Home Office or oversight bodies.[5] In February 2021, three Chinese spies were expelled who were potentially associated with China's Ministry of State Security. President Putin raised the same question of foreign intelligence interference in Russia in the 1990s. He called for greater efforts to undermine foreign spy war on his soil. In 2017, President Putin communicated the threat of foreign intelligence interference in Russia, and said his country needed to stop the work of 52 foreign intelligence agencies. When one talks about security and terrorism in the UK, he comes across many ideas, hypotheses and reports about the government and its agencies' failure to tackle violent extremism, international terrorism and espionage. There are thousands of research papers, essays, speeches and lectures available on the websites of think tanks, newspapers, journals and libraries that address the crisis of national security with different approaches, but lack of professional approach and coordination in these research materials makes the case worse as we have already tested the arrival of new surveillance technologies and their controversial use in our society. Snooper Charter Surveillance and Facial Recognition Technologies by the police have made the lives of citizen's hell. These weapons have badly failed to intercept jihadists joining the ranks of the Islamic State of Iraq and Syria (ISIS) and other groups in the Middle East and South Asia. We also understand that with the introduction of modern communication systems, surveillance and espionage networks have become a global phenomenon.

While we discuss these law enforcement related issues, many new things come to mind that force us to think that surveillance is not the only solution to our social problems. Yes, we know that modern state machinery in the UK ultimately depends on surveillance data but the way surveillance is used against the privacy of citizens has prompted deep frustration and social alienation. On 11 March, 2021, BBC reported (Home Office tests web-spying powers with help of UK internet firms) uneasiness of privacy rights organisations on web-spying business of Home Office: "The power to spy on the websites people visit comes from the Investigatory Powers Act, which critics called it a "snoopers' charter" on account of widespread concerns about its scope. The act gives the secretary of state the power, with a judge's approval, to order internet providers to keep their records for up to a year. Unescorted strategies and measures couldn't help the government in maintaining security and stability unless practical steps are taken on different fronts".[6]

Privacy International (December, 2021) in its report noted strict surveillance measures of Britain and the EU to control population and maintain law and order, but this is not a rational panacea. Surveillance and secretly watching the civilian population and violating privacy cannot help maintain security. Privacy International in its report noted: "In the UK, we have experienced different types of watchdogs, spy networks and private intelligence and intelligence agencies collecting information and data by illegal means".[7] Privacy and human rights organizations filed numerous cases against the state surveillance swords, and tried to convince stakeholders that this way of privacy interference can alienate citizens from the state. If we look into the pool of cyber security strategy (2022-2030), we can find controversies and misunderstandings. We can spotlight the failure of the government to respond professionally to the cyber-attacks of Russia, China and private information warriors. In March 2021, anti-protest measures, or highly controversial covert human intelligence act became law in the UK, while the government proposed a police, crime, sentencing and court bill that contains new powers to clamp down on the right to protest. Statewatch, monitoring the state and civil liberties in Europe (11 March 2021) in its report noted the covert human intelligence sources (Criminal Conduct Act). Covert Human Intelligence agents might be secret police officers, informers and state agents. They will be instructed from police departments and intelligence offices. One of the most controversial aspects of the law, Statewatch noted is the fact that it contains no human rights safeguards of its own, and instead refers to the Human Rights Act 1988:

"With the CHIS Act on the books, the government has now published the Police, Crime, Sentencing and Courts Bill. This contains a whole host of measures, some of which may have positive effects, such as further laws on child abuse. However, it also plans stricter sentencing rules, new stop and search powers, and provisions that would criminalise trespass (currently a civil offence), which appears to be primarily targeted at gypsy and traveller groups but could also have serious negative effects for protesters, ramblers, wild swimmers and many others. The campaign group Friends, Families and Travellers (FFT) notes that: "Whilst the majority of over 26,000 responses to the Government's consultation did not support the proposals, the Government announced that it planned to still go ahead with plans to strengthen police powers against roadside camps. Under the Government's plans, a new criminal offence will be introduced for people living on roadside camps which could result in people being imprisoned, fined or having their home removed from them." Existing powers will also be extended -despite even the police stating that they don't need new powers to deal with unauthorised encampments, FFT underscores. The Bill also contains specific measures to crack down on protests. The government says these new powers will keep people safe and "ensure that they can get on with their daily lives peacefully and without unnecessary interference."[9]

Pakistani ISI openly threatens critics of military establishment and the state, and dances in British cities and towns with impunity. Chinese intelligence agencies are dancing to different tangos and dancing to sound jitterbugs and boogies. The performance of British policing agencies is deeply underwhelming and confounded. British Pakistanis (associated with their country's army and intelligence) are cruising in the EU. States are on a hunt and catch mission to shamelessly target opponents of the state, military and intelligence agencies without fear of British powerful intelligence infrastructure. They openly spy on their army and their country's critics, in streets, towns and counties. Now the question is whether these agents have obtained licenses to kill and spy on British citizens or whether they are so powerful as to challenge the authority of British intelligence agencies.

The Netherlands, Norway, Sweden, and Brussels and French intelligence agencies have lived through different phases of experiments, experiences and participation in the US and NATO war on terrorism in Afghanistan, built professional infrastructures that protected the national security of their states. One thing. I want to elucidate the causes of the failure of intelligence agencies within the EU project. In fact, the lack of adequate intelligence information, trained manpower, flow of low-quality intelligence information purveyed by untrained, illiterate and ill-educated agents, failure to understand modern technology, and proper intelligence sharing with policy makers. The British, French and German intelligence agencies suffer from lack of check and balance and influence. The Danish intelligence infrastructure suffered huge failure when reports of Iranian and Chinese intelligence appeared in newspapers and social media. Iranian and Chinese intelligence agencies had established recruitment centres where educated people were recruited to collect information about Iranian interests. China also spread its blanket to teach some lessons to its cadres. The authorities in other western countries had also uncovered cases of foreign espionage indicating the presence of a threat to their societies. PET assessed the threat from foreign state intelligence activities in Denmark was specific and persistent. The activities include espionage, influence operations, harassment, attempts to illegally procure products, technology and knowledge and, in exceptional cases, outright assassination attempts. The Denmark military intelligence Chief was jailed for sharing sensitive intelligence information with foreign intelligence agencies.[10] On 12 January 2022, analyst Charles Szumski (Danish military intelligence chief jailed for espionage-EURACTIV.com) reported.[11]

Lars Findsen was jailed for a month for leaking classified documents to Danish media. "I plead not guilty," the head of the Danish military intelligence admitted before the judge rendered his verdict. On 9 December, the Danish authorities announced, without revealing their identity, the arrest of four former or current members of the kingdom's two intelligence services. They were accused, among other things, of disclosing "highly confidential information from the intelligence services without authorisation".[12] Expert Nikita Belukhin (The Scandal in Denmark's Military Intelligence: Too Much Transparency? Modern Diplomacy, 25 March 2022) highlighted issue of espionage in Denmark: "The delay in the key five military projects under the 2018-2023 Defence Agreement, including full meaning of the heavy mechanized 1st brigade in the amount of 4000 people, known as the 'fist of the army' and especially, the scandal permeating the Military Intelligence Services of Denmark, which allegedly carried out espionage against German, Dutch, France, Swedish and Norwegian colleagues in favour of the US National Security Agency, have not improved Denmark's standing in alliance either".[12]

Over the past three decades, the UK intelligence agencies have moved from the shadows to a more public-facing role, because their masked faces caused mistrust and misunderstanding that they failed to specify their places in civilian society. Then isolation and solitude generated a negative perception of MI5, MI6 and GCHQ's credibility, performance and community engagement. Today these intelligence agencies have become active in facebook, Twitter, Instagram and newspapers pages to cover up their previous failure. "Social media, public statements, websites and wider media engagement have all become the norm, with more information now available on UK intelligence than any time before. A major theme of agency engagement so far has been the attempt to move beyond traditional James Bond-like clichés or male-dominated workforces and become more representative of the public through their recruitment practices". The Snowden revelation regarding mass surveillance in European Union states and the UK generated an unending debate, while media in 2013 began publishing his documents to inculcate the civilian population about their illegal and shameless intelligence surveillance mechanism and the use of Facial Recognition Technologies. His revelations exposed several states spying on their own citizens. Intelligence war book, Public Perceptions of UK Intelligence: Still in the Dark.[13]

There has been an intense debate in European electronic and print media about the underwhelming Achilles heel operational mechanism and tactics of their intelligence agencies. The involvement of EU agencies in power abuse, over-activation, politics, and corruption has made their performance absurd. Policy experts and intelligence analysts across Europe have recognized the motives of lone actors, and proposed wide-ranging security measures to counter emerging threats. Spain is in deep water. The country has not been exempted from lone-wolves attacks. The

Russian intelligence operation and American intelligence failure are two lessons learnt to understand the role of intelligence in war and peace. Intelligence failure often occurs as a result of weak and wrongly designed strategies. Poor understanding capabilities, and information processes by policymakers are the main reasons intelligence failed. On 30 March 2022, in its yearbook, Swedish intelligence and Security Service warned that Sweden's security was being challenged on several fronts. "We are facing a wider and rapidly changing threat from hostile states and violent extremism, a threat that has therefore become more complex.[14] The crisis of EU intelligence is irksome due to sectarian and ethnic divide. European intelligence agencies lack the confidence of political parties on their mass surveillance system. In Germany, intelligence law does not allow the Federal Intelligence Service (BND) to support police or involve itself in policing business, while in Estonia and Latvia, intelligence plays an important role in policing communities. Targeted surveillance in all EU states is being conducted on different lines. Intelligence agencies of the member states use surveillance but also give importance to human intelligence. In Brussels, Denmark, Finland, France and Italy targeted surveillance of groups and individuals has strong roots in society.

Chapter 5

False Sense of Supremacy: Emerging Technologies, the War in Ukraine, and the Risk of Nuclear Escalation

Marina Favaro and Heather Williams

Abstract

How will emerging technologies impact crisis escalation? What has been the escalatory – or de-escalatory – effect of emerging technologies in contemporary crises? And can the use of emerging technologies increase risks of nuclear use? To answer these questions, we use the ongoing war in Ukraine as a case study to identify how emerging technologies are being used in modern conflicts and the associated escalation risks, including nuclear use. We argue that emerging technologies gave Russia a false sense of supremacy in the lead-up to the war in Ukraine and have largely failed to deliver Russia battlefield victories. As a result, Moscow has increased reliance on nuclear weapons and nuclear threats. This reliance could be exacerbated in the aftermath of the war in Ukraine when Russia is conventionally weakened. Therefore, it is not the technologies themselves that increase risks of escalation, but their impact on decision makers' perceptions of the potential costs of offensive military operations and escalation. Nonetheless, the role of emerging technologies in Ukraine should not inspire complacency because of the impact of new actors, new escalation pathways, and compressed time scales. These trends will have implications for nuclear policy and require more inclusive approaches to risk reduction and arms control, to include an increased focus on behaviors rather than capabilities.

Keywords: emerging technologies crisis stability Ukraine information distortion social media commercial off-the-shelf technologies

Introduction

On 3 May 2023, two drones exploded over the Kremlin in what Russian officials claimed was an assassination attempt on President Vladimir Putin. US Secretary of State Anthony Blinken dismissed these claims and said that anything coming from the Kremlin should be taken with "a very large salt shaker" (Tannehill Citation 2023). Drones and other modern military weapons have been widely employed throughout the war in Ukraine, and their use has raised questions about the wider impacts of emerging technologies on crisis escalation. Many studies examine single technologies in isolation, such as the impact of AI on nuclear decision-making, rather than the intersection of various military capabilities. This relatively narrow focus often comes at the expense of understanding the wider influence of emerging technologies on the nature of warfare, including potential nuclear use. Events in Ukraine offer a first glimpse into whether these capabilities signal a fundamental shift in strategic stability, including risks of crisis escalation, or whether the hype around emerging technologies is just background noise.

We use a definition of emerging technologies from the University of Hamburg, to include "those technologies, scientific discoveries, and technological applications that have not yet reached maturity or are not widely in use but are anticipated to have a major – perhaps disruptive – effect on international peace and security" (Favaro, Reinic, and Kuhn Citation 2022). At the outset, it is important to acknowledge the definitional challenges of "emerging technologies" and ambiguity around when a technology reaches "maturity" and whether or not it has a "disruptive" effect.[1] This definitional issue is particularly challenging against the backdrop of geopolitical and technological competition as states are rapidly advancing their arsenals to incorporate technologies such as artificial intelligence (AI). For the purposes of this paper, we are focused on technologies or technological applications that are still evolving in the context of their impact on international conflict. Essentially, we are tracking a moving target.

How will emerging technologies impact crisis escalation? What has been the escalatory – or de-escalatory – effect of emerging technologies in contemporary crises? And can the use of emerging technologies increase risks of nuclear use? To answer these questions, we use the ongoing war in

Ukraine as a case study to identify how emerging technologies are being used, their impact on tactical and strategic developments, and associated risks of escalation, potentially to include nuclear use. While only Russia possesses nuclear weapons in the crisis, we nonetheless consider it to be a justifiable case study because nuclear weapons have been a strategic consideration throughout the conflict. According to the *New York Times*, Russian military leaders discussed potentially using tactical nuclear weapons in fall 2022 as Russia was losing on numerous fronts (Cooper, Barnes, and Schmitt Citation 2022). This, along with Putin's regular nuclear rhetoric, demonstrates that nuclear weapons can play a role in conflicts with a non-nuclear adversary and still run the risk of escalating to nuclear use. Additionally, NATO has increasingly supported Ukraine in the conflict and includes nuclear possessors, who provide extended nuclear deterrence to members of the alliance. While it has avoided direct military intervention or meeting Russia on the battlefield, NATO's nuclear umbrella and conventional superiority have, arguably, deterred Russia from expanding its military operations beyond Ukraine.

We argue that emerging technologies gave Russia a false sense of supremacy in the lead-up to the war in Ukraine and have largely failed to deliver Russia battlefield victories. As a result, Moscow has increased reliance on nuclear weapons and nuclear threats. This reliance could be exacerbated in the aftermath of the war in Ukraine when Russia is conventionally weakened. Therefore, it is not the technologies that increase escalation risks, but their *perceived* military contributions that could lead states to initiate or escalate conflicts. The limited role of emerging technologies on the battlefields in Ukraine should not inspire complacency. Instead, these technologies and their military applications provide a preview of ways that emerging technologies could contribute to escalation in the future both before and during conflicts.

This article proceeds in three parts. First, we explore various theories on the intersection of emerging technologies and crisis escalation and develop an analytical framework for assessing the potential escalatory impact of emerging technologies. This framework relies on concepts of wormhole escalation, inadvertent escalation, and cost tolerance escalation. Second, we examine the empirical evidence on the role of emerging technologies in Ukraine. We focus on hypersonics, cyber operations, deep fakes, drones, enterprise AI, and anti-satellite capabilities, which are the most novel technologies to be used in the war but have not yet reached maturity and have potentially disruptive effects. Using the analytic framework, we conclude that emerging technologies do not lead to escalation on the battlefield, as often feared in escalation theories; rather they can lead to escalation by giving states a false sense of supremacy, as seems to have been in the case in Russia's invasion of Ukraine. Nonetheless, we identify three ways that emerging technologies could have had a more direct escalatory impact during crises and offer policy recommendations for mitigating these risks.

Theories of Escalation and Emerging Technologies

Risks associated with military technology and crisis escalation are not a new phenomenon for the current age. Traditionally defined, crisis stability refers to a situation in which neither side has an incentive to use nuclear weapons first, out of fear that the other side might retaliate in-kind (Schelling 1966, 234). Another way to approach crisis stability is as scenarios in which "emotion, uncertainty, miscalculation, misperception, or the posture of forces" do not incentivize leaders to strike first, and incentivize leaders "to avoid the worse consequences of incurring a first strike" (Kent and Thaler Citation 1990). This definition emphasizes that, in addition to technical characteristics, other psychological, political, and strategic factors are also relevant to crisis stability. This approach also treats crisis stability more broadly to include reduced incentives to initiate a conflict in the first place, not just relating to nuclear use. Bruusgaard and Kerr (2020) highlight an additional complication to the contemporary definition for crisis stability by adding that "the current information environment presents additional challenges for retaining stability in crisis". This includes new tools of dis- and misinformation and an abundance of unverified data that is available to decision-makers. Conversely, escalation risks refer to factors – such as mistakes and miscalculation, or crisis mismanagement – that could lead to nuclear use (Hersman, Claeys, and Williams Citation 2022). Potential escalation risks are becoming more complicated, including not only technological but also informational and psychological factors.

Arms racing also presents its own set of escalation risks, due to unregulated competition. Acton (Citation 2013, 121) defines arms race stability as the absence of perceived or actual incentives to build up nuclear forces out of fear that in a crisis an opponent would gain a meaningful advantage by using nuclear weapons first. Schelling and Halperin (Citation 1961) noted during the Cold War, "the present arms race seems unstable because of the uncertainty in technology and the danger of a decision break-through. Uncertainty means that each side must be prepared to spend a great deal of money; it also means a constant fear on either side that the other has developed a dominant position, or will do so, or will fear to do so, with the resulting danger of premeditated or pre-emptive attack" (p. 37). More recently, Gottemoeller coined the term "the standstill conundrum" (2021) to refer to the ability of big data analytics and new sensors to render submarines and mobile missiles (i.e. guarantors of second-strike capabilities) vulnerable to detection. New technologies, therefore, could give a real or perceived advantage to offense, by increasing first-strike incentives, but also to defense by potentially undermining legacy strategic systems.

Escalation pathways typically fall into three main categories: inadvertent, accidental, and intentional. Lin (Citation 2012) provides a breakdown of these types: Inadvertent escalation is the result of one side taking deliberate actions that they believe are non-escalatory but are perceived as escalatory by the other side. Accidental escalation results when operational actions have direct unintended effects. And intentional escalation occurs when a side deliberately escalates a conflict to either gain advantage, pre-empt, signal, penalize, or avoid defeat (p. 53). H. Kahn (Citation 1965) proposed that escalation in the Cold War would likely unfold in a series of quasi-predictable steps of increasing risk and intensity, culminating in a 44-rung escalation ladder. Within the escalation ladder there are opportunities for states to manage and reduce risks to prevent further escalation. However, as previously highlighted, escalation today may be more complex, as both states and non-state actors acquire increasingly capable and intrusive digital information technologies and advanced dual-use military capabilities.

Among the growing body of scholarship on emerging technologies, strategic stability, and crisis escalation, there are numerous schools of thought and approaches. From this literature, we identify three broad theories of escalation, some of which overlap: wormhole escalation, inadvertent escalation, and cost tolerance escalation. By no means are these exhaustive, but they do offer useful comparisons into thinking about *how* escalation happens. In using these theories to inform an analytical framework, we assume that states will continue to compete in technological innovation, and emerging technologies will have military applications. The war in Ukraine has demonstrated that the use of these technologies on the battlefield is a new military reality. The focus should not be on whether or not to employ them in warfare; instead, we should focus on how they are employed to explore if certain applications and activities are more escalatory than others. We also assume that technology is neutral; it is neither good nor bad, neither escalatory nor de-escalatory by nature.

Rather, the impact of emerging technologies depends on a host of factors, including their applications, the actors involved, and the stakes at risk. Singer asserts that it is "very clear that technology, and in particular, new technologies matter, and have been incredibly important [in this war], but are they the only important thing? Of course not" (Guyer Citation 2022). Indeed, we must recognize that there are elements of both continuity and change when examining the impact of emerging technologies on warfare.

Turning to three schools of thought about emerging technologies and escalation, the first, "wormhole escalation", focuses on gray zone conflicts and the potential for a non-kinetic conflict to jump "rungs" on the escalation ladder in a non-linear fashion. As described by Hersman, "Holes may suddenly open in the fabric of deterrence through which competing states could inadvertently enter and suddenly traverse between sub-conventional and strategic levels of conflict in accelerated and decidedly non-linear ways". Sub-conventional tactics, such as disinformation and influence campaigns; conflicts at the conventional-nuclear interface, such as a breakdown in escalation firebreaks; and non-linear strategic crises, particularly between regional nuclear actors, all have the potential for emerging technologies to contribute to escalation. With the return of great power competition, Russia and China are actively seeking ways to utilize their perceived asymmetric advantages, such as disinformation campaigns and autocratic decision-making, to challenge American hegemony and the rules-based international order. For example, the 2022 US National Defense Strategy points to a host of strategic challenges, all of which have escalation risks, to include: "emerging technologies; competitor doctrines that pose new threats to the US homeland and to strategic stability; an escalation of competitors' coercive and malign activities in the "grey zone"", along with other factors. To summarize, wormhole escalation happens when emerging technologies prompt crises to quickly jump from one level of conflict, such as non-kinetic, to a higher level, and are non-linear at the regional or strategic levels. Such technologies might include disinformation campaigns, cyberattacks, or other capabilities that muddy the "fog of war".

Second, inadvertent escalation was a concern during the Cold War, and has been revived in recent years largely thanks to the work of James Acton in identifying how the "entanglement" of cyber- and space-based capabilities could escalate crises. In his 1982 study on inadvertent escalation, Barry Posen cautioned:

[I]ntense conventional operations may cause nuclear escalation by threatening or destroying strategic nuclear forces. The operational requirements (or preferences) for conducting a conventional war may thus unleash enormous, and possibly uncontrollable, escalatory pressures despite the desires of American or Soviet policymakers. Moreover, the potential sources of such escalation are deeply rooted in the nature of the force structures and military strategies of the superpowers, as well as in the technological and geographical circumstances of large-scale East-West conflict. (Posen 1982, 28–29)

In the course of conducting a conventional war, an aggressor could threaten attacks on nuclear forces, leading to inadvertent escalation by prompting a response. Lin describes inadvertent escalation as potentially occurring because of incomplete information, a lack of shared definitions, and communication breakdowns. Emerging technologies complicate this scenario because of their reshaping of what constitutes a "conventional" conflict and because of their integration with nuclear command and control. In the specific scenario of "entanglement", Acton captures the risk that attacks on enemy nuclear forces, to include command and control, might not be deliberate but would be interpreted as such (Acton Citation 2018b). To summarize, inadvertent escalation happens when a state targets, either intentionally or not, another's strategic/nuclear assets leading to "use it or lose it" scenarios and forces a response. Emerging technologies can exacerbate inadvertent escalation by creating entanglement scenarios that threaten nuclear command and control or nuclear assets.

Third, a less explored theory of escalation in the context of emerging technologies is cost tolerance, which relies heavily on perceptions of military capabilities and the ability to impose and absorb costs. Unlike the other two theories that focus on how escalation happens once a conflict has begun, a theory of cost tolerance focuses on why states initiate a conflict in the first place. This approach is particularly relevant for questions about a crisis escalating to involve nuclear weapons, as any crisis involving a nuclear possessor inherently comes with the risk of nuclear use. Any conventional conflict, therefore, has an implicit risk of nuclear use being threatened or exercised. There are two main components to a cost tolerance theory of escalation. First, that states will initiate conflicts assuming low costs and/ or resolve to see through their strategic intentions. Patricia Sullivan, for example, has posed the question, "Why Powerful States Lose Limited Wars", and concluded, "strong states become more likely to underestimate the cost of victory as the impact of resolve increases relative to that of war-fighting capacity" (Sullivan 2007, 496). Sullivan focuses on asymmetric wars, wherein "strong states select themselves into armed conflicts only when their pre war estimate of the cost of attaining their political objectives through the use of force falls below the threshold of their tolerance for costs. The more the actual costs of victory exceed a state's prewar expectations, the greater the risk that it will be pushed beyond its cost-tolerance threshold and forced to unilaterally withdraw its forces before it attains its war aims". Emerging technologies could shape pre war estimates, perceptions about military balance, and the likelihood of success.

A second component to this theory of escalation is that actors decide to initiate conflicts with accurate information. States' ability to conduct cost-benefit analyses and understanding of risk tolerance hinges on available information and intelligence, and its credibility. Lawrence Freedman has highlighted the risk of "distortion in political decision-making" and its influence on decisions to initiate military conflict in the first place (Freedman 1991). Our own research supports this conclusion: in a 2021 study drawing on expert surveys, we found that "technologies that distort" are most concerning in terms of nuclear risk, due to their potentially high impact and the high feasibility of their implementation (Favaro Citation 2021). To summarize, a cost tolerance theory of escalation is concerned with why actors initiate crises in the first place and their estimations on likelihood of victory. Emerging technologies have the potential to exacerbate escalation dynamics by shaping decision-makers' perceptions of their military capabilities, i.e. the costs they can impose, strategic advantage, and potential costs they will have to absorb vis-à-vis a potentially weaker adversary.

There are important commonalities across these theories. To avoid nuclear war, avoid conventional war. Information and perception are fundamental factors in whether or not technologies lead to escalation. And emerging technologies add complexity and uncertainty into crisis decision-making. In this article we do not set out to test theories against each other, but rather to use them as frames for exploring the impact of emerging technologies on the war in Ukraine as having escalatory effects by crossing domains, jumping "rungs" on the escalation ladder, increasing risks of misperception, and influencing willingness to accept risk, uncertainty, and costs.

Emerging Technologies in the War in Ukraine

Emerging technologies have been extensively used in the war in Ukraine. Both Russia and Ukraine have deployed a range of innovative military technologies, from armed drones and electronic warfare systems to cyberattacks and AI-enabled intelligence gathering. Many experts expected Russia's larger military and investment in modernizing its forces would give it a technological advantage; however, Ukraine has effectively leveraged emerging technologies to resist and launch counteroffensives. Notwithstanding the tragedy of the situation, the war in Ukraine has given us a new set of datapoints on the role of emerging technologies in warfare. The insights from the role of emerging technologies on the war in Ukraine are not straightforward. On the one hand, this war has been very conventional and exhibited a high degree of *continuity* with warfare of previous decades (or even centuries). On the other hand, emerging technologies have *changed* the character of war by creating new vectors for crisis escalation, new capabilities on the battlefield, and an opportunity for new actors to play a key role in conflict. It is worthwhile to explore many of these technologies in isolation, as a suite of capabilities, and as a wider phenomenon in the war in Ukraine.

Hypersonics

Hypersonic weapon systems are capable of exceeding speeds of Mach 5 within the atmosphere. A combination of speed, maneuverability, stealth, and ability to evade defensive systems makes hypersonic weapon systems unique. Russia has used the air launched hypersonic Khinzal on at least three occasions in Ukraine to hit hardened targets (US News Citation 2022). This may have been a show of force and intended to signal willingness to escalate, but numerous experts suggested this was "serious overkill", wasteful, and an unnecessary show of force (Galeotti Citation 2022). There is speculation that Russia was running out of other missiles (i.e. Iskander and Kalibr) or it was a propaganda tactic. Either way, this very limited use of hypersonics does not seem to have conferred any strategic advantage in the war in Ukraine for Moscow.

Cyber operations

Ukraine's digital infrastructure was hit with cyberattacks hours before any missiles were launched or tanks were moved on 24 February 2022. A Microsoft study from April 2022 found that Russian cyber actors frequently conduct intrusions in concert with kinetic military actions. The study emphasizes the distorting capabilities of cyber operations, noting that "[c]ollectively, the cyber and kinetic actions work to disrupt or degrade Ukrainian government and military functions and undermine the public's trust in those same institutions" (Microsoft Digital Security Unit Citation 2022, 2). Network operations such as wiper attacks have not only degraded the functions of the targeted organizations (i.e. Ukrainian government,

IT, energy, and financial organizations), but "sought to disrupt citizens' access to reliable information … and to shake confidence in the country's leadership" (Microsoft Digital Security Unit Citation2022, 2). While the cyber domain is not a novel threat vector, Russia has allegedly used AI to augment cyberattacks and Ukraine has used AI to augment cyberdefenses (L. Kahn Citation2022; Vectra Citation2022). The use of AI to detect, defend against, and facilitate cyberattacks has the potential to speed up discovery, evaluation, and response processes far beyond human abilities.

Deep fakes

Another widely publicized AI application in this war has been the use of AI for information warfare. AI can be utilized to distort and weaponize information in both peace- and wartime, including in the form of "deep fakes", synthetic media in which an image or video is manipulated. Such techniques have the potential to generate a level of contrived realism that surpasses prior techniques used to falsify information. For example, Russia created and disseminated a deep fake video of Volodymyr Zelensky asking Ukrainian soldiers to lay down their arms and surrender that circulated on social media,2 but it failed to convince viewers of its veracity and was swiftly removed from social media platforms (Simonite Citation 2022). Zelensky doubtlessly benefitted from his high profile and the stakes at play, however, it also underscores that deep fakes are not hugely successful tools for grand deception.

Drones

The Russian military is using a lineup of military-grade unmanned aerial vehicles (UAV) or drones, in this war to conduct intelligence, surveillance, and reconnaissance (ISR) and support combat missions over Ukraine (Bendett and Edmonds Citation 2022). Russia has claimed that it used an AI-enabled (i.e. autonomous) drone, but this claim appears to be all signal and no substance. Though the manufacturer claims in promotional materials that the KUB-BLA can independently identify targets (Knight Citation 2022), there is no evidence that it was used to do so in Ukraine. Ukraine has also been successful in its counter-drone measures and are themselves using UAVs to great effect. Most prominently, the Turkish-made Bayraktar TB2 (i.e. a medium-altitude long-endurance drone) has played a role in targeting and countering Russian military advances, alongside much smaller drones for ISR (McGee Citation 2022; M. Jankowicz Citation 2022). In addition to the military drones that are being used for surveillance purposes and to strike targets on the ground, the scale of commercial UAV usage in Ukraine has become emblematic of Ukraine's "Do It Yourself" methods to counter Russian attacks. Commercial drones are much cheaper than their military counterparts, easy to acquire, and are viewed as disposable, making them attractive to groups that do not have much money. Finally, it is worth noting the presence of the US-made (and donated) Switchblade and Russian-made Lancet and KUB,3 which strike targets in a kamikaze fashion. This is a loitering munition that hovers over battlefields, where they search for a particular class of targets. While humans are often involved in confirming a strike remotely, these operating systems are technologically capable of doing so on their own. Again, there is little evidence that these have independently identified targets in Ukraine, though the difficulty of determining when full autonomy is used in a lethal context is worth flagging.

Enterprise AI

Enterprise AI refers to the way an organization – or, in this case, a military – incorporates AI into its infrastructure. Potential uses include intelligence gathering and analysis, early warning, and just-in-time wargaming/ simulations that generate AI-recommended courses of action. These processes augment and, in some circumstances, replace human perception and judgement. Both Ukraine and Russia are using AI to sift through the data generated by drones with ISR functions and commercial satellite images (Wyrwal 2022). Ukraine has also been using facial recognition technology to identify Russian operatives and soldiers, natural language processing for voice recognition, transcription, and translation services, and predicting Ukraine's ammunition and weapons needs (Tucker Citation2022). Jim Mitre, the director of the International Security and Defense Policy Program at the RAND Corporation and former Defense official was quoted as saying, "It's [Ukraine's] ability to process information at a faster clip than the Russian's that is having a big impact here" (Guyer Citation2022).

Anti-satellite capabilities

Anti-satellite (ASAT) capabilities fall into two categories: ground-to-orbit capabilities, which deliver a kinetic or directed-energy effect from Earth to targets, and co-orbital capabilities, which deny or degrade space assets and enable the covert/overt modification of satellites on orbit. ASAT capabilities are not new technologies, but their use is concerning for the growing number of state and non-state actors who are reliant on a sustainable space environment. Based on publicly available data, many ASAT activities in the war in Ukraine have comprised the use of directed energy to detect, jam, and otherwise thwart signals from satellites. Electronic warfare is integral to how modern militaries fight (Atherton Citation 2022), a fact that was acknowledged by the head of Roscosmos (i.e. the Russian space corporation), who announced in March 2022 that Russia will treat any off lining of its satellites as a justification for war (Reuters Citation 2022b). Nonetheless, Russia conducted a cyberattack against the satellite internet network VIASAT in May 2022 with the intention of disrupting Ukrainian command and control (Reuters Citation 2022b). The hack had immediate knock-on consequences for satellite internet users across Europe. In March 2022, Ukrainian forces reportedly captured a Krasukha-4 electronic warfare system left by the retreating Russian army (Trevithick 2022). Russia has increasingly made use of electronic warfare to detect, intercept, and disrupt communications as cyberattacks and ground strikes against Ukraine's communications infrastructure have proved to have a limited impact (Antoniuk Citation2022).

False Sense of Supremacy and Avoiding Complacency

To better understand the impact of emerging technologies on crisis escalation in Ukraine, we can examine these trends through the lens of the theories of escalation. Looking first to wormhole escalation, emerging technologies did not have a significant escalatory impact on the battlefield in Ukraine once the conflict began. Concerns about jumping "rungs" on the escalation ladder have not (yet) been realized, although Russian military discussions about tactical nuclear weapons use suggest there is potential for wormhole escalation, particularly in situations where Russia faces conventional defeat with few remaining military options. The use of emerging technologies in Ukraine has expanded the war across domains in potentially destabilizing ways. For example, cyberattacks against civilian infrastructure in Ukraine and against NATO members that supply Ukraine risk provoking a wider war. Emerging technologies have also increased uncertainty given their novelty and impact, complicating signaling and the risk of miscalculation. But overall, emerging technologies have not been the decisive factor on the battlefield; for example, Russia's performance in the war is largely being determined by manpower and command issues, rather than any new technologies. This war has resembled warfare of previous centuries to a greater extent than it resembles science fiction.

Turning to inadvertent drivers of escalation, there is little evidence of this in the war in Ukraine. Russia's invasion was decidedly intentional, and not due to misperception of any imminent threat by Ukraine or NATO, nor was it due to any pre-emptive threats to its strategic forces that would have created "use it or lose it scenarios", even at the conventional level. For scenarios of "entanglement", this theory of escalation is somewhat problematic in the case of Ukraine because only Russia, not Ukraine, possesses nuclear weapons; however, with the growing involvement of Western and NATO forces, this risk should nonetheless be taken seriously, and there are other risks of inadvertent escalation aside from "entanglement" scenarios.

Finally, the cost tolerance escalation theory suggests perceptions about supremacy *prior* to a conflict and likelihood of success, to include the impact of emerging technologies, may have had an escalatory effect by emboldening Russia's actions. Prior to February 2022, Russia was perceived to have overwhelming military superiority vis-à-vis Ukraine, including in Western intelligence analyses. To be sure, emerging technologies were not the only factor that contributed to Russian miscalculation. Centralized decision-making, underestimating Ukrainian resolve, and discounting Western support also led to misperceptions in Moscow and elsewhere. Perceived supremacy may have been particularly acute following Russia's military buildup over the previous two years and development of advanced capabilities such as dual-capable hypersonic weapons, disinformation campaigns, and a fleet of drones.

To summarize, emerging technologies did not have a noticeable escalatory nor de-escalatory effect during the Ukraine crisis that would make them unique from other military capabilities and applications. Where emerging technologies potentially did have an escalatory effect was *prior* to the crisis by giving Russia a false sense of supremacy and shaping perceptions in Moscow about the likelihood of success and relatively low costs of invasion. This argument comes with an inherent humility, as no one can know what Putin's perceptions were and Kremlin decision-making is notoriously murky. While the tactical impacts might be limited, the strategic impacts of emerging technologies more broadly point to concerning trends for escalation. Nonetheless, there are other trends in the war in Ukraine that should caution against a false sense of complacency about the escalatory potential of emerging technologies, to include potential for wormhole and inadvertent escalation. Three such trends include new actors, new escalation pathways, and new timescales.

New Actors

Technology companies – to include drone manufacturers, AI companies, commercial space actors, social media companies, and cybersecurity companies – have acted as force multipliers in the Ukrainian war effort on both sides. Gregory Allen from the Center for Strategic and International Studies suggests that this war has highlighted the relevance of commercial-off-the-shelf technology in war: "Across drones, [AI], and space, commercial technology is flexing military muscle to a greater extent than at any time since the end of the Cold War" (Allen Citation 2022). One notable example is the Chinese-made DJI Mavic drones, which have emerged as a key combat multiplier in the war in Ukraine. In another example, civilian researcher Faine Greenwood has used media shared on Twitter, Telegram, YouTube, and other sites to track and log nearly 800 incidents in which consumer drones have been used in Ukraine. In March 2022, Ukraine accused DJI of supplying Russia with its proprietary AeroScope drone detection software to target Ukrainian forces flying the drones. As of April 2022, DJI halted sales in Russia and Ukraine to prevent the use of its drones in combat (Kirton Citation 2022). But DJI are far from the only private sector actors who are playing a role in Ukraine.

In the cyber domain, Ukraine's defensive capabilities have been enhanced by cybersecurity companies and so-called "hacktivists". As regards the former, cybersecurity companies such as Microsoft, Bitdefender, CrowdStrike, and Vectra AI have extended their support to Ukraine to combat Russian ransomware, wipers, spear-phishing, and distributed denial of service (DDoS) attempts. As regards the latter group, the online hacker collective Anonymous declared "cyber war" on Russia when the invasion began (Anonymous 2022) and its members have devoted their skills to activities that range from the banal (e.g. DDoS attacks and data theft) to the imaginative (e.g. creating a massive traffic jam in Moscow by ordering dozens of taxis from the ride-hailing app Yandex Taxi to converge on the same location) (Gordon and Franceschi-Bicchierai Citation 2022). Anonymous comprises part of the "IT army" of Ukrainian volunteers. The role of both private cybersecurity companies and hacktivists reinforces our argument that new actors are playing a role in safeguarding the information ecosystem.

In the space domain, Ukrainian Minister Fedorov sent an appeal via Twitter to the world's commercial satellite companies on 1 March 2022, requesting that they share imagery and data directly with Ukraine. Commercial space capabilities answered the call with a range of providers granting near-real time monitoring of Russian military activities and support to Ukrainian forces, humanitarian organizations, and journalists covering the invasion. The satellite company Planet Labs has played a particularly significant role in this conflict. Satellite imagery can be used to track damages directly (e.g. by spotting fires, changes in the landscape, or direct damage on known sensitive sites) or in combination with social media information (100 Days in Ukraine, 2022). The company also plays a role in the information ecosystem; as recently as August 2022, the company released images that contradicted Russian claims regarding a recent attack on a Russian military base in Crimea (Borowitz Citation 2022). The activities of commercial satellite companies are, of course, on top of private space companies like SpaceX, who provided internet-enabling satellites to Ukraine after their internet was disrupted following Russia's invasion.

The enterprise AI functions mentioned in the previous section, namely the use of AI for facial recognition and natural language processing, have also been enabled by private sector actors. The Ukrainian MoD has been using Clearview AI facial recognition software to build a case for war crimes and identify deceased soldiers. It is also being used at checkpoints and could help reunite refugees with their families. Meanwhile, the AI company Primer has modified their commercial AI-enabled voice transcription and translation service to listen in on intercepted Russian communications and automatically highlight information of relevance to Ukrainian forces in a searchable text database. Both companies have granted Ukraine free access to their software.

Finally, social media companies have acted as gatekeepers for online civic culture in this war. Since its early days, Google, Meta, Twitter, Snapchat, and TikTok have actively removed or demoted Kremlin propaganda or refused to run ads in Russia. Some commentators speculate that these companies are keen to rehabilitate their reputations after facing questions in recent years over violating anti-trust law, infringing on privacy, and spreading toxic and divisive content. This is a point that will be picked up on in the following subsection.

New Escalation Pathways

Social media has emerged as a new vector for information dissemination – both true and false – but also provided an opportunity for social media companies to assume more responsibility for maintaining a healthy online civic culture. From the Russian perspective, social media has played a crucial role in the spread of false claims, assisted by dozens of Russian government Twitter bot accounts. Russian disinformation campaigns have sought to delegitimize Ukraine as a sovereign state, sow doubts and mistruths about Neo-Nazi infiltration in the Ukraine government, spreading "whataboutisms" that downplay the Ukraine invasion by drawing attention to alleged war crimes perpetrated by other countries, and spreading conspiracy theories about US biological weapons laboratories in Ukraine (Graham and Thompson Citation 2023). Russian disinformation campaigns have featured fake and heavily manipulated videos, which were discussed in the previous section.

Ukraine's social media prowess also warrants attention. President Zelensky has made extensive use of social media to broadcast selfie-style videos to the outside world, culminating in the so-called "Zelensky Effect". An actor-turned-politician, Zelensky is a natural messenger for the social media moment. His appeals are complemented by those of Minister Fedorov, who has launched public pressure campaigns that effectively recruited some of the world's most powerful technology companies (e.g. SpaceX, Apple, DJI) to join the Ukrainian war effort (Zakrzewski and De Vynck Citation 2022). More broadly, Ukraine's official media team has used social media to unflinchingly document their grim reality. Some experts maintain that Ukraine's tight focus on social media has been key to its success (Khan Citation 2022).

Whilst social media platforms have emerged as amplification systems for true and false claims, social media companies have simultaneously shown an unusual willingness to take a stand. These companies have prioritized their responsibilities to Ukrainian users and their ties to democratic governments over their desire to remain neutral, even at the cost of being banned in Russia (Oremus Citation 2022). This information blockade appears to be having some success in convincing Russians that the war is justified (Dougherty Citation 2022). Moreover, these decisions have illustrated how internet platforms have been scrambling to adapt content policies built around notions of political neutrality to a wartime context (Oremus Citation 2022). Many commentators have been surprised to witness an industry that has long been reluctant to bend to political demands submit absent any legislation or economic leverage.

New Timescales

Many of the technologies explored here are potentially disruptive because of their speed and ability to compress decisionmaking. It is worthwhile considering how new technologies create new timescales of effects in a crisis. For example, the Russian use of deep fakes has clearly failed to achieve strategic or tactical objectives in the short term. Meanwhile, Ukraine's successes at defending against attacks on their information environment is attributable (at least in part) to the fact that they are well-acquainted with Russian tactics from decades spent under Soviet rule (N. Jankowicz Citation 2020, 128). Political correspondent Vera Bergengruen reaffirms this, asserting that Russia "[floods] the zone with so much information that people don't really know what to believe. And in this case, Ukrainians were able to get ahead of it" (Davies Citation 2022). Ukraine debunked – and even "prebunked" (i.e. warned citizens of the possibility of Russian information operations before they were disseminated) – disinformation narratives before they were able to take root via, *inter alia*, a sophisticated social media outreach strategy.

What this leaves out is the effects of AI-enhanced information operations in the longer term. While synthetic media could theoretically lead to the use of nuclear weapons (e.g. a deep fake video of a head of state ordering their use), several verification measures would need to fail for such an order to be observed. Experts suggest that deep fakes are more likely to complement a kinetic strike or cyberattack (Favaro, Renic, and Kuhn Citation 2022). In these cases, the objective could be to throw the target off-guard before a strike and/or delay a response until it is too late. Perhaps more concerning is the possibility that the compound effect of sustained information operations could create divides in threat perceptions amongst national security staffers, including what information they found credible. This could muddy the strategic waters for decision makers, even if they give more credence to intelligence reports and internal briefings than they do to live news and social media feeds. Finally, this technology could destabilize public opinion and create pressure on decision makers to act quickly in a crisis. On a societal level, one longer-term effect could include the "truth decay" phenomenon, which refers to a diminished reliance on empirics and analysis within society broadly, and especially within political discourse (Kavanagh and Rich Citation 2018). That is, of course, in the absence of initiatives that strengthen societal resilience to disinformation (N. Jankowicz Citation 2020).

Reflecting on what is potentially new or novel about the impact of emerging technologies on the course of the war in Ukraine: The use of drones and satellites in war are not new, however, the use of small, commercial drones and satellites in war are relatively new. Small, commercial drones and satellites being used in a war between two relatively advanced militaries is new. The manufacturers of these drones and satellites being seen as alternately heroic – as in the case of SpaceX's Elon Musk – or suspect – as in the case of Chinese-owned DJI Drones – is new. In summary, the first change caused by emerging technologies are the new actors that are exerting influence on the information ecosystem and the course of the war more generally. Second, emerging technologies have generated new vectors for information diffusion (and thereby for crisis escalation), which includes social media platforms, whose owners find themselves in a content moderation role. The third change prompted by these emerging technologies is the timescales of effects. Not unlike the landmines of previous wars, which continue to cause damage long after war ends, the compound effect of sustained information operations could create a polluted information environment with adverse effects for years to come. Returning to our analytical framework, however, many of these emerging technologies will inform pre-crisis escalation decision making and will likely be assessed as a suite of military capabilities and their applications. It is not a new phenomenon for perceived technological advantage to lead to offensive military action or crisis escalation. But the new actors, new pathways, and new timescales discussed above may increase risks of misperception around the costs and benefits associated with those new technologies.

Implications for Escalation Management, Risk Reduction, and Arms Control

Our primary finding is that emerging technologies could give a false sense of supremacy, could be exacerbated over time and complicate policy options for escalation management, risk reduction, and arms control. Emerging technologies could embolden states to favour offensive action. But they could also lead to countries increasing reliance on nuclear weapons. For example, in the case of Ukraine, Russia will likely increase reliance on nuclear weapons due to its weakened conventional forces as a result of the war and as it rebuilds non-nuclear capabilities in its aftermath. Additionally, nuclear weapons can underpin regional aggression, coercion, or opportunism by states such as Russia and China.

While emerging technologies have highlighted the role of new actors and tools in conflict, it is too soon to conclude whether they have a consistent impact on crisis stability. Many of these technologies remain under-development and their future applications and implications are not yet fully understood. There have been significant investment from major powers like the United States, China, and Russia in military AI applications. These capabilities are expected to play a key role in future wars. However, most of the military AI applications are still in early research, development, or testing phases. Importantly, neither Russia nor Ukraine has deployed

AI-enabled weapons that autonomously select and engage targets in the current conflict (L. Kahn Citation 2022). Even in the cases of enterprise AI functions such as those provided by Clearview and Primer that are being used for intelligence analysis, there is limited publicly available data to meaningfully evaluate their use and impact. The available evidence from Ukraine suggests military AI applications are still too unreliable for combat use or to be trusted by human operators. Russia attempted to showcase advanced weapons like AI-enabled drones and hypersonics in Ukraine. But many of these capabilities either underperformed or were exaggerated by Russian claims. For example, the KUB-BLA drone has autonomous functions but there is no evidence they were used.

Another reason for a more nuanced and balanced approach to the impact emerging technologies on the battlefield is that the majority of scholarship has focused on their offensive applications, but there will also be parallel developments in defensive and protective measures. Russia seemingly had technological superiority and tried to leverage it against Ukraine through cyberattacks and denial of internet access. Ukraine successfully deflected most of these attempts, often with help from private actors like SpaceX. Analysis from June 2022 suggests that only 29% of Russian cyberattacks conducted in the first months of the war were successful (Smith Citation 2022). This is attributable to the fact that Ukraine was well-positioned to fend off cyberattacks, after having endured them for many years. Cybersecurity efforts were also bolstered by companies providing threat intelligence and incident response services. This highlights the many roles private sector actors have played in this war. Russia's poor performance in Ukraine demonstrates that technological superiority alone does not guarantee military gains. Many emerging technologies may offer tactical advantages, but these need to be considered in the broader political context – including external support, asymmetry of stakes, and cost tolerance. One potential lesson is that emerging technologies offer limited strategic advantage and increase reliance on nuclear deterrence for existential scenarios and war termination. This is not a foregone conclusion however, as many technologies like synthetic bio could have much greater strategic impacts as they mature.

A challenge for managing the risks associated with many emerging technologies is the involvement of new actors like the private sector that sit outside traditional arms control mechanisms. To mitigate this challenge, private companies need to be included in discussions and policy development around arms control and risk reduction. For example, Western governments will need to break down silos between the public and private sectors to understand the strategic implications of emerging technologies, where they are proliferating, and how they can be weaponized. More broadly, governments and industry should support inclusive dialogues on the crisis risks of emerging technologies. Private companies like SpaceX or Twitter could sponsor Track 1.5 discussions with experts from industry, think tanks, and governments to identify specific risks. Governments should also break down silos between nuclear and non-nuclear states to develop joint risk reduction tools. Many agree that emerging technologies increase the chance of nuclear use and our research shows this might be the case if technologies give states a false sense of supremacy and embolden offensive action. But multilateral institutions have been slow to address them due to complexity, crowded agendas, and polarization. Initiatives like Creating an Environment for Nuclear Disarmament (CEND) and the Stockholm Initiative may be well-positioned alongside the Non-Proliferation Treaty (NPT) to drive progress on risk reduction and emerging technologies. Non-nuclear states especially have a role to play in countering disinformation and deep fakes.

In addition to including new actors, traditional arms control approaches will need to evolve to address the novel escalation pathways created by emerging tech. Behavioral arms control initiatives like a ban on ASAT tests or limits on manipulating the information environment during crises could help such efforts. A Disinformation Risk Reduction Network could be created for public and private actors to share threat intelligence and coordinate responses. However, the current geopolitical climate makes major new treaties unlikely. In parallel, governments and companies must build resilience to potential manipulation and interference. This should prioritize two domains: social media and satellites. Social media shapes narratives with potentially escalatory effects. Resilience efforts should focus on civic engagement and educating the publics on disinformation. Social media platforms have a key role and responsibility in this. Satellites are also crucial as they provide communications and situational awareness during crises. Ukraine demonstrated the consequences of poor intelligence for Russia. Resilience in space through protected communications and rapid reconstitution/redundancy of satellite capabilities will be critical.

The compressed timescales driven by emerging technologies put a premium on slowing the pace of conflict and maintaining open channels of communication during crises. The demise of critical risk reduction agreements like the INF Treaty is an unfortunate example of what can happen when such channels break down. To avoid this, governments will need to proactively establish lines of communication with private sector leaders. For example, a modern hotline agreement could connect the US President and industry executives during a crisis to coordinate information flow and content moderation. More broadly, all actors should invest in sustained dialogue and signaling well before any triggering events. This will avoid miscalculation and create trusted backchannels to manage any rapid escalation that does occur.

Conclusions

Returning to our initial research questions: How will emerging technologies impact crisis escalation? Thus far, drawing on the case study of the war in Ukraine, emerging technologies have had an emboldening effect by reducing the perceived costs of military escalation for the technologically superior country, Russia. Emerging technologies have the risk of imposing a false sense of supremacy on states considering instigating a military operation or escalating a conflict. Beyond this, there is limited evidence that emerging technologies had an escalatory or de-escalatory effect on the war in Ukraine on the battlefield. What has been the escalatory (or de-escalatory) effect of emerging technologies in contemporary crises? Emerging technologies may have had an emboldening escalatory effect by shaping Russia's perception of costs associated with the invasion of Ukraine and the likelihood of success. The case of the war in Ukraine also points to the role of new actors, new escalation pathways, and new timescales in contemporary conflict, all of which are linked to the impact of emerging technologies. And can the use of emerging technologies increase risks of nuclear use? All three theories of escalation explored here point to the risk that any conventional war has the potential to escalate to nuclear use, albeit along different pathways. By bestowing a false sense of supremacy, emerging technologies could embroil nuclear actors in crises they otherwise would have avoided and result in strategic quagmires with potentially high costs of conflict termination, either politically or militarily.

When interpreting signals of change, skepticism is crucial. On the one hand, the performance of Russia's conventional forces should raise bigger questions about the state of its military-industrial apparatus. Uncertainty surrounding Russia's general technological trajectory and its ability to compete with the United States was already a matter of debate among experts before the war in Ukraine. Given the manifold economic, financial, and technological sanctions imposed on Russia after its renewed attack on Ukraine, the existing barriers to Russia's acquisition and deployment of emerging technologies might only increase in the years ahead. On the other hand, there is cause for skepticism vis-à-vis Ukraine's use of new technologies, such as AI for facial recognition and natural language processing. Who is using these capabilities and to what effect? It seems unlikely that these enterprise AI functions could be seamlessly integrated into existing military structures without substantial changes to doctrine, organization, training, materiel, leadership and education, personnel, and facilities (i.e. DOTMLPF). This calls into question whether this is mere posturing on behalf of Ukraine and/or a successful PR campaign by the AI companies. Moreover, this highlights the role that perceptions play in determining the effects of emerging technologies. Technologies that distort the information environment in particular challenge and confuse perceptions. And emerging technologies can also shape perceptions of likely costs and benefits prior to a crisis.

Acknowledgement: *The authors are grateful to Suzanne Claeys and Reja Younis for their research assistance with this article.* **Disclosure statement:** *No potential conflict of interest was reported by the author(s). Journal for Peace and Nuclear Disarmament. False Sense of Supremacy: Emerging Technologies, the War in Ukraine, and the Risk of Nuclear Escalation. Marina Favaro and Heather Williams. Journal information. Online ISSN: 2575-1654, 2 issues per year, Journal for Peace and Nuclear Disarmament is abstracted and indexed in: Directory of Open Access Journals (DOAJ). Clarivate Analytics' Emerging Sources Citation Index (ESCI) Scopus. Nagasaki University and our publisher Taylor & Francis make every effort to ensure the accuracy of all the information (the "Content") contained in our publications. However, Nagasaki University and our publisher Taylor & Francis, our agents (including the editor, any member of the editorial team or editorial board, and any guest editors), and our licensors make no representations or warranties whatsoever as to the accuracy, completeness, or suitability for any purpose of the Content. Any opinions and views expressed in this publication are the opinions and views of the authors, and are not the views of or endorsed by Nagasaki University and our publisher Taylor & Francis. The accuracy of the Content should not be relied upon and should be independently verified with primary sources of information. Nagasaki University and our publisher Taylor & Francis shall not be liable for any losses, actions, claims, proceedings, demands, costs, expenses, damages, and other liabilities whatsoever or howsoever caused arising directly or indirectly in connection with, in relation to, or arising out of the use of the Content. Journal for Peace and Nuclear Disarmament is an open access, peer-reviewed journal publishing theoretical and practical studies on nuclear disarmament and peace. Aims. "The nuclear threat will not end as long as nations continue to claim that nuclear weapons are essential for their national security." (Nagasaki Peace Declaration, 2017). The main mission of the Journal for Peace and Nuclear Disarmament, edited by the Research Center for Nuclear Weapons Abolition, Nagasaki University (RECNA), is to contribute to furthering nuclear disarmament and peace based on both theoretical and practical* *studies. The journal serves as a vehicle to put forward proposals for policies and other ideas that could contribute to nuclear disarmament, including ways of: Rapidly implementing Article VI of the Nuclear Non-Proliferation Treaty Promoting the norms fully embodied in the Treaty on the Prohibition of Nuclear Weapons Creating a new global governance regime for nuclear activities to facilitate the elimination of nuclear weapons.* © *2023 The Author(s). Published by Informa UK Limited, trading as Taylor & Francis Group on behalf of the Nagasaki University. This is an Open Access article distributed under the terms of the Creative Commons Attribution License (http://creativecommons.org/licenses/by/4.0/), which permits unrestricted use, distribution, and reproduction in any medium, provided the original work is properly cited. The terms on which this article has been published allow the posting of the Accepted Manuscript in a repository by the author(s) or with their consent. CONTACT Heather Williams hwwilliams@csis.org Center for Strategic and International Studies, Washington, D. C., USA*

Chapter 6

The Intelligence Dilemma: Proximity and Politicization–Analysis of External Influences

Beth Eisenfeld

Abstract

The relationship between policy-making and strategic intelligence is a source of ongoing discourse. Although there is an abundance of literature about the relationship between consumers and producers of intelligence, consensus as to the relationship between policy makers and intelligence producers is lacking. The two concepts–proximity and politicization–represent the intelligence dilemma that leads to claims of politicization, a word with many interpretations. Most observers of the democratic policy-making process are familiar with the traditional potential sources of politicization yet those sources are not the only potential sources of politicization and there is a paucity of literature about external influences and the politicization of intelligence. In democracies, governed by the people through their elected representatives, many individuals and groups interact with policymakers to influence decisions. This article provides a framework for understanding sources of politicization external to the intelligence community. It identifies an outside-in influence and uses three examples to show how this type of stimulus contributes to the politicization of intelligence.

Introduction

One of the more thought-provoking aspects of politics is the relationship between policy-making and strategic intelligence. There is an abundance of literature and a variety of opinions about the proper relationship between policymakers, who are consumers of intelligence, and producers of intelligence, who turn raw data into reports to inform policy-making.[1] However, there is a paucity of literature exploring sources of politicization from outside the Intelligence Community (IC), which is necessary to round out the discourse. Indeed, recent news headlines warn about intelligence politicization as the executive branch and the United States Intelligence Community spar publicly over analytic conclusions reached by the IC.[2] For decades, the centre of the discourse about politicization was *proximity*– how close or far apart should consumers and producers operate? The question arose because, as in all relationships, frequent and repeated interactions can be an asset just as much as those interactions can become problematic.

Likewise, amongst scholars and practitioners, there was "no consensus as to what the relationship between intelligence and policy should be."[3] In the political area, intelligence connotes power; proximity to policymakers implies influence; and influence, relative to intelligence, leads to claims of politicization–a word with many interpretations. Most observers of US policy-making processes recognize traditional sources of politicization.[4] Yet these are not the only potential sources.[5] Individual citizens, organizations that provide policy research and advice (think tanks), the media (both traditional and new), and lobbyists contribute to politicized intelligence. Therefore, this article aims to examine how external entities contribute to the politicization of United States domestic intelligence. This article considers the history and definitions of politicization, distinguishes types of politicization, and analyzes three sources of politicization from outside the IC–think tanks, the media, and lobbyists. The article concludes by illuminating the outside-in aspect of politicization so participants and observers of the policy-making process can address this emerging dynamic.

What is Politicization and from Where Does it Come?

According to scholars, the first use of the word politicization was in 1907 when Karl Lamprecht, a German historian, "spoke of *die Politisizerung der Gesellschaft* [the politicizing of society], although in the harmless sense of increasing interest in politics."[6] At some point between 1907 and 1919, the Germans began using the word politicization differently, which "rendered it open to alternatives and controversies and contributed to the rethinking of the concept of politics," and the negative connotations with which politicization is associated today.[7] The word politicization, a derivation of the word *politicize* dating from 1758, did not enter the English vocabulary until after World War I.[8] Despite the relatively recent origin of the word, the concept of politicization has been in existence since Roman times.

Yakobson asserts, "all the elements of politicization known to us from the late [Roman] Republic feature prominently in the descriptions of the elections during the struggle of the orders."[9] In addition, during the second Punic War, according to Futrell,

"Livy [Titus Livius Patavinus, the Roman historian] refers to his [Marcus Aemilius Lepidus'] unsuccessful candidacy for the consulship of 216 [BC]. This is the first known association between the giving of *munera* [gifts] and electioneering for the highest offices would establish a key pattern for the politicization of the gladiatorial combats in the later republic [Roman Republic]."[10]

Palonen asserts, "Politicization means detecting the political potential of some existing changes, shifts, or processes."[11] Although technically an acceptable definition, it results from studying the word's changing use over time, absent the context of its use in national security and intelligence matters or of the intelligence-policy relationship. In this regard, there is little definitional consensus amongst scholars. With the intelligence-policy context added, a conundrum exists with both "the definition and conceptualization of politicization."[12] Depending on how scholars define it, there can be negative connotations as well as the recognition politicization may be a natural component of the intelligence-policy process, and therefore, useful in certain circumstances.[13] Neither the quest for neither a standardized definition nor the concept of politicization leads to definitive conclusions. Rather, the discourse revolves around variations upon themes, which for some authors leads to broad all-encompassing attempts to define politicization, while for others it leads to defining different degrees or types of politicization, further complicating the concept for all actors involved. For example, Johnson defines it as "putting a spin on or 'cooking' intelligence to serve the political needs or beliefs of an intelligence manager or policy official."[14]

Gannon contends it is "the willful distortion of analysis to satisfy the demands of intelligence bosses and policymakers."[15] Rovner defines politicization as "the attempt to manipulate intelligence so that it reflects policy preference."[16] In contrast, Ransom cites multiple meanings including "partisan politicization….a point of contention between organized political parties," "bipartisan politicization" that "generates public debate over ends and means," and "intelligence to please," which occurs when intelligence influences policy.[17] Handel describes politicization as one of four definitions of the word politics, claiming it is the "interference in the intelligence process by leaders and their close aides."[18] However, Treverton suggests that by expanding the definition to include "commitments to perspectives and conclusions, in the process of intelligence analysis or interaction with policy, that suppresses other evidence or views, or blind[s] people to them."[19] Treverton goes on to suggest his definition resulted in five forms of politicization working simultaneously.[20] The five forms are:

➤ Direct pressure from senior policy officials to come to particular intelligence conclusions, usually ones that accord with those officials' policies or policy preferences.

➤ A house line on a particular subject, which shifts the focus of the bias from policy to intelligence. Here, a particular analytic office has a defined view of an issue, and analysts or analyses that suggest heresy are suppressed or ignored.

➤ Cherry picking (and sometimes growing some cherries), in which senior officials, usually policy officials, pick their favorites out of a range of assessments.

➤ Question asking, where, as in other areas of inquiry, the nature of the question takes the analysis a good way if not to the answer, then to the frame in which the answer will lie. A related version of this form occurs when policymakers ask a reasonable question but continue to ask it repeatedly, which distorts analysis—by depriving it of time and effort to work on other questions—even if it does not directly politicize.

➤ A shared mindset, whereby intelligence and policy share strong presumptions. This is perhaps the limiting case; if it is politicization, it is more self-imposed than policymaker-imposed.

Hastedt concluded, "For those who minimize its occurrence politicization involves the overt manipulation of intelligence and the intelligence process. For those who see it as a more pervasive phenomenon it can also take more subtle forms."[21] Finally, Marrin introduced one of the newest phrases based on the idea of "'analytic politicization' (a new term used to distinguish it from other forms of politicization)."[22] Although never defined, Marrin uses the term to dissect various politicization definitions, summing up the definitional debate best by asserting, "the concept of politicization is for the most part analytically useless."[23] Marrin demonstrated that depending on from whose viewpoint–consumer or producer–one person's definition of politicization is another person's standard operating procedure for decision-making in a democratic society.[24]

100

Types of Politicization

In addition to seeking a definition of politicization, scholars struggle with "the issue of the relationship between intelligence and policy making," and the question of what is the appropriate proximity between policymakers and analysts.[25] The two theories, or schools of thought, debated in a similar manner to definitions are the Kent School and the Gates School.[26] Although Kent did not use the word politicization, he was concerned about the policymaker-intelligence relationship and penned one of the earliest articles.[27] Kent contended actors must maintain a certain distance between one another for intelligence to provide proper guidance asserting, "intelligence must be close enough to policy, plans and operations to have the greatest amount of guidance, and must not be so close that it loses all its objectivity and integrity of judgment."[28] In contrast, Betts considered the academic perspective asserting, "objectivity takes precedence over everything," a perspective that provided the modus operandi for the Central Intelligence Agency for over thirty years.[29] By 1980, the Gates School of thought began to emerge because of "critiques of ineffective intelligence contributions to policymaking, and the view that utility is the *sine qua non*."[30]

Gates observed there were some ways in which politicization crept into the intelligence cycle, but said regardless of how it entered the intelligence cycle, both policymakers and intelligence analysts had to work together.[31] His implication was for intelligence to be useful, and to provide policymakers with information necessary to make decisions concerning national security, sensitivity and context linked analysis and policy. Thus, in contrast to the Kent School, the Gates School was about the business of intelligence versus intelligence as an academic endeavour. Westerfield studied both schools and concluded the duality of maintaining both schools of thought, and hence multiple analysis perspectives, was perhaps a "workable–and mutually respectful–a solution for our era," while acknowledging the dual theories might lead to progress but not without difficulty.[32] More recently, Russell, who also studied the merits of both schools, concluded the academic perspective perpetuated by the Kent School was more dangerous in terms of intelligence irrelevance than the Gates School. Given the changing national security needs due to the increased complexity from a more globally connected world in which threats come from nation-states and state-sponsored or independent trans-national actors, the job of intelligence to facilitate decision-making in the name of national security is more multi-faceted than perhaps either

Kent or Gates realized.[33] Having evaluated the definitions and the theories, a multi-dimensional model of politicization emerges. It considers many angles and consists of top-down, bottom-up, bi-directional, and inside-out facets of politicization as described in this paper.[34]

Table 1: Types of Politicization

Type	Description
Top-down	Consumer originated. As Betts contends, it is where "policymakers are seen to dictate intelligence conclusions."[35]
Bottom-up	Producer originated where "coloration of products by the unconscious biases of the working analysts who produce intelligence analyses"[36] occurs, and is the opposite of top down.
Bi-directional	A type in which IC managers who peer review staff analysts' intelligence products providing feedback to shape reports into finished intelligence products before disseminating finished intelligence to consumers.[37]
Inside-out	Originates from individuals working for the government who are not the traditional consumers and producers of intelligence. For example, the Office of Special Plans that was set up by the Department of Defense at the Pentagon in 2002 "whose purpose was to second guess" the civilian IC's Iraq Weapons of Mass Destruction intelligence estimate and to search for and find a link between Saddam Hussein and al Qaeda.[38]

Rovner points out different that facets of politicization are accomplished using direct and indirecmeans.[39] Direct means supply intelligence to please. Indirect means provide a source for actors to receive incentives or disincentives depending on the positions desired. For most of the discourse–definitions, classification, and categorization– there has been little discussion of sources of politicization from outside the IC. Politicization from these sources affects both producers' and consumers of intelligence. Consideration for outside-in politicization–the type that originates from outside government and the IC proper–such as from the media, academia, or private sector businesses is necessary for a well-rounded understanding of the effects that politicization has on intelligence.

Analysis of Politicization External to the Intelligence Community

Up until recently, the literature on politicization focused on traditional sources of politicization such as consumers and producers. Perhaps because intelligence producers primarily relied on information collected using classified methods and sources. However, with the rise of the information economy, both intelligence producers and consumers have instant access to world events. Public sentiment is also immediately available through open information sources such as online foreign and domestic newspapers and social media. All actors have easier access to professional and personal social networks via easy communication vehicles such as email, 24-hour news, and the increased use of social media feeds such as Twitter to promote issues to the top of public consciousness. In a democratic society, these outside stimuli expand horizons beyond those that traditionally informed intelligence. Three of the most prominent non-intelligence sources that influence and contribute to the politicization of intelligence are think tanks, the media, and lobbyists.

Think Tank Influences

According to Haass, "think tanks are independent institutions organized to conduct research and produce independent, policy relevant knowledge."[40] As of 2015, the number of think tank organizations swelled to over 6,840 worldwide, including over 1,835 in the United States alone.[41] The roots of today's think tanks date from the 1830s when Great Britain's Duke of Wellington founded the Royal United Services Institute for Defense and Securities Studies.[42]In the United States, in 1916, Andrew Carnegie founded the Institute for Government Research, which eventually merged with two other organizations to create the Brooking Institution in 1927.[43]

The goal of these organizations was to provide dedicated, professionally trained researchers to study public policy and defence issues to educate and inform policy makers, and the public, through a variety of research products and channels, such as the media. Abelson asserts there are four waves, or generations he defined by time periods in the evolution of think tanks.[44] First-generation think tanks were those that came into existence in the 1900s with the purpose of providing a forum for intellectual and scholarly debate of world issues. Second-generation think tanks evolved after World War II.

Third-generation think tanks took on an *advocacy* character, "combining policy research with aggressive marketing techniques," effectively becoming a central actor in policy debates while seeking to influence "both the direction and content of foreign policy" garnering the attention of policymakers and the public.[45] The fourth-generation think tanks are generally new or start-up companies. Abelson considers this generation *legacy-based* because prominent policymakers, influential scholars, and former presidential administration staffers fund think tanks in an effort to leave a lasting legacy in the public policy arena. As think tanks evolved, so did the underpinning organizational structure of these entities. McGann developed a topology to categorize think tanks to expose the relative independence these organizations purport.[46] The categories included political party affiliated, government affiliated, autonomous and independent, quasi-governmental, quasi-independent, and university affiliated.[47] Each category, named based on the affiliation or sources of funding, contains a number of organizations, many of which now have globally recognizable names. For example, The Hoover Institution is hosted by Stanford University, the Center for Defense Information is quasi-independent; and, the Congressional Research Service, dating from 1914, is a government organization.

Scholarly debates about the purpose of think tanks fall across a spectrum. On one end are self-serving, special-interest organizations promoting a political agenda at the expense of the public, while on the other end think tanks are influential and independent forces, advocating policy research by educating both policymakers and the public on foreign and domestic issues.[48] Those in the middle "sought either to maintain an image of neutrality and distance from policy makers or to finance themselves by producing contract research for the government."[49] Some observers consider think tanks *idea factories*. This is because policymakers, presidents, and Congress engage these quasi-academic institutions to develop agendas to guide political campaigns and runs for the White House with thousand-page documents, which become the basis for a newly elected president and his administration's agenda.[50] For example, Carter, Reagan, Clinton, George W. Bush, and Obama "relied heavily on scholars from think-tanks both during elections and in the transition period that followed."[51]

By way of example, the Heritage Foundation achieved notoriety in 1980 after President Reagan adopted its "'Mandate for Change,' as a blueprint for governing."[52] Singer asserted Reagan gave staffers the 1,100-page book that provided "2,000 recommendations, [of which] roughly 60 percent came to fruition–'which is why Mr. Reagan's tenure was 60 percent successful,' leading conservative William F. Buckley Jr. later quipped.'"[53] Singer also claimed the Center for American Progress (CAP) published a 700-plus page book called "'*Change for America: A Progressive Blueprint for the 44th President*' [that] helped the Obama administration to jump-start its agenda as it came to Washington in early 2009, and more than 50 staff members from CAP have since joined the administration."[54] The Heritage Foundation's release of its "*Blueprint for a New Administration: Priorities for the President*" is a recent example, which illustrates the influence think tanks seek to exert on policy-making.[55] The report provided recommendations and suggested actions for "15 cabinet-level departments and six key executive agencies", including IC elements such as the Office of the Director of National Intelligence.[56]

During wartime, think tanks concentrated on security policy topics using multiple methods for research and analysis that included consideration of alliances, political factors, and economic factors. Following World War II, for example, Brookings Institution was responsible, in part, for "the creation of the Federal government's budget process, civil service system, and Social Security; [and] the development of the Marshall plan."[57] Throughout the years, think tanks also provided guidance and advice to the military. For example, RAND developed many research products for the Army, Air Force, Office of the Secretary of Defense, and the IC.[58] In fact, a search of several think tanks' websites revealed research projects and reports on issues including national security, national defence, domestic policy, and intelligence.[59] The influence think tanks have on foreign and domestic policy issues ranging from intelligence to social security are hard to assess. Metrics are not readily available, funding sources are not always transparent, and measures such as the number of published reports, mentions in the media, or appearances on television are inaccurate at best, because of easy manipulation by marketing. Weidenbaum suggests, "citations in the Congressional Record and in congressional hearings and committee reports may be more indicative of policy impact" than page or document counts, and media mentions.[60] Although consensus on standard measures of think tank influence may not yet exist, the examples previously noted are indicators that think tanks influence the public policy process, including intelligence.[61] In addition, in a study Nicander conducted about the role of think tanks, "the most striking finding was that 94 percent of the respondents thought that think tanks [had] influence and an impact on decisions regarding US security policy."[62]

These organizations are "an important source of information to the media, the government, and to a host of private interest groups."[63] As such, academics and observers of the policy-making process must be aware of the influence think tanks may have on intelligence issues and pay attention to the bias and potential for the introduction of politicization into the public policy-making process because of the proximity and access between think tanks and policymakers. The marketing arms of think tanks will undoubtedly exploit proximity and access to policymakers to the media to influence popular opinion.

Media Influences

For actors seeking to politicize intelligence, the press and other news media outlets had been the traditional communication channels used for information dissemination. As far back as World War II, media outlets, such as the BBC, were not only a source of intelligence, but also a vehicle for politicization, spreading the word policymakers desired the public to hear about war progress.[64] In the United States, prior to 1980, Americans learned of political events and policy through print media or via traditional over-the-air broadcast television networks such as ABC's, CBS's, and NBC's nightly news programs.

The stories broadcast by these network stations were tightly controlled and worded such that the content and the message were politically correct. More importantly, the stories were mostly consistent with the sitting presidential administration's public policy.[65] All this changed when, in 1980, Cable News Network, an all-news channel burst onto the scene, broadcasting news 24 hours a day. Since then, politicized reporting of public policy was thrust onto audiences as pundits and commentators–whether conservative or liberal–opined and changed the course of the American political landscape. In addition to traditional sources such as print media, broadcast, and cable news, the information technology revolution, beginning in the 1990s, also became an outlet for politicized intelligence. According to Denécé, "about 10 million Web pages are created every day, and the total volume doubles every four years."[66] As the frequency and quantity of media reports increase, many sources and channels provide commentary and assessments, which appear more like opinion than the product of credible research or analysis.

Intelligence also faces new challenges from new sources such as social media, an increasingly popular and easily accessible information channel available to anyone with Internet access, including policymakers. With the ability to leverage real-time reports from a variety of social media networks, policymakers have instant access to information. The result has been news media "rais[ing] questions about its [the IC's] ability to provide policymakers anything useful beyond what the new media provide."[67] Further complicating matters, social media companies such as Twitter, Facebook Instagram, Reddit, YouTube, LinkedIn, SnapChat, and Pinterest provide channels where readily accessible information is available to policymakers who are becoming "less dependent on intelligence agencies for updates on current events."[68] For the IC, this is a problem because the window of opportunity in which policy makers consume information is shrinking, leaving little time for the IC to perform its value-added analyses and produce judgments. The volume of available information is an opportunity for policymakers to cherry pick information to support or refute a political position, and the information from which the policymaker can select is virtually unlimited. This increases pressure on the IC to add value to the volume of open source information, and the increased pressure may push some IC leaders to manipulate intelligence to appease policymakers to curb skepticism about the value of the IC. According to Rovner, "in addition, they [IC leaders] might also become willing to deliver intelligence to please to stay in the good graces of policymakers. Politicization will be more likely in this scenario."[69]

Media outlets are a challenge for the IC, which must maintain secrecy while simultaneously educating the public and policymakers about national security threats. With the seemingly unlimited amounts of information available, and the number of professional and armchair journalists, so-called news and information pertaining to national security found on traditional media outlets and social media channels may be misleading, biased, wrong, fake, or intentionally politicized to appeal to the hearts and minds of the public that any actor may strive to influence. For intelligence, "citizens use blogs, journal comments, radio, and TV question and answer (Q&A) sessions to inquire about, comment on, discuss debate, criticize, or favour intelligence issues and developments."[70] This type of communication not only decreases the proximity to policymakers but also influences their thinking. It also leads to "'opinion journalism,' whereby journalists provide their personal opinions, sometimes highly biased and speculative, on a specific issue rather than reporting the facts."[71] Before new media burst onto the scene, the IC had time to vet open source information and fuse it with secret information to differentiate the signals from within the noise, rendering intelligence policymakers used for decision-making.

Today, the politicization of intelligence through traditional media outlets and social media sources is as simple as influencing political leaders through blog posts, Twitter feeds, and YouTube videos that broadcast instantly and "have a major impact on political decision-makers and the public sphere."[72] The relationship intelligence has with the media is "tense but symbiotic" because "the intelligence sector needs media to tell some of its story, while the media need intelligence to get an exciting story."[73] Although Johnson's assessment of intelligence failures and scandals was not about the politicization of intelligence, he correlated a relationship between media coverage and intelligence oversight levels.[74] He explained the influence the media puts on policymakers when he asserted, "extensive media coverage of intelligence seemed to stir interest in a topic amongst executive and legislative officials."[75] In addition, other intelligence practitioners, academicians, and government and journalism experts concur, intelligence and the media have a complex bi-directional relationship.[76] The same holds true for intelligence lobbyists and policymakers.

Lobbyist Influences

According to the Center for Responsive Politics (CRP), an independent, non-partisan, non-profit organization that monitors the money spent on US politics and its effect on public policy, influence is the primary purpose for money flowing through the US political system. The CRP asserts, "corporations and industry groups, labour unions, single-issue organizations– together, they spend billions of dollars each year to gain access to decision-makers in government, all in an attempt to influence their thinking," and their votes.[77] Lobbyists influence public policy across a wide spectrum of topics. Section 6 of the Lobbying Disclosure Act of 1995 (LDA), requires lobbyists to register with the Secretary of the Senate and the Clerk of the House of Representatives based on certain spending thresholds (set for four-year periods) as determined by the Secretary of Labor. According to the LDA Guidance website, "after January 01, 2013, an organization employing in-house lobbyists is exempt from registration if its total expenses for lobbying activities does not exceed and is not expected to exceed $12,500 during a quarterly period," otherwise the lobbyist must register.[78] In addition, the LDA requires active lobbyists to file quarterly activity reports.[79] Information from the filed reports is freely available to the public. To make analysis of lobbying efforts more transparent and easier for the public to understand, the CRP compiles the data and makes it available on its website for anyone to search. For example, as of October 28, 2016, 10,882 lobbyists spent $2.63 billion to influence policymakers' decisions.[80]

In particular, lobbyists focused most of their efforts on both houses of Congress responsible for yearly budget appropriations amongst other items. Since intelligence as a policy issue falls under the purview of several IC elements, lobbyists also spent time courting policymakers and staffers in those respective organizations. In addition, lobbyists also rallied around intelligence as an issue and found a number of opportunities in which to exert influence. In 2016, businesses lobbied Congress for intelligence spending so those businesses could compete for services contracts such as for computer system implementation and integration or advocate agendas related to intelligence issues such as freedom of speech, surveillance, cybersecurity, encryption, and sharing of cybersecurity information. For example, according to the CRP, companies lobbying for intelligence specific issues included Microsoft Corporation, Facebook Inc., Intel Corp, SoftBank Corp., Citigroup Inc., Consumer Technology Association, Twitter, Verizon Communications, Yahoo! Inc., and Zebra Technologies, amongst others.[82] In addition, the CRP data show lobbyists reaching out to policymakers on intelligence issues such as the FY 17 Intelligence Authorization Act, Congressional bills such as H.R. 1037, Global Free Internet Act of 2015, H.R. 1466, The Surveillance State Repeal Act, S. 754, Cybersecurity Information Sharing Act, cybersecurity and encryption technology, and reform issues pertaining to the Electronic Computer Privacy Act.[83]

McKay conducted a study and tested common assumptions about spending related to policymaking by combining new and existing information from a prior survey of lobbyists, which according to her, was "the largest sample of lobbyists ever interviewed by scholars–the Washington Representatives study by Heinz et al. (1990, 1993)."[84] Although McKay's analysis was not specific to intelligence, "the data suggest[ed] that money alone does not buy success, but how it is spent may matter."[85] Whether lobbyists are successful in their endeavours specific to intelligence related matters is an outstanding question worthy of further research. The United States IC, administration officials, and observers of the policy-making process should not only be aware of the vast market related to intelligence lobbying, but also how these lobbyists are proactively guarding against possible politicization attempts or actively pursuing one side of an issue. Conclusion Ransom observed politicization is tied to behaviors such that when "consensus wars" existed, politicization is absent because of "policy neutrality."[86] Yet, when political actors' opinions differ, "the intelligence system tends to become politicized."[87] Handel's first paradox states, "on the one hand,

it is the democracy and the struggle for influence over public opinion that increases politicization of intelligence, but on the other hand it is democratic pressure that contains and limits that politicization."[88] In addition, Handel recognized controlling and opposing political parties might become so embroiled in debates that one way to force resolution was to "market intelligence conclusions...[by taking] them to the media, seeking public opinion in support of policy."[89] Handel was also one of the first scholars to point out "yet another intelligence paradox; namely, that the best professionals are the amateurs."[90] Perhaps he recognized the potential of politicization by non-intelligence actors. Politicization is as old as the intelligence business.[91] It is a continuum and, depending on its use, can have many definitions. Definitions create subtleties and nuances that in certain cases may render politicization a normal part of the political process. Betts concluded "to some degree [politicization is] inevitable, and, in some forms, necessary" and asserted the "paradox...is that the real world of policy makes politicization in one form the worst thing that can happen to intelligence, but, in another form, the best."[92] Politicization is similar to the saying about terrorism, where one man's terrorist is another's freedom fighter. It "exists in the eye of the beholder, and more specifically, the beholder whose political frame of reference differs from the implications of the analysis beheld."[93]

Think tanks are a necessary part of the policy-making process because these organizations augment the capabilities of both the producers and consumers of intelligence. At the same time, all parties must recognize the potential influence and biases these organizations can introduce into the intelligence process. Traditional media had a carefully curated and influential effect on the policy-making process. That changed with the proliferation of communication sources in the Internet age. Instant access to information that is always flowing may influence policy-makers' thinking without the benefit of the value-added and synthesized analyses producers provide to the intelligence process. Lobbyists influence public policy across a wide spectrum of topics. Both producers and consumers of intelligence should become more familiar with the intelligence-related topics and the vast sums of money spent to guard against politicization.

Each of these outside-in aspects of politicization has the potential to affect policy-making and the strategic intelligence process. Intelligence will never be completely free from politics or from the effects of politicization. Both the IC and policymakers must realize in the Information Age, debates will naturally occur in the public's view and are increasingly likely to include a more engaged, but possibly more divided, public due to increased virtual proximity afforded by social media. The secrecy that intelligence once enjoyed has transformed into a more open dialogue about national security. The proximity of the public to policymakers and intelligence leaders is closer than before, if only virtually, enabled by technology. The knowledge that was once difficult to obtain is now more accessible, causing the IC to work harder to add value and compete for policymakers' attention. Unfortunately, debate that is more public will increase opportunities for politicization. Hence, all parties must be aware of the outside-in aspect of politicization and its effects on policy-making and the strategic intelligence process.

Journal of Strategic Security Volume 10 Number 2 Article 6. The Intelligence Dilemma: Proximity and Politicization–Analysis of External Influences. Beth Eisenfeld Henley-Putnam University, beisenfeld@ymail.com. Follow this and additional works at: https://digitalcommons.usf.edu/jsspp. 77-96 Recommended Citation. Eisenfeld, Beth. "The Intelligence Dilemma: Proximity and Politicization–Analysis of External Influences." Journal of Strategic Security 10, no. 2 (2017) : 77-96. DOI:http://doi. org/10.5038/1944-0472.10.2.1583.Available,at: https://digital commons.usf. edu/jss/vol10/iss2/6. This Article is brought to you for free and open access by the Open Access Journals at Digital Commons @ University of South Florida. It has been accepted for inclusion in Journal of Strategic Security by an authorized editor of Digital Commons @ University of South Florida. For more information, please contact digitalcommons@usf.edu. The Journal of Strategic Security (JSS) is a double-blind peer-reviewed professional journal published quarterly by Henley-Putnam School of Strategic Security with support from the University of South Florida Libraries. The Journal provides a multi-disciplinary forum for scholarship and discussion of strategic security issues drawing from the fields of global security, international relations, intelligence, terrorism and counterterrorism studies, among others. JSS is indexed in SCOPUS, the Directory of Open Access Journals, several EBSCOhost databases, EuroPub, and ProQuest databases. Aims & Scope: The Journal of Strategic Security (JSS) is a double-blind peer-reviewed professional journal published quarterly by Henley-Putnam School of Strategic Security with support from the University of South Florida Libraries. The Journal provides a multi-

disciplinary forum for scholarship and discussion of strategic security issues drawing from the fields of global security, international relations, intelligence, terrorism and counterterrorism studies, among others. JSS is indexed in SCOPUS, the Directory of Open Access Journals, and several EBSCOhost and ProQuest databases. The Journal encourages diversity in theoretical foundations, research methods, and approaches. Quantitative and qualitative studies, for example, each offer valuable contributions to the field of strategic security. Academic disciplines of international relations, political science, psychology, sociology, anthropology, criminology, economics, and history are welcome, as are the applied scholarly fields of security studies, strategic studies, and intelligence studies. JSS emphasizes contemporary security issues, so manuscripts focused on great power competition are of particular interest. Topics such as global security threats, multi-domain warfare, artificial intelligence, machine learning, nuclear warfare, space and counterspace threats, intelligence, inter-state armed conflict, military strategy, terrorism and counterterrorism, jihadist ideology, genocide, global policing, insurgencies, irregular warfare, radicalization, risk management, threat assessment, and violent extremism are well suited to the Journal, as are contributions on security threats arising from transnational crime, global climate change, failing states, energy and environmental security issues, and health crises such as pandemics. The Journal of Strategic Security publishes review articles, original empirical research, and analytic/conceptual works that contribute to a better understanding of security-related threats and ways to prevent or mitigate their impact. Each article should analyze and include implications for policy and practice. This journal's content is licensed under a Creative Commons Attribution-NonCommercial 4.0 International License. As a service to the research community, the USF Tampa Library's commitment to true open-access to scholarly information extends to authors. This means that there are no article or submission charges for Journal of Strategic Security. Content is archived in LOCKSS and Portico, and backed up in the bepress Digital Commons system.

Chapter 7

The Social Ties that Bind: Unravelling the Role of Trust in International Intelligence Cooperation

*Pepijn Tuinier, Thijs Brocades Zaalberg
and Sebastiaan Rietjens*

Abstract

International cooperation between intelligence services poses a dilemma. It is an important tool in countering today's complex transnational threats, but at the same time, cooperation is a risky business. Intelligence services can never be sure that a partner will reciprocate in kind. Scholars and practitioners often identify trust as one of the foremost conditions to overcome this dilemma. Yet the notion of trust is seldom conceptualized in these rational-calculative explanations. Contrary to the common view that intelligence services are exceptional in their opportunism and rivalry, social relations and trustworthiness perceptions provide a more dominant explanation for the level of cooperation between intelligence partners than is often assumed by scholars and practitioners. Known reputations, recognized professional standards, and shared traits socially bind intelligence professionals to their community of practice, enabling them to bridge divides like nationality and even conflicting interests. Intelligence services resemble many other organizations in the public and private domains, requiring a de-exceptionalization of their international cooperation.

Often characterized as sinister, the realm of intelligence is instead perhaps the most human of all aspects of government and consists to a large degree of personal relationships. The universal currency is trust.[1]

Scholarly interest in the mechanism of international intelligence cooperation continues to increase.[2] Ever since the start of this increasing interest, in the wake of 11 September 2001, scholars have tended to approach it from a perspective of competition and rivalry. They suggest that cooperation is counter intuitive to intelligence services that only cooperate out of necessity when they feel unable to counter a threat or lack information and resources. When examining the conditions under which international intelligence cooperation occurs, many scholars stress the difficulties in this field. They focus on Machiavellian constructs such as power and hierarchy or highlight functional restraints on cooperative behaviour.[3] Recently, a small group of scholars has started to advocate for a more sociological perspective. They take a relational approach, some even suggesting that intelligence services come close to an international brotherhood.[4] In many of these publications, trust is mentioned as an important facilitator for cooperation. As stated in the opening quote, Richard Aldrich even sees trust as the universal currency in the intelligence domain. In a similar fashion, former director of the Government Communications Headquarters (GCHQ), Sir David Omand, recognizes mutual trustworthiness "as the most valuable attribute of any successful [intelligence] partnership."[5]

Despite its importance, we know little about the underlying conditions shaping trust among services and intelligence personnel. Trust has hardly been conceptualized in relation to intelligence studies.[6] This runs the risk of the debate on international intelligence cooperation getting stuck in oversimplified dichotomies like "friends or foes," "collaboration or competition," and "trust or distrust." This article argues that these dichotomies contribute to the mystification of the intelligence profession, but are not very helpful in understanding the nuanced workings of international intelligence cooperation. Without conceptualization, the notion of trust only becomes a clincher rather than an analytical tool. This article critically examines trust and the underlying perceptions of trustworthiness, and systematically unravels their role in international intelligence cooperation. It first outlines international intelligence cooperation and focuses on the dilemma of cooperation: intelligence organizations often cooperate without being able to rationally calculate their outcome or control the risks involved. Subsequently, the article introduces the role of trust in dealing with this dilemma. Finally, it conceptualizes trust in international intelligence cooperation, identifying the importance of perceptions of trustworthiness and its three conditions: organizational image, organizational culture, and organizational identity. The article demystifies international intelligence cooperation, showing that the role

114

of social relations and trustworthiness perceptions in this activity is much more common than practitioners and scholars have often advocated so far.

Dilemma of international intelligence cooperation

The Reciprocal Benefits of Cooperation

Cooperation, in this article defined as "working together for mutual benefit," is commonplace between organizations, in business, and in public administration, as well as in intelligence. It involves a form of collective action; two or more actors that interact or coordinate their actions. Cooperation between organizations helps them achieve "promotively interdependent goals."[7] Goals that, once reached by one of the participants, have beneficial effects for all. International intelligence cooperation can take many forms. Although most publications on intelligence cooperation focus on information sharing, it can encompass exchanges (sharing), coordination, and coproduction (collaboration); can occur in all phases of the intelligence process; and includes supportive functionalities such as liaison. It covers both formal and informal arrangements in bilateral and multilateral settings.[8] Moreover, it can include knowledge circulation, meant for professional advancement. Mai'a Davis Cross uses such a perspective when examining whether or not the European Union Intelligence and Situation Centre (EU INTCEN) can be seen as an epistemic community, ultimately arriving at the conclusion that this is not the case.[9]

In intelligence, the appeal of international cooperation is relatively straightforward; two can simply achieve more than one. Cooperation is rewarding, as it increases resources and adds valuable expertise. It is widely suggested that cooperation is an essential capability for intelligence services, helping them to face a highly complex and demanding security environment.[10] On the one hand, the current threats are increasingly transnational and non-state. Instead of being adversaries, national services now often win or lose together. On the other hand, notwithstanding their competitive nature, intelligence services need each other to fulfill their national tasking. Alone, not even the joint effort of all U.S. intelligence services, presumably one of the largest and technically most advanced intelligence communities in the world, will be sufficient to deal with the diverse and interdependent range of security threats facing them. For this reason, when confronted with the need for regional intelligence on the Afghan–Pakistan border in their War on Terror, the Central Intelligence Agency (CIA) cooperated with a variety of partners. It represented "a cost-effective way of increasing Human Intelligence (HUMINT) capabilities" by trading information from the technical collection for "local expertise and resources, expensive to acquire and difficult to maintain."[11]

Cooperation is distinct from pure altruism. Whereas both concepts encompass a form of helping others, altruistic behaviour usually implies doing so regardless, or in spite of, the cost this action befalls oneself.[12] Cooperation, although it inflicts costs, ultimately refers to the achievement of a shared aim. Although there is some evidence that people tend to be altruistic by nature, unconditional altruism is quite rare between organizations or states. This does not mean that altruistic features are absent in international intelligence cooperation. Especially in long-standing arrangements between organizations with a history of social interaction, "feelings of interpersonal attachment, sympathy or relational commitment" may very well influence the establishment or maintenance of cooperative behavior.[13] For example, Hager Ben Jaffel's work on Counter-Terrorism and Extremism Liaison Officers in Anglo-French cooperation shows that intelligence liaison officers can be a successful personal bridge between different systems and uphold perceptions of trustworthiness.[14] Nevertheless, on closer inspection, many apparently altruistic forms of exchange are in fact based on expected benefits in the future.[15]

Expectations of reciprocity are at the heart of international intelligence cooperation. Intelligence services will behave cooperatively based on the expectation that their partner will do the same in return. This cooperative behaviour appears easy when it confers direct benefits on all participants in achieving a common goal. The well-known adage of Quid pro Quo (QPQ) in international intelligence cooperation represents this simple, mutually beneficial exchange. Yet when the contributions of both partners differ in quality or quantity, or when a return is not (immediately) guaranteed, this mutualism is asymmetric and imposes relative costs on one of the partners. Many, if not most, forms of international intelligence cooperation constitute postponed and asymmetric arrangements. These arrangements are based not on direct QPQ, but on the more indirect Do ut Des principle; to give with the expectation of receiving a return in the future.[16] Conferring a benefit to another with an expectation of, but not an immediate, return is prominent in cooperation.[17] This can be qualified as a risky business.

The risk of not being rewarded

A much-quoted adage on international intelligence cooperation is that intelligence services have no friends.[18] In this view, intelligence is a harsh and goal-driven activity aimed at a competitive advantage for national decision-makers. As a result, intelligence services constantly strive to outsmart their opponents. In many cases, intelligence services are even perceived as rivals.[19] Instead of only "wanting to be first," actions are aimed at damaging the rival itself.[20] This striving was clearly evident in the fierce (counter) intelligence battle fought between opposing Eastern and Western services during the Cold War. Yet in a weaker form, it can be seen elsewhere as well. It is common knowledge that intelligence services of relatively close allies also spy on each other for strategic and economic purposes. For example, French and American intelligence services are known to have been spying on each other's economic activities for years.[21]

Competition between services seems to be at odds with cooperation. Seeking a competitive advantage, intelligence services are inclined to pursue relative gain for themselves rather than absolute gain for all. Information and knowledge are seen as commodities and treated as property; hard to acquire, precious to poses, and valuable to trade.[22] As a consequence, secrecy, autonomy, and "a culture of wanting to be first" are important obstacles to intelligence cooperation.[23] Moreover, given the secrecy in methods, the uncertainty of results, and the difficulties in assessing the objective value of information, one can seldomly be sure that a partner will be returning the favour in kind. Defection is hard to detect, especially in the case of information sharing and might be committed totally unwillingly. For example, the way fabricated single-source intelligence on the alleged Iraqi biological weapons program found its way through German services to uncritical U.S. decisionmakers in the period 2000 to 2002 shows the serious vulnerability attached to international intelligence cooperation, even in dealing with reliable partners.[24]

Following the logic of competitive advantage, international intelligence cooperation is a beneficial activity that increases capacity. However, it also seems uninviting, as defection by partners is tempting and relatively easy. Intelligence services, therefore, appear to have no choice other than to discount a partner's deliberations and to each pursue their own short-term selfish gain. Some even claim that intelligence services are characterized by a particular organizational culture of distrust, in which "risks of sharing information [...], by any rational calculation, far outweigh the potential benefits." [25] The larger the number of partners included in an arrangement, the greater is that risk. As benefits of cooperation are indivisible and nonexcludable, sharing with many, by definition, means putting aside ambitions of exclusive gain.[26] In addition, more participants mean that it becomes harder to assess the origin of information and make it increasingly difficult to monitor whether or not everyone is contributing. Free-riding, behaving selfishly by parasitizing on the cooperative efforts of others, is a strong temptation in multilateral intelligence cooperation.[27] Moreover, the risk of defection is multiplied in these larger groups. The chances of a group member putting to use the intelligence in a manner not agreed on— or even leaking it to a third, nonparticipating, partner—seem omnipresent.

Intelligence services, trying to minimize risk and maximize their own cost–benefit ratio, tend to shirk full collaboration (e.g., by only sharing second-class information).[28] This will prevent them from reaping the full potential benefits of cooperation. Unwillingly, and apparently, unavoidably, they reach a suboptimal equilibrium.[29] This cooperation dilemma is by no means exclusive to the field of intelligence.[30] Similar problems have been noted in many fields, between organizations as diverse as American, Japanese, and Korean car producers; between Polish tourist firms; and among Italian healthcare institutions.[31] Despite their differences, these organizations share a situation of interdependence where a noncooperative course of action is tempting (as it yields superior, often short-term, outcomes), but if all pursue this noncooperative course of action, all are worse off than if they had cooperated fully. From these cases it becomes clear that organizations can circumvent these difficulties, managing to cooperate despite a degree of conflicting interest, being competitive and cooperative at the same time.

Overcoming the Dilemma

Trying to Reduce the Risk: Rational Calculations and Control

Scholars struggle to understand the conditions under which cooperation is chosen as the preferred strategy. After all, it "entails the risk that others will not reciprocate, leaving the co-operator in the unrewarding position of being exploited."[32] Two distinct agent-based models, or operating mechanisms, can be discerned for achieving cooperative behavior; the mechanism of rational calculations and the mechanism of social relations.[33] Both mechanisms are ways to deal with uncertainty about a partner's behaviour. The first mechanism sticks closely to the dominant cost–benefit approach in intelligence. From this perspective, the most obvious way to increase cooperation is to ensure a partner's returns. That is, to decrease the risk that a partner will defect unexpectedly. In this mechanism, rational calculations can lead to cooperative behaviour when they are sufficiently reliable. The degree of control exercised over the exchange empowers this mechanism. Introducing control as insurance against defection, for example by using contractual safeguards, aims to bring together expectations of reciprocity and actual outcomes.

Control as a condition for cooperative behaviour under circumstances of distrust is a well-known concept in publications on international intelligence cooperation. Especially the concept of hierarchy, introduced by James Igoe Walsh, often figures as a condition for cooperative behaviour between intelligence services. A strong hierarchy between partners can ensure partner compliance as one service has extensive power over the other. It allows the dominant partner to directly manage and oversee the other's intelligence process.[34] As these minor partners are forced into obedience of the wishes of the principal, the chances of them violating expectations are minimized. These expectations can concern the expected outcomes, or include the way these outcomes are reached. The deferential position of the Ministry for State Security (STASI) in relation to the State Committee for Security (KGB) during the Cold War is an example of such a strong hierarchy, part of an "imperial intelligence system centered on the KGB Centre in Moscow." At some point, the first was seen to serve the interests of the latter completely, even keeping a check on their own government for them.[35] Nevertheless, in international intelligence cooperation, these absolute one-sided relations are rare. The junior partner in many cases is able to hold on or gain a degree of self-determination, lessening the control of the principal partner.[36] For example, whereas the former Dutch Domestic Security Service BVD (Binnenlandse Veiligheidsdienst) was seen to accept considerable financial backing from the CIA during the early years of the Cold War, the first was never a "timid partner" in that relationship, sometimes even flatly turning down requests or proposals by the latter.[37] Likewise, although the United States appeared to have bought-in profound influence in the Ethiopian intelligence service in the period from 2000 to 2010, the latter managed to exercise substantial leverage in that asymmetric relationship.[38]

However inviting as the mechanism of rational calculations and control is for the competitive world of intelligence, it has practical flaws with regard to cooperation. First, the presumption of rationality implies that intelligence services are able to fully grasp the indirect and asymmetric cost and benefits of cooperation and adjust their behaviour accordingly. Yet, in practice, this rationality is limited. Social interaction is seen to be affected by incomplete information, cognitive biases, imperfect memory, and an inability to fully analyze the complexities of the environment.[39] Subsequently, the calculation is virtually impossible and acting on its presumption counterproductive. Constantly "asking how well you are doing compared to others is not a good standard [for behaviour] unless your goal is to destroy the other player."[40] Cooperative arrangements need room for uncertainty, interpretation, and error. "Being nice," at least applying a "somewhat forgiving" tit-for-tat-strategy, greatly helps successful and sustained cooperation.[41] Second, seeking control always comes at a cost for the intelligence services involved. To control an exchange relation, it is necessary to dedicate valuable resources in obtaining information not only on targets but on partners as well. Distinguishing among partners and remembering which ones have delivered in the past requires costly and detailed bookkeeping about one's partners, for example, by External Relations branches.[42] Moreover, getting close to a partner in cooperation requires costly counterintelligence and security measures.[43] These measures have to prevent a partner exploiting his privileged position beyond the scope of the agreement or even providing dubious intelligence. In practice, it is hard to imagine a situation in which an intelligence service can have total control over a partner and the environment in which the cooperation takes place. It appears that rational calculations and control alone are insufficient as an explanation for efficient or sustained intelligence cooperation.

Accepting Vulnerability: Social Relations and Trust

Models of rational calculations do not perform well in situations of greater complexity where their predictions are "repeatedly shown to be empirically false."[44] In these situations, uncertainty is a key characteristic of the interaction and exchange. As a consequence, cooperative behaviour always involves a degree of vulnerability.[45] Intelligence systems, with their many participants interacting interdependently at different levels and in different settings simultaneously, qualify as situations of greater complexity.[46] Based on rational calculative considerations alone, international intelligence cooperation is thus fragile and can even be seen to "drive up distrust and defensive positioning, even among relatively close allies."[47] Rationality is unable to mitigate the risk of being (unpleasantly) surprised. To explain durable cooperation between intelligence services, a more resilient mechanism is needed. One that enables participants in the cooperation to expect reciprocity and "rely on each other, despite the presence of uncertainty and risks of partner opportunism and misappropriation."[48] Social relations provide such a mechanism.

Like rational calculations, the mechanism of social relations can invoke cooperative behavior. It helps partners achieve reasonable expectations about each other. Yet social relations do so on an entirely different basis.

They can lead to cooperative behavior when partners accept to be vulnerable in their dealings with a specific counterpart or exchange network. This mechanism thus operates in a far simpler and more efficient way than with rational calculations, as it dodges the need for hard-to-achieve rational prediction and costly objective control measures like monitoring and sanctioning. Social relations are embedded in subjective beliefs and perceptions that enable quick interpretation of a situation and guide the appropriate behaviour.[49] Nevertheless, these beliefs and perceptions are more than mere emotion or intuition. They are an "active sediment of [the] past that functions within [the] present" and reflect best practices for fulfilling expectations of reciprocity.[50] In many, if not most, cases international intelligence cooperation does not occur in a vacuum, nor is it a one-shot "all-or-nothing" exchange. Intelligence services interact not once, but frequently, and they do so in various settings and arrangements. These arrangements open new possibilities for cooperative behaviour. Repeated interaction not only increases the number of chances for reciprocity, it enables a relation, taking a partner's character and behaviour into account when deciding how to act. Studying the guiding beliefs and perceptions of exchange partners or the interdependent network can help explain how cooperation works and develops in these settings.[51]

Trust is generally accepted as a central belief conditioning social relations in cooperation.[52] Interorganizational relations rely heavily on trust, especially in diffuse multilateral settings and among organizations operating in secret.[53] On a micro level, repeated interaction can lead to the development of particular trust between people. This can serve as a "ratchet" for cooperative behaviour. On a macro level, repeated patterns of successful behaviour can in turn lead to a more generalized form of trust between groups, "slow to emerge and decay."[54] The existence or absence of trust is one of the overarching themes in the literature on international intelligence cooperation. Numerous articles name trust as one of the most important determinants of cooperative behaviour in the competitive world of intelligence.[55] They point at the importance of "trust in, and respect for, other agencies" as foremost when deciding on the extent of intelligence-sharing arrangements.[56] Peter Gill, for example, finds mutual trust the premise on which "the whole structure of intelligence cooperation is built."[57] Most take a pessimistic stance though, emphasizing the limitations on cooperation caused by a lack of trust between the partners.[58] Moreover, despite its importance, the notion of trust remains a very murky concept within studies on international intelligence cooperation. Notwithstanding some notable exceptions like Sarah-Myriam Martin-Brûlé's recent article on the role of trust in UN intelligence, it has seldomly been defined or conceptualized.[59]

Trust in international intelligence cooperation

Trust between intelligence services is a form of interorganizational trust, a much-studied concept in sociology and interorganizational relations. It is commonly defined as the extent to which members of one organization hold a collective trust orientation toward one another.[60] Based on various authoritative publications; this study defines trust as "the intentional and behavioural suspension of vulnerability by a trustor on the basis of positive expectations of a trustee."[61] It is seen to hold three dimensions. First, it involves a decision to act in relational exchange. Without the possibility of action, the trust would degrade to mere hope. Second, it involves a degree of vulnerability. Trust enables actors to suspend their vulnerability, not because they are not aware of being vulnerable, but because they believe that their partner will not (overly) exploit this situation. It involves the trustors' belief that their trustees have a responsibility, or even an obligation, to fulfill the trust placed in them. Third, the good reasons underlying these beliefs are based on subjective perceptions of a partner's trustworthiness. Contrary to predictive confidence, trust is not about knowing but about interpreting.[62] It requires a "leap of faith."

From a sociological perspective, the perception of trustworthiness is fundamental for trust and, therefore the key determinant of cooperative behavior.[63] Trust is nothing in or by itself. Whereas many psychological studies at the interpersonal level focus on the individual trust propensity, at the organizational level trust is not considered "trait-like" or unidirectional.[64] In cooperation, trust is based on the belief that a partner will do the right thing. It is relational and reciprocal, requiring interaction with the partner to evolve. Although trustors can begin trusting relationships by a willingness to be vulnerable, it is "trustees [who] determine the success of these relationships."[65] Moreover, trust works in two ways. The roles of trustor and trustee rest simultaneously with both partners. For a positive expectation of behaviour, partners both look at each other's characteristics and interpret why the other would be worthy of trust. This can be the case in particular relations between people or organizations but can concern the trustworthiness of the network as a whole as well. Reciprocal trustworthiness creates a complex system of interdependent relations where "your own behaviour is echoed back to you."[66]

Trustworthiness is spelled out by scholars in a variety of ways. Despite their differences, most include three related conditions for partner trustworthiness.[67] First, partners need to perceive each other as being capable of fulfilling the expectations placed on them. Knowing a partner's competencies is paramount in this, both in achieving operational results and in building and sustaining effective cooperative ties. This is largely cognitive. Second, partners need to perceive each other as possessing integrity. Recognizing a partner's standards as acceptable is regarded as a strong indication that their behaviour will not include unpleasant surprises and that their frame of reference will be understandable. This is largely normative. Third, partners need to perceive each other as benevolent. Having similar attitudes is seen to produce a form of goodwill toward a partner, caring for his welfare and encapsulating his interests. This is mainly effective. From a sociological perspective, the conditions for trustworthiness are "larger than the participants who are in them," based on perceptions of what a collective must be able to achieve, how this ought to be done, and what it stands for.[68] These conditions are often studied in terms of perceived organizational image, culture, and identity. They are seen to work separately, as well as in conjunction, to determine the intensity of cooperation based on trusted relations.[69] From this perspective, intelligence services work together best when they know, recognize, and value each other.

Organizational Image

The first condition for trustworthiness is for partners to hold a favourable image of the other. A durable organizational image in a network, or reputation, is the result of an aggregated process that evolves over time. It refers to a partner's ability to accomplish the specific task at hand effectively, and in cooperation with others.[70] Valuations of numerous individual encounters, on different levels and in varying circumstances, lead to more generalized views about the partner organization as a whole and are transmitted to others. In intelligence, reputation can influence the level of cooperation. Signals intelligence (SIGINT) cooperation between Axis partners Germany and Finland flourished up to and during World War II, as the Germans held Finnish codebreakers at large in high esteem. At the same time, cooperation with the Italians was limited as German officers held the Italians in contempt and qualified them as "temperamentally unfit for serious crypto analysis."[71] More recently, the United Nations (UN)'s reputation for poor information security and lacking professional intelligence standards was found to discourage partners from sharing information, like in the case of the UN Mission to Mali.[72]

A positive reputation is based on previous successful cooperation and helps future cooperation. It is useful, as it attracts other partners or helps to maintain ties with current ones. Organizations with good reputations in a network are seen to be committed to cooperation and unlikely to behave opportunistically, as the latter would destroy their advantageous position. Moreover, as the use of their good reputation is dependent on the network, they tend not only to uphold trustworthiness themselves but also between themselves and others.[73] The effect of reputations on continued cooperation, both on an organizational and a personal level, can be seen in many professional fields where uncertainty and complexity are common, and where there is some competition, like in the case of expertise-sharing networks between firms.[74] It is also present in those cases where (law) enforcement is absent among a variety of anonymous actors with doubtful intentions, like in the dubious example of the crypto market for illegal drugs.[75]

Knowing a partner's reputation requires a basic familiarity with their "professional skills, competencies, and characteristics.[76] Direct feedback, either from own experience or in a network, can foster perceptions of trustworthiness between professionals as they provide a proof of ability that is otherwise difficult to observe."[77] For example, in the case of multilateral intelligence cooperation like in NATO, "some good-natured naming and shaming" can counter free-riding behaviour.[78] Likewise, intelligence services can achieve or maintain a good reputation by directly communicating themselves about their ability to cooperate successfully. A possible case of such direct signaling could be seen in 2018 when the Netherlands Defence Intelligence and Security Service openly communicated about a successful counterintelligence operation against Russian spies allegedly trying to breach into the systems of the Organisation for the Prohibition of Chemical Weapons. This rare public statement of operational results by an intelligence service was made alongside British and American partners, making it clear that international cooperation had been crucial for the result achieved. Put this way, it signaled not only their competence in counterintelligence to a broad audience but made visible their normally unobservable traits as a trustworthy ally as well.[79] Yet these direct forms of communication are rare and, in many cases, direct experience is simply lacking. In these cases, a judgment of ability needs to be based on reputational information that is transmitted indirectly. Jonathan N. Brown and Alex Farrington find that, in international intelligence cooperation, gossip reinforces relational bonds.[80]

Functional divides between services can be the cause of insufficient familiarity, conflicting principles, and incompatible traits, setting the stage for lacking mutual understanding, hampering interoperability, controversy, conflict, and sometimes even rivalries.[81] Yet, at the same time, the intelligence field provides ample opportunity for partners to get familiarized and exchange reputational information. Its patchwork of connections holds numerous interactions in which members of intelligence services come together, in various settings and at various levels. Interagency personal contacts are fostered in collective education, regular meetings, and standardized communications. Together, they create a diverse network of relations between key officials that can be an underpinning for trust.[82] In this manner, the periodical meetings of European heads of Domestic Services in the Club de Berne formed an invaluable fundament for later operational counterterrorism cooperation in Europe.[83] Likewise, the regular encounters between numerous heads of services in NATO's military intelligence committee, and the equivalent body organized by the EU's military staff, can provide fertile ground for operational cooperation. Although perhaps too large a setting to offer direct operational opportunities, they can be of service in "the mutual confidence and understanding and the personal friendships they bring."[84] The importance of personal ties between senior executives of partnering firms for cooperation is well known in the field of business cooperation. For example, in the Taiwanese travel industry, personal ties are often the start of horizontal strategic alliances.[85] When allowed to communicate face to face with each other, many of them are likely, over time, to develop affective ties, based on the likeability of exchange partners, their similar attitudes, and their perceived skills. This effect rubs off on the partner's organization as a whole.

Organizational Culture

The second condition for trustworthiness is for partners to recognize each other's organizational culture, playing the game by clear rules. Organizational culture is associated with integrity, based on a shared system of meaning and similar, or at least acceptable, behavioural norms and values. They provide a generalized set of principles for sensemaking that "influences all aspects of how an organization deals with its primary purpose, its various environments, and its internal operations."[86] Moreover, they reflect what members in an organization find appropriate behaviour in a given situation. For cooperation between organizations, a degree of "value congruence" or "cultural fit" is needed as it limits uncertainty to a predictable and acceptable range of behaviours.[87] Partners will be "most comfortable with others who share the same set of assumptions and very uncomfortable in situations where different assumptions operate because [they] will either not understand what is going on, or, worse, [...] will misperceive and misinterpreted the actions of others."[88] In practice, these assumptions are seldomly articulated and "so taken for granted" that group members will simply find any other premise inconceivable. For example, although cooperating competitors in the very formalized and controlled industry of Polish aviation seldomly identified organizational culture as the leading factor or reason for their cooperation, many implicitly mentioned dissimilarities in norms, standards, and ethics as barriers to sustained relationships.[89]

Many networks have occupational cultures that span the different organizations within them. The intelligence community of practice can offer common standards that reflect the beliefs and values in this occupation and enable recognition of a partner's professional integrity. This espoused institutional framework is a practical reflection of the guiding values and assumptions in the community. Professional standards show the norm on "what is right or wrong, what will work or what will not work." They are often explicitly and repeatedly articulated to guide members in their behaviour, especially when confronted with uncertainty. Although they are sometimes reflected informal rules, these social institutions[90] are informal, and often intangible, frames, part of a durable and recognized pattern of shared practices in a societal group.[91] George Simmel notes that organizations culturally defined by their ordination to be secret, display social restraint and formality to the outside world, mirrored by informality and lack of control on the inside.[92] Moreover, the Intelligence Community (IC) is seen to "harbor deeply embedded institutional and cultural legacies, preferences and biases that favour time-tested tradecraft and practices that they perceive to be the global gold standard."[93] Adhering to established principles, like "need-to-know," "third-party-rule," or "originator-control," can be powerful binding institutions.[94] Culture is considered "one of the most significant relational properties of security networks."[95] On the other hand, differences in professional cultures are seen to be the cause of significant communications problems and conflict, for example in alliances between U.S. pharmaceutical and biotechnology firms. Fundamental differences between their engineering and science cultures on how knowledge is understood and used, leading to diverging normative ideas on principles like research centralization, negatively hampered alliance performance.[96]

When partners are seen to reject or violate some of the professional standards in a community, this will damage their perceived trustworthiness. Anna-Katherine Staser McGill and David Philip Harry Gray find that diverging moral standards (or perceptions thereof) on issues like personal data protection and the treatment of suspected terrorists formed obstacles to cooperation between the United States and some of its partners.[97] Yet what the professional standards are, and which of them carry the most weight, depends on the specific (sub)community of practice, the circumstances at hand, and the backgrounds of the organizations involved. The value of timeliness as a professional intelligence standard gains prominence under circumstances of imminent threat but could be less prominent in strategic intelligence. Similarly, although mendacity is considered a faux pas in the relationship between intelligence services and their political masters or oversight bodies, it can be perfectly acceptable behaviour in the IC itself. A degree of mendacity is even likely to be considered the norm in the secretive world of intelligence, even in the relation between cooperating intelligence services. In 2013, it became apparent that the British GCHQ had breached the infrastructure of the Belgian telecommunications provider Belgacom to use it for their own advantage. The Belgian services were reported not to be involved or notified. The Belgian oversight committee concluded that, at the international level, this meant that trust had taken a blow. They considered it "[no longer clear] who can be considered to be friendly services." Yet, at the organizational level, the Belgian General Intelligence and Security Service pointed out that "reverting to isolationism would not be the right response" and that cooperation had to be maintained.[98] Pragmatism, in this case accepting to be competing and cooperating at the same time, might well be another professional standard in the IC.

In cooperation, maintaining a common professional baseline for interaction is helpful in preserving some order and expectation of reciprocity between partners, even in the face of deep fault lines. Moreover, from these common standards, organizations can subsequently develop shared institutions together that enhance perceived trustworthiness.[99] In the field of intelligence, a normative baseline to support cooperation can be found in shared professional language and modus operandi, like a compatible view of the intelligence cycle, shared technical expertise, a standardized lexicon of qualifying words, or agreeable definitions of intelligence topics.[100] The value of shared technical expertise and practices as a baseline for cooperation can be seen in the development of the MAXIMATOR alliance; a European arrangement for SIGINT cooperation reported on by Bart Jacobs. Not only was admittance to the arrangement based on "close personal ties and a shared high level of technical and cryptanalytical skills," but in the course of its existence, restrictive behaviour between its participants eased.[101] Didier Bigo labels such cross-border communities of practice in the fields of security and intelligence as "transnational guilds." Their shared worldview, vested in practical outings like lifestyle, (body) language, and symbols and shored by similar background and socialization, is what distinguishes them from others and binds them together.[102] Professional recognition allows existing intelligence partnerships to develop incrementally from the grassroots up.[103] Adam Svendsen even notes "something close to international standardization" when describing homogenization in the increasingly globalized IC.[104]

Organizational Identity

The third and final condition for trustworthiness is for partners to possess a shared organizational identity. It refers to how partners perceive and understand who they are and what they stand for as an organization. A collective organizational identity alleviates the fear of a partner's potentially opportunistic behaviour in strategic networks.[105] In intelligence, Daniel Byman names conflicting sense of purpose as an important barrier to cooperation between services that are primarily focused on regime survival and those that derive their raison d'être from supporting decision making in foreign affairs or defence.[106] Social identification, on the other hand, produces benevolence, wanting to do a partner good aside from an egocentric profit motive. This positive assortment distinguishes in-groups, where partners feel attached and care for each other's welfare, from out-groups, where this is less the case. Moreover, it implies a sociological merging, a sense of "we" instead of "you and I," ascribing "group-defining characteristics to the self, and to take the collective's interest to heart."[107] In extremis, continuing the relationship becomes as important as its outcome.

Feelings of shared identity produce affective ties and attachment that go beyond mere cognition and normative concerns. They are a powerful basis for cooperative behaviour. Actors with identical attributes or statuses are seen to form increasingly frequent relationships, compared with those who do not perceive to share characteristics. This tendency of similarity-attraction is also known as the notion of "homophily" in social networks. Experiences in homogenous groups tend to be perceived as less demanding, more agreeable, and more efficient (although not necessarily more effective). In interorganizational relations, patterns of homophily, comfortably sticking to what is known, are remarkably robust.[108] Joseph Soeters and Irina Goldenberg note that in information sharing, people "have a tendency to connect to others who are like them."[109] This can have an inbreeding tendency as well; awareness of an in-group, once found, reinforces awareness of out-groups and leads to intergroup biases.[110] In secret societies, secrecy and the pretense of secrecy are social means for distinguishing from others, signaling superiority, and "building the wall higher."[111] Intelligence services can be seen to have "a sense of being special," deriving a common identity from their specific purpose in national security, their exquisite collection mandates, and the secrecy this involves.[112]

Attachment means that partners see each other as the "object of belonging and commitment, [sufficient] to [...] create meaningful relationships." It requires partners to value each other's identity as (part of) their own. This valuation is supported by categorization and comparison, grouping the identity of oneself and others into a series of social categories. Not only are these categories believed to hold information on what can reasonably be expected from a partner, when partners are perceived to be very similar, but interests also become encapsulated.[113] The U.S.–UK intelligence relationship, the backbone of the five-eyes community, provides an example of such encapsulated interest. The enduring belief "in defending the freedom of democracies" is considered a powerful foundational value. This shared sense of purpose and consciously fostering "a culture of cooperation" that is "handed on from generation to generation" sustains cooperation.[114] In its 70-year existence, despite occasional strategic and operational differences, the partnership proved remarkably resilient.[115] Acknowledging the importance of a shared identity for collaboration, several European countries have recently launched Intelligence College Europe. Its primary aim is not operational exchange, but enhancing a common strategic culture and common understanding within the European IC.[116] It builds on the idea that in the field of European intelligence integration can serve as a stepping stone for cooperation.[117]

A collective identity is the result of the repeated activities of a diverse set of organizations, the emergence of clear patterns of interaction, mutual awareness of participants that they are in a common enterprise, and, eventually, a degree of homogenization. This process is seen in many upcoming industries as well as in more established and enduring alliances. For example, in the case of the American artisanal beer craft industry, identification with traditional production methods first served as a way to contrast (and compete) with large-scale companies like Budweiser, but later became more of a "special way of life" and gradually evolved into a collective trait of character. In the end, cooperation, even between competing firms, had become a core value of what was perceived as a tight-knit community with a collective identity and common sense of purpose.[118] For international cooperation and public administration, similar processes in international bureaucracies have received considerable scholarly attention.[119] For intelligence, Helene L. Boatner points at the "shifting notion of allegiance" with national personnel working in large and long-lived multinational organizations.[120] Nevertheless, although social identification can enable people to bridge organizational and national divides, previous identities are seldomly relinquished entirely. In practice, cooperative arrangements are seen to preserve a dynamic set of multiple subidentities that together form the collective identity and shape cooperative behavior.[121]

Perceptions of a shared organizational identity and feelings of professional attachment are not beholden to formal structures. In fact, they may grow within any "system of cooperative effort and coordinated activities," such as a workgroup, profession, or "other ensemble of individuals in more frequent social interaction than with others."[122] Informal communities of practice, based on "daily, routinized, or patterned production and the extent of shared value, interest, and habit," are seen to develop a sense of belonging, shared identity, and goodwill toward other members that enables them to cooperate and derive resources on the basis of a generalized expectation of reciprocity for that group.[123] In intelligence, small informal clubs can provide a platform for identification and trust-based cooperation. For example, the Counter Terrorism Group provides an intimate and closed locus for cooperation between organizations, centered around a certain shared purpose and common understanding. They operate through a notion of "shared secrecy," where information is exchanged between this small group of participants while being selectively shared with others like EUROPOL and EU INTCEN.[124] Their informality and the decentralized character of these communities do not imply anarchy and ineffectiveness. On the contrary, they are more likely to be practical reflections of an evolved trust-based relationship that enables a high level of risk acceptance and in-depth cooperation between the members.

Conclusion

This article has explored the relationship between trust and cooperation in the international field of intelligence practice. It has demonstrated that unraveling trust provides a valuable, complementary perspective on international intelligence cooperation that nuances our understanding of this activity. Rational calculations on (shared) threats, scarcity of information, and potential benefits, as well as control of information, may all be important drivers for collaboration, but they insufficiently explain efficient and sustained international intelligence cooperation. The mechanism of social relations and trust, based on perceptions of trustworthiness about (a specific set of) partners, enables organizations to cooperate despite the uncertainty and vulnerability inherently present in the process. The conditions for perceived trustworthiness that are known from publications on interorganizational relations are found applicable to the "special," secretive world of intelligence as well.

Cooperation on the basis of social relations seems rare in the international intelligence arena. Trust may be considered important, but intelligence services are seldomly thought of as holding one, shared identity, or encapsulating each other's interests. Many institutional divides exist between them—national, functional, and structural. However, on closer inspection, the intelligence community of practice offers a basis for social identification and trust that can bridge the many conflicting fault lines. Known reputations recognized professional standards, and shared traits socially bind intelligence professionals to their community of practice, allowing them to bridge divides like nationality and even conflicting interests. Moreover, social relations include sources of nonmaterial reciprocity that can be just as important for competitive advantage as material gain. In practice, services and their professionals often cooperate in long-standing arrangements without being able to rationally calculate the outcome or control the risks involved.

By departing from a purely material approach, a more nuanced understanding of cooperative intelligence arrangements comes within reach. Intangible social relations enable partners to cooperate despite the vulnerabilities attached, even allowing them to be simultaneously competitive and cooperative. By conceptually unraveling trust into components of perceived trustworthiness, it becomes possible to study this phenomenon in-depth and examine the role it plays in achieving reasoned expectations in cooperation. From this perspective, particular traits of the IC that are often mentioned as obstacles to cooperation, like pragmatism, secrecy, and informality, can very well be the ties that bind in this diverse community of practice, bolstering social identification. From this perspective, if intelligence services were to have any friends, these would probably be other intelligence services.

Social relations and perceived trustworthiness provide a dominant explanation for cooperative behavior in intelligence. The mechanism behind international cooperation between intelligence agencies is thus much more common than scholars and practitioners themselves tend to suggest. Their practical art differs, and therefore the exact setting and valuation of trust, but conceptually their interaction resembles relations between organizations and professionals in other domains. Trust between them is buttressed by personal relations, evolves over time, and can be sustained despite a degree of competition. We may need to demystify international intelligence cooperation. As a result, using sociological approaches like social network analysis and social psychology for structured analysis of intelligence practice is clearly beneficial to our understanding of international intelligence cooperation. More detailed empirical research into the social dynamics of international intelligence cooperation in specific arrangements, like larger international fusion cells or small informal clubs, would further enhance our knowledge of its workings.

The Social Ties that Bind: Unraveling the Role of Trust in International Intelligence Cooperation. Pepijn Tuinier, Thijs Brocades Zaalberg & Sebastiaan Rietjens. To cite this article: Pepijn Tuinier, Thijs Brocades Zaalberg & Sebastiaan Rietjens (2023). The Social Ties that Bind: Unraveling the Role of Trust in International Intelligence Cooperation, International Journal of Intelligence and CounterIntelligence, 36:2, 386-422, DOI: 10.1080/08850607.2022.2079161. To link to this article: https://doi. org/10.1080/08850607.2022.2079161. © 2022 The Author(s). Published with license by Taylor & Francis Group, LLC Published online: 13 Jul 2022. 2022 The Author(s). *Pepijn Tuinier is a Senior Policy Advisor at the Netherlands Ministry of Defence and a Ph.D. candidate at the Netherlands Defense Academy and Leiden University. The author can be contacted at DH.Tuinier.01@mindef.nl.Thijs Brocades Zaalberg. Thijs Brocades Zaalberg holds a position as an Associate Professor in Intelligence & Security at the Netherlands Defense Academy and an Assistant Professor in Contemporary Military History at Leiden University. He was Director of the research project "Comparing the Wars of Decolonization" at the Netherlands Institute for Advanced Study. The author can be contacted at T.W.Brocades@hum. leidenuniv.nl. Sebastiaan Rietjens is a full professor of Intelligence & Security at the Netherlands Defence Academy as well as a special chair of Intelligence in War & Conflict at Leiden University. He has done extensive fieldwork in military exercises and operations in Afghanistan, Mali, and Greece. The author can be contacted at SJH.*

Rietjens.01@mindef.nl. *Journal information: Print ISSN: 0885-0607 Online ISSN: 1521-0561. 4 issues per year. Abstracted/indexed in: America: History & Life; CSA; EBSCOhost Online Research Databases; ESCI; Historical Abstracts; OCLC; PAIS International; Periodicals Index Online; Scopus; The Lancaster Index; and Ulrichs Periodicals Directory. Taylor & Francis make every effort to ensure the accuracy of all the information (the "Content") contained in our publications. However, Taylor & Francis, our agents (including the editor, any member of the editorial team or editorial board, and any guest editors), and our licensors, make no representations or warranties whatsoever as to the accuracy, completeness, or suitability for any purpose of the Content. Any opinions and views expressed in this publication are the opinions and views of the authors, and are not the views of or endorsed by Taylor & Francis. The accuracy of the Content should not be relied upon and should be independently verified with primary sources of information. Taylor & Francis shall not be liable for any losses, actions, claims, proceedings, demands, costs, expenses, damages, and other liabilities whatsoever or howsoever caused arising directly or indirectly in connection with, in relation to, or arising out of the use of the Content. The International Journal of Intelligence and CounterIntelligence serves as a medium for professionals and scholars to exchange opinions on issues and challenges encountered by both government and business institutions in making contemporary intelligence-related decisions and policy. At the same time, this quarterly serves as an invaluable resource for researchers looking to assess previous developments and events in the field of national security. Dedicated to the advancement of the academic discipline of intelligence studies, the International Journal of Intelligence and CounterIntelligence publishes articles and book reviews focusing on a broad range of national security matters. As an independent, non-partisan forum, the journal presents the informed and diverse findings of its contributing authors, and does not advocate positions of its own. Peer Review Policy: All papers submitted to the International Journal of Intelligence and CounterIntelligence undergoes initial editorial screening. Once deemed suitable, research articles are sent out for double-anonymous peer review by at least two independent referees. Publication office: Taylor & Francis Inc., 530 Walnut Street, Suite 850, Philadelphia, PA 19106*

Chapter 8

The Construction of Secret Intelligence as a Masculine Profession

Eleni Braat

Abstract

The vast majority of intelligence history focuses on operations and executive decision-making rather than attending to, among other topics, analytical work or day-to-day organizational activities in the full (hierarchical) breadth of agencies. Especially in the studies on the Cold War period, one of the major implications of this research focus is that women, in so far as they are not part of top leadership or critical to operations, are excluded from analysis. This article argues that security and intelligence services were constructed as a masculine profession during the Cold War period. The article advances three professional standards that were constructed as masculine: a sense of responsibility, female support, and full-time availability. Empirically, this research focuses on the Dutch Security Service (in-depth interviews and archival research).

This is just a male-dominated environment. The nature of the work, I guess.[1]

For decades, the character who played the head of the Secret Intelligence Service in the James Bond films, M., was a man, and Miss Moneypenny was the only woman within MI6. The American film industry in the 1950s, including earlier films by Hitchcock, portrayed a similar image of a male-dominated intelligence environment.[2] In close collaboration with the Federal Bureau of Investigation, the carefully crafted image of intelligence as a professional environment centered on intelligence officers as "morally irreproachable, authoritative, white, male, and heteronormative" figures.[3]

These men lead adventurous and narcistic lives, "focused on high consumerism and casual sexual conquest." By contrast, in espionage fiction throughout the Cold War period, women occupied secondary, superficial, or negative positions.[4] The 1990s were a turning point for both intelligence fiction and reality. In 1995, in the James Bond films, M. became a woman, portrayed by Judi Dench. And in the forthcoming James Bond film, *No Time to Die*, James Bond will retire, and a woman will be assigned his 007 number, effectively taking over his role. As such, the professional environment of secret intelligence, as portrayed in the James Bond films, has become less masculine: key positions and professional standards in the agency are more diverse regarding gender. During the same period, the Central Intelligence Agency (CIA) leadership made similar attempts to diversify its workforce in higher hierarchical ranks, notably via its "Glass Ceiling Study" in 1992.[5]

While gender diversity may be a remarkable change to the average James Bond film watcher and it may not be a completely novel thought in the American Intelligence Community, the topic of gender has received strikingly little attention in the historical, academic literature on intelligence. Most research focuses on operations and executive decision-making in the Anglo-Saxon world rather than attending to, among other topics, the rest of the organizational activities in the full (hierarchical) breadth of agencies.[6] Especially in research on the Cold War period, one of the major implications of this focus is that women, in so far as they are not part of top leadership or critical to operations, are excluded from analysis. Often, the women who appear in scholarly research on intelligence are recruited agents (spies), usually described as objects of desire, rather than service personnel.[7] Moreover, the omnipresence of men within the services, considered as natural, is not questioned, nor a topic of analysis that merits an evaluation of cause and consequence. As such, Shahan observes, "[G]ender is both an ever present and missing aspect of intelligence studies."[8]

During the Cold War, professional standards in secret intelligence were constructed as masculine, suggesting that a specific ideal type of man was the best fit for work in intelligence. The construction of these so-called masculinities occurs in day-to-day interactions between men and women, and among themselves, on the work floor. They can be observed in particular tacit or well-considered actions, in writing or in informal norms and procedures. This restricted the positions of women and men who did not abide to this dominant image of masculinity. Empirically, this research relies on original in-depth interviews with former personnel from the

Dutch Security Service (DSS) and archival research in the service's internal staff magazine. It unravels debates within the DSS across different levels of the organizational hierarchy on the topic of gender diversity, between the 1960s and 1990s. These debates consist of a dialogue between those who defended intelligence as a typically masculine profession and those who opposed this view. The tenacious construction of intelligence as a masculine profession contributed to restricting women to specific departments and sections of the service, such as administration, counterintelligence, and surveillance, while excluding them from others, such as political extremism. This article builds on a specific body of literature in intelligence studies and advances a conceptual framework that explains how professional standards in intelligence and security services were constructed as masculine. The methodological section addresses the empirical data collection. The empirical analysis of this article discerns three professional standards that were constructed as masculine, and how dialogue on this topic unfolded between men and women within the DSS.

Scholarly relevance

By singling out the construction of gender identities in relation to professional standards in intelligence, this article builds on a recent and exciting body of literature that shifts research interests from operational processes to people, social and organizational identities, and organizational cultures in intelligence.[9] More specifically, this article further substantiates a line of argument in the field of critical intelligence studies that combines gender studies with intelligence studies, emphasizing diversity and inclusion in intelligence.[10] As a forerunner to this specific body of literature, various publications have singled out women spies during the two world wars.[11] Noteworthy is the work of Tammy Proctor, who relates cultural images of the woman spy with the realities of women working in intelligence during World War I, both inside the services and recruited by the services as agents (spies).[12] Only a handful of publications have singled out gender and, more broadly, diversity within intelligence and security services, clearly distinguishing between those who work within the services and those who are recruited by the services.

The work of Jess Shahan and Damien Van Puyvelde focuses exclusively on women (and ethnic and racial minorities) in the services. Shahan uses women's narratives in British and American intelligence to explain how gender influences career progression and experiences in intelligence; for instance, by restricting women to specific types of work.[13] Innovatively, her work takes stock of individual experiences and memories of women to analyze the organizational cultures that shaped their professional opportunities. Van Puyvelde gives important insights into the organizational culture of the CIA, by outlining how the agency has struggled with the position of women and black employees since its foundation in 1947.[14] These publications construct more humane and convincing images of the social fabric that shapes intelligence and security services. By analyzing the construction of masculine professional standards in intelligence, this article demonstrates how gendered professional standards impact both men and women. This theoretical approach provides a useful basis to think about the impact of specific masculine professional standards on a variety of men, although the available empirical material for this research is mostly on women within the DSS.

Gender identities and professional standards

Gender theory offers important tools to better understand the construction of gender identities in professional environments and their relation to professional standards. While sex differences in psychological traits are nonexistent or minor, their social implications—based on the cultural belief in psychological difference—are major. In professional environments such social implications may include unequal responsibilities, unequal incomes, and the restriction or concentration of men or women to specific positions.[15] Gender theory can explain the gendered construction of professional standards, how they normalize and reinforce themselves and, consequently, why the pace of social change is generally slow in this area.

The process through which minor sex differences result in major social gender differences is, according to Connell, "a reproductive arena."[16] Categorizing individuals as either men or women produces these same categories: individuals will feel as either "men" or "women," they will build their identities on these notions, and they will, in turn, reinforce received notions of masculinity and femininity. As such, the construction of gender identities is a performative act; repetition materializes its effect, which consists of the normalization and naturalization of the essence of a specific gender. Widespread, repeated expectations of gender coherence produce these same genders. Judith Butler argues that people are motivated to behave and feel in accordance with what is expected of them because, as such, they live up to a coherent and convincing gendered self that is understood and appreciated by others. These are "the bodies that matter," Butler argues, of which the performativity of gender consists.[17]

Coherent notions of what constitutes a "man" and a "woman," based on various attributed "male" and "female" characteristics, potentially overshadows other individual personality traits, such as cultural, political, and social constituents. Consequently, the process of attributing various "male" and "female" characteristics to individuals simplifies the complexity of an individual's identity and, in professional environments, contributes to restricting an individual's potential to what supposedly befits his or her determined gender: individuals are reduced to their gender.[18] For instance, gender-biased assumptions may consist of the belief that women are less suited for management positions than men. Consequently, in certain professional contexts they are overrepresented in administrative positions.[19] Constructions of gender coherence are usually empirically viable, although theoretically incoherent, according to Butler, when they conform to a binary understanding of gender that restricts gender to men and women only, and to the hierarchical relations between men and women.

The gendered construction of professional standards is from the perspective of masculinity. Masculinity is part of gender theory because it rejects the assumption of predetermined and innate male and female behavior and explains how gender is constructed by means of conformity to cultural norms.[20] It explains the process by which people, both men and women, construct specific personality traits as masculine. This article focuses on the plausible empirical mechanisms that underlie three important conceptual arguments on which the process of masculinity construction is based. First, masculinity is not just a personal idea, but a socially constructed public convention, embedded in institutions, such as families, schools, and (professional) organizations.[21] Second, masculinity has a relational character. It is the product of a dialogue between men and women, and masculinity exists only in relation to its supposed opposite, femininity.[22] This dialogue produces multiple masculinities, which may exist next to each other[23] or which may have one type of masculinity that dominates others (hegemonic masculinity).[24] Finally, masculinity has a dynamic character. It is subject to historical change prompted by, for instance, social movements or organizational leadership. These three conceptual arguments provide focus to the empirical analysis in this article. The analysis centers on the arguments made within actual historical circumstances that contributed to the survival of a specific type of masculinity in the DSS, built on three characteristics: a sense of responsibility, the need of female support, and full-time availability.

Historical Sources

The extent of empirical historical research—the extent to which we can reach into the past—is shaped by the historical primary sources. This article focuses on sources that prioritize individual narratives, either oral or written ones, rather than official sources that are unlikely to explicitly attend to the topic of gender in the organizational culture. The two main types of historical sources are oral history interviews and the personnel magazine of the DSS. In contrast to some of the theory discussed, this article does not engage with how the historical actors related to their assigned gender emotionally and personally, or allow for effective and meaningful non-binary gender identification. As such, inevitably it partly reproduces the binary categories that my historical actors advanced, and it gives a simplified impression of the gender identities that have existed in the agency. This directly results from the sources potentially available, or any other historical source for that matter. Few would effectively enlighten us on identifications that were straightforwardly "unthinkable," let alone discussable, in these historical circumstances. However, while the available empirical data do not give us access to the gender identities of our historical actors, they give us plenty of information on how gender was constructed within the agency and how this construction was intertwined with the professional standards of the agency. Consequently, my empirical focus is on the use of language and the exchange of arguments.

The most relevant historical source is the internal personnel magazine of the agency, *het Spionnetj* [*The Little Spy*]. Its relevance is based on its strikingly informal character until the 1990s, when it became more formal and presumably more controlled. The magazine contained a great amount of discussions between management and staff, and between employees themselves, often signed or, when opposition was fierce, sometimes anonymously. A recurring discussion related to the position of women in the agency, to which contributed men and women, management and staff. A most valuable source on the position of women in the DSS is a 1990 internal report on the topic, containing quantitative material on gender distribution in various departments and sections and changes over time. However, these available quantitative data are fragmented, not longitudinal. Therefore, observations may include the attributions "many" or "some" when this corresponds to the findings in the personnel magazine and the interviews.

The second historical source consists of 37 recorded and transcribed interviews. The author conducted them in 2010 in the framework of a sociocultural history of the agency, which addressed gender as one of the many constituents of the agency's organisational culture. While these interviews addressed some memories on the role of gender in the agency, most interviewees did not have specific recollections on the topic and gave short, factual, sometimes contradictory answers to my questions. This little yield from the oral history interviews does not correspond with the recurring discussions in the personnel magazine. References in this article to the empirical material from the anonymized oral history interviews mention a book of the author on the sociocultural history of the DSS, published in 2012, which includes the analysis of this material. References to the empirical data from the personnel magazine indicate the date and/or edition of the magazine. Both the transcribed oral history interviews and the personnel magazine are in the currently classified archive of the Dutch General Intelligence and Security Service.

Where were the women and men in the security services?

Based on the theoretical literature, this article argues that the specific positions of women and men in the DSS was both the cause and result of the construction of intelligence as a masculine profession. Mainly based on the quantitative data from the 1990 internal report on women in the DSS, it is possible to paint a picture of where women and men in the DSS worked. Women and men were unevenly distributed in the DSS, both horizontally over various departments and sections, and vertically over hierarchical ranks. To a certain extent, this is little surprising in the related historical and geographical context, in which women were relative newcomers to the government labour market. For instance, until 1955, women employees in The Netherlands were forced to resign upon their marriage and, up until the present day, a disproportionally large percentage of women employees in The Netherlands work part time.[25] In the 1970s, more women in the Dutch labor market continued working until the birth of their first child, and in the 1980s more women continued their employment until after their first child's birth.[26] To meet the fast turnover of women employees, the DSS made several attempts to create a day care center for women employees' children. However, these attempts failed in 1965, again in 1973, and finally came to nothing. Consequently, young, married women without children were considered a liability when applying to a position at the DSS. In 1990, the DSS had considerably fewer women (27.3%) than its (parent), the Ministry of the Interior (40%),[27] while its percentage of women was in line with the general Dutch labor market (27.4%).[28]

In the DSS, women, who amounted to 39 percent of the workforce in the DSS, were overrepresented in the administrative sections, while they were nearly absent in higher hierarchical positions and many operational functions. This corresponds to the situation of women in the CIA who, in the early 1990s, constituted nearly 40 percent of CIA personnel while holding 10 percent of senior positions.[29] The large administrative section Afdeling Centrale Documentatie (ACD; Central Documentation Section) had a relatively large proportion of female staff, among whom a disproportionately large percentage originated from the former Dutch East Indies. In 1967, the head of the section ACD explained that "work at the section ACD is specifically female in nature. It consists of producing punch cards, punching and check-punching. It consists of the production of punch concepts, coding, administrating, etc. Personally, I cannot imagine any male employee working at our section, although men are most welcome."[30]

The section EJ, which was responsible for translation and audio work, also attracted women. These administrative tasks belonged to the lower echelons of the organization, while women were "a rarity" higher up the hierarchy.[31] Three notable exceptions were the deputy head of direction C for Counterespionage and the heads of the sections East German and Russian counterespionage, who were both women during a certain period.[32] A comparison between the distribution of men and women by pay scale and hierarchical level in 1977 and 1990 shows in more detail that there was little change over this period. Operational functions—"the rough outside work"—also attracted few women. It is important to note that operational work had a higher professional status than all other positions in the DSS: it was considered the hard core of the DSS. The operational directions B (for political extremism) and C (for counterespionage) competed for which direction was the most important one for the DSS.[33] Operational work included, for instance, running agents, countering foreign espionage, speaking with people for security vetting and clearance procedures, and surveillance.[34]

The surveillance team had its first female member in 1952 already, although she encountered some initial obstacles related to her gender that prevented her, for a while, from doing the job she was supposed to do.[35] At the end of the 1970s, about half the surveillance team consisted of women, which related to clear operational benefits: a man and woman waiting in a car attracted less public attention than two waiting men, and gender diversity in the team allowed it to tail individuals inconspicuously in all kinds of places. For instance, "[I]f someone bursts into a lingerie shop, it would be tricky to go after him or her as a guy alone."[36] Another operational function—running agents—remained entirely male until the first woman appeared in 1989. And the section that was responsible for security vetting and clearance procedures had its first two female interrogators, meaning those who did outside operational work, in 1978.[37] The specific gender distribution within the DSS shows that a great amount of the operational work was male-dominated. The following analysis explains how this gender distribution in the DSS was related to the construction of three masculine professional standards.

Masculine professional standards

The personnel magazine and, to a lesser extent, the oral history interviews, reveal several professional standards that were specifically needed for working with the Dutch Security Service. These were constructed as masculine in their opposition to what was considered feminine. This article discerns three professional standards, unequal in the amount of attention they received, that were constructed as masculine: a sense of responsibility, the need for female support, and full-time availability. These standards remained structurally in place between the 1950s and 1990s, although they became less naturalized throughout the 1970s and 1980s as a result of societal and political changes. In particular, the emancipation policies of the government Den Uyl, implemented by the subsequent government Van Agt, encouraged those employees in the DSS who aimed for change.[38] Nevertheless, change was slow: in 1978, the personnel magazine still stated that women "simply had their shortcomings in our men-oriented world. That's just the way things are."[39]

A Sense of Responsibility

Working with the DSS required a sense of responsibility that women were not willing to assume, according to both men and women who expressed their views in the personnel magazine. Particularly related to management positions, women were less eager to accept the necessary responsibility and pressure, and "they were simply more prone to prioritize their private life."[40] Moreover, they were assumed "to report ill more often and easier," according to various managers in 1990.[41] More importantly, the combination of "work and children causes many women too much physical stress," someone argued in the personnel magazine that same year.[42] And women were supposed to suffer from "oversensitivity to criticism," which made them unfit for responsible work.[43]

The debate on a sense of responsibility as a professional standard started at the occasion of governmental measures in 1962 that aimed at increasing the percentage of women in government agencies. This positive discrimination, which demanded higher qualifications for men than for women, stirred emotions. "Although we support the principle of making government positions more attractive to women," a male contributor wrote indignantly in alleged name of all his male colleagues, "in such a way … NO!"[44] A survey for an internal report on women's emancipation stirred even greater emotions on the same issue of positive discrimination. It would lay the blame with men, according to some, which would be unfair. After all, men in the survey argued, women did not desire any changes in the current division of labour, "because women were unwilling to assume the related responsibilities."[45] One of the first female handlers in the service remembered how, in the 1990s, she was repeatedly set aside each time the handling of her agents "became a bit more difficult or trickier and interventions were needed. In such instances they did not acknowledge my responsibility, because I was a woman, so I was not competent enough to say anything about such issues."[46] In 1990, the internal report on women's emancipation expressed itself on the "unfair" preferential treatment of women in job openings. Discouraged, the female authors of the report concluded that this policy would risk a "boomerang effect" if problems occur with the female candidates. Their solution was to require women to be "at least 10 to 15% better than their male competitors."[47]

Female Support

The support of women, particularly good-looking women, increased the status of men's work. "There were many beautiful girls at the Service," a former employee recollects, who entered the DSS in 1951.[48] Positive discrimination for women in vacancies at the DSS, in combination with a greater degree of independence for women, would impact "private circumstances. The existing division of tasks [at home] will not be obvious anymore."[49] Female support at work, rather than at home, received more attention in the personnel magazine. Such support was tied to women's physical appearance. For instance, the 1959 Christmas edition of the personnel magazine *The Little Spy* commented on the advantages to men of good-looking "girls" in the DSS: For the men in our firm, the start of the month was always particularly nice, because of all these youthful beautiful little faces of our new girls that we encountered in the corridors. […] We will do our best to find female enthusiasts [for our firm]. Otherwise, we will miss them dearly, those sweet little faces on the first floor.[50] The advantages

143

of the presence of the "girls" went further than bringing mere joy to the eye. In September 1968, *The Little Spy* commented on the work of "Eva," meaning all female employees, which presented an important incentive for the work of male colleagues:

Besides showing us statistics, the performance and appearance of the ladies greatly influences the mood, and therefore indirectly the work performances of the employed man in their environment. These ladies can make or break a male civil servant, without being aware of it.[51] This excerpt implies it should be a source of pride for women to be of such influence on their male colleagues, who, in turn, were framed as the driving force of the DSS. In this context of the significance of women's physical appearance we should understand the "Miss BVD" beauty contest in 1965. It was won by the direction Counterespionage. "Congratulations!," *The Little Spy* cheered, while adding that the editorial board had observed "an alarming shortage of high heels" in direction D, which was responsible for internal security.[52] Throughout the 1970s, the personnel magazine ceases to refer to "girls" and "sweet little faces," and there is no trace of any beauty contests. However, in 1988, a female employee calls for a "women's excursion":

Don't you think that it is our turn now, after a men's excursion to the [car manufacturer] DAF, to organize a real women's excursion? For instance, we could go to a Beauty farm. The ultimate beneficiary of such an outing is the Security Service, with all those beautiful, relaxed ladies in the buildings, don't you think? Please send me your reactions.[53] This call shows how the construction of masculine professional standards was the product of a dialogue between men and women. Women contributed to the masculine professional standard of doing work that needed female support. While women's good looks were an asset to men's performances at work, they could be a liability from a counterintelligence and operational perspective. Of special concern were the marriages of "our girls" with "outsiders." From a counterintelligence perspective, the "girls," gullible as they may be, risked sharing confidential information with their husbands, who might have seduced them with this purpose in mind. These "girls" caused the counterintelligence officer "sleepless nights."[54] On the other hand, male employees who married with someone outside the DSS did not seem to be of any counterintelligence concern. From an operational perspective there was also cause for concern. Women in an operational function "would give rise to provocative looks that had to be 'consumed', if necessary," someone warned in the personnel magazine in 1978.[55] The first female member of the surveillance team, young and unmarried, remembered her acquaintance with her ten male colleagues in 1952:

Back then, Jan [...] had to set up the surveillance team. It consisted of only men, [...] and he [thought] that women should be part of it, too. That's when I was hired as the first woman of the team. [...] And I started my job—you won't believe it! [...]—by sewing buttons to the trousers of these men. Just for the fun of it because I had nothing to do. [...] So, I was sitting there, sewing jackets and buttons. Can you believe it? I thought "what a tomfoolery." [...] There wasn't anything for me to do because those guys refused to hit the road with a woman. [...] What else should I have done, my dear? [...] As a starting female member of the team, these men did not accept me because they were married. [...] And they were annoyed that they had to walk outside with me. [...] In the end, after I had spent my time like this for some months, I think, one guy dared to set off with me.[56] A couple of years later, a second woman joined the surveillance team. It was the earliest operational section of the DSS to welcome women, although hesitantly at the start. Women as agent handlers encountered greater reluctance until the 1990s, and it is unclear whether this was due to their physical appearance. Both MI5 and CIA experienced similar longtime reluctance to welcome women as agent handlers.[57] As Pieter de Haan, head of service, explained enigmatically and firmly in 1977:

As far as I know, it has not been proven that we need any women in operational work. Sometimes agents express their preference for an elder civil servant. Never has any agent, not even female agents, expressed any preference for a female agent handler.[58] The 1990s were a turning point when, surprisingly, various managers argued in *The Little Spy* that agent handling would be to the advantage of women. More easily than men, women were supposed to be inquisitive without raising suspicions.[59] The 1980s, and especially the 1990s, were also a period of progress for women's opportunities in the CIA. For instance, in the mid-1980s women as agent handlers were increasingly valued for their different and effective approach to recruiting agents.[60]

Full-Time Availability

A final professional standard, framed as masculine, was full-time availability to work for the DSS. Until the 1970s, part-time employment was only possible in several positions, mostly administrative ones, and only up until a certain hierarchical rank. Consequently, part-time employment was the domain of women. To illustrate this, the authors of the earlier-mentioned internal report on the emancipation of women interviewed 70 women, of whom 68 worked part time.[61] In 1977, an interview in *The Little Spy* with Pieter de Haan, the then newly appointed head of DSS, addressed possibilities to expand part-time employment throughout the DSS. To set the tone, De Haan argued that there is no need for the DSS to keep up with "societal developments." "We do not need to lead the way; in general, the government is not used to running ahead of things."[62] De Haan thought that part-time work goes against the sense of belonging within the DSS, which he associated with the need of the DSS to defend itself. "Within this house," De Haan explained, "we should aim at a strong sense of belonging. This can be our backbone against attacks from the outside. A sense of belonging thrives in a group of people that is constantly in each other's company."[63]

Moreover, De Haan objected to part-time work in operational functions, especially in agent-handling. "You cannot tell an agent, who is trying to get in touch with the Service: 'at this moment Mr so-and-so is not in, he only works in the mornings. The less routine our work becomes, the more difficult." This argument was in line with the internal reputation of direction C, responsible for counterintelligence, as rough, adventurous, risk-taking, and intimate.[64] The editorial comment at the end of the interview with De Haan concluded that "whoever has carefully read the above interview, will have to conclude that the arrival of our new head of service has not improved the chances for women in our service."[65] As a result of this interview, De Haan received a great deal of outraged reactions, of both men and women, that were partly published in *The Little Spy*:

With increasing amazement and repressed anger, I read the interview with [the head of DSS] in our latest *The Little Spy*. It is unbelievable what kind of remarks our head of Service is tossing around in the year 1977. […] The way he simply brushes aside various arguments does not exemplify, in my view, a realistic view on today's (fortunately changing) society.[66] This reaction was signed rather than published anonymously, showing the heated nature of the debate, the personal involvement of employees, and the safe debating platform that *The Little Spy* provided for this topic. Among the many reactions to the interview was a reaction from several typists from the administrative section ACD. They expressed their "feeling of discomfort that has been present with many women typists" on the lack of appreciation for part-time work. The interview with De Haan showed them that "apparently, we are not considered full-fledged employees of the Service."[67] Although the reactions to his interview slightly moderated De

Haan's views on part-time work, his arguments showed his belief that full-time availability as a masculine trait was required for the specific work of the DSS.

A later head of service, Arthur Docters van Leeuwen (1988–1995), thought that problems related to part-time work, which was still associated with women, were never "insurmountable." Women were given the opportunity to reintegrate on a part-time basis after their children had grown up, and he assured his opponents that ambitious women did a whole week's work in three or four days. "Therefore, part-time work is fine," he concluded.[68] Docters van Leeuwen also encouraged the formation of a "women's network" in the DSS. To conclude, arguments on the possibilities of part-time work and its relation to a masculine professional standard of full-time availability changed in the 1970s and then in the 1990s. Those who expressed themselves appeared increasingly more aware of the social and political dimensions of the topic, possibly influenced by governmental emancipation policies during this period.

Conclusion

During the Cold War, professional standards in the realm of secret intelligence were linked to masculinity. The DSS constructed the ideal type of male employee who had a strong sense of responsibility, who needed and was worthy of female support, and who was always available to do the job. This image gradually changed as a result of changes in management (most importantly, the arrival of Arthur Docters van Leeuwen), government emancipation policies, and collective action inside the DSS encouraged by comparisons with the (parent) Ministry of the Interior. The theoretical and empirical contributions, which build on the conditional factors that determine masculinity, are threefold. First, this article has shown that the construction of professional standards intertwined with the construction of received notions of masculinity and femininity. Oral memories and written internal debates on the topic show that employees in the DSS believed in some universal, cross-cultural, unified, and structural basis for what constitutes a woman and a man. They also expressed arguments that showed a hierarchical and patriarchal relationship between men and women. For instance, the available sources show a widespread assumption that women's main contribution to work in the DSS consisted of their support to the work of men. They were in the DSS, but not of the DSS. This confined women to specific positions in the DSS, leading to a long-term insufficient recognition and use of their professional potential. This article shows that, in particular, operational work was a gendered professional

147

environment. And professional standards were constructed in such a way that operational work was more important than other work.

Second, both men and women contributed to the construction of gendered professional standards. Not only men, but also some women in the DSS emphasized specific gendered roles that consolidated the hierarchical relation between men and women, such as the suggestion that women employees should go to a beauty farm with the aim to please and motivate male colleagues. Emphasizing such gendered roles reinforced and reproduced them, and sometimes mockingly challenged them. In some instances, this process even led women to propose greater hierarchical relations than did men, such as the women's response to men's criticism on positive discrimination when hiring new personnel. Third, this research has shown that masculinity in the DSS acquired meaning only relation to what, presumably, it is not: femininity. In the recurring debates on the position of women in the DSS, masculinity was constructed as a neutral space, while femininity was framed as the exception. What employees said and wrote about why female colleagues were, supposedly, not suited for the job, reveals the supposed masculine traits as imagined by these employees that were part of the professional standards of the agency. For instance, male writers assumed women were unsuited for the job because they were unwilling to do responsible work, meaning that male employees are characterized by their willingness to do responsible work.

The conceptual focus of this article on masculinities in the organizational culture of intelligence and security services has various benefits. By analyzing the construction of a dominant type of masculinity, it provides tools to explain the position of women and, more in general, the marginalization of individuals who do not conform to this dominant type of masculinity. Empirically, this article has concentrated on the position of women in the Dutch context of the Cold War. Future research could explore how the construction of masculinity impacted other genders. For instance, a welcome addition to the literature would be the impact on homosexual employees, who were in the Cold War context considered vulnerable to blackmail and therefore a security risk in intelligence. Future research could also explore the validity of the construction of intelligence as a masculine profession in other (non-Western) services than the Dutch one, and whether we can observe similar professional standards. Finally, this historical research shows various slowly changing, structural patterns in the construction of intelligence as a masculine profession. Future research could explore to what extent these patterns are still topical. For instance, Van

Puyvelde observes that memoirs of female CIA employees who served in the 2000s describe the agency as male-dominated where women cope "with prejudices and sometimes harassment."[69] If these memoirs of intelligence as a male-dominated professional environment are representative, can we observe a causal relation with noninclusive professional standards? And presuming that such professional standards prevent the services from capitalizing on the full potential of their employees, what can be practically done about it?

Additional information. Notes on contributors ; Eleni Braat is Associate Professor at Utrecht University. She obtained her Ph.D. from the European University Institute in Florence, Italy. She has been the official historian of the Dutch General Intelligence and Security Service, and she is a member of the executive board of the Netherlands Intelligence Studies Association. The author can be contacted at e.c.braat@uu.nl. Journal information. Print ISSN: 0885-0607 Online ISSN: 1521-0561. 4 issues per year. Abstracted/indexed in: America: History & Life; CSA; EBSCOhost Online Research Databases; ESCI; Historical Abstracts; OCLC; PAIS International; Periodicals Index Online; Scopus; The Lancaster Index; and Ulrichs Periodicals Directory. Taylor & Francis make every effort to ensure the accuracy of all the information (the "Content") contained in our publications. However, Taylor & Francis, our agents (including the editor, any member of the editorial team or editorial board, and any guest editors), and our licensors, make no representations or warranties whatsoever as to the accuracy, completeness, or suitability for any purpose of the Content. Any opinions and views expressed in this publication are the opinions and views of the authors, and are not the views of or endorsed by Taylor & Francis. The accuracy of the Content should not be relied upon and should be independently verified with primary sources of information. Taylor & Francis shall not be liable for any losses, actions, claims, proceedings, demands, costs, expenses, damages, and other liabilities whatsoever or howsoever caused arising directly or indirectly in connection with, in relation to, or arising out of the use of the Content. Terms & Conditions of access and use can be found at http://www.tandfonline.com/page/terms-and-conditions. Aims and scope. The International Journal of Intelligence and CounterIntelligence serves as a medium for professionals and scholars to exchange opinions on issues and challenges encountered by both government and business institutions in making contemporary intelligence-related decisions and policy. At the same time, this quarterly serves as an invaluable resource for researchers looking to assess previous developments and events in the field of national security. Dedicated to the advancement of the academic discipline of intelligence studies, the International Journal of Intelligence and CounterIntelligence publishes articles and book reviews focusing on a broad range of national security matters. As an independent, non-partisan forum, the journal presents the informed and diverse findings of its contributing authors, and does not advocate positions of its own. Peer Review Policy: All papers submitted to the International Journal of Intelligence and CounterIntelligence undergo initial editorial screening. Once deemed suitable, research articles are sent out for double-anonymous peer review by at least two independent referees. Publication office: Taylor & Francis Inc., 530 Walnut Street, Suite 850, Philadelphia, PA 19106. The Construction of Secret Intelligence as a Masculine Profession. Eleni Braat. To cite this article: Eleni Braat (2022) The Construction of Secret Intelligence as a Masculine Profession, International Journal of Intelligence and CounterIntelligence, 35:4, 694-712, DOI:10.1080/08850607.2022.2055429 To link to this article: https://doi.org /10.1080/08850607.2022.2055429.

Chapter 9

Assessing Intelligence Oversight: The Case of Sweden

Dan Hansén

Abstract

The study of intelligence oversight captures the inherently political nature of secret intelligence. However, many studies of intelligence oversight adopt rather instrumentalist views that omit important political aspects of the policy process. Typically, these studies focus on obstacles to effective oversight. This article discusses how the effectiveness of oversight can be assessed by applying broad evaluative categories that contain programmatic, process-related, political, and durability dimensions. Empirically, the study probes the case of Sweden as an illustration. Swedish oversight arrangements have on balance, been successful in some dimensions, particularly the programmatic dimension, which arguably also contributed to its relative longevity.

Introduction

By default, the sub-field of intelligence oversight studies acknowledges the political nature of secret intelligence. The political contexts in the various policy arrangements are paramount in any understanding of intelligence as a phenomenon. This is arguably why intelligence oversight studies gained momentum after the Edward Snowden leaks.[1] The bulk surveillance programmes revealed by Snowden may have been more or less effective from an operational point of view, but they seem to have been politically self-defeating.[2] The ultimate purpose of security and intelligence agencies in western societies is to uphold democracy and the rule of law, which begs the question of why governments, including their intelligence agencies, time and again attempt to push the borders of legitimacy. Most Western democracies have put oversight arrangements in place to tame the power of secrecy. These play an important watchdog role as an intermediary between entrenched government agencies and an open society. However, can we be confident that such arrangements are working? This article discusses how the effectiveness of intelligence oversight can be assessed by probing a framework of broad evaluative categories that contain programmatic, process-related, political, and durability dimensions based on the case of Sweden. The framework originates in scholarship on policy success and failure, and includes a spectrum of outcomes from success to failure in each dimension.

Intelligence oversight arrangements are often studied in terms of their capacity as scrutinisers of the effectiveness, efficiency and propriety of intelligence agencies.[3] Occasionally, the effectiveness of the arrangements as such are also studied. On the US Congress, Amy Zegart contends that 'weak intelligence oversight is a reasonable and useful point of departure'.[4] Some, like Peter Gill, list elements of what would qualify as effective oversight but put analytical weight on obstacles to effectiveness.[5] Njord Wegge and Thorsten Wetzling provide a percipient discussion of the increasingly legalistic nature of intelligence oversight and the challenges overseers face in enacting the laws, let alone those faced by the research community in gaining insight into their functioning: 'Researchers outside the ring of secrecy are often left with little choice but to draw inferences on partial and sometimes politicised information.'[6] Scrutinising intelligence agencies, which is the role and function of overseers, is therefore difficult, while academically assessing the effectiveness of their efforts is just as daunting.

The intelligence studies research community is not unique in finding it challenging to assess the effectiveness of various policy arrangements. Policy scholars have been grappling with similar issues for decades, albeit seemingly without paying much attention to policies related to intelligence affairs. Conversely, references to policy scholars are few and far between in intelligence research. This is probably one reason for the predominantly instrumentalist analyses, which depart from given policy instruments and discuss the difficulties overseers have in using them. There is a certain negativity bias built into the research designs. In order to discuss intelligence oversight effectiveness, this article takes stock of the scholarly debate on policy success and failure. This debate, in turn, developed out of policy evaluation scholarship dominated by a quest to improve policy through evidence-based analyses.[7] Pioneered by Bovens and 't Hart's *Understanding Policy Fiascoes*,[8] the policy success/failure debate involves more dimensions of policy evaluation than the traditional instrumental understanding, and notably contains a political dimension. In essence, what might be a policy failure in terms of immediate service delivery could harbour political and strategic gains for the future, and vice versa. This article aspires to contribute to the flourishing body of intelligence oversight analysis by probing a multidimensional framework. As is further elaborated below, the analysis is explicitly sensitive to nuances of success.

Policymaking on Swedish intelligence oversight serves as an illustrative case study here since it is the case best known to the author. It is, therefore worth mentioning that the point of departure is *not* that the Swedish case necessarily merits the label of policy success; in fact, the success level varies between dimensions, and dilemmas observed elsewhere are certainly also present to varying degrees in Sweden. There is a heuristic value in assessing policy arrangements with eyes sensitive to what works. The dimensions are, therefore broad enough to capture variations in effectiveness.

Looking on the bright side of intelligence policymaking

The extent to which public policies deliver is a pivotal concern for policymakers and academics alike. Much scholarly attention has been paid to policies that have failed to live up to purported goals, such as in the classic works by Pressman and Wildavsky, and Hall.[9] In aspiring to improve the policymaking process, the academic field has developed a culture of seeking to understand and explain failure. More recently, concern that this type of scholarly endeavour has contributed to widespread public mistrust of government has created a counterwave of scholarship preoccupied with mapping and understanding policy success.[10] This is to some extent a new deal for policy scholars, at least when success parameters become selection criteria for case analysis. In this case success is not a selection criterion, but the analytical framework at least dampens the effects of potential negativity bias. Success and failure are polar opposites on a continuum when assessing policy effectiveness. What constitutes success or failure is, of course, inherently contestable. Even if consensus can be reached on a good match between purported policy goals and the ensuing results of the policy intervention, those in a position to have formulated the goals will be more likely to proclaim success.[11] While admitting a slight exaggeration in paraphrasing Clausewitz, Bovens et al. assert that evaluating policy 'is nothing but the continuation of politics by other means'.[12] The analyst must therefore proceed with caution in inventing categories and criteria for evaluation. However, rather than resolving political disagreements on evaluative criteria, which must anyway be a task of the political process, the analyst, according to Majone, would be better 'facilitat[ing] a wide-ranging dialogue among advocates of different criteria'.[13]

To this end, McConnell has made an influential contribution by categorising relatively open dimensions of policymaking that can succeed or fail, or something in between.[14] For each dimension, the framework tries to establish what would qualify as success, and delineates a spectrum of decreasing levels of success until failure, which is then the mirror image of success. The grey areas in-between are *resilient, conflicted* and *precarious* success.[15] The success spectrum certainly reflects a nominal scale intended to facilitate analyses based on judgment, where the nuances serve the purpose of avoiding assessing anything short of a clear success as constituting a failure. This undoubtedly allows for more nuanced analysis and discussion of the effectiveness of public policymaking. The dimensions in question have been refined over the past decade, and this article sets out from the dimensions put forth by Compton and 't Hart, such as programmatic, process, political and endurance dimensions.[16]

These dimensions were constructed to capture policy success and to relate empirical findings to their fit with success criteria. These dimensions are further explored below in the realm of secret intelligence policymaking, or more precisely the policy subfield of intelligence oversight. Here it is, however relevant to point out that the general idea with the dimensions is to enable assessment of different areas, certainly stressing that the political is one of them, and thereby showcasing that policy interventions typically succeed to varying degrees simultaneously, depending on the dimension. Moreover, the relatively broad categories lend themselves more easily to comparison between polities, compared for example to the evaluation of singular policy instruments (the functioning of which may pertain to contextual features in a polity). Within the study of intelligence oversight, the observation that 'comparative research must amount to more than the juxtaposition of a range of single-country studies',[17] may be indicative of the absence of an appropriate framework. The proof of the pudding lies in the extent to which the case study presented in this article can be seen as an implicit comparison.[18]

As a corollary to public administration scholarship's interest in policy failure, the academic field of intelligence studies has developed a strong current around the theme of intelligence failures, which seeks to understand, explain and learn from them. The dearth of cross-referencing between the two research areas could indicate that there are particularities with secret intelligence (as a policy subsystem) that call for particular consideration when analysing effectiveness. However, the heuristic value of keeping an eye on what works is arguably also valid in the intelligence studies subfield of oversight, as it slants towards a focus on what does not.[19]

The secretive nature of intelligence work and politics is arguably what sets it apart from other issue areas. Policy analysts typically engage in high visibility policymaking, such as on healthcare, education or environmental policies – areas that large parts of the population, researchers included, experience first-hand. The abundance of accessible empirics has provided much material for theorising. The toolbox for assessing policy effectiveness owes a lot to policies that are *public* through and through. For researchers interested in analysing the effectiveness of policies on secret intelligence, the scope of possible cases is more limited. Peter Gill depicts the intelligence governance process as comprising control (direction), prior authorisation (supervising) and oversight (scrutinising), arguing that scholars from outside (of the intelligence community) have their best shot at accessing empirics in the latter oversight phase of the process.[20] From a governance perspective, the scrutinising of policy arrangements that include oversight bodies is important in its own right. Governments bestow their secret intelligence organisations with extraordinary mandates, essentially to carry out tasks that would in other circumstances qualify as unlawful. Oversight is hence a crucial policy arrangement that scrutinises the deeds of intelligence organisations at the behest of open society.

Oversight: programmatic, process, political and endurance effectiveness

Any attempt to delineate what intelligence oversight is and what it is not will inevitably also be interspersed with contextual features, most notably regarding the nature of the political system. Just as the US notion relies on the Framers' ideas on checks and balances,[21] the Swedish notion falls back on control and supervision ('oversight' does not translate easily into Swedish).[22] Such cultural aspects are integral to expectations of what oversight ought to achieve. To exemplify, a fairly common view of intelligence oversight is that, '[i]t suggests something looser than control in the sense of day-to-day management of the operations of the agencies'.[23] This seems to hold for systems where the legislature is the premier overseer, but arguably less so where expert bodies within the executive branch perform the role, at least spot-checking on day-to-day activities. Not surprisingly, therefore, the more oversight arrangements are subject to comparison, the broader the scope of oversight tends to be. Oversight can hence be understood as something that happens before (i.e., authorising), during, or after an intelligence operation.[24] It can encompass scrutiny by the executive and/or the legislature, as well as the actual legislating.[25] Emphasis can be put on effectiveness, efficiency (cost-benefits), or propriety (the quality of the laws and lawfulness of the agencies). This is what Gill refers to as the trilemma of scrutiny, since it is difficult to fulfil more than two of the above at a time without renouncing the third.[26] This is not an exhaustive account of definitional variations. The point here is that the catch-all nature of the concept is useful for the purpose of this study. The many ways in which intelligence oversight have been constructed informs the policy dimensions of what could qualify as more or less successful.

Programmatic effectiveness

This dimension straightforwardly examines the relation between policy goals, the theory of change that underpins them, and the policy instruments selected to achieve the goals.[27] Policy arrangements can by design have more or less auspicious prospects of success. In the realm of secret intelligence oversight, the institutional set-up is frequently implied to be pivotal to achieving efficiency and effectiveness.[28] Policy goals are often vague, and intelligence oversight is no exception. Across polities they revolve around the general idea of safeguarding democratic scrutiny of agencies with extraordinary mandates. The variation is rather to be found in institutional design and the selected policy instruments. Since these are contextually constructed, the task is to analyse their viability in any given polity. To be successful, there must be tangible evidence that what was once problematic is now considerably less so. Governments have a range of policy instruments to choose from when designing and redesigning oversight arrangements.

In the mid–1970s, the introduction of oversight arrangements proliferated, especially in western democracies,[29] which indicates that governments are impressionable and learn from each other in this policy domain. Intelligence oversight can be kept together in a designated legislative committee or in a committee external to the legislature, or be dispersed in various bodies with varying relations to the legislature and the executive. Expertise in intelligence work can be mixed with expertise in law and technology, and with lay persons' perspectives. Mandates can be specific and narrow or wide-ranging and all-encompassing. Do intelligence agencies need to be better at abiding by the law, or is the legitimacy of their actions being questioned? Arguably, the question somehow insinuates a false dichotomy, since consistently ignoring the law decreases legitimacy. However, keeping the oversight capacity close to the legislature is often seen as enhancing legitimacy,[30] whereas oversight by the executive, be it a ministry or an external authority, restrains the illegality of agencies.[31] Intentionally or not, different designs convey different problem representations.

Process effectiveness

The effectiveness of a policy programme or arrangement must take account of the design and procedural organisation of decision-making and implementation. To be successful an oversight arrangement must confer legitimacy on the policy. The design process needs to carefully take into consideration the mix of policy instruments that would be contextually appropriate, to be perceived as correct and fair. Different stakeholders should ideally be given the opportunity to influence the policymaking process before choices are made. Process effectiveness also implies striking a balance between acceptable costs and adequate levels of funding, and agreeing on realistic timelines.[33]

Parliamentary ownership has in a comparative study by Born & Wetzling emerged 'as a decisive condition for the overall success of intelligence control'.[34] The argument rests on the premise of independence of the legislature vis-à-vis the executive (including the agencies). It also presupposes an engagement and commitment by legislators, which is harder to achieve (see next section). Rather than independence, which in parliamentary systems are characterised by shades of grey, the nature of the relation between overseers and overseen may be telling as to the process effectiveness. According to Wegge, security service staff in north-western Europe caution that overseers, especially if they are parliamentarians aligned with the incumbent executive, sometimes use secret information for their own political purposes rather than to safeguard national security.[35] In general, there is an information asymmetry between the secret intelligence agencies and their overseers, since the latter rely on the former to obtain information. As long as the attitude among the secret services is one of mistrust of the overseers' precautions taken with secret information, they are likely to veer on the minimalistic side of cooperation. Undoubtedly, such a relationship seriously hampers the effectiveness of the oversight arrangement.

Oversight arrangements have become commonplace in recent decades, and part of the normal in secret intelligence agencies in democracies. The two parties have developed different relations depending on the context.

Some intelligence agencies have learned that keeping the overseers happy can turn them into patrons, which is particularly useful if the overseers have any influence over budgets.[36] From an effectiveness perspective, there is obviously a risk that the overseers might be co-opted by the agencies in 'the subtle process by which watchdogs are transformed into lapdogs'.[37]

In order to be effective, overseers obviously need resources in terms of both investigative powers and mandates. For a mandate to qualify as successful, it must allow the overseer to dig as deeply as it finds pertinent. At the very minimum, overseers must not be able to complain about weak mandates. However, a strong mandate does not get very far if its owners do not know where to look or what to ask. Some level of expertise is therefore necessary for oversight bodies to be effective, but also sufficient time to absorb the culture and probe relevant factors.[38] In some countries oversight is chiefly conducted by the legislature, in the case of the US Congress by subcommittees in the Senate and the House of Representatives. Amy Zegart has reported on the difficulties in attaining an acceptable level of expertise, especially in the House of Representatives which has biennial elections.[39] A key to developing the expertise required to ask relevant questions of the right people and for the right documents is a relatively slow turnover of staff and organised handovers. Perhaps the major drawback with having inexperienced overseers is that the overseen agencies can more easily keep up a lip-serving facade, behind which nothing really changes, or what Rittberger and Goetz call an organised hypocrisy and Hijzen refers to as a ritual dance.[40]

Political effectiveness

For a policy arrangement to be politically successful, it needs to garner a broad coalition of supporters among policymakers and representatives in authority. It needs to ramp up the reputation of its initiators, or at least to be largely unchallenged.[42] Mustering legislative commitment to secret intelligence work presents challenges as incentives are largely absent. The political payoff is too small and the issue area complex and time-consuming to penetrate.[43] A political reluctance to engage with secret intelligence affairs clearly detracts from the effectiveness of the policy area, not least in terms of its legitimacy. Politicians, Loch Johnson observes, however tend to devote much attention to accountability and turn to firefighting mode when intelligence failures break open or when scandals erupt, only to gradually fall back to a low-intensity patrolling once the intelligence shock has lost topicality.[44] Success in this dimension would entail visibility on the political agenda and the political will to engage with the complexities of secret intelligence, thereby heightening the political status of secret intelligence as a tool in the service of democracy.

Endurance effectiveness

The longevity of a policy arrangement is an essential but insufficient indicator of success. As social and politico-administrative environments gradually evolve, arrangements must also adapt and learn in order to deliver on the initially purported core objective: to excel at dynamic conservatism.[46] There is nothing about this policy dimension that is particular to secret intelligence. All organisations and institutions periodically face surprises and critical events, and at times must endure heavy criticism for not having been vigilant enough. To be successful in this dimension, actors within the oversight arrangement will need to perform pre-emptive adaptation in order to absorb new circumstances and to protect the core institutions. If the core objective of the arrangement is to increase the legitimacy of secret intelligence, adaptations should ideally enhance legitimacy. A pertinent question, however, is how long a rope is in this context; what would qualify as policy longevity? Typically, a full policy cycle, including agenda-setting, decision-making, implementation, and evaluation based on feed-back loops, takes about a decade (or more).[47] Success criteria can therefore relate to the policy cycle. By the end of it, even initial core institutions may be in need of reassessment.

Intelligence oversight in Sweden: A Success Story?

In the case of Sweden, secret intelligence encompasses both defence and law enforcement agencies, with foreign as well as domestic remits. The foreign/defence side comprises four intelligence agencies, two of which – the Swedish Armed Forces Intelligence and Security Agency (MUST) and the National Defence Radio Establishment (NDRE) – actively collect intelligence. The other two, the Swedish Defence Research Agency and the Defence Materiel are passive consumers of intelligence, and therefore of lesser interest to overseers and in terms of this paper. The defence intelligence agencies are overseen by the Foreign Intelligence Inspectorate (FII). On the domestic/law enforcement side, the Security Service, the National Police, the Public Prosecutor, Swedish Customs and the Swedish Economic Crime Authority are overseen by the Swedish Commission on Security and Integrity Protection. The Swedish National Audit Organisation scrutinises all authorities, including the defence and security sector, with a focus on efficiency. The Swedish Authority for Privacy Protection supervises authorities' adherence to rules on personal data. The focus of this article is on oversight arrangements in relation to foreign/defence intelligence.

Analysis of the programmatic dimension

By the turn of the millennium, when the Cold War seemed far away and international terrorism and other non-military menaces had largely replaced military threats, at least from the Swedish horizon, the time was ripe for a review of the tasks of the intelligence agencies and their ways of working. The wider security agenda that had been generally embraced called for a shift in the centre of gravity from traditional military warning of an armed invasion, and from comprehensive tactical and operative military forewarning, to strategic, non-military intelligence, as well as more selective monitoring of military operations in the near abroad and a greater focus on broader and longer term security policy analysis.[49] Intelligence agencies were therefore supposed to be alert to international terrorism and international organised crime, as well as the potential risks related to migration flows and climate change. To this end, the Government proposed replacing the concept of *military* intelligence with the broader concept of *defence* intelligence. Essentially, all foreign threats should be assessed and analysed by the intelligence agencies in support of Swedish foreign, security and defence policies, and in order to identify external military threats to the country. Activities should also assist Sweden's participation in international security cooperation.[50] This transition happened without much fanfare, arguably because it made sense to make use of available resources more effectively and adapt to the new realities.

Controversial adaptations

The intelligence oversight arrangement remained unchanged until the second half of the first decade of the new century, when a new government proposed changes to the intelligence legislation. In June 2007, the government proposed deleting the word *military* from section 2 of the Swedish Law (2000:130) on defence intelligence operations so that intelligence agencies would now identify external threats to the country as opposed to external military threats, which parliament found unproblematic. The government also drafted a new Signals Intelligence Act, empowering the National Defence Radio Establishment (NDRE) to intercept data traffic in fibre optic cables. Previously, they could only listen to signals in the ether, which made their job less and less effective since so much traffic had moved to cables.[51] In sharp contrast to the enlargement of the remit of intelligence agencies, considerable controversy surrounded extending the means by which the signals intelligence agency could gather information. Wire-tapping cables obviously raised the possibility of mass surveillance of data traffic, such as e-mail, which caused considerable public discontent. Even though the government had a parliamentary majority, parliament put the proposed Signals Intelligence Act on hold for twelve months. When a slightly amended version of the Act was tabled for parliamentary discussion and a vote in June 2008 it passed; however parliament stated that the law should be further amended. The government was asked to specify *how* the law would act to protect the privacy of individuals, and to confirm that the authorising body for signals intelligence operations would be organisationally separate from the oversight body and have similar procedures to a court.[52] The Signals Intelligence Act became law on 1 January 2009. The tapping of cables was supposed to start on 1 October 2009 but was delayed until 1 December due to the 'extensive and meticulous treatment of the Parliament's suggested amendment to the Signals Intelligence Act'.[53] Even though the basic structures of the intelligence oversight body were more or less settled by the initial 2007 Government proposition, the ensuing political process emphasized the importance of its free-standing role and strong powers.

Historical reasons for controversy

The Foreign Intelligence Inspectorate replaced its predecessor, the Intelligence Committee (Underrättelsenämnden), an organisation within the Swedish Armed Forces which had been established in 1976 following a scandal that emerged in 1973.[54] Two journalists had published a story about the military intelligence organisation's special operations branch, the IB (Information Bureau). Part of their story revolved around the domestic activities of IB, and that part became highly politicised. The article suggested that military intelligence had infiltrated political parties on the far-left and other lawful organisations, and had kept files on 20,000 individuals.[55] In particular, the purported links between the IB and the Social Democratic Party, which by 1973 had ruled Sweden for 41 years, fuelled its politicisation. The so-called IB affair gave rise to an investigation by the Parliament Defence Committee, a government investigation and an investigation by the Justice Ombudsman.[56] The Intelligence Committee was thus a product of these investigations. The Justice Ombudsman confirmed that the IB had spied on people living in Sweden, often by infiltrating political organisations, but found that this was not directed by the Social Democratic Party.[57] However, the IB affair lingered in Swedish political life, and official reports were published in 1976, 1979, 1980, 1998 and 2002. The affair became an issue in the general election campaigns of 1973, 1988, 1991 and 1998, and has been the subject of numerous books and documentaries.[58] A 2002 report established that the IB and the Social Democratic Party were to some extent entangled, and that the party benefited from this entanglement.[59] It is therefore important to keep in mind that the 1973 IB affair was not just a historical event when the revamped signals intelligence legislation became politicised at the end of the 2000s. The process of amendment clarified the objectives of signals intelligence – as a tool for the acquisition of foreign intelligence – and specified the procedure for authorisation of operations and the destruction of information.[60]

Hence, the current oversight arrangement with regard to defence intelligence stems from December 2009, when the Signals Intelligence Act took practical effect. The arrangement consists of an authority, the Foreign Intelligence Inspectorate (FII),[61] but also of a privacy protection representative (integritetsskyddsombud) based at the Foreign Intelligence Court (Försvarsunderrättelsedomstolen), an authorising body, and a Privacy Protection Council located at the Signals Intelligence Agency (NDRE), appointed by the government with a mandate to observe the measures taken to ensure the integrity of individuals involved in signals intelligence operations. Thus, apart from the external authority, there are also elements of what Born & Wetzel call embedded human rights in intelligence affairs.[62]

Programmatic Assessment

The fact that FII was made an independent authority outside the armed forces is undeniably a step in the right direction for obtaining independent scrutiny. The creation of an authorising Foreign Intelligence Court, and the division of labour between it and the FII are also important for avoiding compromising the integrity of the scrutiniser. The iteration process leading up to the amended legal framework at the end of the decade almost exclusively considered safeguarding the protection of individual privacy from potentially intrusive intelligence agencies, implying that the theory of change was based on legitimacy. Most of the legitimisation however relates to the legal framework, which in a way boxes in what oversight should mean. On balance, however, given the period of amendments, Swedish intelligence oversight arrangements qualify as a resilient success on this dimension.

Analysis of the process-related dimension

The Intelligence oversight arrangement

Signals intelligence gathering in particular became more regulated under the new legislation and new authorities, so the oversight arrangement also needed to be revamped, with a core objective to ensure that the actions of the defence intelligence agencies were lawful. However, their mandate also included ensuring that defence intelligence was conducted in accordance with directives, to scrutinise signals and human intelligence work carried out by special means, to scrutinise other means and methods for collecting information, and to review the principles for recruiting and training personnel. The FII must also oversee MUST's and the NDRE's treatment of personal data, respond to allegations from the general public that intelligence agencies have unduly intercepted their messages (i.e., ex post facto reviews), and control the agencies' usage of qualified protected identities. In addition, FII has the exclusive right to give the NDRE access to signals bearers when authorised by the Foreign Intelligence Court and a mandate to discontinue information gathering that is not authorised by this court.[63]

The FII comprises up to seven committee members, of whom the president and vice president are experienced judges and the rest are nominated by the parliamentary party groupings, but appointed by the government for a term of at least four years. (Most commonly, they are former parliamentarians.) The authority also has a secretariat of five to six people working full time, while the committee convenes when called on by its chair or at the request of one of the defence intelligence agencies. The FII conducts some 20 to 30 investigations per year, and is free to decide for itself what to investigate. The Swedish intelligence oversight arrangement is more ambitious than the one in place before the 2008 regulations and the 2009 amendments. In addition to increased resources intended to reflect the increased mandate bestowed on the Signals Intelligence Agency, it was also given a more independent role in relation to the agencies it is supposed to oversee and enhanced investigative powers. The FII is not an isolated entity. The ordinances governing its functioning state that it can call on experts in its deliberations when needed.[64] In its annual reports, it regularly chronicles having paid study visits to peer organisations abroad and in Sweden, especially to peers overseeing the domestic arena.[65]

Domestic reassurance

The Swedish National Audit Office (NAO) investigated the FII in 2015 and, from an effectiveness perspective, its report was rather comforting. Among other things, it observed that the FII has been well funded from the start. In fact, the FII had not spent its entire budget in a single year since its inception[66]; and that holds up until fiscal year (FY) 2021.[67] The Swedish NAO also found that the FII had been fulfilling its obligations according to the law and ordinances.[68] The Swedish NAO believes that the agencies under the FII's scrutiny are attentive to the latter's opinions and recommendations.[69] In the period 2010–21, the FII conducted 303 examinations, 29 of which led to opinions and recommendations (16 to the NDRE and 13 to MUST). In its annual reports, the FII writes of having a good rapport with the agencies it scrutinises, based on dialogue and a will to guide them on legally difficult balancing acts.[70] To the extent that trends can be identified with such low numbers, the most recent six-year period has seen a decrease in opinions, as about 6 percent of all examinations led to the issuance of opinions compared to about 11 per cent in the first six years.[71] This might be indicative of intelligence agencies learning from scrutiny, and in that sense also becoming more effective in their work.

An International Reality Check

The NGO Centrum för rättvisa (Center for Justice) first reported the Signals Intelligence Act to the European Court of Human Rights in 2008. It took until May 2021 for the Grand Chamber of the ECHR to deliver its verdict, which found the state of Sweden and the Signals Intelligence Act in breach of Article 8 of the European Convention: the right to respect for private and family life, home and correspondence. In large part, the ECHR found the legislation to be of high quality, but the arrangement nonetheless suffered from three shortcomings: the absence of a clear rule on destroying intercepted material which [does] not contain personal data; the absence of a requirement in the Signals Intelligence Act or other relevant legislation that, when deciding to transmit intelligence material to foreign partners, consideration [is] given to the privacy interests of individuals; and the absence of an effective *ex post facto* review.[72]

The last point constitutes unadorned disapproval of Swedish intelligence oversight arrangements as far as ex post facto reviews are concerned. This is what the FII does at the request of individuals who want to know whether their communications have been intercepted by the NDRE. In the period 2010–21 such a request occurred on 171 occasions, and in none of them did the FII find any undue interception by the NDRE.[73] The problem that the ECHR pointed out is that it cannot be ruled out that the FII might have incentives not to find undue interceptions, since this would mean that their oversight of the NDRE had at some point been at fault. The dual roles are in principle incompatible.[74]

The Government communicated an action plan to the ECHR in May 2022, according to which any shortcomings would be addressed in a forthcoming government inquiry, which would be a fundamental review of the Signals Intelligence Act. The same went for the absence of an effective ex post facto review, even though the government referred to the independence enjoyed by the Swedish authorities which meant that it was up to the FII to interpret laws and ordinances. The government announced the remit of the inquiry in June 2022. It will make recommendations on the issues addressed by the ECHR in April 2023 and complete its work in April 2024.[75] The FII does not mention the ECHR ruling in its 2021 annual report. It does, however, discuss the difficulties of measuring the effectiveness of secret intelligence oversight. It maintained that it is not only through its opinions and recommendations that it exerts influence–the fact that the intelligence agencies know that they are being regularly scrutinised also has an impact.[76]

Parliament discusses signals intelligence in early March each year, based on the report that the FII submits to the MoD in February, which is then passed on to the Parliamentary Defence Committee. In 2022, this discussion took place on 2 March, only days after the Russian military invaded Ukraine. Only one representative of the Moderate Party (opposition, right wing) and the Social Democratic Party (minority government) respectively took part in the debate, and the discussion revolved around the upcoming government inquiry into the Signals Intelligence Act. The Moderate Party member lamented that it had not started years ago, since he regarded it as paramount to increase the capacity of signals intelligence. He also made a case for more transparency when it comes to international cooperation among intelligence agencies, thereby touching on the second point of criticism by the ECHR. The Social Democrat parliamentarian, a former president of the FII, said that the inquiry would start in due course. Both professed the importance of strong and capable intelligence agencies, and praised the functioning of the highly important oversight arrangements.[77]

Process assessment

The process leading up to the legislative framework and institutional set-up seems to have conferred legitimacy on the arrangement. This was arguably paramount in order to satisfy a sense of fairness and of the correctness of the arrangement, given the nature of the debate at the time. The 2015 (domestic) reality check by the Swedish NAO consolidated intentions of a well-funded and authoritative FII that actually works. The mandates are wide and the expertise is developing. In light of the continuously underutilised budget, one however wonders why they have not assumed a larger assignment. Is there nothing more to scrutinise? The financial suit was adjusted after the Swedish NAO's investigation, but is still oversized, which allows for the interpretation that a balance has been struck between acceptable costs and appropriate funding, including some growth potential. When looking only at the domestic arena, the process dimension is a clear success. Obviously, the verdict from the ECHR does not speak in favour of a successful assessment of the legislative framework, even though the ruling also said that for the most part it was sound. From the perspective of the international herald of guiding principles on legal security, the verdict is arguably somewhere between resilient and conflicted success.

Analysis of the Political Dimension

Political engagement and complacency

Compared to many other western democracies, the Swedish Parliament plays a fairly unobtrusive role as an overseer of secret intelligence. Oversight authorities are responsible to the government, and for defence intelligence to the Ministry of Defence. This means that oversight is an arrangement within the executive branch. Naturally, the government is responsible to parliament so the Ministry of Defence submits a report to parliament on an annual basis on the oversight of defence intelligence, which is debated first in the Defence Committee and then in a plenary session. When the Signals Intelligence Act was amended in 2008–2009, however, parliament asked the government for annual reports only on oversight of the Signals Intelligence Act. For this reason, the annual reports and the parliamentary discussion only concern that legislation; not how the intelligence agencies operate more generally. Of the FII's 303 investigations in the period 2010–21, 82 had a bearing on the Signals Intelligence Act, yielding six opinions and recommendations.[78] Of the rest of the FII's activities, the 221 examinations that led to 23 opinions have by arrangement not been of visible interest to parliament. In fact, not even the oversight of signals intelligence led to much discussion in parliament.

Every year since 2010, the Defence Committee has endorsed the report from the Ministry of Defence and rejected the few motions raised, and this has been endorsed in the plenary. Motions have been issued by the Sweden Democrats, which argues that the fact that not all parliamentary parties are represented in the FII is a democratic deficiency. The Left Party laments the NDRE's close ties with US intelligence agencies, especially in the light of the Snowden revelations. The Moderates, Christian Democrats and Liberals have generally pushed for a wider mandate for the NDRE. The overall impression however is that the political establishment as a whole, including the government of the day and parliament, is highly complacent with regard to the intelligence agencies and the oversight arrangement set up to scrutinise them. There is no intelligence committee in parliament so defence intelligence is discussed in the Parliamentary Defence Committee. On the one hand, the broader scope of the committee reduces the risk of disincentivised parliamentarians, as discussed by Zegart,[79] but consideration of intelligence affairs might also be diluted in the sea of defence-related issues.

Political assessment

The Swedish political establishment regularly reiterates the importance of a vigorous oversight arrangement for preserving public trust in the intelligence agencies, not least given the secrecy surrounding the matters they are working on. The Swedish arrangement gives the impression of having the necessary checks and balances in place and there is little or no evidence of dissatisfaction among stakeholders. Within the Swedish bubble, there is a strong narrative that the intelligence oversight arrangements are a success story, as the legal framework is rigorous, it champions the rule of law, and it encourages the intelligence agencies to be effective within legal parameters. This self-confident self-image does not seem to have been particularly harmed by the 2021 ruling by the ECHR. It is as if we are all excellent when we mark our own homework. On the domestic arena, there is however nothing much that detracts from success criteria, even though the disinterest shown by Parliament in intelligence matters beyond the working of the Signals Intelligence Act rather testifies to a complacent indifference.

Analysis of the endurance dimension

Changing requirements

One of the 2008–2009 amendments involved a specification as to which agencies should be able to direct NDRE operations. The original 2008 law left this up to the government to decide but the amendment allows only the government, the Government Offices and the armed forces to direct NDRE operations. This has consequences for law enforcement authorities, which also need signals intelligence on foreign targets. An official government inquiry and a ministerial inquiry investigated policing needs and their conclusions led to a government proposition that was accepted by parliament, which means that of 1 January 2013 the Security Services and the National Police can direct the NDRE's signals intelligence.[80] As a result of the 7 April 2017 terrorist attack in Stockholm, a cross-coalition agreement between six of the eight parliamentary parties (excluding the Sweden Democrats and the Left party) paved the way for the police and the Security Services to direct the NDRE during ongoing criminal investigations,[81] which had been explicitly ruled out in the 2009 amendment.[82] In 2021, the principle that signals intelligence operations could be allowed only where at least one party (sender or receiver) was located abroad was nibbled around the edges, since it was made inapplicable if the signals pertain to foreign military personnel, foreign state ships, foreign state aircraft or foreign military vehicles.[83] In November 2021, parliament also decided that signals intelligence could under certain circumstances be gathered at the behest of international parties, even in the absence of a threat to Sweden or Swedish interests.[84] Slowly, the reservations that once set the tone for the 2009 amendments have given way to empowering secret intelligence agencies.

Endurance assessment

Once up and running, the Swedish intelligence oversight arrangements have remained intact in terms of structure, mandate and resources since 1 December 2009. At the same time, the legislative framework that governs the intelligence agencies has undergone incremental change, to some extent rolling back the 2009 amendments. From a strict controlling-the-legality perspective, it is possible to argue that enhancing the mandates of the agencies made it easier for them to stay within the law, thereby lowering the burden on the oversight arrangement. In a way, the arrangement may be seen to have protected the agencies from scrutiny. Indeed, the number of opinions from the FII has decreased over the years, although this could also be attributable to learning and adaptation processes in the FII. At least by its own account, the FII has improved its methods over the years and developed expertise in how to control and encourage the agencies, which speaks to a developing effectiveness not only of the FII, but also of the intelligence community. Worth mentioning is also that the Snowden revelations, a potential pusher for overhaul of intelligence-related policies everywhere, did not leave any traces on Swedish intelligence oversight. In terms of durability, the arrangements have been successful.

Concluding Remarks

It is one thing to compare intelligence oversight policy instruments with the conditions on their use by overseers and be disappointed, but this was never the objective of this study. Rather, by applying broader dimensions of policy evaluation that in and of themselves maintain a distance from politicised assessments, it has sought to disentangle evaluative categories and allow a more nuanced view of success. Overall, however, it is difficult to avoid the assessment that Swedish intelligence oversight arrangements are in a better state today than they were before 2009. That is not to say that there is no room for further improvement, but the direction of travel is promising. In a nutshell, the relative longevity of Swedish intelligence oversight arrangements is probably attributable to the legitimacy given to them by the iterative process that led to their inception, that is, the theory of change. Most domestic observers seem to find the policy instruments appropriate and purposeful. Whether the political enthusiasm is genuine or merely reflects a lack of interest, however, is hard to tell. The fact that the signals intelligence legislation, including the oversight arrangements, is up for review after 12 years could be testament to a dynamic conservatism or to a hands-off approach until internal and external circumstances call for change.

This type of analysis deliberately omits some of the difficulties that overseers might run into when implementing policy instruments, and instead focuses on policy arrangements. It adds value because it complements analyses of a more instrumentalist nature, and perhaps inspires a focus on the bright side of secret intelligence policymaking. It is, after all, not certain that the relative success of Swedish intelligence oversight arrangements had been identified at all within more traditional analyses. That being said, adopting the analytical framework has also implied some challenges, which may provide fruit for thought in future refinements. In particular, the issue of from whose vantage point assessment should depart has proved somewhat problematic. Intelligence oversight is domestically oriented, which made it difficult to accommodate the outsider's view, in this case the verdict from the ECHR. The secret nature of intelligence also made it problematic to assess political effectiveness, at least in the absence of scandals or intelligence failures that could have distilled engagement from complacency. However, the lack of intelligence shocks may testify to the effectiveness of the oversight arrangement.

Acknowledgements: I want to thank Tom Lundborg for insightful comments on an early draft of this article, and the two anonymous reviewers who provided very constructive criticism. Disclosure statement. No potential conflict of interest was reported by the author(s). Additional information. Notes on contributors. Dan Hansén is Associate Professor of Political Science at the Swedish Defence University. He has an interest in the politics of intelligence, in particular in relation to crisis management, which includes crisis decision-making as well as accountability and learning aspects that inform subsequent preparedness. He has published numerous articles and book chapters in journals such as Journal of Public Administration Research and Theory, Journal of Contingencies and Crisis Management, Public Administration, and with publishers including Routledge and Cambridge University Press.Journal information: Print ISSN: 0268-4527 Online ISSN: 1743-9019. 7 issues per year. Intelligence and National Security is covered by the following abstracting, indexing and citation services: ABC-CLIO - Historical Abstracts; ABC-CLIO - America: History and Life; World Political Science Abstracts; Historical Abstracts and America: life and history; CSA Political Science and Government and British Humantities Index; Lancaster Index to Defence; International Security Literature and Sociological Abstracts. Taylor & Francis make every effort to ensure the accuracy of all the information (the "Content") contained in our publications. However, Taylor & Francis, our agents (including the editor, any member of the editorial team or editorial board, and any guest editors), and our licensors, make no representations or warranties whatsoever as to the accuracy, completeness, or suitability for any purpose of the Content. Any opinions and views expressed in this publication are the opinions and views of the authors, and are not the views of or endorsed by Taylor & Francis. The accuracy of the Content should not be relied upon and should be independently verified with primary sources of information. Taylor & Francis shall not be liable for any losses, actions, claims, proceedings, demands, costs, expenses, damages, and other liabilities whatsoever or howsoever caused arising directly or indirectly in connection with, in relation to, or arising out of the use of the Content. Terms & Conditions of access and use can be found at http://www.tandfonline.com/page/terms-and-conditions. Aims and scope."The premier journal of intelligence studies" Eliot A. Cohen, Foreign Affairs. Intelligence has never played a more prominent role in international politics than it does now in the early years of the twenty-first century. National intelligence services are larger than ever, and they are more transparent in their activities in the policy making of democratic nations. Intelligence and National Security is widely regarded as the world's leading scholarly journal focused on the role of intelligence and secretive agencies in international relations. It examines this aspect of national security from a variety of perspectives and academic disciplines, with insightful articles research and written by leading experts based around the globe. Among the topics covered in the journal are: the historical development of intelligence agencies, representations of intelligence in popular culture, public understandings and expectations related to intelligence, intelligence and ethics, intelligence collection and analysis, covert action and counterintelligence, privacy and intelligence accountability, the outsourcing of intelligence operations the role of politics in intelligence activities, international intelligence cooperation and burden-sharing, the relationships among intelligence agencies, military organizations, and civilian policy departments. Assessing intelligence oversight: the case of Sweden. Dan Hansén. To cite this article: Dan Hansén (2023): Assessing intelligence oversight: the case of Sweden,Intelligence and National Security, DOI: 10.1080/02684527.2023.2222534. To link to this article: https://doi.org/10.1080/02684527.2023.2222534.© 2023 The Author(s). Published by Informa.UK Limited, trading as Taylor & Francis Group. Published online: 11 Jun 2023.

Chapter 10

The Spy Power, Technological Innovations, and the Human Dimensions of Intelligence: Recent Presidential Abuse of America's Secret Agencies

Loch K. Johnson

Introduction

The purpose of national security intelligence is to provide policy officials with an advantage in the making of effective policy, based on the collection and analysis of accurate information from around the world that can help to illuminate a decision. Foreknowledge is invaluable in the service of a nation's security; and, in the gathering of useful information, technological innovations in the world of intelligence can result in a stronger shield to protect citizens against the many dangers that lurk across the continents in this uncertain and hostile world. Among the technological innovations that have allowed the United States to forge one of the most sophisticated intelligence capabilities in history have been: Ever greater resolution for cameras on surveillance satellites orbiting the earth or hovering over a battlefield; Listening and sensing devices placed on omnibus, as well as niche, satellites in space that can pick up conversations, electronic and radioactive emissions, and other insightful data from the ground below; Sea-based sonar devices that can track submarines deep within the seven seas and far beyond the horizon; Increasingly capable Unmanned Aerial Vehicles (UAVs) or drones that come in a variety of sizes, from insect and hummingbird dimensions to large aircraft with multiple collection capabilities—all with ever quieter engines, higher resolution cameras, prolonged hovering abilities, and, when necessary, devastating missilery. Messaging devices that have come a long way from the secret notes once fastened to the legs of pigeons, relying now on microsecond burst transmissions from asset-to-handler via satellite linkages; Communications equipment that now appears to be a harmless packet of cigarettes or a shampoo bottle, rather than a bulky radio transmitter; Better-than-Hollywood disguises that can magically transform a James Bond into a Beatrix Potter.

Upgraded tools for lock-picking, state-of-the-art computer hacking skills, and listening wires that make the Soviet bug inside the U.S. embassy seal in Moscow during the Cold War look as primitive as a Model-T Ford.[2] The list goes on, especially at a classified level where technological breakthroughs can be found that are far more astonishing than even these remarkable advances known to the public. Despite all the marvels of modern espionage tradecraft, the governments that rely on them must still deal with the human side of intelligence activities. Unfortunately, arrogance, shortsightedness, laziness, frenetic schedules, and the corrosive influences of power (among other flaws) often lead policy officials to ignore or warp the advantages they could accrue from advanced intelligence spycraft, if they would only use these sources and methods properly. This article examines some of the problems that imperfect human behaviour has created for intelligence in the United States at the highest levels of government over the past two decades.

The US Leadership and the Spy Power

While impressive achievements have been made by the United States and other nations with respect to "techint" (technical intelligence), the men and women in high office for whom this information is intended have frequently failed to appreciate its value; worse still, they have abused the secret agencies that are the sources of the information. These leaders have turned to the intelligence organizations in inappropriate ways or, just as foolishly, they have discounted their relevance altogether. This article presents a capsule chronicle of key human deficiencies that have detracted from the technological successes of the U.S. spy agencies during the three most recent White House administrations, led by Presidents George W. Bush, Barack Obama, and Donald J. Trump.

One of the most important, and disquieting, aspects of the human shortcomings associated with intelligence activities is the gravest threat to any democratic society: the aggrandizement of power within the hands of a single leader—a drift toward autocracy. All too frequently, recent presidents have rejected the prescriptions of the U.S. Constitution, whose drafters went to great lengths in 1789 to ensure that power would never accumulate into the hands of another tyrant, now that the new nation had fought its way out from under the heavy hand of King George III. In place of autocratic rule, power in the new Republic would be dispersed among three branches of government: the executive, legislative, and judicial. "Ambition would be made to counteract ambition," as the leading drafter of the Constitution, James Madison, put it.[3]

Above every other goal, the purpose of the Constitution was to hold executive power in check, by the rule of law and the establishment of other centers of governance—Congress and the courts—to share in the making of decisions that would guide the nation's destiny. Under Presidents Bush II, Obama, and Trump, this bedrock principle of "separate institutions sharing power" experienced a troubling erosion, as the United States began a slide toward excessive presidential discretion over intelligence operations— over the spy power, the most secretive and, therefore, the most potentially dangerous of all governmental authorities in a democracy.[4]

Abuses of the Spy Power in the United States

The war power, the treaty power, and the spy power—each has played an important role in America's relations with the world. The first two were central in the writing of the Constitution.[5] The spy power, though, remained outside the normal framework of government at the time and, indeed, for the next 186 years. Not until 1975 did investigators on the Church Committee (led by Frank Church, D, Idaho) persuasively argued in the Senate, in the wake of a domestic spy scandal in the United States, that intelligence agencies should be "brought in from the cold" (a British intelligence expression meaning, in this instance, to make the spy agencies more acceptable in a democratic society by insisting that they conduct themselves within the law and honour moral guardrails) (Johnson, 1985). Congress acted in a bipartisan manner to subject the Central Intelligence Agency (CIA) and its fellow organizations in the Intelligence Community (IC) to the same checks-and-balances imposed by the Constitution on the rest of the government.[6]

Lawmakers created new laws and regulations to ensure that America's espionage services were properly harnessed and responsive to the same rules of accountability faced by every other government entity in Washington, D.C. The notion of "intelligence exceptionalism"—secret agencies operating outside the framework of the Constitution—was discarded, out of a concern that the nation's spies and analysts had become too isolated

174

from American values and emphasis on the rule of law. The U.S. intelligence agencies benefit from having invaluable partners in the development of technological innovations for espionage: the techint companies that manufacture surveillance satellites, along with reconnaissance drones, other spy planes, and a wide array of additional equipment for watching and listening around the globe. They are known generally as "Beltway Bandits," although not all of these corporations have their headquarters buildings located along the traffic loop that circumvents the District of Columbia. At the very time these two vital segments of American society—the IC and the techint companies—were working in tandem to develop important intelligence advances for the United States based on the latest technology, the manner in which presidents were dealing with their veiled agencies was beginning to slip backwards. This retrogression at the highest levels of government took the form of a retreat from the application of constitutional principles to intelligence, as well as an increasingly faulty comprehension displayed by presidents and members of the National Security Council (NSC) about the value-added capabilities—facts and thoughtful assessments—the spy agencies could bring to the table.

The New Era of Intelligence Accountability in the United States

In 1975 the Church Committee uncovered, among other shocking disclosures, that the CIA had engaged in espionage operations directed against anti-Vietnam War protesters—American citizens demonstrating peacefully within their country, in accordance with First Amendment guarantees (Operation CHAOS); the FBI had adopted covert schemes to ruin the lives of these protesters, plus individuals involved in the civil rights movement (Operation COINTELPRO); and the National Security Agency (NSA) had resorted to wiretapping the telephones of American citizens (Operation MINARET) and reading their international cables (Operation SHAMROCK). The CIA, known by insiders as "The Agency," accumulated files on 1.5 million American citizens; infiltrated media, academic, and religious groups inside the United States; and plotted assassinations against foreign leaders in third-world countries. The smear tactics adopted by the FBI in COINTELPRO were intended to blacken the reputations of antiwar and civil rights activists, from the lowliest volunteers to the top leaders, even pressuring the preeminent civil rights leader in the United States, Dr. Martin Luther King, Jr., to take his own life.[7]

Moreover, the NSA leaned on flimsy executive orders from the days of the Truman administration in its conduct of MINARET and SHAMROCK. These operations targeted anti-war protesters and other perceived "subversives" in the United States throughout the next five presidencies (1953-1977: Eisenhower, Kennedy, Johnson, Nixon, and Ford)—never mind Article I of the Constitution that protects peace demonstrations and free speech. Not once did the NSA seek renewed authority for its ongoing surveillance operations from any of the White Houses or from Congress once President Harry S. Truman had left office. In the aftermath of the Church Committee inquiry, lawmakers moved quickly and in a bipartisan fashion to stretch the constitutional canvas over the full framework of American government, so that it covered the hidden parts as well as the visible ones. The Hughes-Ryan Amendment, enacted in the waning days of 1974, forced the president to shed the doctrine of plausible deniability. Henceforth, all significant covert actions—the means by which the CIA attempts to manipulate foreign nations and the course of history through the use of secret propaganda, political and economic machinations, and paramilitary (warlike) activities around the globe—would be formally approved by a president. Further, these approvals had to be reported to the Senate and the House "in a timely fashion" (two days was the understanding).[8]

Then, at the end of its inquiry in 1976, the Church Committee successfully advocated the creation of a permanent standing committee for intelligence accountability, known as the Senate Select Committee on Intelligence (SSCI, pronounced "sissy"). The next year the House followed suit by establishing its counterpart: the House Permanent Select Committee on Intelligence (HPSCI, or "hip-see"). The Congress enacted additional legislation to give these two panels meaningful authority to conduct intelligence reviews. The most important was the Intelligence Oversight Act of 1980. This brief, but far-reaching, statute required the executive branch to report to Congress not only on CIA covert actions but *all* other significant intelligence activities conducted by each of the spy agencies (as well as any other "entities" assigned intelligence responsibilities, including the staff of the National Security Council or NSC), and *prior* to their implementation. Here was the powerful *ante facto* reporting, rather than the earlier Hughes-Ryan standard of an *ex post facto* informing of Congress. Lawmakers had become genuine partners in the nation's intelligence activities, just as the Constitution had prescribed for every other policy arena.[9]

The vigour and success of congressional accountability over intelligence activities fluctuated throughout the five presidencies that followed the Church Committee investigation (from 1977-2001, which included the Carter, Reagan, George H.W. Bush, and Clinton administrations). The most serious setback to accountability occurred with the Iran-*contra* scandal during the Reagan years, followed by NSA violations of the law revealed in 2013 by Edward J. Snowden; and the CIA's adoption of a torture program disclosed by SSCI the following year. These intelligence excesses occurred in the crucible of fear in the United States that followed the devastating 9/11 terrorist attacks.[10] By the advent of the George W. Bush administration in 2001, Congress had become well-establish in the exercise of intelligence oversight. The difference between the pre-Church Committee era of benign neglect toward the America's secret agencies and the post-Committee existence of SSCI and HPSCI was as stark as night and day. With the exception of the Iran-*contra* scandal in the mid-1980s, the new intelligence accountability was working out—although exactly how well this experiment in bringing democracy to the dark side of government would fare during the tenures of Presidents Bush II, Obama, and Trump remained a question mark. As events in these administrations unfolded, relations between the governmental branches with regard to the spy power would prove to be fraught.

The Spy Power in the Bush II, Obama, and Trump Administrations

Presidents Bush II, Obama, and Trump were all less than robust in their embrace of the institutional sharing between the executive and legislative branches of national security powers; the approach prescribed for good governance by the Constitution and successfully promulgated by the Church Committee for Intelligence activities.[11] This institutional sharing is often referred to as the Madisonian model of governance since the eponym, one of the founders and the nation's fourth president, played such a major role in drafting the democratic safeguards found in the Constitution. Bush and Trump especially pushed the boundaries of executive authority over national security intelligence in a manner designed to ensure White House political control over the secret agencies, thereby undermining their credibility and effectiveness as independent, fact-seeking organizations and relegating Congress to the sidelines.[12]

The Bush II Administration

The government led by George W. Bush (2001-2008) opened the door to a stark executive branch aggressiveness toward the espionage function of government. Its responses to Iraq provide the most blatant illustrations. The administration:

177

➤ Attempted, in the lead-up to the 2003 U.S. war against Iraq, to influence the CIA toward adopting the view that Iraq possessed weapons of mass destruction (WMD), with Vice President Cheney visiting the Agency eleven times, always pushing on behalf of this hypothesis (no other vice president had ever visited the CIA even once);

➤ Placed into the State of the Union address in 2002 a reference to a supposed purchase by Iraq's leader, Saddam Hussein, of forty tons of yellow-cake uranium from Niger to construct nuclear weapons, even though CIA research had debunked this rumour (which originated in a flawed Italian intelligence report shared with the United States and

➤ The United Kingdom) and had urged the president to drop the reference in the speech;

➤ Never ordered the writing of a National Intelligence Estimate (NIE) on Iraq before the invasion, which should have been standard protocol—and was finally demanded by lawmakers, but the document was then too hastily prepared and ambiguous to affect public opinion on the proposed invasion;

➤ Too readily accepted the pro-WMD testimony of Iraqi émigrés in the United States who had escaped the Saddam regime, one of whom claimed to have personally knowledge of unconventional weaponry in Iraqi—only to be revealed as an ambitious politician-in-exile who hoped the United States could bring about regime change and install him as president of the new government in Baghdad;

➤ Failed to listen to important IC agencies in the Departments of Defense, Energy, and State who had significant reservations, based on advanced technological capabilities of the NSA and the National Geospatial-Intelligence Agency (NGA), about some of the "evidence" supporting the WMD argument that should have been further explored before an invasion (as urged unsuccessfully by German and French allies);

➤ Ignored a CIA report, originally prepared in 1995 (and dismissed by the Clinton administration, as well) and updated each year, that warned "aerial terrorism" might come to the United States, with terrorists hijacking and flying U.S. commercial airliners into city skyscrapers—yes, 1995; and,

➢ Waved off further warnings by the outgoing Clinton administration that Al Qaeda was now Threat No. One to the United States, with the Bush national security team failing to hold a NSC meeting on the subject until nine months later (on September 4, 2001).[13]

An additional aspect of the administration's reaction to 9/11 was to encourage the NSA director to flaunt the Foreign Intelligence Surveillance Act (FISA) of 1978, another Church Committee initiative.[14] Here again, Vice President Cheney played a major role in pushing the President (and the NSA) toward the stance of unilateral White House action in security affairs—a posture often referred to as the "unitary theory" of the presidency.[15]Cheney ordered the NSA chief, Air Force Lt. Gen. Michael V. Hayden, to return to his agency and unleash its surveillance powers against suspected terrorists, without bothering about warrants beforehand (as lawfully required by FISA). The General returned to NSA Headquarters at Ft. Meade, Maryland, and informed his Office of Legal Counsel that "the President is going to do this on his own hook. Raw Article 2, commander-in-chief stuff. No new legislation" (Hayden, 2016, p. 68). Neither the director nor his lawyers bothered to object that this order from the White House flew directly in the face of FISA rules and fell outside the white line of the law. The technological prowess of the NSA is legendary; on this occasion (and others), its constitutional sensitivities proved primordial.

All of these failures of law and protocol were driven by hubris in the White House, fueled by the belief of Cheney and the so-called neo-conservatives ("neo-cons") in the administration that they knew best, and the President could proceed with war and illegal surveillance, other considerations—such as Article I of the Constitution or FISA requirements—to the contrary notwithstanding. Throughout the build-up to this second invasion of Iraq (the first had taken place in 1990-91), the Congress was of little more use to the body politic than the vermiform appendix is to the human body. Like his father George H.W. Bush, an outspoken critic of the Church Committee reforms, Bush II preferred the era before lawmakers became equal partners in the use of, and supervision over, the nation's secret agencies—the "good old days" when presidents could blithely direct, or ignore, their secret agencies according to the whims and wishes of the White House.

The Obama Administration

President Obama (2009-2016) had minimal interest in working with Congress when it came to matters of intelligence. For example, he objected to the idea of keeping lawmakers in the "witting circle" on highly sensitive intelligence operations, such as the Osama bin Laden take-down.16 During SSCI's investigation into the CIA's use of torture against suspected terrorists, Obama time and again resisted providing documents to investigators—indeed, by executive order, he bottled up over 10,000 pages highly relevant to the inquiry. Further, when the Committee wrote a report despite the President's lack of cooperation, the President refused to declassify even an executive summary of the panel's findings for public consumption, let alone the full report. In addition, Obama moved to lock SSCI's torture report away forever from the public; and, he refused to have even a discussion about the CIA's practice of torture with the Senate's chief investigator on the topic, fellow Democrat Dianne Feinstein (California). These missteps seemed to have been based on misguided advice from former CIA Director John Brennan, who had become Obama's White House adviser on intelligence and related matters.

Similarly, this President was slow to work with Capitol Hill on developing proper procedures for the use of drones in warfare. This included the establishment of appropriate approval procedures for placing suspected terrorists on the targeting roster (the "kill" or "goodbye" list), even though the use of CIA drone-fired missiles had become the tip of the spear in America's struggle against global terrorism. At the Agency, drones had evolved into the most lethal form of covert action in U.S. history, with these silent killers unleashed in a rising number of attacks in the Middle East, South Asia, and North Africa—often without a partnership role with lawmakers or review by a judicial panel (as required by FISA for wiretaps) in deciding when and where these aerial robots would be deployed (Fuller, 2017). It was a legal oddity: judicial review and warrants for wiretaps, but not for killing people overseas. An example: Obama ordered CIA drones and other surveillance planes to track down the Libyan leader, Muammar el-Qaddafi. Once found, he was executed by local rebel forces. The Obama administration also authorized, via White House decree, the killing of American citizens abroad (including Anwar al-Awlaki) who were suspected of terrorist activities against the United States, but who were never tried in a court of law.17

The Trump Administration

No president has played as fast and loose with America's intelligence agencies as President Trump (2017-2021). The application of constitutional principles to the spy power requires judging secret operations according to democratic tenets, just as happens with the more open agencies and departments. Even before the dramatic intelligence oversight reforms advanced by the Church Committee, certain norms of integrity and honesty guided intelligence professionals. Although a few strayed into illegal domestic surveillance activities, as revealed by the Church Committee probes into Operations CHAOS, COINTELPRO, MINARET, and SHAMROCK, most of these men and women obeyed the law and sought to provide presidents and other policymakers with accurate, timely, and objective intelligence, based on the latest technological capabilities for collection-and-analysis. Yet President Trump began to undermine even these basic expectations. Trump's first dubious position came early during his presidential campaign in 2016 when, on the analysis side of intelligence, he rejected traditional CIA daily briefings provided to leading candidates.

These briefings are a sensible development from the 1960s, based on the notion that a successful contender for the White House ought to arrive at 1600 Pennsylvania Avenue on Day One with a solid knowledge of world affairs, ready to lead the United States in a spiky global environment. President Trump found the briefings unhelpful. Sometimes, in fact, intelligence reports do echo what one has already read in the newspapers or heard on CNN; but almost always they include, as well, information derived from clandestine sources that government leaders can benefit from learning. Once in office, President Trump initially rejected delivery to him of the most important intelligence report prepared by the Intelligence Community, the *President's Daily Brief* (*PDB*).[18]He later relented, but said he preferred to have an oral briefing rather than read the actual document. As a result of refusing to peruse the *PDB* (which is only about twenty-five, easily read pages, with figures and graphs in four colors, as well as interesting satellite- and human intelligence-derived photography), President Trump lost much of the detail and texture, wherein can lie the truth. The President also said, early in his administration, that neither the chair of the Joint Chiefs of State (C/JCS), the Director of Central Intelligence (D/CIA), or the Director of National Intelligence (DNI) would be welcome at most sessions of the National Security Council, where their presence had been routinely expected and valued by previous administrations. Trump later changed his mind about this prohibition as well, but he still paid only marginal attention to these officials—except for D/CIA Mike Pompeo, a former member of Congress from Kansas who had become his Polonius.

On the eve of his failed re-election bid in November of 2020, President Trump—in a funk over his defeat—cancelled all meetings in the Oval with top CIA briefers, favouring instead a reliance on intelligence reporting from his political appointees. Foremost among them was the newly confirmed DNI, John Ratcliffe, a former Republican member of Congress from Texas. Holding a seat on HPSCI while in Congress, Ratcliffe had a reputation for seldom attending the panel's briefings and hearings. In Washington, he was widely considered the least qualified person to be a leader in the Intelligence Community since the founding of the modern espionage establishment in the United States in 1947. A former CIA officer described the new DNI as a D.C. politician viewed "first and foremost as a political ally [of President Trump] and someone who is on the president's team" (Barnes & Goldman, 2020). Further, in a marked breach of tradition and a staggering display of sour grapes after his loss in the 2020 election, Trump refused to allow CIA intelligence briefings for his victorious opponent, Joe Biden, even though these information sessions have been the norm in past presidential transitions. This unprecedented halt to the president-elect briefings placed U.S. national security in jeopardy, by limiting the ability of Joe Biden to be fully prepared to serve as the next chief executive should be.

Trump was criticized as well, early in his presidential tenure, for selecting an arch right-wing ideologue to serve as D/CIA. Mike Pompeo had been a leader of the Tea Party faction in the House of Representatives and a resolute attack dog against Secretary of State Hilary Clinton. President Trump chose another politician, Dan Coates (R, Indiana), as DNI—although the former Senator and SSCI member turned out to be less partisan than Pompeo. More than anything else, intelligence is expected to be politically neutral, dedicated to fact-finding and not policy recommendations or partisan stances. Pompeo was not the first politician to head the CIA, but the number has been few and the results have almost always been regrettable. Examples from the past of such appointments include: George H.W. Bush, a former director of the Republican National Committee and a member of the House (R, Texas), selected by President Gerald R. Ford (1976); William J. Casey, the former national presidential campaign director for Ronald Reagan and appointed by the new President (1981); George J. Tenet, a Democrat and former SSCI staff director, chosen by President Bill Clinton (1997); Porter J. Goss, another former House member and HPSCI chair (R, Florida), appointed by President Bush II (2004); and, finally, Leon E.

Panetta, a former House member (D, California), placed at the CIA by President Obama (2009). This sums to six individuals, counting Pompeo, who have been former or current politicians picked to serve as CIA chief, out of a total of twenty-three directors since 1947.

Of these men, George H.W. Bush and Panetta usually honored the neutrality principle. Casey, though, was rabidly partisan; Tenet fell into overly friendly relations with the White House; and Goss used the CIA as a bully pulpit to carry on his long-standing public loathing of Hilary Clinton. As for Pompeo, as D/CIA during the Trump administration, he often appeared to be more of a White House aide and policymaker than he was an unbiased spymaster—even calling for regime change in North Korea, as if he were secretary of state or defense rather than the CIA Director.[19] Soon, in fact, Trump did appoint him as Secretary of State. Thus, by past standards of respect for political neutrality among intelligence leaders, Pompeo was a sharp departure, in the manner of William Casey, the chief architect of the Iran-*contra* intelligence scandal in the 1980s. One of the more widely admired intelligence directors, Richard Helms (1966-1973) observed that in high-level meetings at the White House what was needed was someone in the room "who was not trying to formulate a policy, carry a policy, or defend a policy; someone who could say: 'Now listen, this isn't my understanding of the facts'" (as cited in Johnson, 2018, p. 471).

Pompeo's extreme political views, coupled with his policy pronouncements as CIA chief, disqualified him as the trustworthy fact-provider in the room.

Furthermore, unlike any other president, soon after he settled into office Donald Trump lashed out at the CIA and the FBI (in particular, but also the IC writ large). From time to time, other presidents have complained about the intelligence agencies, too, especially when these organizations have delivered bad news to the White House ("The war in Vietnam is failing," was an unwanted message from DCI Helms during the era of President Lyndon B. Johnson); or if they had been unable to anticipate a major calamity (9/11, for example). None, however, had done so as publicly—or as savagely—as President Trump.

Among Trump's accusations against the IC: it had leaked a secret dossier that alleged he had engaged in sexual improprieties while in Moscow in 2013 (as a private citizen); and, as a consequence, he may have been compromised by Russian intelligence. The allegations in this dossier have yet to be substantiated, nor the source of the leak confirmed. The

President claimed, further, that the Obama administration and the FBI had carried out an illegal surveillance against him during the 2016 presidential campaign. This suggestion of political spying by the Obama administration was strongly denied by former President Obama and the Bureau. Clearly, though, and rightly so, an inquiry had been initiated by the Department of Justice and the FBI during the Obama years to examine the validity and implications of widely reported ties between Trump's senior election staff and Russian intelligence officers. Not to have looked into this relationship would have qualified as gross negligence with respect to the FBI's counterintelligence responsibilities. The findings of the Bureau's investigation remain classified.

Further, while the CIA had sworn off waterboarding against suspected terrorists—the subject of the searing inquiry by SSCI's Democratic staffers during the Obama years mentioned earlier—President Trump sang the praises of this form of "enhanced interrogation" as an intelligence gathering technique. He proclaimed during the presidential campaign: "I would bring back waterboarding, and I'd bring back a hell of a lot worse than waterboarding" (Bruck, 2016, p. 34). President Trump was over the top, as well, in his scathing, ongoing denigration of, and jousting with, America's spy agencies. While visiting Langley (the home of CIA Headquarters in Northern Virginia) in early 2017, he claimed that the intelligence services of the United States were involved in behind-the-scenes plots against him that reminded the President of approaches used by Adolf Hitler to defame adversaries during the Third Reich. This comparison astonished and demoralized intelligence officers at the CIA. They had been called nasty things before, but never Nazis. The world of America's spies under this President had fallen into pronounced turmoil.

On the question of how the Trump administration measured up to the post-Church Committee standards of strong intelligence accountability, the story grows grimmer still. Created in 1976, the purpose of HPSCI and SSCI was to stand as checks against the abuse of spy power within the executive branch. Yet HPSCI's chair during the early years of the Trump presidency, Devin Nunes (R, California), seemed to become an extension of the White House within the inner sanctums of the House of Representatives. He met regularly with the President's staff to plan how, as chair, he might best divert the attention of his Committee away from a thorough investigation into possible collusion by Trump with the Russians in derailing Hilary Clinton's presidential campaign in 2016; and whether Trump had known about Russian intelligence efforts to manipulate that election in his favor. The

House Committee was being torn asunder by this coordinated jockeying between the White House and the HPSCI chair. At least on the Senate side of Capitol Hill, the Democratic and Republican leaders at SSCI's helm were attempting to achieve some degree of bipartisan cooperation in that panel's separate inquiry into these topics. The involvement of both committees in these matters was supplementary to another probe being conducted by special prosecutor Robert S. Mueller III, a former FBI Director.

When it came to the spy power, then, President Trump acted in a more unilateral and anti-intelligence manner than any previous president in the modern era. Arguably his departure from tradition was, at any rate, less dangerous than when President Richard M. Nixon endorsed the Huston Spy Plan in 1970, a scheme concocted by the White House to spy on and disrupt antiwar protests inside the United States.[20] Still, the cozy relationship of the Trump administration with Chairman Nunes was chilling, bordering on what had all the trappings of an attempted coverup regarding ties between the President, his family, and top aides, on the one hand, and the Russian government and its intelligence services, on the other hand. At the same time that SSCI displayed a devotion to seeing its Russia-probe through to completion without partisan ranker, HPSCI continued to disintegrate along party lines—with Nunes even ordering the construction of a wall between the offices of Democratic and GOP staffers. Further, the Congress passed the USA Liberty Act in 2017, with little debate and a willingness to grant the President broadly delegated discretion over the surveillance of suspected terrorists inside the United States, often without a warrant requirement. This law represented a return to the same old "the president knows best" philosophy that haunted a supine Congress in the years prior to the Church Committee investigation—the time that had led to Operations CHAOS, COINTELPRO, and the other domestic spying calamities, not to mention two of the most ill-conceived covert action initiatives in U.S. history: the Cuban Bay of Pigs fiasco in 1961, and the toppling of the Salvador Allende's democratic government in Chile during the early 1970s.

In addition, the President's advocacy of torture and his renewal of indefinite terms of imprisonment for suspected terrorists at Guantanamo (who were being held without proper legal counsel, let alone a fair trial), along with his ordering of a dramatic increase in the number of drone attacks against suspected terrorists in Somalia and elsewhere, raised further questions about Trump's stewardship over the hidden side of America's government. At the same time, he was interested in having the secret agencies vigorously use their drones and torture skills against suspected terrorists overseas; he often seemed to believe that these organizations comprised a nefarious "deep state" opposed to his administration and committed to its own agenda. The White House brimmed with paranoia and distrust toward the intelligence agencies, while at the same time pursued highly aggressive CIA paramilitary operations—indeed, more so than any other administration in American history.[21]

The Spy Power in Suspension

The three presidencies examined in this article each exhibited a tendency toward a rejection of Madisonian constitutional principles for policymaking. Each pushed Congress away and embraced a more unilateral presidential approach to foreign policy, national security, and intelligence activities. In the instances of Bush II and Trump, the tendencies toward executive aggrandizement in the realm of intelligence were tethered to a fervent belief in the "unitary presidency," a model of White House supremacy over Congress in all matters related to national security and foreign policy. Even the former constitutional scholar President Obama ended up in this camp, though sometimes more by necessity when a polarized Congress made a policy partnership between the executive and legislative branches difficult, if not impossible, to achieve on some issues. Often Obama's heart and legal mind seemed to bend toward Madison, although his actions largely remained in the camp of Article II devotees.

What would a respect for Madisonian principles have looked like in these three administrations? It would have required fealty to the Constitution's basic requirement of sharing power between the Congress and the executive, with the courts as occasional arbiters. If serious disagreements occurred between the two action branches, then the executive should have backed away from its policy objectives; without the support of the American people, as reflected in the stances of their representatives in the House and Senate, a president should keep clear of major initiatives in the national security and foreign policy domains. Furthermore, this leadership triad should have named non-political figures, or at least non-ideological lawmakers or former lawmakers (like George H.W. Bush, Coats, and Panetta), to head the intelligence agencies, instead of individuals at the extreme wings of their party. Pompeo was an especially dubious pick, allowing a Tea Party stalwart to lead the non-partisan CIA. At every opportunity, the presidents should have placed intelligence above politics-as-usual.

Also, Bush II, Obama, and Trump could have worked more closely with lawmakers on improving procedures for the approval of drone targeting lists, especially when American citizens were in the crosshairs. Moreover, the presidents could have shared intelligence across the board with SSCI and HPSCI, in a more systematic, regularly, and timely manner. President Trump, in particular, was in violation of the legal reporting requirements laid out in the 1980 and 1991 Intelligence Oversight Acts when he failed to consult with senior SSCI and HPSCI members (the "Gang of Eight") before the assassination of the Iranian senior policy official Qasem Soleimani in January of 2020—an extreme covert action against a non-combatant, and a rash act that invited retaliation against U.S. officeholders. Soleimani was a non-combatant and this hit should have been a CIA responsibility with reporting under Hughes-Ryan to the senior lawmakers (a so-called Article 50 assassination, named after its number in the legal code of intelligence statutes), instead of using a military drone that requires no congressional reporting (Article 10).[22] As well, Trump should have stayed far away from trying to turn HPSCI chair Nunes into a fifth column for the administration.

These are serious defects that marred all three administrations. The evocation of an imperial presidency tilted America's government far away from a focus in the White House on important technological innovations in intelligence and the important products these advances can yield. Human foibles hindered the value-added potential of the secret agencies, buffeted as they have been by political disputes; attempts to cherry-pick their assessments; clashes between the branches over intelligence accountability; verbal attacks by President Trump against former D/CIA Brennan and DNI Clapper, as well as the incumbent DCIA Gina Haspel; the President's firing of the DNI's Inspector General; and a cavalier attitude in the White House toward the usefulness of the secret agencies in decision-making.[23] The end result: a waste of the nation's investment in intelligence innovations and activities that can provide presidents and lawmakers with cat's eyes in the dark.

Part of the problem stemmed from the fact that these three presidents had little knowledge about intelligence prior to their election to the nation's highest office, especially Trump (who seemed to have limited knowledge about *any* function of modern government). When individuals like George Washington and Dwight David Eisenhower have been in the White House (military personnel who understood that battles are won with superior intelligence), or George H.W. Bush (the only president to have served as the nation's spymaster and, therefore, arriving at the White House with a hands-on knowledge of the value of these agencies), the secret agencies receive the attention they deserve as deep reservoirs of knowledge about international events and conditions.

Presidents who appreciate the gift of reliable information have turned to their intelligence agencies every day with attentiveness to their reports, realizing that the data and analysis they provided is based in large part on cutting edge technology that is unique in the world. The American electorate would do well to evaluate their presidential candidates according to how well these men and women are likely to appreciate and manage these vital wellsprings of global information. Absent a serious level of interest from the White House in national security intelligence, the $80 billion secret agencies become just so many self-licking ice cream cones.

Intelligence and Democracy

What direction will the United States take in the future when it comes to the spy power? Will the constitutional model advanced by Madison and his colleagues attract the respect it has enjoyed for most of America's history; or will the Richard Nixons, Dick Cheneys, and Donald Trumps of the world hold sway, allowing presidents to become ever more imperial? In his magisterial study of the Roman Empire, the British historian Edward Gibbon cautioned that "constitutional assemblies form the only balance capable of preserving a free-constitution against enterprises of an aspiring prince" (Gibbon, 1952, p. 85). America's founders understood this historical truth and enshrined it in the Constitution. That document's safeguards against the abuse of power were their greatest innovation, and the most important gift they gave to the young Republic. Whether current and future generations in the United States will appreciate and honor these safeguards in the realm of intelligence is a matter of ongoing debate from Hawaii to Maine.

The "unitary" theory of the presidency and its strident worshipers of centralized authority are always hovering near and sometimes in control of the White House—and, ironically, even key positions in the Congress, the very institution created by the founders to guard America's freedoms against the accumulation of powers into the hands of a president. The United States, Canada, and other countries will continue to push forward on the boundaries of techint innovation, as the search goes forward for better ways to protect the democracies against enemies at home and abroad. But will the democracies choose leaders who understand and appreciate the technological-based capabilities of their secret services and the advantages

188

these capabilities can provide for improved decision-making? And will they honor the idea of accountability for the secret agencies, even in—most especially in—the darkest corridors of power?

Chapter 11

Cyber-Enabled Tradecraft and Contemporary Espionage: Assessing the Implications of the Tradecraft Paradox on Agent Recruitment in Russia and China

Kyle S. Cunliffe

Abstract

The acquisition of clandestine human sources–or agents – inside Russia and China likely remains the key priority for Western HUMINT agencies, and yet their ability to do this safely is quickly waning. This paper considers the utility of cyberspace for espionage recruitment in these two hard target states, and assesses its value as a potential solution to emerging surveillance threats. With the aid of history, this paper proposes that hard target espionage is fundamentally afflicted by a tradecraft paradox, one that will severely curtail the utility of cyberspace to agent recruitment.

Introduction

Espionage, or what is more often known as human intelligence, is fundamentally about people, yet this paper aims to assess its relationship with cyberspace. Merely convincing a foreign official to walk a path that too often ends in execution or imprisonment is a delicate task, while the personal foibles which intelligence officers exploit to recruit spies seem just as likely to sow the seeds of distrust and doubt.[1] As such, at the heart of spying lies the trusting bonds between those who spy and the operatives who enable them. Those bonds, as with all relationships, are best developed face-to-face, but personal meetings are 'almost always the most precarious and dangerous part' of any operation.[2] In the past, the perils of street

190

surveillance, meaning the physical observation of foreign intelligence officers, led to new innovations in 'tradecraft', the methods used to recruit and handle spies.[3] But as the espionage world enters into a changing security landscape, one defined by a new age of street surveillance threats, innovation is rising up the agenda. This paper is thus a study of cyber-enabled tradecraft, as a solution to a problem that intelligence officers cannot easily resolve.

Tradecraft is often regarded as more of an art than a science, 'a combination of common sense and imagination'.[4] The CIA even recruited magician, John Mulholland, to write operational manuals using established theories of deception.[5] But common sense and imagination are not enough to overcome the challenges of hard target states, meaning intelligence officers must make informed decisions about the tools and technologies to apply to their work. This was exemplified in the Cold War, where the seemingly impenetrable city of Moscow forced intelligence officers to rethink the tried and tested tradecraft of the past.[6] It kick-started a cultural transformation, whereby for the first time in history, technology's role in espionage shifted from a minor aid to a vital function in operational affairs.[7] But despite being armed with a repertoire of tools, from cutting-edge listening devices to million-dollar spy cameras built in the garages of Swiss watchmakers, neither the CIA nor SIS ever reclaimed any significant advantage over the Soviet KGB.[8] Only a handful of agents, mainly volunteers such as Oleg Penkovsky and Adolf Tolkachev, were successfully operated within the confines of Moscow, while others, including Oleg Gordievsky, were merely kept 'on ice' (meaning operational acts were avoided) whenever they returned to the capital.[9] This brief history lesson is important, because as the US and its allies enter what pundits are calling the 'New Cold War', with Russia and China at the very peak of national security concerns, today's practitioners face a new hard target problem.[10]

The invasion of Ukraine and rising tensions over Taiwan, echo the fact that the West has entered a new age of nation-state rivalry, one in which intelligence must be at the forefront of an effective defence. But while technical intelligence remains a key form of collection, when it comes to discerning Russia and China's most guarded secrets, including the plans and intentions of Putin and Xi, a clandestine human source–an agent, or spy–is required.[11] The problem, is that in seeking to recruit and handle those spies, intelligence officers must grapple with a new era of 'Moscow and Beijing Rules'.[12] The original Moscow Rules, derived from the Cold War, denoted conditions in which peacetime operations were beleaguered by the ever present threat of the KGB's street surveillance, to the extent that personal meetings were largely prohibited.[13] Today, aided by new developments including biometric checkpoints and smart CCTV, burgeoning and increasingly hostile armies of watchers tasked by Russia's Federal security Service (FSB) and China's Ministry of State Security (MSS) are able to identify undercover operatives and observe their movements with unparalleled speed and precision.[14] In turn, while espionage is fundamentally about people, meetings between intelligence officers and foreign officials inside Moscow and Beijing are once again becoming a prohibitively dangerous act.[15]

But according to Alex Younger, the former chief of SIS, espionage in the cyber era faces not just an 'existential threat', but also a *'golden opportunity'*.[16] Practitioners argue that by harnessing the benefits of cyberspace, new tradecraft can be developed to reduce or even eliminate, the need for personal meetings. Former CIA officer, David Gioe – who sees cyberspace as carrying profound revisions to tradecraft – makes a strong case that meetings will almost always have some role to play in espionage, because they offer an unrivalled means for intelligence officers to assess their agents.[17] But, if cyber-enabled tradecraft can reduce dependency on face-to-face encounters to the minimum (perhaps even to a single meeting per case), it could shift the advantage in the intelligence officers' favour. The CIA and SIS are already spending huge sums to modernise their methods, as exemplified in 2015 when the CIA revealed its first new directorate in over fifty years, *The Directorate of Digital Innovation*, for the purpose of researching and identifying technological threats and opportunities.[18] This is not an encroachment on the turf of NSA, but rather an effort to harness digital and cyber technology for espionage purposes, as the then serving CIA director argued, 'human interactions take place in that digital domain. So the intelligence profession needs to flourish in that domain. It cannot avoid it'.[19]

That being said, even if cyberspace is a powerful aid to espionage in most contexts, its utility when turned against authoritarian regimes is open to doubt. It must be considered that Russia and China are counterintelligence states, who will seek to undermine whatever advantages cyberspace affords to their opponents.[20] And if cyberspace cannot aid in the penetration of Moscow and Beijing, intelligence officers may be forced to follow in the footsteps of their Cold War predecessors, by pursuing the bulk of their sources on safer soil. In the last century, the challenges encountered in Moscow forced intelligence officers to pursue their quarry outside of the

Eastern Bloc, detrimentally reducing access to the Kremlin's most senior ranks.[21] Today, Russian and Chinese officials – especially those in Putin and Xi's inner circle – are largely prohibited from travelling abroad, shifting the focus onto Moscow and Beijing.[22] Therefore, this paper assesses the value of cyberspace in recruiting agents with high level placement and access who reside in Russia and China, to determine whether it offers US and UK intelligence officers the advantage they require to pierce these hard target states. This focus on agent recruitment, rather than handling, is due to the fact it is often the most difficult stage of espionage, not least because there is no pre-existing trust between the intelligence officer and the person they aim to recruit.

It bears note that contemporary tradecraft remains one of the more opaque areas of intelligence scholarship. However, while practitioners are unlikely to be forthcoming about their knowledge of cyber affairs, the control and exploitation of cyberspace within Russia and China have been subjects of growing journalistic and academic interest. Meaning the research challenge is not in acquiring new data, but in making sense of the data that already exists. As such, owing to recent declassifications and a growing body of literature documenting the tradecraft challenges of the time, there is no period more fitting for deriving lessons that can aid this study than the West's efforts to penetrate Soviet Moscow. In turn, this paper will show that an increasing need for trust constrains the application of tradecraft in hard target conditions. Specifically, this paper hypothesizes that:

Justifying the risks of tradecraft in hard target conditions requires greater trust in the prospective spy. However, in such conditions, the odds of failure are vastly increased since, without alternative tradecraft at their disposal, intelligence officers have few means to develop that trust.

The crux of this argument rests on the premise that any risks inherent in tradecraft increase the odds of an operational failure or, worse, increase the probability that the candidate for recruitment is a counterintelligence 'dangle' sent to waste intelligence officers' time and resources or lure them into a provocation. As these risks increase, so too does the need to justify operational acts by gathering supplementary assessment information, allowing varying degrees of trust to be developed in the prospective recruitment candidate. The problem, is that there are no clear solutions to acquiring that information without access to secure tradecraft, leading to a paradoxical situation that goes some way to explaining why high risk operational acts can be justified in some situations (e.g., where trust has been built) but not others. Herein, just as it hindered the recruitment of spies in the Cold War, this paper aims to show that through a catalogue of mounting risks and a rising need for trust, the tradecraft paradox looks set to hinder agent recruitment in the cyber era.

Spotting and assessment

Unless a source volunteers their own services, all espionage begins with the gathering of spotting and assessment data, to determine who has access to the secrets sought, what might motivate them to consider a career as a spy, and whether they are ultimately suited for clandestine work. During the Cold War, contacts and agents provided some of this data, often by supplying classified phone books containing lists of government employees.[23] Further information would be learned through interactions with foreign officials, or from operatives discretely following their targets to observe their daily habits.[24] The most intrusive insights into a person's private affairs, however, were often learned through bugging, better known as technical or audio surveillance.[25] As Easter argues, the planting of hidden listening devices in the embassies and residences of foreign officials revealed a person's 'weaknesses', 'exposing unhappy marriages, homosexual inclinations, money problems, or doubts about their own government', and in turn, it offered access to plethora of deeply personal information that could aid in discerning a target's value and motive.[26]

Despite its usefulness, planting a listening device was often a hazardous undertaking, especially in hard target conditions. During most of the Cold War, bugging operations typically required lengthy installation periods, foreknowledge of the premises targeted, and a human asset to alert operatives whenever the occupant vacated the building (or to plant the bug themselves), all of which needed to be repeated whenever installed devices were detected and neutralised by 'sweeping' equipment deployed by opposing security personnel.[27] In fact, the KGB would even go so far as redecorating the residences of its foreign officials, 'baffling the effectiveness of any bugs that may have been installed'.[28] Only when technological advances enabled so-called 'quick-plant' operations in the later years of the Cold War (meaning a hidden listening device could be placed by single individual in a short amount of time), were bugging operations permitted inside Moscow, albeit even these did not eliminate the unpredictable risks of surreptitiously entering a foreign official's apartment or workplace.[29]

Any mistake in the bugging process could have exposed the recruitment target to counterintelligence, but if the bug was found, security personnel might have kept it in place, utilising the device for deceptive purposes such as seeding a dangle.[30] Gordievsky, for example, who knew his Copenhagen embassy was likely bugged by Danish intelligence, telephoned his wife to complain about the Soviet invasion of Czechoslovakia, sending his 'first, deliberate signal to the West', in an act that could just as feasibly have been used by the trained KGB officer to lure operatives into a provocation.[31] This leads into the first observation of the tradecraft paradox in action, as justifying a hazardous bugging operation required some degree of trust in a target's prospective value, as well as their likelihood of revealing information that would facilitate their recruitment.[32] Indeed, bugging was not guaranteed to reap rewards, not least because Eastern Bloc officials, who were primarily concerned with being subjected to technical surveillance by their own security services, often acted with high a degree of discretion, which somewhat helps to explain why, throughout the Cold War, only a fraction of the CIA's bugging operations returned meaningful results.[33] As former CIA officer, Henry Crumpton, concluded after his high risk, six- month bugging operation achieved zero results, in future missions he would gather assessment information to better understand his target.[34] He would study his target's 'propensity for gab', and consult with the CIA's expert psychological assessments, adding that it 'was dumb to take risks without better understanding the odds of success'.[35]

Cyberspace, however, has opened up the prospect of gathering spotting and assessment data from a distance, without the hazards of a surreptitious entry. As Gioe argues, '[it] is not hyperbole to acknowledge that the twin cyber giants of social media and malicious hacking have revolutionized the ways in which intelligence services seek, locate, assess, and vet their quarry'.[36] But while it is true that by perusing spaces such as Facebook and LinkedIn, personal details can be gleaned that might otherwise have taken 'weeks or even months of personal meetings to elicit', Gioe adds that governments often regulate what their employees share online, as underscored by Britain's 'Think before you share' campaign.[37] Similar, if not stricter, measures should be expected in Russia and China; the Kremlin, for example, has banned servicemen from using smartphones (or other devices), posting photos online, or writing about the military while on duty, with culprits facing a two week jail sentence.[38] In that sense, Russia put its soldiers on similar footing to its security services, whose officers were already banned from posting about themselves or their work online (although it is worth bearing in mind that, as demonstrated throughout the war in Ukraine and the numerous leaks from within Russia via social media platforms such as Telegram, this rule appears to be frequently broken, at least by junior ranking military personnel who seem oblivious to, or undeterred by, the consequences).[39]

By contrast, the hacking of databases and personal devices offers a pathway to information that a person would not otherwise wish to share. Gioe underscores this point through the 2014 US Office of Personnel Management hack, a largescale breach by Chinese intelligence which 'lay bare troves of personal information that would save any intelligence service untold amounts of time in seeking the right approach to recruit the right person, in the right agency, at the right time'.[40] The value of the OPM hack to Chinese intelligence was echoed by the former US counterintelligence chief, Michelle Van Cleave:

The Chinese now have a detailed roster of most if not all American contractors and government employees who have access to classified information, plus a roster of their friends, colleagues or co-workers who may be useful conduits or potential assets in their own right . . . [they] also have a treasure trove of data that can be used to coerce, blackmail or recruit U.S. sources'.[41]

While the OPM hack was a devastating blow for the US, it was also indicative of the type of rewards database hacking can afford to any actor, including for the CIA's efforts to gather personal information about Russian or Chinese employees. As acknowledged by the former Director of National Intelligence, James Clapper: '[you] have to kind of salute the Chinese for what they did. If we had the opportunity to do that, I don't think we'd hesitate for a minute'.[42] Equally tempting databases exist in the private sector, where companies sometimes place profits ahead of security; here, recruiters might find all manner of useful information, ranging from financial data to more scandalous revelations. When the dating website tailored specifically for adulterers, known as Ashley Madison, was hacked in 2013, British intelligence trawled the disclosed files to identify potential sources, as well as to ensure that their own people had not been compromised.[43]

That being said, largescale breaches are a growing concern for governments around the world, including Russia and China. Since 2015, the Kremlin has directed its scientific resources (and a small army of coerced hackers) toward strengthening national networks and databases.[44] It has also forced improvements in the private sector, by enacting strict legislation such as changing the state's definition of critical infrastructure to include healthcare, communication, banking, energy, transport and other strategically valuable sectors.[45] This means, as Sergey Sukhankin of the Jamestown

Foundation contends, that 'the Russian state will be able to exercise even greater control over public and private entities employing IT technologies and infrastructure'.[46] Every company affected is obliged to bolster its cyber defences and report all detected intrusions to the government. And any company that uses insecure foreign software has been warned, by Putin himself, that they will be banned from working with government agencies.[47]

Similar steps have been taken in China, which has expanded the umbrella of critical infrastructure to include a vast swathe of companies that manage Chinese citizens' personal information, thus giving the government greater leverage to improve its cyber defences across the board.[48] Despite these measures, there has been a boom in personal information being sold on black markets in Russia and China, indicating that both governments are struggling to fully protect their citizens data.[49] One case from 2022, revealed that around one billion Chinese citizens were compromised in a database breach of the Shanghai National Police, containing criminals records pertaining to cases such as fraud and sexual assault.[50] On the one hand, the sheer scale of the breach underscores that even a regime as rich as China cannot protect all government systems from abuse (although it is worth noting that the system was not hacked; rather, a back door had been left open that allowed anyone to access the database if they knew where to look).[51] On the other hand, incidents of this kind are likely to encourage even greater efforts to protect critical networks, with President Xi immediately calling for public bodies to 'defend information security . . . to protect personal information, privacy and confidential corporate information'.[52]

The strengthening of defences inevitably raises the cost and time involved in committing a large scale breach, but, at a time when Western states are keen to dissuade their competitors from hacking their own systems, political implications must also be considered. In 2020, Chinese security firm Qihoo, released evidence tying Langley to a series of breaches against airlines and industries throughout China, only a month after the US government indicted four Chinese hackers for similar charges, implying that Beijing is willing to use evidence of hacking for political leverage.[53] Moreover, there is always a risk that a breach may incur some form of retaliation. Obama's administration instructed the NSA to hack Russian networks in response to the 2016 DNC breach, and some US politicians called for a similar response to China over OPM.[54] As such, there exists the possibility that Russia and China will retaliate in kind to a significant breach, regardless of the intention behind the intrusion. That will not deter intelligence agencies from largescale database hacking altogether, but the potential for political fallout cannot be overlooked.

By comparison, the risks of political fallout are substantially reduced if personal information is acquired by hacking individuals, rather than databases. In 2017, a batch of documents released by WikiLeaks, called Vault 7, showed that Langley had developed a catalogue of tools for hacking popular smartphones and other personal devices.[55] Some of these hacking tools could bypass the encryption of popular instant messengers, including WhatsApp, Telegram, and Signal, lifting the cleartext logs from a target's phone.[56] Langley could even siphon a smartphone's audio, video, and geo-locational data without alerting the device's operator.[57] The prospect of turning a recruitment target's personal device into a mobile surveillance platform is undoubtedly a tempting one, as one former US diplomat affirmed, '[everything] with bugs has been tried, phones are better'.[58] And as more people connect 'smart' devices into their home networks, through the widening 'Internet of Things', the potential for this type of personalized hacking continues to grow. WikiLeaks, as a case in point, revealed a range of CIA hacking toolkits aimed at everything from smart televisions to smart cars.[59] One of these toolkits, 'Weeping Angel', targeted Samsung televisions, allowing access to their embedded microphones while harvesting Wi-Fi details and passwords to facilitate further penetration of the home network.[60]

Still, hacking individuals is not without risks. While Langley's hacking tools have inevitably evolved over time, the Vault 7 leaks revealed that the CIA's hacking capabilities were heavily dependent on 'zero day' exploits.[61] Zero day exploits are considered one of the most powerful tools in a hacker's arsenal, because they utilize flaws in code which are unknown to 'software makers and to the antivirus vendors'.[62] And since nobody knows that the flaw in the code exists, it is much harder to detect or block hackers who utilise them. The downside for intelligence agencies is that zero-day exploits are highly sought after by the defending side.[63] This is especially true for popular consumer brands, with mainstream companies willing to pay enormous fees (including six figure sums) for any uncovered flaws in their code.[64] Hence, in a lucrative market, the most sought after zero days are likely to be more difficult to discover while yielding shorter lifespans, making personal devices harder to hack and significantly increasing the time and resources required to do so. Indeed, both Apple and Google were quick to reassure their customers that the zero day exploits disclosed in the Vault 7 files were patched years before the leak.[65]

This challenge, along with increasingly prevalent training and awareness programmes designed to educate employees on the need to update security software as well as in how to avoid typical hacking tactics such as phishing, can render many expensive toolkits obsolete.[66] This helps explains why the Vault 7 files revealed that the CIA often required physical access to the devices they were trying to hack, to the extent that they set up a specialised 'Physical Access Group'.[67] The point about physical access is important, because, from a technical perspective, it is often easier to infect a device physically (e.g., plugging a thumb drive into a target's computer) than it is to brute force hack or 'phish' a target. In select cases, it seems that Langley managed to physically infect some devices with relatively low levels of risk. According to reports, some 'factory fresh' devices were infected by 'interdicting mail orders and other shipments . . . leaving the United States or otherwise', while one document suggested gifting an infected 'MacBook Air' to a target.[68]

But if gifting or interdicting a device is not possible, the obstacle of gaining physical access to a target's devices is not an easy one to resolve. Security specialist Sean Sullivan, suggests that the CIA might infect somebody's phone as they pass through airport security, while even wider promise was underscored through a GCHQ programme called 'Royal Concierge' (as revealed in the Snowden files), which intercepted booking emails from over 350 international upscale hotels.[69] Royal Concierge became an 'enabler' for espionage, allowing intelligence officers to arrive on the ground ready to meet arriving guests, and even created opportunities to bug their rooms and infect their devices.[70] However, when it comes to physically infecting the devices of Moscow and Beijing residents, intelligence officers might have little recourse other than to enter a target's home or workplace, raising similar challenges to planting a traditional hidden listening device.

Still, the level of risk and cost entailed in hacking a target's devices depends, to an extent, on whether that person (or organisation) is sensible enough to adopt best-practice security measures. In this respect, no one, not even officials in Russia and China's highest levels of state, are fully immune to the fallibility of human error, which may open up hacking opportunities. In 2019, various members of Russia's political and business elite were exposed in a cache of hacked documents known as the 'Dark Side of the Kremlin'.[71] Over one hundred gigabytes of data were released, including the personal communication logs of arms dealers, oligarchs, defence personnel, and Kremlin officials. The leaks prove that even Russia's elite are vulnerable to the consequences of incompetence, and according to *Meduza*, in some instances, Russian politicians' correspondences were being hacked due to shoddy security practices by individual officials, with victims using insecure instant messengers when discussing sensitive affairs, rather than the government's encrypted RSNet email system.[72] Still, proper training and disciplinary actions, which, in the current climate, are likely to be encouraged, can address many of these incompetencies, pushing hacking operations toward more challenging avenues of access and exploitation.

Especially if physical access to the target device is necessary for a breach to succeed, the above factors increase the likelihood of counterintelligence discovering a hacking operation before it reaches fruition. If counterintelligence detects a breach, they might opt for an immediate shut down, removing any malware but not before learning from its technical signatures to prevent reoccurrence. However, in some cases it may be advantageous for security personnel to allow the breach to continue, to better understand the opposing side's targets and interests, and to use that information against them. As Althoff argues, the Internet can be used to 'ferret out opponents by posing as sympathisers to their cause', and while he refers specifically to social media, the planting of fraudulent information on networks and devices is an increasingly common tactic in the defence against hackers.[73] Following a tip-off from the NSA, Emmanuel Macron's campaign team created a string of fake emails and fake information, designed to lure (and waste the time of) hackers during a significant breach in 2017, a tactic that if adopted by Russia and China, could be just as feasibly used to lure, as well deter, foreign intelligence officers.[74] Hence, given the likelihood of a breach being discovered, operatives cannot rule out the possibility that what they concurrently see or hear may be designed to attract their attention and seed a dangle.

In light of these concerns, today's intelligence officers, like their predecessors, will be better served by ascertaining whether hacking will yield actionable results, to better justify the risks that such a high risk operational act affords. Meaning, in addition to knowing the value of their target, they will want some degree of preliminary trust in the target's tendency towards indiscretion. According to US intelligence officials, senior ranking members of the Kremlin are 'guarded in their use of phones, computers and other devices', fearing they might be compromised.[75] Judah claims that these type of measures are common among Russia's elite, many of whom are fearful of being targeted in the next 'wave of sackings, arrests or even purges'.[76] Those 'privy to sensitive information no longer carry smartphones', and instead resort to 'simple old cell phones and now remove the battery – to make sure the phone is dead – when they talk about Kremlin politics among themselves', steps allegedly taken out of fear that the FSB might be eavesdropping.[77] Measures of this kind, which are likely to be echoed by China's own increasingly fearful political elite, reflect the fact that a hacking operation, even if undiscovered by counterintelligence, is hardly guaranteed to provide information that operatives can leverage for recruitment, an outcome that must call into question the wisdom of running such an operation in the first place.[78] Thus, it is arguably difficult to justify a high risk hacking operation in Moscow and Beijing conditions without , at minimum, a degree of confidence in the target's tendency to overshare, particularly in the presence of their devices.

Cultivation and five-minute pitches

Upon identifying an ideal target, the next stage (unless they volunteer) is to convince that person to become a spy. There are two approaches to recruiting an agent; one approach is to cultivate close trusting bonds with a candidate (known as a 'developmental') before a pitch – 'would you be willing to work for the CIA?' – is delivered, while the other approach is to circumvent this process altogether by delivering a pitch without any prior cultivation (known as a 'five minute pitch').[79] Throughout the Cold War, pursuing either of these approaches without revealing the recruiter's intelligence affiliations proved challenging, with contact relying primarily on personal meetings supplemented, on occasion, by secure telephone conversations. As revealed in the accounts of former CIA officer, Richard Holm, it was not abnormal for intelligence officers to initiate contact by phone, the distance of which reduced any immediate risks to the operative, before a pitch was delivered face-to-face so as to better assess and mitigate the target's reaction.[80]

Leveraging the telephone in this way was far more challenging in Moscow, due to widespread telephonic eavesdropping throughout the Soviet Union. Accounting for the extraordinary hazards of meeting a boding source, all telephone lines 'into the offices and apartments of foreigners were tapped and monitored around the clock by a virtual army of eavesdroppers.'[81] Intelligence officers could get around this problem by losing their surveillance tails and calling from payphones, but if they were observed by the KGB using public phone booths, their calls may have been traced.[82] All payphones in Moscow 'were numbered', meaning the KGB 'could easily ask for an immediate trace' of any phone call made from a specific booth.[83] Further complicating matters, should they have reached a public phone without being spotted, operatives still had to account for the fact that the telephones belonging to 'any Soviet citizen in a sensitive position' were sometimes monitored by the KGB, upping the odds of exposure.[84]

Even outside of Moscow, the workplace and apartment telephones of Eastern Bloc officials were routinely monitored by their own security services, pushing up the risks of a call's interception and, as a result of that compromise, of the target falling under counterintelligence control.[85] When attempting to recruit a Polish consulate worker, dubbed Adamski, in Turkey, the former CIA officer Duane Clarridge remained concerned about his target's proclivity for telephoning his apartment. He noted that 'hostile coverage of our meeting could already be in place if Adamski were a double agent, or if he had been careless or naïve enough to call from a phone monitored by his security personnel'.[86] This leads to the second observation of the tradecraft paradox in action, as while in Clarridge's case, the use of the telephone was out of his control, it was generally wise to develop a degree of trust in whether a candidate was worth pursuing, and likely to respond positively to a pitch, before injecting further risks. This point was all the more acute for shorter recruitment attempts, as without the development of close interpersonal bonds, a pitch was more likely to be rejected; as noted by former KGB officer, Victor Cherkashin, five minute pitches placed `great psychological pressure on a target, and often failed'.[87] Hence, as Wallace et al argue, '[operational] circumstances determined whether an individual was the subject of extended development or a cold pitch, but in either case, the assessment conducted before the question was asked loaded the dice in favour of the case officer'.[88]

But while today, meetings or telephone calls (even by smartphone or burner phone) retain many of their traditional insecurities, online social communications are seen to have opened pathways to cultivate sources without, as Wallace argues, 'revealing the hand of an intelligence service'.[89] The security of online social communications, which by nature are not covert, rests partly on the premise that cyberspace is drowning in data, meaning incriminating communications are less likely to be noticed by the opposing side's Internet surveillance. This much was illustrated, ironically, by Edward Snowden, the NSA leaker who released thousands of documents about mass surveillance. As Omand notes, Snowden's disclosures indicate that the NSA, with its enormous resources, was only capable of looking at '0.00004 per cent of the world's traffic in conducting their mission', inferring that even one of the most competent and heavily resourced technical intelligence agencies in the world, struggled to monitor the sheer volume of communications sent and intercepted via the Internet.[90]

CYBER-ENABLED TRADECRAFT AND CONTEMPORARY ESPIONAGE

Moreover, an increasing number of social communications utilise end-to-end encryption, meaning messages can only be read by the sender and receiver. WhatsApp, for example, encrypts the messages of over a billion users to a standard that continues to frustrate intelligence and security agencies around the world.[91]

These factors have certainly worked to the advantage of the West's competitors. In 2017, the German federal security service, the BfV, accused China of targeting over 10,000 German citizens through 'networks like LinkedIn'.[92] As *Newsweek* reported, Chinese intelligence officers posed as 'academics, business consultants and policy experts' to cultivate relations with 'high profile politicians and business leaders'.[93] Yet the BfV struggled to counter China's activities on LinkedIn, because it had little way to differentiate between the communications 8 of which reduced any immediate risks to the operative, before a pitch was delivered face-to-face so as to better assess and mitigate the target's reaction.

of Chinese intelligence officers and those of ordinary LinkedIn users, as the agency acknowledged, '[the] infections are difficult to detect, since network connections between service providers and their customers aren't suspicious. This gives the attack an even better disguise than before'.[94] However, one report released by Snowden, shows that Western intelligence officers, in the right conditions, are equally prepared to cultivate targets online. Written for GCHQ's *Joint Threat Intelligence Group* (JTRIG), the report reveals how GCHQ uses cyberspace to conduct a wide variety of missions.[95] Most of these missions appear to be focused on influencing behaviours rather than espionage, but JTRIG occasionally tried to cultivate human sources:

Some of JTRIG's staff have conducted online HUMINT operations. Such operations typically involve establishing an online alias/personality that has a Facebook page, and membership of relevant web forums, etc. The target is then befriended (or the target befriends the alias). Interactions with the target may be informed by a combination of analysis of SIGINT . . . monitoring of the target's online behaviour, and intelligence from SIS "on-the-ground". The goal may be to collect intelligence and/or to facilitate SIS contact in order to disrupt, delay, deceive, deter, or dissuade.[96]

In short, GCHQ conducts the groundwork, cultivating online relationships in forums and social networks, before passing the reigns to SIS for the target to be further developed. In theory, any online social medium could be utilised for agent cultivation. Snowden's files, for example, revealed that various agencies, including the FBI and CIA, ran 'HUMINT operations' inside 'massively multiplayer' online video games, to the extent that they even considered establishing a 'deconfliction and tipping group' to avoid overlap and improve collaboration.[97] Another leaked memo, produced by GCHQ and read by *The Guardian*, claimed that World of Warcraft, a massively multiplayer online game with several million players, contained a rich list of targets, including 'telecom engineers, embassy drivers, scientists, the military and other intelligence agencies'.[98]

But the outlook of online cultivation must be weighed against the fact that Russia and China continue to expand surveillance of the Internet, ironically through laws designed to protect their citizens from Western Internet surveillance.[99] China is well known for its tight control of the Internet, having blocked its citizens from accessing foreign services such as Google and Facebook through the 'Great Firewall'.[100] Snowden's 2013 mass surveillance disclosures, however, served as the ideal excuse for Beijing to further tighten its grip over cyberspace. Since 2015, China has enacted sweeping legislation forcing companies to relocate Chinese data into the mainland, curbing US eavesdropping by ensuring that data is held in servers that cannot be accessed by Western intelligence agencies.[101] Similar measures followed in Russia, where the introduction of the 2015 Data Localization Act claimed to protect Russian citizens from the 'misuse of their personal data by foreign companies and surveillance by foreign governments'.[102] The government blocked access to LinkedIn in 2016 for refusing to relocate its servers into Russia, while further threats supposedly resulted in the compliance of at least Google and Apple.[103] It also bears note that since the invasion of Ukraine, Russia has completely blocked access to Facebook, Twitter, and Instagram, cutting off its citizens access to some of the world's most popular social platforms.[104]

Although data localization protects citizens from foreign surveillance, it also makes them more vulnerable to eavesdropping by their own governments. While surveillance of the Internet is thought to be widespread throughout China, much of which is relegated to the private sector, a similar outlook is emerging in Russia. Prior to the Localisation Act, Russian officials saw the 'uncontrolled use' of foreign services such as 'Skype, Gmail, and Hotmail' as potential challenges to state security, because their servers were located abroad where they could not be accessed by the FSB.[105] Now, any major company with servers located in Russia is compelled to install SORM black boxes, a technical eavesdropping system that feeds data, including telephone, email, and social media traffic, to FSB facilities across the country.[106] That information can be accessed at the FSB's discretion, without any need to give a warrant to the company holding the data.[107] As one FSB officer told *Wired*, they 'can use SORM to take stuff off their servers behind their backs'.[108] Russian citizens are placed on SORM watchlists for a variety of indiscretions, including attending anti-regime demonstrations or for expressing support for Putin's opponents on social media.[109] Official figures show that in a mere six years, annual SORM intercepts doubled, rising to 539,864 cases by 2012.[110] And yet, this figure could be far higher, since it does not include the number of people targeted by SORM surveillance for counterintelligence purposes.

These are not problems that can be fixed by something as simple as deleting a message, since communication logs (including content and metadata) are likely to be stored for a substantial length of time. In 2016, Russia introduced a bill better known as Yarovaya's Law, obligating companies to store communication data for six months and metadata for three years (in a move criticised for its high financial costs), vastly extending the timeframe in which an incriminating message could be uncovered.[111] And since Yarovaya's Law forces companies to provide communication data on request, it essentially outlawed end-to-end encryption applications such as WhatsApp. But despite being delegitimised, Russia has not been wholly successful in blocking encrypted messengers. The Kremlin tried to block Telegram–a Russian made encrypted messenger that is widely used by privacy activists, criminals, and the political and economic elite–in 2018, but it was unable to do so without disrupting other services including Google and Amazon.[112] Nonetheless, the Kremlin has not given up on its efforts, levelling threats at a wide range of popular applications (including WhatsApp), with one official asserting that any company who failed to comply with Yarovaya's Law 'will be blocked sooner or later'.[113] Likewise, China fully blocked access to WhatsApp in 2017, and the only remaining encrypted platform in the country – Apple messenger – remains under doubt. To date, Apple has been accused of making compromises in terms of its customers security in order to comply with China's security laws, as one experts notes, the 'Chinese are serial iPhone breakers'.[114]

These ongoing efforts demonstrate that Russia and China are fully determined to shut down or control any potential pathway to privacy in cyberspace, regardless of medium. Even video games have not gone unscathed, with China reportedly attempting to ban all interaction with foreigners in online games, due to what it perceives as a key security loophole.[115] Likewise, the widely popular online game, League of Legends, briefly suspended all voice chat functionality for its Russian players, because its developers were unable to find the capacity to store that data as dictated by Yarovaya's Law.[116] Moreover, a key part of the problem facing any Russian and Chinese citizen in cyberspace, let alone the operatives seeking to recruit them, is that it is increasingly difficult to determine what is secure and what is not. Telegram, for example, is consistently lauded as a relatively secure app in Russia, one that is used by a significant number of Russian citizens who oppose Putin.[117] However, since the war in Ukraine, there are growing numbers of reports suggesting that Telegram may have been compromised by Russian security services, but it remains unclear as to how, if it all, the Russian security services have achieved this goal.[118]

The sheer outreach of this surveillance – not to mention the risks that a target's personal devices might be monitored by their own security services – calls into question the wisdom of sustained online contact. This much was demonstrated in a case reported in Chinese state media, involving a low-level agent known as 'Li', who was recruited online by a foreign operative dubbed 'Feige'.[119] In one respect, the fact that Li (a low-ranking agent, sentenced to ten years in prison) was run for several years through China's 'QQ' messenger, suggests, as Mattis argues, that despite the government's vast surveillance powers, its security services still have 'trouble tracking the flow of information'.[120] And yet, in what should serve as a dire warning for other recruiters, it is reported that once the authorities narrowed their investigation, Feige's historic communication logs unmasked around forty additional 'suspected spies'.[121] Still, the evidence certainly suggests that, in the right circumstances, operatives are willing to use a minimal amount of online interaction to facilitate a swift recruitment, even in hard target conditions, as illustrated by the CIA's efforts to lure Iranian candidates over the border using fake online job websites.[122] Such a move is less effective against officials who cannot travel abroad freely, but a single introductory message sent to a Russian or Chinese official by a medium such as Telegram or Apple Messenger, may be sufficient to elicit enough information about a person's whereabouts and availability in order to arrange a daring meeting, without creating enough noise so as to attract the attention of Internet surveillance. Nonetheless, doing so securely would depend on whether the target accessed their messages from a secure device (as opposed, for example, to a work computer), as well as the degree to which that person, as well as their devices, was already under scrutiny by their own security services.

Thus, today's intelligence officers face significant challenges when pitching spies, as even a seemingly innocuous online relationship can compromise a case and increase the risk of a target falling under counterintelligence control. No matter how brief, any contact stands a chance of being monitored by Internet surveillance, but when the nature of a relationship becomes more personal, or the content of the interaction raises potential red flags (such as attempts to elicit information), the risks only mount. Once alerted, counterintelligence may opt to put an end to a growing relationship, or, if a dangle operation is preferred, security personnel can take control of a person's online accounts and impersonate them, turning the operation back against the intelligence officer doing the recruiting. This was illustrated by the fate that befell one Russian operative who was duped by US security officials posing as the Russian's own recruitment target.[123] Specifically, the Russian operative attempted to pressure a US diplomatic official by email, and when the official reported the incident, 'American security officials impersonated the diplomat in a reply email and arranged their own meeting with the Russian, turning the game back on him'.[124]

In light of these issues, before initiating contact with Russian or Chinese officials in cyberspace, it is essential that today's operatives, not unlike their predecessors, justify such an operational act by developing some degree of trust in their target. Compared to a slow burning developmental, a five minute pitch would involve less contact time but also require robust assurances that the target is worth pursuing and is willing to cooperate with a proposal to engage in espionage. Moreover, because counterintelligence concerns are high in these countries, any out of the ordinary online interaction may only add to the psychological pressures that a short recruitment affords. China, for example, runs various public awareness campaigns, forewarning its citizens, particularly those with access to sensitive or classified information, about the threat of ostensibly friendly foreigners using cyberspace to recruit spies and elicit information, cultivating a culture of awareness that potentially increases the probability of a target rejecting an intelligence officer's advances.[125] When it comes to staving off such concerns, by building trust, Grey argues that today's recruiters are armed with so much prior assessment information that a pitch can be 'accelerated' with a greater' chance of success'.[126] However, at least where hard targets are concerned, this perspective appears somewhat optimistic. If that preliminary assessment information cannot be obtained by other means (such as hacking), meaning operatives cannot develop sufficient trust before the pitch is delivered, then it is difficult to perceive how any recruitment attempt aided by cyberspace can be justified in Moscow or Beijing conditions.

Volunteers

The complications encountered in cultivation, could be skipped altogether if a source volunteers their own services. In the Cold War, volunteers in most parts of the world pitched their desire to spy by entering or telephoning foreign embassies, where they could speak directly to diplomatic officials. However, in Moscow, round-the-clock physical and technical surveillance of embassies made it difficult for people to offer their services, with the handful of known successes – Adolf Tolkachev and Oleg Penkovsky – approaching foreign nationals in the street, in the hope that someone would relay their messages to the West.[127] When an offer to volunteer was received, formulating a response presented its own challenges. Short telephone calls (made from payphones) offered more security for the officer making the response than a personal meeting, but these came at the expense of endangering the person on the receiving end.[128] For instance, while responding to Tolkachev by telephone – who was instructed to pick up a dead-drop containing secret writing equipment for further communication – posed few complications, CIA officers viewed a failed attempt to telephone Penkovsky as 'totally useless . . . dangerous and stupid'.[129]

Intelligence officers viewed volunteers in Moscow with a heightened degree of suspicion, but the inherent risks of their approach (as well as any means of response) furthered concerns about candidates falling under the scrutiny or control of counterintelligence.[130] The CIA assessed that even if Tolkachev was bona fide initially, his high risk method of approaching cars with American license plates in gas stations increased the probability of him being monitored or controlled by the KGB, leading Langley to reject initial proposals by its officers in Moscow to arrange a meeting.[131] This leads into the third observation of the tradecraft paradox in action, as in light of such concerns, justifying a response required greater trust in a candidate's existing and potential access to classified information, their suitability for spy work, as well as the motivating factors that might have driven them to take such significant risks.[132] Some volunteers established this trust as part of their initial pitch, if they were willing to share incriminating information over insecure channels. From the onset, Penkovsky provided bona fides strong enough to prompt officers into various daring attempts to respond. At the same time, Tolkachev resisted, sharing only a small amount of evidence in his early attempts to contact the CIA.[133] That finite evidence was viewed with a heightened degree of scepticism. Still, despite not convincing Langley to approve his immediate request for a meeting, it did justify approval for a less risky (for the intelligence officer) telephone response.[134]

But while entering or phoning foreign embassies, or even approaching foreign officials, remains a hazardous act for Moscow or Beijing residents, it is now possible for candidates to volunteer their services online.[135] Both SIS and the CIA provide online contact forms on their websites, allowing interested parties to pitch directly to intelligence agencies. According to the CIA's website, sources can use this system if they want to share information that may be useful to its foreign intelligence collection mission.[136] This method of contact proved useful in the 2009 case of Roman Ushakov, of Russia's Interior Ministry (MVD), who initiated contact through the CIA's website, becoming 'a kind of spotter' for the agency.[137] Ushakov, a low-ranking officer of Russia's Interior Ministry (MVD), offered insider access to his own agency, as well as the identities of around a dozen FSB officers. Similarly, Yevgeny Chistov, a former Russian police officer, is thought to have pitched his services online around 2011, securing a response from the CIA in ten days.[138]

And yet, approaching intelligence agencies in this way is not without its risks, since, as SIS warns, connections to intelligence agency websites are 'monitored by most governments'.[139] To an extent (and very much depending on the environment), this problem can be mitigated by taking precautionary steps, including, as SIS recommends, messaging from disposable devices or Internet cafes.[140] The CIA has even set up an online contact site in the dark web, which can be accessed using The Onion Router (Tor) for an extra layer of security.[141] But the safest online approach, according to SIS, is to 'not contact us from inside your own country, or from a country likely to share security information with your country'.[142] But even if a message is received, the feasibility of a secure response will very much depend on the technical aptitude of the person making the offer. In 2013, one CIA officer, named Ryan Fogle, was caught in Russia trying to a deliver a letter to a would-be source, which included instructions to continue contact by Gmail.[143] This may sound promising, but as Russia and China have tightened their grip over cyberspace, a response of this kind is dangerous. And while the risks can be mitigated if a person provided clear instructions for a more secure reply (such as using Tor from a disposable device), it only takes a single laps in tradecraft by either party to draw the attention of counterintelligence.

These risks likely exacerbate broader concerns about operational compromise and provocations. Regardless of whether the volunteer was bona fide initially, any attempt to contact an agency website (or respond accordingly) significantly increases the odds of counterintelligence involvement. Once again, officers must assume that if opposing security personnel were to identify the culprit, they would put an end to their efforts or take control of their online persona and run their own operations in their stead. Heightening these concerns is the ease at which Russian and Chinese security services can exploit intelligence agency websites to their advantage. In 2016, Russian media claimed that two Russian fraudsters had emailed the CIA's website offering fake military secrets, spurring on the CIA's curiosity and leading officers 'up the garden path'.[144] Incidents of this nature, some of which may be manufactured by the opposition to waste their time and resources, have somewhat soured intelligence officers' expectations of anyone contacting an agency website, as candidly put by former CIA officer, Colin Thompson, 'the CIA should view any Russian volunteer using that channel as a likely provocation or, if not, a fool who should be ignored'.[145] Until recently, the CIA even included the follow warning on its website: 'Attention: If you are a citizen of the Russian Federation, please do not contact us via this site'.[146]

In turn, it is likely that today's intelligence officers, in parallel to their Cold War counterparts, will want strong assurances about the prospective spy's placement, access, suitability and motive, before initiating a high risk response. It bears note, for example, that in the cases of Roman Ushakov and Yevgeny Chistov, both agents were reportedly able to meet with CIA officers abroad, under circumstances that allowed for a safer assessment. However, in the absence of such conveniences, and when entirely dependent upon inherently insecure means of contact, the need for a degree of preliminary trust before initiating a hazardous reply is arguably more significant.[147] Here, it is impossible to determine whether high value volunteers will be willing to share bona fides across blatantly insecure channels, since the interception of personal information could ultimately expose the would-be spy to their own security services. Of course, some volunteers will be savvy enough to securely communicate (perhaps through Tor) some degree of personally identifiable information, but that is entirely dependent on the aptitude, and willingness, of the individual in question; arguably, the high risks of a compromise through any degree of online interaction are likely to deter a growing number of cautious candidates from doing so. However, should such assessment information be unobtainable by other means, it is hard to see how operatives can develop the necessary trust to justify responding, either online or in person, to Moscow or Beijing residents pitching their services through intelligence agency websites.

The tradecraft paradox

Consequently, this paper demonstrates the recurring challenges embedded in agent recruitment. In one respect, cyberspace is a tradecraft game-changer, opening up capabilities that profoundly alter how targets are found and recruited. But in another respect, the risks inherent to cyber-enabled tradecraft are very much a continuation of the risks encountered in the past. The result, as initially hypothesised, is that *the risks of tradecraft in hard target conditions require greater trust in the prospective spy. However, in such conditions, the odds of failure are vastly increased since, without alternative tradecraft at their disposal, intelligence officers have few means to develop that trust.* Indeed, when it comes to recruiting agents with high level placement and access in Moscow and Beijing, this tradecraft paradox seems likely to undermine whatever advantages cyberspace affords, just as it undermined the benefits of tradecraft and technology in the Cold War.

In the last century, the inability of operatives on the ground to develop sufficient trust to justify their tradecraft, left few options to recruit spies beyond the handful of high value volunteers who were willing to provide assessment information on their own initiative. In parallel, under mounting risks, tradecraft enabled by cyberspace simply cannot be justified without ensuring that those risks – including the fact that any misstep in tradecraft increases the probability that the person being pursued for recruitment is a counterintelligence dangle – are not being undertaken needlessly. This situation places today's intelligence officers in the same dilemma as their predecessor, since they cannot develop necessary assurances without recourse to secure tradecraft. Undoubtedly, the mere prospect that a person has access to valuable intelligence, even without proof, may be enough to spur some risk-taking operatives into action without developing sufficient trust to justify an operational act, but doing so would increase the odds of failure, put lives in danger, push up the probability of recruiting a dangle, and reduce operational successes to luck and intuition, none of which offers a sustainable or ethical strategy for moving forwards.

No doubt, there will be occasional exceptions – SIS officers might discover a target with poor digital hygiene and a proclivity for gossip, before hacking his devices and using that data to run a five-minute pitch arranged online, or perhaps a tradecraft-savvy officer of China's Ministry of State Security might pitch her services to the CIA's website, providing strong bona fides and instructions for a secure response. But when pitted against aggressive and heavily resourced counterintelligence, opportunities of this fashion are likely to be rare, and unless there are radical changes to cyberspace as a whole, the tradecraft paradox is unlikely to be resolved. Operatives are more likely to achieve success by recruiting the bulk of their sources on safer soil, yet doing so cuts off access to the majority of desired agents in the highest ranks of government, especially those in Putin and Xi's inner circles who are forbidden from foreign travel. That said, by pursuing agents outside the hazardous confines of Moscow and Beijing, where the tradecraft paradox offers little reprieve, intelligence officers are better able to harness the advantages that cyberspace affords. Nevertheless, without a sufficient means to develop trust, Russia and China's most guarded – and most valued – secrets are likely to remain hidden.

Cyber-enabled tradecraft and contemporary espionage: assessing the implications of the tradecraft paradox on agent recruitment in Russia and China Kyle S. Cunliffe To cite this article: Kyle S. Cunliffe (2023): Cyber-enabled tradecraft and contemporary espionage: assessing the implications of the tradecraft paradox on agent recruitment in Russia and China, Intelligence and National Security, DOI:10.1080/02684527.202 3.2216035. To.link.to.this.article: https://doi.org/10.1080/02684527.2023.2216035 © 2023 The Author(s). Published by Informa UK Limited, trading as Taylor & Francis Group. Published online: 02 Jun 2023. CONTACT Kyle S. Cunliffe k.s.cunliffe@ salford.ac.uk INTELLIGENCE AND NATIONAL SECURITY https://doi.org/ 10.1080/02684527.2023.2216035 © 2023 The Author(s). Published by Informa UK Limited, trading as Taylor & Francis Group. This is an Open Access article distributed under the terms of the Creative Commons Attribution-NonCommercial-NoDerivatives License (http://creativecommons.org/licenses/by-nc-nd/4.0/), which permits non-commercial re-use, distribution, and reproduction in any medium, provided the original work is properly cited, and is not altered, transformed, or built upon in any way. The terms on which this article has been published allow the posting of the Accepted Manuscript in a repository by the author(s) or with their consent. Journal information. Print ISSN: 0268-4527 Online ISSN: 1743-9019. 7 issues per year. Intelligence and National Security is covered by the following abstracting, indexing and citation services: ABC-CLIO - Historical Abstracts; ABC-CLIO - America: History and Life; World Political Science Abstracts; Historical Abstracts and America: life and history; CSA Political Science and Government and British Humantities Index; Lancaster Index to Defence; International Security Literature and Sociological Abstracts. Taylor & Francis make every effort to ensure the accuracy of all the information (the "Content") contained in our publications. However, Taylor & Francis, our agents (including the editor, any member of the editorial team or editorial board, and any guest editors), and our licensors, make no representations or warranties whatsoever as to the accuracy, completeness, or

Chapter 12

The Ambiguity of Cyber Security Politics in the Context of Multidimensional Uncertainty

Andreas Wenger and Myriam Dunn Cavelty

In a world of rapid socio-technical transformation and increasing fragmentation of political power and authority, cyber security has firmly established itself as one of the top national security issues of the 21st century. Managing cyber insecurities will most likely further increase in complexity and political significance in the next decade, co-produced by an acceleration of the ongoing socio-technical transformations, on the one hand, and the changing dynamics of the related political responses, on the other. The first part of the book recorded the ongoing geographic expansion of cyberspace into outer space, anticipated how emerging technologies will increase the interconnectedness of infrastructures and services, and projected how in a context of ever tighter coupled and integrated socio-technical systems cyber threat narratives will inevitably expand to more policy fields at both the national and international levels. The second part of the book discussed how in cyberspace state actors need to find the right balance between restraint and exploitation, why they need to uphold their efforts to control the risk of escalation, and why governments increasingly share responsibility with actors from economy and society. The current state of cyber security politics is very much a reflection of the interplay between the underlying forces of great power competition and the dynamics of socio-technical and socio-economic globalization processes.

From the interplay of these two processes emerge the two key factors – multidimensional uncertainty and socio-political ambiguity – that characterize the current context of cyber security politics at both the national and international levels, as highlighted in Figure 16.1. Multidimensional uncertainty plays a key role in the emergence of cyber insecurity as a wicked problem and shapes – and is shaped by – the ambiguity of cyber security politics. The ambiguity of cyber security politics encompasses the two dimensions of cyber security outlined in the introductory chapter (Dunn Cavelty and Wenger 2022): First, the international dimension of cyber security politics concentrates on how state actors shape and use cyberspace in accordance with their strategic goals, while at the same time struggling to uphold the stability of their strategic relationships. The interactive search for an acceptable balance between the strategic utility of and the strategic stability in cyberspace is represented in the upper left (possibilities of (geo)political (mis)use) and lower right (conflictive/ cooperative government responses) corners. Second, the broader dimension of cyber security politics focuses on how state, industry, and societies negotiate their respective roles in governing cyberspace, while at the same time competing in the tech innovation process that affects the continued transformation of cyberspace.

The interactive search for norms of responsible behaviour in an uncertain and ambiguous socio-technical and sociopolitical context is represented in the lower left (fragmented trans-sectoral/transnational governance responses) and upper right (emerging digital technologies) corners. This concluding chapter, building on the individual contributions to this book, highlights four key debates that together encapsulate the complexities and paradoxes of the current thinking about the future of cyber security politics from a Western perspective. The first section asks how much political influence states can achieve via cyber operations and what context factors condition the (limited) strategic utility of such operations. A second section discusses the role of emerging digital technologies in cyber security politics and notes how the dynamics of the tech innovation process reinforce the fragmentation of the governance space around them. A third section asks how states attempt to uphold stability in cyberspace, and in their strategic relations more general, highlighting three interconnected challenges – escalation, deterrence, and intelligence – of this interactive quest. A fourth and final section focuses on the shared responsibility of state, economy, and society for cyber security and calls attention to the continuing renegotiation processes about their respective roles in an increasingly trans-sectoral and transnational governance space.

The strategic utility of cyber operations

The debate about the strategic utility of cyber operations arises in a context characterized by the interplay between the rapid emergence of new digital technologies and the politics of their use and misuse. Over time, the debate evolved considerably, as cyber security issues transformed from a technical risk management issue discussed by a limited circle of experts into a key challenge of national security debated at the highest level of governments (Dunn Cavelty 2008; Dewar 2018). In its early stages, the debate focused on "doomsday" cyberattack scenarios that centered on the strategic exploitation of increasingly interconnected and vulnerable infrastructures (Clarke and Knake 2010). As out-of-the-blue cyber war failed to make its expected appearance, experts began to shift their attention to the political and strategic implications of low-level cyber conflict (Baezner 2018; see also Rid 2012; Lindsay 2014/15), on the one hand, and to the increase of computer network attack campaigns linked to covert state involvement (Dunn Cavelty 2015), on the other.

At the current point in time in the history of cyber security politics the empirical picture is characterized by "dogs that did not bark" at the high end of conflict and persistent cyber operations and instability at the low end of conflict (Schulze 2020; Harknett and Smeets 2020; Lupovici 2021). Within this context, the chapters in this volume point to three interconnected aspects of the enduring debate about the strategic utility of cyber operations: A first subsection concentrates on the difficulty of achieving a controlled strategic effect under multidimensional uncertainty. The focus here is on explaining why most cyber operations so far seem not very escalatory and appear unlikely to result in visible changes in the existing balance of power between great powers. A second subsection focuses on the utility of cyber operations as a tool of subversion and mild sabotage. Here the focus is on understanding how the ambiguity of involved actors and the opaqueness of cyber operations can be manipulated in specific strategic contexts by some powers for asymmetric influence. A third subsection deals with the assumed asymmetrical vulnerability of democracies to disinformation as the latest cyber threat focus in Western (security) politics. Here the debate centers on the question if a strategic effect can be achieved via cyber influence operations that aim at undermining social cohesion and trust in democratic political institutions.

The difficulty of achieving a controlled strategic effect under multidimensional uncertainty

Several chapters in this volume engage with the notion that cyber operations are of limited strategic utility in terms of transforming the balance of economic and military power at the level of interstate relations or, more specifically, in terms of an adversary changing its rival's political goals (Gomez and Whyte 2022; Baezner and Cordey 2022). The authors do not explicitly dispute the conclusion of the strategic studies literature that a strategic impact of cyber operations might be elusive (Smeets 2018; Borghard and Lonergan 2017: 477; Kostyuk and Zhukov 2017; Valeriano and Maness 2015: 183; Gartzke 2013). Yet they are concerned, albeit for different reasons, that the insights of this literature might translate into policies that underestimate the escalatory risk of persistent engagement and defend forward (see also Devanny 2021; Healey and Jervis 2020; Healey 2019; Cavaiola et al. 2015). We will come back to the problem of upholding strategic stability under multidimensional uncertainty below. Operating strategically in cyberspace, so much seems to be clear, is far more technically and operationally demanding than the "cheap and easy" metaphor suggests (Lindsay 2013; Slayton 2017; Lewis 2018). "Causing a specific, targeted cyber effect, at a designated point in time, which achieves a strategic purpose, and outweighs the impact of negative consequences, is hard", Max Smeets notes in a forthcoming book (Smeets forthcoming). Resources constrain the overall utility expected from cyber operations.

This is a point reinforced by the economic logic of cyber influence, as Jon R. Lindsay has argued (Lindsay 2017). He holds that setting up cyber exploitations is generally more expensive than countering them, which increases the incentive to keep the target at risk over longer periods of time, turning cyber conflict into primarily an intelligence game (cf. Chesney and Smeets forthcoming; Chesney and Smeets 2020; Rovner 2019). These technical, organizational, and economic challenges all reflect the structural features of cyberspace. Achieving a controlled strategic impact via cyber operations is challenging because cyberspace as an operating environment is characterized by multidimensional uncertainty and sociopolitical ambiguity. On the one hand, cyberspace is marked by a high degree of interconnectedness. This very feature makes it very difficult to fully control the strategic effects of cyber operations since some unintended side-effects in the sense of collateral damage beyond the intended target seem almost unavoidable (Smeets 2018). On the other hand, cyberspace is characterized by constant political contestation. This makes it very difficult to achieve a stable political outcome in which an adversary changes their political goals. According to the same logic, attribution of cyber operations to specific political actors remains time-consuming and often inconclusive (Rid and Buchanan 2015).

Neither states nor cyber intelligence firms have enough of an incentive to fully share the data, methods, and tools behind their attribution claims (Egloff 2020a, Egloff and Wenger 2019). As a consequence, many attribution processes lack transparency and credibility, making it difficult to build broad and stable political support for response strategies based on inherently contested attribution claims (Egloff and Dunn Cavelty 2021). In the context of political competition, cyber operations lack strategic utility as a stand-alone tool to gain an enduring political or military advantage. In actual practice, however, they are linked to and integrated with a broad range of other foreign and security policy instruments. The covert nature of cyber operations means that elites use them as instruments that signal resolve while minimizing escalation risks (Poznansky and Perkoski 2018). The second subsection turns to the question how certain actors attempt to manipulate cyber operations in certain strategic contexts for limited asymmetric influence.

The power to subvert: Manipulating "grey zones" while minimizing the risk of escalation

Most cyber operations take place below the threshold of war, Marie Baezner and Sean Cordey (2022) note in their chapter. Mapping the practical use of such operations in a series of cyber conflict case studies, they confirm that especially influence operations fall into a zone which goes beyond conventional diplomacy and stops short of conventional war, which Lucas Kello describes as "unpeace" (Kello 2017). Taking this empirical puzzle as a starting point for their analysis, the chapter asks why some actors see such operations as attractive and efficient tools of power projection and influence. The (limited) strategic utility of cyber (influence) operations, the two authors conclude, depends on the characteristics of the strategic context and the operational environment in which they are employed and on the nature of the strategic actor employing such operations. At a strategic level, the increasingly pervasive use of cyber (influence) operations in international affairs reflects the current dynamics of great power competition. Together, the increasing costs of conventional war and the realities of economic interdependence create incentives, especially for great powers, to gain asymmetric influence through cyber operations, in particular in their spheres of interest, without however unduly undermining the strategic stability of great power relations.

At an operational level, the use of cyber influence operations reflects an operational environment that is characterized by legal ambiguity and political contestation, opacity of the parties involved and blurred boundaries between the private and public domains. Referring to the concept of and literature on "gray zones", Baezner and Cordey argue that revisionist powers use cyber operations as tools to operate below the threshold of armed combat to gain an asymmetric advantage in their relationship with other political actors, especially in view of the global (military) dominance of the United States. Based on a series of case studies, Baezner and Cordey note that the following operational assumptions about cyber (influence) operations seem to make them attractive tools for many to intervene in gray zone conflicts. First, the majority of the cyber technologies used in such contexts are widely available at relatively low cost. Patriotic hackers or opaque criminal groups with ties to domestic or foreign elites use them opportunistically for disruption and mild sabotage rather than for destruction. Second, cyber espionage and influence operations are increasingly used to influence the information environment of a conflict and gain an asymmetric advantage.

They work in tandem with a wider set of economic, political, and military coercive tools. Third, the legal uncertainty surrounding intelligence operations allows state actors to avoid formal condemnation and uphold a posture of plausible deniability. The opaqueness of actors and operations makes it unlikely that a verdict of attribution would be as transparent and credible as to justify a military response. The importance of the strategic context and the nature of the strategic actor employing cyber (influence) operations are confirmed by Aaron Brantly (2022) in his chapter on Ukraine. He analyzes Ukraine as a case of how to confront a larger aggressive adversary employing cyber and information warfare in its considered sphere of influence at a time of extreme domestic vulnerability amid violent regime change. Before the 2014 Euromaidan revolution, widespread rent-seeking behavior of criminal–political patronage networks and extensive penetration of Ukraine's state structures by Russia's intelligence service made Ukraine vulnerable to foreign cyber and influence operations. The revolution reversed Ukraine's foreign policy alignment from Russia to the West and began a slow process of domestic legal, organizational, and policy transformation that however remains contested by entrenched elites.

Both the relative success of Russia's cyber and information warfare as well as the relative success of Ukraine's response to Russian cyberattacks and disinformation campaigns, Brantly notes, must be assessed in the context of broader patterns of domestic political contestation, on the one hand, and the countries' international orientation and dependence, on the other. Cyber operations in "gray zone" strategic contexts should be conceptualized less as a means of warfare and more appropriately as a tool of political power projection, Marie Baezner and Sean Cordey conclude.

The two authors see such operations as both a novel, efficient and effective tool for disruption (and, to a lesser extent, sabotage) and an "enhancer and transformer" of traditional espionage and covert intelligence operations (Baezner and Cordey 2022: 25). Although their strategic utility will remain elusive, they argue, actors operating in the "gray zones" of modern conflict will likely continue to invest into cyber operations and use them in order to gain an asymmetric advantage. Yet the widely shared assumption that cyber (influence) operations carry a limited risk of escalation might be misplaced and should be reconsidered, the two authors argue. As long as there is a lack of consensus among great powers about norms of acceptable espionage and as long as their definitions of cyber security diverge, the risks of unintentional escalation remain worrisome.

Disinformation as a new threat focus: Asymmetrical vulnerability of democracies?

In cyberspace "the power to subvert seems to trump both the power to coerce and the power to attract" (Dunn Cavelty and Wenger 2019: 15). Subversive power is especially relevant in strategic contexts in which the perceived spheres of interest by rising powers overlap with the geopolitical interests of ruling powers that uphold the status quo (Maschmeyer 2021). But to what degree can revisionist powers use cyber influence operations also as effective tools to undermine the social cohesion and the political stability of democracies? This concern has turned into one of the most relevant cyber threat narratives in Western policy circles, ever since US authorities have attributed the cyber campaigns targeting the US election in 2016 to Russia (Egloff 2020b). Western policymakers increasingly perceive disinformation and cyber influence campaigns by Russia and China as a major threat to liberal democracies, Wolf J. Schünemann (2022) notes in his chapter. Analyzing the threat frames used in Western policy documents, he shows that Western policymakers conceptualize disinformation campaigns that target democratic elections as strategic tools used by Russia and China in the context of great power competition. According to the threat narrative that emerges from these policy documents, foreign actors are actively exploiting the bias of liberal democracies against media control.

They actively manipulate the ambiguities between public diplomacy and coordinated disinformation campaigns to target and potentially distort national elections. Such a threat narrative is often connected to a policy response that aims at strengthening the state's strategic communication capacities. This, however, Schünemann cautions, might have unintended side-effects. Expanding the control of the state over the information sphere might weaken a democracy's best barriers against disinformation: public discourse and public opinion. The political context of the alleged asymmetrical vulnerability of democracies is characterized by uncertainty and a lack of knowledge about the actual impact of disinformation. There is very little robust empirical evidence, Schünemann notes, that foreign disinformation campaigns have a substantial long-term effect on public discourse and public policy. The potential macro effects on political discourses are very difficult to understand and to prove, not least because the digital public sphere and the mass media system are themselves in the middle of a structural transformation. Several phenomena associated with this transformation – for example, echo chambers and automated social bots – are seen as facilitating factors for the spread of disinformation. Yet there is little robust evidence about how they influence the processes of political opinion formation at the macro level (also see Maschmeyer et al. forthcoming). Understanding how the attack surface – the public sphere and public discourse – is changing in the context of digitalization is a precursor for the study of the impact that disinformation might have on political discourse and electoral processes at the national level.

New digital tools such as social media have a potential – with or without outside interference – to erode social trust and increase political fragmentation in (democratic) societies. The use of new socio-technical tools, however, is not predetermined, as Jasmin Haunschild, Marc-André Kaufhold, and Christian Reuter demonstrate in their chapter (Haunschild et al. 2022). This means, they argue, that new socio-technical countermeasures can be designed and developed that ameliorate the potentially negative effects of social and political bots. New technologies can be used to increase social cohesion or to exploit existing grievances. And while tech race dynamics can be strong – for example, between automated bot configuration and automated bot detection – social intervention will remain decisive. Their chapter highlights that the micro-politics of business and civilian actors designing the right social-technical tools might be as important for the resilience of democratic societies against disinformation campaign as the macropolitical responses of state (security) organizations. The effectiveness of foreign disinformation and propaganda is linked to the exploitation of preexisting social distrust and political grievances.

On this, the authors of Chapters 3 and 4 agree. Successful disinformation campaigns exploit existing vulnerabilities of the public discourse and as such must be reduced from within, Schünemann notes. Uncertainty about the potential negative effect of foreign disinformation, he concludes, "must not let us stumble into a new phase of international threat politics and of securitisation of cyberspace with potentially detrimental effects on liberal democratic values and international peace" (Schünemann 2022: 33). Increasing the resilience of democratic societies against foreign disinformation campaigns remains a shared responsibility of civil society, the private and the public sectors.

Emerging technologies and the future of cyber security politics

Ever since cyber security issues have appeared on the agenda of national and international politics, Jon R. Lindsay (2022) argues in his chapter on the ambiguity of a cryptologic advantage, two analytically distinct perspectives have informed the debate about their relevance for cyber security politics. A first perspective builds on the premise that technology determines politics. Anticipating the transformative potential of emerging technologies, this view tends to extrapolate dramatic consequence for security politics. We have already reviewed early expert assumptions along the line that the nature of cyberspace is destabilizing and favours the offence. A second perspective starts from the opposite end of the relationship and assumes that politics determines technology. Such an analytical perspective translates into expectations that the sociopolitical context mitigates the supposed advantages of cyber offence and reinforces established power relationships (cf. Dunn Cavelty and Wenger 2019). We argue throughout the volume that a perspective that combines the two views and unpacks the co-constitution and co-dependency of technology and politics provides a more productive analytical lens for studying the ambiguous implications of rapid technological change on cyber security politics and vice versa.

Within this context, the chapters in this volume discuss three key insights on the interrelationship between emerging technologies and the future of cyber security politics. A first subsection concentrates on tech race dynamics as drivers of cyber threat perceptions. The focus here is on the interplay between global market and geopolitical dynamics under multidimensional uncertainty and how these dynamics feed into threat narratives. A second subsection highlights that the sociopolitical context conditions the strategic utility of emerging technologies. Here the focus is on how social and institutional factors shape the influence that emerging technologies have on the balance between the offense and the defense. A third subsection deals with the growing role of private actors in digital innovation in general and in securing cyberspace more specifically. The focus here is on how the multiplication of actors increases the socio-technical uncertainty and the sociopolitical ambiguity of the governance space around emerging technologies.

Tech race dynamics as drives of cyber threat perceptions

The dynamic and emergent trajectory of technology development is a key factor shaping the interplay between technology and politics. Multidimensional uncertainty – about the scope and tempo of the technological development and about market dynamics and social acceptance – is a key driver of the innovation process. Technology firms are exposed to market pressures and driven by profit. They make their design and development decisions, including complex trade-offs between the performance and the safety and transparency of their products and services, in the shadow of a potential first-mover advantage and the promise of huge economies of scale. Conversely, governments influence the innovation process via the formulation and implementation of technology strategies that specify national levels of ambition. Such strategies aim at incentivizing the domestic uptake of new technologies and creating a regulatory environment that fits their societies' institutional and normative contexts while positioning their countries in the best possible way in the emerging global innovation space (Bonfanti 2022).

As new technological possibilities – linked to the development of artificial intelligence, quantum computing, or space technologies – appear on the horizon, both governments and corporations focus on their potentially transformative capacities, and, more specifically, anticipate what role these technologies will play in shaping cyber security. Most technologies discussed in the chapters of this volume are dualuse technologies and as such might influence the global economic and military balance. As a consequence, great powers tend to treat such technologies as a potential strategic resource. Out of these technical, economic, and (geo)political dynamics an ambiguous political interaction dynamic evolves that fits the logic of the security dilemma (Jervis 1978): The means – in this case, maneuvring to attain or sustain an advantage in critical technologies – by which a state tries to maximize its national interests and security threatens the interests and relative security of other states. From a political perspective, it is problematic if the technology development process is dominated by only a few dominant economic (global tech firms) and political actors (great powers).

A concentration of technical resources in the hands of a few actors might affect the global distribution of economic and military power and create or deepen asymmetric economic and political dependencies. A context of an intensifying technology competition creates incentives for states to influence the innovation process and the proliferation of new technology in their narrow national interest (Fischer and Wenger 2019). Conversely, technology race dynamics act as drivers of national threat perceptions and tend to feed doom scenarios. State actors see themselves increasingly caught in a global race for AI or quantum dominance (Lindsay 2022; Bonfanti 2022). From the perspective of science and technology studies, such threat narratives are co-constituted by the micro-politics of design decisions in competitive global markets and the macropolitics of great powers that act strategically in a competitive international system (Fischer and Wenger 2021).

The strategic utility of emerging technologies depends on the sociopolitical context

The insight that the balance between offense and defense in intelligence has always depended more on institutional factors and strategic context than on technological architecture represents the key message of Chapter 6 in this volume. Analyzing the tumultuous relationship between cryptologic technology and political advantage, Jon R. Lindsay (2022) highlights the fundamental political paradox between cryptography (code-making) and cryptanalysis (code-breaking): They must cooperate to compete and respect the constraints of a cooperatively produced cryptosystem. As a consequence, cryptology turns into an organizational contest and as such heavily depends on social factors. It does not come as a surprise against this background that one of the central insights of cryptologic history is that "gullible humans are the Achilles Heel of classical cryptology" (Lindsay 2022: 89). This again, Lindsay argues, makes it reasonable to expect that humans "will also be the undoing of quantum cryptology" (Lindsay 2022: 89). A working quantum computer should be able to crack the current cryptographic protocols that are vital for cyber security. Anticipating a one-sided technological breakthrough easily translates into fear that a breakthrough in quantum computing might compromise the existing public key infrastructure. As China began to heavily invest into quantum technology, a threat narrative evolved in Western states that perceived the great powers to be locked into a global race to gain a quantum advantage.

A quantum breakthrough would have major repercussion for security and defense, so the arguments went, since one's own intelligence would be locked out while the first-movers' communication would become impenetrable. Should this indeed happen, policymakers and strategists feared, global stability could be at risk. Yet the implications of the interaction between technology and politics will likely be more ambiguous, Lindsay argues. First, such a perspective overlooks that the search for quantum safe protocols begins parallel to the development of a quantum computer that would be able to break the current cryptographic protocols. Second, quantum computing would not change the reliance of cryptology on social factors. Intelligence remains fundamentally a contest between human organizations. The current golden age of cyber espionage was not enabled by a mathematically and technically weak public key infrastructure. It can be traced back to an overly complex organizational setup of the infrastructure and poor cyber hygiene among computer users. Third, even if one side in a geopolitical contest would develop a cryptographic advantage, how this advantage would translate into a political outcome is not predetermined by technology. Rather it would be contingent on the overarching strategic context and the specifics of institutional decision-making.

A cryptanalytic success, Lindsay notes, can make a bargain more likely or a surprise attack more attractive, and it may even provide a false sense of security. In his chapter, Matteo E. Bonfanti (2022) in a similar vein discusses the implications of emerging AI technologies for the offense–defense balance in cyber security. These implications are difficult to predict, he argues, because the context is characterized by widespread uncertainty and ambiguity. Most AI tools can be used in support of both cyber defense as well as cyber offense. AI-based cyber capabilities will affect both the logical (software) dimension as well as the semantic (content) dimension of cyberspace. That AI will have major implications for cyber security is undisputed among experts. Yet who will be the winner – offense or defense, states security agencies or private threat intelligence firms, democracies or autocracies – remains to be seen. The eventual outcome of the integration of AI technologies into cyber security depends on the strategic and sociopolitical context and the risk-benefit calculations of many different public and private cyber security stakeholder.

Private actor innovation increases socio-technical uncertainty and sociopolitical ambiguity

The growing role of private actors in cyber security and in the digital innovation process is noted in most chapters of the book. Big technology companies make key contributions to the development and operation of cyberspace. Private companies act as operators of networks, designers of products and suppliers of services (Eggenschwiler 2022). Small and large technology companies drive the AI innovation process (Bonfanti 2022).

Private actors make smaller and more efficient satellites and have turned into key players in the integration of cyberspace and outer space. The growing role of private actors in outer space was enabled by legal changes in the United States and other states that in the context of a neoliberal vision of state-business relationship opened dual-use space projects to private investment and research and development (Erikkson and Giacomello 2022). Over the past 30 years, the global technology innovation system has increasingly been shaped by the twin forces of globalization and commercialization.

While during the Cold War, the development of nuclear, chemical, and biological dual-use technologies was dominated by state investment and national security concerns, the tide began to turn toward a private sector lead as the development of digital technologies began to take off during the 1990s when the first mobile phones and the internet were made available to the broader public (Fischer 2021). The multiplication of actors in digital innovation and cyber security had ambiguous implications, as the incentive structure of widely heterogonous and increasingly transnationally active technology companies increased the prevailing socio-technical uncertainties. Private technology firms are primarily driven by profit and economies of scale. Although their collective business success depends on high levels of social trust in digital technologies and infrastructures, individual firms have a structural motivation to protect their trade secrets and not to fully disclose all their data and algorithms. Private actors are not only a key innovator of digital technologies, but they have also dramatically expanded their role in securing cyberspace. Brenden Kuerbis, Farzaneh Badiei, Karl Grindal, and Mitlon Mueller (2022) show in their chapter that private threat intelligence firms have turned into key attribution actors. The forensic capabilities of some of the bigger transnational firms are more advanced than those of many states.

Yet their attribution claims lack transparency and public legitimacy (Egloff and Wenger 2019). Moreover, it is unclear why they would contribute to a transnational attribution authority, Kuerbis et al. (2022) note. Conversely, the average dependence of critical public security services on private technology companies providing specialized services in the area of big data analytics and AI-based automated evaluation and assessment will likely grow in the future. Already today, technology consultancy firms provide critical services for states' intelligence services, military (cyber) commands, and national police forces. All of these systems need to be maintained and further developed on a continuous basis. As a consequence, specialized private firms will be drawn ever deeper into the operational work of state security services, further increasing sociopolitical ambiguities. During the golden years of globalization, liberals hoped that global technology norms and regulatory standards would increasingly converge. But while the technology innovation space increasingly expanded around the globe, alternative technology norms and regulatory standards began to emerge in the 21st century, based on a different vision of state-business relationship. China heavily invested in so-called national technology champions, installed a "Civil Military Fusion" mechanism (Bitzinger 2021), and began to actively influence the development of international technology standards (US-China Business Council 2020; Li and Chen 2021). As Western states increasingly perceived China as a geopolitical competitor, they began to set up foreign direct investment screening mechanisms and broadened their dual-use export control systems with the aim of limiting China's access to the West's technology innovation space.

In parallel, they began to look for new ways of how best to secure their states' – and especially their security services' – access to their national technology base. As Danny Steed (2022) argues in his chapter, the Snowden revelations substantiated the extent to which Western technology firms shared data with the US state in the name of national and international security. The upshot of these developments is that the governance space around emerging technologies has become increasingly fragmented and plagued by socio-technical and sociopolitical ambiguity. Cyberspace was originally created as a politically open space with governance structures limited to its technical architecture. As Steed notes in his chapter, the existing sovereignty gap in cyberspace "is not the source of fragmentation, it is the growing [geopolitical] competition to fill the gap that is". The same applies to the growing interconnectedness between cyberspace and outer space, as Johan Eriksson and Giampiero Giacomello (2022) show in their chapter. Private actors increasingly drive the space technology innovation process, as an increasing number of (cyber) infrastructures depends on space-based satellite services. Yet at the same time, state militarization and politicization of outer space accelerates, as an ever-growing number of states use satellite technologies to modernize their security services. The coming together of these two trends creates new vulnerabilities and new types of treats (e.g. anti-satellite weapons, space debris). At the same time, it increases political fragmentation. The diversification of private and state actors raises the old question with new urgency if and how publicprivate partnerships can secure technological reliability and long-term investment.

Strategic stability under multidimensional uncertainty

The assumed revolutionary potential of cyberspace, Miguel A. Gomez and Christopher Whyte (2022) note in their chapter, was the product of the twin uncertainties about the scope and tempo of the technical innovation and the related social and political responses. As new technological possibilities emerged, politics began to catch up in a process of sociopolitical normalization. As a consequence, state behaviour evolved over time. In the absence of a demonstrable strategic utility of cyber operations and a strategic context characterized by a puzzling co-existence of restraint at the high end of conflict and persistent low-level cyber conflict, key states started to increasingly move away from deterrence to cyber conflict management. In 2018, the United States issued a new cyber strategy signaling a shift to persistent engagement and defend forward. The logic of the new approach emphasized that the characteristics of the operational environment in cyberspace – a space of constant contact – demand a continuing engagement and degradation of adversarial cyber capabilities and operations wherever they were found (US Cyber Command 2018; US Department of Defense 2019). This shift away from deterrence might be premature and underestimate the potential of (unintended) escalation, Gomez and Whyte argue.

Moreover, it is still unclear why states invest substantial technical, financial, and organizational resources in using the domain offensively if cyber operations are indeed of limited strategic utility only. Within this context, the chapters in this volume focus on three interconnected aspects of upholding strategic stability under multidimensional uncertainty. A first subsection concentrates on the micro-dynamics of decision-making that might drive escalation under uncertainty and ambiguity. The focus here is on how prior beliefs and cognitive biases might influence the response decisions of elite stakeholders in varying national strategic cultures. A second subsection deals with the ambiguities of attribution as a precondition for a credible deterrence threat. The focus here is on how policymakers perceive cyberspace as a completely human-built domain and how this translates into political apprehension about the applicability of deterrence in cyberspace. A third subsection analyzes the growing role of intelligence in cyberspace. The focus here is on how the digitalization of intelligence changed its strategic and operational role and what (un)intentional consequences this had for cyber insecurity, on the one hand,

and for great powers' views on (un)acceptable behavior of intelligence services in cyberspace, on the other.

Escalation: The micro-dynamics of decision-making in varying sociopolitical contexts

Precisely because it is difficult to control the strategic effects of cyber (influence) operations, more research is needed on the micro-dynamics of decision-making that may drive unintended escalation. Contributing to the behavioural turn in cyber security research, Miguel A. Gomez and Christopher Whyte (2022) investigate the effects of uncertainty on judgment in the context of (crisis) decision-making under cyberattack. In such situations, the ambiguity of diffuse actors and malicious actions increases the uncertainty of decision-makers about both the intent behind and the consequences of cyber (influence) operations. The authors use war gaming as a pseudo-experimental method to determine if and how decision-makers use well-known heuristic mechanisms such as prior beliefs and analogical reasoning to discern intent and consequences behind cyber operations. The authors find distinct evidence in support of the notion that decision-makers, when faced with digital insecurity and the use of adversarial cyber operations, fall back on non-cyber situations to make their task simpler.

The degree to which heuristic shortcuts interfere with objectivity and results in more or less severe responses depends on distinct national (strategic) cultures. Gomez and Whyte discuss evidence of cross-national cultural variations influencing the response decision among elite stakeholders. The socio-institutional correlates of civil–military relations in a given democracy stand out to have a unique impact on decision-making processes. Based on their observations from cross-national war games, they conclude that the interaction between the microfoundations of decision-making in a given cultural and institutional setting "might ultimately have some effect on the strategic calculations states make around signaling and adversary behavior" (Gomez and Whyte 2022: 125). The fact that unintended escalation due to prior beliefs, cognitive biases of decision-makers, and/ or bureaucratic politics cannot be excluded in strategic context characterized by uncertainty and ambiguity highlights the advantage of deterrence as a conflict management tool: As a theory of interdependent decision-making, it might prevent militarization and escalation (Schelling 1966).

Deterrence: The ambiguity of attribution in the context of cyber conflict management

Over the years there has been considerable work invested at the science-policy interface in adapting deterrence to the ambiguous context of cyberspace. The scope of the practical applicability of the tenets of deterrence to cyberspace is considerably more limited than in more traditional conventional and nuclear deterrence settings (Soesanto and Smeets 2020). At the same time, deterrence attempts in cybersecurity and cyber defence span a wide spectrum of threats, including cybercrime, cyber espionage, and operational cyberattack. From a conceptual point of view, the attention at the lower end of conflict shifted to criminological conceptions of deterrence and from punishment to denial mechanisms converging on target hardening through cyber resilience (Wenger and Wilner 2021). In such settings, though, deterrence approaches are typically integrated with other coercive and non-coercive tools into a broader conflict management strategy. Conversely, at the higher end of conflict the attention of strategists has shifted to the concept of cross domain deterrence (Lindsay and Gartzke 2019). The focus here is on adversaries that apply ambiguous "gray zone" strategies that integrate military and non-military coercive instruments while evading attribution. Cross domain deterrence tends to include both positive inducements and negative threats and brings the concept of deterrence "back to the broader coercive diplomacy literature from which it originally emerged" (Sweijs and Zilinick 2021: 152).

In his chapter on the limited reliance of Israel on cyber deterrence, Amir Lupovici (2022) explores how new digital technologies enter into doctrine and strategy. Acknowledging the methodological difficulties of studying cyber deterrence, he deliberately shifts the focus from studying what makes deterrence effective in a given strategic context to analyzing how the cyber domain is embedded in Israel's strategic culture and identity. From such a viewpoint, Lupovici argues, it is puzzling that Israel has so far not developed a clear cyber deterrence strategy, given the prominent role deterrence has played in Israel's strategy and the country's "deterrer identity" (Lupovici 2016). Israeli policymakers, he concludes, seem to recognize the uncertainty and ambiguity involved in establishing a deterrence balance in cyberspace and consequently shy away from formulating a declaratory cyber deterrence strategy. From an operational point of view, Lupovici (2022) argues, Israel's repeated use of offensive cyber operations against the Iranian and Syrian nuclear programs have been interpreted by some experts as attempts to establish cumulative deterrence through the actual use of force, a concept which is deeply ingrained in Israeli strategic culture (Adamski 2021).

Yet the effectiveness of such a strategy remains in dispute, Lupovici insists, and whatever deterrent threat might get through to the adversary is communicated in an indirect and implicit way only. From a conceptual perspective, the US strategy of persistent engagement and defend forward seems to share some of the tenets of the Israeli concept of cumulative deterrence (Tor 2015; Kello 2017). Yet the concept of cumulative deterrence was customarily rejected by most US strategists and policymakers, since in the context of nuclear deterrence the use of force was seen as a symptom of deterrence failure, signaling a shift from a policy of influence to a policy of control (Adamsky 2021). It is quite telling that two of the leaders in thinking about and in practicing deterrence in their different strategic contexts have come to accept the limits of deterrence in cyberspace. The way US and Israeli policymakers and strategist conceptualize the cyber domain – as an operating environment with a high degree of technical interconnectedness (increasing uncertainty) and constant political contestation (increasing ambiguity) – seems to be part of the explanation why they, respectively, moved away from cyber deterrence (United States) and never declared a clear deterrence strategy (Israel).

Although cyberspace is conceptualized as the fifth domain of warfare, its structural characteristics differ from the other four domains. Cyberspace is completely human-built, shaped by technology companies, and operating in it will always be hard and only partially under control of any one actor (Seebeck 2019). Precisely because cyberspace is completely designed by humans, states can shape it according to their interest. Yet as in cryptology they must cooperate to compete and accept the constraint of a cooperatively produced network of networks. The economic and political logic of cyberspace as something completely designed by humans might explain why states seem to perceive cyberspace as a domain of intelligence rather than warfare. As discussed above, the fact that setting up cyber exploitation is more expensive than countering released exploitation translates into an incentive to keep the target at risk. From a political point of view, transparent attribution as a precondition of a credible deterrence threat is difficult. Relating an intrusion set to a politically responsible party, Kuerbis et al. (2022) argue, remains challenging because it includes a judgment about the relation between victim and adversary. As such, it should be interpreted as "a product more of political science or intelligence studies than computer science" (Kuerbis et al. 2022: 222).

Intelligence: The growing operational role of intelligence as a source of cyber insecurity

In the context of the multidimensional uncertainty prevailing in cyberspace, intelligence agencies have turned into one of the most dominant actors in this human-built domain (Buchanan 2020; Egloff 2022). Their role in cyber conflict is a paradox and highly ambiguous one: They represent both the biggest threat and the most capable provider of security and safety. Such an outcome is not without irony, because the technical transformation from an analog to a digital world exposed them to a mortal threat: going dark. In his chapter on the consequences of the digital disruption of the second oldest profession, Danny Steed (2022) discusses how US and British intelligence "mastered the internet". In the process, he concludes, they not only transformed their role in security and defense, but unintentionally exacerbated cyber insecurity. As global information flows began moving into fiber optics, US and British intelligence adapted their skillset to one that could penetrate digital codes and infrastructure (Buchanan 2020). Exploiting the sovereign geographic access to the submarine cables through which the bulk of the internet traffic traversed, was a key factor for success, as was a close partnership with numerous technology companies that facilitated access and sharing of meta-data. The solution to the old intelligence adage – to find the needle in the haystack – was found in technical innovation, as Steed explains:

The two intelligence services temporarily collected the whole haystack in a buffer system, which allowed them to sort out relevant information and meta-data via automated analysis. This unique access to large volumes of internet traffic created intelligence dependencies even among close allies, as Stefan Steiger (2022) shows in his chapter on Germany's cyber security politics. Once the Snowden leaks highlighted that foreign intelligence was an accepted state practice even among allies, the German government in a partnership with Brazil invested into a new submarine cable across the Atlantic. Intelligence services are the most purposefully ambiguous tools of statecraft. The legal ambiguity of intelligence in domestic and international law was for a long time based on the reciprocal assumption of great powers that intelligence services would help decision-makers guard against a military fait accompli and uphold strategic stability. The purpose of the limited intrusion into the sovereign affairs of another state was to provide enough transparency to avoid rapid escalation. In the context of their digital transformation, Danny Steed (2022) contends, their strategic relevance increased considerably. At the same time, their operational focus increasingly shifted from assessing uncertainty to eliminating uncertainty.

The shift to a more operational role needs to be seen in the context of a unipolar world, in which the management of transnationally networked threats – terrorism, extremism, organized crime, cyberattacks, WMD proliferation – dominated Western policy and strategy. In the post-9/11 context, operational intelligence and close (bilateral) cooperation among asymmetrically dependent intelligence services played a preeminent role in the global management of the then dominant security challenges. With the return of geopolitical rivalry between great powers and in the context of the pro-active use of intelligence and cyber (influence) operations by rising powers, international disagreement about what should be considered acceptable use of espionage began to multiply, as noted above in section one. From the perspective of great power politics, it seems essential that states sort out the difference between mutually acceptable espionage in support of strategic stability and inacceptable meddling in the internal political and economic affairs of another state.

The 2015 mutual agreement between China and the United States, in which both states committed to not conducting or supporting economic cyber espionage (Baezner and Robin 2017), and the recent agreement between Biden and Putin to conduct "experts-level talks" on red lines for cyberattacks on "critical" sectors (Hirsh 2021), might be read as early beginnings of a long haul toward a tacit understanding of acceptable behavior of intelligence services in cyberspace. It seems highly unlikely, however, that talks at the diplomatic level will result in a breakthrough any time soon. For this to happen, the differences of acceptable surveillance at the domestic level are simply too big. Societies need to know how their intelligence services work in cyberspace, because their tools and practices set practical norms with far-reaching effects on state, society and economy (Georgieva 2020). For authoritarian states, the priority is to control citizens' access to information, while for democracies the priority is to protect individual privacy and intellectual property rights. Questions about privacy, security, information are at the heart of the political struggle about cyber security and this makes the quest for global norms of responsible behavior in cyberspace a slow and difficult one. The manner in which intelligence services mastered the internet, Danny Steed (2022) convincingly argues, created additional socio-technical uncertainty and exacerbated the cyber security challenge.

Digitalization made intelligence more visible, because unlike in an analog world spies now worked within the same digital infrastructure as all other social, economic, and political actors. As a consequence, intelligence intrusion could be exposed much faster than before, which made intelligence far more visible. When whistle-blowers brought their activities into the spotlight, domestic and international political contestation about their role multiplied. As a corollary of the exposure of intelligence methods, intelligences services turned into inadvertent proliferators of malicious code and zeroday exploits. As a consequence, more people were enabled to use intelligence tools for malicious purposes – compared to intelligence services, with no oversight whatsoever. Some of these tools were later deployed in two global malware attacks – WannaCry and NotPetya–further increasing the ambiguity of action in cyberspace and the uncertainties of attribution.

Emerging governance responses: Policy coordination and norms formation

The socio-technical expansion of cyberspace is led by private technology firms, yet state actors shape the tighter coupling of technical systems with sociopolitical institutions. This in turn means that governments share the responsibility to secure cyberspace with actors from the economy and society. In the process of these socio-technical and sociopolitical transformations, emerging cyber governance responses unfold in an increasingly transnational and trans-sectoral policy space. The vision of a wireless, satellite-based internet accessible to everyone propagated by private business actors and the parallel reality of state actors that are increasingly politicizing and militarizing outer space is set to further expand cyberspace as a transnational policy space. As a network of interdependent information technology infrastructures, cyberspace is connected across state borders and through global satellite-based communications services. At the same time, cyberspace as a trans-sectoral policy space also expands rapidly.

The tighter coupling of ever more socio-technical systems increases the interconnectedness of cyberspace. As a consequence, cyber security affects a rapidly growing number of different policy fields. The key governance challenge in cyberspace is how to overcome fragmentation of authority and accountability. Within the context of a trans-sectoral and transnational policy space, the chapters in this volume highlight three aspects of the ongoing re-negotiation processes among state, society, and economy about their roles and responsibilities in cyberspace. A first subsection deals with the significant expansion of state responsibilities in cyberspace over the past decades. The focus is on how state actors fine-tuned their multidimensional role across different policy fields in a process that was influenced by distinct patterns of interaction between domestic contestation and international orientation and dependence. A second subsection concentrates on the increasingly prominent role of private and civil society actors in the search for new forms of transnational governance in cyberspace. The focus here is on the norm-based activities of big tech companies, on the one hand, and a series of proposals for a global platform for transnational attribution, on the other. A third subsection brings the attention back to state actors, shedding light on the critical role of intelligence services in (in)securing cyberspace. As long as great powers disagree about what constitutes acceptable behavior of intelligence services in cyberspace, the systemic levels of insecurity in cyberspace will likely not materially decrease.

Growing role of governments: Shifting patterns of domestic and international governance

The tech pioneers had built the internet based on the vision of an open technical governance infrastructure with minimal involvement of government. Yet as cyberattacks were becoming more persistent, more targeted, more expensive, and more disruptive, governments began to significantly expand their roles and responsibilities in cyberspace. Ever since states find themselves in the midst of two interlinked re-negotiation processes of their roles and responsibilities in (securing) cyberspace. While at the level of domestic politics they renegotiate their role in securing cyberspace as a shared responsibility with society and industry, at the level of international politics they renegotiate the patterns of international governance with states, private and civil actors. In his chapter, Stefan Steiger (2022) analyzes how Germany's cyber security policies evolved over time, shaped by the complex interactions between domestic and international negotiation processes. He employs a role theoretical two-level game to analyze how domestic and international factors influenced the development of German cyber security policy. Isolating four interconnected policy domains – critical infrastructure protection (CIP); law enforcement; intelligence services; military – he discusses how varyingly fragmented national and international actors reached four distinct, but still connected policy outcomes.

The CIP and law enforcement domains of German cyber security policy comprise the most distinct international and regional cooperation patterns, Steiger concludes. In the CIP domain, domestic CIP policies emerged first, based on a model of public-private partnerships that delegated the primary responsibility for cyber security to the private sector. Over time, however, the federal government strengthened its supervisory role considerably. The German government promoted the protection of critical infrastructures also internationally, primarily in the EU and the OSCE, reflecting the physical interconnectedness of critical infrastructure across borders. In the domain of law enforcement, EU members successfully harmonized criminal law, without however weakening the central authority and sovereignty of the (German) state. The intelligence and military domains of German cyber security policy remain intergovernmental policy domains, in which the German government accepted no self-binding regulations. The intelligence domain exhibits the most paradoxical interaction patterns between national and international re-negotiation processes, Steiger notes. On the one hand, Germany's early call for international restraint in cyberspace was facilitated by the intelligence dependence on the United States.

Once the Snowden revelations showed that digital surveillance was an accepted state practice even among allies, the role of intelligence was hotly contested at the domestic level. As a consequence, Germany expanded the legal basis for foreign surveillance, began to stockpile zero-day exploits, and expanded its access to the transatlantic internet traffic. In parallel, this expanded foreign mandate of German intelligence was balanced with stronger domestic control mechanisms and special protection rights for German and EU citizen. In the military domain too, Germany, because of its commitment to NATO, began to move away from international restraint, established a cyber-command, and prepared for the use of offensive cyber capabilities. Chapters 11 and 12 in this volume offer two additional case studies discussing the cyber security policies of two states that are located at the periphery of Europe and want to move closer to Western institution. The evolution of their cyber security policies too is characterized by distinct patterns of interaction between domestic institutional transformation and international orientation and dependence. We have already discussed the case of Ukraine above. Ukraine represents the extreme case of a small state with weak cyber capacity that sits on the geopolitical fault lines between Russia and the West.

Exposed to persistent Russian cyberattacks and massive information operations, the country recently lived through a domestic revolution linked to an abrupt reorientation of its foreign policy alignment from Russia to Europe and the West. In his chapter, Aaron Brantly (2022) shows that the pattern of domestic contestation and international reorientation resulted in a fairly successful response of the country to Russia's information warfare, aimed at undermining the social and political fabric of Ukraine. He explains this as the result of a combination of a series of top-down government initiatives – including restrictive moves against Russian-dominated web platforms and broadcast channels and the introduction of a Ministry of Information Policy – with a series of bottom-up initiatives by journalist and externally sponsored NGOs–focusing on fact checking, disclosure of foreign propaganda, and the training of journalists and civil society. Less successful, however, were the country's efforts to increase its resilience against cyberattacks. Although the country aligned the legal and organizational foundations of its cyber security policies with EU and NATO standards, the new cyber security structures are not yet functional on their own, Brantly concludes. He points to the dominance of old bureaucratic cultures–especially in the security services–and dependence on external assistance and funding as the two main reasons for weak policy implementation. Albania represents another interesting case of a small state with weak cyber capabilities that is transforming toward democracy and wants to move closer to Western institutions.

In his chapter, Islam Jusufi (2022) discusses how both the cyber threat frames and the policy responses visible in Albania's policy documents diffused from the international level – especially from US, UK, EU, and NATO sources. This policy diffusion process to the national level had two notable consequences, the author argues: First, cyber security was preemptively upgraded to a national threat level, i.e. not in response to national incidents. Second, the new policy introduced the concept of multi-stakeholder governance that represented a shift from Albania's traditional state-centered governance model. In combination, these two developments resulted in a somewhat paradoxical outcome: While the dependence of a technologically weak state on foreign actors increased, the introduction of new international policy concepts augmented the fragmentation of domestic authority in cyber security. Moreover, this outcome highlights a certain time-inconsistency problem in international policy coordination. It is not without irony that Western states in parallel began to reclaim authority and sovereignty in certain policy domains–as demonstrated in the German case above – and expanded the protector role of the government in cyberspace.

Toward new forms of transnational governance: Norms and institutions

The search for new forms of transnational governance reflects a realization that digital technologies and the services they provide are increasingly connected across state borders and into outer space. Why do private and civil society actors play an increasingly prominent role in the development of norms and institutions that aim to regulate human behavior in cyberspace? First, cyber norms and institutions remain contested at the level of international politics. The inability of states to make progress in the direction of a common understanding of cyber norms, especially at the United Nations, provided the context for a growing engagement of non-state actors. Second, a series of large-scale data breaches and malware strikes undermined social trust – a critical success factor for the business models of transnationally operating tech firms – in the socio-technical systems that constitute cyberspace. Third, the mostly private creators of cyber space possess key engineering expertise that is essential to ensure that new governance approaches are anchored in a tacit understanding of research and development and broader business practices.

In turn, civil society has the potential to provide additional benefits in terms of transparency, privacy, and equality. In her chapter, Jacqueline Eggenschwiler (2022) evaluates the norm-based activities of big tech companies, including Kaspersky Lab, Siemens, Telefónica, and Microsoft. She introduces norms approaches as appropriate regulatory approaches to tackle the contextual ambiguities of fast-moving environments, which preempt costly–and from the viewpoint of tech firms unwanted – changes to legal frameworks. With their voluntary engagement in support of the development of cyber security norms of responsible behavior, technology firms aim to define responsible product development and engineering practices and establish trust in social interactions enabled by digital technologies. The norm-based activities of big tech have been partially successful insofar as they have converged on a number of widely shared normative ideas and design principles and injected these ideas and principles into a number of regional and international political processes. The procedural effects of a greater inclusion of private and civil society actors in norm development processes will likely be enduring, Jacqueline Eggenschwiler concludes. Yet big tech's push for cyber security norms has not resulted in a substantial reduction of cyber insecurity. Not only the development of cyber security norms will be a long process, the same is

238

true for the institutionalization of a recognized transnational attribution process, Brenden Kuerbis, Farzaneh Badiei, Karl Grindal, and Milton Mueller (2022) argue in their chapter. Cyber attribution as a socio-technical and highly interdisciplinary endeavor is a precondition for the deterrence of cyberattacks and a precursor for stable social relations in cyberspace.

The current attribution claims of threat intelligence firms and national security services are however often based on limited evidence and the reputation of the attributing actor, and, as a consequence, lack transparency and credibility. However, new advances in attribution that combine better algorithm-driven technical attribution with better understanding of the institutional condition under which attribution might occur, Kuerbis et al. note, may in the future improve the baseline for institutionalizing transnational attribution. The chapter discusses various proposals from private actors and academic institutions on how a global platform for transnational attribution could be set up and what the scope of its activities should be. The following two major challenges on the way toward implementation stand out in most of them: A first key question is how to ensure the technical independence of such a platform and the professionalism of the participants. There is still a lot of research needed to define the scientific and methodological standards, including transparency, reproducibility, and falsifiability, of the practice of attribution. In addition, it remains unclear why private tech firms with advanced forensic capabilities would participate in such a platform. A second key question is how to guarantee the judicial independence of such a platform and what governance form would be effective in aligning the participants' incentives. The spectrum of conceivable solutions ranges from hierarchically organized institutions to loosely organized forms of networked governance. In the final analysis, however, the success of private and civil sector–driven cyber security norms processes as well as of initiatives aimed at the institutionalization of transnational attribution critically depend on the political will of state actors, especially great powers, to agree upon norms of responsible behavior as the ultimate enforcer.

Great powers as ultimate enforcers: Re-negotiation, the ambiguous norms of espionage

States cannot govern cyberspace on their own, they need to integrate economic and social actors into a wider cyber security governance framework. Yet no stable cyber security governance framework will evolve without greater convergence among great powers on responsible state behavior as ultimate enforcers. It is therefore vital for non-state and state actors to work closer together and aid one another in their behavior-shaping efforts in order to decrease the systematic levels of cyber insecurity, Jacqueline Eggenschwiler (2022) argues in her chapter. As long as emerging (information) technologies are perceived as a geopolitical battleground, limited progress will be possible. States need to negotiate a tacit understanding about what constitutes a mutually acceptable balance between restraint in and exploitation of cyberspace. As discussed above, a critical component of such an understanding is linked to the behavior of state intelligence services in the digital domain. The great power's views on what forms of espionage and interference in the political processes and socioeconomic activities of other societies through cyberspace are acceptable need to converge before the systemic levels of cyber insecurity will materially decrease.

Conclusion

The chapters in this book discussed the ambiguity of current cyber security politics in an uncertain context characterized by rapid socio-technical transformation and increasing fragmentation of political authority. In this concluding chapter, we highlighted four key debates in current thinking about cyber security, all of them linked to the interplay between technological possibilities and political choices in cyberspace. An analytical perspective that emphasizes the co-constitution and co-dependency of technology and politics provides an especially productive lens for studying the complexities and paradoxes of cyber security politics. The key reason for this is found in the nature of cyberspace as a domain completely designed and built by humans – with a high degree of technical interconnectedness and constant political contestation. As a consequence, state, economy and society must cooperate to compete in cyberspace and accept the constraints of a cooperatively produced network of networks. A key insight that such an analytical perspective offers is that both evolving cyber threat narratives and emerging cyber governance responses are co-produced by state and non-state actors in a rapidly changing trans-sectoral and transnational policy space. Emerging cyber threats are co-constituted by the micro-politics of technology design decisions in competitive global markets, the meso-politics of technology norms choices in competitive regulatory environments, and the macro-politics of great powers that act strategically in a competitive international system. Within this broader context, the chapters in this book highlight a series of interaction mechanisms between technology and politics that influence cyber threat politics in different strategic contexts: Tech race dynamics around emerging dual-use technologies clearly leave a mark in the national threat politics of great powers.

Actors in "gray zone" conflicts attempt to manipulate the opaqueness of cyber (influence) operations. And in democracies policymakers are increasingly concerned about the asymmetrical vulnerability of their socio-technical public sphere to foreign disinformation and cyber influence campaigns. That cyber threat perceptions are co-constituted by technology and politics also means that their realization is not predetermined. Both state and non-state actors can contribute to a decrease of the level of insecurity in cyberspace. States need to establish red lines, uphold strategic stability, and develop norms of responsible state behavior in cyberspace. Actors from society and economy need to develop norms of responsible behavior for the creators and users of emerging technologies as the bedrock of societies' trust in socio-technical systems. Yet the effectiveness of their individual responses to cyber threats depends on their mutual interplay. States and societal actors need to negotiate how public authority is exercised in cyberspace. A stable governance framework for cyber security can only emerge if great powers develop a tacit understanding on what represents a responsible use of cyber operations in state interactions, and societal actors successfully navigate the normative space around technology, information, privacy, and security.

Researchers can contribute to the search for a functioning governance framework: They can highlight the less visible actors in cyberspace, design and evaluate new socio-technical institutions to secure cyberspace or monitor, and analyze publicly available data about cyber operations. A key conceptual challenge for cyber security research is linked to the integration of theoretical knowledge from different disciplines that allows to analyze the many interactions between the international dimension of cyber security politics and the broader dimension of cyber security politics (Dunn Cavelty and Wenger 2019). Those who study the former tend to build on approaches from IR, security, and intelligence studies, but increasingly recognize broader contributions from critical security studies and practice theory. Those who study the latter, leverage an even broader array of theoretical perspectives including approaches from IPE, governance studies, and the IR norms literature. A practical challenge is how to overcome the dominance of Western perspectives both in politics as well as in academia. We tend to see only the peak of an iceberg of malicious activities in cyberspace that is linked to the political and economic interests of Western states and threat intelligence firms. The empirical focus of most chapters in this book is informed by the geostrategic rivalry between Western democracies and Russia and China as their main authoritarian contender. It is this strategic context and the differences in the domestic institutional setup of the leading great powers that guide large parts of the analyses of cyber conflict in this volume. Yet at the same time, individual chapters point to interesting variances in the cyber security policies among traditional (United States, Israel) and aspiring (Albania, Ukraine) democracies, on the one hand, and to the important role of cross-national cultural variations in cyber decision-making, on the other. Cyber security is increasingly negotiated at the global level and this is why we need to better understand how different regions and cultures think about the interplay of technology and politics in cyberspace.

OPEN ACCESS, Creative Commons, CC BY-NC-ND, Book. Cyber Security Politics Socio-Technological Transformations and Political Fragmentation Edited ByMyriam Dunn Cavelty, Andreas Wenger. Edition1st Edition. First Published2022, eBook Published16 February 2022, Pub. LocationLondon, ImprintRoutledge, DOIhttps:// doi.org/10.4324/9781003110224, Pages286. eBook ISBN9781003110224. SubjectsPolitics & International Relations, Taylor & Francis ebooks is a single destination platform with ebooks in science, technology, engineering, medical, humanities and social science. It includes a librarian dashboard, which provides quick access to MARC and KBART reports, usage data, entitlements and much more. Researchers have a single point of discovery for eBook content, multiple search options, and more. Access to the platform will allow users to: search ebook content at both the book and chapter level, filter search results by subject area, publication date and year published, and create citations in APA format. Flexible purchase options, subject collections, and free trials are available. Bring a World of Knowledge to Your Organization. Request a trial of Taylor & Francis ebooks, giving you access to a vast collection of ebooks across a range of subject areas. To request a free trial, you will first need to create an account and then complete an online request form. If you are a librarian, once we have received a trial request we will be in touch about setting up your trial. If you are a faculty member or a student we will contact the library at your organisation. About Taylor & Francis. Taylor & Francis Group publishes books for all levels of academic study and professional development, across a wide range of subjects and disciplines. We publish Social Science and Humanities books under the Routledge, Psychology Press and Focal Press imprints. Science, Technology, and Medical books are published by CRC Press. We publish textbooks for emerging subject areas as well as the most established and for students at all stages of their studies. Our books for professional development are written by recognized experts in their field. Our reference works and encyclopedias have earned an outstanding reputation for their accuracy and reliability and are used extensively world-wide. Our research program consists of single and multi-authored books and edited collections, and is characterized by dynamic interventions into established subjects and innovative studies on emerging topics. https://www. taylorfrancis.com/books/oa-edit/10.4324/9781003110224/cyber-security-politics-andreas-wenger-myriam-dunn-cavelty?context=ubx&refId=7bcd3915-608b-4f7d-89a4-2d65a5afe047. This book examines new and challenging political aspects of cyber security and presents it as an issue defined by socio-technological uncertainty and political fragmentation. Structured along two broad themes and providing empirical examples for how socio-technical changes and political responses interact, the first part of the book looks at the current use of cyberspace in conflictual settings, while the second focuses on political responses by state and non-state actors in an environment defined by uncertainties. Within this, it highlights four key debates that encapsulate the complexities and paradoxes of cyber security politics from a Western perspective – how much political influence states can achieve via cyber operations and what context factors condition the (limited) strategic utility of such operations; the role of emerging digital technologies and how the dynamics of the tech innovation process reinforce the fragmentation of the governance space; how states attempt to uphold stability in cyberspace and, more generally, in their strategic relations; and how the shared responsibility of state, economy, and society for cyber security continues to be re-negotiated in an increasingly trans- sectoral and transnational governance space. This book will be of much interest to students of cyber security, global governance, technology studies, and international relations. Myriam Dunn Cavelty is deputy head of research and teaching at the Center for Security Studies (CSS), ETH Zurich, Switzerland. Andreas Wenger is professor of international and Swiss security policy at ETH Zurich and director of the Center for Security Studies (CSS), Switzerland. The CSS Studies in Security and International Relations series examines historical and contemporary aspects of security and conflict. The series provides a forum for new research based upon an expanded conception of security and will include monographs by the Center's research staff and associated academic partners. Series Editor: Andreas Wenger. Center for Security Studies, Swiss Federal Institute of Technology (ETH), Zurich. Cyber Security Politics Socio-Technological Transformations and Political Fragmentation. Edited by Myriam Dunn Cavelty and Andreas Wenger. First published 2022 by Routledge. 4 Park Square, Milton Park, Abingdon, Oxon OX14 4RN and by Routledge 605 Third Avenue, New York, NY 10158. Routledge is an imprint of the Taylor & Francis Group, an informa business.

and are used only for identification and explanation without intent to infringe. British Library Cataloguing in Publication Data A catalogue record for this book is available from the British Library Library of Congress Cataloging in Publication Data Names: Dunn Cavelty, Myriam, editor. | Wenger, Andreas, editor. Title: Cyber security politics: socio-technological transformations and political fragmentation/ edited by Myriam Dunn Cavelty and Andreas Wenger.

Chapter 13

Artificial Intelligence and EU Security: The False Promise of Digital Sovereignty

Andrea Calderaro & Stella Blumfelde

Abstract

EU Digital Sovereignty has emerged as a priority for the EU Cyber Agenda to build free and safe, yet resilient cyberspace. In a traditional regulatory fashion, the EU has therefore sought to gain more control over third country-based digital intermediaries through legislative solutions regulating its internal market. Although potentially effective in shielding EU citizens from data exploitation by internet giants, this protectionist strategy tells us little about the EU's ability to develop Digital Sovereignty, beyond its capacity to react to the external tech industry. Given the growing hybridisation of warfare, building on the increasing integration of artificial intelligence (AI) in the security domain, leadership in advancing AI-related technology has a significant impact on countries' defence capacity. By framing AI as the intrinsic functioning of algorithms, data mining and computational capacity, we question what tools the EU could rely on to gain sovereignty in each of these dimensions of AI. By focusing on AI from an EU Foreign Policy perspective, we conclude that contrary to the growing narrative, given the absence of a leading AI industry and a coherent defence strategy, the EU has few tools to become a global leader in advancing standards of AI beyond its regulatory capacity.

Keywords: Digital sovereignty, artificial intelligence, EU security, EU foreign policy.

Introduction

The call for EU Digital Sovereignty identifying the need to build free and safe, yet resilient cyberspace is increasingly at the centre of the EU agenda. These issues are consistent with the broader EU ambition to achieve "strategic autonomy", first announced in 2013 in regards to the defence industry (European Council, Citation 2013), and later adopted for broader defence and security purposes with the launch of the European Union Global Strategy (EUGS) in 2016 (European External Action Services 2016). Clustered around the need to strengthen the EU's capacity and ability to protect itself as an actor in global politics as well as its citizens (European Commission Citation 2020a) both within and outside its borders (Bellanova and Glouftsios 2022, Martins et al. Citation 2022), this priority has developed over the years of challenging external circumstances. The Snowden case, first, increased public concern with state-sponsored mass surveillance strategies, and digital privacy became a priority of a nascent EU digital agenda (Hintz et al. Citation 2019). The subsequent Cambridge Analytica scandal, further highlighted the dominant role of digital intermediaries over states and society (Kapczynski 2019), with the increasing trend of economic exploitation of data (Zuboff 2019), and their interfering capacity in states' democratic equilibrium (York 2021). The market influence of private actors in what is traditionally state affairs pushed the EU to demand stronger regulations over digital services. Then, with growing tension in the transatlantic relationship during the Trump presidency, the EU initiated a string of initiatives to gain independence from the US-led digital market and assert a claim to EU Digital Sovereignty.

The emerging claim to Digital Sovereignty has been coupled with vibrant discussions on the role of AI, including on data mining, algorithms accountability and leadership in the tech industry, which has become a prominent feature in European efforts to achieve strategic autonomy. The 2022 Strategic Compass sets out the EU's ambition to become a global leader in AI by reducing the dependency on external actors for emerging technologies, increasing the production of high-performance computer processors and the establishment of an independent data space. Moreover, the document highlights how AI in the EU is expected to be a key component of a new European security and defence strategy as it shall be a part of future weapon systems (European Commission Citation2021a, European External Action Service,2022).

However, the growing narrative on EU Digital Sovereignty and the intensification of initiatives aiming at building EU leadership on AI, tell us little about the EU's actual capacity to achieve this goal. AI is still a foggy concept, turning the debate in the field into a cacophony of perspectives from both scholars and policymakers. Without a convincing framework of what AI really means, it is still difficult to identify what global leadership in AI implies and how it could be achieved. The EU is not immune to the general confusion in the field, and it has addressed sovereignty over AI in an increasing number of statements and strategies ranging from protectionist practices, claims to gain technology and innovation superiority, and ambition to achieve "tech-deterrence". However, as we argue in this article, we have little evidence that the EU will be able to pursue Digital Sovereignty and global leadership in the AI domain given the lack of major digital tech industry and investments when compared to the intensity in efforts by the leading actors in the AI domain, notably the US and China (Archibugi and Mariella Citation2021).

This article addresses how the EU is positioning itself in the race to dominate technological developments, and focuses on the implications of such positioning. In particular, we explore how the EU's ambition to lead technological developments in the field of artificial intelligence (AI) map onto the nascent concept of Digital Sovereignty. We approach AI as the intrinsic functional combination of three key elements: data, algorithms and hardware, which in the specific case of AI is referred to as computational power, and we argue that any country's ambition to gain sovereignty over AI is bound to its capacity to be sovereign over each of these elements. By adopting this lens to the EU case, this approach enables us to highlight the limited tools that the EU has to pursue its coveted global leadership in AI, and questions what kind of Digital Sovereignty the EU could achieve given the limited available tools.

The findings of the paper point to discrepancies between the EU's normative and legislative approach to protecting its digital market, on the one hand, and the practical steps taken towards the development of an EU global leadership in AI, on the other. As such, it highlights internal tension and possibly contradictions in the EU's understanding of Digital Sovereignty. We first look at the strategies that the EU has implemented to advance Digital Sovereignty by protecting its internal digital market and EU citizens' data from third countries-based tech industry. By focusing on the global rush to implement AI in defence strategies, we then compare the EU approach to other global competitors in this domain. With this approach, we emphasise how the lack of an EU-leading tech industry is not the only weakness for overcoming the current technological gap where the EU is cornered. While other countries are boosting their advancement in the tech sector by building on their security framework, the EU suffers from the lack of a consistent defence strategy. We, therefore, conclude that the EU is trying to overcome this gap and lack of short-term solutions by implementing protectionist regulatory tools, an approach that enables the EU to influence a field without being able to contribute to shape it.

The EU approach to Digital Sovereignty

In the EU context, Digital Sovereignty is often addressed under the umbrella of a broader initiative on "strategic autonomy" (Timmers Citation2019). The concept of strategic autonomy was introduced in the EU's global strategy in 2016 in which sovereignty was mainly used in the context of military, security and defensive discourse (European External Action Services Citation 2016). Digital Sovereignty, however, entails a much wider meaning (see introduction to this issue Bellanova et al. Citation 2022). European sovereignty has been referred to as the need to put the EU's "destiny into its own hands" and to the ambition to develop "the capacity to play a role in shaping global affairs" (Juncker Citation 2018), yet it remains unclear how Digital Sovereignty is defined and operationalised. The concept is often used intercheangibly with "technological sovereignty", mostly relating to normative and prescriptive ideas of control, autonomy and independence (Couture and Toupin Citation 2019, Pohle and Thiel Citation2020). In particular, the Strategic Compass refers to Technological Sovereignty instead than Digital Sovereignty, as a key tool for mitigating strategic dependencies and preserving intellectual property (European External Action Service Citation 2022).

Despite the lack of a consistent and clear definition, the call for Digital Sovereignty builds on the full dependency of the EU on external digital intermediaries and tech companies. So far, the lack of major EU tech companies has prevented the EU and its member states from being proactive in the race to technological global leadership. As a consequence, the EU strategy to achieve Digital Sovereignty has been sought with the intention not only to generate imaginaries of an EU leadership in the field (Csernatoni Citation 2022, Lambach and Monsees Citation 2022), but also by implementing protectionist initiatives, by which we mean the series of regulations designed to protect its internal digital market. As a result, EU Digital Sovereignty has been mostly tied to the idea of the EU as a regulatory actor in the international digital environment (Bradford Citation 2020, Micklitz et al. Citation2021, Farrand and Carrapico Citation 2022), impacting on the monopoly of US digital service providers and

Chinese tech companies in the European market only. We can identify early initiatives aiming at empowering the EU competencies over non-EU tech companies even before the more recent growing call for EU Digital Sovereignty. In line with the approach, we propose to frame AI Sovereignty, as the sovereignty over its core intrinsic elements, i.e. data, algorithms and hardware. We observe how the EU has traditionally adopted a regulatory approach to protect its digital market to be influential in the domain of digital innovation despite the lack of leadership in this sector.

Data. Looking at what we identify as the first core element of AI, sovereignty over data, with the 2012 European Data Protection Regulation, launching the discussion on the "right to be forgotten" (European Parliament Citation2012), one of the most significant steps to develop EU digital standards on privacy was implemented. This regulation has impact not only within, but also beyond EU borders, and in particular it enables the EU to impose digital privacy standards on US-based internet service. A few years later, the Snowden case further boosted the EU efforts to gain sovereignty by protecting EU citizens' data. The exposure of EU citizens' data to the US' mass surveillance strategy leaked by Snowden, pushed the EU to develop a concrete EU model of data mining to reinforce a European digital privacy framework against the so far Laisse-fair approach of the US. With the General Data Protection Regulation (GDPR) in 2016, the EU equipped itself with an additional tool to impose its standards over the data mining capacity of the private sector (Bradford Citation 2020). In this case too, by focusing on the protection of privacy of EU citizens, the GDPR has a significant impact on internet standards given that any company, regardless of where it is based and accessed by EU citizens, should comply with the law (Li et al. Citation 2019). The GDPR is a key example of how the EU has been able to overcome a lack of global leadership in the digital sector by implementing protectionist regulations targeting its digital market but simultaneously influencing the global debate on how to develop a human rights-based approach to digital strategies.

Algorithms. The proliferation of online Hate Speech generated concerns over the power of algorithms in locking the public's knowledge building into filter bubbles (Flaxman et al. Citation 2016). Its impact on global security became evident when in the early 2010s the Islamic State of Iraq and Syria (ISIS) exploited such filter bubbles to boost its ideological propaganda and recruitment strategy (European Parliament and Council of the European Union Citation 2018, Marsden et al. Citation 2020). A few years later, the ensuing Cambridge Analytica scandal linked to the economic models

249

adopted by US-based tech giants like Google and Facebook, illustrated the uncontrolled pattern of online user data exploitation and surveillance for commercial, health and political purposes (Woolley and Howard Citation2018). The Cambridge Analytica case shed light on the detrimental consequences of the dominant role of US-based tech giants not only over the privacy of EU citizens but also on the EU electoral system. The centrality that Tech Giants have gained in channelling the political debate was tied to their power in boosting misinformation campaigns with the consequent direct impact on EU electoral processes. In addition to data mining, the Cambridge Analytica case shifted attention to the second pillar of AI consisting of algorithms accountability and the weak EU control of these processes. The concurrent tensions in the US-Europe partnership during the Trump presidency provided further incentives to seek alternative ways to the status quo situation on AI. Not only because of the reluctance of the Trump administration to negotiate solutions aiming at solving the growing EU concerns related to the dominance of US-based digital intermediaries. Moreover, by announcing the charging of different tariffs on European imports and actual rejection of elements of the multilateral trading system (Azmeh et al. Citation 2020), Trump effectively pushed the EU to further prioritise its ambition to build EU Digital Sovereignty by gaining independence from the US-led digital market.

Hardware. A more explicit call for EU Digital Sovereignty was laid out in a 2017 report by the European Union Agency for Cybersecurity (ENISA) before the release of the Digital Single Market. It warned about the critically high dependency of the EU on third country technology and the detected cases of state-sponsored surveillance and espionage, and called for protecting the EU's privacy, security and data through law and development of core products and competencies (ENISA Citation 2017). In addition to the dominant position of US-based digital intermediaries in the EU digital market, the lack of algorithm accountability and transparency of data mining policy, attention shifted also to the potential threats emerging from non-EU digital tech hardware and related computational power, here identified as the third element of AI. In particular, the European Parliament expressed concerns about the potential security threats of embedded backdoors in 5G equipment provided by two key Chinese companies, Huawei and ZTE, that could allow unauthorised access to sensitive data and telecommunications (Friis and Lysne Citation 2021). The statement supported the concern over third-country equipment vendors and emphasised the need to "develop a strategy aimed at reducing Europe's dependency on foreign technology in the field of cybersecurity" (European Parliament Citation 2019). In order to react to the rapidly evolving debate on the urgency to achieve EU Digital Sovereignty, the European Commissioner, Ursula von der Leyen, launched her presidency in 2019 by emphasising that technological sovereignty can be achieved by having digital capacities such as quantum computing, 5G and AI, which are based on European values (von der Leyen Citation 2019). Shortly later, the European Council followed up by stressing the need to ensure technological sovereignty through a digital single market, global regulatory power and strategic digital capacity and infrastructure (European Council Citation 2020). These points were elaborated further in the Coordinated Plan on the Development of AI in Europe approved in 2021 (European Commission Citation 2021b).

However, in contrast to this emerging narrative of a forceful EU en route to solidifying its control over Digital Sovereignty across the three core dimensions, AI's technical nature points to a very different picture. In particular, given the European tech industry's lack of ability to compete with the dominant US and Chinese companies, the EU appears disarmed in achieving the claimed global leadership in the AI domain (Mazzucato and Perez Citation 2015). For this reason, the current Digital Sovereignty strategy of the EU (European Commission Citation 2020b) largely mirrors the objectives and tools to achieve their goals set out in the Digital Single Market Strategy of 2015 and more recently renewed by the EU Commissioner for the internal market, Thierry Breton. The three pillars of the Digital Sovereignty announced by Breton (2020) are Data, Microelectronics, and Connectivity, referring to the EU ambition to gain more control over data mining and cloud services, develop an EU industry microchip industry, and secure its connectivity infrastructure. These priorities have been reinforced by the European Council calling for more rules, advancing technological capacity and safeguarding of European values to reach greater security (European Council Citation 2020). The only difference between the previous and new strategies is the technology identified, which besides mentioning big data and cloud computing now also include AI, quantum computing and other recent technological developments (European Commission Citation 2020b). Furthermore, the Digital Strategy redundantly reaffirms the objectives and strategic steps to be taken towards greater autonomy, as already outlined in the digital agenda (European Commission Citation 2021c).

Overall, according to initiatives that the EU has taken to achieve Digital Sovereignty, the economic pillar of the digital strategy is the most significant at achieving Digital Sovereignty as it foresees investment as an important part of the dependency problem. The announced investments could certainly provide results, but only in the long term, leaving the EU with little capacity to quickly bridge the technological gap with the US and China, and gain independency from them. In the short and medium term, similarly to the initiatives taken in the near past and discussed above, the EU can mostly rely on proxy measures consisting of regulatory tools adopted to protect the Digital Single Market.

From Normative Power Europe to the Brussels Effect

Building on the growing debate on norms shaping the EU context, by proposing the concept of Normative Power of the European Union, Manners (Citation 2002) aimed to build-up on the existent knowledge and offer a greater understanding of the European integration processes. Even though normative power has been acknowledged as having been exercised by different actors such as the US, the EU is seen as an exceptional case based on its historic background which builds on "exceptional" failures and crimes of the past such as colonialism, world wars and holocaust (Manners and Diez Citation 2007). By defining Normative Power Europe (NPE), Manners (Citation 2002) introduced normative power as an exclusive EU "ability to shape or change what passes for normal in international relations". Ever since the concept has been broadly applied across multiple dimensions of the EU's emerging areas of influence, exposing the concept to revision, adaptation and critique (Onar and Nicolaïdis Citation2013). It is however noteworthy how "sticky" this term has been, including among EU policy makers.

More recently, the "Brussels Effect" has been proposed in reference to the EU's unilateral capacity to regulate products and processes in global markets. Given its specific focus, the Brussels Effect could be more explicity adopted to address the EU Digital Market, including the EU approach to data mining and their storage (Bygrave Citation 2021, Renda Citation 2022). In contrast to the NPE, the Brussels Effect refers to a specific capacity of soft power potentially acquirable by any jurisdiction depending upon the size, behaviour and market forces (Bradford Citation 2020). Here, what moves the spread of EU regulations worldwide is the size and attractiveness of its market. At the same time, the externalisation of its regulatory agenda seems to be a protectionist strategy for its domestic economic goals. This interpretation of the EU actorness is in line with the regularly announced intention of the European Union to emerge as a "global market rule maker" (European Commission Citation 2007, Citation 2017). Parallel to these aspirations, the EU has steadily emphasised the importance to promote European values for global standards of data privacy laws (European Commission Citation 2010, European Council Citation 2010). Departing from the extensive debate on the degrees of authority and power that an institution might have in pursuing this goal, in this paper the discussion around NPE and the Brussels Effect contributes to expand our understanding on the EU struggle for legitimacy and leadership in global governance. Here the focus is on the EU capacity in influencing global digital innovation, beyond the traditional realist perspective on great powers and instead consider also the struggle over who governs.

AI and Security

Although most of the contemporary debate on AI is related to regulation, innovation and the digital market, the development of AI is tied to the history of warfare and security. The concept of AI builds on Turing's pioneering work "Can Machines Think?" (Turing Citation 1950), with which he developed reflections derived from his effort in designing the so-called "Turing Bomb". This electro-mechanical device was commissioned by the UK Government during the Second World War to decode the German cryptographic language generated by the first-ever designed electro-mechanical device Enigma. Both machines were built to process algorithms able to code and decode data to perform military operations. This early implementation of AI is representative of how the rush to gain computational capacity has been traditionally led by the willingness of countries to strengthen their national security. Since Turing's work on AI, the latest advancement in the field reflects the recently acquired access to "big data", developments in machine learning approaches, and increased computer processing power. Today, AI consists of a set of elements including data, sensors, algorithms, actuators, and machine learning, that can emulate human cognition in reasoning, learning and autonomously taking actions as a response. These latest progresses in AI have and will continue to have enormous impact on international security. Therefore, due to the digital, physical and political security threats arising from the competition between AI in military applications, private digital innovations and scientific development (Johnson Citation 2019), normative and legal frameworks are seen as crucial to sustain international stability (UNIDIR Citation 2019).

The security dimension of AI has been on the agenda of various international organisations such as the G7, the Organisation for Economic Co-operation and Development (OECD) and Asia-Pacific Economic Cooperation (APEC). However, it is in the context of the UN with the

"Convention on Certain Conventional Weapons framework on Lethal Autonomous Weapons Systems" that we can identify one of the first attempts to consider the role of AI in a military context in international cooperation (High Contracting Parties CCW Citation 2019). AI impacts on security in several domains. In the context of cybersecurity, AI can be used for discovering and exploiting vulnerabilities while patching their own ones, therefore, creating a defence against external cyberattacks (Brown Citation 2019, DARPA Citation 2019). AI has attracted concerns in the context of disinformation campaigns (Marsden et al. Citation 2020). While AI provides tools for eroding social trust through fast and broad dissemination of credible disinformation and deep fakes (Whyte Citation 2020), machine learning can be applied to detect, analyse and destroy undesired propaganda content. As an economic and financial tool of statecraft, AI can be applied to strengthen counter operations against illicit funds that are the terrorism and Weapons of Mass Destruction runoff (Kirkos et al. Citation 2007).

In the context of defence, AI systems might also be used in logistics by facilitating the analysis of data to predict various components like equipment maintenance, service member performance and others (Taddeo Citation 2019). Moreover, due to the potential adoption of AI in combat, autonomous systems have been increasingly applied in military systems across the globe with the Lethal Autonomous Weapon Systems (LAWS), capable of independently identifying and destroying a target without human interaction (Haner and Garcia Citation 2019, Horowitz Citation 2019). Due to the accessible nature of AI, also individuals and non-state actors are obtaining the possibility to use the technology (Rassler Citation 2018). Meanwhile, for diplomacy and humanitarian missions, AI could reshape diplomatic practices through its capacity to identify vulnerabilities within personnel and advance communication by lowering language barriers, as well as forecasting political, economic and social trends (Hoadley and Lucas Citation 2018). Finally, AI enhances various daily life operations and other benefits, yet AI systems themselves are faced with threats and therefore need to be secured. Among the possible threats to AI, ENISA (Citation 2020) lists malicious acts to ICT infrastructure to steal, alter, or destroy a target; interception of communication without consent; physical attacks; insufficient functioning of assets; and finally, unexpected disruptions.

In addition to the various elements and security applications of AI, there are just as many variances in national security approaches, reports and initiatives (UNIDIR Citation 2019). Today, 48 countries have official national strategies or plans for AI of which 21 are EU Member States[1] (OECD.AI Citation 2021). While every government has the intention to build its AI capabilities and foster economic growth through a safe and ethical environment, the AI application to the military is limited to the acknowledgement that emerging technologies are crucial to integrate into the national security and defence systems. Nonetheless, by boosting their investments for the implementation of AI in their national security strategies, the US, China and Russia are leading the rush to the adoption of AI for military ambitions (Taddeo and Floridi Citation 2018, Boulanin et al. Citation 2020, Bendett et al. Citation 2021).

The militarisation of AI: US, China and Russia

We may identify four basic strategies, guided by resources and competencies available, that major international actors might adopt (Danilin Citation 2018). Two of them apply to state actors. Technological and innovative superiority is the approach adopted by key global actors through intensified development of emerging technologies through defensive and commercial perspectives. The US has held an indisputable global leadership role, firmly set in its "Artificial Intelligence Strategy" (US Department of Defense Citation 2019). China is also actively engaging in adopting the strategy of technological superiority, notably through the "Made in China 2025" initiative (The State Council of People's Republic of China Citation 2021) and has been slowly catching up. However, other actors might have limited resources to compete in the race to emerging technology leadership, and therefore might adopt a "tech-deterrence" strategy or support the revision of regional or world order. This typology of strategy is supported either by the development of both defence and commerce, or only defence.

The US perceives military capabilities as essential to the national security agenda that aims to both prevent and respond to conflict. This mirrors the fact that the US has been one of the first countries to carry out an AI-enabled DoD military project "Algorithmic Warfare" also known as "Project Maven" in partnership with Google, aimed to be used for drone footage analysis in operations against non-state actors (Crofts and van Rijswijk Citation 2020). Automated intelligence processing to collect data and identify hostile activity for targeting has been used against ISIS (Deputy Secretary of Defense Citation 2017). The priority of a technologically empowered military is highlighted also by strong investments in research and development (Briscoe and Fairbanks Citation 2020). Political and military leaders of the US have often mentioned a Third Offset deterrence strategy that aims to counter and overcome military modernisation and technological advances made by China and Russia (Lange Citation 2016, Pellerin Citation 2016, Work Citation 2016). This has been emphasised with the establishment of "The Office of Digital and Artificial Intelligence" in February of 2022, which is led by a Chief Officer who oversees DoD's strategy development for data, analytics and AI (US Department of Defense Citation 2022). While the US leads global research and development, different recent reports and indexes demonstrate that other countries are quickly catching up (National Science Board Citation 2020, UNESCO Institute for Statistics Citation 2021).

China is the US' most ambitious and dynamic competitor in AI. In 2017, China released its "Next Generation AI Development Plan" in which AI was described as a "strategic technology" (State Council of China Citation 2017). The document outlines the aim for China to become the leading centre of AI by 2030, based on an innovation-driven strategy for both the civilian and military sectors. As is also mentioned in the strategy, while China has achieved important breakthroughs in various fields of AI innovation and has a considerable number of published scientific papers and innovation patents, there are still various shortcomings that China must address in its quest for domination of AI, such as human capital, key equipment, research and development layout and others (Demchak Citation 2019). Moreover, the plan emphasises the importance of cooperating with internationally leading AI institutes by encouraging domestic enterprises to provide their services to foreigners and to encourage also foreign AI enterprises to establish research centres in China. This tendency can be observed in China's increasing investments in the US AI market (Cheung et al. Citation 2016). Vital to achieving the strategy is perceived civil–military integration. There is evident progress and competition among such Chinese technology companies as Baidu, Alibaba and Tencent. Several similar enterprises are increasingly challenging the US in innovation. As for the AI integration within the military, China is following the military concepts of the US. Besides seeking to enhance battlefield decision-making, China is investing in research of autonomous vehicles and AI tools for cyber defence and attack (Kania Citation 2021).

Russia's strategy for AI is heavily based on its application in the defence sector, specifically targeting the roboticisation of the military through various conferences and organisations. The most well-known projects are unmanned ground vehicles capable of carrying machine guns that have a multi-use purpose in combat, intelligence gathering and logistic roles

(Horowitz Citation 2018). Additionally, similarly to the US and China, also the Russian military is planning to incorporate AI into other vehicles to make them autonomous and evolve the capability of swarming (Bendett Citation 2017). To counter the US leadership in emerging technologies, Russia is developing Intercontinental Ballistic Missiles (ICBMs) and modernising its nuclear arsenal. Research, development and cooperation with like-minded countries on AI and emerging technologies have been actively taken upon by the Advance Russian Force (Kashin and Raska Citation 2017). While Russia could be perceived as another rival in the pursuit of AI leadership due to its technological developments, as well as policy statements, it lags behind in investments in research and AI. Moreover, until 2019, Russia was the only large country without a strategy for AI development (Petrella et al. Citation 2021).

While research in the field usually focuses on Western technological innovation, history on the Chinese and Arab advancement in the field of AI demonstrates that Western superiority over technology is a recent trend. Technology bends to changes, so an environment that seems inoperable, could prove revolutionary in another time (Headrick Citation 2010). Technological superiority, encapsulated in the first-mover advantage in AI, has been and still is the key pillar of US national and military power and global competitiveness, however, China is persistently exercising its strategy of becoming the technological leader. The development of an offensive strategy of innovation, which defines the current competition between the US and China (Kania Citation 2017), typically enhances strategic mobility and global influence. A defensive strategy of innovation on the other hand serves to reassert the autonomy of smaller political entities (Goldman and Andres Citation 1999). Brooks (Citation 2017) observes that no state, including the great powers, can remain the leader in military technology unless internationalisation of production is pursued.

The EU, like other actors, views AI from the perspective of global leadership and its strategic and transformative potential (European Commission Citation 2018, High-Level Expert Group on Artificial Intelligence Citation 2019, von der Leyen Citation 2019). However, in the following section, we address how in contrast to other leading actors, notably the US, China and Russia, EU ambitions are not built on solid basis. In particular, what distinguishes the EU is not only the lack of a leading global EU tech industry, which weakens the EU's capacity to lead technological advancements in the field, and causes significant brain drain in the sector (Docquier and Rapoport Citation2012). It is also very much the nature of the EU itself, and looking at AI from a security perspective, we discuss how the announced ambition to achieve EU Digital Sovereignty is also constrained by the traditional weaknesses of EU defence strategy more broadly.

EU Sovereignty over AI

Since the approval of the Treaty on the European Union, EU member states have agreed on the need for a collective commitment to the creation of a coherent defence policy environment (Whitman Citation 1998). However, historically, EU institutions have had a limited reach on defence matters (Zielonka Citation 1998, Nicolaïdis and Howse Citation 2002). While some EU members are seeking greater collaboration and reflection on the role of AI for defence through their national strategies and initiatives, others remain wary of specifying their stance on AI and of incorporating defence use of it in national funding and defence planning. Meanwhile, earlier in 2022, the European Commission released a roadmap on critical technologies which affirms how significant their development is in affecting the global security landscape (European Commission Citation 2022a).

This ambiguous approach to AI in the security sector reflects the existing traditional disagreement about the need for the EU to equip itself with a unique defence strategy shared among member states. Although there have been increasing efforts to work towards the capacity to act autonomously in the military field, liberal theories of international politics do not predict for the EU to have a defence project (Posen Citation 2006). Historically, the goal of the EU has been to improve member states economies to achieve such a level of interdependence that would not permit the development of individual military aspirations. Consequently, technological development and ambitions to establish a supranational technological capability in the EU context has suffered from a lack of unified EU defence among its member states (Citi Citation 2014). The absence of an EU approach to AI is widening the technological capability gaps between EU Member States, and generating inconsistencies in approaching AI across the EU. Although several EU Member States have adopted a national AI strategy, only France has released a specific AI military strategy. With this document, France equiped itself with a guideline on AI-enabled military applications and sets the framework for the creation of various bodies with the role of adopting national military AI (AI Task Force Citation 2019). Moreover, it has been actively promoting its national AI defense and technological superiority goals by establishing such AI-enabled military systems as nEUROn – an unmanned combat air vehicle (Barela Citation 2016). Given the intrinsic relationship between AI and security as discussed above, contrary to the

258

US, China and Russia, the lack of this perspective in the development of an EU AI agenda further weakens the EU's ambition to achieve Digital Sovereignty.

More recently, with the establishment of the European Defence Agency (EDA) and Permanent Structured Cooperation in Defence (PESCO), the EU intends to have a greater impact on fostering transnational collaboration. Although cautiously, security and strategic autonomy are set within the frameworks of the EDA. In this context, the former High Representative of the Union for Foreign Affairs and Security Policy Federica Mogherini stressed the primary role of EDA in building a consensus on compliance with international law and the use of AI-enabled weapons (European Defence Agency Citation 2020a). While there has been a certain wariness in releasing a definitive strategy and guidelines, EDA Chief Executive Jiří Šedivý (Citation 2021) underpinned that "for the EU to be a credible security provider and a trusted partner in defence [Artificial Intelligence] must be in the centre of our capability development". The EDA has actively been approving various projects involving AI for radar systems (European Parliament Citation 2021a), data collection through simulation training (European Defence Agency Citation2020b), autonomous drone detectors (European Parliament Citation 2021a) and more. These projects contributing to strategic autonomy are funded by the European Defence Fund (EDF). Out of 60 PESCO projects, Maritime Unmanned Anti-Submarine System (MUSAS) is the only one that directly mentions AI as a part of its agenda. However, while not mentioning AI nor the degree of a system›s autonomy, 9 PESCO projects are based upon unmanned systems and their operability.[2]

Despite this latest development, the lack of heterogeneity in defence cooperation is mirrored in low R&D (Soare Citation 2021). While the EU defence investment and expenditure have been constantly growing, only 16.9% of the total investments were spent to fund collaborative defence R&D being "the lowest level of collaborative spending ever measured by EDA" (European Defence Agency Citation 2021, p. 14). The rest has been utilised to procure military equipment and technologies. The EDA has been increasingly working towards developing a joint response on AI capability development but without an officially published plan yet. AI technology and its safety will have an impact on the future developments of capability in the military, industrial and civil sectors. A lack of coordinated security and defence strategy raises the risk of AI capability gaps and issues with interoperability.

Private investments provide little support to improve this situation. European external AI investments reached 4 billion USD in 2016 compared to 12 billion USD in Asia and 23 billion USD in North America (Bughin et al. Citation 2017). US private investment in AI companies from 2013–2021 was significantly higher than those of other actors standing at 52 billion USD, while those of China at 17 billion USD, and the EU trailing behind with 6 billion (Zhang et al. Citation 2022). American private firms are investing more in AI R&D than European ones – 70 billion EUR and 9 billion EUR respectively (European Investment Bank Citation 2021). Overall, in 2019, the EU is estimated to have spent almost 9 billion EUR in AI investments, and half of them were targeted at skills and capacity building (European Parliament Citation 2021b).

These investments explain the latest picture on the AI Worldwide Ecosystem offered by the EU Joint Research Centre (JRC). In its latest TES Analysis mapping the techno-economic segment of AI, the JRC reports that the US is the leader in the absolute numbers of AI industrial players globally (Samoili et al. Citation 2020). The same analysis reports China in second place in the context of total AI players, with the highest number of research institutions in AI, as well as the highest number of patent applications. However, for others the granted number of patents worldwide is instead dominated by North America (Zhang et al. Citation2022). In comparison to US and China, the EU has a stronger position in the research output. However, the EU's lower propensity of AI industrial actors' innovative activities suggests a slower penetration of the technology when compared to the other leading global powers (Samoili et al. Citation 2020). Castro et al. (Citation 2019) have compared talent, research, development, adoption, data and hardware in the context of AI between China, the US and the EU. Overall, their analysis confirms the US as the absolute leader in AI in talent, research, development and hardware, while China is seen as catching up and is the leader in AI adoption and data, and the EU trailing behind with no leading position in any of the categories operationalised.

We can conclude that global investments in AI and the industry of security and defence are dominated by the US and China, with figures that are incomparable to other countries. Massive investments for AI and robotics defence systems are observed also for Israel and Russia. Saudi Arabia, Japan and South Korea on the other side, invest in large-scale procurement of these enabling systems. In the EU context, the long-time awaited Strategic Compass for the EU's security and defence policy (2022) does not offer a clear vision on the future strategic development of AI. Throughout the 64 pages of the document, "artificial intelligence" is mentioned only four times acknowledging it as one of the "critical dependencies" (European External Action Service Citation2022, p. 48), as well as stating its importance for the improvement of military mobility and innovation (European External Action Service Citation2022, pp. 31, 47) and operations within the cyber domain (European External Action Service Citation2022, p. 45).

Finally, given the limited investments vis-à-vis other countries, the lack of an EU global leading tech industry, and no support from a coherent defence strategy, the EU seems short of tools to achieve the announced Digital Sovereignty by becoming a global leader in the AI sector. However, as detailed above, since the early implementation of regulatory initiatives targeting its digital market, the EU has triggered standards that not only have protected its citizens but also have imposed an EU view on digital services over the tech industry and third countries (Calderaro et al. Citation2014). We can identify a similar approach also in setting ethical standards in the implementation of AI in the defence industry.

EU Digital Sovereignty: global leadership or normative power?

We have discussed the various challenges that the EU is facing to achieve Digital Sovereignty at the centre of the ambition to develop strategic autonomy. The lack of a Digital Tech industry and other forms of investments coming from the defence sector, prevents the EU from playing a proactive role in the rush to global tech supremacy. In particular, the EU is lagging behind in the domain of AI, while main competitors are constantly moving ahead of the technological boundaries in data mining, algorithms complexity and computational capacity led by the development of quant-computers. In the current scenario, it is difficult to foresee the EU catching up in the nearest future. To the economic, security and geo-political consequences of this situation, we should also consider that in a domain where technology evolves quicker than the capacity to develop norms, policy and regulations, countries in the lead of the current technological developments will also be in a position of advantage to set standards on the use and impact of these technologies (Calderaro and Craig Citation2020). Consequently, the EU might face future scenarios of declining control and autonomy in this area.

At the same time, we have also discussed how the EU is trying to overcome its dependency of technological dominance by implementing regulations for the protection of its digital market and EU citizens, that have indirectly set an EU view on industry and technology. The emerging voice of the EU in the digital domain is in line with its core values established with Article 3-5, Reform Treaty 2007, clustered around the principles of protection of its citizens and human rights, support to global stability via peace, security, the protection of the Global environment, solidarity and free and fair trade (Cremona Citation 2004, Lucarelli and Manners Citation 2006, Fahey et al. Citation 2020).

Similar to the initiatives taken to protect its Digital Market and EU citizens, looking at the relevant implementation of AI in the military sector, the EU has presented a common position on human control over AI-enabled systems at the UN debate on LAWS (Boulanin et al. Citation 2020). Following the increased global concern related to the adoption of AI in the defence industry and the consequent use of such weapons (Asaro Citation 2013), in 2017 the UN established a Group of Governmental Experts (UNGGE) on Emerging Technologies in the Area of LAWS. With the goal to identify principles and norms formalised in the context of the UN, due also to the proactive role of EU member states, the UNGGE has identified humanitarian principles in the use of LAWS (Cath et al. Citation 2018). In line with this resolution, in early 2021, the European Parliament adopted a text on non-binding guidelines for military and non-military use of AI, placing AI as subject to international public law as is the use of conventional weapons in conflicts. This new resolution identifies the legitimate use of AI in the military sector (Horowitz Citation 2018). Notably, it recognises the utility of AI via the mass processing of health monitoring and environmental risk projection, as well as the possibility for military personnel to stay at a distance in operations in high-risk environments, for mine clearance and defence against drone swarms. This resolution follows a preliminary consensus achieved by the European Parliament in 2018, calling for the ban of LAWS (European Parliament Citation 2018). Although this outcome was not binding, it offered an EU perspective on the adoption of AI in the military realm. Nonetheless, this ban was turned into practice with the launch of the EDF in 2019. On this occasion, the EDF's budget was approved by members of the parliament under the condition that no funds can be allocated on R&D on LAWS, in respect of the 2018 resolution banning their adoption (Boulanin et al. Citation 2020).

A similar position concerning ethical application of dual-use technologies was already expressed in 2015, when the EU Parliament adopted the resolution on "Human rights and technology: the impact of intrusion and surveillance systems on human rights in third countries" (European

Parliament Citation2015). Two years later, in 2017, the EP Committee for International Trade (INTA) adopted a position promoting the update of the EU regulation concerning the export control of dual-use technologies entitled "Union Regime for the Control of Exports, Transfer, Brokering, Technical Assistance and Transit of Dual-Use Items" (Committee on International Trade Citation 2017). In May of 2022, the EP adopted recommendations provided by its Special Committee on AI in a Digital Age (AIDA), which highlighted an urgent need for the EU to act "as a global standard-setter in AI" in the light of the AI's potential in human labour, as well as the risk of global standards being developed and sustained by undemocratic actors (European Parliament Citation 2022). We can conclude that where EU Member States' often offer fragmented ideas about what AI is and what role it should play in the defence sector, unity prevailed when developing a collective response to the concerns related to the unethical adoption of AI.

The EU perspective on regulation and protection of individual rights has been seen as hindering aspects of AI development as it makes innovation and data gathering strenuous (Brattberg et al. Citation 2020). This criticism could be reverted if the EU implements its regulations with clarity and good guidance (Roberts et al. Citation 2021). We have already discussed how Manners (Citation 2002) interpreted the EU's capacity to intervene in international affairs by exporting its core values as "normative power". These and subsequent debates on EU external governance and its norms-based approach to foreign policy, have highlighted the capacity of the EU to play a key role in international challenges in line with the EU treaties designed around the idea of protection of civilians and human rights.

In line with the perspectives offered by the NPE and Brussels Effects, that helps us to interpret the EU trying to overcome its lack of leadership in the AI industry and its related security sector, with the promotion of ideas, norms and regulations, the EU is increasingly emphasising the importance of cooperating with other like-minded actors in response to military and security aspects of AI (European Parliament Citation 2022). This is particularly evident in the cyber security domain, where the EU is growing its ambition to play a central role in international cooperation (Calderaro Citation 2021, Barrinha and Christou Citation 2022, Farrand and Carrapico Citation 2022). As a result, the EU is intensifying the establishment of partnerships by expanding its cyber diplomatic approach beyond the realm of security (Marzouki and Calderaro Citation 2022). One of them has been a reinforced cooperation with Brazil on the digital economy through the Digital Economy Dialogue, which ought to discuss also AI (European Commission Citation 2021d). A similar partnership has been reinforced also with Singapore which provides a framework for future cooperation in emerging areas with transformative economic potential, including AI (European Commission Citation 2022b). Finally, the first officialised digital partnership the EU has signed with a partner country was at the EU-Japan Summit in May of 2022 with Japan (European Commission Citation 2022c). In the context of AI, the cooperation between the two actors shall focus on safe and ethical applications of the technology.

As discussed in this article, even if we may observe coherence between EU initiatives taken to gain Digital Sovereignty and protection of core EU values, we have also noted that in the digital domain, the EU has few other options. Contrary to the US' free market-driven development of AI, and the Chinese rush to gain military dominance in the AI sector, without tools to play in this domain, the EU is constrained to adopt an ethical approach to AI. By doing so, it renders distinct its role in the global debate on sustainable digital developments and protect itself from external digital giants. Yet whether it is compatible with the ambition to gain Digital Sovereignty is less evident.

Conclusion

Given that the EU is expanding its competencies in policy fields as diverse as energy, security and development, recent efforts to gain competencies on cross-cutting issues on AI call for developing a better understanding of the relationship between EU digital strategies and strategic positioning in international politics. At the same time, due to its complex political structures and lack of a global leading Digital Tech industry, the EU is facing several challenges in attempting to gain international legitimacy in this domain. With the goal to understand whether and how the EU is developing Digital Sovereignty in the area of AI, this paper has evidenced the significant challenges that the EU is facing in its ambition to successfully gain leadership and strategic autonomy in foreign and security politics specifically. By process tracing EU initiatives in the domain of AI, this paper has, first, discussed how the EU's ambition to gain Digital Sovereignty is currently pursued through regulatory tools aiming at protecting the digital single market. Second, the comparison between the EU's approach and AI strategies of the US and China provides additional evidence on the limited tools that the EU has in pursuing its ambitions of digital sovereignty. Contrary to leading state actors placing their AI industries at the centre of national security, the lack of a coherent EU defence strategy prevents the EU from approaching AI in a similar fashion. However, we have also discussed how, where no agreement could be achieved in identifying a commonly shared tangible approach on AI across EU institutions and its member states, the EU has successfully designed ethical standards in the adoption of AI in its internal market and defence strategy, which does project influence on a global scale.

European Digital Sovereignty comes at a moment where there is no time left as other actors and technologies are rapidly progressing and developing. European Digital Sovereignty is a core part of the aim to advance the strategic autonomy of the EU. It may be a mistake to hinge its success on the adoption of AI capabilities. Not only because of the major and long-term investment this will entail, but also because it would potentially change the fabric of the EU's actorness altogether. Its largely civilian, regulatory and "benevolent" identity is perhaps the reason for its existence in the first place. Equipped with an advanced AI-based security and defence strategy, it will begin to look like a rather different beast.

Journal information: Print ISSN: 0966-2839 Online ISSN: 1746-1545. 4 issues per year. European Security is indexed in: CSA - Political Science Abstracts; The International Bibliography of the Social Sciences; National Library of China; Naver; University of Bremen and Clarivate Analytics © Social Sciences Citation Index. Taylor & Francis make every effort to ensure the accuracy of all the information (the "Content") contained in our publications. However, Taylor & Francis, our agents (including the editor, any member of the editorial team or editorial board, and any guest editors), and our licensors, make no representations or warranties whatsoever as to the accuracy, completeness, or suitability for any purpose of the Content. Any opinions and views expressed in this publication are the opinions and views of the authors, and are not the views of or endorsed by Taylor & Francis. The accuracy of the Content should not be relied upon and should be independently verified with primary sources of information. Taylor & Francis shall not be liable for any losses, actions, claims, proceedings, demands, costs, expenses, damages, and other liabilities whatsoever or howsoever caused arising directly or indirectly in connection with, in relation to, or arising out of the use of the Content. Terms & Conditions of access and use can be found at http://www.tandfonline.com/page/terms-and-conditions. Disclosure statement. No potential conflict of interest was reported by the author(s). Correction Statement. This article has been corrected with minor changes. These changes do not impact the academic content of the article. Additional information. Funding. This work was supported by the Economic and Social Research Council [grant number 520791]. Aims and scope: European Security is a forum for discussing challenges and approaches to security within the region as well as for Europe in a global context. The journal seeks to publish critical analyses of policies and developments in European institutions and member states, their relations with European and other immediate neighbours, and their relations with the wider world, including other regional and international organisations. It is also interested in non-European perspectives on Europe in a global context. Whilst the journal is particularly interested in stimulating debate between varied theoretical approaches, it strongly encourages policy debates on topical issues that combine conceptual and empirical analyses. Within this broad framework the journal invites submissions in the following areas: Theoretical and methodological approaches to the study of security in Europe, Comparative and in-depth studies of European states and national defence policies, European organisations as security providers, Conflict prevention, peacekeeping, conflict resolution, and crisis management as reactions to regional insecurity, Security and geo-politics of Europe and the wider world. Artificial intelligence and EU security: the false promise of digital sovereignty. Andrea Calderaro & Stella Blumfelde. aDepartment of Politics and International Relations, Cardiff University, Cardiff, UK; Department of Political and International Science, University of Genoa, Genoa, Italy. Contact: Andrea Calderaro CalderaroA@Cardiff.ac.ukTo cite this article: Andrea Calderaro & Stella Blumfelde (2022) Artificial intelligence and EU security: the false promise of digital sovereignty, European Security, 31:3, 415-434,DOI:10.1080/09662839.2 022.2101885To.link to this article:https://doi.org/10.1080/09662839.2022.210188 5.© 2022 The Author(s). Published by Informa. UK Limited, trading as Taylor & Francis. Group. Published online: 09 Sep 2022. This article has been corrected with minor changes. These changes do not impact the academic content of the article. © 2022 The Author(s). Published by Informa UK Limited, trading as Taylor & Francis Group This is an Open Access article distributed under the terms of the Creative Commons Attribution License (http://creativecommons.org/licenses/by/4.0/), which permits unrestricted use, distribution, and reproduction in any medium, provided the original work is properly cited.

Chapter 14

Towards Democratic Intelligence Oversight: Limits, Practices, Struggle

Ronja Kniep, Lina Ewert, Bernardino Léon Reyes, Félix Tréguer, Emma Mc Cluskey and Claudia Aradau

Abstract

Despite its common usage, the meaning of 'democratic' in democratic intelligence oversight has rarely been spelled out. In this article, we situate questions regarding intelligence oversight within broader debates about the meanings and practices of democracy. We argue that the literature on intelligence oversight has tended to implicitly or explicitly follow liberal and technocratic ideas of democracy, which have limited the understanding of oversight both in academia and in practice. Thus, oversight is mostly understood as an expert, institutional and partially exclusive arrangement that is supposed to strike a balance between individual freedom and collective security, with the goal of establishing the legitimacy of and trust in intelligence work in a national setting. 'Healthy' or 'efficient' democratic oversight then becomes a matter of technical expertise, non-partisanship, and the ability to guard secrets. By analysing three moments of struggle around what counts as intelligence oversight across Germany, the UK, and the US, this article elucidates their democratic stakes. Through a practice based approach, we argue that oversight takes much more agonistic, contentious, transnational, and public forms. However, these democratic practices reconfiguring oversight remain contested or contained by dominant views on what constitutes legitimate and effective intelligence oversight.

Keywords: intelligence oversight, democracy, surveillance, litigation, whistleblowing, advocacy.

Introduction

I would definitely describe my work holding governments and intelligence agencies to account as a form of oversight . . . Activism, advocacy, litigation; it's just a different language to talk about the same thing; it's all various forms of oversight.[1]

In 2013, the revelations by whistleblower Edward Snowden that intelligence agencies were routinely gathering and sharing data on citizens precipitated a crisis of legitimacy for the bodies in charge of holding these agencies to account. The reason why the disclosures were seen as subversive by many oversight and intelligence actors was not so much because, as many have claimed, that they threatened 'national security'. Even former NSA director Michael S. Rogers downplayed the impact of the Snowden disclosures on national security, saying that the 'sky did not fall' as a consequence of his actions.[2] Rather, as some observers have pointed out, the leaks made clear the structural failures of institutional oversight.[3] From this perspective, the practices that Snowden documented were not an 'aberration', but a form of systemic abuse to which oversight structures were – at least to some degree–complicit. How can we then understand the meaning of 'democratic oversight' amidst such systemic failure? In this paper, we propose to approach this question through the analysis of struggles around three elements of intelligence oversight. Firstly, who is included as a democratic protagonist of oversight? Should oversight be confined to formal bodies legally tasked with that role (parliaments, courts, or administrative agencies)?

If not, who should be included? As one of our interlocutors pointed out, the forms of advocacy, activism and litigation in which they were engaged as a member of civil society in the aftermath of the Snowden disclosures were for them a de facto form of overseeing intelligence agencies. Secondly, what role does 'secrecy' as a defining feature of intelligence policy – and particularly the fact of being positioned within the so-called 'ring of secrecy–play? By consequence, can forms of 'radical transparency'[4] like public whistleblowing be seen as a means of legitimate democratic oversight, enabling disclosure, visibility and public debate? Thirdly, how does contestation shape how 'democratic oversight' is practised? To what extent does oversight rely on consensual practices, trust and impartiality? The paper takes these questions as a point of departure to interrogate three sites of non-official intelligence oversight–litigation, whistleblowing and advocacy–to identify the dominant ways of construing 'democracy' and 'oversight', and challenges to those. Academic discussions of intelligence

268

oversight have mainly taken place within the field of intelligence studies, a field historically derived from a strong Anglo-American state-policy lineage and grounded within functionalist, state-centric epistemologies.[5] As Hager Ben Jaffel, Alvina Hoffmann, Oliver Kearns and Sebastian Larsson have argued in a recent article, this sociological context has narrowed the scope of the field to the promulgation of 'theories for, rather than of, intelligence'.[6]

Although the intellectual genealogy of intelligence oversight is slightly more heterogeneous than this diagnosis suggests, we argue that these debates have been underpinned by certain normative assumptions, centring on liberal, functionalist and technocratic views at the expense of more radical and agonistic understandings of democracy.[7] As we unpack further down, these assumptions in turn limit the range of democratic practices deemed to enact legitimate forms of intelligence oversight. While the discipline of international relations (IR) has seen numerous debates about theories and practices of democracy, an engagement with the kinds of democracy practised through intelligence oversight has been largely absent from intelligence studies.[8] We propose to unpack the versions of democracy 'at work' in intelligence oversight in order to understand what other versions of democracy are silenced, left unsought or excluded. Rather than starting with a taxonomy of democracy, we draw out the normative assumptions about democracy by attending to practices, thus bringing to the fore the limits of liberal democracy and the struggles for other forms of democracy.

The dominance of liberal understandings of democracy in intelligence studies can be seen as the consequence of two factors: the proximity of intelligence scholars to the agencies (either former intelligence officers or policymakers) and a wider trend in academia to increasingly focus on professional skills. A community of practitioner-scholars or 'pracademics' emerged from the common socialisation of intelligences scholars and practitioners.[9] What Ben Jaffel and Larsson call 'endogamy' has come to structure the limits of the field of intelligence studies, either through formal outreach mechanisms such as the CIA's Office for Academic Affairs,[10] or through the establishment of visiting professorships on prominent intelligence programmes. Taken together, these dynamics explain the lack of 'critical distance' required to break with the pre-given notions of the intelligence field.

Most scholarly discourse on intelligence oversight has thus led to the disqualification of more agonistic critiques of intelligence, and more radical modes of oversight. To this day, the dominant frame of oversight as a well-ordered, institutionalised and secret arrangement often masks how the history of intelligence oversight has largely been driven by scandals unleashed by whistleblowers, and struggles by activists or investigative journalists, with new oversight structures often being created in response to public pressure and following the delegitimation of intelligence agencies' practices. An early prominent example is the establishment of the so-called 'Church Committee' in the US, following several press revelations in the early 1970s. 1975–often termed the 'Year of Intelligence' – marked a moment when intelligence oversight was institutionalised through various pieces of legislation and formal bodies. In the literature on intelligence oversight, the Church Committee is typically seen as having curtailed the power of US intelligence, setting the standard for other countries to follow. As Loch Johnson has put it, 'the Church Committee did nothing less than revolutionise America's attitudes toward intelligence supervision.'[11]

However, the Church Committee cannot be seen in isolation from a decade-long series of scandals and radical opposition to the work of and abuses by intelligence actors.[12] In the view of such radical opposition– one that has been largely overlooked by intelligence studies –, the Church Committee also sought to re-establish consensus around intelligence through a legal framework that supposedly guaranteed that intelligence would now stick to the rule of law. But the new oversight professionals populating these structures came to view their work primarily as abiding by secrecy and representing intelligence within parliament. Their insertion in the realm of secrecy displaced the boundary between intelligence and its critics, excluding more radical engagements which appeared less legitimate. Soon enough, they could be co-opted by the executive branch to help build consensus around intelligence policy, passing regressive intelligence reforms and codifying expansive intelligence powers, construing their oversight role as a matter of checking conformity of rule by law, rather than rule of law.[13]

Although strong differences remain in the national histories of intelligence oversight, similar processes of scandal-driven institutionalisation took place in other countries like the UK, France, and Germany from the 1970s and 1980s onwards. Taking as a point of departure practices of oversight rather than its policy representation, the article unpacks the everyday struggles involved in the constitution of 'democratic intelligence oversight'. It reveals ways in which practising 'oversight' can take much more agonistic, contentious, transnational, and public forms than most of literature on oversight suggests, or that applicable policy frameworks acknowledge. As with the theoretical discussions on oversight, however, these heterogeneous practices of oversight are similarly contested or contained by dominant views on what constitutes legitimate oversight.

Methodologically, we approach oversight practices in situations of struggle in the wake of scandals about the activities of intelligence agencies. The analysis includes different national contexts (the USA, Germany, and the UK), formal oversight bodies, and civic practices of disputing and challenging intelligence powers. Our choice of empirical sites is driven by attention to three modes of agonistic practices–litigation, whistleblowing and advocacy–that brings to light three distinct limits and practices of liberal democracy: exclusion/inclusion, secrecy/publicity and contestation/consensus. While situated against national backgrounds, these practices emerged in the wake of the transnational circulation of the Snowden disclosures, public concern and mobilisation about mass surveillance.[14] The paper also brings together authors with different disciplinary backgrounds and working on distinct empirical fields, which means that the methods pursued in our empirical research reflect this heterogeneity, combining archival analysis, textual analysis of legal documents and oral history interviews with key actors involved in contesting surveillance legislation.

To trace what democracy does in these practices and struggles, we proceed in three steps. First, we examine the tension over what we call the 'dual exclusion' of who is regarded as a legitimate actor of oversight, and whose communication is deemed to deserve oversight. To unsettle these lines of inclusion/exclusion, we investigate strategic litigation by a transnational constellation of German non-governmental organisations (NGOs) and foreign journalists against the foreign intelligence service of Germany, the Bundesnachrichtendienst (BND). Second, we revisit the struggle over secrecy and publicity in democratic oversight by placing Snowden's public disclosures of routine mass surveillance in relation to current whistleblowing and national security laws in the US. Third, we turn to the tension between contestation and consensus in what is considered legitimate and effective democratic oversight. The analysis of an advocacy campaign by a coalition of NGOs against the UK's 2016 Investigatory Powers Act reveals how this tension plays out in practice. We conclude with a set of reflections on the practices of 'democratic oversight' and how our approach to oversight and democracy as practices offers both an agenda for research for intelligence studies and IR more broadly, and a political intervention in debates about meanings and practices of oversight.

Inclusion and Exclusion: Pluralising Oversight Protagonists

The dual exclusion of actors and non-citizens

Who are the protagonists of oversight? By attending to who is seen as a legitimate oversight actor and who is not, we can unpack how oversight and democracy are intertwined through the dynamics of inclusion/exclusion. Different understandings of representative or participatory democracy underpin various oversight architectures and constellations of actors. These may vary with regards to the involvement of civil society actors and their potentially more contentious oversight practices, or the centrality of professional and legally established overseers. The institutionalisation of oversight went along with another, generally accepted, form of exclusion. In most Western democracies, data collection on foreigners has been either completely or largely excluded from established regulations of intelligence and oversight structures.[15] By concentrating intelligence laws and their oversight on national citizens or national territory, it not only determined who is entitled to make claims against the surveillance of their communication, but also who and whose communication deserves to be subjected to oversight to begin with. Being considered 'fair game', non-nationals have been the primary targets of large-scale surveillance but not subjects of protection through institutional oversight.

This dual exclusion is by and large mirrored in the academic literature on intelligence oversight.[16] Oversight scholars have indeed remained largely silent on the foreign-national distinction in intelligence practices and oversight, replicating a territorialised understanding of liberal democracy. After the Snowden disclosures, it was legal scholarship that either opposed the exclusion of foreigners from oversight by promoting a human rights approach,[17] or asked for granting at least some protection to foreigners.[18] With respect to the exclusion of unofficial oversight actors, many intelligence scholars iterate the historical trajectories of oversight by emphasising formal, public bodies as oversight protagonists.[19]

Some authors locate civil society as external to the official oversight system of legislative, executive, and expert bodies, stating that civil society organisations and the media play some role in oversight without further definition.[20] Here, democracy veers towards representative institutions and balance of powers, with oversight understood in terms of scrutiny or control. Other intelligence scholars employ a broader understanding of oversight, integrating practices of civil society actors as 'public oversight[21] 'informal oversight'[22] or 'civil society oversight'[23] Civil society actors are envisaged to provide input for official oversight, restrain intelligence agencies' power and offer a secondary accountability mechanism to scrutinise the overseers' activities.[24]In this literature, oversight comprises different levels or layers, with so-called 'soft' or 'informal' oversight framed as the outermost layer, while remaining within the same space of formal oversight institutions. These informal overseers become intermediaries acting on behalf of and being responsive to a wider (and rather abstract) public.[25] Others even see them as a means for the political participation of citizens.[26] It is this 'acting for'[27]that necessitates the inclusion of leverage under the direct influence of the public, namely through elected representatives.[28]

More recently, several authors have criticised the focus on representative institutions as too narrow and bureaucratic in comparison with wider democratic 'accountability', which can entail 'assertive verification in advance of proposed action, or report or correction once an action has been taken'.[29] As the transnationalisation of intelligence agencies has limited formal accountability structures in many countries,[30] Richard J. Aldrich has described civil society as the sole locus of transnational efforts to control the agencies, noting that 'accountability now seems to flow from a globalised network of activists and journalists, not from parliamentary oversight committees'.[31] Understood in this broader sense of 'accountability', oversight mobilises a wider array of actors. Such flexible conceptualisations see an 'informal network of researchers, journalists and lawyers in civil society' acting to some extent in symbiosis with formal oversight,[32] positioning civil society in a loose configuration with official oversight actors, while entrenching a temporal dimension in which formal oversight comes first. Consequently, it cannot but act as a 'fire alarm' to, as opposed to a 'police patrol' of, intelligence practices.[33]

This temporal distanciation is supplemented through a spatial distanciation, as these actors are situated on the margins of the social space inhabited by formal oversight actors, which means that actors acting from outside oversight institutions are only partially included – or putting it differently, they continue to be partially excluded. Ultimately, representative democracy comes first, with participatory and agonistic forms of democracy as supplementary and secondary. Despite acknowledging that actors from civil society play a role in intelligence oversight, there have been no studies of the practices of actors such as the media or NGOs through the lens of oversight. While the oversight literature has acknowledged that courts play an increasingly important role in intelligence oversight, and that these judicial corrective practices depend on litigation to get underway,[34]there has been almost no attention to how legal challenges to the dual exclusions we have located can contribute to oversight as democratic practice. Yet, strategic litigation–the collective mobilisation of law by civil society actors–can perform a watchdog function, advocating for marginalised groups, and stirring public discourse.[35] In the following section, we analyse strategic litigation by two German NGOs to account for practices of oversight that challenge the dual lines of inclusion/exclusion outlined above.

Struggles over inclusion/exclusion in practice: the case of litigation

In 2017, two German NGOs, Gesellschaft für Freiheitsrechte e.v. (GFF) and Reporters without Borders (RSF Germany) as well as six investigative journalists from different countries lodged a case against the intelligence law that authorises the BND to conduct foreign intelligence. The plaintiffs challenged the hitherto largely unchecked surveillance of foreigners and particularly the attachment of protection against surveillance to nationality and state territory. They argued that what was at stake was not only the privacy of communications but also press freedom, since the BND law did not foresee protective mechanisms for journalists and their sources.[36]Referring to international law, the collective of NGOs and journalists argued that foreigners may claim fundamental rights vis-à-vis German authorities, since the latter are bound by constitutional law when acting on behalf of the German state, no matter where these actions take place. The German government and the BND defended the opposite view, claiming that the scope of applicability was limited to national territory.[37]

In May 2020, the constitutional court ruled against the government, requiring reform of the intelligence law. This decision against the status quo was made despite former intelligence officers publicly disqualifying the claimants as 'fools' ('Hansel')[38] and framing the lawsuit as a national security threat.[39] The case entails two related struggles over inclusion/exclusion: who is allowed to participate in oversight and who deserves protection, and thus oversight. For decades, the rationale 'we only spy on foreigners' has become entrenched in the logic of mass surveillance in liberal democracies. This rationale helped intelligence agencies justify blanket data collection and enabled the partly automated exchange of indiscriminately collected data of foreigners among intelligence agencies of different countries.[40] As a consequence of foreigners' exclusion from protection, their data has become a currency in the transnational economy of surveillance.

Rather than being clearly articulated in a legal statute, the distinction between foreigners and nationals has operated as a taken-for-granted legal interpretation and as a practice that has been institutionalised in the organisation of intelligence, technical surveillance infrastructures and oversight regimes. Therefore, most of the surveillance conducted by agencies like the British GCHQ, the German BND, and the French DGSE is subject to much looser independent oversight than domestic surveillance. Following the Snowden disclosures, a discourse emerged through transnational constellations of actors that transformed the blanket interception of foreign data from a silent, institutionalised practice of the field to a publicly contested principle. In the immediate aftermath of the first Snowden leaks, a transnational network of NGOs published a working version of the 'Necessary and Proportionate' principles, providing an analysis of international human rights and its application to communications surveillance. The text made clear that human rights applied 'extraterritorially', meaning that they covered both domestic surveillance conducted on the residents and foreign nationals whose data might be scooped in the context of large-scale surveillance.[41] The text was presented at the UN Human Rights Council in Geneva in September 2013 and subsequently endorsed by more than 400 organisations across the world.

After this initial push, 2014 was marked by several 'critical moments',[42] i.e. moments of dispute that required justification and contributed to breaking the silence on the previously taken-for-granted assumption of foreigners being 'fair game' for mass surveillance. In the US, the Obama administration adopted the 'Presidential Policy Directive 28' (PPD28), which promised to grant privacy protections to all humans 'regardless of their nationality or wherever they might reside'.[43] Following an initiative by Germany and Brazil and the engagement of various NGOs, the UN published its resolution 'Right to Privacy in the Digital Age', which reconfigured data subjects as data citizens through the language of human rights.[44] In Germany, the critical moment took place through a confrontation of the BND's practices with the legal discourse of constitutional lawyers in the parliamentary 'NSA inquiry panel'. The right to privacy, Article 10 of the German constitution, protects all humans, the lawyer's claimed.[45]

Yet, after its reform in 2016, the revised BND law did not take this constitutional and human rights perspective into account. With a growing transnational discourse on the foreign-national distinction providing momentum, GFF and RSF Germany challenged the foreign-national distinction through the litigation process. While the question of who enjoys privacy rights and who deserves oversight could be relevant for everyone in a transnationally connected world, they chose to focus on consequences for journalists. Due to their work on sensitive issues like corruption and other forms of abuse, the plaintiffs suspected that they had been of interest to intelligence agencies – not necessarily by the BND itself, but its foreign partner agencies. They were concerned about the consequences of uncontrolled data sharing among intelligence agencies from different countries, both for their own safety and the protection of their sources. By tackling this mix of unregulated gathering and sharing of foreign communication by the BND, the claimants illustrated the transnational implications of data collection and expanded the democratic values that are at stake under the BND surveillance, from privacy as a universal right to press freedom.

The ruling of Germany's constitutional court was a landmark decision. The judges acknowledged the vulnerable situation of journalists and lawyers abroad, demanding a quasi-judicial oversight body to authorise the surveillance of these professional groups as well as the sharing of insights about them with foreign state authorities. However, regarding the foreign-national distinction, the judges adopted an ambivalent interpretation. On one hand, they agreed that neither privacy nor press freedom are bound to nationality. On the other hand, the ruling ultimately legalised the distinction foreign national, as it justified lower standards of protections for foreigners. The judges deduced the theoretical inclusion and practical exclusion of foreigners from protective safeguards in two steps. First, they followed the claimants' line of argumentation to include foreigners in the realm of basic rights by anchoring the applicability of the German constitution not in the location of the object of state action, but the state actor itself. Like a leash, there is a binding effect of fundamental rights for state actors acting beyond borders, including intelligence agencies, with a claim to democratic legitimacy.[46]

Nonetheless, the judges argue that in contrast to foreigners, German citizens are to a greater extent exposed to interventions by German state authorities, and, therefore more easily subjected to follow-up action when surveilled by the BND.[47] Regarding foreigners abroad, the BND's lack of 'operational powers' in conjunction with spatial distance is seen as a buffer that lessens the potential impact of communications surveillance on foreigners abroad.[48] What follows from this line of argument is a differential treatment that leaves foreigners with little benefit from their newly granted right to private communication. For instance, in contrast to nationals, foreigners are not deemed 'notification worthy' since they could not seek legal remedy and their notification would allegedly not foster democratic discourse on communications surveillance.[49]

The litigation showed how established boundaries and mechanisms of exclusion embedded in intelligence oversight can be partially re-opened and re-negotiated. First, the exclusion of foreigners from oversight was declared unconstitutional. Yet, boundaries are not dissolved but displaced, as the foreigner-national distinction is upheld and legalised. Second, civic collectives used strategic litigation to circumvent established oversight bodies, becoming themselves oversight actors against delegitimising strategies of intelligence and government officials. The transnational constellation of claimants –NGOs and affected journalists from abroad– transcended boundaries of who was allowed to make claims about surveillance and reversed the primacy of representative over participatory democracy. In 2015, a lawsuit by RSF Germany had been rejected on the grounds that, as national claimants, they were not able to construct a case of affectedness.

Foreigners alone had also not been able to challenge BND's surveillance. The strategic alliance of nationals and foreigners was able to address a vacuum of oversight that transnational surveillance by intelligence agencies had created and upheld. This transnational push can be seen as part of what Alvina Hoffmann has described as 'a new imaginary and set of resistance practices', in which civil society facing surveillance by intelligence agencies has started to make claims with reference to universal rights, 'not just as citizens' of their own country'.[50] These practices are connected to a second tension, that between secrecy and publicity, to which we now turn.

Secrecy and Publicity: Whistleblowing As Democratic Practice

The 'circle of secrecy' in oversight and intelligence Intelligence

Intelligence is a field of state secrecy par excellence, where secrecy reinforces the exclusion of outsiders by depriving them of knowledge about the reality of intelligence work. This secretive nature is at odds with demands for control of governmental conduct and publicity, rendering intelligence oversight a special oversight case.[51] In intelligence studies, the answer out of this conundrum of democratic values then usually becomes that of a 'balance' to be reached between secrecy and publicity. This idea of 'balancing' secrecy and publicity has, in recent years, been subjected to greater scrutiny within critical IR literature on security.[52] Within these conversations, secrecy is conceptualised not in opposition to publicity, but as a mutable and fluctuating category of international politics, able to reorganise socio-political relations in particular ways.[53] What William Walters has tentatively described as a 'secrecy turn' in the study of security practices has seen secrecy examined as a social space,54 in relation to subjectivity,[55] as a form of non-knowledge,[56] and as a terrain to navigate in relation to methods and methodology.[57]

Far from seeing secrecy as antagonistic to publicity, this literature reconceptualises the relation between the two 'poles' as a dynamic terrain of contested knowledge practices.[58] Following Walters' invitation to 'inject mobility, struggle, and material transformation into the way we theorize secrecy'[59,] we approach whistleblowing as struggles over the relations between secrecy, publicity and democracy. 'Public' whistleblowing is a democratic practice whereby insiders with access to secret information 'go public', bringing that special knowledge–e.g. knowledge about abuse committed by intelligence professionals–to the media, NGOs, or lawyers who can then further investigate, advocate, and/or litigate. At least since the 1960s, whistleblowing has been a key driver in enabling public debate around intelligence. But where special laws were adopted to regulate whistleblowing in the field of national security (first in the US and much more recently in France), it was confined to institutional channels, effectively limiting the role of whistleblowers to that of 'organisational de-fenders' rather than public advocates against intelligence abuse.[60]

Such reports to institutional oversight institutions, however, have proved unable to generate reform or address abuse, which might be partly explained by the fact that these entities address governmental institutions, not publics.[61] In other words, struggles about whistleblowing in intelligence affairs constitute another stage where the opposition to agonistic and more participatory democracy plays out. Therefore, governments have tried to delegitimise or suppress public whistleblowing under laws around state secrecy and counterespionage. Take, for instance, a piece of legislation adopted in the US: the 1998 Intelligence Community Whistleblower Protection Act. This law was introduced not to protect insiders going public but ultimately to reinforce the protection of secrecy, making public whistleblowing a federal crime for those with access to classified information. This piece of legislation was sponsored by Porter Goss, former CIA agent who served as chairman of the House Permanent Select Committee on Intelligence between 1997 and 2004. In his congressional role, Goss can be seen as what intelligence scholar Loch K. Johnson calls a 'cheerleader' for the agencies, by which Johnson means a type of overseer who promotes the rationale, demands and overall interests of intelligence agencies.[62]After being appointed by George W. Bush to head the CIA, Goss would stick to the same line regarding whistleblowing:

(...) those who choose to bypass the law and go straight to the press are not noble, honorable or patriotic. Nor are they whistleblowers. Instead they are committing a criminal act that potentially places American lives at risk. It is unconscionable to compromise national security information and then seek protection as a whistleblower to forestall punishment.[63]

One might object that Goss and others have simply sought to defend legislation that regulates official secrets. However, as many journalists have pointed out, elected officials have no problem leaking sensitive information as long as they obtain political credit from it[64]with the US Department of Justice showing far less interest in these leaks. These efforts to criminalise public whistleblowing undermine the ability to denounce fundamental rights violations. In the academic literature on intelligence oversight, several authors have offered more nuanced justifications for this historically sedimented structure of exclusion. While acknowledging systemic oversight failure, Mark Phythian bemoans that, with public whistleblowing, 'we are dependent on a moral compass emanating from sources outside of government'.[65]Recently, Melina Dobson has also expressed worry about a 'continuing trend to "publish and be damned"'.[66]Johnson adopts a similar view. While acknowledging that 'far too much information–some 85 percent–is unnecessarily classified by intelligence and military bureaucrats in the first place' and that 'the significance and danger of leaks have been exaggerated'[67]he still frames public whistleblowing as illegitimate.

For him, the priority lies in improving internal whistleblowing channels so as 'to make sure whistle-blowers have a chance to make their case in a responsible manner, without having to go to jail or abandon their country'.[68] Some intelligence scholars, however, recognise that public whistleblowing can address oversight failures. Damien Van Puyvelde writes that 'whistleblowers are particularly valuable because they provide alternative sources of information that, by definition, are not controlled by the government'.[69] For Claudia Hillebrand too, 'media outlets can provide a channel for leaking information that might not have been taken into account by formal oversight bodies, or when individuals felt unable to approach formal oversight bodies and instead approached journalists'.[70] Finally, Aldrich points out that 'regulation by revelation' has seen activists and media pressure groups performing a de facto, albeit problematic oversight role, in that 'these organisations have no democratic mandate and are not concerned with effectiveness'.[71]

While some authors advocate granting oversight bodies the power to declassify information and to hold public hearings on intelligence matters[72] many of those we interviewed dismissed the desirability and even the legitimacy of these oversight bodies going public. Overall, the focus lies in ensuring better access for oversight agencies to information exchanged within intelligence agencies. This is the Janus face of access: it expands the inner circle of secrecy and closes off that space for everyone else. Thus, oversight officials become the guardians of secrets. This idea is a common, even if sometimes subtle, thread in oversight literature. This is, for instance, the case when authors write that 'in the USA the requirement that all involved in oversight bodies sign non-disclosure agreements neuters most effective exposure should wrongdoing be detected',[73] or that 'the ability of the Committee to demonstrate the basis for its conclusions is restricted by the fact that it operates within the ring of secrecy, and does not itself have the competence to declassify secret information'.[74] Generally, secrecy is normatively defended (e.g. 'the committees have proven themselves reliable keepers of the nation's highest secrets;'[75] after September 11, 2001, it became widely acknowledged that a legitimate requirement for secrecy exists').[76]

The struggle over secrecy and publicity: The Snowden case

When Snowden decided to go public, he knew that he would be subjected to many attacks on the part of US state actors and media. The cases of Chelsea Manning, Thomas Drake, and other intelligence whistleblowers who had faced prosecution provided a clear indication that he would be demonised and even risk incarceration. Along with these recent cases, official warnings by intelligence professionals had long signalled what would happen to those who break the rule of secrecy. Take for instance the warning by Goss in 2006 to 'investigate these cases of unauthorised disclosures aggressively'.[77] While attacks by prominent intelligence officials were to be expected, a more surprising reaction was that of many leading media who attacked Snowden, particularly in the US and the UK. There were two main kinds of disqualifications: those that accused Snowden of endangering national security 'beyond repair', and those that rather focused on particular personality traits, insisting on his pathological solitary character[78] or his 'narcissistic' personality.[79] The common thread to both types of attacks was clear: Snowden was no hero and deserved no praise because he did not follow the proper channels to raise his concerns.

These efforts to delegitimise Snowden were echoed amongst intelligence scholars. When six members of the Church Committee wrote a letter to then President Barack Obama asking him to pardon Snowden, arguing that the 'lack of disclosure can cause just as many, if not more, harms to the nation than disclosure',[80] one of its most visible representatives, Loch K. Johnson, refused to sign. While recognising Snowden's contribution to public debates, Johnson considered that he did not use the proper institutional channels and, more importantly, went too far in releasing 'granular details about intelligence budgets and very sensitive programs'.[81] In more than a dozen interviews that our team conducted, intelligence scholars argued that Snowden endangered national security and that whistleblowers should have gone through official channels. They considered it too dangerous to defer to the whistleblower's moral standards and to journalists to decide what was of legitimate public interest. However, such disqualifications of public whistleblowing by virtue of the unreliability of their individual values contradicts the same scholars' insistence that, at the end of the day, the effectiveness of oversight institutions largely lies in overseers' own personality and ethics.[82]

Snowden's disclosures did not only undermine the legitimacy of intelligence agencies. They also, albeit less directly, delegitimised oversight bodies like parliamentary committees, secret courts like the Foreign Intelligence Surveillance Court (FISC), and the people working in these institutions. If, as most intelligence scholars argue, overseers have only worked as reactive 'fire fighters' instead of a preemptive 'police patrol', Snowden started a fire that forced these officials to face their own shortcomings. As Snowden recalls in his memoirs, he had sought to report these abuses internally only to be turned down by his superiors.[83] Therefore, his case proved that insiders worried about the vast expansion of surveillance powers could not hope to see these practices reformed without relying on external public pressure. It highlighted the structural failures of institutional oversight.

Long-standing attempts at containing whistleblowing to institutional channels neglect the history of public investigations and their role in keeping intelligence in check. With no press, there would have been no 'Year of Intelligence' in 1975, nor many other fundamental public debates about intelligence policy, violence and abuse. This is why; in contrast to dominant views in the field of intelligence oversight and against governments' attempts at suppression, the right to public whistleblowing has been claimed time and time again. When Daniel Ellseberg leaked the

Pentagon Papers in 1971 and the Nixon administration sought to prevent their publication, Supreme Court Justice Hugo Black stressed that:

> *in the absence of the governmental checks and balances present in other areas of our national life, the only effective restraint upon executive policy and power in the areas of national defense and international affairs may lie in an enlightened citizenry – in an informed and critical public opinion which alone can here protect the values of democratic government.*[84]

A few weeks after Snowden's first disclosures, the European Court of Human Rights also stressed the importance of the right for whistleblowers to 'go public' with public-interest information. The case at hand related to an intelligence agent who revealed in the press widespread practices of illegal political surveillance of communications by the Romanian intelligence service.[85]Further initiatives took place transnationally, as NGOs and academic experts issued the 2013 Tshwane Principles on Transparency and National Security,[86] which were reproduced by the Council of Europe in a resolution on 'national security and access to information'[87] Principle 37 for example recalls the need to protect whistleblowers for reporting a wide range of abuses and other 'wrongdoing' that they witness, both in the context of internal procedures (Principle 39) as well as in the context of public disclosures–for example via the press. This is particularly the case when, following an internal alert, the 'person has not received reasonable and appropriate results within a reasonable time' or where 'the person has reasonable grounds to believe that there is a significant risk that an internal disclosure and/or disclosure to an independent oversight body will result in the destruction or concealment of evidence, interference with witnesses or retaliation against the person or a third party' (Principle 40).

Current laws surrounding whistleblowing in national security contexts remain disconnected from these international standards, effectively creating a chilling effect for potential whistleblowers. Similarly, we have not seen these principles taken up, or even discussed, in intelligence studies. This gap underlines the fact that, although it is arguably one of the most important forms of oversight over intelligence abuse, 'public' whistleblowing remains a contested practice, one that is effectively repressed and delegitimised by dominant approaches to intelligence oversight. The struggles around whistleblowing illustrate a clash between agonistic democratic claims and the defence of the prevailing consensus in intelligence affairs, one that most intelligence studies and state officials work to protect. Whistleblowing asks us to revisit democratic tensions between secrecy and publicity and reformulate publicity beyond the discourse of the balance between security and privacy, secrecy and transparency. By approaching whistleblowing as a practice of 'going public', we have shown how democratic publics are not pre-given or limited to electoral moments, but enacted by challenging the boundaries of secrecy and revealing the failures of oversight institutions.

Consensus and Contestation: Limits On Civil Society Engagement

Consensus through impartiality and trust

Past scandals and ensuing legitimation strategies have led to a widespread view that radical critiques of intelligence agencies are illegitimate. For instance, this was the case in the US, where anti-war activist engagement with intelligence policies in the 1960s and 1970s came to be disqualified and delegitimised. However, the US has not been unique in this regard. In the UK, for example, with the establishment of the first Intelligence and Security Committee (ISC) in the Parliament in 1994, inaugural chairperson Lord Tom King described in his memoirs the need to ensure that parliamentarians (MPs) selected to serve on the committee were not 'ideologically predisposed' to an anti-agency viewpoint.[88] That state of play is by and large reflected in the academic literature on intelligence oversight, which tends to privilege a consensual view of democracy. Scholarship in intelligence studies often shares a presupposition that oversight bodies have to collaborate with and not confront the agencies.[89]

As Anne Karalekas, author of one of the first books on the CIA, puts it, 'The intelligence committees are heavily dependent on the agencies for the information required to execute their oversight responsibilities, creating strong incentives to establish cooperative relationships.'[90] Even when contestation is acknowledged, as in the conflict over the definition of democratic values like transparency, or between courts and intelligence agencies, it is integrated within an architecture of consensus and largely limited to the institutions of representative democracy. This architecture of consensus takes two forms. One of these is trust understood as a mediator of relations between oversight bodies and intelligence agencies. Scholars writing at the intersection of intelligence studies and intelligence policy often hold this view. For instance, Anthony Glees and Phillip Davies, both university professors and frequent media commentators on intelligence matters, argue that the ISC must win 'the trust of the secret agencies, and in particular their heads, in order to be able to 'oversee' them.'[91]

This alleged need of trust suggests both that oversight is in a position of inferiority vis-à-vis the security and intelligence services (who can provide or deny access to their workings) and that a relation of companionship may arise between these two services. As echoed by Fred Schreier, the 'critical issue of oversight is the balance between committee independence and criticism on the one hand, and the maintenance of a working relationship between the committee and the intelligence agencies on the other hand'.[92]As we have seen with the delegitimation of whistleblowing as a challenge to the taken-for-granted 'circle of secrecy', trust promotes a consensual understanding of democracy, where contestation is seen as unproductive and conflict to be avoided. Trust also represents oversight as politically neutral or impartial. This has led some authors on oversight to highlight and argue that cases in which oversight was politicised entailed negative effects. For example, Johnson describes the decade between 1992 and 2001 as the 'partisan' era, showing how power struggles of political parties have negatively affected the control of agencies.[93]

In this vein, the political partisanship of oversight is assumed to undermine its effectiveness, since finding a common ground for investigations is harder and intelligence officials might doubt the intentions of political actors turned overseers.[94]As Gill points out, in the 1960s and 1970s there was a widespread fear that 'legislatures would not be appropriate, for example because of their tendency to partisanship and to leak information for political advantage'.[95]It is against an agonistic understanding of democracy that understandings of neutrality, a politics or impartiality promote an aura of deliberation and came to be seen as desirable. Subsequently, these were supplemented by an emphasis on trust. In discussing congressional oversight in the US, Jennifer Kibbe goes as far as calling for 'appointing intelligence committee chairs who are moderate, responsible, dedicated and committed to the notion of nonpartisan oversight'.[96]These arguments are also echoed in reference to European oversight, where scholars caution against the dangers of parliamentary scrutiny as the 'security sector may be drawn into party political controversy – an immature approach by Parliamentarians may lead to sensationalism in public debate, and to wild accusations and conspiracy theories being aired under parliamentary privilege'.[97]

Given these assumptions about political impartiality and the need for trust relations, it is not surprising that the understanding of democratic politics as consensual is extended to civil society. As we will see further down in the analysis of the 'Don't Spy on Us' campaign in the UK, more conflictual forms of oversight come to be disqualified. This was also the case of the media, which was sometimes framed in a rather suspicious light as it might be leveraged for partisan power struggles.[98] However, we have seen that civil society actors can be a 'surprisingly effective sentinel' driving inquiries in intelligence activities and calls for public accountability.[99] Whilst this may be true in some contexts, the stance that often dominates in the literature fails to problematise the limits of established oversight agencies, both theoretically and practically. Not only does it overlook the process whereby accountability is triggered (publicly politicising wrongdoing through a scandal); it also dismisses most conceptions of democracy and democratic politics as a locus for conflict. In so doing, these views merely reflect existing power relationships in the actual practice of intelligence oversight, as our final case illustrates.

Contestation and its constraints

The 'Don't Spy on Us' Coalition came together to contest the new UK legislation, the Investigatory Powers Bill, which was subsequently passed into law in 2016. A coalition of NGOs campaigning for privacy, freedom of expression, and digital rights, Don't Spy On Us made a series of recommendations for legislative overhaul following the Snowden revelations. The purpose of forming a coalition was to ensure that arguments were gaining maximum traction, that goals were aligned and strategically communicated, and that a consistent message was formulated. The campaign's aims were twofold: raising public awareness of the harms of mass surveillance legalised and extended by the Investigatory Powers Bill, and lobbying parliamentarians to amend the bill along specific lines. However, after the bill was passed, the Don't Spy On Us Coalition disbanded, leaving a sombre epitaph: 'The UK Parliament has passed the Investigatory Powers Act, the most extreme surveillance law in our history'.[100]

The advocacy practices of the Don't Spy On Us coalition embodied both conflictual and consensual styles of democratic practice in its campaigns and within legislative struggles. Their practices shed light on another limit of what counts as 'democracy' in intelligence oversight, namely the role of more radical contestations in democracy. Drawing on interviews with actors involved in this coalition, as well as MPs, peers and expert witnesses who engaged with these NGOs, we trace how dynamics of contestation transform into consensual practices through the foreclosing of debate around specific sites. As the campaign progressed, conflictual modes of engagement that resonate with agonistic and radical democratic approaches gave way to more consensus-based advocacy. This is partly because contestations of mass surveillance can be seen as constrained within certain dynamics, parameters and 'norms of sayability' which dictate what could be accepted as 'realistic' or 'legitimate' critique by other actors, including members of civil society themselves.[101]

At the same time, these advocacy practices lent credibility to the idea, which intelligence services, the government, and official oversight actor's endorsed, that the UK was setting a 'global gold standard' of surveillance legislation. At the start of the campaign, Don't Spy On Us agreed on six demands for UK legislation on surveillance: no surveillance without suspicion; transparent laws, not secret laws; judicial not political authorisation; effective democratic oversight; the right to redress and a secure internet for all. While mobilising key principles of liberal democracy around the rule of law, transparency and separation of powers, the framing of this initial contestation of mass surveillance was increasingly limited in two ways: first, around what claims were deemed 'realistic', and second, around what claims were deemed 'legitimate'. One of the initial cleavages as the coalition came together was around formulating a strategic position: did the coalition want to engage and improve safeguards, or try to kill the entire practice of mass surveillance altogether? One member of the coalition we interviewed remembers this to be the single most contentious issue throughout the passing of the bill through Parliament. For Don't Spy On Us, the legislative struggle over the IPA came after a previous legislative victory of sorts against extending state surveillance.

The 2012 Draft Communications Data Bill had been thrown out after being vetoed by then Deputy Prime Minister Nick Clegg. Within this campaign, NGOs had argued that older, much broader legislation was out of date and that new legislation was needed to better guard against abuse by the agencies. As one of our interlocutors explained,

> Everybody called for the IP Act effectively; they called for a better version of RIPA the (old) regulation of investigatory powers act. So, you can't scrap that. All you can do to my mind is improve it, improve transparency, improve oversight, improve mechanisms so that the wins are going to be very slight . . . .[102]

After the Snowden disclosures, a review of the use of bulk powers in the UK by David Anderson, the Independent Reviewer of Terrorism Legislation, deemed these powers of 'vital utility' to security and intelligence agencies, the use of which could not be matched by data acquired through targeted means.[103] His main issue with RIPA was that it was 'incomprehensible to all but a tiny band of initiates.[104] To occupy a position of trying to scrap the powers altogether was seen as somewhat unrealistic from the outset:

There were people civil society activists who felt that they would win the argument through the sheer conviction that they were right on a moral level, which anybody who's worked in politics for more than a day knows is wrong.[105] When I went to Parliament to say to people who want to work in Parliament, do you want to obliterate every boulder? Or are you prepared to just chip away at the boulder so that you might be able to squeeze round it to get to the other side of the path? And anyone who said I want to obliterate the boulder I knew was not cut out for this.[106]

In this demarcation of what was deemed a 'realistic' position for the government to engage with, opposing mass surveillance was reduced to tactical dimensions of safeguards and limitations. Some campaigners would refuse to engage with specific sections of the bill on bulk data collection, deciding instead to brief backbench MPs on specific language they could use to temper some of the more wide-ranging powers.[107] Struggles around what counted as 'realistic' also took place around public advocacy and campaigns, with different imaginaries of 'the public' enacted to mobilise public opinion against the bill. A widely circulated poster campaign likened then UK Home Secretary Theresa May to well-known dictators, such as Putin and Xi Jinping, calling on her to 'stop giving them ideas'.[108] Appealing to critiques of surveillance based around the totalitarian-democratic binary was seen as 'out of touch' by fellow campaigners, who argued that a campaign based around government incompetence and fear of the 'tax-man' having access to this data would be more effective: The poster campaign they ran was just inept! The public don't respond well to being told that their government is like China and Russia, because it's not, it's nonsense. And I think it was just embarrassing that this went ahead.[109]

Advocacy around the IP Bill embodied conflictual and agonistic understandings of democracy. It also raised questions about what mass surveillance means for understandings of democracy–does liberal democracy have the tools to hold it in check, or does it risk morphing into illiberal or even totalitarian forms? However, contestation was also constrained by who or what was deemed to be a legitimate actor. For instance, in the evidence submitted to the Intelligence and Security Committee of the UK Parliament, former GCHQ Director David Omand deemed the reactions to the Snowden disclosures 'a quite unnecessary moral panic over privacy' and strove to clearly distinguish what he called 'bulk access to the internet' from 'mass surveillance'.[110] Omand's play with categories and claim of 'category error' was successful to the extent that both Tory and Labour MPs came to reject 'mass surveillance' in debating the Investigatory Powers Bill only a few years later.[111]More agonistic understandings of democratic practice were thus reserved for public campaigning. However, actors who engaged in more public forms of advocacy were often deemed illegitimate by MPs, peers, and some expert witnesses. Campaigners who held a more radical message were delegitimated as 'sensationalist' or considered to instrumentalise the debate on behalf of the NGOs to gain more funding. In this vein, particular campaigning and highly visible strategies were deemed as 'street theatre' or 'self-congratulatory' and lacking nuance.

> I mean, you have obviously got people who are more active and rather keen on the publicity aspect of it. But there are others who are going to take a more nuanced and thoughtful approach. You know, that is that you have to speak to the detail of it.[112]

Rather than an integral aspect of agonistic democracy, publicity was equated with performance and spectacle. Parliamentarians involved in the Investigatory Powers Bill debates mentioned taking care with formulating their interventions in language which did not connect them to particular groups which were deemed 'fringe', which they argued would delegitimise their intercession. MPs and peers trying to limit these data collection and retention powers spoke about having more credibility with fellow parliamentarians if they adopted a position of being in dialogue with the needs of the security services rather than presenting arguments put forward by civil society, particularly civil society groups deemed too radical or extreme.[113] The advocacy practices of the Don't Spy on Us coalition show how more conflictual and agonistic versions of democratic practices become constrained within parameters which narrow the terms of engagement and reflect dominant understandings of what is considered 'realistic' and 'legitimate' in liberal terms of rule of law and institutional arrangements.

They are also indicative of the fact that democratic contestation is not easily opposed to consensus, but that various actors operated at the interstices of more contestatory or more consensual politics. However, normative assumptions about consensual democracy, and the delegitimation of actors as radical or too 'unrealistic', limit the form and content of contestation. This resonates with understandings of effective oversight being seen as apolitical within much of the literature. Although members of the coalition took pride in making some gains (particularly around the inclusion of a judicial 'double lock' mechanism before certain powers can be used), many took a more ambivalent stance, describing these struggles as a moment in time, part of the ever-shifting relations between freedom, democracy and surveillance.

Conclusion

Taking as a point of departure the diverging answers to the key question of what makes intelligence oversight democratic; this paper has focused on practices that contest mass surveillance by intelligence agencies across various national settings. Our aim has been to make a two-pronged contribution to critical approaches in intelligence studies and international relations more broadly. By contrasting the dominant ways of construing 'intelligence oversight' as democratic in the academic and policy literature with three case studies of litigation, whistleblowing, and advocacy, we have shown how competing understandings of democracy play out in the everyday struggles of actors engaged in legitimising and contesting intelligence surveillance, highlighting how these practices were usually excluded from the remit, justifications, and modes of institutionalised oversight. Rather than starting from a taxonomy of theories of democracy, we looked at messy practices where different elements of what counts as 'democracy' co-exist, compete or dominate. Moreover, our analysis of practices of litigation, whistleblowing and advocacy suggests there isn't a single model of democracy that informs these struggles – whether liberal, civic republican, deliberative or agonistic. Rather, different elements are combined to challenge the exclusions, secrecy and consensus that subtend practices of liberal democracy and its taken-for-granted dominance in academic and policy engagements with intelligence oversight.

The first case of the litigation against the BND has tackled two boundaries of liberal democracy: that of legitimate actors and territorial limits to the rule of law. We have shown how actors from civil society became meaningful oversight protagonists by collectively mobilising to litigate against the exclusion of foreigners from the purview of oversight. Here, although still constrained by dominant positions and views on what is needed to protect intelligence work, oversight can be seen as democratic through pluralising and including more actors in the process, thereby also extending oversight not just within but across borders. The second case on the contested practice of whistleblowing revisited tensions between secrecy and publicity, particularly the acceptance of 'secrecy' as a security practice in liberal democracies. By claiming 'publicity' and enacting 'publics', public whistleblowing practices simultaneously revealed the failures of institutionalised oversight and made the boundaries of secrecy more fluid, subject to mobilisation and struggle over the limits of knowledge. The third case about the UK's Don't Spy On Us coalition has illustrated how advocacy oscillates between conflictual and consensual styles of democratic practice, being channelled towards consensus through the delegitimation of critique that is deemed to go beyond what is accepted as 'legitimate' or 'realistic'.

Of course, these localised instances of struggles inscribed in transnational networks are just three of the many that we could have investigated to show how clashing visions of democracy play out in intelligence oversight practices. Other sites could have been addressed – and should be considered in future research –, from open-source journalistic investigations such as those conducted by Bellingcat to the tensions surrounding the work of the United Nations in intelligence policy. What we hope to have conveyed is how meanings and practices of democracy that emerge through oversight practices move along a spectrum, from liberal and deliberative-functionalist understandings of democracy to participatory and radical-agonistic ones.[114] In the former, legitimate actors of intelligence oversight are construed as 'reasonable overseers' who agree on the relevance and acceptability of intelligence agencies and state surveillance, and where bounded public discussions on intelligence affairs are supposed to help achieve a consensus around intelligence policy based on a stabilised 'balance' of values. In the latter, these functionalist views as well as the legal and institutional structures of exclusion giving them prominence are challenged by more radical and often excluded actors hoping to convey a more systemic critique over the merits and motives of intelligence policy in democracy. What emerges out of these struggles are strategies of compromise, of tinkering and hybridization, so that really-existing intelligence oversight remains heterogeneous and contested.

What then are the theoretical and political implications of these heterogeneous practices of oversight and meanings of democracy that our paper has shown to be fundamental to the everyday practices of holding intelligence agencies to account? Firstly, our intervention comes as an invitation to reflect on the normative assumptions about democracy that underpin the practices of secret services and oversight actors. We have argued that moving towards plural democratic forms of intelligence oversight would require political imaginaries and policies to accommodate more radical claims and practices and better articulate the different actors engaged in oversight practices. In parallel to such a pluralisation of intelligence oversight practice, this paper suggests that intelligence oversight scholarship needs to open up to a wider range of views and disciplinary approaches. As we have shown, the literature on intelligence oversight has tended to either explicitly or implicitly work with liberal and functionalist ideas of democracy that reproduce technocratic institutional arrangements, the rule of law within territorial boundaries, the necessity of secrecy to intelligence agencies, and the priority of consensus through representative institutions. In so doing, these implicit and explicit assumptions about what counts as 'democratic' shape and limit the understanding of oversight both in academia and in practice.

Addressing these limitations requires taking studies of intelligence practices and secret services beyond the confines of a field of study and connecting it with broader political questions of democracy, struggles, contestation and agency, which have been at the core of critical approaches in international relations. These conversations have often taken place in subdisciplinary silos, fragmented and neatly delimited, precluding the construction of bridges or transversal social enquiry between these different imaginaries of democracy. Building on the analysis developed here, struggles around surveillance, intelligence and oversight can be reformulated in the broader terms of struggles around exclusion/inclusion, secrecy/publicity and consensus/ contestation, paying attention to how these were formed and evolved in different national and transnational settings. Therefore, the boundaries of intelligence studies as a subfield need to be dismantled so that the theoretical and political concerns of international relations and interdisciplinary research come to reshape the questions, concerns and methods at work in the field.

Secondly, our practice-based approach to intelligence oversight can contribute to discussions of security, surveillance and contestation in international relations more broadly. Oversight as a practice that limits and mediates security and intelligence practices has received little attention in IR. Oversight both overlaps with and slightly differs from control, scrutiny, or accountability, which constitute an important conceptual and practical apparatus of democratic practice that needs to be further unpacked. In constraining struggles over security, rights and democracy, oversight is worthy of attention in its own right. When oversight and accountability are increasingly invoked in key sites of international politics, from borders to Artificial Intelligence, our analysis raises a cautionary note and offers a methodological investigation to both specify practices and analyse what a call for oversight means in relation to the multiplicity of democratic practices, meanings and political subjectivities. Furthermore, as we have seen, oversight also mediates practices of legitimation and delegitimation.

Future research will need to attend to practices of intelligence oversight as an important locus in the process of state-making and state legitimation as well.

Thirdly, our research recasts questions about democracy and IR. While democracy has been key to many theoretical approaches in IR, dichotomous conceptions of democracy have often been mobilised to unsettle the irenic vision of liberal democracy and even dismantle its dominance: lib-eral/ illiberal democracy, liberal/imperial, state/global, liberal/cosmopolitan, representative/participatory, antagonistic/agonistic, representative/ deliberative, liberal/civic republican and the list could go on. Through a practice based methodology, we have shown that different elements which do not belong to one coherent theory or model of democracy are mobilised in struggles over the limits of democracy. In working through a set of dichotomies that are seen as constitutive of liberal democracy, we have shown how practices of 'going democratic' make these limits visible and challenge them. Rather than privileging a particular theory of democracy, we have proposed to take democracy seriously as 'the paradoxical regime which – as much as possible – admits and accepts the risk of its own internal critique – in any case the critique of its own power-holders'.115 This is neither to revere nor reject certain versions of democracy, but to acknowledge practices that are messy, disputed and replete with paradoxes.

Acknowledgements

We are grateful to the three anonymous reviewers for their thoughtful engagement with the article and enjoining us to further develop our understanding of democracy. We would also like to thank the civil society actors who have generously shared their insights with us. This collaborative research was made possible through joint funding under the Open Research Area for the GUARDINT project ('Oversight and Intelligence Networks: Who guards the guardians?'). In France, this work was funded by the French National Research Agency (Grant n° 18-ORAR-0006-01). In Germany, it was supported by Deutsche Forschungsgemeinschaft (DFG, German Research Foundation, Grant n° HO 5317/5-1). In the UK, this research was supported by the Economic and Social Research Council (Grant n° ES/S015132/1). Towards democratic intelligence oversight: Limits, practices, struggles. Ronja Kniep, L. Ewert, Bernardino León-Reyes, Félix Tréguer, Emma Mc Cluskey, Claudia Aradau. To cite this version: Ronja Kniep, L. Ewert, Bernardino León-Reyes, Félix Tréguer, Emma Mc Cluskey, et al.. Towards democratic intelligence oversight: Limits, practices, struggles. Review of International Studies, 2023, 39p.10.1017/S0260210523000013. hal-03952695v4. HAL Id: hal-03952695 https://hal-sciencespo.archives-ouvertes.fr/ hal-03952695v4.Submitted on 30 May 2023. HAL is a multi-disciplinary open access

Chapter 15

Between a Rock and a Hard Place: The Precarious State of a Double Agent during the Cold War

Eleni Braat & Ben de Jong

Abstract

While scholarly literature has paid attention to human intelligence professionalism from the perspective of the agent handler, we know relatively little about the precarious positions in which (double) agents often find themselves and what their ensuing needs from their handlers consist of. This article suggests that (double) agents desire a reciprocal, affect-based relationship with their handlers, involving trust and gratitude, more than just a negotiated relationship based on (financial) agreements. This article explains the importance of such a relationship. The main source of this research consists of original, in-depth oral history interviews with former double agent "M." He operated from the 1960s through the 1990s for the Dutch Security Service and the Central Intelligence Agency against the East German Ministerium für Staatssicherheit. The article analyzes the varying degrees of appreciation that these services showed for his work, and it investigates their consequences on the psychological well-being of the double agent.

Double agents may yield important operational benefits for the service running them by tasking them with acquiring specific information on the personnel, operations, and modus operandi of the adversary service. However, running a double agent requires a high degree of professionalism in the field of human intelligence (HUMINT), entailing much effort, patience, understanding, tact, and firmness. A double agent often operates in a dangerous environment, being in close proximity to the adversary service and, in many instances, with few options for protection when operating in hostile territory. A double agent "works as an agent for one intelligence service but reports to and is loyal to another intelligence service as its agent."[1] Indeed, it could be said that more than a regular agent, the double agent is potentially mistrusted by the adversary service, which always reckons with the possibility that he may be working for the other side. While scholarly literature has paid attention to HUMINT professionalism from the perspective of the agent handler,[2] relatively little is known about the precarious position a double agent often finds himself in and what his ensuing needs from his handlers consist of. This research suggests that (double) agents desire a reciprocal, affect-based relationship with their handlers, involving trust and gratitude, more than just a negotiated relationship based on (financial) agreements. What explains the importance of such a relationship?

This research is based on unique empirical data, derived from original, in-depth oral history interviews with a former double agent. He prefers to remain anonymous and, hence, this article refers to him as "M." To contextualize the interviews, the authors of this article have requested archival material from the Dutch Intelligence and Security Service on the same operation. The service has denied them access. Double agent M. operated from the 1960s through the 1990s, initially for the Dutch domestic security service Binnenlandse Veiligheidsdienst (BVD) and from 1981 for the CIA, against the East German Ministerium für Staatssicherheit (MfS, Ministry of State Security).[3] This article analyzes the varying degrees of gratitude that these services showed for his work, such as personal attention, verbal expressions of gratitude, and material gifts. It also discusses the role of trust in their dealings with M. and investigates how the various signs of gratitude and trust affected the relationships. This article aims to enrich the literature on agent-handler relationships from an empirical and theoretical perspective. It advances a theoretical framework that explains the importance of socially embedded relationships in secretive professional environments. The methodological section explains how the authors collected and used the empirical data, primarily through oral history interviews. The empirical analysis centers on M.'s different relationships with the BVD, the CIA, and the MfS.

Agent-handler relationship in intelligence literature

Literature on intelligence history has an overriding interest in the historical reconstruction of operations and is less inclined to analytically single out specific operational themes. Consequently, the topic of this article is mostly treated implicitly rather than explicitly in the relevant literature. This article identifies three factors in the relationship between an agent and his handler that to a large extent also apply to the relationship between the double agent and his handlers, in this case from both services.[4]

First, trust and distrust, fear and danger play a major role. A double agent usually operates against experienced intelligence officers of an adversary service. He has regular meetings with them, during which they will always look for indications in his behavior that he might be under the control of another service. If the meetings with the adversary service take place on their turf, as was often the case with double agent M., that evidently adds an extra dimension of fear and insecurity to the situation. During the Cold War, meetings of Western double agents with their Soviet and East European adversaries sometimes took place behind the Iron Curtain, during which they basically risked their lives. The Federal Bureau of Investigation (FBI) double agent Morris Childs, for instance, who had first been recruited by the KGB, went on 52 missions behind the Iron Curtain in the 1960s and 1970s, in most cases for several weeks. On multiple occasions, he was subjected to harsh interrogations by the State Committee for Security (KGB) in Moscow after the Russians became suspicious about his loyalty.[5] In another, rather extreme case in 1975, an FBI double agent who worked against the KGB was lured to Vienna by the Russians and subsequently abducted and killed.[6]Additionally, the literature on the Double-Cross System is rife with references to British double agents who potentially put themselves in grave danger during World War II when they traveled to Portugal or occupied Western Europe, sometimes for a period of many weeks, to be debriefed by their Abwehr masters.[7] Even though Portugal was strictly speaking a neutral country during the war, the Abwehr had a strong presence there.

A second factor in the relationship between agent and handler is the dependence of the former on the latter, which is reinforced by the agent's social isolation. It contributes to the security of the operation if nobody, not even the agent's spouse, is aware of his operational activities. However, the presence of a supportive partner, who is at least partially in the know, can make it much easier for a double agent to cope with the psychological strain that is often part of an operation.[8] From an agency's perspective, preferably, the handler is the most trusted person for an agent, a dependence that infuses the relationship between them with a certain "therapeutic" quality. Ideally, the agent should have the opportunity to bring up any issue he is wrestling with in his daily life, even if it is not directly related to his spycraft.[9] When it comes to letting the agent know about the value and importance of his work, the well-known case from the early 1960s of the British-American agent, the Main Intelligence Directorate (GRU) officer Oleg Penkovsky, offers a striking example. On his request, the CIA and the British intelligence service MI6, who together ran Penkovsky as an agent, officially made him a colonel in both of their armies at a secret meeting in a London hotel in July 1961. He dressed in a British and an American army uniform and was photographed in both to show appreciation and recognition for the work that he undertook at great personal risk. For Penkovsky his two American and two British handlers [...] were his lifeline. While he worked hard to be accepted [by them] as a professional intelligence officer, he also craved their personal acceptance and respect. He wanted them to accept him as a friend, to share and support his emotional needs. Despite his bravado and single-minded sense of purpose, Penkovsky had no place or person to turn to except his case officers [handlers].[10] It also makes sense to keep in touch with an agent after an operation has ended, to show appreciation for his service or to check how he is doing, financially or otherwise.[11] As we shall see in the case of double agent M., agents sometimes can become extremely dissatisfied with the way an agency treats them after an operation has been terminated.

Finally, the literature shows that financial issues often play an important role in any agent operation, but in a double agent operation especially. Double agents find themselves in the perverse position that they are paid by each of the sides they work for. To eliminate temptation, American and Dutch services do not allow their double agents to keep the money given to them by the adversary service and it seems likely that other services do likewise. After all, if the double agent would be allowed to keep it, he could easily be lured to switch sides, especially if the adversary service pays him more than his own side. Characteristically, the FBI double agent Joe Cassidy did not even know how much the GRU was paying him. The money was left at dead drops by the GRU inside artificial rocks that he handed over to the FBI without opening them.[12] In situations like this, it is easy to imagine how a suspicion could arise whether the double agent really handed over the money he received from the other service.[13] As we shall see in the story of double agent M., money became a major irritant in his relationship with the Dutch service.

Secretive professional environment induce socially embedded relationshiop

M. specifically emphasizes the nature of the relations he had with the various services with which he dealt and also emphasizes that he directly associates the quality of these relations with his well-being. Relationships in secretive professional environments, such as those involving intelligence and security services, are characterized by social isolation from friends and family, an ensuing dependence of the agent on his handler, and an often precarious situation that involves deception, exploitation, and risk. These characteristics, this article theorizes, reinforce the importance of socially embedded relationships, characterized by trust and reciprocity, rather than relationships solely based on negotiated financial agreements.

Secrecy separates those who know from those who do not know.[14] It creates a barrier with the "outside" world because it limits the possibilities to seek and maintain proximity to social contacts outside the professional environment of intelligence. There is always the impediment of not being able to speak freely about one's work, and once the intelligence officer or agent has to invoke his obligation to observe secrecy, openly or not, he distances himself from his family members, friends, or acquaintances. Henceforward, two individuals will not communicate on the same level, as the noninitiated individual may be aware that his initiated interlocutor knows more than he does and possibly even knows much about him personally. Such restrictions in the establishment and maintenance of social contacts outside the intelligence environment increase the dependency of the agent on his handler, not only from a professional and operational perspective but also from a personal one.

Relationships in secretive professional environments are characterized by precarious situations, involving deception, exploitation, manipulation, and risk (sometimes including physical danger).[15] Intelligence and security services manipulate their own agents to a greater or lesser degree, to maneuver them in a position to obtain relevant intelligence. Double agents are exposed to additional layers of potential deception, amplifying the uncertainty of the circumstances in which they operate. In the case of M., traveling regularly behind the Iron Curtain for his debriefing sessions with the MfS each time put him in an extraordinarily hazardous position. Operating in such uncertain circumstances made him more likely to seek stable relations or a network of trusted partners from the other side, i.e., from the Dutch service or the CIA.[16] Such relations instigate a sense of security and safety.[17] For M., his agent handlers were the human faces of the intelligence services that loomed as mountains of unfathomable scale. M. desired a reciprocal, socially embedded relationship with his handlers, characterized by trust and reciprocity rather than a relationship governed by negotiated (financial) agreements.[18] A reciprocal relationship, in this case, would have consisted of a fair balance between, on the one hand, the dangers to which M. was exposed on behalf of the services he worked for and, on the other, the gratitude that his handlers expressed for his efforts.[19] Even if the expression of gratitude was partially financial, the uncertainty of the circumstances in which M. operated intensified the significance of a socially embedded relationship.

It is useful to conceptualize agent handlers as "attachment figures": supportive persons in an individual's life.[20] If an attachment figure is sensitive and responsive for better or for worse and recognizes the individual's feelings, the individual is likely to view himself as worthy and others as reliable. He will feel secure and will be better able to cope with stressful situations, drawing on his own resources and those of others. On the other hand, an unavailable or unresponsive attachment figure evokes a feeling of insecurity. The individual may become anxious, acquires a negative self-image, and becomes overdependent on the unresponsive attachment figure. Alternatively, the individual may downplay the importance of the relationship and may become more self-reliant and more distant toward his unresponsive attachment figure.[21]

Conceptualizing agent handlers as "attachment figures" has the potential to explain, first, why M. ascribed such importance to the presence of supportive, caring, and sensitive agent handlers from all sides he worked for—and against. Second, it explains the significance M. attached to a reciprocal relationship with the services he worked for, including expressions of gratitude and recognition, either verbal or material, for his efforts, his ideological motivation, and the personal dangers he was exposed to. In the secretive, isolated, and threatening environment of intelligence, the attachment style of an agent toward his handler may harbour expectations that are more akin to attachment mechanisms in childhood than to those in professional environments.[22] Tellingly, M. told about a confusing and disconcerting period when he noticed his East German handlers suddenly appeared less responsive: "[T]hose kinds of services offered you, after all, security and support. They represented the love of the mother, to put it in Freudian terms. You need them, they are your footing."[23]

Methodology

M. is a tall man, calm and sociable, carefully observing the people he talks to and their reactions to what he tells them. He is eager to tell his story. The authors of this article met M. in 2019 and agreed to interview him on his espionage past, under the condition that certain data would be anonymized.[24] Throughout 2019, they interviewed him four times. Each of the sessions lasted between four to five hours, they were structured around open-ended questions, and they were voice recorded. Generally, M. took the lead and shared his experiences in chronological order, organically emphasizing his relationships with his handlers.[25] Oral history methods are particularly suited to researching individual memories of historical developments and phenomena. Memories, either individual or collective, are by definition fluid, incomplete, and subjective, as all historical primary sources are in various ways. Therefore, their interpretation consists not only of what the respondent says, but is also determined by how he says it, why he says it, what he might mean to say, and what he does not say (or attempts not to say).[26] Consequently, in the transcription and analysis of the interviews, the authors of this article were not only interested in the literal reading of what M. told them; they were equally interested in silences, hesitations, humour and laughter, irony, consistencies and inconsistencies within and between interviews, emphasis on certain aspects (for instance, by banging his fist on the table), and attempts to avoid specific topics.[27]

The authors also asked themselves why M. chose to share his memories with them. First, they distinguish his growing disillusionment in recent years with the ways the former BVDF[28] and the CIA responded to his requests for psychological assistance and access to his files. Only the archives of the former MfS granted him partial permission, while the legal successor of the BVD granted him limited access and only after several attempts, and the CIA granted him no access at all. The conceptualization of these intelligence services and their agent handlers as "attachment figures" to M. explains his disillusionment with their unresponsiveness. M. considered such (partial) refusal even more painful given the considerable personal dangers he faced on behalf of these two services. This has undoubtedly strengthened M.'s need to share his story with a wider public. A second, related, reason why M. shared his memories is his preoccupation with the possibility of having been betrayed from within the CIA. Since 1994, it is known that, in the mid-1980s, CIA officer Aldrich Ames passed information to the KGB on CIA and FBI agents, including double agents, who operated against the KGB and their allies.[29] M. connects Ames' betrayal to the sudden change around 1988 in his cordial relationship with his handlers of the Hauptverwaltung (Chief Directorate) A, the foreign intelligence service of the MfS.[30] This important turning point, which at the time was inexplicable to him, intensified his need to understand what has happened. The possible reconstruction of the events around 1988 has been a recurring topic in the interviews.

Finally, as is rather common for those who had a career in secrecy, either as an intelligence officer or an agent, the authors observe with M. a need to break his silence, in his case mostly regarding the psychological costs of his operational past. A career in intelligence usually entails the deliberate creation of a rather dull image of oneself vis-à-vis family and friends with the aim to attract as little attention as possible. Intelligence officers can compensate for the ensuing lack of professional recognition in their personal and social environment with a tightly knit professional environment and, upon retirement, by associating with former colleagues.[31] However, (former) agents usually have few such outlets to vent professional tensions. Hence, it is plausible that M. was motivated to share his story with the aim to obtain recognition for his extraordinarily lengthy and perilous espionage career. While the interviews with M. are the primary historical source, this article also refers to the correspondence between M. on the one hand, and the CIA, the AIVD, and the MfS record agency on the other, in the context of his requests to inspect his files. In 2015, the Stasi Records Agency confirmed in a letter to M. that he was indeed registered as an agent of the MfS in their archives.[32] Additionally, the authors of this article have also filed requests to inspect M.'s files at the AIVD, but, repeatedly, have been denied access.

Who is double agent

M. grew up in a working-class family in the Netherlands. After spending a year at an American high school, he obtained a degree in higher education in his home country. He fulfilled his military service, started a career with a large multinational company, and lived in several European, African, and Asian countries. His familiarization with intelligence dates from his military service and subsequent studies. The services he came in touch with initially tasked him to infiltrate on their behalf local anti-communist, fascist, and radical rightwing organizations that were part of international networks.[33]"It was challenging, interesting," M. recalls. "I did not consider myself as someone who was deceiving others. I was a soldier in the Cold War. [...] In that sense, the word 'deception' is a misnomer. [...] I did not support their philosophies," M. explains, "I was an infiltrator tasked to figure out what was going on there."[34] It is clear from what he said that M. also felt a sense of excitement and satisfaction about his role as a double agent and soldier in the fight against communism.

During an internship in Israel, as part of his studies in the winter of 1967–1968, a somewhat older man introducing himself as "Gerber" approached M. and invited him for dinner. He was interested in M.'s background, the year he had spent at an American high school, and, a rather unusual topic for a casual conversation among strangers, Israeli nuclear developments in the Negev desert.[35] M. did not give a reason why this first contact with the East Germans was made in Israel; his internship there was not related to any nuclear issues. Later, in West Germany, "Herr Gerber" sent him his regards via a stranger who approached M. in the street. M.'s intelligence contacts in the Netherlands correctly interpreted this approach as a recruiting attempt by the MfS, especially because the location of the proposed meeting with "Herr Gerber" that the stranger gave was in East Berlin. M.'s Dutch handlers encouraged him to respond favorably.[36] A successful "recruitment" would allow the Dutch services to increase their knowledge of the operational methods, personnel, and targets of the MfS in the Netherlands and elsewhere.

Shortly afterward, in the beginning of 1968, the MfS formally recruited M., registering him with the codename JANSEN.[37] He became a double agent of several Dutch intelligence and security services consecutively and later for the BVD, operating initially against the Hauptabteilung (Chief Department) II of the MfS, while continuing his employment in the Netherlands for a large multinational company.[38] "Gerber," who had approached him in Israel and West Germany, was in fact a codename for Erhard Schierhorn, who became his first handler on behalf of the Hauptabteilung II, Abteilung [Department] 2 (HA II/2).[39]In 1973, the HV A took over the offensive tasks of the Hauptabteilung II, M. was transferred from HA II/2 to the Abteilung IX of the HV A (HV A IX).[40] During most of the following period, Harry Schütt headed HV A IX.[41] M.'s longtime handlers were Wolfgang Koch and Heinz Nötzelmann. Both worked with a subunit of HV A IX that operated especially against the services of the United States, United Kingdom, France, and Israel.[42]

In 1981, the BVD handed M. over to the CIA. By this time, M.'s residence in Asian and African countries did not correspond anymore with the BVD's national operational remit. The Americans would run him until the early 1990s. While his subsequent CIA handlers would change often, he would still occasionally meet his first handler, who remained a presence as a mentor in the background. In 1985, M.'s operational position became extra complicated when his CIA handlers proposed a new twist to the ongoing operation, in response to the attempts of his HV A handlers to "dangle" him before the CIA with the aim to have the Americans "recruit" him as an agent.[43] According to this plan, M. would then pretend to the East Germans to work for them as a double agent against the CIA. That way the CIA would get information about the intelligence requirements of the HV A as they pertained to the CIA. This plan was implemented by the CIA in cooperation with M. in the following years.

M. met his East German handlers and their couriers all over the world, but never in the Netherlands, partly depending on where he was based for his regular employment. Among the locations of the meetings with the MfS were East Berlin, Leipzig, Zürich, Vienna, Budapest, Kuala Lumpur, Singapore, Muscat, New Delhi, and Jakarta. Personal meetings occurred five or six times a year in safe houses (often in the German Democratic Republic [GDR]), in public spaces, or in hotels. While M. saw his handlers in Eastern Europe for long debriefings that lasted several days, outside Eastern Europe—adversarial territory for his East German handlers—he had only brief meetings or brush contacts with their couriers.[44] The MfS supplied him with Dutch, American, Swiss, British, and West German passports, which enabled him to travel inconspicuously under different names. He also communicated with the MfS through dead drops and by written or oral messages via East German embassies, which he visited secretly on a few occasions. He also received messages from the MfS through short-wave radio transmissions from Magdeburg in the GDR.[45]

Double agents often have a relatively short "shelf life" of about two to three years. Thereafter, the hostile service is likely to ask for more intelligence than the service that runs the double agent is willing to provide. Moreover, the psychological strains as a result of the agent's double life may become unbearable. There are relatively few known double agent operations that have lasted for a period as long as M.'s operation: 22 years.[46] If an operation lasts that long, it usually means that the double agent does not have direct access to top secret information.[47] Still, M.'s professional mobility and his many international contacts gave him access to information that was clearly of operational importance to the HV A.[48] Moreover, M.'s ability to infiltrate ideological communities, especially those on the far right, was also very valuable in the view of the HV A,[49] as was his easy access to individuals living in the Netherlands who traveled to Eastern Europe and the USSR.[50] When M. was stationed in several parts of the world for his career with a large multinational company, the MfS remained interested in him as a "mole" within the company, and for his access to individuals of operational interest in the countries where he was stationed.[51]

Relationship with the the MFS: Attachment to the adversary

Paradoxically, M. maintained a friendly relationship with the adversary he deceived. The relationship between M. and his East German handlers involved recognition and gratitude on their part for the yield of his work and for the related dangers to which M. was supposedly exposed on their behalf. His handlers appeared responsive to his needs, always cordially receiving him at meetings. They took him on day trips, inquired about his well-being, and offered him gifts. Hence, the sudden change in their attitude around 1988 worried and confused M. considerably. Until then, M's East German handlers treated him as a trustworthy comrade. "We are in this together," he paraphrases them saying, "you are our Mitarbeiter [coworker] in our fight for peace, you belong to us."[52]Yet, when M. met his handlers, they usually tried to educate him ideologically. Obviously, they also debriefed him, gave him new assignments, trained him technically, introduced him to new contacts,[53] and settled financial accounts. Debriefings usually lasted three to ten days. "The atmosphere was friendly," M. recalls, but he found these stays exhausting. "We visited nightclubs or a museum in Leipzig, we went for rides. [...] In Budapest we went to those hot baths on the Margareteninsel [Margaret Island]."[54] Alternatively, they went to saunas, restaurants, they drank Georgian cognac together, and once had tea with the renowned SONYA in East Berlin.[55] Besides debriefing M., the goal of these meetings was also to appease and reward him as a valuable asset, to guide him psychologically, and to check how sincere he was.

M. is still ambivalent about his relationship with his East German handlers, while he was also touched by their signs of gratitude and appreciation for his efforts. On some level, he personally sympathized with them. "Sometimes," M. tells us, "I really liked those East Germans from the HV A as human beings, even though I deceived them. Their company was actually quite pleasant." They were "genuinely cordial, we bonded as men."[56] M. and his handlers addressed each other in the familiar German du and, although they did not meet each other's spouses and families, their relationship was informal.[57]

M. felt his handlers knew him through and through, "to a certain degree of course," not only because of their personal interest in him, but also because they hardly alternated throughout the years.[58]His long-term handlers,

"Heinz" and "Wolfgang," as M. knew them,[59] usually assumed "the roles of good cop, bad cop." At times M. found bad cop Koch hard to fathom, in particular his body language. Koch had a competitive, "aggressive and distrustful personality," he was "pushy" and at times almost hostile, M. remembers.[60] Nötzelmann, "somewhat more corpulent and easy-going," used to play good cop.[61] He was a "bon vivant,"[62] more flexible, calm and relaxed, more empathetic than a leader, and more of a go-getter than an intellectual.[63] Despite his recurring musings about his personal relationship with his East German handlers, M. concludes that "the question whether you personally like someone is, of course, not decisive. You simply need to do business with someone, just like in the business world, and in such a framework, feelings of sympathy are not really decisive."[64]

Koch and Nötzelmann lavishly showed their appreciation for M. Besides all visits and trips they did together, they also capitalized on M.'s personal material interests. For instance, they took him to toyshops where—at their expense—he could indulge in his love for model trains. They gave him specific books that corresponded to his interests,[65] and on the occasion of his marriage, they gave him an exquisite Bohemian vase.[66] Most importantly, in 1985 the MfS awarded him a Golden Distinguished Service Medal of the National People's Army (Verdienstmedaille der Nationalen Volksarmee).[67] The HV A presented him with this medal in a remote safehouse not far from East Berlin. M. recollects how Markus Wolf, the elusive, long-term head of the HV A, arrived in a Swedish-made Volvo, escorted by motorcyclists at the front and rear of the vehicle. "We shook hands and talked. I found him a very friendly, amicable man."[68] However, the day had started much less amicably when M. was put through the wringer of a mock arrest, an ordeal allegedly meant to prove his loyalty to the MfS, which had lasted from the early morning hours until the afternoon.

During the first couple of interviews in 2019, M. had mentioned this experience only in passing, averting the additional questions of the authors of this article while switching to another subject. In the last interview, after the authors shared their observation that he seemed unwilling to expand on this particular episode, M. explained why, after 34 years, he still found it painful to talk about. He agreed to disclose what happened that day, albeit clearly holding back on specific details. On an early spring day, around 4 AM, while still asleep in a safe house somewhere close to East Berlin, M. was woken up very rudely by a special squad of the MfS that shouted, "Staatssicherheit. Sie sind verhaftet!" [State security. You're under arrest!] Abducted while still in his pajamas, he was stuffed into a van with blacked-out windows and taken to Hohenschönhausen prison in East Berlin, the MfS penitentiary notorious for its use of torture and psychologically intimidating interrogation techniques. It was early spring and pretty cold. Their behavior was rough, to say the least. After they have taken you in, they examine you. You are ordered to undress completely. All body openings are being inspected rather roughly. They threw me in a prison cell, and after a while they took me out again. Naked through the corridors on my way to the interrogation room. The corridors were lit. And if somebody would arrive from the opposite direction, they would push your face against the wall. [...] It was overwhelming, to put it mildly.[69]

M. continues in the second rather than the first person singular. "You become totally demoralized, you cannot do anything anymore and you feel absolutely defenseless. They deprive you, as it were, of your identity and any form of humanity." His predicament was exacerbated by the knowledge that his wife was home alone and that the CIA was unlikely to find his precise location. I was naked, tied to a hard chair with handcuffs. Three or four burly fellows in uniform are standing around me, one of them behind me with a truncheon. [...] "Sie sind ein Verräter!" [You are a traitor!], they snap. [...] They did not beat or abuse me. It was pure intimidation.[70] Mentally, he recited the mantra, "Keep denying, do not give in. Keep insisting that as a foreigner you devoted yourself to the good cause, to socialism [...], that you had expected something better than this inhuman treatment." They poured cold water over him repeatedly, and after a while, he lost sense of time and place.[71] When he thought his ordeal would last forever, suddenly "Wolfgang" and "Heinz" entered the room. "Congratulations!" they exalted him, adding that he had passed the test and that he was now a real "Kundschafter."[72] But M. was "still in a kind of trance," thinking, "Piss off, I want to get away from this world. I am fed up!" They released him from his chair, returned his clothes to him, and guided him to a room where he could freshen up. That same afternoon M. received his gold medal from Markus Wolf, probably as a direct result of resisting the pressure of the mock arrest. That day proved to be a schizophrenic, traumatic experience for him.

During a meeting in Zagreb in 1988, M. clearly realized he had fallen into disfavor with his East German handlers, in a way that made him suspect treason within the CIA. To his American handlers, he had described Wolfgang Koch as someone whom the CIA could possibly try to recruit. In his descriptions of Koch, M. had emphasized not only Koch's behavior and personality but also his brown eyes as a distinguishing physical trait. To

M.'s dismay, at the three-day meeting in Zagreb Koch asked unexpectedly, aggressively, and in English: "You don't like brown eyes, do you?" M. was clearly shocked by this turn of events: "You try not to lose your cool, but all alarm bells start ringing. You're on edge."[73] He mentioned this remark by Koch in each of the interviews conducted for this research. It ushered in a period when both Koch and Nötzelmann became more distant. The male bonding and the toasting were over, their body language had changed, and their friendly relationship had derailed.[74] M. kept wondering whether he had made some sort of error, whether something had gone wrong in communications, or whether there was treason within the ranks of the CIA. The end of his reciprocal relationship with his East German handlers, "the insecurity and threat that it generated," had a considerable impact on M.'s well-being. It contributed to his ensuing depression, for which he later received treatment.[75] In one of the interviews for this research in 2019, M. showed the authors of this article the last telegram from his East German handler, dated 13 February 1990, in which they canceled their planned meeting in Budapest. "That was the last time I heard from them." According to M., this abrupt farewell, sharply contrasted with their earlier lavish expressions of gratitude, clearly showed that they knew he had been deceiving them.[76]

Relationship with the BVD

M.'s reciprocal relationship with his East German handlers, whom he probably managed to deceive for a long period, was as paradoxical as his much more distant, negotiated relationship with his Dutch handlers, under whose authority he operated in extremely dangerous circumstances. M. was specifically tasked to acquire information about his East German handlers and their modus operandi, including, for instance, methods of communication with agents and the use of concealment devices. The cordial meetings with the East Germans and their lavish expressions of recognition and gratitude for his efforts contrasted starkly with the sober, bureaucratic relationship between him and his Dutch handlers. M. remains intrigued by the many differences between his Dutch and East German handlers, shown by his frequent comparisons during the interviews. While he discusses his East German handlers independently, he mentions his Dutch handlers mostly in comparison to their East German counterparts.

While working for the BVD over the years, M. was in touch with five or six men whom he knew by their fictitious last names only. They addressed each other by their last name and the formal u rather than the informal jij, which can be explained partially by the common forms of address in

307

the 1960s and 1970s in the Netherlands. Another explanation, however, is the handlers' age and social background, both of which contributed to a distant, paternalistic, bureaucratic relationship in M.'s recollection: My handlers at the BVD were rather aloof, mostly elderly men who had taken part in the resistance against the German occupation during World War II. They weren't great intellectuals. Some of them were civil servants who had come from the [Dutch East] Indies, people with a somewhat bureaucratic mindset. They were above 50 and I was in my mid-twenties, so our relationship resembled the one between father and son. [...] They showed little psychological empathy, rather a certain arrogance along the lines of "We have seen it all." They didn't guide me psychologically by asking, for instance, "How did you experience it?" or "How did you feel?" Such guidance didn't suit them. [...] I got assignments [...], I reported back to them. Everything was very businesslike.[77]

Some of his handlers, M. thought, were of strict reformed protestant upbringing. His impression corresponds to our knowledge of the postwar generation of BVD officials, which included disproportionally many members of the Dutch reformed church.[78] To M., their reformed and wartime background transpired through their reactions to certain topics and their sensitivities. For instance, M. noticed that his handlers sometimes talked about "godless communism," and that they had extensive knowledge of arms, munition, and transmitters.[79] The most striking difference, according to M., between his East German and Dutch handlers was the appreciation and gratitude they showed for his work. "The Dutch never gave me any sign of appreciation or reward, not even a ballpoint," M. recollects resentfully.[80] Although, on a later occasion, he acknowledges that he received an occasional bottle of wine on top of his regular remuneration. The BVD approached its double operation with M. as a cost-neutral endeavour, both in the reimbursement of expenses and the remuneration. Besides his reimbursement of expenses, M. received payment for his work both from his East German and Dutch handlers. He had to hand over the East German remuneration to his Dutch handlers, who repaid him the same amount and also matched any raise in the East German amount.[81] This financial arrangement had operational and financial benefits for the BVD: it prevented M. from becoming financially dependent on his East German handlers and it made this double operation free of charge for the Dutch service.

M.'s BVD handlers strictly checked up on his bookkeeping.[82] For instance, once they called M. to account for declaring an excess of fl. 40,-in expenses.[83] On regular occasions, they also reminded M. that they were spending taxpayers' money by reimbursing his expenses and taking him out for the occasional dinner. One of his handlers, himself a volunteer with the Red Cross, even advised M. to refrain from declaring any expenses.[84] What struck and disappointed M. most when reading parts of his BVD files in 2016 was a report of a meeting of the BVD management team in which M.'s recent marriage was discussed. The managers had decided not to buy him a wedding present because, as they concluded, M. had already claimed enough expenses.[85] In May 1981, the BVD handed over their double agent to the CIA.[86] The transfer took place over dinner in a restaurant in Rotterdam, in the presence of a couple of BVD officers, who M. was familiar with, and three CIA representatives, who were stationed at the American embassy in The Hague.[87] During this meeting, the BVD formally distanced itself from M., which fits in with M.'s recollection of their negotiated relationship, by asking him to sign a letter renouncing any future BVD responsibilities. While this letter did not make a particularly strong impression on him in 1981, he was struck by its contents when inspecting his BVD files in 2016.[88] "The BVD abandoned me completely," M. recounts. "After all those years that I had risked my life for you," he continues, addressing the former BVD. "In this world, you are being fooled on the spot."[89]

Relationship with the CIA

During the interviews, M. regularly refers to his relationship with the CIA as casual and informal. Money was not an issue, contrary to the relationship with the BVD and similar to the one with the MfS. However, he appears less attached to his American than to his East German handlers. Similar to his disillusionment regarding the BVD, feelings of abandonment and rejection also dominate M.'s memory of the ending of his relationship with the CIA. After the transfer meeting in Rotterdam, M.'s second meeting with the CIA was in Frankfurt am Main where he took a polygraph test. He was given another polygraph a couple of years later.[90] The CIA instructed M. in techniques that were developed to recruit KGB intelligence officers who might know about penetrations in the U.S. Intelligence Community.[91] The operation started in 1987 against the background of investigations into the "1985 losses" the FBI and the CIA had suffered in a wave of arrests among their agents in the USSR.[92]

Potential approaches of KGB officers were preceded by detailed logging of their whereabouts and psychological assessments that could estimate their willingness to collaborate. These assessments also provided clues on how to compromise or manipulate them. M. was tasked by the CIA to analyze his East German handlers' behavior with these techniques. This was preliminary work for a possible future approach by someone else. The operation, codenamed RACKETEER by the CIA, used the Personality Assessment System (PAS) designed by former CIA star psychologist John Gittinger. The CIA mainly applied PAS to focus on deviant traits that might indicate individuals who rejected the values of their society, which allowed the agency to understand the vulnerabilities of such individuals. For practical operational purposes, the Gittinger staff developed a list of 30 to 40 character traits that a skilled observer could look for.[93] The CIA trained and instructed M. in observing the behavior of Wolfgang Koch and Heinz Nötzelmann. M. showed the authors of this article a document entitled "Traits to Look For," that his CIA contacts had given him. It included traits like "ignores danger; exuberant; outgoing; enjoys humor; drives aggressively; socially pushy; interested in the unusual; very ambitious; drinks heavily; openly critical of others; open, playful about sex; rapid bodily actions; highbrow tastes."[94] In his descriptions of Koch to his American handlers, M. often mentioned the distinctive color of Koch's brown eyes. Hence, in 1988, when Koch suddenly asked M., "You don't like brown eyes, do you?" M. became convinced "they knew more about me than they should have."[95]

M. remembers his CIA handlers as easygoing and personable; they often used their real names. Contrary to his Dutch and certainly his East German handlers, some of them introduced him to their families, invited him to their homes, and they regularly met their partners.[96] Because of his work for a large multinational company, M. had legitimate reasons to be in touch with American embassies and firms abroad and, M. notes, his American contacts blended seamlessly with his contacts with other expats.[97] His wife sometimes joined him in his meetings with the Americans, partly because as a couple they would raise fewer suspicions than M. alone, but also because the CIA was interested in knowing, reassuring, and supporting his wife.[98] These gatherings with his CIA handlers and his wife were purely social, with much small talk. His wife knew, for instance, that she was meeting a CIA officer, but she did not know any details about her husband's operations. The CIA gave her an emergency number that she could reach in case of need, and she had to call specific phone numbers with cryptic messages to let the CIA know each time her husband had returned from Eastern Europe.[99] In general, M. remembers, his American handlers never displayed any shortage of money when showing their appreciation for his work.

"You are meeting a lot of our people," one of M.'s American handlers once told him grudgingly. Indeed, M.'s handlers changed frequently, due to the fact that M. often relocated to different parts of the world, but also because CIA handlers rotated roughly once every four years. The frequent change of his handlers may have contributed to the little personal attachment M. showed toward them. However, M. developed a longer-term and closer relationship with his first CIA handler, whom he knew by his real name and with whom he reconnected in 2015. However, in 1988, when Wolfgang Koch made his disconcerting remark about M.'s presumed dislike of brown eyes he realized how overly dependent he was on his American handlers. "The party you need to trust, that needs to back you up, that you can call upon in case of need, that party is being betrayed from within."[100] M. decided not to report Koch's remark to his American handlers, isolating himself in his fear of betrayal. This was a turning point in his relationship with his American handlers. No longer being able to trust the only party he was supposed to trust resulted in "total solitude, helplessness, confusion and alienation," and the feeling of being "a pawn in a manipulative, well-oiled power machine." He felt he was forced to dissolve his "maternal" bond of trust with his American handlers and subsequently experienced a "process of mourning."[101] The end of the Cold War further accelerated his separation from the CIA in a way that reminded him of his separation from the BVD a decade earlier.

Farewell to his handler

In the 22 years that M. operated against the MfS for the BVD and CIA, his position over time became increasingly complicated, confusing, and lonely.[102] When the suspicion of treason arose, his position became almost unbearable. I could no longer trust anyone. [...] I had to be constantly alert and wary. [...] To remain in this position over such a long period of time requires much stamina. [...] There is a line of appreciation, trust, but also of abandonment. [...] You are being used as a pawn by something amorphous, by an entity that you cannot enter. No, they will approach you. [...] You are appreciated for your efforts, but [these services] remain a dark cloud that you cannot enter. They guide you. You have no input.[103] The BVD in 1981, and the MfS and CIA after the end of the Cold War, abruptly ended their relationship with M. These sudden endings placed him in a situation that was "Kafkaesque," a term he himself used when reflecting on his psychological state.[104] He did not know what the MfS would do to his files and whether they had shared them with their Russian allies.[105] Moreover, he was no longer able to reach his former handlers. "There was nobody left to share everything with," M. recollects.[106] He felt abandoned. "You do not have any colleagues in espionage," he explains.

You are left entirely to your own devices. [The separation from my handlers] was really a turning point. Until then I was engaged in all kinds of geopolitical developments, I was right on top of them. I had interesting contacts. And then suddenly, all this ended, and I was sitting at home. That was a shock.[107]In 2016, M. experienced acute emotional problems and he spent a night in a hospital emergency ward. He asked the AIVD, the legal successor of the BVD, for assistance in getting treatment from an agency "with experience in treating the emotional burdens of a long-time double agent." After a week, M. received an answer from the AIVD's legal department (which the authors have seen) saying that "at the Ministries of Internal Affairs and/or Defence there are no facilities for the psychological help you requested. I advise you to contact your GP, so he/she can put you in touch with a regular therapist."

Conclusions

This research suggests that (double) agents prioritize a reciprocal, affect-based relationship with their handlers, involving trust and gratitude. They are less interested in a negotiated relationship based on financial agreements unless financial rewards become one the few means through which an agent perceives recognition for his work. In such cases, financial compensation risks becoming a source of friction, as the relationship between M. and the BVD has shown. Agents' prioritization of a reciprocal, affect-based relationship with their handlers is explained by emphasizing the professional and personal dependence of the agent on his handler. This is a result of, first, the agent's social isolation and, second, the dangers he is exposed to. First, operational secrecy isolates agents from their social environments. The case of M. shows that, although his wife knew M. was operationally active, he could not share any operational details with her. His handlers were the only individuals he could confide in and, as such, they developed into attachment figures: central individuals in his life, who made him feel secure and enabled him to cope with stressful situations. The disruptive abandonment M. felt when his handlers broke off contact abruptly confirms how vital his handlers had become in his life.

Second, the dangerous environment in which an agent operates deepens the agent's dependence on his handler. An affect-based relationship was of special significance to M. because of his numerous debriefings by the MfS on enemy territory, behind the Iron Curtain, where he was in a very vulnerable position. The tension and fear that M. often felt in his dealings with the East Germans was partly compensated by feelings of excitement and personal satisfaction because of the success of the operation. His perception of his Dutch handlers as unavailable and unresponsive attachment figures, however, contributed to his anxiety, which became apparent by the way he downplayed the importance of their relationship. He deliberately became more self-reliant, and more distant toward them. Paradoxically, M.'s East German handlers, rather than his Dutch or American handlers, emerged as his most responsive attachment figures. This contradiction between his ideological loyalty as a "soldier" in the Cold War and his personal sympathies made an already tense operational environment even more contradictory and alienating.

Clearly, reactions toward unresponsive attachment figures increase the risk that agents' loyalty toward the adversary outstrips their loyalty toward their home service. From an operational perspective, if the BVD had offered M. at least a higher rather than similar remuneration to the MfS, as a sign of recognition for his work, it could have strengthened M.'s commitment to the BVD. One could even argue that this double agent deserved a higher remuneration from the Dutch service than from the MfS, given the fact that he put himself in potentially grave danger every time he had his meetings with his East German handlers behind the Iron Curtain. M.'s memories sketch a predominantly bleak picture of his operational past. They overshadow feelings of excitement and satisfaction that, most probably, were of decisive importance to continue his operational activities on behalf of the West. Throughout his years as a double agent, he did feel strongly that he was engaged on the right side in the fight against communism in the Cold War. This was in spite of his negative feelings about his BVD handlers. Arguably, the abrupt abandonment by his handlers and the subsequent laborious process of accessing his files have shaped his present memories. Further research into the relationship between agents and their handlers could explore the period after an operation has ended. More specifically, it could delve into the attention and aftercare (or lack thereof) a service offers its former agents, including how it deals with their desire to access their files and other sensitive issues.

Acknowledgment

The authors are grateful to Dan Mulvenna, a twenty-year veteran of the Security Service of the Royal Canadian Mounted Police, for his comments on an earlier version of this article. They also thank the participants of the Cold War Research Network

(Utrecht University, Leiden University, and the University of Amsterdam) for their valuable comments on a presentation of this research in January 2021. References: Eleni Braat is an Associate Professor in the History of International Relations at Utrecht University. She obtained her Ph.D. from the European University Institute in Florence, Italy (2008). She has been the official historian of the Dutch General Intelligence and Security Service, and she is a member of the executive board of the Netherlands Intelligence Studies Association. The author can be contacted at e.c.braat@uu.nl. Ben de Jong is a retired Assistant Professor from the University of Amsterdam. He is a Researcher at the Institute of Security and Global Affairs at Leiden University. His most recent publication is on the life and times of a former Dutch security service official: Op de bres voor de rechtsstaat in het Verzet en bij de BVD: Ad de Jonge 1919–2002 [In defense of democracy with the Resistance and the BVD: Ad de Jonge 1919–2002].Journal information: Print ISSN: 0885-0607 Online ISSN: 1521-0561. 4 issues per year. Abstracted/indexed in: America: History & Life; CSA; EBSCOhost Online Research Databases; ESCI; Historical Abstracts; OCLC; PAIS International; Periodicals Index Online; Scopus; The Lancaster Index; and Ulrichs Periodicals Directory. Taylor & Francis make every effort to ensure the accuracy of all the information (the "Content") contained in our publications. However, Taylor & Francis, our agents (including the editor, any member of the editorial team or editorial board, and any guest editors), and our licensors, make no representations or warranties whatsoever as to the accuracy, completeness, or suitability for any purpose of the Content. Any opinions and views expressed in this publication are the opinions and views of the authors, and are not the views of or endorsed by Taylor & Francis. The accuracy of the Content should not be relied upon and should be independently verified with primary sources of information. Taylor & Francis shall not be liable for any losses, actions, claims, proceedings, demands, costs, expenses, damages, and other liabilities whatsoever or howsoever caused arising directly or indirectly in connection with, in relation to, or arising out of the use of the Content. Aims and scope: The International Journal of Intelligence and CounterIntelligence serves as a medium for professionals and scholars to exchange opinions on issues and challenges encountered by both government and business institutions in making contemporary intelligence-related decisions and policy. At the same time, this quarterly serves as an invaluable resource for researchers looking to assess previous developments and events in the field of national security. Dedicated to the advancement of the academic discipline of intelligence studies, the International Journal of Intelligence and CounterIntelligence publishes articles and book reviews focusing on a broad range of national security matters. As an independent, non-partisan forum, the journal presents the informed and diverse findings of its contributing authors, and does not advocate positions of its own. Peer Review Policy: All papers submitted to the International Journal of Intelligence and CounterIntelligence undergo initial editorial screening. Once deemed suitable, research articles are sent out for double-anonymous peer review by at least two independent referees. Publication office: Taylor & Francis Inc., 530 Walnut Street, Suite 850, Philadelphia, PA 19106. Readership: Current and former intelligence and national security professionals in government, business, and the military, as well as academics studying intelligence and foreign policy, members

of the media covering foreign and domestic affairs, and interested members of the public. Authors can choose to publish gold open access in this journal. International Journal of Intelligence and CounterIntelligence. ISSN: (Print) (Online) Journal homepage: https://www.tandfonline.com/loi/ujic20. Between a Rock and a Hard Place: The Precarious. State of a Double Agent during the Cold War. Eleni Braat & Ben de Jong. To cite this article: Eleni Braat & Ben de Jong (2023) Between a Rock and a Hard Place: The Precarious State of a Double Agent during the Cold War, International Journal of Intelligence and CounterIntelligence, 36:1, 78-108, DOI: 10.1080/08850607.2022.2088951. To link to this article: https://doi.org/1 0.1080/08850607.2022.2088951 © 2022 The Author(s). Published with license by Taylor & Francis Group, LLC Published online: 25 Jul 2022. 2022 The Author(s).

 acknowledgement.The authors are grateful to Dan Mulvenna, a twenty-year veteran of the Security Service of the Royal Canadian Mounted Police, for his comments on an earlier version of this article. They also thank the participants of the Cold War Research Network (Utrecht University, Leiden University, and the University of Amsterdam) for their valuable comments on a presentation of this research in January 2021.

Chapter 16

Enemy image? A comparative analysis of the Russian Federation's role and position in the leading national security documents of Estonia and the Czech Republic

Monika Gabriela Bartoszewicz & Michaela Prucková

Abstract

States are security-seekers vis-a-vis 'significant others' who are cast as enemies in the international system. Usually, the study of the enemy image is connected with relative equilibrium concerning power capabilities. Less attention was given to a situation of a decisive power imbalance. Thus, a question arises whether such a situation will lead to a uniform enemy image? Concomitantly, what is the impact of the enemy image on security-related behaviour and policy preferences? To shed light on this problem, we analyse the strategic security documents of the Czech Republic and the Republic of Estonia to explore how they project the Russian Federation into their security discourses. By engaging the broader question of the discursive construction of the enemy in the national security documents, we seek to contribute to how vernacular perspectives feed into the regional dynamic of Central Eastern Europe understood either as an EU region or as NATO's Eastern Flank.

Keywords: Enemy image, strategic documents, security policy, the Czech Republic, Estonia

Introduction

Even before the 2022 invasion on Ukraine, it was acknowledged that for the states on Europe's eastern borders, the Russian Federation (the RF, or Russia) epitomises a primary security threat (Bartoszewicz Citation2021; Pezard et al. Citation 2018) and therefore performs the symbolic and functional role of an enemy. Bachleitner (Citation 2021) shows that states are not only spatial but also temporal security seekers vis-a-vis a 'significant historical other' from their past. However, a question arises whether it is indeed the case that collective memory of a former foe leads to contemporary enemy image projection, and if so, whether such projection leads to a uniform enemy image in these states. To this end, we conduct two case studies, focusing on Russia's role and position in the leading national security documents of the Czech Republic and Estonia. The comparative perspective adds greater analytical diversity via a deductive approach (Sodaro and Collinwood Citation 2004). Against 'the problem of selection bias', as Landman (Citation 2002, 81) puts it, our cases are two European countries that share similar historical experiences, a method which has been used by other scholars (Kazharski and Makarychev Citation 2021). In our analysis, the dependent variable is the centre of attention, as we focus on the question of the RF's role and image in the two countries' leading national security documents.

At the international system level, states might be considered unitary actors, but as Herrmann and Fischerkeller (Citation 1995, 427) notice, they are not anthropomorfic entities. Our explorative work is based on the premise that national documents reflect the state's mentality as the document is not a product of an individual but rather a tangible result of invisible human interactions. Thus, it can be argued that strategic security documents reflect the collective attitudes of decision-makers and offer insights into the undertows of the national security discourse. This angle anchors our inquiry in the social constructivist paradigm and at the same time offers a fresh perspective diverging from the more popular scholarship on othering, societal debates or foreign policy preferences. For instance, even an excellent Yarhi-Milo's (Citation 2014) work on determining another country's foreign policy plans looks into indicators such as capabilities, behaviours or strategic military doctrine, awhile discounting the strategic security documents. This begs another question: Is there coherence between the written security policy guideline and actual policymaking?

The leading national security documents at the centre of attention of this paper are the *Security Strategy of the Czech Republic* (Strategy), adopted in (Citation2015), and the *National Security Concept of Estonia* (Concept), adopted in (Citation2017). Since these documents represent the highest expression of security policy objectives and the aims of the states, they as a consequence decisively form the policy of the state (Frank and Melville Citation1988). Despite their similarities, both states exhibit significant differences in how they refer to the Russian Federation in their strategic documents. By engaging the broader question of the discursive construction of the enemy in the national security documents, we seek to contribute to how vernacular perspectives feed into the regional dynamic of Central-Eastern Europe, as understood as an EU region or as NATO's Eastern Flank.

Our aim is to understand the dynamic of enemy image construction and its variation vis a vis power imbalances and policy praxis. Consequently, the paper begins with the exploration of how Russia is perceived in the two states according to the public reports published by their intelligence agencies. We thus treat the Estonian and Czech security discourse as intertextual, produced in tight nexus with the input of the state's 'eyes and ears' as per a structural and systemic approach (Skocpol Citation 1979). Secondly, we take stock of how the enemy image is constructed in the official security documents of both countries in order to explore what these images might look like and how they might differ. This allows for a comparative analysis of the key security documents in terms of direct and indirect references to the Russian Federation, which allows for elaboration on the strategic positioning of Russia via interpretive content analysis (Ahuvia Citation2001; Ginger Citation 2006) focusing on the frequency of mentions, indirect innuendos and the choice of adjectives in terms of their denotations and connotations (i.e. basic meanings of the word versus something suggested by the word in addition to its simple meaning).

Imagining the enemy

To develop our argument, we turn to the 'enemy image' concept which moves away from the rationalist utility-maximising model of the state that focuses on large, structural drivers (Dodge Citation 2012) into the cognitive realm. The enemy image implies a negative portrayal of adversaries. Identifying the enemy is deeply connected to the notions of 'self' and 'the other', which creates a dichotomy endowed with a sense of threat. However, the enemy should not be conflated with the concept of the 'other' especially that unlike the latter (Bartoszewicz Citation 2014; Diez Citation 2004, Prozorov Citation2011; Mouffe Citation 1993; Neumann Citation 1996; Wæver Citation 1993), the former has not received an equal measure of scholarly attention in the post-Cold War world. While the concept of the 'enemy image' was neglected after the end of the Cold War, now with the arrival of a hot one, it is more timely than ever.

The enemy symbolizes the antithesis of core values and beliefs regarding human needs, such as belongingness and security, as well as attitudes toward authority. He is a part of the polarized world which all men create, and reflects man's two-sided prism of beliefs and disbeliefs - that which is accepted as true and good and which is rejected as false and evil. There are, in other words, cognitive processes of adjustment, balance and strain for congruence which tend to cause and sustain ideas of enemies. (Finlay, Holsti, and Fagan Citation 1967,7). Thus, the enemy image that conveys very simplified beliefs about individual characteristics on the basis of ascribed group belonging, and as Petersson (Citation 2009) demonstrates, it has more far-reaching implications than the more commonly encountered negative stereotypes of strangers. So far, the emergence and salience of this phenomenon has been scrutinised in movies (Burke Citation2017) and newspapers (Mandelzis Citation 2003; Ottosen Citation 1995) – since media representations are closely linked to policy and the media play a vital role akin to negative political advertising (Bahador Citation 2015; Muižnieks Citation2008; Osipian Citation 2015)–in social networks (Zheltukhina, Krasavsky, and Ponomarenko Citation 2016), and as an inseparable element contributing to the formation of national identity (Kryvda and Storozhuk Citation 2020). We explore this concept through the textual lens of official government security-oriented documents via empirically-driven comparative analysis of how Russia features as an enemy trope in the political discourse of the Czech Republic (Czechia) and the Republic of Estonia (Estonia).

In our study, the enemy image refers to a belief held by a state that 'its security and basic values are directly and seriously threatened' (Luostarinen Citation1989, 125). Ottosen (Citation 1995, 98) links the national processes of defining other nations or states as 'the other' to Carl Schmitt, who considers the friend-enemy distinction is the ultimate, defining distinction of politics to which every political action and motive can be reduced (Schmitt Citation 2008, 26). As such, projections of enemy images are a substantial part of politics. In addition to biological and psychological explanations (Eckhardt Citation 1991; Fromm Citation 1955; Keen Citation 1991), there are also strategic and functional dimensions of this concept as enemy image is frequently used to fuel various mobilisation efforts (Gerő et al. Citation 2017). Specifically, in political science, enmification of countries (Jung et al. Citation2002) can emerge when two actors compete for the same goal. In such a scenario, their interactions may escalate into the perception of each other as national enemies (Holt Citation 1989), which is dangerous for the stability and security of international relations (Frank and Melville Citation1988) as it is believed to be a prerequisite in preparedness for war (Oppenheimer Citation 2006). Consequently, the explanations of this dynamic can be sought in the events and tensions between the actors or in the internal situation determining the image formation.

Czechia and Estonia share similar historical experiences regarding Russia (Brüggemann and Kasekamp Citation 2008; Hakauf Citation 2011; Piotrowski Citation2018; Runnel, Pruulmann-Vengerfeldt, and Reinsalu Citation2009; Sierzputowski Citation 2019; Stoneman Citation 2015), coupled with occasional recent confrontational episodes with Russia (e.g. the Bronze Soldier incident in Estonia and the munitions explosion in Czech Vrbětice). Estonia believed itself to be a victim of Russia's cyber capabilities unleashed vengefully after the relocation of the Bronze Soldier. However, despite many accusations and clues, these cyber campaign was never officially attributed to the RF. The involved culprits were labelled as 'patriotic hackers' who were supposed to have acted autonomously (Dong Citation 2019, 47). On the other hand, Czech-Russian ties are strained in other areas. Czechia remained a favourite place for Russian spies (Schindler Citation 2017) as a base to obtain security-related information about NATO and the EU. For example, there was an equal number of Russian diplomats in Czechia as in the United Kingdom.

In 2017, there were 140 Russian diplomats in Czechia, a large number for such a small country. The Czech counterintelligence agency acknowledged in 2020 that the activities of Russian intelligence operatives were concealed 'under diplomatic cover' (Bezpečnostní informační služba Citation2020, 9). In 2014, the US security agencies assumed there were up to 400 Russian spies located in Czechia (Baret Citation 2014). In 2018, Czechia expelled three Russian diplomats in reaction to the murder attempt of a former Russian spy, Sergej Skripal, in the United Kingdom (Kopecký Citation 2018). A year later, in 2019, Russia debated a law that would have recognised the Soviet troops in the occupation of 1968 as war veterans (ČT24 Citation 2019), which resulted in a minor diplomatic dispute. Finally, in the same year, a monument to Marshal Koněv became a point of contention, as the RF did not want the Czechs to move the statue of a Russian war hero situated in Prague. The whole affair was eerily similar to the 2007 incident in Estonia. Only this time, no cyber attacks occurred, even though Czech agencies prepared for this scenario (Ministry of Foreign Affairs of the Czech Republic Citation2020). Due to these similar negative historical experiences, we take the former as a constant and allow for a variance in the latter, i.e. the role and position of the Russian Federation vis-a-vis the two selected cases.

Undoubtedly, images of other, external actors are complex constructs that are but an element of a wider meaning system (Szalay and Mir-Djahali Citation1991) that helps to organise and simplify the political environment of the state on the basis of mirrored value-guided attributions (Sande et al. Citation1989). Building on this notion, Cottam (Citation2000) observes that imagining other states to be enemies or allies is merely a cognitive device that simultaneously serves as an information filter. Frank and Melville (Citation1988) notice that enemy images are by no means monolithic, and thus interpreting the enemy image helps to illuminate patterns of how the feedback between image creation and strategic discourses influence state policy. The motives of the enemy are judged to be evil – but will the perceptions always be the same? There are scant premises to assume uniformity, hence the need to look within the image construction and explore the variance. In this regard, our study is meant to introduce empirical information on subjective images as they vary across the broad spectrum of state actors.

Furthermore, since the enemy images derive from selective perception and biased attribution, for analytical purposes they can be categorised into ideal types (Ottosen Citation 1995, 99). While capturing the mechanisms and dynamics of social reality, by their nature archetypes offer certain simplified versions of the real world. Indeed, Herrmann and Fischerkeller (Citation1995, 415) theorise that these archetypical enemy images can be used to predict how state actors will perceive and define strategic situations. They define the images as a 'cognitive construction or mental representation of another actor in the political world' (Herrmann and Fischerkeller Citation 1995, 415). When it comes to strategic security choices, power imbalances and situational contexts notwithstanding, possible policy options are rarely reduced to one default position. For this reason, the image of the other actor is a pivotal help in navigating the policy waters. Cottam (Citation 2000) posits that state interactions are largely determined on the basis of the characteristic associated with the image, hence the question of the impact of the enemy image on behaviour and policy preferences.

We proceed from the observation that central to the enemy image in its ideal-typical form is the judgment concerning the threat (or opportunity) that a given external actor represents. Unsurprisingly, societal debates on enmification and perceptions of threat have received the lion's share of scholarly attention; therefore, the enemy image has been well-articulated and well-studied (Herrmann and Fischerkeller Citation 1995, 423–424) in the context of the strategic behaviours it provokes. Secondly, the study of the enemy image is also connected with the relative power capabilities of the concerned actors. It is usually assumed that for the functional enemy image to emerge, both actors will be on par when it comes to power distribution, i.e. that both actors are roughly comparable in capability and not too distinct in terms of cultural sophistication (Cottam Citation 2000). This is not the case here: Russia is undoubtedly much stronger than either Estonia or the Czech Republic, regardless of the metric. This is important for two reasons. Firstly, Herrmann and Fischerkeller (Citation 1995, 425) claim that the enemy image is directly related to the consequent security strategy, which will range from direct attack (should the other state be considered much weaker), to containment in the case of a power balance, to appeasement if 'the other' is believed to be much stronger. Can we, however, unequivocally argue that this is always the case? Secondly, the above review of the enemy image literature reveals that the majority of studies concerning state actors focus on the great powers, usually the mutual enemy image dynamic of the Cold War-era bipolar system (Silverstein Citation 1989). Contrarily, we are looking into a situation of decisive power imbalance, and we are interested in the weaker actors' strategic perspectives, thus contributing to the existing repository of knowledge.

Leading national security documents: an overview

Given the similarities of the 'Russian experience' in historical perspective, it is not surprising that both countries repeatedly frame the RF as a threat actor or aggressive actor in their public counter-intelligence services reports. The Estonian Foreign Intelligence Service (EFIS Citation 2021) and the Estonian Internal Security Service (KaPo) pay close attention to Russia's behaviour. KaPo's public reports, called the 'Annual Review', date back to 1998 and are usually published at the beginning of the year they cover. Therefore, they mix analysis of previous events and the current security environment with predictions of what might happen during that year. The 2016 report mentions the RF 150 times; 154 times in 2017; 203 times in 2018; and 157 times in the joint report for 2019 and 2020 (KaPo Citation 2016, Citation 2017, Citation 2018, Citation 2020). According to KaPo, the RF's intelligence agents are active on the ground, carrying out 'espionage against Estonia' and recruiting 'ordinary people and criminals for secret collaborations' (Kapo Citation 2016). The influence of Russian 'government-controlled media' was accentuated in the 2017 report, along with a statement that the 'most likely and serious threat to constitutional order continues to arise from Russia's aggressive foreign-policy objectives' (Kapo 2017, 4–5).

In Czechia, the act on the intelligence services of the Czech Republic defines three actors – the Security Information Service (BIS), the Office for Foreign Relations and Information (ÚZSI), and Military Intelligence (VZ). Unlike their Estonian counterparts, the Czech agencies publish their reports retrospectively, and are therefore based mainly on analysis of recent past events. While established in 1994, BIS's annual reports date to 1996, when the first public report was published. In the BIS annual report for 2015, Russia is mentioned 30 times; 49 times in 2016; 40 times in 2017; 40 times in 2018; and 41 times in 2019 (Bezpečnostní informační služba Citation 2016, Citation 2017, Citation 2018, Citation 2019, Citation 2020). The reports repeatedly stress the Russian intelligence agencies' activity on the ground, which is, along with China's activity, the most significant for state security. It should be taken into consideration that the Czech reports tend to be much shorter than those from Estonia.

The National Security Concept of Estonia ('Eesti julgeolekupoliitika alused') represents the basic Estonian framework of security policies.[1] Its existence and form are based on the National Defence Act passed in 2015, being in force since 2016. The document sets up the way of responding to security threats. Therefore, it provides the country's security policy with objectives, principles, and directions. The current version replaced the Concept from 2010 (Concept 2017, 2). As opposed to the leading Czech security document, the Concept is not based on addressing threats; it primarily addresses the measures through which security can be strengthened–e.g. diplomacy, military defence, law enforcement, crisis management, cyber and economic security.

In the 22-page text, there is a grand total of 13 mentions of Russia.[2] In all of them, the RF is seen as a dangerous actor, a source of security problems that 'has become more aggressive in the past decade' (Concept 2017, 10). In addition to direct mentions, the document is interspersed with several innuendoes that refer to Russia without naming it. For instance, the reference to the increasing 'violations in cyberspace', attacks launched by individuals or groups that are 'too often supported and directed by states'

(Concept 2017, 5). This appears to refer to the 2007 DDoS campaign. The RF is also alluded to in a paragraph referring to Estonian responsibility 'for guarding the European Union's border' and 'maintaining the reliability of the Schengen area'. However, despite the numerous side references to Russia, the number of direct mentions in the Concept is sufficient for the primary analysis.

Starting with European security, the Concept frames Russian military activity as increasing in terms of intensity and aggression, being 'interested in restoring its position as a great power' for which it will not hesitate to come 'into a sharp opposition' with the Western and the Euro-Atlantic countries (Concept 2017, 4). The Concept recognises Western values (democracy, the market economy, the rule of law, human rights) are in decline; thus, the threats coming from the neighbouring actor are grave and must be clearly identified. As for specific threats, the Concept mentions Russian airspace violations, offensive military exercises, and nuclear threats. Another threat related to Russia's behaviour is the 'weakening of the ties' that keep the EU members together. According to Estonia, this weakening could Russia's embolden confidence, leading to even more aggressive power politics (Concept 2017, 5). Threats regarding the global energy market and energy supply between the EU and the RF are discussed, too, being a possible influencer of the Estonian economy and economic security. As for bilateral relations, Estonia sees itself as occupying a negotiator position due to its geographic position and border-sharing. As Estonia puts it, it will 'cooperate with Russia on a practical level', trying to keep the dialogue open in its own interest as well that of the EU and NATO (Concept 2017, 10).

The main security policy conceptual document of Czechia is the Security Strategy of the Czech Republic ('Bezpečnostní strategie České republiky'), currently in force since 2015 (when the Strategy from 2011 was updated). Since the Czech Strategy is now eight years old, some recent threats and risks are missing. On the other hand, it is supposed to be a longitudinal document that does not have to be updated with every incident and international event. Its principal *raison d'être* is to articulate the nation's fundamental security aims and describe the main threats to them. The security aims are divided into three groups: vital, strategic, and other important interests (Strategy 2015, 7). Based on this approach and design, Czechia's Strategy is a very general document that does not identify specific actors or events. In stark contrast to its Estonian counterpart, no name-and-shame policy is present, so the document can be seen as a little vague and detached. However, indirect references are there to be deciphered by the careful reader.

According to the Strategy, the security environment in Europe is increasingly unpredictable. Without any specific reference, the document warns against a 'direct threat to the territory of some NATO and EU member states', especially those on the margins (Strategy 2015, 8). Given its geographic location and geographical predisposition, and the conflict in eastern Ukraine, where Russian troops have taken control of Crimea, claiming to fulfil the popular will to become part of the RF, Russia can be indicated as the suggested culprit. What can be undoubtedly connected to Russia are the warnings of the 'power aspirations of some states', which 'stopped respecting international arrangements and basic principles of international law' (Strategy 2015, 8). The ongoing territorial conflict between the RF and Ukraine that erupted in early 2014 is an obvious example of this phenomenon.

In this context, the Strategy marks the 'weakening of the cooperative security mechanisms' as a threat (Strategy 2015, 11). It further enumerates the conventional, non-conventional, and non-military tools that can be used to support this weakening – propaganda, disinformation actions led by foreign intelligence entities, cyber attacks, political and economic pressure, and deployment of unidentified armed forces. The 'threat of instability and regional conflicts in and around the Euro-Atlantic area' is also described (Strategy 2015, 11). Another anticipated threat is the 'interruption of supplies of strategic raw materials or energy' (Strategy 2015, 12). Unlike the Concept, which attributes the danger of possible interruptions of this kind to EU-RF relations, the Strategy is limited to acknowledging that 'ensuring energy and raw material security is becoming increasingly important'.

Divergent security narratives

The first thing that strikes the reader of the Czech document is how carefully worded it is to ensure obscurity regarding the identity of potential enemies. While the strategy acknowledges vulnerability 'in the border regions of Europe' (Strategy 2015, 6), there is no hint as to whether this refers to the eastern or any other border. Similar abstruseness is noticeable when the document discusses potential direct threats only with regard to 'the territory of some NATO and EU member states' (Strategy 2015, 8) without any further specification of whether the state in question is Greece or rather Latvia. More importantly, the word 'ambiguous' is used not only with respect to identifying threats, but a similar ambiguity characterises the discussion of potential remedies and tools that can be used for alleviating the risks. For instance, the Strategy (2015, 8) indicates that good relations with neighbouring countries are the primary tool for threat elimination without ever specifying which countries are pertinent in this regard.

Whereas Czechia is careful and somewhat bashful if not hesitant, Estonia is very precise in terms of language and confident of its diagnosis, and thus does not employ any vaguely diplomatic manoeuvres. Where Czechia chooses a cautious writing style, avoiding naming particular threat actors or events, Estonia, in contrast, chooses a name-and-shame policy approach towards the RF, even though its Concept makes clear that 'Estonia's security policy is not directed against any other state' (Concept 2017, 2). Simultaneously, the Concept states candidly that 'Estonia will defend itself in any case, no matter how overwhelming the opponent might be' (Concept, 2017, 3), and a quick look at the map is enough to understand that there is only one potential enemy with an overwhelming power disparity. This impression is further reinforced by a declaration that 'if the state temporarily loses control over a part of its territory, Estonian citizens will engage in organised resistance in that area' (Concept 2017, 3). Again, even though Russia is not named per se, there is no doubt that a possible territorial dispute might come only from one direction. Indeed, Russia's 'increased military activity and aggressive behaviour' (Concept 2017, 4) is presented as threatening not only to Estonia but the whole of European security.

The deliberate semantic vagueness of the Czech Strategy leaves a lot of space for strategic manoeuvring. In this sense, the document is opportunistic as it does not lay out and then commit to one security strategy but rather is keen on a multi-vectoral policy whose direction can be chosen and amended as circumstances arise, balancing both 'the benefits of collective defense and security, as well as a commitment to contribute to common defence and security' (Strategy 2015, 6). It concludes with a statement that 'the security system of the Czech Republic needs to be perceived as an open system that continuously adapts to the current security situation' (Strategy 2015, 23). On the other hand, even the brief 'shopping list' of security threats in the document leaves no doubt that Czechia knows precisely what ought to be done and how, but simply cannot follow the route. The political and everyday reality – especially when it comes to the Czech-Russia relationship – goes almost against some parts of the text. For instance, the commitment 'to gradually increase the defense budget to 1.4% of GDP by 2020' (Strategy 2015, 3) is just a very opportunistic move trying to make a failure shine like success since in 2014 during the Wales Summit, the Allies pledged to increase their defence spending to two per cent of GDP by 2024.

In contrast to Czechia's opportunist stance, Estonia is very pragmatic in its approach. The Concept states matter-of-factly that 'being responsible for guarding the European Union's border, Estonia plays an important role in maintaining the reliability of the Schengen area' (Concept 2017, 5). While it is said plainly that Russia is the main enemy, there is no ideological tenaciousness involved. On the contrary, the Concept (2017, 10) makes it clear that Estonia wants to maintain good relationships with all its neighbours, and it will 'cooperate with Russia on a practical level as much as necessary and will keep the options for dialogue open. The development of democracy and the rule of law in Russia would serve Estonia's interests'. Simultaneously, one would be mistaken to regard Estonia as a lone wolf that is not restricted by others in its security-seeking behaviour. On the contrary, the Concept mentions several international institutions from the UN to OSCE to NATO to the EU whose efficiency and activity are deemed to be 'in Estonia's interests' and 'help to cope with security issues' (Concept 2017, 9). Efforts to show unity with other relevant actors are present and frequently referred to in the Concept (2017 3, 9, 11, 12). In a way, Estonia sets a perfect example for Czechia. This is how a small, vulnerable state ought to behave in terms of reaching an international compromise in line with its security interests.

In the Czech case, if we talk about compromise, it is more of a domestic nature. The Strategy, written as a collaborative task guided by the Ministry of Foreign Affairs, is a result of negotiations between the Parliament, government, and the wider security community of the Czech Republic, including 'the state and non-state spheres' (Strategy 2015, 4). We can expect these involved actors to differ in their goals and perceptions, which means that the purely political motives of some were confronted with expert views on the one hand and bureaucratic objectives on the other. However, the Strategy also recognises that 'the security policy of the Czech Republic is guided not only by specific interests but also by solidarity with allies in NATO and the EU' (Strategy 2015, 6) and thus cannot be separated from the Euro-Atlantic dimension of security. In fact, an entire chapter in the Strategy focuses on the 'collective dimension of defence and security'. However, while the document admits that 'it is often necessary to protect the security interests of the Czech Republic far beyond the borders of allied states', let alone the Czech borders (Strategy 2015, 6), no particulars are provided.

The Enemy images: invisibility cloak and a red flag

The first striking characteristic of the Czech enemy image is that it is barely there. The defining trait of the document's negative portrayal of Russia is that it remains invisible to a large extent. Since no direct mention of Russia or any specific Russia-related security incident appears in the Strategy, one could even think Russia is a non-issue in the Czech security dilemma (Holzer and Mareš Citation 2019). The Strategy sounds very ardent and proactive. By the contents of the text, one can assume that Czechia is genuinely working hard and contributes to the region's increased security. The Strategy does not sound like a document written by a state that is exploited for espionage, treated as a gateway to the West, or allows foreign operations on its territory. Nevertheless, against the invisibility of the potential enemy, these things have happened. Therefore, we can conclude that the coherence and connection between how the enemy image is cast in the written security strategy and the state's security policy actually looks like it is missing in the case of Czechia.

In its Strategy, Czechia does not acknowledge itself to be in any toxic relationship with any international or state entity. Which, of course, does not mean there is none. This takes us back to the detached and ambiguous style of writing when describing the security threats, aims and objectives. In a way, the Strategy surreptitiously points a finger at Russia hiding behind the 'some states' euphemism. We can read about the problem of the 'power aspirations of some states, which are increasingly ceasing to respect the international order and the basic principles of international law' (Strategy 2015, 8). Further, there are also 'growing ambitions of some actors, who are ready to use military force'. There are also some states who 'are seeking to revise the current international order' (Strategy 2015, 11) through a variety of means. An avid observer of international relations will know that there are not that many states who can perform this role of 'some states', especially when the range of threats is clarified as encompassing 'conventional and unconventional military means with non-military instruments (traditional and new media propaganda, intelligence disinformation, cyber-attacks, political and economic pressure, deployment of unidentified members of the armed forces'.

This implies that while Czechia knows Russia is not a friend, it maintains ties and hopes not to be stabbed in the back. The treacherous and recurring nature of this toxic relationship is perhaps best represented by the image of an abusive ex-husband that still can be seen in family photos or an alcoholic father whose problem everyone knows but no one talks about. Similarly, while Russia is repeatedly probing how far it can go by putting pressure on Czechia and using it to its benefit, the Strategy does not comment upon this as if in indifference. On the contrary, the indifferent approach helps to sustain this state of affairs. Consequently, when a toxic behaviour occurs, an indifferent (weak or absent) reaction follows as if Czechia knows that what has happened will happen again but hopes it will have the smallest harm and consequences – a sign of toxicity. At the same time, Russia knows it can do something again, precisely because of the indifferent reaction.

Where the Czech enemy is invisible, the Estonian adversary is simply unavoidable, if only for geographic reasons. Russia is 'on Estonia's border' and is seen as 'unpredictable, aggressive and provocative' (Concept 2017, 4). The word aggressive is used frequently to describe both Russia itself as well as its policies. Next to being a possible source of threat and offensive behaviour, the RF is also seen as a country lacking democracy and the rule of law. Such a deduction can be derived from various mentions in the Concept, especially when it says that the 'development of democracy and the rule of law in Russia would serve Estonia's interests' (Concept 2017, 4). Even though the Concept does not precisely frame Russia as a non-democratic country, the signs of inefficient democratic practices are present there. Also, the Ukrainian situation since 2014 and especially after February 2022 is a source of alarm for the Estonians, who are well aware that they could find themselves in the very same situation if it were not for their NATO and EU membership.

In contrast to Czechia, which seems not to be noticing the elephant in the room, Estonian documents make it clear that Russia is problematic, to say the least. In this regard, the Concept (2017, 4) portrays the RF as a great power already involved in conflicts and standing in sharp opposition to the West and the Euro-Atlantic collective security system. Therefore, we can conclude that there is a coherence between Estonian written and actual policy and state of affairs.

Discussion and Conclusions

The shared history of enmity between Czechia and Estonia has unsurprisingly influenced their intelligence agencies to repeatedly perceive the Russian Federation as a threat. This study tentatively affirms that the memory of a former foe contributes to contemporary enemy image projection, thus answering the first research question positively. However, as we delve deeper, the situation becomes more complex. Our conceptual overview of enmification suggested that apparent enmification should lead to similar, if not uniform, national security approaches. Although the Czech and Estonian national security documents were adopted two years apart, both aim for longitudinal perspective. The expressed perceptions of the security environment are firmly anchored in the international structures both countries share as well as their identical geopolitical and strategic orientations, coupled with occasional confrontational episodes with Russia. Hence, even though the documents differ by country and year of writing, the shared initial conditions – allies, collective security structures, threat perception – are undeniably evident upon careful analysis. However, the analysis also reveals differences in the style of the leading national security documents, indicating that even though enemy image projections are present, they do not lead to a uniform or archetypical enemy image, as proposed by Herrmann and Fischerkeller (Citation 1995).

When comparing the content and wording of the documents, it becomes evident that despite the similarities in threat perceptions, the most striking difference lies in how the security policy is formulated. Estonia's National Security Concept adopts a precise and straightforward 'name-and-shame' policy approach towards the RF, explicitly naming it as the alleged threat actor while enumerating possible dangers. In contrast, the Security Strategy of the Czech Republic adopts a more cautious and diplomatic writing style, avoiding specific mention of Russia as a potential threat actor. Instead, it provides a general and non-specific description. This suggests that the differences in enemy images are reflected in the formulation of security policy. Estonia's approach is pragmatic and confrontational, while Czechia adopts a careful and opportunist stance, allowing room for strategic maneuvering if necessary. The feedback loop between image creation and strategic discourse necessitates a more nuanced understanding of the influence of enemy images on state policy, going beyond a simple yes/no answer.

We show that no single uniform enemy image emerges from these documents, as it is not only the style but also the view of Russia that varies dramatically between them. The Czech enemy is invisible to a large extent, which is exacerbated by the fact that Russia is not mentioned by name even once. On the contrary, the image is blurred by ambiguous references to 'some states', which are revisionist and increasingly hostile. The Estonian enemy is not hiding under an invisibility cloak. Here, a red flag is raised to indicate an enemy which is as unavoidable as it is unpredictable, aggressive and provocative. The Estonian security Concept frequently uses the word 'aggressive' to describe both Russia and Russian policies. Therefore, we can conclude that the differences in enemy images are reflected in how security policy is formulated: Estonia chooses a name-and-shame policy approach towards the RF, which is precise and straightforward, yet very pragmatic, whereas Czechia chooses to use a careful and diplomatic writing style, avoiding naming particular threat actors or events. The carefully worded security Strategy ensures opacity regarding potentially hostile actors and at the same time grants ample space for strategic manoeuvring should the need arise.

This brings us to perhaps the most important ramification of the divergent enemy images. These documents indicate the position the state should take in the international arena. It is only natural that the security documents are not prepared outside of the societal, political, economic and geographic context of each country. However, we observe a lack of coherence and connection between how the enemy image is portrayed in the written security strategy and the actual policymaking in the case of Czechia. In contrast, congruity between the written and actual security policy behavior is palpable in Estonia. This implies that the theoretical dilemma of power disparity, often highlighted by existing literature, is less relevant than commonly assumed. Our study challenges the notion that appeasement is a default policy response in the face of inherent power imbalances. Even though Czechia is geographically insulated and seemingly less vulnerable, it takes a relatively less appeasing stance compared to Estonia, which directly faces its alleged enemy.

Furthermore, while Czech document is more circumspect than Estonian, neither can be called appeasing even in the broadest sense. However, this reluctance to pursue containment, at least in a latent form, might be subverted. It is worth noting that strategic repositioning can occur, potentially leading to a shift in enemy image and future strategy documents. As evidenced by the Czech government's recent public declaration of Russia's responsibility for explosions at ammunition depots resulting in some strong political statements regarding Russia's action to be an 'act of state terrorism' (iROZHLAS.cz Citation 2021), new approaches may emerge. Such developments may result in different wording and expression styles in future strategy documents, resembling Estonia's more explicit depiction of the enemy image. Nevertheless, a provocative question arises: if leading national security documents do not directly translate into policy action, why do we have them at all? Are security strategies becoming obsolete in the dynamic 21st-century environment?

It is crucial to acknowledge that the ongoing Russian aggression against Ukraine has dramatically altered the situation, prompting both countries to initiate the process of preparing new Security Strategies. Until these new strategies are approved, the current documents remain valid and binding, shaping national security policies to some extent. They serve as the foundation for all other sector- or topic-based security documents. However, our study also reveals that national security can rely on outdated material, which cannot be entirely disregarded as it represents a system baseline. Despite the dynamic transformation of the international milieu, our research offers valuable insights that can be applied in various settings where two actors have a difficult history but are not officially engaged in war or open conflict, In conclusion, this exploratory inquiry provides valuable insights into the divergent enemy images and their impact on security policy formulation and behavior. It emphasizes the complex interplay between enemy image projection, security strategy, and actual policymaking, challenging traditional assumptions and highlighting the contextual nuances at play. By shedding light on the significance of enemy images and their potential implications, this study contributes to our understanding of navigating strategic policy choices in uncertain and challenging circumstances.

Disclosure statement: No potential conflict of interest was reported by the author(s). Journal information. Print ISSN: 1478-2804 Online ISSN: 1478-2790. 4 issues per year. Journal of Contemporary European Studies is abstracted/indexed in: ANVUR (Class A) Clarivate Social Sciences Citation Index. CSA Worldwide Political Science Abstracts (Cambridge Scientific Abstracts). Current Abstracts, Humanities International Index. OCLC. SCOPUS. Sociological Abstracts. Taylor & Francis make every effort to ensure the accuracy of all the information (the "Content") contained in our publications. However, Taylor & Francis, our agents (including the editor, any member of the editorial team or editorial board, and any guest editors), and our licensors, make no representations or warranties whatsoever as to the accuracy, completeness, or suitability for any purpose of the Content. Any opinions and views expressed in this publication are the opinions and views of the authors, and are not the views of or endorsed by Taylor & Francis. The accuracy of the Content should not be relied upon and should be independently verified with primary sources of information. Taylor & Francis shall not be liable for any losses, actions, claims, proceedings, demands, costs, expenses, damages, and other liabilities whatsoever or howsoever caused arising directly or indirectly in connection with, in relation to, or arising out of the use of the Content. Terms & Conditions of access and use can be found at http://www.tandfonline.com/page/terms-and-conditions . Aims and scope: Journal of Contemporary European Studies (JCES) is a multidisciplinary journal for the empirical study of European societies, politics and cultures and is committed to the encouragement and promotion of debate on these topics. The central area focus of the journal is European in its broadest geographical definition and articles are welcomed from both cross-national and single-country specialists in European studies. The JCES differentiates itself from other European Studies journals in that it is not EU focused - its focus and interests extend beyond the EU - and in that it also provides a forum for debate about the theory and practice of 'area studies' and the advantages, scope and limitations of interdisciplinary. Furthermore, the Journal is enhanced by non-European perspectives. Research and review articles are published in the JCES, as well as an extensive section containing reviews on recently published books relating to European areas and themes. The journal publishes articles from a variety of disciplines within the humanities and social sciences, including sociology and social policy, politics and economics. Recent issues have considered a range of themes including: gender, migration, labour, identity and integration. Thematic issues are regularly published and the Editorial Board welcomes critical replies to articles that have appeared in earlier issues. of Contemporary European Studies. ISSN: (Print) (Online) Journal homepage: https://www.tandfonline.com/loi/cjea20. Enemy image? A comparative analysis of the Russian federation's role and position in the leading national security documents of Estonia and the Czech Republic. Monika Gabriela Bartoszewicz & Michaela Prucková. To cite this article: Monika Gabriela Bartoszewicz & Michaela Prucková (2023): Enemy image? A comparative analysis of the Russian federation's role and position in the leading national security documents of Estonia and the Czech Republic, Journal of Contemporary European Studies, DOI: 10.1080/14782804.2023.2224237. To link to this article: https://doi.org/10.1080/1 4782804.2023.2224237. © 2023 The Author(s). Published by Informa UK Limited, trading as Taylor & Francis Group. Published online: 14 Jun 2023. CONTACT Monika Gabriela Bartoszewicz monika.bartoszewicz@uit.no Department of Technology and Safety, UiT The Arctic University of Norway, Tromso, Norway. JOURNAL OF CONTEMPORARY EUROPEAN STUDIES. https://doi.org/10.1080 /14782804.2023.2224237. © 2023 The Author(s). Published by Informa UK Limited, trading as Taylor & Francis Group.

Notes to Chapters

Introduction

1. Associate Fellow at the Manohar Parrikar Institute for Defense Studies and Analyses, New Delhi. Swasti Rao: Europe's Re-awakening: The Arduous Task of Re-linking Security Concerns-May 09, 2023.

2. John Keiger, (The French riots threaten the state's very existence, The Spectator-02 July 2023

3. Yellow Vests Protests, 29 November 2018

4. Daniel Shapiro as a PhD student in Political Science at the University of Pennsylvania (Where do former Soviet countries stand? Euro-Atlantic Security Policy Brief. The European Leadership Network, June 2023.

5. Lilia Rzheutska noted (Ukraine: What's the worst-case scenario for Zaporizhzhia?

6. Drago Bosnic. The Ukraine Counteroffensive has Stalled: Failures of Germany's 'Leopard-2' Battle Tanks, Global Research, June 16, 2023

7. Expert, Jonathan Cook, author of three books on the Israeli-Palestinian conflict, and a winner of the Martha Gellhorn Special Prize for Journalism 'Russia-Ukraine War: Another Act of Terror Met by Western Media Silence Coverage of the destruction of the Kakhovka dam and Nord Stream pipelines shows a western media willing to priorities anti-Russian propaganda over facts. Global Research, 18 June, 2023.

8. Evening Standard, 30 June 2023

9. 06 July 2023, TASS News Agency

10. Dr. Gordon M. Hahn 'Dangerous Crossroads: The Zaporozhiya Nuclear Plant, Zelenskiy's Next Simulacra? Impending "False-Flag". Global Research, July 05, 2023. Russian & Eurasian Politics 4 July 2023.

11. Research Fellow at the Manohar Parrikar Institute for Defense Studies and Analyses, New Delhi, Rajneesh Singh (Retd) in his research paper (The Wagner Group: A Tool of Hybrid Warfare-May 31, 2023

Chapter 1: The Wagner Rebellion, Spetsnaz, GRU, the Chechen Militia, and the War in Ukraine

1. Russia's use of semi-state security forces: the case of the Wagner Group-Kimberly Martin, Post-Soviet Affairs, 27 February, 2019

2. 27 June 2023, TASS News Agency

3. 24 June 2023, Kommersant newspaper

4. President Putin addressed the nation

5. 24 February 2022, the head of MI6 tweet

6. Huw Dylan and Thomas J. Maguire (Secret Intelligence and public diplomacy in the Ukraine War-Survival Global Politics and Strategy-02 August 2022.

7. Ibid

8. Ambient Accountability: Intelligence Services in Europe and the Decline of State Secrecy. Professor Richard J. Aldrich and Daniela Richterova-PAIS, University of Warwick.

9. Dr Mark Galeotti (Russian intelligence is at (political) war-NATO Review 12 May 2017

10. Biometrics and Surveillance Camera Commissioner statement

11. The Home Office Biometrics and Surveillance Camera Commissioner survey in the second half of 2022

12. Ibid

13. Mark Gill in his well-documented analysis, (What does the UK government know about you? Comparitech a pro-consumer website-20 May, 2021

14. Kyle S. Cunliffe (Cyber-Enabled Tradecraft and Contemporary Espionage: Assessing the Implications of the Tradecraft Paradox on Agent Recruitment in Russia and China

15. Dylan, H.; Maguire, T.J. Secret Intelligence and public diplomacy in the Ukraine War. Survival, 64(4), 33-74.Survival, 02 Aug 2022

16. Kyle S. Cunliffe in his paper (Cyber-Enabled Tradecraft and Contemporary Espionage: Assessing the Implications of the Tradecraft Paradox on Agent Recruitment in Russia and China.

17. Intelligence and Security Committee of Parliament-Russia-21 July 2020

18. Sedat Laçine. The Effects of the Ukraine War on the European Balance of Power: From Dream World to Reality Modern Diplomacy, June 22, 2023.

19. Ibid

20. Ibid

21. Russian report-2020

22. Catarina P Thomson in her paper (Foreign Policy Attitudes and National Alignments in Times of Chinese and Russian Threats: Public Opinion across Three NATO Members, The RUSI Journal, 29 Jun 2022.

23. The UK National Cyber Security Centre

24. Ibid

25. Óscar Fernández, Marie Vandendriessche, Angel Saz-Carranza,Núria Agell and Javier Franco in their research paper, The impact of Russia's 2022 invasion of Ukraine on public perceptions of EU security and defence integration: a big data analysis, Journal of European Integration. Volume 45, 2023-Issue 3: 02 May 2023

26. Melina J. Dobson (The Last Forum of Accountability: State Secrecy, Intelligence and Freedom of Information in the United Kingdom

27. CONTEST: The United Kingdom's Strategy for Countering Terrorism-Presented to Parliament by the Secretary of State for the Home Department-June 2018

28. Integrated Review Refresh 2023: Responding to a more contested and volatile world, Presented to Parliament by the Prime Minister by Command of His Majesty- March 2023.

29. Loch K. Johnson:Pegasus affair: the end of privacy and cybersecurity?)

30. Secret, Confused and Illegal: How the UK Handles Personal Data under Prevent-2022

31. Director of the Surveillance Studies Centre, and professor of sociology at Queen's University, Kingston-Ontario, David Lyon (Security, Surveillance and Privacy, the Centre for International Governance Innovation (CIGI).

32. Director of the Surveillance Studies Centre, and professor of sociology at Queen's University, Kingston-Ontario, David Lyon (Security, Surveillance and Privacy, the Centre for International Governance Innovation (CIGI).

33. 24 May 2023, the EU Agency for Fundamental Rights releases a report-24 May 2023-Surveillance by intelligence services: Fundamental rights safeguards and remedies in the EU

34. Ibid

35. The FRA report of 2017

36. European Union Agency for Fundamental Rights-2023, an expert organization of intelligence and surveillance oversight in its recent report highlighted intelligence surveillance and oversight mechanisms in the European Union. This report is a partial update of the 2015 and 2017 European Union Agency for Fundamental Rights (FRA) reports entitled Surveillance by intelligence services: Fundamental rights safeguards and remedies in the EU

37. Ibid

38. Withdrawal Symptoms: party factions, political change and British foreign policy post-Brexit.Benjamin Martill, Journal of European Public Policy-2023

39. Dr Miah Hammond-Errey, Director of the Emerging Technology Program at the United States Studies Centre at the University of Sydney-09 February 2023

40. Surveillance Technology Challenges Political Culture of Democratic States. Inez Miyamoto

41. Artificial intelligence and EU security: the false promise of digital sovereignty. Andrea Calderaro & Stella Blumfelde

42. Professor Richard J. Aldrich and Daniela Richterova in their paper (Ambient Accountability: Intelligence Services in Europe and the Decline of State Secrecy. Professor (PAIS, University of Warwick

Chapter 2: Spyware-Pegasus, Surveillance and the EU Court of Human Rights

1. Mateusz Kolaszyński (Secret surveillance in Poland after Snowden Between secrecy and transparency

2. Ibid

3. Barbara Grabowska-Moroz in her paper (The Polish surveillance regime before the ECHR-about:intel-Stiftung Neue Verantwortung.

4. Editor of Notes from Poland (Critics of Polish government "systematically surveilled with spyware", finds EU report

5. Mateusz Kolaszyński in his research paper (Overseeing Surveillance powers-the Cases of Poland and Slovakia

6. Surveillance, Legal Restraints and Dismantling Democracy: Lessons from Poland Marcin Rojszczak-18 November 2020.

7. Surveillance, Legal Restraints and Dismantling Democracy: Lessons from Poland-Democracy and Security, Volume 17, 2021 - Issue 1, 18 November-2020), expert Marcin Rojszczak.

8. France's National Intelligence and Counterterrorism Coordinator, Laurent Nuñez-Belda (May 16, 2022, How Intelligence Supports EU Security-Internationale Politik Quarterly.

9. Professor Richard J. Aldrich and Daniela Richterova (Ambient Accountability: Intelligence Services in Europe and the Decline of State Secrecy-PAIS, University of Warwick.

10. Chris Jones (Analysis: Secrecy reigns at the EU's Intelligence Analysis Centre

11. Press Release: Marco Rubio, Senate Intel Republicans Demand Answers from Intelligence Community on Biden Laptop Letter- 01 June 2023.

12. Huw Dylan & Thomas J. Maguire (Secret Intelligence and public diplomacy in the Ukraine War-2022

13. Alex Younger, C of MI6, acknowledgement

14. The British Intelligence Services in the public domain: Thesis submitted in partial fulfilment of the requirements for the degree of PhD Department of International Politics Aberystwyth University 2019.

15. The Last Forum of Accountability: State Secrecy, Intelligence and Freedom of Information in the United Kingdom. Melina J. Dobson.

16. Professor Richard J. Aldrich and Daniela Richterova. Ambient Accountability: Intelligence Services in Europe and the Decline of State Secrecy -PAIS, University of Warwick.

17. Chapter 12: Why a militantly democratic lack of trust in state surveillance can enable better and more democratic security. Miguelángel Verde Garrido, Trust and Transparency in an Age of Surveillance Edited ByLora Anne Viola, Paweł Laidler-Taylor and Francis Group, 2021.

18. Miguelángel Verde Garrido. Chapter 12: Why a militantly democratic lack of trust in state surveillance can enable better and more democratic security. Miguelángel Verde Garrido, Trust and Transparency in an Age of Surveillance Edited ByLora Anne Viola, Paweł Laidler-Taylor and Francis Group, 2021.

19. Sune J. Andersen, Martin Ejnar Hansen & Philip H. J. Davies has noted some important aspects of intelligence oversight in their paper (Oversight and governance of the Danish intelligence community, Intelligence and National Security-04 January 2022.

20. Anton Mardasov. Al monitor April 22, 2023

21. Leaked Documents Reveal Depth of U.S. Spy Efforts and Russia's Military Struggles: The information, exposed on social media sites, also shows that U.S. intelligence services are eavesdropping on important allies. New York Times, April 8, 2023.

Chapter 3: The US Leaked Documents, President Trump Punch on the Face of US Intelligence Management, Artificial Intelligence Technologies, and the British Counter-Extremism and Counter-Intelligence Capabilities

1. The Intelligence War, Musa Khan Jalalzai, India, 2023

2. Spying with Little Eye. Musa Khan Jalalzai, India, 2023.

3. Ibid

4. Daily Telegraph London

5. Ibid

6. UK Research and Innovation

7. Artificial Intelligence Technologies: Regulation Volume 732: debated on Wednesday 3 May 2023, House of Common

8. The UK Big-3, Musa Khan Jalalzai, 2022 New Delhi India

9. The Times, 22 May 20110.

10. BBC 06 March 2023

11. Attacks in London and Manchester, Guardian, March 2017

12. A highly classified document explores how the Ukraine war could spill over into war with Iran. Ken Klippenstein, Murtaza Hussain, Intercept-April 13 2023.

13. How Trump's attacks on the intelligence community will come back to haunt him. Daniel Benjamin. January 12, 2017

14. Trump-Era Politicization: Code of Civil–Intelligence behaviour is Needed. John A. Gentry, International Journal of Intelligence and Counter-Intelligence, 01 Sep 2021.

15. 09 June 2023, former President Donald Trump was indicted on seven counts related to classified papers case. TASS News Agency and Reuter reported the indictment of Donald by a federal grand jury for retaining classified government documents and obstruction of justice.

16. 09 June 2023, Al Jazeera

17. Daniel Benjamin in his paper (How Trump's attacks on the intelligence community will come back to haunt him. Brookings, January 12, 2017

18. The politics of intelligence failures: power, rationality, and the intelligence process, Tom Lundborg, Intelligence and National Security 04 Dec 2022.

19. 01 June 2023, Modern Diplomacy

20. 01 June 2023. Intercept-April 13 2023

21. Ken Klippenstein and Murtaza Hussain in their analysis noted that these documents appeared abruptly while conflict in Ukraine and ongoing tensions in the Middle East are becoming more closely linked.

22. Fight against Mass Surveillance and Security Sector Reforms in Britain and the European Union.

23. On 4 March 2018, Sergei Skripal, a former Russian military officer and his daughter, Yulia Skripal, were poisoned in the city of Salisbury with a Novichok nerve agent

24. Chapter-1 of Fight against Mass Surveillance, and Security Sector Reforms in Britain and the European Union

25. Integrated Review Refresh 2023: Responding to a more contested and volatile world. Responding to a more contested and volatile world, Presented to Parliament by the Prime Minister by Command of His Majesty- March 2023.

26. Ibid

27. Ibid

28. Overview of the review noted that "the 2021 Integrated Review, Global Britain in a Competitive Age (IR2021).

29. Moreover, in 2023, the Integrated Review strongly responded 'to Russia's illegal invasion of Ukraine. Putin's act of aggression has precipitated the largest military conflict, refugee and energy crisis in Europe since the end of the Second World War.

30. Chapter-2 of Fight against Mass Surveillance, and Security Sector Reforms in Britain and the European Union

31. On 21 July 2020, Intelligence and Security Committee published a Russian report and warned government to take immediate action to effectively counter Russian espionage networks.

32. The Pentagon confirmed the leak's authenticity, while the documents were available online for months, U.S. officials weren't aware of the leak until April 6, 2023, the day it was reported by the New York Times. (What Secrets Are in the Leaked Pentagon Documents-and Who Leaked Them? Chas Danner.

33. The Associated Press reported that one document, March 9, 2023

34. New Statement, 13 October 2021

35. Doctor, journalist, editor, and broadcaster, Kamran Abbasi. Covid-19: politicisation, "corruption," and suppression of science, BMJ, 13 November 2020

36. Privacy International, December, 2021

37. Cyber security strategy. 2022-2030

38. Kingston Reif and Shannon Bugos- April 2021

39. Introduction. Fight against Mass Surveillance system and Security Sector Reforms in Britain and the European Union. Musa Khan Jalalzai. April 2021.

40. Manage Death Instead of Managing Live. Pp: 44

Chapter-4: Boris Johnson's Mismanagement of the State, Cross border Mobility, Interoperability, Interactivity and Interface of Different Policing and Intelligence Agencies, Foreign Espionage, MI5 and a Shift from Silhouette to a more Public-Facing role

1. Manage Deaths Instead of Managing Life the UK Government's Failure to Protect Communities and Care Homes during the Covid-19 Pandemic

2. Ibid

3. 13 January 2022, Al Jazeera

4. Intelligence war book, 2023, BBC-30 November 2021

5. On 25 July 2022, Human Rights Organization Liberty told the investigatory power tribunal that MI5 had breached surveillance laws since 2010, and provided false information to unlawfully obtain bulk surveillance warrants against the public.

6. 11 March, 2021, BBC reported (Home Office tests web-spying powers with help of UK internet firms) uneasiness of privacy rights organisations on web-spying business of Home Office.

7. Privacy International. December, 2021

8. Statewatch, monitoring the state and civil liberties in Europe (11 March 2021) in its report noted the covert human intelligence sources (Criminal Conduct Act).

9. Ibid

10. The Danish intelligence report-PET Report

11. Ibid

12. Nikita Belukhin (The Scandal in Denmark's Military Intelligence: Too Much Transparency? Modern Diplomacy, 25 March 2022

13. Daniel W B Lomas &Stephen Ward.

14. On 30 March 2022, in its year book, Swedish intelligence and Security Service warned that Sweden's security was being challenged on several fronts.

Chapter 5: False Sense of Supremacy: Emerging Technologies, the War in Ukraine, and the Risk of Nuclear Escalation. Marina Favaro and Heather Williams

1   An alternate definition comes from North Atlantic Treaty Organization (NATO) as denoting those technologies or scientific discoveries that are expected to reach maturity in the period 2020–2040; and are not yet widely in use or whose effects on defense [and] security are not entirely clear (NATO Science and Technology Organization [STO]).

2   It is unsurprising that we have seen deep fake technology deployed by Russia in the war in Ukraine, due it its lower price tag (relative to other emerging technologies surveyed in our study) and its confluence with Russia's subthreshold warfare doctrine. Furthermore, using AI to enhance active measures and influence campaigns is a natural outgrowth of Russia's history of information operations.

3   In June 2022, the Russian military admitted that it is also using Lancet in Ukraine, possibly adding more fuel to the debate about the use of AI in this war, considering that this particular munition was advertised as "highly autonomous" for target identification and destruction (Tass Citation2022).

References

Acton, J. M. 2013. Reclaiming Strategic Stability. Carnegie Endowment for International Peace. https://carnegieendowment.org/2013/02/05/reclaiming-strategic-stability-pub-51032. [Google Scholar]

Acton, J. M. 2018b. "Escalation Through Entanglement: How the Vulnerability of Command-And-Control Systems Raises the Risks of an Inadvertent Nuclear War." International Security 43 (1): 56–99. https://doi.org/10.1162/isec_a_00320. [Crossref], [Web of Science ®], [Google Scholar]

Allen, G. C. 2022. Across Drones, AI, and Space, Commercial Tech is Flexing Military Muscle in Ukraine. Center for Strategic and International Studies. https://www.csis.org/analysis/across-drones-ai-and-space-commercial-tech-flexing-military-muscle-ukraine. [Google Scholar]

Antoniuk, D. 2022. How electronic warfare is reshaping the war between Russia and Ukraine The Record by Recorded Future. https://therecord.media/how-electronic-warfare-is-reshaping-the-war-between-russia-and-ukraine/ [Google Scholar]

Atherton, K. D. 2022. The US Could Get a Peek into Russia's Electronic Warfare Secrets Thanks to Ukraine. Popular Science. https://www.popsci.com/technology/russian-electronic-warfare-equipment-ukraine/. [Google Scholar]

Bendett, S., and J. Edmonds. 2022. "Russian Military Autonomy in Ukraine: Four Months In." CNA. https://www.cna.org/reports/2022/07/russian-military-autonomy-in-ukraine-four-months-in [Google Scholar]

Borowitz, M. 2022. War in Ukraine highlights the growing strategic importance of private satellite companies - especially in times of conflict. Space.com, August 29, 2022. https://www.space.com/ukraine-war-strategic-importance-private-satellites [Google Scholar]

Cooper, H., J. Barnes, and E. Schmitt. 2022. "Russian Military Leaders Discussed Use of Nuclear Weapons, U.S. Officials Say." New York Times, November 2, 2022. https://www.nytimes.com/2022/11/02/us/politics/russia-ukraine-nuclear-weapons.html. [Google Scholar]

Davies, D. 2022. "Ukraine is Inventing a New Way to Fight on the Digital Battlefield." NPR, March 31, 2022. https://www.npr.org/2022/03/31/1089660395/ukraine-is-inventing-a-new-way-to-fight-on-the-digital-battlefield [Google Scholar]

Dougherty, J. 2022. "Russians in the Dark About True State of War Amid Country's Orwellian Media Coverage." CNN, April 3, 2022. https://edition.cnn.com/2022/04/03/media/russia-media-ukraine-cmd-intl/index.html [Google Scholar]

Favaro, M. 2021. Weapons of Mass Distortion. Centre for Science & Security Studies. https://www.kcl.ac.uk/csss/assets/weapons-of-mass-distortion.pdf. [Google Scholar]

Favaro, M., N. Renic, and U. Kuhn. 2022. "New Research Report: Forecasting the Future Impact of Emerging Technologies on International Stability and Human Security." Institut für Friedensforschung und Sicherheitspolitik (IFSH). https://ifsh.de/en/news-detail/new-research-report-forecasting-the-future-impact-of-emerging-technologies-on-international-stability-and-human-security [Google Scholar]

Galeotti, M. 2022. "Why is Putin Firing a Hypersonic Missile in Ukraine?" The Spectator, March. https://www.spectator.co.uk/article/why-is-putin-firing-a-hypersonic-missile-in-ukraine- [Google Scholar]

Gordon, A., and L. Franceschi-Bicchierai. 2022. "Hackers Create Traffic Jam in Moscow by Ordering Dozens of Taxis at Once Through App." VICE, September 2, 2022. https://www.vice.com/en/article/y3pbgy/hackers-create-traffic-jam-in-moscow-by-ordering-dozens-of-taxis-at-once-through-app [Google Scholar]

Graham, T., and J. D. Thompson. 2023. "Russian Government Accounts are Using a Twitter Loophole to Spread Disinformation." The Conversation, March 15, 2022. https://theconversation.com/russian-government-accounts-are-using-a-twitter-loophole-to-spread-disinformation-178001 [Google Scholar]

Guyer, J. 2022. "The West is Testing Out a Lot of Shiny New Military Tech in Ukraine." Vox, September 21, 2022. https://www.vox.com/2022/9/21/23356800/us-testing-tech-ukraine-russia-war [Google Scholar]

Hersman, R., S. Claeys, and H. Williams. 2022. "Integrated Arms Control in an Era of Strategic Competition." Nuclear Network. https://nuclearnetwork.csis.org/integrated-arms-control-in-an-era-of-strategic-competition/. [Google Scholar]

Jankowicz, M. 2022. "Ukraine Posts Videos It Says Show Bayraktar Drones Blowing Up Russian Armor, Further Cementing Their Heroic Status." Yahoo! News. March 15, 2022. https://news.yahoo.com/ukraine-posts-videos-says-show-170137072.html?guccounter=1. [Google Scholar]

Jankowicz, N. 2020. How to Lose the Information War. I.B. Tauris, Bloomsbury Publishing Plc. https://doi.org/10.5040/9781838607715. [Crossref], [Google Scholar]

Kahn, H. 1965. On Escalation. Abingdon-on-Thames, Oxfordshire: Routledge. [Google Scholar]

Kahn, L. 2022. "How Ukraine is Remaking War." Foreign Affairs, September 1, 2022. https://www.foreignaffairs.com/ukraine/how-ukraine-remaking-war [Google Scholar]

Kavanagh, J., and M. D. Rich. 2018. "Truth Decay: An Initial Exploration of the Diminishing Role of Facts and Analysis in American Public Life". Santa Monica, CA: RAND Corporation. https://www.rand.org/pubs/research_reports/RR2314.html [Google Scholar]

Kent, G. A., and D. E. Thaler. 1990. First-Strike Stability: A Methodology for Evaluating Strategic Forces. Santa Monica, CA: Rand. [Google Scholar]

Khan, I. 2022. "Zelenskyy Humanizes Ukraine's Plight in His Social Media Messaging." CNET, March 17, 2022. https://www.cnet.com/news/politics/zelenskyy-humanizes-ukraines-plight-in-his-social-media-messaging/ [Google Scholar]

Kirton, D. 2022. "China's DJI Halts Russia, Ukraine Sales to Prevent Use of Its Drones in Combat." Reuters, April 27, 2022. https://www.reuters.com/technology/chinese-drone-maker-dji-suspends-business-activities-russia-ukraine-2022-04-26/ [Google Scholar]

Knight, W. 2022. "Russia's Killer Drone in Ukraine Raises Fears About AI in Warfare." Wired, March 17, 2022. https://www.wired.com/story/ai-drones-russia-ukraine/ [Google Scholar]

Lin, H. 2012. "Escalation Dynamics and Conflict Termination in Cyberspace." Strategic Studies Quarterly 6 (3). http://www.jstor.org/stable/10.2307/26267261. [Google Scholar]

McGee, W. 2022. "Video: Ukrainian Forces Take Out Russian Equipment with Turkish Drones." Newsweek, March 25, 2022. https://www.newsweek.com/video-ukrainian-forces-take-out-russian-equipment-turkish-drones-1691952 [Google Scholar]

Microsoft Digital Security Unit. 2022. An overview of Russia's cyberattack activity in Ukraine. Microsoft. https://query.prod.cms.rt.microsoft.com/cms/api/am/binary/RE4Vwwd [Google Scholar]

Oremus, W. 2022. "Analysis | Social Media Wasn't Ready for This War. It Needs a Plan for the Next One."|"analysis | Social Media Wasn't Ready for This War. It Needs a Plan for the Next One." The Washington Post, March 26, 2022. https://www.washingtonpost.com/technology/2022/03/25/social-media-ukraine-rules-war-policy/ [Google Scholar]

Reuters. 2022b. "Russia Space Agency Head Says Satellite Hacking Would Justify War -Report." Reuters. March 2, 2022. https://www.reuters.com/world/russia-space-agency-head-says-satellite-hacking-would-justify-war-report-2022-03-02/. [Google Scholar]

Schelling, T. C., and M. H. Halperin. 1961. Strategy and Arms Control. Eastford, CT: Martino Publishing. [Google Scholar]

Simonite, T. 2022. "A Zelensky Deepfake Was Quickly Defeated. the Next One Might Not Be." Wired, March 17, 2022. https://www.wired.com/story/zelensky-deepfake-facebook-twitter-playbook/ [Google Scholar]

Smith, B. 2022. Defending Ukraine: Early Lessons from the Cyber War. Microsoft On the Issues. https://blogs.microsoft.com/on-the-issues/2022/06/22/defending-ukraine-early-lessons-from-the-cyber-war/. [Google Scholar]

Tannehill, B. 2023. "What the Drone Strikes on the Kremlin Reveal About the War in Ukraine." The Atlantic, May 4, 2023. https://www.theatlantic.com/

ideas/archive/2023/05/ukraine-drones-long-range-munitions-alternative-kremlin-attack-accusation/673951/ [Google Scholar]

Tass. 2022. "Kamikaze Drones Successfully Used in Russia's Special Operation in Ukraine - Defense Firm." TASS, June 8, 2022. https://tass.com/defense/1462311 [Google Scholar]

Tucker, P. 2022. "US Working on AI to Predict Ukraine's Ammo and Weapons Needs." Defense One, September 20, 2022. https://www.defenseone.com/technology/2022/09/us-working-ai-predict-ukraines-ammo-and-weapons-needs/377429/ [Google Scholar]

US News. 2022. "Russia Says It Has Deployed Kinzhal Hypersonic Missile Three Times in Ukraine." US News, August 21, 2022. https://www.usnews.com/news/world/articles/2022-08-21/russia-says-it-has-deployed-kinzhal-hypersonic-missile-three-times-in-ukraine [Google Scholar]

Vectra. 2022. "As the War in Ukraine Spirals, Vectra AI Announces Free Cybersecurity Services: #microsoft: #hacking: #cybersecurity." National Cyber Security News Today, February 28, 2022. https://www.vectra.ai/news/as-the-war-in-ukraine-spirals-vectra-ai-announces-free-cybersecurity-services [Google Scholar]

Zakrzewski, C., and G. De Vynck. 2022. "The Ukrainian Leader Who is Pushing Silicon Valley to Stand Up to Russia." The Washington Post, March 3, 2022. https://www.washingtonpost.com/technology/2022/03/02/mykhailo-fedorov-ukraine-tech/ [Google Scholar]

Chapter 6: The Intelligence Dilemma: Proximity and Politicization–Analysis of External Influences. Beth Eisenfeld

1   Uri Bar-Joseph, "The Politicization Of Intelligence: A Comparative Study," International Journal of Intelligence and CounterIntelligence 26:2 (2013): 347-369, doi:10.1080/08850607.2013.758000; Richard K. Betts, "Politicization of Intelligence Costs and Benefits," in Paradoxes of Strategic Intelligence: Essays in Honor of Michael I. Handel, eds. Richard K. Betts and Thomas G. Mahnken (London: Frank Kass, 2003), 57-76, available at:http://people.exeter.ac.uk/mm394/Richard%20Betts%20Paradoxes%20of%20Intelligence%20Essays%20in%20Honor%20of%20Michael%20I.%20Handel%20%202003.pdf; Richard K. Betts, Enemies of Intelligence: Knowledge and Power in American National Security (New York: Columbia University Press, 2007); Robert M. Gates, "Guarding Against Politicization," Studies in Intelligence 36:1 (1992): 5-13, available at:https://www.cia.gov/library/center-for-the-study-of-intelligence/kent-csi/volume-36-number-1/pdf/v36i1a01p.pdf; Arthur S. Hulnick, "The Intelligence Producer–Policy Consumer Linkage: A Theoretical Approach," Intelligence and National Security 1:2 (1986): 212-233, doi:10.1080/02684528608431850; Sherman Kent, Strategic Intelligence for American World Policy (Princeton: Princeton University Press, 1949); Mark M. Lowenthal, Intelligence: From Secrets to Policy, 6th

ed. (Los Angeles: CQ Press, 2015); Steven Marrin, "At Arm's Length or at the Elbow? Explaining the Distance Between Analysts and Decisionmakers," International Journal of Intelligence and CounterIntelligence 20:3 (2007): 401-414, doi:10.1080/08850600701249733; Joshua R. Rovner, "Intelligence-Policy Relations and the Problem of Politicization," (doctoral dissertation, MIT, 2009), available at: http://dspace.mit.edu/handle/1721.1/46633; Richard L. Russell, "Achieving All-Source Fusion in the Intelligence Community," in Handbook of Intelligence Studies, ed. Loch K. Johnson (New York: Routledge, 2007), 189-199; Gregory F. Treverton and Wilhelm Agrell, National Intelligence Systems: Current Research and Future Prospects (New York: Cambridge University Press, 2009).

2   Jeet Heer, "The Danger of Politicizing Intelligence," The New Republic, December 12, 2016, available at: https://newrepublic.com/article/139275/danger-politicizing-intelligence.

3   Stephen Marrin, "Revisiting Intelligence and Policy: Problems with Politicization and Receptivity," Intelligence and National Security 28:1 (2013): 4, doi:10.1080/02684527.2012.749063.

4   Betts, "Politicization of Intelligence;" Michael I. Handel, "The Politics of Intelligence," Intelligence & National Security 2:4 (1987): 5-46, doi:10.1080/02684528708431914; Hulnick, "The Intelligence Producer;" Russell, "Achieving All-Source Fusion;" Betts and Mahnken, Paradoxes of Strategic Intelligence; Gates, "Guarding Against Politicization;" Kent, Strategic Intelligence; Lowenthal, Intelligence: From Secrets to Policy; Stephen Marrin, "Rethinking Analytic Politicization," Intelligence and National Security 28:1 (2013), 32-54, doi:10.1080/02684527.2012.749064; Rovner, "Intelligence-Policy Relations"; Treverton and Agrell, National Intelligence Systems.

5   Maciej Bartkowski, "The Study of Politicization: The Case of the UN," Rubikon (2001): 1-11, availableat: http://webcache.googleusercontent.com/search?q=cache:xQ2ML_VjuA4J:maciejbartkowski.com/wp-content/uploads/2013/10/Maciej-Bartkowski.-The-Study-of-Politicization.-The-Case-of-the-UN.pdf+&cd=1&hl=en&ct=clnk&gl=us; Jonathan Craft and Michael Howlett, "The Dual Dynamics of Policy Advisory Systems: The Impact of Externalization and Politicization on Policy Advice," Policy & Society 32:3 (2013): 187- 197, doi:10.1016/j.polsoc.2013.07.001; Saville R. Davis, "Documentary Study of the Politicization of UNESCO," Bulletin of the American Academy of Arts and Sciences 29:3 (1975): 6-20, doi:10.2307/3824003; Cynthia R. Farina et al., "Rulemaking in 140 Characters or Less: Social Networking and Public Participation in Rulemaking," Pace Law Review 31:1 (2011): 382-468, available at: http://digitalcommons.pace.edu/plr/vol31/iss1/8/; Michael Howlett and Andrea Migone. "Searching for Substance: Externalization, Politicization and the Work of Canadian Policy Consultants 2006-2013," Central European Journal of Public Policy 7:1 (2013): 112-133, available at: http://www.cejpp.eu/index.php/ojs/article/view/143/110;

Brandon Rottinghaus, "'Dear Mr. President': The Institutionalization and Politicization if Public Opinion Mail in the White House," Political Science Quarterly 121:3 (2006): 451- 476, doi:10.1002/j.1538-165X.2006.tb00578.x; Peter W. Singer, "Washington's Think Tanks: Factories to Call Our Own," The Brookings Institution, (August 12, 2010): 1-9, available at: http://www.brookings.edu/research/articles/2010/08/13-think-tanks-singer; Jose D. Villalobos and Justin S. Vaughn. "Presidential Staffing and Public Opinion: How Public Opinion Influences Politicization.

6   Kari Palonen, "Four Times of Politics: Policy, Polity, Politicking, and Politicization,"Alternatives: Global, Local, Political 28:2 (2003): 181, available at:http://www.jstor.org/stable/40645073; See also Roger Chickering, Karl Lamprecht: A German Academic Life (1856-1915), (New Jersey: Humanities Press), 315.

7   Ibid., 181.

8.   Ibid., 182; "Politicize," Online Etymology Dictionary, available at:http://www.etymonline.com/index.php?term=politicize&allowed_in_frame=0.

9   Alexander Yakobson, Elections and Electioneering in Rome: A Study in the Political System of the Late Republic (Stuttgart: F. Steiner, 1999), 180.

10   Alison Futrell, Blood in the Arena: The Spectacle of Roman Power (Austin: University of Texas Press, 2001), 23.

11   Palonen, "Four Times of Politics," 182.

12   Marrin, "Revisiting Intelligence and Policy," 2.

13   Scholars writing about negative connotations include Betts, "Politicization of Intelligence," Handel, "The Politics of Intelligence," and Kent, Strategic Intelligence. Scholars writing about politicization from the intelligence-policy process perspective include Betts, Enemies of Intelligence; Glenn Hastedt, "The Politics of Intelligence and the Politicization of Intelligence: The American Experience," Intelligence and National Security 28:1 (2013): 5-31, doi:10.1080 /02684527.2012.749062; Marrin, "Rethinking Analytic Politicization;" Joshua R. Rovner, "Is Politicization Ever a Good Thing?" Intelligence and National Security 28:1 (2013): 55-67, doi:10.1080/02684527.2012.749065, and Nathan Woodard, "Tasting the Forbidden Fruit: Unlocking the Potential of Positive Politicization," Intelligence and National Security 28:1 (2013): 91-108, doi:10.1080/02684527.2012.749066.

14   Loch Johnson, "Bricks and mortar for a theory of intelligence," Comparative Strategy 22:1 (2003): 11, doi:10.1080/0149593039013048111.

15   John C. Gannon, "Managing Analysis in the Information Age," in Analyzing intelligence: Origins, Obstacles, and Innovation, eds. Roger Z. George and James B. Bruce (Washington, D.C.: Georgetown University Press, 2008), 221.

16 Joshua R. Rovner, Fixing the Facts: National Security and the Politics of Intelligence (Ithaca: Cornell University Press, 2011), 5.

17 Harry H. Ransom, "The Politicization of Intelligence," in Intelligence and the Intelligence Policy in a Democratic Society, ed. Stephen. J. Cimbala (Dobbs Ferry, NY: Transnational Publishers, Inc., 1987), 26.

18 Handel, "The Politics of Intelligence," 6.

19 Gregory F. Treverton, "Intelligence Analysis: Between 'Politicization' and Irrelevance," in Analyzing intelligence: Origins, Obstacles, and Innovation, eds. Roger Z. George and James B. Bruce (Washington, D.C.: Georgetown University Press, 2008), 93.

20 Ibid.

21 Hastedt, "The Politics of Intelligence," 5-6.

22 Marrin, "Rethinking Analytic Politicization," 34.

23 Ibid., 32.

24 Ibid.

25 Treverton and Agrell, National Intelligence Systems, 201.

26 Betts, "Politicization of Intelligence;" Betts, Enemies of Intelligence; Jack Davis, "Sherman Kent and the Profession of Intelligence Analysis," Kent Center Occasional Papers 1:5 (2002): 1-16, available at: https://www.cia.gov/library/kent-centeroccasional-papers/pdf/OPNo5.pdf; Russell, "Achieving All-Source Fusion;" H. Bradford Westerfield, "Inside Ivory Bunkers: CIA Analysts Resist Managers' 'Pandering'–Part II," International Journal of Intelligence & Counterintelligence 10:1 (1997), 19-54, doi:10.1080/08850609708435332

27 Kent, Strategic Intelligence.

28 Ibid., 180.

29 Betts, Enemies of Intelligence, 76.

30 Ibid.

31 Gates, "Guarding Against Politicization."

32 Westerfield, "Inside Ivory Bunkers," 52.

33 Russell, "Achieving All-Source Fusion" Kent, Strategic Intelligence; Gates, "Guarding Against Politicization."

34 Note: Bar-Joseph in "The Politicization of Intelligence" considers the top-down portion of the model; Betts in "Politicization of Intelligence," contemplates the top-down, bottomup, and bi-directional positions, and Riste considers the inside out aspect in Olav Riste, "The Intelligence-Policy Maker Relationship and the Politicization of Intelligence," in National Intelligence Systems: Current Research and Future Prospects, eds, Gregory F. Treverton and Wilhelm Agrell, (New York: Cambridge University Press, 2009), 179-209.

35 Betts, "Politicization of Intelligence," 58.

36 Betts, "Enemies of Intelligence," 77.

37 Betts, "Politicization of Intelligence," 59.

38 Riste, "The Intelligence-Policy Maker Relationship," 181.

39 Rovner, "Is Politicization Ever;" Joshua R. Rovner, "Intelligence in the Twitter Age,"International Journal of Intelligence and CounterIntelligence 26:2 (2013): 260-271, doi:10.1080/08850607.2013.757996.

40 Richard N. Haass, "Think Tanks and U.S. Foreign Policy: A Policy-Maker's Perspective," in The Role of Think Tanks in U.S. Foreign Policy, ed. Michael T. Scanlin, U.S. Foreign Policy Agenda 4:3 (2002): 5.

41 James G. McGann, 2016 Global Go to Think Tank Index Report (Philadelphia: Think Tanks and Civil Societies Program, University of Pennsylvania, January 26, 2017), 25-26, available at:http://repository.upenn.edu/cgi/viewcontent. cgi?article=1011&context=think_tanks.

42 Donald D. Abelson, "Old World, New World: The Evolution and Influence of Foreign Affairs Think-Tanks," International Affairs 90:1 (2014): 125-142, doi:10.1111/1468-2346.12099.

43 Ibid.

44 Ibid.

45 Ibid., 11.

46 McGann, 2016 Global Go to Think Tank Report, 7.

47 Ibid.

48 Abelson, "Old World, New World."

49 Andrew Rich, "The Politics of Expertise in Congress and the News Media," Social Science Quarterly 82:3 (2001): 585, doi:10.1111/0038-4941.00044.

50 Abelson, "Old World, New World;" Haass, "Think Tanks and U.S. Foreign Policy;"McGann, 2016 Global Go to Think Tank Report; Andrew Rich. Think Tanks, Public Policy, and the Politics of Expertise (Cambridge: Cambridge University Press, 2004); Michael T. Scanlin, ed., "The Role of Think Tanks in U.S. Foreign Policy," U.S. Foreign Policy Agenda 4:3 (2002).

51 Abelson, "Old World, New World," 138.

52 Haass, "Think Tanks and U.S. Foreign Policy," 7.

53 Singer, "Washington's Think Tanks," 2.

54 Ibid.

55 The Heritage Foundation, Blueprint for a New Administration: Priorities for the President (Washington, D.C.: The Heritage Foundation,

2016). Available at:http://thf_media.s3.amazonaws.com/2016/BlueprintforaNewAdministration.pdf.

56 "Blueprint for a New Administration: Priorities for the President," The Heritage Foundation, November 1, 2016, available at:http://www.heritage.org/conservatism/report/blueprint-new-administrationpriorities-the-president.

57 Strobe Talbott, "The Brookings Institution: How a Think Tank Works," in The Role of Think Tanks in U.S. Foreign Policy, ed. Michael T. Scanlin, U.S. Foreign Policy Agenda 4:3 (2002): 19.

58 Haass, "Think Tanks and U.S. Foreign Policy;" Michael D. Rich, "RAND: How Think Tanks Interact with the Military," in The Role of Think Tanks in U.S. Foreign Policy, ed. Michael T. Scanlin, U.S. Foreign Policy Agenda 4:3 (2002).

59 To validate this assertion, the author conducted searches using terms such as national security, national defense, domestic policy, and intelligence on the websites of 10 randomly selected think tanks. These included Center for a New American Security, Belfer Center for Science and International Affairs, Brookings Institution, Cato Institute, Center for American Progress, Center for Strategic and International Studies, Council on Foreign Relations, Hoover Institution, RAND, and The Heritage Foundation.

60 Murray Weidenbaum, "Measuring the Influence of Think Tanks," Society 47:2 (2010):135, doi:10.1007/s12115-009-9292-8.

61 Abelson, "Old World, New World," 138; Haass, "Think Tanks and U.S. Foreign Policy;"Singer, "Washington's Think Tanks," 2.

62 Lars Nicander, "The Role of Think Tanks in the U.S. Security Policy Environment," International Journal of Intelligence & Counterintelligence 28:3 (2015): 494 doi:10.1080/08850607.2015.1022462.

63 Weidenbaum, "Measuring the Influence of Think Tanks," 136.

64 Laura M. Calkins, "Patrolling the Ether: US-UK Open Source Intelligence Cooperation and the BBC's Emergence as an Intelligence Agency, 1939-1948," Intelligence and National Security 26 no. 1 (2011): 1-22, available at: doi:10.1080/02684527.2011.556355.

65 Rovner, "Intelligence in the Twitter Age."

66 Eric Denécé, "The Revolution in Intelligence Affairs: 1989–2003," International Journal of Intelligence and CounterIntelligence 27:1 (2014): 34, doi:10.1080/08850607.2014.842796.

67 Rovner, "Intelligence in the Twitter Age," 261.

68 Ibid., 263.

69 Rovner, "Intelligence in the Twitter Age," 268.

70 Florina C. Matei, "The Media's Role in Intelligence Democratization," International Journal of Intelligence and CounterIntelligence 27:1 (2014): 81, doi:10.1080/08850607.2014.842806.

71 Ibid., 95.

72 Felicitas Macgilchrist and Ines Bohmig, "Blogs, Genes and Immigration: Online Media and Minimal Politics," Media, Culture & Society 34:1 (2012): 84, doi:10.1177/0163443711427201.

73 Matei, "The Media's Role," 92.

74 Loch K. Johnson, (2014) "Intelligence Shocks, Media Coverage, and Congressional Accountability, 1947–2012," Journal of Intelligence History 13, no.1 (2014), 1-21, doi:10.1080/16161262.2013.811905

75 Ibid., 7.

76 Robert Dover and Michael Goodman (eds.). Spinning Intelligence: Why Intelligence Needs the Media, Why the Media Needs Intelligence. (New York: Columbia University Press, 2009.

77 Influence & Lobbying, The Center for Responsive Politics, accessed January 17, 2017, available at: https://www.opensecrets.org/influence/.

78 US House of Representatives Lobbying Disclosure Notices and Announcements website accessed January 17, 2017, available at: http://lobbyingdisclosure.house.gov/.

79 Ibid.

80 Lobbying Database, The Center for Responsive Politics, accessed January 18, 2017, available at: https://www.opensecrets.org/lobby/.

81 The author created this graphic using the data as coded and categorized by the CRP. According to the CRP, lobbyists report activities on the LD-2 Disclosure forms under one of 80 issue areas. The author relied on the CPR to code issues properly. The CRP also makes individual reports filed available to the public via its website. To confirm coding for intelligence issues, the author inspected a random sample of reports from the elements in Figure 1, searching through disclosure forms looking specifically at the category Intelligence (as an issue) and the code "INT" to validate lobbying for intelligence related topics. Random samples of disclosure forms for other categories also revealed the "INT" coding. While it is difficult to ascertain the topic of discussions lobbyists conducted with respective parties without having been present at the meetings, the number of clients and the number of files noted serve as proxy measures indicating proximity and influence analogous to methods suggested by Weidenbaum, McKay, and Nicander.

82 The Center for Responsive Politics, Intelligence Issue Profile, January 18, 2017, available at: https://www.opensecrets.org/lobby/issuesum.php?id=INT&year=2016.

83 Ibid., available at:https://www.opensecrets.org/lobby/issue_spec. php?id=INT&year=2016. For more information on these legislative matters, see https://www.congress.gov/.

84 Amy McKay, "Buying policy? The Effects of Lobbyists' Resources on Their Policy Success," Political Research Quarterly 65:4 (2012): 910, doi:10.1177/1065912911424285.

85 Ibid., 908.

86 Ransom, "The Politicization of Intelligence," 44.

87 Ibid., 44.

88 Handel, "The Politics of Intelligence," 13.

89 Ibid., 9.

90 Ibid., 24.

91 Gates, "Guarding Against Politicization."

92 Betts, "Politicization of Intelligence," 59.

93 Ibid., 58.

References

Barnes, J. E., & Goldman, A. (2020, October 31). Trump is said to set aside intelligence career intelligence briefer to hear from advisers instead. New York Times. https://www.nytimes.com/2020/10/30/us/politics/trump-intelligence-briefings.html

Bruck, C. (2016, August 1). The Guantánamo failure. The New Yorker.

Fuller, C. J. (2017). See it/shoot it: The secret history of the CIA's lethal drone program. New Haven, Connecticut: Yale University Press.

Gibbon, E. (1952). The decline and fall of the Roman Empire. New York: Viking.

Hayden, M. V. (2016). Playing to the edge: American intelligence in an age of terror. New York: Penguin.

Johnson, L. K. (1985). A season of inquiry: The senate intelligence investigation. Lexington: University Press of Kentucky.

Johnson, L. K. (2018). Spy watching: Intelligence accountability in the United States. New York: Oxford University Press.

Footnotes

1 For illustrations in the public literature of modern techint in the domain of satellite camera-surveillance (imint or "imagery intelligence"), see Bruce Berkowitz, The National Reconnaissance Office at 50 Years: A Brief History (Chantilly, VA: U.S National Reconnaissance Office, Center for the Study of National Reconnaissance, Washington, D.C., 2011); Dino A. Brugioni, From Balloons to Blackbirds: Reconnaissance, Surveillance and Imagery

intelligence, How It Evolved, The Intelligence Professional Series, No. 1 (McLean, VA: Association of Former Intelligence Officers, 1993); on listening and sensing devices in space, Matthew M. Aid, The Secret Sentry: The Untold History of the National Security Agency (New York: Bloomsbury Press, 2009), and underwater, James Bamford, The Puzzle Palace: Inside the National Security Agency (New York: Penguin, 1983), and Jeffrey T. Richelson, The US Intelligence Community, 7th ed. (Boulder, Colorado: Westview, 2016); on drones as intelligence-collection platforms, Sarah E. Kreps, Drones: What Everyone Needs to Know (New York: Oxford University Press, 2016); on asset communications with their handlers, Frederick P. Hitz, The Great Game: The Myth and Reality of Espionage (New York: Knopf, 2004); and on CIA disguises, Antonio J. Mendez with Malcolm McConnell, The Master of Disguise: My Secret Life in the CIA (New York: Morrow, 2000). Insightful general works on techint include: Robert M. Clark, The Technical Collection of Intelligence (Washington, D.C: CQ Press, 2011); Mark M. Lowenthal, Intelligence: From Secrets to Policy 7th ed (Thousand Oaks, CA: CQ Press/SAGE, 2017); Mark M. Lowenthal and Robert M. Clark, eds., The Five Disciplines of Intelligence Collection (Washington, D.C.: CQ Press, 2016); and Robert Wallace and H. Keith Melton, with Henry Robert Schlesinger, Spycraft: The Secret History of the CIA's Spytechs, from Communism to Al-Qaeda (New York: Penguin Plume Book, 2009).

2   On the Soviet spy caper against the U.S. Embassy in Moscow during the Cold War, see George F. Kennan, Memoirs, 1950–1963, Volume II (New York: Little, Brown & Co., 1972): 155-56.

3   "Paper No. 51," The Federalist (New York: Modern Library, 1937): 335-41.

4   This description is from the famed presidential scholar, Richard E. Neustadt, Presidential Power (New York: Wiley, 1960): 33.

5   See Loch K. Johnson, American Foreign Policy and the Challenges of World Leadership: Power, Principle, and the Constitution (New York: Oxford University Press, 2015).

6   Final Report, Select Committee to Study Governmental Operations with Respect to Intelligence Activities (Church Committee), Report No. 94-755, U.S. Senate, 94th Cong., 2d Sess. (April 23, 1976). The author served as a senior aide to Senator Church during this inquiry.

7   On these and the following controversial intelligence operations, see the Church Committee, Final Report, ibid.

8   An amendment to the Foreign Assistance Act of 1974, Pub. L. No. 93-559, 32, 88 Stat. 1795, 1804 (1974).

9   Title V of the National Security Act of 1947 (50 U.S.C. 413), Accountability for Intelligence Activities: The Intelligence Oversight Act of 1980), Pub. L. No. 96-450, 94 Stat. 1975 (1981).

10 See Karen J. Greenberg, Rogue Justice: The Making of the Security State (New York: Crown, 2016); Loch K. Johnson, Spy Watching: Intelligence Accountability in the United States (New York: Oxford University Press, 2018).

11 See Johnson, Spy Watching, ibid.

12 For a provocative analysis that is highly pessimistic about the chances that Madisonian checks-and-balances can stand up successfully against forces in Washington, D.C. that favor government authority centralized into the hands of the executive branch, see Michael J. Glennon, National Security and Double Government (New York: Oxford University Press, 2015).

13 On these points, see Richard A. Clarke, Against All Enemies: Inside America's War on Terror (New York: Simon & Schuster, 204), pp. 229, 237; Robert Jervis, Why Intelligence Fails: Lessons from the Iran Revolution and the Iraq War (Ithaca: Cornell University Press, 2010); and Loch K. Johnson, The Threat on the Horizon: An Inside Account of America's Search for Security after the Cold War (New York: Oxford University Press, 2011).

14 50 U.S.C. 1801-1811 (Supp. V 1981), enacted in 1978.

15 For this theory of the presidency, see John Yoo, The Powers of War and Peace: The Constitution and Foreign Affairs after 9/11(Chicago: University of Chicago Press, 2010).

16 See Leon Panetta [CIA Director in the Obama Administration] and Jim Newton, Worthy Fights: A Memoir of Leadership in War and Peace (New York: Penguin, 2014): 299.

17 For a case study of the al-Awlaki assassination, see Scott Shane, Objective Troy: A Terrorist, a President, and the Rise of the Drone (New York: Tim Duggan Books, 2015).

18 While serving as a senior aide to former Secretary of Defense Les Aspin when he chaired the Aspin-Brown Presidential Commission on Intelligence in 1995, the author reviewed many PDBs for the commissioners, comparing these top-secret documents with leading newspaper reporting (see Johnson, Horizon, op.cit.).

19 Remarks, Aspen Institute Forum, Aspen, Colorado (July 20, 2017).

20 See Loch K. Johnson, America's Secret Power: The CIA in a Democratic Society (New York: Oxford University Press, 1989).

21 PBS News Hour reported on the increase in drone attacks (February 26, 2018); see also, Greg Jaffe, "Trump Administration Reviewing Ways to Make It Easier to Launch Drone Strikes," Washington Post (March 13, 2017), p. A1. For a comparison of the frequency with which covert actions have been adopted by these administrations, see Johnson, Spy Watching, op.cit.

22 See Johnson, Spy Watching, op.cit.

23 An illustration of the Trump family's disdain for intelligence officers could be seen in a remark by Donald J. Trump, Jr., who on Twitter referred to CIA Director Haspel as a "trained liar" [Julian E. Barnes, "An Intramural Republican Fight Breaks Out Over the C.I.A. Director's Fate," New York Times (November 11, 2020): A16].

Chapter-7: The Social Ties that Bind: Unravelling the Role of Trust in International Intelligence Cooperation. Pepijn Tuinier, Thijs Brocades Zaalberg and Sebastiaan Rietjens

1 Richard J. Aldrich, "US–European Intelligence Co-Operation on Counter-Terrorism: Low Politics and Compulsion," The British Journal of Politics and International Relations, Vol. 11, No. 1 (2009), p. 124.

2 Pepijn Tuinier, "Explaining the Depth and Breadth of International Intelligence Cooperation: Towards a Comprehensive Understanding," Intelligence and National Security, Vol. 36, No. 1 (2021); Timothy W. Crawford, "Intelligence Cooperation," in Oxford Research Encyclopedia of International Studies (Oxford University Press, 2010).

3 Stéphane Lefebvre, "The Difficulties and Dilemmas of International Intelligence Cooperation," International Journal of Intelligence and CounterIntelligence, Vol. 16, No. 4 (2003), pp. 527–542; Jennifer E. Sims, "Foreign Intelligence Liaison: Devils, Deals, and Details," International Journal of Intelligence and CounterIntelligence, Vol. 19, No. 2 (2006), pp. 195–217; James Igoe Walsh, The International Politics of Intelligence Sharing (New York: Columbia University Press, 2010); Tore Vestermark, "International Intelligence Liaison in the Afghan Theatre of War: Strategic Interests and Hierarchical Relations," The International Journal of Intelligence, Security, and Public Affairs, Vol. 19, No. 2 (2017), pp. 112–33; Aviva Guttmann, "Turning Oil into Blood: Western Intelligence, Libyan Covert Actions, and Palestinian Terrorism (1973–74)," Journal of Strategic Studies (2021), advance online publication, https://doi.or g/10.1080/01402390.2020.1868995; Björn Müller-Wille, "EU Intelligence Co-Operation. A Critical Analysis," Contemporary Security Policy, Vol. 23, No. 2 (2002), pp. 61–86; Björn Fägersten, Sharing Secrets: Explaining International Intelligence Cooperation (Lund: Department of Political Science, Lund University, 2010).

4 Bridget Rose Nolan, "A Sociological Approach to Intelligence Studies," in Researching National Security Intelligence: Multidisciplinary Approaches, edited by Stephen Coulthart, Michael Landon-Murray, and Damien Van Puyvelde (Washington, DC: Georgetown University Press, 2019), pp. 79–97; Hager Ben Jaffel, "Britain's European Connection in Counter-Terrorism Intelligence Cooperation: Everyday Practices of Police Liaison Officers," Intelligence and National Security (13 June 2020), pp. 1–19; Marie-Helen Maras, "Overcoming the Intelligence-Sharing Paradox: Improving Information Sharing through Change in Organizational Culture," Comparative Strategy,

Vol. 36, No. 3 (2017), pp. 187–197; Richard J. Aldrich, "Dangerous Liaisons," Harvard International Review; Cambridge, Vol. 24, No. 3 (2002), p. 50; Adam D. M. Svendsen, "Contemporary Intelligence Innovation in Practice: Enhancing 'Macro' to 'Micro' Systems Thinking via 'System of Systems' Dynamics," Defence Studies, Vol. 15, No. 2 (2015), pp. 105–123; Didier Bigo, "Sociology of Transnational Guilds," International Political Sociology, Vol. 10, No. 4 (2016), pp. 398–416; Adam D. M. Svendsen, Understanding the Globalization of Intelligence (Basingstoke: Palgrave Macmillan, 2012).

5   Sir David Omand, How Spies Think; 10 Lessons in Intelligence (New York: Penguin, 2020), pp. 167, 168–169.

6   This argument is central in the Ph.D. project that one of the authors (Tuinier) is currently working on at Leiden University. It concerns the role of social relations in international intelligence cooperation, focusing on the European Union, and is expected to be ready in 2023.

7   Eric A. Smith, "Human Cooperation," in Genetic and Cultural Evolution of Cooperation, edited by Peter Hammerstein (Cambridge, MA: The MIT Press, 2003), p. 402; Samuel Bowles and Herbert Gintis, A Cooperative Species: Human Reciprocity and Its Evolution (Princeton, NJ: Princeton University Press, 2011), p. 2.

8   Michael Herman, Intelligence Power in Peace and War (Cambridge: Royal Institute of International Affairs, 1996); H. Bradford Westerfield, "America and the World of Intelligence Liaison," Intelligence and National Security, Vol. 11, No. 3 (1996); Martin Rudner, "Hunters and Gatherers: The Intelligence Coalition Against Islamic Terrorism," International Journal of Intelligence and CounterIntelligence, Vol. 17, No. 2 (2004), pp. 193–230; Sims, "Foreign Intelligence Liaison"; Richard J. Aldrich, "International Intelligence Cooperation in Practice," in International Intelligence Cooperation and Accountability, edited by Hans Born, Ian Leigh, and Aidan Wills (London; New York: Routledge, 2011).

9   Sophia Hoffmann, "Circulation, Not Cooperation: Towards a New Understanding of Intelligence Agencies as Transnationally Constituted Knowledge Providers," Intelligence and National Security, 1 July 2021, pp. 1–20; Mai'a K. Davis Cross, "The Limits of Epistemic Communities: EU Security Agencies," Politics and Governance; Lisbon, Vol. 3, No. 1 (2015), n.a.; Mai'a K. Davis Cross, Security Integration in Europe: How Knowledge-Based Networks Are Transforming the European Union (Ann Arbor: University of Michigan Press, 2011); Mai'a K. Davis Cross, "A European Transgovernmental Intelligence Network and the Role of IntCen," Perspectives on European Politics and Society, Vol. 14, No. 3 (2013), pp. 388–402.

10   Didier Bigo, "Shared Secrecy in a Digital Age and a Transnational World," Intelligence and National Security, Vol. 34, No. 3 (2019), p. 384; Marcos Degaut, "Spies and Policymakers: Intelligence in the Information Age," Intelligence

and National Security, Vol. 31, No. 4 (2016), p. 510; Gregory F. Treverton, "The Future of Intelligence: Changing Threats, Evolving Methods," in The Future of Intelligence: Challenges in the 21st Century, edited by Ben de Jong, Joop van. Reijn, and Isabelle Duyvesteyn (Routledge, 2014), pp. 27–30; David Tucker, The End of Intelligence: Espionage and State Power in the Information Age (Redwood City, CA: Stanford University Press, 2014), p. 13; Zakia Shiraz and Richard J. Aldrich, "Globalisation and Borders," in Routledge Companion to Intelligence Studies, edited by Robert Dover, Michael S. Goodman, and Claudia Hillebrand (London; New York: Routledge, 2013), pp. 266–267; Richard J. Aldrich, "Global Intelligence Co-Operation versus Accountability: New Facets to an Old Problem," Intelligence and National Security, Vol. 24, No. 1 (2009), p. 33; Omand, How Spies Think, p. 162.

11 James J. Wirtz, "Constraints on Intelligence Collaboration: The Domestic Dimension," International Journal of Intelligence and CounterIntelligence, Vol. 6, No. 1 (1993), p. 248; Derek S. Reveron, "Old Allies, New Friends: Intelligence-Sharing in the War on Terror," Orbis, Vol. 50, No. 3 (2006), p. 456.

12 Bowles and Gintis, A Cooperative Species, pp. 8, 202; Brian C. Rathbun, Trust in International Cooperation: International Security Institutions, Domestic Politics and American Multilateralism (Cambridge: Cambridge University Press, 2011), p. 35; L. Lehmann and L. Keller, "The Evolution of Cooperation and Altruism—A General Framework and a Classification of Models," Journal of Evolutionary Biology, Vol. 19, No. 5 (2006), p. 1367.

13 Paul van Lange et al., Social Dilemmas: Understanding Human Cooperation (Oxford University Press, 2014), p. 73; Carlos Alós-Ferrer and Michele Garagnani, "The Cognitive Foundations of Cooperation," Journal of Economic Behavior & Organization, Vol. 175 (July 2020), p. 72.

14 Ben Jaffel, "Britain's European Connection in Counter-Terrorism Intelligence Cooperation," pp. 9, 11.

15 Martin Mathews, "Gift Giving, Reciprocity and the Creation of Trust," Journal of Trust Research, Vol. 7, No. 1 (2017), pp. 95–96, 102; Bowles and Gintis, A Cooperative Species, p. 52; Samuel Bowles and Herbert Gintis, "22 Origins of Human Cooperation," in Genetic and Cultural Evolution of Cooperation, edited by Peter Hammerstein (Cambridge, MA: MIT Press, 2003), pp. 429–44; Smith, "Human Cooperation," pp. 402–413; Robert Axelrod, The Evolution of Cooperation. Rev. ed. (New York: Basic Books, 2006), pp. vii, 4, 7, 74, 87, 10–112.

16 Belgian Standing Intelligence Agencies Review Committee, "Activity Report 2018" (Belgian Standing Intelligence Agencies Review Committee, n.d.), pp. 31–32; Omand, How Spies Think, p. 174; Sims, "Foreign Intelligence Liaison," pp. 197–200.

17 James Walker and Elinor Ostrom, Trust and Reciprocity: Interdisciplinary Lessons for Experimental Research (Russell Sage Foundation, 2003), pp. 4, 9;

Bart Nooteboom, Trust: Forms, Foundations, Functions, Failures and Figures (Cheltenham: Edward Elgar Publishing, 2002), pp. 72–74.

18 Mark M. Lowenthal, Intelligence: From Secrets to Policy, 7th ed. (Washington, DC: SAGE, CQ Press, 2017), pp. 163–178; Aldrich, "Dangerous Liaisons."

19 Omand, How Spies Think, p. 178.

20 Ibid.; Morton Deutsch, "A Theory of Co-Operation and Competition," Human Relations, Vol. 2, No. 2 (1949), p. 130–132.

21 Gustavo Díaz Matey, "From Cooperation to Competition: Economic Intelligence as Part of Spain's National Security Strategy," International Journal of Intelligence and CounterIntelligence, Vol. 29, No. 1 (2016), pp. 154–157; Duncan L. Clarke and Robert Johnston, "Economic Espionage and Interallied Strategic Cooperation," Thunderbird International Business Review (1 July 1998), pp. 415–418.

22 Maras, "Overcoming the Intelligence-Sharing Paradox," pp. 189–191; Thorsten Wetzling, "European Counterterrorism Intelligence Liaisons," in PSI Handbook of Global Security and Intelligence: National Approaches, edited by S. Farson, P. Gill, and S. Shpiro (Santa Barbara, CA: ABC-CLIO, LLC, 2008; Intelligence and the Quest for Security Series), pp. 498–529. Jeffrey T. Richelson, "The Calculus of Intelligence Cooperation," International Journal of Intelligence and CounterIntelligence, Vol. 4, No. 3 (1990), pp. 307–323.

23 Gregory F. Treverton, CSIS Strategic Technologies Program, and Center for Strategic and International Studies, "New Tools for Collaboration: The Experience of the U.S. Intelligence Community" (Washington, DC, 2016); Müller-Wille, "EU Intelligence Co-Operation. A Critical Analysis"; Oldrich Bures, "Intelligence Sharing and the Fight against Terrorism in the EU: Lessons Learned from Europol," European View; Heidelberg, Vol. 15, No. 1 (2016): 57–66; Raphael Bossong, "The Eu's Mature Counterterrorism Policy—A Critical Historical and Functional Assessment" (London School of Economics, 2008).

24 Reveron, "Old Allies, New Friends," p. 458; Derek S. Reveron, "The Impact of Transnational Terrorist Threats on Security Cooperation," n.d., p. 34.

25 Otwin Marenin and Arif Akgul, "Theorizing Transnational Cooperation on the Police and Intelligence Fields of Security," in Emerging Transnational (in) Security Governance: A Statist-Transnationalist Approach, edited by Ersel Aydinli (New York: Routledge, 2010), pp. 115–116.

26 Robert Boyd and Peter J. Richerson, The Origin and Evolution of Cultures (Oxford University Press, 2005), pp. 137, 160; Robert Axelrod, The Complexity of Cooperation: Agent-Based Models of Competition and Collaboration (Princeton, NJ: Princeton University Press, 1997), p. 41; Michael Taylor, The Possibility of Cooperation, Repr, Studies in Rationality and Social Change (Cambridge: Cambridge University Press, 1997), pp. 7–8, 43, 36, 58.

27 Alós-Ferrer and Garagnani, "The Cognitive Foundations of Cooperation," p. 71; Bowles and Gintis, A Cooperative Species, pp. 11, 64; Nora Bensahel, "A Coalition of Coalitions: International Cooperation Against Terrorism," Studies in Conflict and Terrorism, Vol. 29, No. 1 (2006), pp. 35–49; Lefebvre, "The Difficulties and Dilemmas of International Intelligence Cooperation"; Elinor Ostrom, "Toward a Behavioral Theory Linking Trust, Reciprocity, and Reputation," in Trust and Reciprocity: Interdisciplinary Lessons for Experimental Research, edited by James Walker and Elinor Ostrom (Russell Sage Foundation, 2003), p. 20.

28 Richard J. Aldrich, "Transatlantic Intelligence and Security Cooperation," International Affairs, Vol. 80, No. 4 (2004), p. 3.

29 The most famous game-theoretical model describing this situation is probably the Prisoners Dilemma as put forward by Robert Axelrod. It shows how two rational egoists faced with uncertainty will both choose to defect from full cooperation, their (lack of) cooperative behavior balancing them in a suboptimal outcome.

30 van Lange et al., Social Dilemmas, pp. 3–9; Martin A. Nowak, "Evolving Cooperation," Journal of Theoretical Biology, Vol. 299 (2012), p. 1; Axelrod, The Evolution of Cooperation, pp. 7–9; Ostrom, "Toward a Behavioral Theory Linking Trust, Reciprocity, and Reputation," pp. 20–21; A. Diekmann and S. Lindenberg, "Cooperation: Sociological Aspects," in International Encyclopedia of the Social & Behavioral Sciences (Elsevier, 2001), pp. 1–3; Douglas D. Heckathorn, "Sociological Rational Choice," in Handbook of Social Theory, edited by George Ritzer and Barry Smart (London: SAGE Publications, 2001), pp. 275–278; Martin A. Nowak and Karl Sigmund, "Cooperation versus Competition," Financial Analysts Journal, Vol. 56, No. 4 (1 July 2000), pp. 13–22. Taylor, The Possibility of Cooperation, pp. 2–3, 19.

31 Jeffrey H. Dyer and Wujin Chu, "The Determinants of Trust in Supplier–Automaker Relationships in the US, Japan, and Korea," Journal of International Business Studies, Vol. 42, No. 1 (2011), pp. 10–27; Katarzyna Czernek and Wojciech Czakon, "Trust-Building Processes in Tourist Coopetition: The Case of a Polish Region," Tourism Management, Vol. 52 (2016), pp. 380–394; Antonio Barretta, "The Functioning of Co-Opetition in the Health-Care Sector: An Explorative Analysis," Scandinavian Journal of Management, Vol. 24, No. 3 (2008), pp. 209–220.

32 Alós-Ferrer and Garagnani, "The Cognitive Foundations of Cooperation," p. 72; van Lange et al., Social Dilemmas, pp. 58–68; Joseph Henrich, "Cultural Evolution of Human Cooperation," in The Origin and Evolution of Cultures, edited by Robert Boyd and Peter Richerson (Oxford University Press, 2005), pp. 251–252; Rick L. Riolo, Michael D. Cohen, and Robert Axelrod, "Evolution of Cooperation without Reciprocity," Nature, Vol. 414, No. 6862 (2001), p. 441; Nowak and Sigmund, "Cooperation versus Competition," p. 14; Axelrod, The Complexity of Cooperation, p. 15.

33   T. K. Das, Bing-Sheng Teng, and Baruch College, "Between Trust and Control: Developing Confidence in Partner Cooperation in Alliances," The Academy of Management Review, Vol. 23, No. 3 (1998), pp. 493–497.

34   James I. Walsh, "Defection and Hierarchy in International Intelligence Sharing," Journal of Public Policy; Cambridge, Vol. 27, No. 2 (2007), p. 161.

35   Richard J. Popplewell, "The KGB and the Control of the Soviet Bloc: The Case of East Germany," in Knowing Your Friends: Intelligence inside Alliances and Coalitions from 1914 to the Cold War, edited by Martin S. Alexander (London: Frank Cass, 1998), pp. 255–257.

36   Diana Bolsinger, "Not at Any Price: LBJ, Pakistan, and Bargaining in an Asymmetric Intelligence Relationship," Texas National Security Review (Winter 2021/2022), https://tnsr.org/2021/11/not-at-any-price-lbj-pakistan-and-bargaining-in-an-asymmetric-intelligence-relationship/ (accessed 18 November 2021); İ. Aytaç Kadıoğlu and Egemen B. Bezci, "Small State Intelligence: New Zealand in SEATO Security Affairs," Pacific Focus, Vol. 35, No. 1 (2020), pp. 5–28; Sobukwe O. Odinga, Irving Leonard Markovitz, and City University of New York Political Science, "Looking For Leverage: Strategic Resources, Contentious Bargaining, and US-African Security Cooperation" (New York: City University of New York, 2016).

37   Bob de Graaff and Cees Wiebes, "Intelligence and the Cold War behind the Dikes: The Relationship between the American and Dutch Intelligence Communities, 1946–1994," Intelligence and National Security, Vol. 12, No. 1 (1997), pp. 44–47.

38   Sobukwe Odinga, "'We Recommend Compliance': Bargaining and Leverage in Ethiopian-US Intelligence Cooperation," Review of African Political Economy, Vol. 44, No. 153 (2017), pp. 434–435, 443–444.

39   van Lange et al., Social Dilemmas, pp. 60–61; Bowles and Gintis, A Cooperative Species, pp. 68–70, 76; Reinhard Bachmann and Akbar Zaheer, "Trust in Inter-Organizational Relations," in The Oxford Handbook of Inter-Organizational Relations, edited by Steve Cropper et al. (Oxford University Press, 2008), p. 537; Axelrod, The Evolution of Cooperation, pp. 11–12, 17–18, 140; Kevin A McCabe, "A Cognitive Theory of Reciprocal Exchange," in Trust and Reciprocity: Interdisciplinary Lessons for Experimental Research, edited by James Walker and Elinor Ostrom (Russell Sage Foundation, 2003), pp. 149, 160; Ostrom, "Toward a Behavioral Theory Linking Trust, Reciprocity, and Reputation," pp. 9–10, 23; Nooteboom, Trust, pp. 20–22; Nowak and Sigmund, "Cooperation versus Competition," pp. 15–16; Herbert A. Simon, "Bounded Rationality in Social Science: Today and Tomorrow," Mind & Society, Vol. 1, No. 1 (2000), pp. 25–29; Axelrod, The Complexity of Cooperation, pp. 6–7, 14–15, 47; Bernard Williams, "Formal and Social Reality," in Trust: Making and Breaking Cooperative Relations, edited by Diego Gambetta (Oxford: Basil Blackwell, 1988), p. 4.

40 Axelrod, The Evolution of Cooperation, pp. 110–111.

41 Ibid., pp. 35–44; Bowles and Gintis, A Cooperative Species, p. 59; Ernst Fehr and Urs Fischbacher, "Social Norms and Human Cooperation," Trends in Cognitive Sciences, Vol. 8, No. 4 (2004), p. 186; Nowak and Sigmund, "Cooperation versus Competition," p. 17; Axelrod, The Complexity of Cooperation, pp. 34–35.

42 Svendsen, Understanding the Globalization of Intelligence, p. 91.

43 Reveron, "Old Allies, New Friends," p. 457.

44 Ostrom, "Toward a Behavioral Theory Linking Trust, Reciprocity, and Reputation," pp. 23–25; Bowles and Gintis, A Cooperative Species, pp. 9–10.

45 Bowles and Gintis, A Cooperative Species, pp. 22–23, 88–89, 92; Robert Boyd and Peter J. Richerson, "Culture and the Evolution of Human Cooperation," Philosophical Transactions of the Royal Society B: Biological Sciences, Vol. 364, No. 1533 (2009), p. 3283; Boyd and Richerson, The Origin and Evolution of Cultures, p. 135; Ostrom, "Toward a Behavioral Theory Linking Trust, Reciprocity, and Reputation," pp. 38–39; Taylor, The Possibility of Cooperation, pp. 62, 85, 105.

46 Aldrich, "International Intelligence Cooperation in Practice," pp. 1, 24–25; Jelle Van Buuren, "Analysing International Intelligence Cooperation: Institutions or Intelligence Assemblages?," in The Future of Intelligence: Challenges in the 21st Century, edited by Ben de Jong, Joop van Reijn, and Isabelle Duyvesteyn (London; New York: Routledge, 2014), pp. 84–89; Svendsen, "Contemporary Intelligence Innovation in Practice," pp. 106–109.

47 Crawford, "Intelligence Cooperation," p. 2; Jan Ballast, "Merging Pillars, Changing Cultures: NATO and the Future of Intelligence Cooperation Within the Alliance," International Journal of Intelligence and CounterIntelligence, Vol. 31, No. 4 (2018), p. 735; Müller-Wille, "EU Intelligence Co-Operation," pp. 73–74; Loch K. Johnson and Annette Freyberg, "Ambivalent Bedfellows: German-American Intelligence Relations, 1969–1991," International Journal of Intelligence and CounterIntelligence, Vol. 10, No. 2 (1997), p. 175.

48 Tatbeeq Raza-Ullah and Angelos Kostis, "Do Trust and Distrust in Coopetition Matter to Performance?," European Management Journal (October 2019), p. 2; Emanuela Todeva and David Knoke, "Strategic Alliances and Corporate Social Capital," Kölner Zeitschrift Für Soziologie Und Sozialpsychologie, Organisations-Sociologie, 25 August 2003, p. 23; Tung-Mou Yang and Terrence A. Maxwell, "Information-Sharing in Public Organizations: A Literature Review of Interpersonal, Intra-Organizational and Inter-Organizational Success Factors," Government Information Quarterly, Vol. 28, No. 2 (2011), p. 169; Peter Kollock, "The Emergence of Exchange Structures," in Organizational Trust, edited by Roderick M. Kramer (Oxford; New York: Oxford University Press, 2006), pp. 189–190, 195.

49 Martin Schulz, "Logic of Consequences and Logic of Appropriateness,"
    in The Palgrave Encyclopedia of Strategic Management, edited by Mie
    Augier and David Teece (Palgrave Macmillan, 2015), pp. 1–9; Marc A.
    Cohen, "Genuine, Non-Calculative Trust with Calculative Antecedents:
    Reconsidering Williamson on Trust," Journal of Trust Research, Vol. 4, No.
    1 (2014), pp. 52–53; Ulrike Malmendier, Vera L. te Velde, and Roberto A.
    Weber, "Rethinking Reciprocity," Annual Review of Economics, Vol. 6, No. 1
    (2014), p. 364; Bowles and Gintis, A Cooperative Species: Human Reciprocity
    and Its Evolution, pp. 4, 9, 12, 32–35, 89; Jeffrey H. Dyer and Wujin Chu,
    "The Role of Trustworthiness in Reducing Transaction Costs and Improving
    Performance: Empirical Evidence from the United States, Japan, and Korea,"
    in Organizational Trust, edited by Roderick M. Kramer (Oxford; New
    York: Oxford University Press, 2006), pp. 207–225; Oliver E. Williamson,
    "Calculativeness, Trust, and Economic Organization," in Organizational
    Trust (Oxford; New York: Oxford University Press, 2006), pp. 65–73; Karen
    S. Cook, Russell Hardin, and Margaret Levi, Cooperation without Trust
    (Russell Sage Foundation, 2005), p. 52; Reinhard Bachmann, "Trust and
    Power as Means of Coordinating the Internal Relations of the Organization:
    A Conceptual Framework," in The Trust Process in Organizations, edited by
    Bart Nooteboom and Frédérique Six (Cheltenham: Edward Elgar Publishing,
    2003), pp. 59–62; Guido Möllering, "The Nature of Trust: From Georg Simmel
    to a Theory of Expectation, Interpretation and Suspension," Sociology, Vol.
    35, No. 2 (2001), pp. 403, 409–410; K. G. Smith, S. J. Carroll, and S. J. Ashford,
    "Intra- and Interorganizational Cooperation: Toward a Research Agenda,"
    Academy of Management Journal, Vol. 38, No. 1 (1995), pp. 17–18; Todeva
    and Knoke, "Strategic Alliances and Corporate Social Capital," pp. 21–22.

50 Pierre Bourdieu, The Logic of Practice, 15th ed. (Cambridge: Polity Press,
    2019), pp. 52–65; Alós-Ferrer and Garagnani, "The Cognitive Foundations
    of Cooperation," p. 72; Joe O'Mahoney and Steve Vincent, "Critical Realism
    as an Empirical Project," in Studying Organizations Using Critical Realism:
    A Practical Guide, edited by Paul K. Edwards, Joe O'Mahoney, and Steve
    Vincent (Oxford University Press, 2014), pp. 2–3; Bachmann and Zaheer,
    "Trust in Inter-Organizational Relations," pp. 538, 541–544; Barry Barnes,
    "Practice as Collective Action," in The Practice Turn in Contemporary
    Theory, edited by Theodore R Schatzki, Karin Knorr Cetina, and Eike Von
    Savigny (Taylor & Francis Group, 2001), pp. 25–26; Nick Crossley, "The
    Phenomenological Habitus and Its Construction," Theory and Society, No. 30
    (2001), pp. 85; Theodore R. Schatzki, "Practice Theory," in The Practice Turn in
    Contemporary Theory, edited by Theodore R. Schatzki, Karin Knorr Cetina,
    and Eike Von Savigny (Taylor & Francis Group, 2001), p. 12; Margaret Archer,
    "Realism in the Social Sciences," in Critical Realism Essential Readings, edited
    by Margaret Archer et al. (Taylor & Francis Group, 1998), p. 196; Douglas V.
    Porpora, "Four Concepts of Social Structure, in Critical Realism: Essential

Readings, edited by Margaret Archer et al. (Taylor & Francis Group, 1998), pp. 339–354.

51 Maria Bengtsson and Tatbeeq Raza-Ullah, "A Systematic Review of Research on Coopetition: Toward a Multilevel Understanding," Industrial Marketing Management, Vol. 57 (2016), pp. 28–29; van Lange et al., Social Dilemmas, pp. 64–65; Bowles and Gintis, A Cooperative Species, pp. 22–23, 59; Axelrod, The Evolution of Cooperation, pp. 12, 59, 102–103, 187–188; Cook, Hardin, and Levi, Cooperation without Trust, p. 3, 188; Diekmann and Lindenberg, "Cooperation," pp. 1, 4–5; Linda Molm, "Theories of Social Exchange and Exchange Networks," in Handbook of Social Theory, edited by George Ritzer and Barry Smart (London: SAGE Publications, 2001), pp. 269–270; Taylor, The Possibility of Cooperation, pp. 31, 62, 85; Smith, Carroll, and Ashford, "Intra- And Interorganizational Cooperation," pp. 17–18, 34.

52 Jon Reiersen, "Drivers of Trust and Trustworthiness," International Journal of Social Economics, Vol. 46, No. 1 (2019), p. 2; van Lange et al., Social Dilemmas, p. 63; Donald L. Ferrin, Michelle C. Bligh, and Jeffrey C. Kohles, "It Takes Two to Tango: An Interdependence Analysis of the Spiraling of Perceived Trustworthiness and Cooperation in Interpersonal and Intergroup Relationships," Organizational Behavior and Human Decision Processes, Vol. 107, No. 2 (2008), p. 161; Russell Hardin, "Gaming Trust," in Trust and Reciprocity: Interdisciplinary Lessons for Experimental Research, edited by James Walker and Elinor Ostrom (Russell Sage Foundation, 2003), p. 8 Smith, "Human Cooperation," pp. 10–11; Walker and Ostrom, Trust and Reciprocity, p. 6; Russell Hardin, Trust (Polity Press, 2006), p. 18.

53 Dagmara Lewicka and Agnieszka Zakrzewska-Bielawska, "Interorganizational Trust in Business Relations: Cooperation and Coopetition," in Contemporary Challenges in Cooperation and Coopetition in the Age of Industry 4.0: 10th Conference on Management of Organizations' Development (MOD), edited by Agnieszka Zakrzewska-Bielawska and Iwona Staniec, Springer Proceedings in Business and Economics (Cham: Springer International Publishing, 2020), pp. 155–157; Angelos Kostis and Malin Harryson Näsholm, "Towards a Research Agenda on How, When and Why Trust and Distrust Matter to Coopetition," Journal of Trust Research (17 December 2019), pp. 1–15; Martin Parker, "Secret Societies: Intimations of Organization," Organization Studies, Vol. 37, No. 1 (2016), p. 109; Rathbun, Trust in International Cooperation, pp. 2, 4; Yang and Maxwell, "Information-Sharing in Public Organizations," p. 169; Janaina Macke et al., "The Impact of Inter-Organizational Social Capital in Collaborative Networks Competitiveness: An Empirical Analysis," in Collaborative Networks for a Sustainable World, edited by Luis M. Camarinha-Matos, Xavier Boucher, and Hamideh Afsarmanesh, vol. 336, IFIP Advances in Information and Communication Technology (Berlin, Heidelberg: Springer Berlin Heidelberg, 2010), pp. 3–4, 10; Bachmann and Zaheer, "Trust in Inter-Organizational Relations," pp. 536–537; Cook, Hardin,

and Levi, Cooperation without Trust, p. 51; Möllering, "The Nature of Trust," pp. 404, 407–410.

54 Axelrod, The Evolution of Cooperation, p. 177; Reiersen, "Drivers of Trust aTrustworthiness," p. 4; Bachmann and Zaheer, "Trust in Inter-Organizational Relations," p. 538; Ferrin, Bligh, and Kohles, "It Takes Two to Tango," pp. 171, 173, 175; Todeva and Knoke, "Strategic Alliances and Corporate Social Capital," p. 25; Nooteboom, Trust, pp. 63–65; Birgitta Nedelmann, "The Continuing Relevance of Georg Simmel: Staking Out Anew the Field of Sociology," in Handbook of Social Theory, edited by George Ritzer and Barry Smart (London: SAGE Publications, 2001), pp. 67–72; Cormac MacFhionnlaoich, "Interorganizational Cooperation: Towards a Synthesis of Theoretical Perspectives" (The 15th Annual IMP Conference, Dublin, 1999), pp. 4–5; Peter Smith Ring and Andrew H. van de Ven, "Developmental Processes of Cooperative Interorganizational Relations," Academy of Management Review, Vol. 19, No. 1 (1994), pp. 101–105.

55 See, for example, Aldrich, "Transatlantic Intelligence and Security Cooperation"; Sir Stephen Lander, "International Intelligence Cooperation: An Inside Perspective," Cambridge Review of International Affairs, Vol. 17, No. 3 (2004), pp. 481–493; Oldrich Bures, "Informal Counterterrorism Arrangements in Europe: Beauty by Variety or Duplicity by Abundance?," edited by Christian Kaunert and Sarah Léonard, Cooperation and Conflict, Vol. 47, No. 4 (2012), pp. 495–518; Reveron, "Old Allies, New Friends"; Ballast, "Merging Pillars, Changing Cultures"; Shlomo Shpiro, "The Communication of Mutual Security: Frameworks for Euro-Mediterranean Intelligence Sharing," NATO Academic Fellowship Program (2001). Available at: https://www.nato.int/acad/fellow/99-01/shpiro.pdf (accessed 16 June 2022); Björn Fägersten, For EU Eyes Only? Intelligence and European Security (Paris: Institute for Security Studies, 2016); Svendsen, Understanding the Globalization of Intelligence, pp. 14, 91, 102.

56 Lefebvre, "The Difficulties and Dilemmas of International Intelligence Cooperation," pp. 528–529.

57 Peter Gill, "Rendition in a Transnational Insecurity Environment," in Emerging Transnational (in)Security Governance: A Statist-Transnationalist Approach, edited by Ersel Aydinli (Abingdon, UK: Routledge, 2010), p. 74.

58 See, for example, Treverton et al., "New Tools for Collaboration"; Sims, "Foreign Intelligence Liaison"; Georgios X. Protopapas, "European Union's Intelligence Cooperation: A Failed Imagination?," Journal of Mediterranean and Balkan Intelligence (2014), p. 9; Scott E. Jasper, "U.S. Cyber Threat Intelligence Sharing Frameworks," International Journal of Intelligence and CounterIntelligence, Vol. 30, No. 1 (2017), pp. 53–65.

59 Sarah-Myriam Martin-Brûlé, "Competing for Trust: Challenges in United Nations Peacekeeping-Intelligence," International Journal of Intelligence and CounterIntelligence, Vol. 34, No. 3 (2021), pp. 494–524.

60 Akbar Zaheer and Jared Harris, "Interorganizational Trust," in Handbook of Strategic Alliances (Thousand Oaks, CA: SAGE Publications, 2006), p. 170.

61 Peter Oomsels and Geert Bouckaert, "Studying Interorganizational Trust in Public Administration: A Conceptual and Analytical Framework for 'Administrational Trust,'" Public Performance & Management Review, Vol. 37, No. 4 (2014), pp. 578–584; Ferrin, Bligh, and Kohles, "It Takes Two to Tango," p. 174; Paul W. L. Vlaar, Frans A. J. Van den Bosch, and Henk W. Volberda, "On the Evolution of Trust, Distrust, and Formal Coordination and Control in Interorganizational Relationships: Toward an Integrative Framework," Group & Organization Management, Vol. 32, No. 4 (2007), pp. 5–6; Walker and Ostrom, Trust and Reciprocity, p. 6; Russell Hardin, Trust and Trustworthiness, The Russell Sage Foundation Series on Trust; Vol. 4 (New York: Russell Sage Foundation, 2002), pp. 1–27, 81; Aaron M. Hoffman, "A Conceptualization of Trust in International Relations," European Journal of International Relations, Vol. 8, No. 3 (2002), pp. 376–377; Nooteboom, Trust, pp. 36–61; Möllering, "The Nature of Trust," pp. 404, 412–413; Denise M. Rousseau et al., "Not So Different After All: A Cross-Discipline View of Trust," Academy of Management Review, Vol. 23, No. 3 (1998): pp. 394–395; Ring and van de Ven, "Developmental Processes of Cooperative InterOrganizational Relations," p. 93; Roger C Mayer, James H. Davis, and F. David Schoorman, "An Integrative Model of Organizational Trust," Academy of Management Review, Vol. 20, No. 3 (1995), pp. 712–714.

62 This explicitly leaves out "calculative trust," a form of trust mostly mentioned in economic scholarship. In this concept, trust is ideally based on prediction and objectively decreases vulnerability. It is based on negative expectations about a partner; from a sociological perspective qualified as distrust. It resembles the mechanism presented above depicting rational calculations and control. Although calculative trust is shown to affect cooperative behavior, it is distinct from the social–relational concept of trust here. The latter is seen to have its own, separate effect on cooperative behavior. In intelligence studies both concepts are often used intermingled and without distinction, adding other terms like "confidence" and "reliability." This diffuses the clarity of the mechanisms at work.

63 Onora O'Neill, "Linking Trust to Trustworthiness," International Journal of Philosophical Studies, Vol. 26, No. 2 (2018), pp. 293–295; Reiersen, "Drivers of Trust and Trustworthiness," pp. 3–4, 11; Nava Ashraf, Iris Bohnet, and Nikita Piankov, "Decomposing Trust and Trustworthiness," Experimental Economics, Vol. 9, No. 3 (2006), p. 204; Hardin, Trust and Trustworthiness, pp. 29–32.

64 F. David Schoorman, Roger C. Mayer, and James H. Davis, "An Integrative Model of Organizational Trust: Past, Present, and Future," Academy of Management Review, Vol. 32, No. 2 (2007), pp. 344–345; Rathbun, Trust in International Cooperation, p. 39; Hardin, "Gaming Trust," p. 295.

65 Hoffman, "A Conceptualization of Trust in International Relations," p. 381.

66 Axelrod, The Evolution of Cooperation, pp. 121–122; Hardin, "Gaming Trust," pp. 92–95; Walker and Ostrom, Trust and Reciprocity, p. 8; Hardin, Trust and Trustworthiness, pp. 21–22.

67 Mayer, Davis, and Schoorman, "An Integrative Model of Organizational Trust," pp. 716–720; Schoorman, Mayer, and Davis, "An Integrative Model of Organizational Trust"; Reiersen, "Drivers of Trust and Trustworthiness," pp. 4–5; Oliver Schilke and Karen S. Cook, "Sources of Alliance Partner Trustworthiness: Integrating Calculative and Relational Perspectives," Strategic Management Journal, Vol. 36, No. 2 (2015), pp. 277, 283, 289–290; Bill McEvily and Marco Tortoriello, "Measuring Trust in Organisational Research: Review and Recommendations," Journal of Trust Research, Vol. 1, No. 1 (2011), pp. 4–5; Ferrin, Bligh, and Kohles, "It Takes Two to Tango," p. 163; Jason A. Colquitt, Brent A. Scott, and Jeffery A. LePine, "Trust, Trustworthiness, and Trust Propensity: A Meta-Analytic Test of Their Unique Relationships with Risk Taking and Job Performance," Journal of Applied Psychology, Vol. 92, No. 4 (2007), pp. 909–911, 918; Risto Seppänen, Kirsimarja Blomqvist, and Sanna Sundqvist, "Measuring Inter-Organizational Trust—A Critical Review of the Empirical Research in 1990–2003," Industrial Marketing Management, Project Marketing and the Marketing of Solutions, Vol. 36, No. 2 (2007), pp. 250–256; Hardin, "Gaming Trust," pp. 83–84; Yang and Maxwell, "Information-Sharing in Public Organizations," p. 169; Nooteboom, Trust, pp. 85–89.

68 Rathbun, Trust in International Cooperation, pp. 39, 25–26.

69 Mary Jo Hatch and Majken Schultz, "Relations between Organizational Culture, Identity and Image," European Journal of Marketing, Vol. 31, No. 5/6 (1997), pp. 356, 360–362; Mary Jo Hatch and Majken Schultz, "The Dynamics of Organizational Identity," Human Relations, Vol. 55, No. 8 (2002), pp. 989–1015; Schilke and Cook, "Sources of Alliance Partner Trustworthiness," pp. 280–283; Nuzhat Lotia and Cynthia Hardy, "Critical Perspectives on Cooperation," in The Oxford Handbook of Inter-Organizational Relations, edited by Steve Cropper et al. (Oxford University Press, 2008), p. 369; Colquitt, Scott, and LePine, "Trust, Trustworthiness, and Trust Propensity," p. 922; Mayer, Davis, and Schoorman, "An Integrative Model of Organizational Trust," pp. 717–722.

70 Dennis A. Gioia, Aimee L. Hamilton, and Shubha D. Patvardhan, "Image Is Everything," Research in Organizational Behavior, Vol. 34 (2014), pp. 133–134; Schoorman, Mayer, and Davis, "An Integrative Model of Organizational

Trust," pp. 345–346, 350; Mayer, Davis, and Schoorman, "An Integrative Model of Organizational Trust," pp. 717–718; Hatch and Schultz, "The Dynamics of Organizational Identity," pp. 990, 994–995.

71   David Alvarez, "Axis Sigint Collaboration: A Limited Partnership," Intelligence and National Security, Vol. 14, No. 1 (1999), pp. 4–9.

72   Martin-Brûlé, "Competing for Trust," pp. 506–507; Sebastiaan Rietjens and Floribert Baudet, "Stovepiping Within Multinational Military Operations: The Case of Mali," in Information Sharing in Military Operations, edited by Irina Goldenberg, Joseph Soeters, and Waylon H. Dean (New York: Springer Berlin Heidelberg, 2016); Per Martin Norheim-Martinsen, and Jacob Aasland Ravndal, "Towards Intelligence-Driven Peace Operations? The Evolution of UN and EU Intelligence Structures," International Peacekeeping, Vol. 18, No. 4 (2011), pp. 457–461; A. Walter Dorn, "The Cloak and the Blue Beret: Limitations on Intelligence in UN Peacekeeping," International Journal of Intelligence and CounterIntelligence, Vol. 12, No. 4 (1999), pp. 416–417.

73   David G. Rand and Martin A. Nowak, "Human Cooperation," Trends in Cognitive Sciences, Vol. 17, No. 8 (2013), pp. 417–419; Nowak, "Evolving Cooperation," p. 2; Ostrom, "Toward a Behavioral Theory Linking Trust, Reciprocity, and Reputation," p. 43; Todeva and Knoke, "Strategic Alliances and Corporate Social Capital," pp. 5–6; Hoffman, "A Conceptualization of Trust in International Relations," p. 390; Nowak and Sigmund, "Cooperation versus Competition," p. 20; Partha Dasgupta, "Trust as a Commodity," in Trust: Making and Breaking Cooperative Relations, edited by Diego Gambetta (Oxford: Basil Blackwell, 1988), p. 53; David Good, "Individuals, Interpersonal Relationships and Trust," in Trust: Making and Breaking Cooperative Relations, edited by Diego Gambetta (Oxford: Basil Blackwell, 1988), p. 38; Bowles and Gintis, A Cooperative Species, pp. 31–32.

74   A. Tiwana and A. A. Bush, "Continuance in Expertise-Sharing Networks: A Social Perspective," IEEE Transactions on Engineering Management, Vol. 52, No. 1 (2005), pp. 85–101; Helge Svare, Anne Haugen Gausdal, and Guido Möllering, "The Function of Ability, Benevolence, and Integrity-Based Trust in Innovation Networks," Industry and Innovation, Vol. 27, No. 6 (2020), p. 598; Dong Chen, Li Dai, and Donghong Li, "A Delicate Balance for Innovation: Competition and Collaboration in R&D Consortia," Management and Organization Review, Vol. 15, No. 1 (2019), pp. 145–76; Yadong Luo, "A Coopetition Perspective of Global Competition," Journal of World Business, Vol. 42, No. 2 (2007), pp. 129–144.

75   Wojtek Przepiorka, Lukas Norbutas, and Rense Corten, "Order without Law: Reputation Promotes Cooperation in a Cryptomarket for Illegal Drugs," European Sociological Review, Vol. 33, No. 6 (2017), pp. 752–764.

76   Schilke and Cook, "Sources of Alliance Partner Trustworthiness," pp. 280, 290–291; Hardin, "Gaming Trust," pp. 92–93; Nooteboom, Trust, pp. 12–15;

Todeva and Knoke, "Strategic Alliances And Corporate Social Capital," p. 24; Stefan Volk, "The Evolution of Trust and Cooperation in Diverse Groups. A Game Experimental Approach" (University of St. Gallen, 2009), p. 79.

77   Bowles and Gintis, A Cooperative Species, pp. 71–72; Yang and Maxwell, "Information-Sharing in Public Organizations," p. 165; Ranjay Gulati and Maxim Sytch, "Does Familiarity Breed Trust? Revisiting the Antecedents of Trust," Managerial and Decision Economics, Vol. 29, No. 2–3 (2008), pp. 167–169, 185; Axelrod, The Evolution of Cooperation, pp. 150–151; Smith, "Human Cooperation," p. 414; Ranjay Gulati, "Does Familiarity Breed Trust? The Implications of Repeated Ties for Contractual Choice in Alliances," Academy of Management Journal, Vol. 38, No. 1 (1995), p. 105.

78   Omand, How Spies Think, p. 170.

79   Ank Bijleveld, "Russian Cyber Operation, Remarks Minister of Defence, 4 October in The Hague," Home News & Speeches, 4 October 2018, https://english.defensie.nl/topics/cyber-security/documents/publications/2018/10/04/remarks-minister-of-defense-4-october-in-the-hague; Junhui Wu, Daniel Balliet, and Paul A. M. Van Lange, "Reputation, Gossip, and Human Cooperation: Reputation and Cooperation," Social and Personality Psychology Compass, Vol. 10, No. 6 (2016), pp. 352–354.

80   Jonathan N. Brown and Alex Farrington, "Democracy and the Depth of Intelligence Sharing: Why Regime Type Hardly Matters," Intelligence and National Security, Vol. 32, No. 1 (2017), pp. 68–84; Wu, Balliet, and Van Lange, "Reputation, Gossip, and Human Cooperation," p. 354; Malmendier, te Velde, and Weber, "Rethinking Reciprocity," p. 365; Rand and Nowak, "Human Cooperation," pp. 414–415; Roderick M. Kramer, "Trust and Distrust in Organizations: Emerging Perspectives, Enduring Questions," Annual Review of Psychology; Palo Alto, Vol. 50 (1999), pp. 576–577.

81   Aldrich, "Dangerous Liaisons," p. 51; Wirtz, "Constraints on Intelligence Collaboration."

82   Omand, How Spies Think, pp. 169–171; Stefanie Pleschinger, "Allied Against Terror: Transatlantic Intelligence Cooperation," Yale Journal of International Affairs, Vol. 2, No. 1 (2006), pp. 55–67; Shpiro, "The Communication of Mutual Security," p. 35.

83   Aviva Guttmann, "Combatting Terror in Europe: Euro-Israeli Counterterrorism Intelligence Cooperation in the Club de Berne (1971–1972)," Intelligence and National Security, Vol. 33, No. 2 (2018), p. 159; Shpiro, "The Communication of Mutual Security," p. 21.

84   Lander, "International Intelligence Cooperation," p. 489; Ballast, "Merging Pillars, Changing Cultures," p. 724; Aldrich, "Transatlantic Intelligence and Security Cooperation," pp. 18–19; Artur Gruszczak, Intelligence Security in the European Union: Building a Strategic Intelligence Community. New Security Challenges (London: Palgrave Macmillan, 2016), p. 105.

85 Ying Hu and Tor Korneliussen, "The Effects of Personal Ties and Reciprocity on the Performance of Small Firms in Horizontal Strategic Alliances," Scandinavian Journal of Management, Vol. 13, No. 2 (1997), pp. 159–173; Sheng-Hshiung Tsaur and Chih-Hung Wang, "Personal Ties, Reciprocity, Competitive Intensity, and Performance of the Strategic Alliances in Taiwan's Travel Industry," The Service Industries Journal, Vol. 31, No. 6 (2011), pp. 911–928; Charlotte Schlump and Thomas Brenner, "Firm's Cooperation Activities: The Relevance of Public Research, Proximity and Personal Ties—A Study of Technology-Oriented Firms in East Germany," Working Papers on Innovation and Space, n.d.

86 Edgar H. Schein and Peter A. Schein, Organizational Culture and Leadership (New York: John Wiley & Sons, 2016), pp. 6, 9–11; Schilke and Cook, "Sources of Alliance Partner Trustworthiness," p. 279; Yang and Maxwell, "Information-Sharing in Public Organizations," p. 166; Boyd and Richerson, The Origin and Evolution of Cultures, p. 206; David B. Drake, Nicole A. Steckler, and Marianne J. Koch, "Information Sharing in and Across Government Agencies: The Role and Influence of Scientist, Politician, and Bureaucrat Subcultures," Social Science Computer Review, Vol. 22, No. 1 (2004), pp. 69, 81; Ostrom, "Toward a Behavioral Theory Linking Trust, Reciprocity, and Reputation," pp. 40–41; Hatch and Schultz, "Relations Between Organizational Culture, Identity, and Image," p. 358; Hatch and Schultz, "Dynamics of Organizational Identity," 996–997.

87 Mayer, Davis, and Schoorman, "An Integrative Model of Organizational Trust," pp. 719–720; Kramer, "Trust and Distrust in Organizations," pp. 579–581; Axelrod, The Complexity of Cooperation, pp. 145, 151–152; Kim S. Cameron and Sarah J. Freeman, "Cultural Congruence, Strength, and Type: Relationships to Effectiveness," Research in Organizational Change and Development, No. 5 (1991), pp. 24–25, 52; Marc Ulco Douma, "Strategic Alliances: Fit or Failure" (Enschede, University of Twente, 1997), p. 581, https://research.utwente.nl/en/publications/strategic-alliances-fit-or-failure

88 Schein and Schein, Organizational Culture and Leadership, pp. 21–22; Good, "Individuals, Interpersonal Relationships and Trust," pp. 44–45.

89 Patrycja Klimas, "Organizational Culture and Coopetition: An Exploratory Study of the Features, Models and Role in the Polish Aviation Industry," Industrial Marketing Management, Vol. 53 (2016), pp. 91–102.

90 Social institutions as depicted in this article differ from the institutions generally talked about in liberal institutionalist theory: the consciously designed, formal organizations for dealing with various problems in international affairs.

91 Schein and Schein, Organizational Culture and Leadership, pp. 4, 19; Reiersen, "Drivers of Trust and Trustworthiness," p. 6; Barry (Barry G.) Buzan, From International to World Society?: English School Theory and

the Social Structure of Globalisation, Cambridge Studies in International Relations; 95 (Cambridge: Cambridge University Press, 2004), pp. 166, 181; Andrea Herepath, "In the Loop: A Realist Approach to Structure and Agency in the Practice of Strategy," Organization Studies, Vol. 35, No. 6 (2014), pp. 859–860; MacFhionnlaoich, "Interorganizational Cooperation," pp. 12–13.

92 Georg Simmel, "The Sociology of Secrecy and of Secret Societies," The American Journal of Sociology (n.d.), pp. 470–473, 482; Peter M. Haas, "Introduction: Epistemic Communities and International Policy Coordination," International Organization, Vol. 46, No. 1 (1992), p. 20; Joseph Soeters, Sociology and Military Studies (Routledge, 2018), p. 58.

93 CSIS Technology and Intelligence Task Force, "Maintaining the Intelligence Edge" (Center for Strategic and International Studies, January 2021), p. 6.

94 Georg Simmel, "The Sociology of Secrecy and of Secret Societies," pp. 445–446, 462; Geert Hofstede, "Dimensionalizing Cultures: The Hofstede Model in Context," Online Readings in Psychology and Culture, Vol. 2, No. 1 (December 2011), p. 20, https://scholarworks.gvsu.edu/orpc/vol2/iss1/8/ (accessed 16 June 2022). Thierry Balzacq and Benjamin Puybareau, "The Economy of Secrecy: Security, Information Control, and EU-US Relations," West European Politics, Vol. 41, No. 4 (2018), pp. 897–899; Omand, How Spies Think, p. 173.

95 Chad Whelan, "Security Networks and Occupational Culture: Understanding Culture within and between Organisations," Policing and Society, Vol. 27, No. 2 (2017), pp. 114, 118–120; Schein and Schein, Organizational Culture and Leadership, p. 18.

96 David G. Sirmon and Peter J. Lane, "A Model of Cultural Differences and International Alliance Performance," Journal of International Business Studies, Vol. 35, No. 4 (2004), pp. 306–319.

97 Anna-Katherine Staser McGill and David Philip Harry Gray, "Challenges to International Counterterrorism Intelligence Sharing," Global Security Studies, Vol. 3, No. 3 (2012), pp. 77–81, 84.

98 Belgian Standing Intelligence Agencies Review Committee, "Activity Report 2014–2015" (Belgian Standing Intelligence Agencies Review Committee, 2014), pp. 32–39.

99 Juan Almandoz, Christopher Marquis, and Michael Cheely, "Drivers of Community Strength: An Institutional Logics Perspective on Geographical and Affiliation-Based Communities," in The SAGE Handbook of Organizational Institutionalism (2nd ed.), edited by Royston Greenwood et al. (Los Angeles: SAGE Reference, 2017), pp. 192–197; Maciek Chudek, Wanying Zhao, and Joseph Henrich, "Culture-Gene Coeveolution, Large-Scale Cooperation, and the Shaping of Human Social Psychology," in Cooperation and Its Evolution, edited by Kim Sterelny et al. (Cambridge, MA: MIT Press, 2013), p. 438, 442–444; Bowles and Gintis, A Cooperative Species, p. 90; Barretta,

"The Functioning of Co-Opetition in the Health-Care Sector," pp. 217–219; Douglas Hartmann and Joseph Gerteis, "Dealing with Diversity: Mapping Multiculturalism in Sociological Terms," Sociological Theory, Vol. 23, No. 2 (2005), p. 223; Henrich, "Cultural Evolution of Human Cooperation," p. 253; Möllering, "The Nature of Trust," p. 406; Nooteboom, Trust, pp. 64–65; Taylor, The Possibility of Cooperation, p. 23.

100 Ilkka Salmi, "Why Europe Needs Intelligence and Why Intelligence Needs Europe: 'Intelligence Provides Analytical Insight into an Unpredictable and Complex Environment,'" International Journal of Intelligence and CounterIntelligence, Vol. 33, No. 3 (2020), p. 466; Omand, How Spies Think, pp. 163–164, 166–167; John M. Nomikos and A. Th. Symeonides, "Coalition Building, Cooperation, and Intelligence: The Case of Greece and Israel," International Journal of Intelligence and CounterIntelligence, Vol. 32, No. 4 (2019), p. 684.

101 Bart Jacobs, "Maximator: European Signals Intelligence Cooperation, from a Dutch Perspective," Intelligence and National Security, Vol. 35, No. 5 (2020), pp. 1–4, 8.

102 Bigo, "Sociology of Transnational Guilds," pp. 399–400, 405, 410; Bigo, "Shared Secrecy in a Digital Age and a Transnational World."

103 Guttmann, "Combatting Terror in Europe," p. 159; Adam D. M. Svendsen, "Developing International Intelligence Liaison Against Islamic State: Approaching 'One for All and All for One'?," International Journal of Intelligence and CounterIntelligence, Vol. 29, No. 2 (2016), pp. 260–261, 268; Svendsen, Understanding the Globalization of Intelligence, p. 91; Aldrich, "US–European Intelligence Co-Operation on Counter-Terrorism," p. 126.

104 Svendsen, Understanding the Globalization of Intelligence, p. 47; Adam D. M. Svendsen, "The Globalization of Intelligence Since 9/11: The Optimization of Intelligence Liaison Arrangements," International Journal of Intelligence and CounterIntelligence, Vol. 21, No. 4 (2008), pp. 661–678; Adam D. M. Svendsen, The Professionalization of Intelligence Cooperation: Fashioning Method out of Mayhem (Basingstoke: Palgrave Macmillan, 2012).

105 Hatch and Schultz, "The Dynamics of Organizational Identity," pp. 996–1001; Majken Schultz, Mary Jo Hatch, and Mogens Holten Larsen, "Scaling the Tower of Babel: Relational Differences between Identity, Image, and Culture in Organizations," The Expressive Organization: Linking Identity, Reputation, and the Corporate Brand, edited by Majken Schultz, Mary Jo Hatch, and Mogens Holten Larsen (Oxford University Press, 2002), pp. 9–35; Marko Kohtamäki, Sara Thorgren, and Joakim Wincent, "Organizational Identity and Behaviors in Strategic Networks," Journal of Business & Industrial Marketing, Vol. 31, No. 1 (2016), pp. 36–43.

106 Daniel Byman, "US Counterterrorism Intelligence Cooperation with the Developing World and Its Limits," Intelligence and National Security, Vol. 32, No. 2 (2017), pp. 145–160.

107 Daan van Knippenberg and Ed Sleebos, "Organizational Identification versus Organizational Commitment: Self-Definition, Social Exchange, and Job Attitudes," Journal of Organizational Behavior, Vol. 27, No. 5 (2006), p. 572; Yang and Maxwell, "Information-Sharing in Public Organizations," p. 167; Colquitt, Scott, and LePine, "Trust, Trustworthiness, and Trust Propensity," p. 911; Cook, Hardin, and Levi, Cooperation without Trust, pp. 42–43; Mayer, Davis, and Schoorman, "An Integrative Model of Organizational Trust," pp. 718–719; Deutsch, "A Theory of Co-Operation and Competition," pp. 149–150; Michael Tomasello et al., Why We Cooperate (Cambridge, MA: MIT Press, 2009), pp. 57–58.

108 Soeters, Sociology and Military Studies, p. 52; Ozan Aksoy, "Effects of Heterogeneity and Homophily on Cooperation," Social Psychology Quarterly, Vol. 78, No. 4 (2015), pp. 339–341; Carlos Lozares et al., "Homophily and Heterophily in Personal Networks. From Mutual Acquaintance to Relationship Intensity," Quality & Quantity, Vol. 48, No. 5 (2014), p. 2658; Bowles and Gintis, A Cooperative Species, pp. 3, 24; Sandra G. L. Schruijer, "The Social Psychology of Inter-Organizational Relations," in The Oxford Handbook of Inter-Organizational Relations, edited by Steve Cropper et al. (Oxford University Press, 2008), pp. 427–28; Bowles and Gintis, "22 Origins of Human Cooperation," pp. 437–438; Miller McPherson, Lynn Smith-Lovin, and James M. Cook, "Birds of a Feather: Homophily in Social Networks," Annual Review of Sociology, Vol. 27, No. 1 (2001), pp. 416–417, 428–429; Riolo, Cohen, and Axelrod, "Evolution of Cooperation without Reciprocity," pp. 441, 443.

109 Joseph Soeters and Irina Goldenberg, "Information Sharing in Multinational Security and Military Operations. Why and Why Not? With Whom and with Whom Not?," Defence Studies, Vol. 19, No. 1 (2019), p. 40.

110 Volk, "The Evolution of Trust and Cooperation in Diverse Groups," pp. 16–17; Hatch and Schultz, "The Dynamics of Organizational Identity," pp. 1006–1010; Blake E. Ashforth and Fred Mael, "Social Identity Theory and the Organization," Academy of Management: The Academy of Management Review; Briarcliff Manor, Vol. 14, No. 1 (1989), pp. 31–33.

111 Georg Simmel, "The Sociology of Secrecy and of Secret Societies," pp. 486, 490; Soeters, Sociology and Military Studies, p. 57; Jana Costas and Christopher Grey, "Bringing Secrecy into the Open: Towards a Theorization of the Social Processes of Organizational Secrecy," Organization Studies, Vol. 35, No. 10 (2014), pp. 1436–1438.

112 Soeters, Sociology and Military Studies, p. 58; CSIS Technology and Intelligence Task Force, "Maintaining the Intelligence Edge," p. 6.

113 John C. Turner and Katherine J. Reynolds, "Self-Categorization Theory," in Handbook of Theories of Social Psychology, edited by Paul Van Lange, Arie Kruglanski, and E. Higgins (London: SAGE Publications, 2012), pp. 3–6; Bowles and Gintis, A Cooperative Species, p. 35; Rathbun, Trust in International Cooperation, pp. 38–39; Schruijer, "The Social Psychology of Inter-Organizational Relations," p. 419; Cook, Hardin, and Levi, Cooperation without Trust, pp. 4–5, 85; Hardin, "Gaming Trust," pp. 82–83; Kramer, "Trust and Distrust in Organizations," pp. 577–578; Taylor, The Possibility of Cooperation, p. 153; Ashforth and Mael, "Social Identity Theory And The Organization," pp. 21, 23.

114 Omand, How Spies Think, pp. 163, 168.

115 Anthony R. Wells, Between Five Eyes; 50 Years of Intelligence Sharing (Casemate, 2020), pp. 135, 202–203.

116 Damien Van Puyvelde, "European Intelligence Agendas and the Way Forward," International Journal of Intelligence and CounterIntelligence, Vol. 33, No. 3 (2020), p. 3; Yvan Lledo-Ferrer and Jan-Hendrik Dietrich, "Building a European Intelligence Community," International Journal of Intelligence and CounterIntelligence, Vol. 33, No. 3 (2020), pp. 446–447.

117 Mai'a K. Davis Cross, "EU Intelligence Sharing and Joint Situation Centre: A Glass Half-Full" (2011), pp. 388, 400, https://www.offiziere.ch/wp-content/uploads/3a_cross.pdf

118 Blake D. Mathias et al., "An Identity Perspective on Coopetition in the Craft Beer Industry," Strategic Management Journal, Vol. 39, No. 12 (2018), pp. 3086–3115.

119 Rafael Biermann, "The Role of International Bureaucracies," in Palgrave Handbook of Inter-Organizational Relations in World Politics, edited by Rafael Biermann and Joachim A. Koops (Palgrave Macmillan, 2017), pp. 248–253.

120 Helene L. Boatner, "Sharing and Using Intelligence in International Organizations: Some Guidelines," National Security and the Future, Vol. 1, No. 1 (2000), p. 12.

121 Paula Ungureanu et al., "Collaboration and Identity Formation in Strategic Interorganizational Partnerships: An Exploration of Swift Identity Processes," Strategic Organization, Vol. 18, No. 1 (2020), pp. 200–202; Graham Dietz, Nicole Gillespie, and Georgia T. Chao, "Unravelling the Complexities of Trust and Culture," in Organizational Trust, edited by Mark N. K. Saunders et al. (Cambridge: Cambridge University Press, 2010), pp. 17–19; Volk, "The Evolution of Trust and Cooperation in Diverse Groups," pp. 37, 68; William B. Swann et al., "Finding Value in Diversity: Verification of Personal and Social Self-Views in Diverse Groups," Academy of Management Review, Vol. 29, No. 1 (2004), pp. 16–22; Ashforth and Mael, "Social Identity Theory and the Organization," p. 22.

122 Bowles and Gintis, A Cooperative Species, p. 48; Smith, Carroll, and Ashford, "Intra- and Interorganizational Cooperation," p. 8; Walter W. Powell and Achim Oberg, "Networks and Institutions," in The SAGE Handbook of Organizational Institutionalism, edited by Royston Greenwood et al., 2nd ed. (Los Angeles: SAGE Reference, 2017), pp. 346–347.

123 Almandoz, Marquis, and Cheely, "Drivers of Community Strength," p. 192; Joachim A. Koops, "Theorising Inter-Organisational Relations: The 'EU–NATO Relationship' as a Catalytic Case Study," European Security, Vol. 26, No. 3 (2017), pp. 329–331; Nina Graeger, "European Security as Practice: EU–NATO Communities of Practice in the Making?," European Security, Vol. 25, No. 4 (October 2016), p. 481; Bowles and Gintis, A Cooperative Species, pp. 169–170; Etienne Wenger, Beverly Trayner, and Maarten de Laat, "Promoting and Assessing Value Creation in Communities and Networks: A Conceptual Framework," Report 18 (Open Universiteit, Ruud de Moor Centrum, 2011), p. 63; Etienne Wenger, Communities of Practice: Learning, Meaning, and Identity (Cambridge: Cambridge University Press, 1998); Haas, "Introduction," pp. 3, 26; Paul J. DiMaggio and Walter W. Powell, "The Iron Cage Revisited: Institutional Isomorphism and Collective Rationality in Organizational Fields," American Sociological Review, Vol. 48, No. 2 (1983), pp. 148–154; Taylor, The Possibility of Cooperation, p. 23; Powell and Oberg, "Networks and Institutions," pp. 447–448; Royston Greenwood et al., "Institutional Complexity and Organizational Responses," Academy of Management Annals, Vol. 5, No. 1 (2011), pp. 346–347.

124 Bigo, "Shared Secrecy in a Digital Age and a Transnational World," pp. 379–380; Volk, "The Evolution of Trust and Cooperation in Diverse Groups," p. 15; Ashforth and Mael, "Social Identity Theory and the Organization," pp. 20, 22, 26; Dominic Abrams et al., "Knowing What to Think by Knowing Who You Are: Self-Categorization and the Nature of Norm Formation, Conformity and Group Polarization," British Journal of Social Psychology, Vol. 29, No. 2 (1990), pp. 97–119; Dora C. Lau and I. Keith Murnighan, "Demographic Diversity and Faultlines: The Compositional Dynamics of Organizational Groups," Academy of Management Review, Vol. 23, No. 2 (1998), p. 17; Monica Bakker, "The Importance of Networks and Relationships," in Managing Authentic Relationships: Facing New Challenges in a Changing Context, edited by Jean Paul Wijers et al. (Amsterdam: Amsterdam University Press, 2019), p. 32; Lozares et al., "Homophily and Heterophily in Personal Networks," p. 2658; Crawford, "Intelligence Cooperation," p. 20; Nicolas Labasque, "The Merits of Informality in Bilateral and Multilateral Cooperation," International Journal of Intelligence and CounterIntelligence, Vol. 33, No. 3 (2020), pp. 493, 495; Fägersten, For EU Eyes Only?, p. 2; Lefebvre, "The Difficulties and Dilemmas of International Intelligence Cooperation"; Aldrich, "Transatlantic Intelligence and Security Cooperation"; Björn Müller-Wille, "The Effect of International Terrorism on EU Intelligence Co-Operation," JCMS: Journal of Common Market Studies, Vol. 46, No. 1 (2008), pp. 49–73; Mary Manjikian,

"But My Hands Are Clean: The Ethics of Intelligence Sharing and the Problem of Complicity," International Journal of Intelligence and CounterIntelligence, Vol. 28, No. 4 (2015), pp. 692–709; Svendsen, "Contemporary Intelligence Innovation in Practice"; David Schaefer, "Intelligence Cooperation and New Trends in Space Technology: Do the Ties Still Bind?," Australian Journal of International Affairs; Canberra, Vol. 72, No. 4 (2018), pp. 364–370.

Chapter 8: The Construction of Secret Intelligence as a Masculine Profession. Eleni Braat

1   Oral history interview with a former employee of the Dutch Security Service, 2010, anonymously cited in Eleni Braat, *Van oude jongens, de Dingen die Voorbij Gaan* (Zoetermeer: Algemene Inlichtingen- en Veiligheidsdienst, 2012), p. 164.

2   While the spy novel originated from Britain, the genre of the spy film was mostly an American product. Among the few European exceptions is *Spione* (1928) from Fritz Lang, which gave importance to women in intelligence, in contrast to the American film industry. Alan R. Booth observes the persistently "ancillary, superficial and generally negative roles" women have played in the espionage film, both inside and outside the American film industry. Alan R. Booth, "The Development of the Espionage Film," in *Spy Fiction, Spy Films and Real Intelligence*, edited by Wesley K. Wark (London: Frank Cass, 1991), p. 136–160.

3   Simon Willmetts, *In Secrecy's Shadow: The OSS and CIA in Hollywood Cinema, 1941–1979* (Edinburgh: Edinburgh University Press, 2016), p. 128.

4   Booth, "The Development of the Espionage Film," pp. 150, 157.

5   Damien Van Puyvelde, "Women and Black Employees at the Central Intelligence Agency: From Fair Employment to Diversity Management," *Cambridge Review of International Affairs* (2020). doi:10.1080/09557571.2020.1853052, pp. 16–19; Amy J. Martin, "America's Evolution of Women and Their Roles in the Intelligence Community," *Journal of Strategic Security*, Vol. 8, No. 3 (Suppl., 2015), pp. 99–109.

6   Damien Van Puyvelde and Sean Curtis, "'Standing on the Shoulders of Giants': diversity and scholarship in Intelligence Studies," *Intelligence and National Security*, Vol. 31, No. 7 (2016), pp. 1040–1054; Lenn Scott and Peter Jackson, "The Study of Intelligence in Theory and Practice," *Intelligence and National Security*, Vol. 19, No. 2 (2004), pp. 139–169.

7   Kathryn S. Olmsted, "Blond Queens, Red Spiders, and Neurotic Old Maids: Gender and Espionage in the Early Cold War," *Intelligence and National Security*, Vol. 19, No. 1 (2004), pp. 78–94; Sandra C. Taylor, "Long-Haired Women, Short-Haired Spies: Gender, Espionage, and America's War in Vietnam," *Intelligence and National Security*, Vol. 13, No. 2 (1998), pp. 61–70; Tammy Proctor, *Female Intelligence: Women and Espionage in the First World*

War (New York and London: New York University Press, 2004); Deborah van Seters, "'Hardly Hollywood's Ideal': Female Autobiographies of Secret Service Work, 1914-1945," *Intelligence and National Security*, Vol. 7, No. 4, 1992, pp. 403-424. Juliette Pattinson, "The twilight war: gender and espionage, Britain, 1900-1950," Simona Sharoni, Julia Welland, Linda Steiner, and Jennifer Pedersen eds., *Handbook on Gender and War* (Cheltenham: Edward Elgar, 2016), pp. 66-85. Confusingly, some literature treats intelligence employees and recruited agents (spies) together, even if agents do not contribute to the organizational culture of intelligence and security services.

8   Jess Shahan, "'Don't Keep Mum': Critical Approaches to the Narratives of Women Intelligence Professionals," *Intelligence and National Security*, Vol. 36, No. 4 (2021), p. 570.

9   For example, see Hamilton Bean, "Rhetorical and Critical/Cultural Intelligence Studies," *Intelligence and National Security*, Vol. 28, No. 4 (2013), pp. 495–519; Eleni Braat, "Self-Reinforcing Secrecy: Cultures of Secrecy within Intelligence Agencies," in *Transparency and Secrecy in European Democracies. Contested Trade-offs*, edited by Dorota Mokrosinska (London and New York: Routledge, 2021), pp. 118–134; Van Puyvelde, "Women and Black Employees at the Central Intelligence Agency."

10   Daniel W. B. Lomas, "#ForgetJamesBond: Diversity, Inclusion, and the UK's Intelligence Agencies," *Intelligence and National Security*. doi:10.1080/026845 27.2021.1938370, 2 July 2021; Jess Shahan, "'Don't Keep Mum.'"

11   The references in reference 6 mostly relate to women agents during the two world wars.

12   Proctor, *Female Intelligence*.

13   Shahan, "'Don't Keep Mum.'" This article is based on a part of Shahan's Ph.D. thesis (Jessica Renee Shahan, *Spying Gender: Women in British Intelligence 1969–1994*, Aberystwyth University, 2019).

14   Van Puyvelde, "Women and Black Employees at the Central Intelligence Agency."

15   R. W. Connell, *Masculinities* (Berkeley, Los Angeles: University of California Press, 2005), pp. 21–23.

16   *Ibid.*, p. 71.

17   Judith Butler, *Gender Trouble* (New York and London: Routledge, 2007), p. 11, 34; Melissa Tyler and Laurie Cohen, "Spaces that Matter: Gender Performativity and Organizational Space," *Organization Studies*, Vol. 31, No. 2 (2010), p. 179.

18   Butler, *Gender Trouble*, pp. 10–11, 24.

19   Yvonne Due Billing and Mats Alvesson, "Questioning the Notion of Feminine Leadership: A Critical Perspective on the Gender Labelling of Leadership," *Gender, Work & Organization*, Vol. 7, No. 3 (2000), pp. 144–157.

20   This definition is workable in the context of this article. However, it falls short of the long-term debates on definitions of masculinity in the related literature (e.g., Janwillem Liebrand, *Masculinities among Irrigation Engineers and Water Professionals in Nepal*, Ph.D. thesis Wageningen University 2014, p. 1, 14); Judith Halberstam, "Female Masculinity," in *Literary Theory. An Anthology*, edited by Julie Rivkin and Michael Ryan (Oxford: Blackwell, 2004), pp. 935–936.

21   Connell, *Masculinities*, pp. 28–29.

22   Butler, *Gender Trouble*, p. 13.

23   Eric Anderson and Rory Magrath, *Men and Masculinities* (London & New York: Routledge, 2019).

24   Connell, *Masculinities*; Jeff Hearn, "From Hegemonic Masculinity to the Hegemony of Men," *Feminist Theory*, Vol. 5. No. 1 (2004), pp. 49–72.

25   Joyce Outshoorn, "Half werk. Vrouwenbeweging, emancipatie en politiek in Nederland, 1950–1990," *Leidschrift*, Vol. 17, No. 2 (2002), pp. 35–51.

26   Kea Tijdens, *Een wereld van verschil: arbeidsparticipatie van vrouwen, 1945–2005*, inaugural lecture Erasmus University Rotterdam, 3 March 2006, p. 3.

27   Internal report on the emancipation of women, 1990, archive Dutch General Intelligence and Security Service.

28   F. M. van der Meer and L. J. Roborgh, *Ambtenaren in Nederland: omvang, bureaucratisering en representativiteit van het ambtelijk apparaat* (Alphen aan den Rijn: Samson H.D. Tjeenk Willink, 1993).

29   Van Puyvelde, "Women and Black Employees at the Central Intelligence Agency," p. 17.

30   Personnel magazine *Het Spionnetje*, January 1967, archive Dutch General Intelligence and Security Service.

31   Oral history interview with former intelligence officer, 2010, anonymously cited in Braat, *Van oude jongens*, p. 167.

32   Oral history interview with former employee of the Dutch Security Service, 2010, anonymously cited in Braat, *Van oude jongens*, pp. 167–168.

33   Eleni Braat, *Van oude jongens*, pp. 114–118 on the reputations of the operational directions B (political extremism) and directions C (counterespionage).

34   Vetting and surveillance were not part of directions B and C.

35   Oral history interview with former employee of the Dutch Security Service, 2010, anonymously cited in Braat, *Van oude jongens*, p. 169.

36 *Ibid.*

37 Personnel magazine *Het Spionnetje*, January/February 1982, archive Dutch General Intelligence and Security Service.

38 The Cabinet Den Uyl (1973–1977), headed by social democrat Joop den Uyl, was one of the most leftwing and progressive governments in Dutch parliamentary history. Its successor was the Cabinet Van Agt I (1977–1981), headed by Christian democrat Dries van Agt.

39 Personnel magazine *Het Spionnetje*, first quarter 1978, archive Dutch General Intelligence and Security Service.

40 Braat, *Van oude jongens*, p. 168. A 1953 internal report of the CIA, the "Petticoat" Report, which studied career opportunities for women within the agency, expressed similar gender biases (Van Puyvelde, "Women and Black Employees at the Central Intelligence Agency," p. 7).

41 Internal report on the emancipation of women, 1990, archive Dutch General Intelligence and Security Service.

42 *Ibid.*

43 *Ibid.*

44 Personnel magazine *Het Spionnetje*, November 1962.

45 Internal report on the emancipation of women, 1990, archive Dutch General Intelligence and Security Service.

46 Oral history interview with former intelligence officer, 2010, anonymously cited in Braat, *Van oude jongens*, p. 171.

47 Internal report on the emancipation of women, 1990, archive Dutch General Intelligence and Security Service.

48 Oral history interview with former employee of the Dutch Security Service, 2010, anonymously cited in Braat, *Van oude jongens*, p. 163.

49 Internal report on the emancipation of women, 1990, archive Dutch General Intelligence and Security Service.

50 Personnel magazine *Het Spionnetje*, Christmas edition 1959, archive Dutch General Intelligence and Security Service.

51 Personnel magazine *Het Spionnetje*, September 1965, archive Dutch General Intelligence and Security Service.

52 *Ibid.*

53 Personnel magazine *Het Spionnetje*, November 1988, archive Dutch General Intelligence and Security Service.

54 Personnel magazine *Het Spionnetje*, June 1965, archive Dutch General Intelligence and Security Service.

55 Personnel magazine *Het Spionnetje*, first quarter 1978.

56 Oral history with former intelligence officer, 2010, anonymously cited in Braat, *Van oude jongens*, p. 169.

57 Jess Shahan, "'Don't Keep Mum,'" pp. 576–577.

58 Personnel magazine *Het Spionnetje*, December 1977.

59 Internal report on the emancipation of women, 1990, archive Dutch General Intelligence and Security Service.

60 Van Puyvelde, "Women and Black Employees at the Central Intelligence Agency," pp. 16–19.

61 Internal report on the emancipation of women, 1990, archive Dutch General Intelligence and Security Service.

62 Personnel magazine *Het Spionnetje*, archive Dutch General Intelligence and Security Service, December 1977.

63 *Ibid.*

64 *Ibid.* See also Braat, *Van oude jongens*, pp. 116–118.

65 Personnel magazine *Het Spionnetje*, archive Dutch General Intelligence and Security Service, December 1977.

66 Personnel magazine *Het Spionnetje*, archive Dutch General Intelligence and Security Service, first quarter 1978.

67 *Ibid.*

68 Oral history interview with former head of service Arthur Docter van Leeuwen, 2010, as cited in Braat, *Van oude jongens*, p. 166.

69 Van Puyvelde, "Women and Black Employees at the Central Intelligence Agency," p. 23.

Chapter 9: Assessing Intelligence Oversight: the Case of Sweden, Dan Hansén

1. Leigh & Wegge "Introduction" to *Intelligence oversight in the twenty-first century*, p. 1.

2. See e.g., Wright & Kreissl "European responses to the Snowden revelations: A discussion paper"

3. See e.g., Cayford, Pieters and Hijzen "Plots, murders, and money: oversight bodies evaluating the effectiveness of surveillance technology", and Dietrich 'Of Toothless Windbags, Blind Guardians and Blunt Swords: The Ongoing Controversy about the Reform of Intelligence Services Oversight in Germany'.

4. Zegart *Eyes on Spies*, p. 20; see also Holt *Secret Intelligence and Public Policy: A Dilemma of Democracy*, pp. 230–236

5. Gill 'Of intelligence oversight and the challenge of surveillance corporatism'.

6. Wegge & Wetzling "Contemporary and future challenges to effective intelligence oversight", p. 28

7. For a succinct overview of the debate, see Marsh & McConnell 'Towards a Framework for Establishing Policy Success'. See also FitzGerald et al. 'Policy success/policy failure: A framework for understanding policy choices'

8. Bovens & 't Hart *Understanding Policy Fiascoes*

9. Pressman & Wildavsky *Implementation*; Hall *Great Planning Disasters*

10. Douglas et al. "Rising to Ostrom's challenge: an invitation to walk on the bright side of public governance and public service"; Compton & 't Hart *Great Policy Successes*

11. Marsh & McConnell "Towards a Framework for Establishing Policy Success"; FitzGerald et al. 'Policy success/policy failure: A framework for understanding policy choices'

12. Bovens, 't Hart & Kuipers (2006, p. 319), cited in Marsh & McConnell "Towards a Framework for Establishing Policy Success", p. 569

13. Majone (1989, p. 183), cited in Marsh & McConnell "Towards a Framework for Establishing Policy Success", p. 570

14. McConnell "Policy Success, Policy Failure and Grey Areas In-Between".

15. Ibid.

16. Compton & 't Hart *Great Policy Successes*. McConnell (Citation2010) also elaborates with process, program and political dimensions.

17. Defty "From committees of parliamentarians to parliamentary committees" p. 369. Defty in turn refers to Gill, P. "'Knowing the Self, Knowing the Other": The Comparative Analysis of Security Intelligence'. In Handbook of Intelligence Studies, edited by L. K. Johnson, 82–90. London: Routledge, 2009.

18. For more on implicit comparisons, see George & Bennett's discussion on structured, focused comparison in Case Studies and Theory Development, chapter 3.

19. Zegart *Eyes on Spies; Spies, Lies, and Algorithms*; Dietrich 'Of Toothless Windbags, Blind Guardians and Blunt Swords'; Wegge "Intelligence Oversight and the Security of the State"

20. Gill 'Of intelligence oversight and the challenge of surveillance corporatism', p. 972.

21. Zegart *Eyes on Spies*

22. The same goes for Danish, see Andersen et al. "Oversight and governance of the Danish intelligence community", p. 243.

23. Leigh 'More Closely Watching the Spies: Three Decades of Experience', p. 7.

24. Wegge 'Intelligence Oversight and the Security of the State'.

25. Hillebrand 'Intelligence Oversight and Accountability'.

26. Gill 'Of intelligence oversight and the challenge of surveillance corporatism', p. 974.

27. Compton & 't Hart *Great Policy Successes*, p. 5

28. Gill 'Of intelligence oversight and the challenge of surveillance corporatism'; Wegge 'Intelligence Oversight and the Security of the State'; Hijzen 'More than a ritual dance. The Dutch practice of parliamentary oversight and control of the intelligence community'; Aldrich & Richterova 'Ambient accountability: Intelligence services in Europe and the decline of state secrecy'.

29. Hillebrand "Intelligence Oversight and Accountability".

30. Gill 'Of intelligence oversight and the challenge of surveillance corporatism'; Zegart *Spies, Lies, and Algorithms*

31. Hillebrand "Intelligence Oversight and Accountability".

32. The table is a modification and simplification of McConnell's "Policy Success, Policy Failure and Grey Areas In-Between", p. 354, also inspired by Compton & 't Hart *Great Policy Successes, p.5*

33. McConnell "Policy Success, Policy Failure and Grey Areas In-Between"; Compton & 't Hart *Great Policy Successes*, p. 5; FitzGerald el al 'Policy success/ policy failure'

34. Born, Hans & Thorsten Wetzling "Intelligence accountability" p. 318

35. Wegge "Intelligence Oversight and the Security of the State".

36. Holt *Secret Intelligence and Public Policy*

37. Holt *Secret Intelligence and Public Policy*, p. 232

38. Gill 'Of intelligence oversight and the challenge of surveillance corporatism'.

39. Zegart *Spies, Lies, and Algorithms*

40. Rittberger & Goetz "Secrecy in Europe, West European Politics", p. 838–839; Hizen 'More than a ritual dance'

41. The table is a modification and simplification of McConnell's "Policy Success, Policy Failure and Grey Areas In-Between", p. 352, also inspired by Compton & 't Hart *Great Policy Successes, p.5*

42. Compton & 't Hart *Great Policy Successes*, p. 5; McConnell 'Policy Success, Policy Failure and Grey Areas In-Between'

43. Gill 'Of intelligence oversight and the challenge of surveillance corporatism',; Zegart *Spies, Lies, and Algorithms*

44. Loch Johnson "A shock theory of congressional accountability for intelligence".

45. The table is a modification and simplification of McConnell's 'Policy Success, Policy Failure and Grey Areas In-Between', p. 356, also inspired by Compton & 't Hart *Great Policy Successes, p.5*

46. Compton & 't Hart *Great Policy Successes*, p. 5; Ansell et al. 'Dynamic conservatism: How institutions change to remain the same'

47. Sabatier Paul, "Toward better theories of the policy process".

48. The table is inspired by Compton & 't Hart *Great Policy Successes, p.5* and uses the spectrum categories developed by McConnell's 'Policy Success, Policy Failure and Grey Areas In-Between', p. 352–6

49. Swedish Government proposition (Citation1999).

50. Swedish Law (2000:130) on defence intelligence operations.

51. Swedish Government proposition (Citation2007).

52. Swedish Parliament (Citation2008), see also Nohrstedt 'Shifting Resources and Venues Producing Policy Change in Contested Subsystems: A Case Study of Swedish Signals Intelligence Policy'

53. Swedish Parliament Citation(2009b).

54. Swedish Parliament (Citation1976).

55. Bratt, P. & J. Guillou "Sveriges spionage"

56. Swedish Parliament (Citation1973); Swedish Government 1976; Swedish Justice Ombudsman (Citation1975)

57. Swedish Justice Ombudsman (Citation1975).

58. Swedish Government 2002, p. 17 (on election campaigns); p. 19 (on official inquiries and books/documentaries).

59. Swedish Government 2002, p. 509.

60. Swedish Government 2009b.

61. FII, in Swedish: Statens inspektion för försvarsunderrättelseverksamhet, Siun, lit.: the state's inspectorate for defence intelligence operations.

62. Born, Hans & Thorsten Wetzling "Intelligence accountability" p. 320

63. Swedish Law (2008:717); Compilation of FII annual reports retrieved from FII web page (2022).

64. Swedish Parliament Citation(2009b).

65. Compilation of FII annual reports retrieved from FII web page 2022.

66. Swedish National Audit Organisation (Citation2015), p. 3

67. In FY 2010–16, FII spent 61–68 per cent of their budget, and in FY 2017–21 they spent 84–90 per cent of a somewhat decreased budget. Compilation of FII annual reports retrieved from FII web page 2022

68. Swedish National Audit Organisation (Citation2015), p. 10
69. Ibid.
70. Compilation of FII annual reports retrieved from FII web page 2022.
71. Ibid.
72. European Court of Human Rights 2021, p. 92.
73. Compilation of FII annual reports retrieved from FII web page 2022.
74. European Court of Human Rights 2021, p. 93.
75. Government Offices of Sweden 2022.
76. FII annual report 2022.
77. Swedish Parliament 2022, § 10, p. 35–38
78. Compilation of FII annual reports retrieved from FII web page 2022.
79. Zegart *Spies, Lies, and Algorithms*, pp. 212–215
80. Swedish Government official report (Citation2009); Swedish Justice Ministry report (Citation2011); Swedish Government proposition (Citation2012).
81. Swedish Government proposition 2018.
82. Swedish Parliament (Citation2008).
83. Swedish Law 2021:1173.
84. Swedish Parliament 2021.

References

Aldrich, R. J., and D. Richterova. "Ambient Accountability: Intelligence Services in Europe and the Decline of State Secrecy." West European Politics 41, no. 4 (2018): 1003–1024. doi:10.1080/01402382.2017.1415780. [Taylor & Francis Online], [Web of Science ®], [Google Scholar]

Andersen, S. J., M. Ejnar Hansen, and P. H. J. Davies. "Oversight and Governance of the Danish Intelligence Community." Intelligence & National Security 37, no. 2 (2022): 241–261. doi:10.1080/02684527.2021.1976919. [Taylor & Francis Online], [Web of Science ®], [Google Scholar]

Ansell, C., A. Boin, and M. Farjoun. "Dynamic Conservatism: How Institutions Change to Remain the Same." Research in the Sociology of Organizations 44 (2015): 89–119. [Google Scholar]

Born, H., and T. Wetzling. "Intelligence Accountability: Challenges for Parliaments and Intelligence Services." In Handbook of Intelligence Studies, edited by L. Johnson, 315–328. London and New York: Routledge, 2007. [Google Scholar]

Bovens, M., and H. Paul 't. Understanding Policy Fiascoes. New Brunswick, NJ: Transaction Press, 1996. [Google Scholar]

Bratt, P., and J. Guillou. "Sveriges spionage" [Sweden's Espionage]." Folket i Bild/ Kulturfront 2, no. 9 (1973). [Google Scholar]

Cayford, M., W. Pieters, and C. Hijzen. "Wolter Pieters & Constant Hijzen "Plots, Murders, and Money: Oversight Bodies Evaluating the Effectiveness of Surveillance Technology." Intelligence & National Security 33, no. 7 (2018): 999–1021. doi:10.1080/02684527.2018.1487159. [Taylor & Francis Online], [Web of Science ®], [Google Scholar]

Compton, M. Paul 't Hart Great Policy Successes: Or, a Tale About Why It's Amazing That Governments Get so Little Credit for Their Many Everyday and Extraordinary Achievements as Told by Sympathetic Observers Who Seek to Create Space for a Less Relentlessly Negative View of Our Pivotal Public Institutions. Oxford: Oxford University Press, 2019. [Google Scholar]

Defty, A. "From Committees of Parliamentarians to Parliamentary Committees: Comparing Intelligence Oversight Reform in Australia, Canada, New Zealand and the UK." Intelligence & National Security 35, no. 3 (2020): 367–384. doi:10.1080/02684527.2020.1732646. [Taylor & Francis Online], [Web of Science ®], [Google Scholar]

Dietrich, J.-H. "Of Toothless Windbags, Blind Guardians and Blunt Swords: The Ongoing Controversy About the Reform of Intelligence Services Oversight in Germany." Intelligence & National Security 31, no. 3 (2016): 397–415. doi:10.1080/02684527.2015.1017246. [Taylor & Francis Online], [Web of Science ®], [Google Scholar]

Douglas, S., T. Schillemans, H. Paul 't, C. Ansell, L. B. Andersen, M. Flinders, B. Head, et al. "Rising to Ostrom's Challenge: An Invitation to Walk on the Bright Side of Public Governance and Public Service." Policy Design and Practice 4, no. 4 (2021): 441–451. doi:10.1080/25741292.2021.1972517. [Taylor & Francis Online], [Web of Science ®], [Google Scholar]

European Court of Human Rights, Grand Chamber, Centrum för Rättvisa v. Sweden, Application no. 35252/08, Judgement, Strasbourg, 25 May 2021. [Google Scholar]

FII 2022a, retrieved from Fii's Web Page Siun.Se on 1 November 2022 [Google Scholar]

FII 2022b, in Swedish Only: Siun, Årsredovisning 2021 [FII, Annual Report 2021], Stockholm 18 February 2022 [Google Scholar]

FitzGerald, C., E. O'Malley, and D. Ó Broin. "Policy Success/Policy Failure: A Framework for Understanding Policy Choices." Administration 67, no. 2 (2019): 1–24. doi:10.2478/admin-2019-0011. [Crossref], [Web of Science ®], [Google Scholar]

George, A., and A. Bennett. Case Studies and Theory Development in the Social Sciences. Cambridge, Ma: MIT Press, 2004. [Google Scholar]

Gill, P. "Of Intelligence Oversight and the Challenge of Surveillance Corporatism." Intelligence & National Security 35, no. 7 (2020): 970–989. doi:10.1080/026 84527.2020.1783875. [Taylor & Francis Online], [Web of Science °], [Google Scholar]

Government Offices of Sweden: Action Plan: Case of Centrum För Rättvisa. V. Sweden (Application 35252/08), Judgment of 25 May 2021, Final on 25 May 2021, Stockholm 25 May 2022a. [Google Scholar]

Hall, P. Great Planning Disasters. Berkeley, CA: University of California Press, 1982. [Crossref], [Google Scholar]

Hijzen, C. "More Than a Ritual Dance. The Dutch Practice of Parliamentary Oversight and Control of the Intelligence Community." Security and Human Rights 24, no. 3–4 (2013): 227–238. doi:10.1163/18750230-02404002. [Crossref], [Google Scholar]

Hillebrand, C. "Intelligence Oversight and Accountability." In Routledge Companion to Intelligence Studies, edited by R. Dover, M. S. Goodman, and C. Hillebrand, 305–312. London & New York: Routledge, 2015. [Google Scholar]

Holt, P. M. Secret Intelligence and Public Policy: A Dilemma of Democracy. Washington: Congressional Quarterly Inc, 1995. [Google Scholar]

Johnson, L. "A Shock Theory of Congressional Accountability for Intelligence." In Handbook of Intelligence Studies, edited by L. Johnson, 343–360. London and New York: Routledge, 2007. [Crossref], [Google Scholar]

Leigh, I. "More Closely Watching the Spies: Three Decades of Experience." In Who's Watching the Spies? Establishing Intelligence Service Accountability, edited by H. Born, L. K. Johnson, and I. Leigh, 3–11. Nebraska: Potomac Books, 2005. [Google Scholar]

Leigh, I., and N. Wegge. "Introduction." In Intelligence Oversight in the Twenty-First Century: Accountability in a Changing World, edited by I. Leigh and N. Wegge, 1–4. London & New York: Routledge, 2020. doi:10.4324/9781351188791-1. [Crossref], [Google Scholar]

Marsh, D., and A. McConnel. "Towards a Framework for Establishing Policy Success." Public Administration 88, no. 3 (2010): 564–583. doi:10.1111/j.1467-9299.2009.01803.x. [Crossref], [Google Scholar]

McConnell, A. "Policy Success, Policy Failure and Grey Areas In-Between." Journal of Public Policy 30, no. 3 (2010): 345–362. doi:10.1017/S0143814X10000152. [Crossref], [Web of Science °], [Google Scholar]

Nohrstedt, D. "Shifting Resources and Venues Producing Policy Change in Contested Subsystems: A Case Study of Swedish Signals Intelligence Policy." Policy Studies Journal 39, no. 3 (2011): 461–484. doi:10.1111/j.1541-0072.2011.00417.x. [Crossref], [Web of Science °], [Google Scholar]

Pressman, J., and A. Wildavsky. Implementation: How Great Expectations in Washington are Dashed in Oakland; Or, Why It's Amazing That Federal Programs Work at All, This Being a Saga of the Economic Development Administration as Told by Two Sympathetic Observers Who Seek to Build Morals on a Foundation. Berkeley, CA: University of California Press, 1973. [Google Scholar]

Rittberger, B., and K. H. Goetz. "Secrecy in Europe." West European Politics 41, no. 4 (2018): 825–845. doi:10.1080/01402382.2017.1423456. [Taylor & Francis Online], [Web of Science ®], [Google Scholar]

Sabatier, P. "Toward Better Theories of the Policy Process." PS: Political Science and Politics 24, no. 2 (1991): 147–115. doi:10.2307/419923. [Crossref], [Web of Science ®], [Google Scholar]

Swedish Government official report 1976, in Swedish only: Den militära underrättelsetjänsten, betänkande från 1974 års underrättelseutredning SOU 1976:19 [The military intelligence: report from the 1974 intelligence inquiry, SOU 1976:19] [Google Scholar]

Swedish Government official report 2002, in Swedish only: Det grå brödraskapet. En berättelse om IB, SOU 2002:92 [The Grey Brotherhood: A Story About IB, SOU 2002:92] [Google Scholar]

Swedish Government official report 2009, in Swedish only: Signalspaning för polisiära behov SOU 2009:66 [Signals intelligence for the police's needs, SOU 2009:66] [Google Scholar]

Swedish Government proposition 1999, in Swedish only: Regeringens proposition 1999/2000:25 Lag om forsvarsunderrättelseverksamhet [Government proposition 1999/2000:25 Law on defence intelligence operations] [Google Scholar]

Swedish Government proposition 2007, in Swedish only: Regeringens proposition 2006/07:63 En anpassad försvarsunderrättelseverksamhet [Government proposition 2006/07:63 An adapted defence intelligence function] [Google Scholar]

Swedish Government proposition 2009, in Swedish only: Regeringens proposition 2008/09:201 Förstärkt integritetsskydd vid signalspaning [The Govenment's proposition 2008/09:201 Enhanced integrity protection in signals intelligence.] [Google Scholar]

Swedish Government proposition 2012, in Swedish only: Regeringens proposition 2011/12:179 Polisens tillgång till signalspaning i försvarsunderrättelseverksamhet [The Government's proposition 2011/12:179 The police's access to signals intelligence in defence intelligence operations.] [Google Scholar]

Swedish Government proposition 2019, in Swedish Only: Polisens Tillgång Till Underrättelser Från Försvarets Radioanstalt, Prop. 2018/19: 96 [The Police's Access to Intelligence from the National Defence Radio Establishment, Proposition 2018/19: 96] [Google Scholar]

Swedish Justice Ministry report 2011, in Swedish Only: Departementsserien Och Promemorior Från Justitiedepartementet: Polisens Tillgång Till Signalspaning I Försvarsunderrättelseverksamhet Ds 2011: 44 [Ministerial Series and Memos from the Ministry of Justice: The Police's Access to Signals Intelligence in Defence Intelligence Operations Ds 2011: 44] [Google Scholar]

Swedish Justice Ombudsman 1975, in Swedish Only: Jo: S Ämbetsberättelse 1975/76 [Jo's Official Report 1975/76.] [Google Scholar]

Swedish Law 2000:130, in Swedish only: Lag 2000:130 om försvarsunderrättelseverksamhet [Law 2000:130 on defence intelligence operations.] [Google Scholar]

Swedish Law 2008:717, in Swedish Only: Lag 2008: 717 Om Signalspaning I Försvarsunderrättelseverksamhet [Law 2008/717 on Signals Reconnaissance in Defence Intelligence Operations.] [Google Scholar]

Swedish Law 2021:1173, in Swedish Only: Lag 2021: 1173 Om Ändring I Lagen (2008: 717) Om Signalspaning I Försvarsunderrättelseverksamhet [Law 2021: 1173 on Changes of the Law (2008: 717) on Signals Intelligence in Defence Intelligence Operations.] [Google Scholar]

Swedish National Audit Organisation 2015, in Swedish with a summary in English: Kontrollen av försvarsunderrättelseverksamheten, RiR 2015:2 [Control of defence intelligence operations, RiR 2015:2] [Google Scholar]

Swedish Parliament, in Swedish Only: Riksdagsskrivelse 2021/22: 45 [Parliamentary Letter 2021/22: 45], 24 November 2021. [Google Scholar]

Swedish Parliament 1973, in Swedish only: FöU 1973:25 Försvarsutskottets betänkande angående den militära underrättelsetjänsten mm. [The Parliament Defence Committee's report on the military intelligence etc.] [Google Scholar]

Swedish Parliament 1976, in Swedish only: Förordning (1976:498) med instruktion för försvarets underrättelsenämnd [Ordinance (1976:498) with instructions to the armed forces' intelligence committee]. [Google Scholar]

Swedish Parliament 2008, in Swedish Only: Försvarsutskottets Betänkande 2007/08: FöU15 Lag Om Signalspaning M.M. (Förnyad Behandling) [Parliament Defense Committee Report 2007/2008: FöU15 Signals Intelligence Act Etc. (Renewed Tratment)] [Google Scholar]

Swedish Parliament 2009a, in Swedish only: Förordning (2009:969) med instruktion för Statens inspektion för försvarsunderrättelseverksamheten. [Ordinance (2009:969) with instructions to the Foreign Intelligence Inspectorate] [Google Scholar]

387

Swedish Parliament 2009b, in Swedish only: Försvarsutskottets betänkande 2008/09:FöU11 Ändrad tidpunkt för signalspaning i kablar [Parliament Defence Committee report 2008/2009:FöU11 Changed time for signals intelligence in cables] [Google Scholar]

Swedish Parliament, in Swedish Only: § 10 Integritetsskydd Vid Signalspaning I Försvarsunderrättelseverksamhet [§ 10 Integrity Protection in Defence Intelligence Operations], Protocol 2 March 2022b. [Google Scholar]

Wegge, N., and Wegge. "Njord "Intelligence Oversight and the Security of the State." International Journal of Intelligence & CounterIntelligence 30, no. 4 (2017): 687–700. doi:10.1080/08850607.2017.1337445. [Taylor & Francis Online], [Web of Science *], [Google Scholar]

Wegge, N., and T. Wetzling. 2020. "Contemporary and Future Challenges to Effective Intelligence Oversight" Leigh & WeggeEds., Intelligence Oversight in the Twenty-First Century: Accountability in a Changing World, London & New York: Routledge, 25–39. 10.4324/9781351188791-3 [Crossref], [Google Scholar]

Wright, D., and R. Kreissl "European Responses to the Snowden Revelations: A Discussion Paper," Increasing Resilience in Surveillance Societies, December 2013. [Google Scholar]

Zegart, A. B. Eyes on Spies: Congress and the United States Intelligence Community. Stanford, Ca: Hoover Institution Press, 2011. [Google Scholar]

Zegart, A. B. Spies, Lies, and Algorithms: The History and Future of American Intelligence. Princeton: Princeton University Press, 2022. [Google Scholar]

Chapter 10: Spy power, Technological Innovations, and the Human Dimensions of intelligence: Recent Presidential Abuse of America's Secret Agencies

Barnes, J. E., & Goldman, A. (2020, October 31). Trump is said to set aside intelligence career intelligence briefer to hear from advisers instead. New York Times.https://www.nytimes.com/2020/10/30/us/politics/trump-intelligence-briefings.html

Bruck, C. (2016, August 1). The Guantánamo failure. The New Yorker. Fuller, C. J. (2017). See it/shoot it: The secret history of the CIA's lethal drone program. New Haven, Connecticut: Yale University Press.

Gibbon, E. (1952). The decline and fall of the Roman Empire. New York: Viking.

Hayden, M. V. (2016). Playing to the edge: American intelligence in an age of terror. New York: Penguin.

Johnson, L. K. (1985). A season of inquiry: The senate intelligence investigation. Lexington: University Press of Kentucky.

Johnson, L. K. (2018). Spy watching: Intelligence accountability in the United States. New York: Oxford University Press.

Footnotes

1 For illustrations in the public literature of modern techint in the domain of satellite camera-surveillance (imint or "imagery intelligence"), see Bruce Berkowitz, The National Reconnaissance Office at 50 Years: A Brief History (Chantilly, VA: U.S National Reconnaissance Office, Center for the Study of National Reconnaissance, Washington, D.C., 2011); Dino A. Brugioni, From Balloons to Blackbirds: Reconnaissance, Surveillance and Imagery intelligence, How It Evolved, The Intelligence Professional Series, No. 1 (McLean, VA: Association of Former Intelligence Officers, 1993); on listening and sensing devices in space, Matthew M. Aid, The Secret Sentry: The Untold History of the National Security Agency (New York: Bloomsbury Press, 2009), and underwater, James Bamford, The Puzzle Palace: Inside the National Security Agency (New York: Penguin, 1983), and Jeffrey T. Richelson, The US Intelligence Community, 7th ed. (Boulder, Colorado: Westview, 2016); on drones as intelligence-collection platforms, Sarah E. Kreps, Drones: What Everyone Needs to Know (New York: Oxford University Press, 2016); on asset communications with their handlers, Frederick P. Hitz, The Great Game: The Myth and Reality of Espionage (New York: Knopf, 2004); and on CIA disguises, Antonio J. Mendez with Malcolm McConnell, The Master of Disguise: My Secret Life in the CIA (New York: Morrow, 2000). Insightful general works on techint include: Robert M. Clark, The Technical Collection of Intelligence (Washington, D.C: CQ Press, 2011); Mark M. Lowenthal, Intelligence: From Secrets to Policy 7th ed (Thousand Oaks, CA: CQ Press/SAGE, 2017); Mark M. Lowenthal and Robert M. Clark, eds., The Five Disciplines of Intelligence Collection (Washington, D.C.: CQ Press, 2016); and Robert Wallace and H. Keith Melton, with Henry Robert Schlesinger, Spycraft: The Secret History of the CIA's Spytechs, from Communism to Al-Qaeda (New York: Penguin Plume Book, 2009).

2 On the Soviet spy caper against the U.S. Embassy in Moscow during the Cold War, see George F. Kennan, Memoirs, 1950–1963, Volume II (New York: Little, Brown & Co., 1972): 155-56.

3 "Paper No. 51," The Federalist (New York: Modern Library, 1937): 335-41.

4 This description is from the famed presidential scholar, Richard E. Neustadt, Presidential Power (New York: Wiley, 1960): 33.

5 See Loch K. Johnson, American Foreign Policy and the Challenges of World Leadership: Power, Principle, and the Constitution (New York: Oxford University Press, 2015).

6 Final Report, Select Committee to Study Governmental Operations with Respect to Intelligence Activities (Church Committee), Report No. 94-755, U.S. Senate, 94th Cong., 2d Sess. (April 23, 1976). The author served as a senior aide to Senator Church during this inquiry.

7   On these and the following controversial intelligence operations, see the Church Committee, Final Report, ibid.

8   An amendment to the Foreign Assistance Act of 1974, Pub. L. No. 93-559, 32, 88 Stat. 1795, 1804 (1974).

9   Title V of the National Security Act of 1947 (50 U.S.C. 413), Accountability for Intelligence Activities: The Intelligence Oversight Act of 1980), Pub. L. No. 96-450, 94 Stat. 1975 (1981).

10 See Karen J. Greenberg, Rogue Justice: The Making of the Security State (New York: Crown, 2016); Loch K. Johnson, Spy Watching: Intelligence Accountability in the United States (New York: Oxford University Press, 2018).

11 See Johnson, Spy Watching, ibid.

12 For a provocative analysis that is highly pessimistic about the chances that Madisonian checks-and-balances can stand up successfully against forces in Washington, D.C. that favor government authority centralized into the hands of the executive branch, see Michael J. Glennon, National Security and Double Government (New York: Oxford University Press, 2015).

13 On these points, see Richard A. Clarke, Against All Enemies: Inside America's War on Terror (New York: Simon & Schuster, 204), pp. 229, 237; Robert Jervis, Why Intelligence Fails: Lessons from the Iran Revolution and the Iraq War (Ithaca: Cornell University Press, 2010); and Loch K. Johnson, The Threat on the Horizon: An Inside Account of America's Search for Security after the Cold War (New York: Oxford University Press, 2011).

14 50 U.S.C. 1801-1811 (Supp. V 1981), enacted in 1978.

15 For this theory of the presidency, see John Yoo, The Powers of War and Peace: The Constitution and Foreign Affairs after 9/11(Chicago: University of Chicago Press, 2010).

16 See Leon Panetta [CIA Director in the Obama Administration] and Jim Newton, Worthy Fights: A Memoir of Leadership in War and Peace (New York: Penguin, 2014): 299.

17 For a case study of the al-Awlaki assassination, see Scott Shane, Objective Troy: A Terrorist, a President, and the Rise of the Drone (New York: Tim Duggan Books, 2015).

18 While serving as a senior aide to former Secretary of Defense Les Aspin when he chaired the Aspin-Brown Presidential Commission on Intelligence in 1995, the author reviewed many PDBs for the commissioners, comparing these top-secret documents with leading newspaper reporting (see Johnson, Horizon, op.cit.).

19 Remarks, Aspen Institute Forum, Aspen, Colorado (July 20, 2017).

20 See Loch K. Johnson, America's Secret Power: The CIA in a Democratic Society (New York: Oxford University Press, 1989).

21 PBS News Hour reported on the increase in drone attacks (February 26, 2018); see also, Greg Jaffe, "Trump Administration Reviewing Ways to Make It Easier to Launch Drone Strikes," Washington Post (March 13, 2017), p. A1. For a comparison of the frequency with which covert actions have been adopted by these administrations, see Johnson, Spy Watching, op.cit.

22 See Johnson, Spy Watching, op.cit.

23 An illustration of the Trump family's disdain for intelligence officers could be seen in a remark by Donald J. Trump, Jr., who on Twitter referred to CIA Director Haspel as a "trained liar" [Julian E. Barnes, "An Intramural Republican Fight Breaks Out Over the C.I.A. Director's Fate," New York Times (November 11, 2020): A16].

Chapter 11: Cyber-Enabled Tradecraft and Contemporary Espionage: Assessing the Implications of the Tradecraft Paradox on Agent Recruitment in Russia and China. Kyle S. Cunliffe

1. Wilder, 'The Psychology of Espionage', 19–34.

2. Gioe, "'The More Things Change'", 220.

3. Ibid.

4. Holm, The Craft we Chose, 275.

5. Wallace and Melton, C.I.A. Manual of Trickery and Deception, 15.

6. C Mendez, Mendez, and Baglio. The Moscow Rules, 20–21.

7. Wallace, et al, Spycraft, 36–40.

8. Russel, Sharpening Strategic Intelligence, 51–52.

9. See for example Gioe, 'Handling HERO' and Hoffman, The Billion Dollar Spy.

10. National Security Strategy, 6–9.

11. Cunliffe, 'Hard Target Espionage', 1019.

12. Ibid, 1028.

13. Mendez, Mendez, and Baglio. The Moscow Rules, 19–21.

14. Cunliffe, 'Hard Target Espionage', 1019–1028.

15. Ibid.

16. 'CIA-GW intelligence conference'.

17. Gioe, "'The More Things Change'", 221.

18. Cunliffe, 'Hard Target Espionage', 1025–1026.

19. Reuters, 'Digitizing the CIA: John Brennan's Attempt to Lead America's Spies Into the Age of Cyberwar'.

20. According to Dziak, referring to the Soviet Union, in a counterintelligence state 'the discovery and elimination of perceived conspiracies and enemies characterized the motives and behavior of an intermeshed party and state security apparat'. Dziak, 'The Soviet System of Security and Intelligence', 41.

21. Russel, Sharpening Strategic Intelligence, 51–52.

22. Cunliffe, 'Hard Target Espionage', 1020–1021.

23. Gioe, '"The More Things Change"', 219.

24. Wallace, et al, Spycraft, 367–368.

25. Ibid, 365.

26. Easter, "Soviet Bloc and Western Bugging of Opponents', 31.

27. Wallace, et al, Spycraft, 230; Crumpton, The Art of Intelligence, 67–70; Dulles, The Craft of Intelligence, 63–64.

28. Marchetti and Marks, The CIA and the Cult of Intelligence, 190.

29. Wallace, et al, Spycraft, 159 and 228–229.

30. Dulles, The Craft of Intelligence, 64.

31. Gordievsky, Next Stop Execution, Ch. 7.

32. Crumpton, The Art of Intelligence, 70.

33. Aldrich, GCHQ, 3; Wallace, et al, Spycraft, 231.

34. Crumpton, The Art of Intelligence, 70.

35. Ibid.

36. Gioe, '"The More Things Change"', 218.

37. Ibid.

38. Lokhov, 'How and Why the Russian Military Puts Soldiers in Jail for Using Smartphones and Social Media'.

39. BBC News, 'Russian Soldiers Face Ban on Selfies and Blog Posts'.

40. Gioe, 'The More Things Change', 218.

41. Van Cleave, 'Chinese Intelligence Operations and Implications for U.S. National Security', 1.

42. Pepitone, 'China is "Leading Suspect" in OPM Hacks, Says Intelligence Chief James Clapper'.

43. Farmer, 'British Spies Trawl Ashley Madison Leak for Intelligence'.

44. Baranovskaya, 'Moscow's Cyber-Defense'.

45. Sukhankin, 'Russia on the Verge of a "Cyber Purge?"'.

46. Ibid.

47. Reuters, 'Putin Tells Russia's Tech Sector: Ditch Foreign Software or Lose Out'.

48. Yang, 'China's Cyber Security Law Rattles Multinationals'.

49. Feng, 'In China, a New Call to Protect Data Privacy'.; Zakharov, 'Russian Data Theft: Shady World Where all is for Sale'.

50. Tidy, 'Security Warning after Sale of Stolen Chinese Data'.

51. Ibid.

52. Ibid.

53. Satter, 'Chinese Cybersecurity Company Accuses CIA of 11-Year-Long Hacking Campaign'.

54. Miller et al, 'Obama's Secret Struggle to Punish Russia for Putin's Election Assault'.; Sanger, 'U.S. Decides to Retaliate Against China's Hacking'.

55. WikiLeaks. 'Vault 7: CIA Hacking Tools Revealed'.

56. Barrett, 'Don't Let WikiLeaks Scare You off of Signal and Other Encrypted Chat Apps'.

57. WikiLeaks. 'Vault 7: CIA Hacking Tools Revealed'.

58. Matthew and Bodner. 'Spy Games'.

59. Greenberg, 'How the CIA Can Hack Your Phone, PC, and TV (Says Wikileaks)'.

60. Wikileaks, 'Weeping Angel (Extending) Engineering Notes'.

61. Greenberg, 'How the CIA Can Hack Your Phone, PC, and TV (Says Wikileaks)'.

62. Zetter, Countdown to Zero Day, 8.

63. Ibid, 110.

64. Greenberg, 'Here's a Spy Firm's Price List for Secret Hacker Techniques'.

65. Burgess, 'Wikileaks Drops "Grasshopper" Documents, Part Four of Its CIA Vault 7 Files'.

66. A good example of this is the FBI's Know the Risk Raise Your Shield programme. For more information, see ODNI. 'Know the Risk Raise Your Shield'.

67. WikiLeaks. 'Vault 7: Projects'.

68. CIA. 2009. 'DarkSeaSkies 1.0 User Requirements Document'.

69. The Telegraph. 'British and US Spies at Risk After Wikileaks Publishes Top-secret CIA Spyware Document'.; Poitras, et al. "GCHQ Monitors Diplomats' Hotel Bookings".

70. Poitras, et al. "GCHQ Monitors Diplomats' Hotel Bookings".

71. Mackinnon, 'Hackers Turn the Tables on Russia'.

72. Baranovskaya, 'Moscow's Cyber-Defense'.

73. Althoff, 'Human intelligence', 75.
74. Nossiter, Sanger, and Perlroth, 'Hackers came, but the French Were Prepared'.
75. Miller, 'As Russia Reasserts Itself, U.S. Intelligence Agencies Focus Anew on the Kremlin'.
76. Judah, 'Putin's Coup'.
77. Ibid.
78. CNN, 'What Happened to China's Former Leader Hu Jintao?'.
79. Wallace, et al, Spycraft, 364.
80. Holm, The Craft we Chose, 292.
81. Mendez and McConnell, The Master of Disguise, 221.
82. Hoffman, the Billion Dollar Spy, Ch. 4.
83. Ibid.
84. Mendez and McConnell, The Master of Disguise, 221.
85. A Spy for all Seasons, 139.
86. Ibid.
87. Cherkashin and Feifer, Spy Handler, 120.
88. Wallace, et al, Spycraft, 364.
89. Wallace, 'A time for counterespionage', 113.
90. Omand, 'Understanding Digital Intelligence and the Norms That Might Govern It', 3.
91. Kelion, 'WhatsApp's Privacy Protections Questioned After Terror Attack'.
92. Cuthbertson, 'China Is Spying on the West Using LinkedIn, Intelligence Agency Claims'.
93. Ibid.
94. Ibid.
95. Dhami, 'Behavioural Science Support for JTRIG's (Join Threat Research and Intelligence Group) Effects and Online HUMINT Operations', 9–11.
96. Ibid.
97. NSA, 'Exploiting Terrorist Use of Games & Virtual Environments'.
98. Ball, 'Xbox Live among Game Services Targeted by US and UK Spy Agencies'.
99. Sargsyan, 'Data Localization and the Role of Infrastructure for Surveillance, Privacy, and Security', 2225–2229.
100. Deibert, Black Code, 62.

101. Zhou, 'China's Comprehensive Counter-Terrorism Law'.; Wong, 'China Adopts Cyber Security Law in Face of Overseas Opposition'.

102. Daniel and Byhovsky, 'Privacy and Data Protection in Russia', 241–242.

103. Lunden, 'Russia Says "Nyet" Continues LinkedIn Block after It Refuses to Store Data in Russia'.

104. Bond and Allyn, 'Russia is Restricting Social Media. Here's What We Know'.

105. Lowenthal, Intelligence: From Secrets to Policy. Ch. 17.

106. Soldatov and Borogan, The Red Web. Ch. 8.

107. Soldatov and Borogan, 'Russia's Surveillance State', 24–25.

108. Soldatov and Borogan. 'In Ex-Soviet States, Russian Spy Tech Still Watches You'.

109. Morgus, 'The Spread of Russia's Digital Authoritarianism', 90–91.

110. Soldatov and Borogan, I, 'Russia's surveillance state', 25.

111. Meduza. 'Russia's State Duma just Approved some of the most Repressive Laws in Post-Soviet History'.

112. Burgess, 'This Is Why Russia's Attempts to Block Telegram Have Failed'.; Loucaides, 'The Kremlin Has Entered the Chat'.

113. Sudakov, 'Russia May Block Whatsapp, Viber, Telegram Even Tomorrow'.

114. Ibid.

115. Yang, 'China to Ban Online Gaming, Chatting with Foreigners outside Great Firewall'.

116. Heath, 'Riot Finally Enables Voice Chat for Russian Players in VALORANT'.

117. Loucaides, 'The Kremlin Has Entered the Chat'.

118. Ibid.

119. Brookes, 'Is China Swarming with Foreign Spies?'.

120. Mattis, 'Virtual Espionage Challenges Chinese Counterintelligence'.

121. Brookes, 'Is China Swarming with Foreign Spies?'.

122. Dorfman and McLaughlin. 'The CIA's Communications Suffered a Catastrophic Compromise. It Started in Iran'.

123. Matthew and Bodner. 'Spy Games'.

124. Ibid.

125. Liao, 'China's Education Group Released a Cartoon Encouraging Kids to Embrace Counterespionage'.

126. Grey, S. The New Spymasters, 277.

127. Victor Sheymov described contacting the American embassy in Moscow as 'out of the question'. For more details, see: Sheymov, Tower of Secrets, 288; Duns, Dead Drop, Ch. 2; Hoffman, The Billion Dollar Spy, Ch. 2, 3 & 4.

128. Hoffman, The Billion Dollar Spy, Ch. 3.

129. Ashley, CIA SpyMaster, Ch. 10.

130. The Billion Dollar Spy, Ch. 4.

131. Ibid.

132. Ibid; Duns, Dead Drop, Ch. 2.

133. Hoffman, The Billion Dollar Spy, Ch. 4.

134. Ibid.

135. Althoff, 'Human intelligence', 75.

136. SIS. 'Sharing Information Securely'.

137. Stein, 'The Russian Spy Who Came in through the Email'.

138. Merzlikin, "'I'd Be Willing to Work against This Government with Satan Himself" We Talked to a Suburban Russian Policeman Who Spied for the CIA, Fought in Eastern Ukraine, and Got Sentence to 13 Years for Treason'.

139. SIS. 'Sharing Information Securely'.

140. Ibid.

141. Newman, 'The CIA Sets Up Shop on Tor, the Anonymous Internet'.

142. SIS. 'Sharing Information Securely'.

143. The Telegraph, 'CIA Agent "detained in Moscow": His "letter" in Full'.

144. Yahoo! News. "Russia Busts Pair 'Trying to Sell CIA Fake Secrets".

145. Stein, 'The Russian Spy Who Came in Through the Email'.

146. CIA. 'Contact Us'.

147. Stein, 'The Russian Spy Who Came in through the Email'.; Merzlikin, "'I'd Be Willing to Work against This Government with Satan Himself" We Talked to a Suburban Russian Policeman Who Spied for the CIA, Fought in Eastern Ukraine, and Got Sentence to 13 Years for Treason'.

Bibliography

Aldrich, R. J. GCHQ: The Uncensored Story of Britain's Most Secret Intelligence Agency. London: Harper Press, 2010. [Google Scholar]

Althoff, M. "Human Intelligence." In The Five Disciplines of Intelligence Collection, edited by M. Lowenthal and R. M. Clark, 45–80. Thousand Oaks: CQ Press, 2016. [Google Scholar]

Ashley, C. CIA Spymaster: Kisevalter, the Agency's Top Case Officer, Who Handled Penkovsky and Popov. Gretna: Pelican Publishing Company, 2004. [Google Scholar]

Ball, J. "Xbox Live Among Game Services Targeted by US and UK Spy Agencies." The Guardian, December 9, 2013. https://www.theguardian.com/world/2013/dec/09/nsa-spies-online-games-world-warcraft-second-life. [Google Scholar]

Baranovskaya, S. "Moscow's Cyber-Defense: How the Russian Government Plans to Protect the Country from the Coming Cyberwar." Meduza (July 19, 2017). https://meduza.io/en/feature/2017/07/19//moscow-s-cyber-defense [Google Scholar]

Barrett, B. "Don't Let WikiLeaks Scare You off of Signal and Other Encrypted Chat Apps". Wired, March 7, 2017. https://www.wired.com/2017/03/wikileaks-cia-hack-signal-encrypted-chat-apps/. [Google Scholar]

BBC News. "Russian Soldiers Face Ban on Selfies and Blog Posts." October 5, 2017. http://www.bbc.co.uk/news/world-europe-41510592?ocid=socialflow_twitter. [Google Scholar]

Bond, S., and B. Allyn. "Russia is Restricting Social Media. Here's What We Know." NPR, March 21, 2022. https://www.npr.org/2022/03/07/1085025672/russia-social-media-ban. [Google Scholar]

Bradsher, K. "China Blocks WhatsApp, Broadening Online Censorship." The New York Times, September 25, 2017. https://www.nytimes.com/2017/09/25/business/china-whatsapp-blocked.html. [Google Scholar]

Brookes, A. "Is China Swarming with Foreign Spies?" Foreign Policy, November 4, 2014. http://foreignpolicy.com/2014/11/04/is-china-swarming-with-foreign-spies/. [Google Scholar]

Burgess, M. "This is Why Russia's Attempts to Block Telegram Have Failed." Wired, April 18, 2018. https://www.wired.co.uk/article/telegram-in-russia-blocked-web-app-ban-facebook-twitter-google. [Google Scholar]

Burgess, M. "WikiLeaks Drops 'Grasshopper' Documents, Part Four of Its CIA Vault 7 Files." Wired, May 7, 2017. https://www.wired.co.uk/article/cia-files-wikileaks-vault-7. [Google Scholar]

Cherkashin, V., and G. Feifer. Spy Handler, Memoir of a KGB Officer. New York: BasicBooks, 2005. [Google Scholar]

CIA. "Contact Us." July 1, 2021. https://www.cia.gov/cgi-bin/forlang_form.cgi. [Google Scholar]

CIA. 2009. "DarkSeaskies 1.0 User Requirements Document." January. Published by WikiLeaks, March, 23, 2017. https://wikileaks.org/vault7/darkmatter/document/DarkSeaSkies_1_0_URD/DarkSeaSkies_1_0_URD.pdf. [Google Scholar]

Clarridge, D. R., and D. Diehl. A Spy for All Seasons: My Life in the CIA. New York: Scribner, 1997. Kindle. [Google Scholar]

CNN. "What Happened to China's Former Leader Hu Jintao?" October 28, 2022. https://edition.cnn.com/2022/10/28/china/china-party-congress-hu-jintao-new-video-intl-hnk/index.html. [Google Scholar]

Crumpton, H. A. The Art of Intelligence: Lessons from a Life in the Cia's Clandestine Service. New York: Penguin Books, 2012. [Google Scholar]

Cunliffe, K. S. "Hard Target Espionage in the Information Era: New Challenges or the Second Oldest Profession." Intelligence & National Security 36, no. 7 (2021): 1018–1034. doi:10.1080/02684527.2021.1947555. [Taylor & Francis Online], [Web of Science *], [Google Scholar]

Cuthbertson, A. "China is Spying on the West Using LinkedIn, Intelligence Agency Claims." Newsweek, December 11, 2017. http://www.newsweek.com/china-spying-west-using-linkedin-743788. [Google Scholar]

Deibert, R. J. Black Code: Inside the Battle for Cyberspace. Toronto: McClellend & Stewart, 2013. [Google Scholar]

Dhami, M. K. "Behavioural Science Support for Jtrig's (Join Threat Research and Intelligence Group) Effects and Online HUMINT Operations." Statewatch, June 22, 2015. 9–11, https://www.statewatch.org/media/documents/news/2015/jun/behavioural-science-support-for-jtrigs-effects.pdf. [Google Scholar]

Dorfman, Z., and J. Mclaughlin. "The Cia's Communications Suffered a Catastrophic Compromise. It Started in Iran." Yahoo News, November 2, 2018. https://uk.finance.yahoo.com/news/cias-communications-suffered-cata-strophic-compromise-started-iran-090018710.html. [Google Scholar]

Dulles, A. W. The Craft of Intelligence: America's Legendary Spy Master on the Fundamentals of Intelligence Gathering for a Free World. New York: The Lyons Press, 2006. [Google Scholar]

Duns, J. Dead Drop: The True Story of Oleg Penkovsky and the Cold War's Most Dangerous Operation. London: Simon & Schuster, 2013. [Google Scholar]

Dziak, J. J. "The Soviet System of Security and Intelligence." In Security and Intelligence in a Changing World, edited by A. S. Farson, D. Stafford, and W. K. Wark, 25–45. New York: Routledge, 2021. [Google Scholar]

Easter, D. "Soviet Bloc and Western Bugging of opponents' Diplomatic Premises During the Early Cold War." Intelligence & National Security 31, no. 1 (2016): 28–48. doi:10.1080/02684527.2014.926745. [Taylor & Francis Online], [Web of Science *], [Google Scholar]

Farmer, B. "British Spies Trawl Ashley Madison Leak for Intelligence." The Telegraph, August 31, 2015. http://www.telegraph.co.uk/news/uknews/defence/11830594/British-spies-trawl-Ashley-Madison-leak-for-intelligence. html. [Google Scholar]

Feng, E. "In China, a New Call to Protect Data Privacy." NPR, January 5, 2020. https://www.npr.org/2020/01/05/793014617/in-china-a-new-call-to-protect-data-privacy?t=1600710014451. [Google Scholar]

Garrie, D., and I. Byhovsky. "Privacy and Data Protection in Russia." Journal of Law and Cyber Warfare 5, no. 2 (2017): 241–242. https://www.jstor.org/stable/26441276. [Google Scholar]

Gioe, D. V. "Handling HERO: Joint Anglo-American Tradecraft in the Case of Oleg Penkovsky." In An International History of the Cuban Missile Crisis, edited by D. V. Gioe, L. Scott, and C. Andrew, 135–175. London: Routledge, 2014. [Crossref], [Google Scholar]

Gioe, D. V. "'The More Things Change': HUMINT in the Cyber Age." In The Palgrave Handbook of Security, Risk and Intelligence, edited by R. Dover, H. Dylan, and M. Goodman, 213–228. London: Palgrave Macmillan, 2017. [Crossref], [Google Scholar]

Gordievsky, O. Next Stop Execution: The Autobiography of Oleg Gordievsky. London: Endeavour Media, 2018. [Google Scholar]

Greenberg, A. "Here's a Spy Firm's Price List for Secret Hacker Techniques." Wired, November 18, 2015. https://www.wired.com/2015/11/heres-a-spy-firms-price-list-for-secret-hacker-techniques/. [Google Scholar]

Greenberg, A. "How the CIA Can Hack Your Phone, PC, and TV (Says WikiLeaks)." Wired, March 7, 2017. https://www.wired.com/2017/03/cia-can-hack-phone-pc-tv-says-wikileaks/. [Google Scholar]

Greenwald, G., and E. MacAskill. "NSA Prism Program Taps in to Use Data of Apple, Google and Others." The Guardian, June 7, 2013. https://www.theguardian.com/world/2013/jun/06/us-tech-giants-nsa-data. [Google Scholar]

Grey, S. The New Spymasters: Inside Espionage from the Cold War to Global Terror. New York: Viking, 2015. [Google Scholar]

Heath, J. "Riot Finally Enables Voice Chat for Russian Players in VALORANT." Dot Esports, June 9, 2021. https://dotesports.com/valorant/news/riot-enables-voice-chat-for-russians-players-valorant. [Google Scholar]

Hoffman, D. E. The Billion Dollar Spy: A True Story of Cold War Espionage and Betrayal. London: Icon Books, 2017. Kindle. [Google Scholar]

Holm, R. The Craft We Chose: My Life in the CIA. Oakland: Mountain Lake Press, 2011. [Google Scholar]

Judah, B. "Putin's Coup: How the Russian Leader Used the Ukraine Crisis to Consolidate His Dictatorship." Politico, October 19, 2014. https://www.politico.com/magazine/story/2014/10/vladimir-putins-coup-112025_full.html#. WJo84H9yXE9. [Crossref], [Google Scholar]

Kelion, L. "WhatsApp's Privacy Protections Questioned After Terror Attack". BBC News, March 17, 2017. https://www.bbc.co.uk/news/technology-39405178. [Google Scholar]

Kupfer, M., and M. Bodner. "Spy Games: How the Spectre of Surveillance Impacts Moscow's Foreigners." The Moscow Times, January 19, 2017. https://themoscowtimes.com/articles/spy-games-how-the-spectre-of-surveillance-impacts-the-lives-of-moscows-foreigners-56865. [Google Scholar]

Lewis, J. "How Spies Used Facebook to Steal NATO Chiefs' Details." The Telegraph, March 10, 2012. https://www.telegraph.co.uk/technology/9136029/How-spies-used-Facebook-to-steal-Nato-chiefs-details.html. [Google Scholar]

Liao, S. "China's Education Group Releases a Cartoon Encouraging Kids to Embrace Counterespionage." The Verge, November 7, 2017. https://www.theverge.com/2017/11/7/16617494/china-national-security-spying-propaganda-cartoon-education. [Google Scholar]

Lokhov, P. "How and Why the Russian Military Puts Soldiers in Jail for Using Smartphones and Social Media." Meduza, August 6, 2019, https://meduza.io/en/feature/2019/08/06/how-and-why-the-russian-military-puts-soldiers-in-jail-for-using-smartphones-and-social-media. [Google Scholar]

Loucaides, D. "The Kremlin Has Entered the Chat." Wired, February 2, 2023. https://www.wired.com/story/the-kremlin-has-entered-the-chat/. [Google Scholar]

Lowenthal, M. M. Intelligence: From Secrets to Policy. 7th ed Kindle. Thousand Oaks: CQ Press, 2017 [Google Scholar]

Lunden, I. "Russia Says 'Nyet' Continues LinkedIn Block After It Refuses to Store Data in Russia." TechCrunch, March 7, 2017. https://techcrunch.com/2017/03/07/russia-says-nyet-continues-linkedin-block-after-it-refuses-to-store-data-in-russia/?guccounter=1. [Google Scholar]

Mackinnon, A. "Hackers Turn the Tables on Russia." Foreign Policy, January 28, 2019. https://foreignpolicy.com/2019/01/28/hackers-turn-the-tables-on-russia-hacking-leaking-cyber-documents-wikileaks/. [Google Scholar]

Marchetti, V., and J. D. Marks. The CIA and the Cult of Intelligence. London: Jonathan Cape, 1974. [Google Scholar]

Mattis, P. "Virtual Espionage Challenges Chinese Counterintelligence." The Jamestown Foundation, May 7, 2014. https://jamestown.org/program/virtual-espionage-challenges-chinese-counterintelligence/. [Google Scholar]

Mazetti, M., and J. Elliot. "Spies Infiltrate a Fantasy Realm of Online Games." The New York Times, December 9, 2013. http://www.nytimes.com/2013/12/10/world/spies-dragnet-reaches-a-playing-field-of-elves-and-trolls.html?mtrref=onlinelibrary.wiley.com&gwh=EE5694212E9FCD4467863E6 2E311F74E&gwt=pay. [Google Scholar]

McLaughlin, J., and Z. Dorfman. "At the CIA, a Fix to Communications Systems That Left Trail of Dead Agents Remains Elusive." The Huffington Post, December 6, 2018. https://www.huffpost.com/entry/at-the-cia-a-fix-to-communications-system-that-left-trail-of-dead-agents-remains-elusive_n_5c09 4117e4b069028dc7696a. [Google Scholar]

Meduza. "Russia's State Duma Just Approved Some of the Most Repressive Laws in Post-Soviet History." June 24, 2015. https://meduza.io/en/feature/2016/06/24/russia-s-state-duma-just-approvedsome-of-the-most-repressive-laws-in-post-soviet-history. [Google Scholar]

Mendez, A. J., and M. McConnell. The Master of Disguise: My Secret Life in the CIA. New York: Harper Collins, 2007. Kindle. [Google Scholar]

Mendez, A. J., J. Mendez, and M. Baglio. The Moscow Rules: The Secret CIA Tactics That Helped America Win the Cold War [Google Scholar]

Merzlikin, P. "'I'd Be Willing to Work Against This Government with Satan Himself' We Talked to a Suburban Russian Policeman Who Spied for the CIA, Fought in Eastern Ukraine, and Got Sentenced to 13 Years for Treason." Meduza, July 31, 2019. https://meduza.io/en/feature/2019/07/31/i-d-be-willing-to-work-against-this-government-with-satan-himself. [Google Scholar]

Miller, G. "As Russia Reasserts Itself, U.S. Intelligence Agencies Focus Anew on the Kremlin." The Washington Post, September 14, 2016. https://www.washingtonpost.com/world/nationalsecurity/as-russia-reasserts-itself-us-intelligence-agencies-focus-anew-on-thekremlin/2016/09/14/cc212c62-78f0-11e6-ac8ecf8e0dd91dc7_story.html?postshare=371473956824384&tid=ss_twbottom&utm_term=.d8941ad4f02e#comments. [Google Scholar]

Miller, G., E. Nakashima, and A. Entous. "Obama's Secret Struggle to Punish Russia for Putin's Election Assault." The Washington Post, June 23, 2017. https://www.washingtonpost.com/graphics/2017/world/nationalsecurity/obama-putin-election-hacking/?utm_term=.73bfdde12b13. [Google Scholar]

Morgus, R. "The Spread of Russia's Digital Authoritarianism." In Artificial Intelligence, China, Russia and the Global Order, edited by N. D. Wright, 89–97. Maxwell: Air University Press, 2019. [Google Scholar]

National Security Strategy, The White House, 2022. https://www.whitehouse.gov/wp-content/uploads/2022/10/Biden-Harris-Administrations-National-Security-Strategy-10.2022.pdf. [Google Scholar]

Newman, L. H. "The CIA Sets Up Shop on Tor, the Anonymous Internet." Wired, May 7, 2019. https://www.wired.com/story/cia-sets-up-shop-on-tor/#:~:text=On%20Tuesday%2C%20the%20CIA%20announced,that%20uses%20its%20own%20URLs. [Google Scholar]

Newton, C. "How China Complicates Apple's Chest-Thumping About Privacy." The Verge, October 25, 2018. https://www.theverge.com/2018/10/25/18020508/

how-china-complicates-apples-chest-thumping-about-privacy. [Google Scholar]

Nicas, J., R. Zhong, and D. Wajabayashi. "Censorship, Surveillance and Profits: A Hard Bargain for Apple in China." The New York Times, June 17, 2001. https://www.nytimes.com/2021/05/17/technology/apple-china-censorship-data.html. [Google Scholar]

Nossiter, A., D. E. Sanger, and N. Perlroth. "Hackers Came, but the French Were Prepared." The New York Times, May 9, 2017. https://www.nytimes.com/2017/05/09/world/europe/hackers-came-but-the-french-were-prepared.html. [Google Scholar]

NSA. "Exploiting Terrorist Use of Games & Virtual Environments." Published by Cryptome, December 9, 2013. Accessed June 15, 2022. https://cryptome.org/2013/12/nsa-spy-games.pdf. [Google Scholar]

Office of the Director of National Intelligence. "Know the Risk Raise Your Shield: NSCS Awareness Materials." June 15, 2022. https://www.dni.gov/index.php/ncsc-how-we-work/ncsc-know-the-risk-raise-your-shield. [Google Scholar]

Of Justice, D. "United States of America V. Jun Wei Yeo, Also Known as Dickson Yeo." Accessed June 15, 2022. https://www.justice.gov/opa/press-release/file/1297486/download. [Google Scholar]

Omand, D. "Understanding Digital Intelligence and the Norms That Might Govern It". In Global Commission on Internet Governance Paper Series: No. 8, 2015. https://www.cigionline.org/sites/default/files/gcig_paper_no8.pdf. [Google Scholar]

Panel at Third Ethos and Profession of Intelligence Conference held at the George Washington Center for Cyber and Homeland Security. 2016. "CIA-GW Intelligence Conference: Panel on the View from Foreign Intelligence Chiefs." September 20. Youtube video, 57: 48. https://www.youtube.com/watch?v=yefBv7Q3sv0. [Google Scholar]

Pepitone, J. "China is 'Leading Suspect' in OPM Hacks, Says Intelligence Chief James Clapper." NBC News, June 25, 2015. http://www.nbcnews.com/tech/security/clapper-china-leading-suspect-opm-hack-n381881. [Google Scholar]

Poitras, V. L., M. Rosenbach, and H. Stark. "GCHQ Monitors Diplomats' Hotel Bookings." Der Spiegel, November 17 2013. http://www.spiegel.de/international/europe/gchq-monitors-hotel-reservations-to-trackdiplomats-a-933914.html. [Google Scholar]

Reuters, "Digitizing the Cia: John Brennan's Attempt to Lead America's Spies into the Age of Cyberwar." November 2, 2016. https://www.reuters.com/investigates/special-report/usa-cia-brennan/. [Google Scholar]

Reuters, "Putin Tells Russia's Tech Sector: Ditch Foreign Software or Lose Out." September 8, 2017. https://www.reuters.com/article/russia-it-software-idUSL8N1LP4IC. [Google Scholar]

Russel, R. L. Sharpening Strategic Intelligence: Why the CIA Gets It Wrong and What Needs to Be Done to Get It Right. New York: Cambridge University Press, 2007. Kindle. [Crossref], [Google Scholar]

Samuel, H. "Chinese Spies Fooled 'Hundreds' of Civil Servants and Executives, France Reveals." The Telegraph, October 23, 2018. https://www.telegraph.co.uk/news/2018/10/23/chinese-online-spies-fool-hundreds-totally-unprepared-top-french/. [Google Scholar]

Sanger, D. E. "U.S. Decides to Retaliate Against China's Hacking." The New York Times, July 31, 2015. https://www.nytimes.com/2015/08/01/world/asia/us-decides-to-retaliate-against-chinas-hacking.html. [Google Scholar]

Sargsyan, T. "Data Localization and the Role of Infrastructure for Surveillance, Privacy, and Security." International Journal of Communication, no. 10 (2016): 2225–2229. https://ijoc.org/index.php/ijoc/article/viewFile/3854/1648. [Google Scholar]

Satter, R. "Chinese Cybersecurity Company Accuses CIA of 11-Year-Long Hacking Campaign." Reuters, March 3, 2020. https://www.reuters.com/article/us-china-usa-cia-idUSKBN20Q2SI. [Google Scholar]

Sheymov, V. Tower of Secrets: A Real Life Spy Thriller. New York: Harper, 2012. [Google Scholar]

SIS. "Sharing Information Securely." March 29, 2023. https://www.sis.gov.uk/share-information-securely.html. [Google Scholar]

Soldatov, A., and I. Borogan. "In Ex-Soviet States, Russian Spy Tech Still Watches You." Wired, December 21, 2012. https://www.wired.com/2012/12/russias-hand/. [Google Scholar]

Soldatov, A., and I. Borogan. "Russia's Surveillance State." World Policy Journal 30, no. 3 (2013): 23–30. doi:10.1177/0740277513506378. [Crossref], [Google Scholar]

Soldatov, A., and I. Borogan. The Red Web: The Struggle Between Russia's Digital Dictators and the New Online Revolutionaries. New York: Public Affairs, 2015. Kindle. [Google Scholar]

Stein, J. "The Russian Spy Who Came in Through the Email." Newsweek, July 3, 2015. https://www.newsweek.com/russian-spy-through-email-312104. [Google Scholar]

Sudakov, D. "Russia May Block Whatsapp, Viber, Telegram Even Tomorrow.", Pravda, May 2, 2017. http://www.pravdareport.com/business/companies/02-05-2017/137639-messaging_service_russia-0/. [Google Scholar]

Sukhankin, S. "Russia on the Verge of a 'Cyber Purge?'" The Jamestown Foundation, February 9, 2017. https://jamestown.org/program/russia-verge-cyber-purge/. [Google Scholar]

The Telegraph. "British and US Spies at Risk After Wikileaks Publishes Top-Secret CIA Spyware Document". May 20, 2017. https://www.telegraph.co.uk/news/2017/05/20/british-us-spies-risk-wikileaks-publishes-top-secret-cia-spyware/. [Google Scholar]

The Telegraph, "CIA Agent 'Detained in Moscow': His 'Letter' in Full." May 14, 2013. http://www.telegraph.co.uk/news/worldnews/europe/russia/10056972/CIA-agent-detained-in-Moscow-his-letter-in-full.html. [Google Scholar]

Tidy, J. "Security Warning After Sale of Stolen Chinese Data." BBC News, July 8 2022. https://www.bbc.co.uk/news/technology-62097594. [Google Scholar]

Turovsky, D. "Moscow's Cyber-Defense: How the Russian Government Plans to Protect the Country from the Coming Cyberwar." Meduza, July 19 2017. https://meduza.io/en/feature/2017/07/19/moscow-s-cyber-defense. [Google Scholar]

Van Cleave, M. "Chinese Intelligence Operations and Implications for U.S. National Security." Statement for the Record for U.S. China Economic and Security Review Commission, 2019, 1–10. http://www.uscc.gov/sites/default/files/Michelle%20Van%20Cleave_Written%20Testimony060916.pdf. [Google Scholar]

Wallace, R. "A Time for Counterespionage." In Vaults, Mirrors, & Masks: Rediscovering U.S. Counterintelligence, edited by J. E. Sims and B. Gerber, 101–124. Washington: Georgetown University Press, 2008. [Google Scholar]

Wallace, R., and H. K. Melton. C.I.A. Manual of Trickery and Deception. London: Harper Collins, 2009. [Google Scholar]

Wallace, R., H. K. Melton, and H. R. Schlesinger. Spycraft: Inside the Cia's Top Secret Spy Lab. London: Bantam Press, 2008. [Google Scholar]

Watkins, A. "China Grabbed American as Spy Wars Flare." Politico, November 10, 2017. https://www.politico.com/story/2017/10/11/china-spy-games-espionage-243644. [Google Scholar]

WikiLeaks. "Vault 7: CIA Hacking Tools Revealed". Accessed June 15, 2022. https://wikileaks.org/ciav7p1/index.html. [Google Scholar]

Wikileaks. "Vault 7: Projects". Accessed June 15, 2022. https://wikileaks.org/vault7/. [Google Scholar]

Wikileaks, "Weeping Angel (Extending) Engineering Notes." Accessed January 15, 2023. https://wikileaks.org/ciav7p1/cms/page_12353643.html. [Google Scholar]

Wilder, U. M. "The Psychology of Espionage." Studies in Intelligence, CIA 61, no. 2 (2017): 19–36. [Google Scholar]

Wong, S. -L., and M. Martina. "China Adopts Cyber Security Law in Face of Overseas Opposition." Reuters, November 7, 2016. https://www.reuters.com/article/us-china-parliament-cyber/china-adopts-cyber-security-law-in-face-of-overseas-opposition-idUSKBN132049. [Google Scholar]

Yahoo! News. "Russia Busts Pair 'Trying to Sell CIA Fake Secrets." September 20, 2016. https://news.yahoo.com/russia-busts-pair-trying-sell-cia-fake-secrets-182012535.html. [Google Scholar]

Yang, S. "China to Ban Online Gaming, Chatting with Foreigners Outside Great Firewall: Report." Taiwan News, April 15, 2020. https://www.taiwannews.com.tw/en/news/3916690. [Google Scholar]

Yang, Y. "China's Cyber Security Law Rattles Multinationals." Financial Times, May 30, 2017. https://www.ft.com/content/b302269c-44ff-11e7-8519-9f94ee97d996. [Google Scholar]

Zakharov, A. "Russian Data Theft: Shady World Where All is for Sale." BBC News, May 27, 2019. https://www.bbc.co.uk/news/world-europe-48348307. [Google Scholar]

Zetter, K. Countdown to Zero Day: Stuxnet and the Launch of the World's First Digital Weapon. New York: Crown Publishers, 2014. [Google Scholar]

Zhou, Z. "China's Comprehensive Counter-Terrorism Law." The Diplomat, January 23, 2016. https://thediplomat.com/2016/01/chinas-comprehensive-counter-terrorism-law/ [Google Scholar]

Chapter-12: The Ambiguity of Cyber Security Politics in the Context of Multidimensional Uncertainty Andreas Wenger and Myriam Dunn Cavelty

Adamsky, D. D. (2021). Deterrence by Denial in Israeli Strategic Thinking. In A. Wenger and A. Wilner (eds), Deterrence by Denial: Theory and Practice. Amherst, NY: Cambria Press, 163–190.

Baezner, M. (2018). Hotspot Analysis: Synthesis 2017: Cyber-Conflicts in Perspective. Zurich: Center for Security Studies (CSS).

Baezner, M., and Cordey, S. (2022). Cyber in the Grey Zone: Influence Operations and other Conflict Trends. In M. Dunn Cavelty and A. Wenger (eds), Cyber Security: Socio-Technological Uncertainty and Political Fragmentation. London: Routledge, pp. 17–31.

Baezner, M., and Robin, P. (2017). Hotspot Analysis: Strategic stability between Great Powers: the Sino-American Cyber Agreement. Zurich: Center for Security Studies (CSS).

Bitzinger, R. A. (2021). China's Shift from Civil-Military Integration to Military-Civil Fusion. Asia Policy, 28(1): 5–24. https://doi.org/10.1353/asp.2021.0001.

Bonfanti, M. E. (2022). Artificial Intelligence and the Offence-Defence Balance in Cyber Security. In M. Dunn Cavelty and A. Wenger (eds), Cyber Security: Socio-Technological Uncertainty and Political Fragmentation. London: Routledge, pp. 64–79.

Borghard, E. D., and Lonergan, S. W. (2017). The Logic of Coercion in Cyberspace. Security Studies, 26(13): 452–458.

Brantly, A. (2022). Battling the Bear: Ukraine's Approach to National Cyber and Information Security. In M. Dunn Cavelty and A. Wenger (eds), Cyber Security: SocioTechnological Uncertainty and Political Fragmentation. London: Routledge, pp. 157–171.

Buchanan, B. (2020). The Hacker and the State: Cyber Attacks and the New Normal of Geopolitics. Harvard: Harvard University Press.

Cavaiola, L. J., Gompert, D. C., and Libicki, M. (2015). Cyber House Rules: On War, Retaliation and Escalation. Survival, 57(1): 81–104.

Chesney, R., and Smeets, M. (2020). Roundtable: The Dynamics of Cyber Conflict and Competition. Texas National Security Review, 3(4): 4–7. https://doi.org/10.26153/tsw/10964.

Chesney, R., and Smeets, M. (forthcoming). Deter, Disrupt or Deceive: Assessing Cyber Conflict as an Intelligence Contest. Washington: Georgetown University Press.

Clarke, R. A., and Knake, R. K. (2010). Cyber War. New York: Ecco.

Devanny, J. (2021). 'Madman Theory' or 'Persistent Engagement'? The Coherence of US Cyber Strategy under Trump. Journal of Applied Security Research. Retrieved August 19, 2021, from: https://www.tandfonline.com/doi/abs/10.1080/19361610.2021.1872359.

Dewar, R. S. (ed.). (2018). National Cybersecurity and Cyberdefense Policy Snapshots. Zurich: Center for Security Studies (CSS).

Dunn Cavelty, M. (2008). Cyber Security and Threat Politics: US Efforts to Secure the Information Age. London: Routledge.

Dunn Cavelty, M. (2015). The Normalization of Cyber-International Relations. In O. Thränert and M. Zapfe (eds), Strategic Trends 2015: Key Developments in Global Affairs. Zurich: Center for Security Studies (CSS), pp. 81–98.

Dunn Cavelty, M., and Egloff, F. J. (2019). The Politics of Cybersecurity: Balancing Different Roles of the State. St Antony's International Review, 15(1): 37–57.

Dunn Cavelty, M., and Wenger, A. (2019). Cybersecurity Meets Security Politics: Complex Technology, Fragmented Politics, and Networked Science. Contemporary Security Policy, 41(1): 5–32.

Dunn Cavelty, M., and Wenger, A. (2022). Introduction: Cyber Security between SocioTechnological Uncertainty and Political Fragmentation. In M. Dunn Cavelty and A. Wenger (eds), Cyber Security: Socio-Technological Uncertainty and Political Fragmentation. London: Routledge, pp. 1–13.

Eggenschwiler, J. (2022). Big Tech's Push for Norms to Tackle Uncertainty in Cyberspace. In M. Dunn Cavelty and A. Wenger (eds), Cyber Security: Socio-Technological Uncertainty and Political Fragmentation. London: Routledge, pp. 186–204.

Egloff, F. J. (2020a). Contested Public Attributions of Cyber Incidents and the Role of Academia. Contemporary Security Policy, 41(1): 55–81. https://doi.org/1 0.1080/13523260.2019.1677324.

Egloff, F. J. (2020b). Public Attribution of Cyber Intrusions. Journal of Cybersecurity, 6(1): 1–12. https://doi.org/10.1093/cybsec/tyaa012.

Egloff, F. J. (2022). Semi-State Actors in Cybersecurity. Oxford: Oxford University Press.

Egloff, F. J., and Dunn Cavelty, M. (2021). Attribution and Knowledge Creation Assemblages in Cybersecurity Politics. Journal of Cybersecurity, 7(1): tyab002. https://doi.org/10.1093/cybsec/tyab002.

Egloff, F. J., and Wenger, A. (2019). Public Attribution of Cyber Incidents. In F. Merz (ed.). CSS Analyses in Security Policy, 244. Zurich: Center for Security Studies (CSS), pp. 1–4.

Eriksson, J., and Giacomello, G. (2022). Cyberspace in Space: Fragmentation, Vulnerability, and Uncertainty. In M. Dunn Cavelty and A. Wenger (eds), Cyber Security: SocioTechnological Uncertainty and Political Fragmentation. London: Routledge, pp. 95–107.

Fischer, S.-C. (2021). The Mobilization of Commercial Technology Companies: Explaining the Pursuit of U.S. Technological Superiority vis-à-vis China in a Private Sector-Driven and Globalized Innovation System. Unpublished PhD Manuscript. Zurich: Center for Security Studies (CSS).

Fischer, S.-C., and Wenger, A. (2019). A Politically Neutral Hub for Basic AI Research. CSS Policy Perspectives, 7(2). Zurich: Center for Security Studies (CSS).

Fischer, S.-C., and Wenger, A. (2021). Artificial Intelligence, Forward-Looking Governance and the Future of Security. Swiss Political Science Review, 27(1): 170–179. https://doi .org/10.1111/spsr.12439.

Gartzke, E. (2013). The Myth of Cyberwar. Bringing War in Cyberspace Back Down to Earth. International Security, 38: 41–73. https://doi.org/10.1162/ ISEC_a_00136.

Georgieva, I. (2020). The Unexpected Norm-Setters: Intelligence Agencies in Cyberspace. Contemporary Security Policy, 41: 33–54. https://doi.org/10.1080 /13523260.2019.1677389.

Gomez, M. A., and Whyte, C. (2022). Cyber Uncertainties: Observations from CrossNational Wargames. In M. Dunn Cavelty and A. Wenger (eds), Cyber Security: Socio-Technological Uncertainty and Political Fragmentation. London: Routledge, pp. 111–127.

Harknett, R. J., and Smeets, M. (2020). Cyber Campaigns and Strategic Outcomes. Journal of Strategic Studies, Ahead of Print: 1–34. https://doi.org/10.1080/0 1402390.2020.1732354.

Haunschild, J., Kaufhold, M.-A., and Reuter, C. (2022). Cultural Violence and Peace in Social Media: Technical and Social Interventions. In M. Dunn Cavelty and A. Wenger (eds), Cyber Security: Socio-Technological Uncertainty and Political Fragmentation. London: Routledge, pp. 48–63.

Healey, J. (2019). The Implications of Persistent (and Permanent) Engagement in Cyberspace. Journal of Cybersecurity, 5(1): tyz008. https://doi.org/10.1093/ cybsec/tyz008.

Healey, J., and Jervis, R. (2020). The Escalation Inversion and Other Oddities of Situational Cyber Stability. Texas National Security Review, 3(4): 30–53. https://doi.org/10.26153/tsw/10962.

Hirsh, M. (2021, July 8). Putin Is Testing Biden's Cyber Resolve. Foreign Policy. Retrieved August 19, 2021, from: https://foreignpolicy.com/2021/07/08/ putin-biden -cyber-security-attacks-ransomeware/.

Jervis, R. (1978). Cooperation under the Security Dilemma. World Politics, 30(2): 167–214.

Jusufi, I. (2022). Uncertainty, International Obligations, Fragmentation and Sovereignty: Cyber Security in Albania. In M. Dunn Cavelty and A. Wenger (eds), Cyber Security: Socio-Technological Uncertainty and Political Fragmentation. London: Routledge, pp. 172–185.

Kello, L. (2017). The Virtual Weapon and International Order. New Haven: Yale University Press.

Kostyuk, N., and Zhukov, Y. M. (2017). Invisible Digital Front: Can Cyber Attacks Shape Battlefield Events? Journal of Conflict Resolution, 63(2): 317–47.

Kuerbis, B., Badiei, F., Grindal, K., and Mueller, M. (2022). Understanding Transnational Cyber Attribution: Moving from 'Whodunit' to Who Did it. In M. Dunn Cavelty and A. Wenger (eds), Cyber Security: Socio-Technological Uncertainty and Political Fragmentation. London: Routledge, pp. 220–238.

Lewis, J. A. (2018). Rethinking Cyber Security: Strategy, Mass Effects, and States. Washington, DC: Center for Strategic and International Studies.

CoLi, X., and Chen, D. (2021, April 15). Should the West Fear China's Increasing Role in Technical Standard Setting? The Diplomat. Retrieved from: https:// thediplomat.com /2021/04/should-the-west-fear-chinas-increasing-role-in-technical-standard-setting/.

Lindsay, J. R. (2013). Stuxnet and the Limits of Cyber Warfare. Security Studies, 22(3): 365–404.

Lindsay, J. R. (2014/2015). The Impact of China on Cybersecurity: Fiction and Friction. International Security, 39(3): 7–47.

Lindsay, J. R. (2017). Restrained by Design: The Political Economy of Cybersecurity. Digital Policy, Regulation and Governance, 19: 493–514. https://doi.org/10.1108/DPRG-05-2017-0023.

Lindsay, J. R. (2020). Cyber Conflict vs. Cyber Command: Hidden Dangers in the American Military Solution to a Large-Scale Intelligence Problem. Intelligent and National Security, 36(2): 260–278. https://doi.org/10.1080/02684 527.2020.1840746.

Lindsay, J. R. (2022). Quantum Computer and Classical Politics: The Ambiguity of Cryptologic Advantage. In M. Dunn Cavelty and A. Wenger (eds), Cyber Security: Socio-Technological Uncertainty and Political Fragmentation. London: Routledge, pp. 80–94.

Lindsay, J. R., and Gartzke, E. (2019). Cross-Domain Deterrence: Strategy in an Era of Complexity. Oxford: Oxford University Press.

Lupovici, A. (2016). The Power of Deterrence. Emotions, Identity, and American and Israeli Wars of Resolve. Cambridge: Cambridge University Press.

Lupovici, A. (2021). The Dog that Did not Bark, the Dog that Did Bark, and the Dog that Should Have Barked: A Methodology for Cyber Deterrence Research. International Studies Review, viab032. https://doi.org/10.1093/isr/viab032.

Lupovici, A. (2022). Uncertainty and the Study of Cyber Deterrence: The Case of Israel's Limited Reliance on Cyber Deterrence. In M. Dunn Cavelty and A. Wenger (eds), Cyber Security: Socio-Technological Uncertainty and Political Fragmentation. London: Routledge, pp. 128–140.

Maschmeyer, L. (2021). The Subversive Trilemma: Why Cyber Operations Fall Short of Expectations. International Security, 46(2): 51–90.

Maschmeyer, L., Abrahams, A., Pomerantsev, P., and Yermolenko, V. (forthcoming). Donetsk Don't Tell. Hybrid War in Ukraine and the Limits of Digital Influence Operations.

Poznansky, M., and Perkoski, E. (2018). Rethinking Secrecy in Cyberspace: The Politics of Voluntary Attribution. Journal of Global Security Studies, 3(4): 402–416. https://doi.org/10.1093/jogss/ogy022.

Rid, T. (2012). Cyber War Will Not Take Place. Journal of Strategic Studies, 35(1): 5–32.Rid, T., and Buchanan, B. (2015). Attributing Cyber Attacks. The Journal of Strategic Studies, 38(1–2): 4–37.

Rovner, J. (2019, September 16). Cyber War an Intelligence Contest. War on the Rocks. Retrieved August 19, 2021, from: https://warontherocks.com/2019/09/cyber-war-as-an-intelligence-contest/.

Schelling, T. C. (1966). Arms and Influence. New Haven: Yale University Press.

Schulze, M. (2020). Cyber in War: Assessing the Strategic, Tactical, and Operational Utility of Military Cyber Operations. In 2020 12th International Conference on Cyber Conflict. Retrieved August 19, 2021, from: https://www.ccdcoe.org/uploads/2020/05/CyCon_2020_10_Schulze.pdf.

Schünemann, W. (2022). A Threat to Democracies? An Overview of Approaches to Measuring the Effects of Disinformation. In M. Dunn Cavelty and A. Wenger (eds), Cyber Security: Socio-Technological Uncertainty and Political Fragmentation. London: Routledge, pp. 32–47.

Seebeck, L. (2019, September 5). Why the Fifth Domain is Different. The Strategist, ASPI (Australian Stratic Policy Institute). Retrieved from: https://www.aspistrategist.org.au/why-the-fifth-domain-is-different/.

Slayton, R. (2017). What is the Cyber Offense-Defense Balance? Conceptions, Causes, and Assessment. International Security, 41: 72–109. https://doi.org/10.1162/ISEC_a_00267.

Smeets, M. (2018). The Strategic Promise of Offensive Cyber Operations. Strategic Studies Quarterly, 12(3): 90–113.

Smeets, M. (2022). No Shortcuts: Why States Struggle to Develop a Military Cyber-Force. London: Hurst Publishers.

Soesanto, S., and Smeets, M. (2020). Cyber Deterrence: The Past, Present, and Future. In F. Osinga and T. Sweijs (eds), NL ARMS Netherlands Annual Review of Military Studies 2020. The Hague: T.M.C. Asser Press. https://doi.org/10.1007/978-94-6265-419-8_20.

Steed, D. (2022). Disrupting the Second Oldest Profession: The Impact of Cyber on Intelligence. In M. Dunn Cavelty and A. Wenger (eds), Cyber Security: SocioTechnological Uncertainty and Political Fragmentation. London: Routledge, pp. 205–219.

Steiger, S. (2022). Cyber Securities and Cyber Security Politics: Understanding Different Logics of German Cyber Security Policies. In M. Dunn Cavelty and A. Wenger (eds), Cyber Security: Socio-Technological Uncertainty and Political Fragmentation. London: Routledge, pp. 141–156.

Sweijs, T., and Zilincik, S. (2021). The Essence of Cross-Domain Deterrence. In F. Osinga and T. Sweijs (eds), NL ARMS Netherlands Annual Review of Military Studies 2020.

The Hague: T.M.C. Asser Press. https://doi.org/10.1007/978-94-6265-419-8_8.

Tor, U. (2015). 'Cumulative Deterrence' as a New Paradigm for Cyber Deterrence. Journal of Strategic Studies, 40(1–2): 92–117.

US-China Business Council (USCBC). (2020). China in International Standards Setting. USCBC Recommendations for Constructive Participation. Retrieved from: https://www.uschina.org/sites/default/files/china_in_international_standards_setting.pdf.

US Cyber Command. (2018). Achieve and Maintain Cyberspace Superiority: Command Vision for US Cyber Command. Retrieved from: https://www.cybercom.mil/Portals /56/Documents/USCYBERCOM%20Vision%20 April%202018.pdf?ver=2018-06-14 -152556-010.

US Department of Defense. (2019). Cyber Strategy 2019: Summary. Retrieved from: https://media.defense.gov/2018/Sep/18/2002041658/1/1/1/CYBER_ STRATEGY_SUMMARY_FINAL.PDF.

Valeriano, B., and Maness, R. C. (2015). Cyber War versus Cyber Realities: Cyber Conflict in the International System. Oxford: Oxford University Press.

Wenger, A., and Wilner, A. (eds). (2021). Deterrence by Denial: Theory and Practice. Amherst, NY: Cambria Press

Chapter 13: Artificial Intelligence and EU Security: the False Promise of Digital Sovereignty. Andrea Calderaro & Stella Blumfelde

AI Task Force. 2019. Artificial intelligence in support of defence. Paris: Ministère des Armées. [Google Scholar]

Archibugi, D., and Mariella, V., 2021. Is a European recovery possible without high-tech public corporations? Intereconomics, 56 (3), 160–166. [Crossref], [Google Scholar]

Asaro, P., 2013. On banning autonomous weapon systems: human rights, automation, and the dehumanization of lethal decision-making. Cambridge: Cambridge University Press. [Google Scholar]

Azmeh, S., Foster, C., and Echavarri, J., 2020. The international trade regime and the quest for free digital trade. International studies review, 22 (3), 671–692. [Crossref], [Web of Science °], [Google Scholar]

Barela, S.J., 2016. Legitimacy and drones: investigating the legality, morality and efficacy of UCAVs. London: Routledge. [Crossref], [Google Scholar]

Barrinha, A., and Christou, G., 2022. Speaking sovereignty: the EU in the Cyber Domain. European Security, 31 (3), 356–376. [Taylor & Francis Online], [Google Scholar]

Bellanova, R., Carrapico, H., and Duez, D., 2022. Digital/sovereignty and European security integration. An introduction. European Security, 31 (3), 337–355. [Taylor & Francis Online], [Google Scholar]

Bellanova, R., and Glouftsios, G., 2022. Formatting European security integration through database interoperability. European security, 31 (3), 454–474. [Taylor & Francis Online], [Google Scholar]

Bendett, S. 2017. Red robots rising. Real Clear Defense. [Google Scholar]

Bendett, S., et al., 2021. Advanced military technology in Russia. London: Chatham House. [Google Scholar]

Boulanin, V., et al. 2020. Responsible military use of artificial intelligence: can the European Union Lead the way in developing best practice? SIPRI. [Google Scholar]

Bradford, A., 2020. The Brussels effect: how the European Union rules the world. New York: Oxford University Press. [Crossref], [Google Scholar]

Brattberg, E., Csernatoni, R., and Rugova, V. 2020. Europe and AI: leading, lagging behind, or carving its own way? Carnegie Endowmnet for International Peace. [Google Scholar]

Briscoe, E., and Fairbanks, J., 2020. Artificial scientific intelligence and its impact on national security and foreign policy. Orbis, 64 (4), 544–554. [Crossref], [Google Scholar]

Brooks, S.G., 2017. Producing security: multinational corporations, globalization, and the changing calculus of conflict. Princeton, NJ: Princeton University Press. [Google Scholar]

Brown, M. 2019. Statement by Michael Brown, Director of the Defense Innovation Unit, Before the Senate Armed Services Committee Subcommittee on Emerging Threats and Capabilities Hearing on "Artificial Intelligence Initiatives Within The Defense Innovation Unit". National Security Archive. [Google Scholar]

Bughin, J., et al., 2017. Artificial intelligence: the next digital frontier? Mckinsey Global Institute. [Google Scholar]

Bygrave, L.A., 2021. The 'strasbourg effect' on data protection in light of the 'brussels effect': logic, mechanics and prospects. Computer law & security review, 40, 105460. [Crossref], [Web of Science ®], [Google Scholar]

Calderaro, A., 2021. Diplomacy and responsibilities in the transnational governance of the cyber domain. In: H. Hansen-Magnusson, and A. Vetterlein, eds. The Routledge handbook of responsibility in world politics (pp. 394–405). London: Routledge. [Crossref], [Google Scholar]

Calderaro, A., and Craig, A.J.S., 2020. Transnational governance of cybersecurity: policy challenges and global inequalities in cyber capacity building. Third world quarterly, 41 (6), 917–938. [Taylor & Francis Online], [Web of Science ®], [Google Scholar]

Calderaro, A., Gollatz, K., and Wagner, B., 2014. Internet & human rights in foreign policy : comparing narratives in the US and EU internet governance agenda. Working Paper. Florence: European University Institute. [Google Scholar]

Castro, D., McLaughlin, M., and Chivot, E. 2019. Who is winning the AI race: China, the EU or the United States? Center for Data Innovation. [Google Scholar]

Cath, C., et al., 2018. Artificial intelligence and the 'good society': the US, EU, and UK approach. Science and engineering ethics, 24 (2), 505–528. [PubMed], [Web of Science *], [Google Scholar]

Cheung, T.M., et al. 2016. Planning for innovation: understanding China's plans for technological, energy, industrial, and defense development. U.S.- CHINA. ECONOMIC and SECURITY REVIEW COMMISSION. University of California - Institute on Global Conflict and Cooperation. [Crossref], [Google Scholar]

Citi, M., 2014. Revisiting creeping competences in the EU: the case of security R&D policy. Journal of European integration, 36 (2), 135–151. [Taylor & Francis Online], [Web of Science *], [Google Scholar]

Committee on International Trade, E.P. 2017. Proposal for a regulation of the European Parliament and of the Council setting up a Union regime for the control of exports, transfer, brokering, technical assistance and transit of dual-use items (recast) (COM(2016)0616 – C8-0393/2016–2016/0295(COD)). [Google Scholar]

Couture, S., and Toupin, S. 2019. What does the notion of "sovereignty" mean when referring to the digital?. New Media & Society, 21 (10), 2305–22. [Google Scholar]

Cremona, M., 2004. The union as a global actor: roles, models and identity. Common market law review, 41, 553–573. [Crossref], [Web of Science *], [Google Scholar]

Crofts, P., and van Rijswijk, H., 2020. Negotiating 'evil': google, Project Maven and the corporate form. Law, technology and humans, 2 (1), 75–90. [Crossref], [Google Scholar]

Csernatoni, R., 2022. The EU's hegemonic imaginaries: from European strategic autonomy in defence to technological sovereignty. European security, 31 (3), 395–414. [Taylor & Francis Online], [Google Scholar]

Danilin, I.V., 2018. Emerging technologies and their impact on international relations and global security. Washington, DC: Hoover Institution. Text. [Google Scholar]

DARPA. 2019. Automated Rapid Certification of Software (ARCOS). [Google Scholar]

Demchak, C.C., 2019. China: determined to dominate cyberspace and AI. Bulletin of the atomic scientists, 75 (3), 99–104. [Taylor & Francis Online], [Web of Science *], [Google Scholar]

Deputy Secretary of Defense, 2017. Establishment of an algorithmic warfare cross-functional team (Project Maven). Washington, DC: US Department of Defense. [Google Scholar]

413

Docquier, F., and Rapoport, H., 2012. Globalization, brain drain, and development. Journal of economic literature, 50 (3), 681–730. [Crossref], [Web of Science ®], [Google Scholar]

ENISA. 2020. Artificial intelligence cybersecurity challenges. Report/Study. [Google Scholar]

ENISA, E.U.A. for C. 2017. Principles and opportunities for a renewed EU cyber security strategy. [Google Scholar]

European Commission. 2007. The external dimension of the single market review - a single market for 21st century Europe. [Google Scholar]

European Commission. 2010. A comprehensive approach on personal data protection in the European Union. [Google Scholar]

European Commission, 2017. White paper on the future of Europe. Brussels: European Commission. Text. [Google Scholar]

European Commission. 2018. Coordinated plan on artificial intelligence. [Google Scholar]

European Commission. 2020a. Digital Economy and Society Index (DESI) 2019. Country Report: Italy. [Google Scholar]

European Commission. 2020b. Shaping Europe's digital future. [Google Scholar]

European Commission. 2021a. Fostering a European approach to artificial intelligence. [Google Scholar]

European Commission. 2021b. Coordinated plan on artificial intelligence 2021 review, shaping Europe's digital future. [Google Scholar]

European Commission. 2021c. Europe's digital decade: digital targets for 2030. [Google Scholar]

European Commission. 2021d. EU and Brazil to reinforce cooperation ahead of 12th Digital Economy Dialogue. Shaping Europe's digital future. [Google Scholar]

European Commission. 2022a. Roadmap on critical technologies for security and defence. Strasbourg, Text. [Google Scholar]

European Commission, 2022b. Joint statement: EU and Singapore agree to accelerate steps towards a comprehensive digital Partnership. European Commission. [Google Scholar]

European Commission. 2022c. EU-Japan summit: strengthening our partnership. European Commission. [Google Scholar]

European Council. 2010. The Stockholm Programme — an open and secure Europe serving and protecting citizens. [Google Scholar]

European Council. 2013. Conclusions of the European Council of 19/20 December 2013. EUCO 217/13. [Google Scholar]

European Council. 2020. European Council conclusions, 1-2 October 2020. [Google Scholar]

European Defence Agency. 2020a. ESA and EDA joint research: advancing into the unknown. [Google Scholar]

European Defence Agency, 2020b. Artificial intelligence: Joint quest for future defence applications. European defence matters (19), 34–37. [Google Scholar]

European Defence Agency. 2021. Defence Data 2018-2019: Key findings and analysis. [Google Scholar]

European External Action Service, 2022. A strategic compass for security and defence: for a European Union that protects its citizens, values and interests and contributes to international peace and security. Brussels: The European External Action Service. [Google Scholar]

European External Action Services. 2016. Shared vision, common action: a stronger Europe. A global strategy for the European Union's foreign and security policy. [Crossref], [Google Scholar]

European Investment Bank. 2021. Artificial intelligence, blockchain and the future of Europe: How disruptive technologies create opportunities for a green and digital economy. [Google Scholar]

European Parliament. 2012. Human rights in the world and the European Union's policy on the matter including implications for the EU's strategic human rights policy - P7_TA(2012)0126. [Google Scholar]

European Parliament. 2015. Human rights and technology in third countries. [Google Scholar]

European Parliament. 2018. Autonomous weapon systems. 2020/2684(RSO). [Google Scholar]

European Parliament. 2019. Security threats connected with the rising Chinese technological presence in the EU and possible action on the EU level to reduce them. [Google Scholar]

European Parliament. 2021a. Artificial intelligence: questions of interpretation and application of international law. [Google Scholar]

European Parliament. 2021b. Artificial intelligence funding under the European Defence Fund. [Google Scholar]

European Parliament. 2022. Artificial intelligence: MEPs want the EU to be a global standard-setter. [Google Scholar]

European Parliament and Council of the European Union. 2018. Proposal for a Regulation of the European Parliament and the Council on preventing the dissemination of terrorist content online A contribution from the European Commission to the Leaders' meeting in Salzburg on 19-20 September 2018. COM/2018/640 final. [Google Scholar]

Fahey, E., et al. 2020. The EU as a Good Global Actor. [Google Scholar]

Farrand, B., and Carrapico, H., 2022. Digital sovereignty and taking back control: from regulatory capitalism to regulatory mercantilism in EU cybersecurity. European security, 31 (3), 435–453. [Taylor & Francis Online], [Google Scholar]

Flaxman, S., Goel, S., and Rao, J.M., 2016. Filter bubbles, echo chambers, and online news consumption. Public opinion quarterly, 80 (S1), 298–320. [Crossref], [Web of Science *], [Google Scholar]

Friis, K., and Lysne, O., 2021. Huawei, 5G and security: technological limitations and political responses. Development and change, 52 (5), 1174–1195. [Crossref], [Web of Science *], [Google Scholar]

Goldman, E.O., and Andres, R.B., 1999. Systemic effects of military innovation and diffusion. Security studies, 8 (4), 79–125. [Taylor & Francis Online], [Web of Science *], [Google Scholar]

Haner, J., and Garcia, D., 2019. The Artificial Intelligence arms race: trends and world leaders in autonomous weapons development. Global policy, 10 (3), 331–337. [Crossref], [Web of Science *], [Google Scholar]

Headrick, D.R., 2010. Power over peoples: technology, environments, and western imperialism, 1400 to the present. Princeton, NJ: Princeton University Press. [Google Scholar]

High Contracting Parties CCW. 2019. Meeting of the high contracting parties to the convention on prohibitions or restrictions on the use of certain conventional weapons which may be deemed to be excessively injurious or to have indiscriminate effects. United Nations. [Google Scholar]

High-Level Expert Group on Artificial Intelligence. 2019. Policy and investment recommendations for trustworthy AI. European Commission. [Google Scholar]

Hintz, A., Dencik, L., and Wahl-Jorgensen, K., 2019. Digital citizenship in a datafied society. Cambridge: Polity Press. [Google Scholar]

Hoadley, D.S., and Lucas, N.J., 2018. Artificial intelligence and national security. Washington, DC: US Congress, Congressional Research Service. [Google Scholar]

Horowitz, M.C., 2018. Artificial Intelligence, international competition, and the balance of power. Texas national security review, 1 (3), 22. [Google Scholar]

Horowitz, M.C., 2019. When speed kills: lethal autonomous weapon systems, deterrence and stability. Journal of Strategic studies, 42 (6), 764–788. [Taylor & Francis Online], [Web of Science *], [Google Scholar]

Johnson, J., 2019. Artificial intelligence & future warfare: implications for international security. Defense & security analysis, 35 (2), 147–169. [Taylor & Francis Online], [Web of Science *], [Google Scholar]

Juncker, J.-C. 2018. State of the Union 2018: Annual State of the EU address by President Juncker at the European Parliament. [Google Scholar]

Kania, E.B. 2017. Battlefield singularity: artificial intelligence, military revolution, and China's future military power. Center for a New American Security. [Google Scholar]

Kania, E.B., 2021. Artificial intelligence in China's revolution in military affairs. Journal of strategic studies, 44 (4), 515–542. [Taylor & Francis Online], [Web of Science *], [Google Scholar]

Kapczynski, A., 2019. The law of informational capitalism review. Yale law journal, 129 (5), 1460–1515. [Web of Science *], [Google Scholar]

Kashin, V., and Raska, M. 2017. Countering the U.S. third offset strategy: Russian perspectives, responses and challenges. S. Rajaratnam School of International Studies. [Google Scholar]

Kirkos, E., Spathis, C., and Manolopoulos, Y., 2007. Data mining techniques for the detection of fraudulent financial statements. Expert systems with applications, 32 (4), 995–1003. [Crossref], [Web of Science *], [Google Scholar]

Lambach, D., and Monsees, L., 2022. Digital sovereignty, geopolitical imaginaries, and the reproduction of European identity. European Security, 31 (3), 377–394. [Taylor & Francis Online], [Google Scholar]

Lange, K. 2016. 3rd Offset strategy 101: what it is, what the tech focuses are. The Department of the Navy's Information Technology Magazine. [Crossref], [Google Scholar]

Li, H., Yu, L., and He, W., 2019. The impact of GDPR on global technology development. Journal of global information technology management, 22 (1), 1–6. [Taylor & Francis Online], [Web of Science *], [Google Scholar]

Lucarelli, S., and Manners, I., 2006. Values and principles in European Union foreign policy. New York, NY: Routledge. [Crossref], [Google Scholar]

Manners, I., 2002. Normative power Europe: a contradiction in terms? JCMS: Journal of common market studies, 40 (2), 235–258. [Crossref], [Web of Science *], [Google Scholar]

Manners, I., and Diez, T., 2007. Reflecting on Normative Power Europe. In: F. Berenskoetter, and M.J. Williams, eds. Power in world politics. New York: Routledge, 173–188. [Google Scholar]

Marsden, C., Meyer, T., and Brown, I., 2020. Platform values and democratic elections: how can the law regulate digital disinformation? Computer law & security review, 36, 105373. [Crossref], [Web of Science *], [Google Scholar]

Martins, B.O., Lidén, K., and Jumbert, M.G., 2022. Border security and the digitalization of sovereignty: insights from EU borderwork. European security, 31 (3), 475–494. [Taylor & Francis Online], [Google Scholar]

Marzouki, M., and Calderaro A., 2022. Internet diplomacy: shaping the global politics of cyberspace. New York, NY: Rowman & Littlefield. [Google Scholar]

Mazzucato, M., and Perez, C., 2015. Innovation as growth policy: the challenge for Europe. In: J. Fagerberg, S. Laestadius, and B.R. Martin, eds. The triple challenge for Europe: economic development, climate change, and governance. Oxford: Oxford University Press, 229–253. [Crossref], [Google Scholar]

Micklitz, H.-W., et al., 2021. Constitutional challenges in the algorithmic society. Cambridge: Cambridge University Press. [Crossref], [Google Scholar]

National Science Board. 2020. The State of U.S. Science and Engineering 2020. [Google Scholar]

Nicolaïdis, K., and Howse, R., 2002. 'This is my EUtopia...': narrative as power. JCMS: Journal of common market studies, 40 (4), 767–792. [Crossref], [Web of Science ®], [Google Scholar]

OECD.AI. 2021. Database of national AI policies. Available from: https://www.oecd.ai/dashboards. [Google Scholar]

Onar, N.F., and Nicolaïdis, K., 2013. The decentring agenda: Europe as a postcolonial power. Cooperation and conflict, 48 (2), 283–303. [Crossref], [Web of Science ®], [Google Scholar]

Pellerin, C. 2016. Deputy Secretary: third offset strategy Bolsters America's Military Deterrence. U.S. Department of Defense. [Crossref], [Google Scholar]

Petrella, S., Miller, C., and Cooper, B., 2021. Russia's artificial intelligence strategy: the role of state-owned firms. Orbis, 65 (1), 75–100. [Crossref], [Google Scholar]

Pohle, J., and Thiel, T., 2020. Digital sovereignty. Internet policy review, 9 (4), 1–19. [Crossref], [Google Scholar]

Posen, B.R., 2006. European Union security and defense policy: response to unipolarity? Security studies, 15 (2), 149–186. [Taylor & Francis Online], [Web of Science ®], [Google Scholar]

Rassler, D. 2018. The Islamic State and drones: supply, scale, and future threats. United States Military Academy. [Google Scholar]

Renda, A., 2022. Beyond the Brussels effect. leveraging digital regulation for strategic autonomy. Brussels: Foundation for European Progressive Studies. [Google Scholar]

Roberts, H., et al., 2021. Achieving a 'Good AI society': comparing the aims and progress of the EU and the US. Science and engineering ethics, 27 (6). [Crossref], [PubMed], [Web of Science ®], [Google Scholar]

Samoili, S., et al. 2020. TES analysis of AI Worldwide Ecosystem in 2009-2018. [Google Scholar]

Soare, S.R., 2021. European Defence and AI: game-changer or gradual change? RSIS commentary, 51, 4. [Google Scholar]

State Council of China. 2017. A next generation artificial intelligence development plan. [Google Scholar]

The State Council of People's Republic of China. 2021. Made in China 2025. [Google Scholar]

Taddeo, M., 2019. Three ethical challenges of applications of artificial intelligence in cybersecurity. Minds and machines, 29 (2), 187–191. [Crossref], [Web of Science *], [Google Scholar]

Taddeo, M., and Floridi, L., 2018. Regulate artificial intelligence to avert cyber arms race. Nature, 556 (7701), 296–298. [Crossref], [PubMed], [Web of Science *], [Google Scholar]

Timmers, P., 2019. Ethics of AI and cybersecurity when sovereignty is at stake. Minds and machines, 29 (4), 635–645. [Crossref], [Web of Science *], [Google Scholar]

Turing, A.M., 1950. Computing machinery and intelligence. Mind, LIX (236), 433–460. [Crossref], [Google Scholar]

UNESCO Institute for Statistics. 2021. Science,technology and innovation. United Nations. [Google Scholar]

UNIDIR. 2019. The 2019 innovations dialogue report: digital technologies & international security. [Google Scholar]

US Department of Defense. 2019. Harnessing AI to advance our security and prosperity. [Google Scholar]

US Department of Defense. 2022. DoD Announces Dr. Craig Martell as Chief Digital and Artificial Intelligence Officer. U.S. Department of Defense. [Google Scholar]

von der Leyen, U., 2019. A Union that strives for more: my agenda for Europe : political guidelines for the next European Commission 2019-2024. Brussels: Publications Office of the European Union. [Google Scholar]

Whitman, R.G., 1998. From civilian power to superpower? : the international identity of the European union. Basingstone: Macmillan. [Crossref], [Google Scholar]

Whyte, C., 2020. Deepfake news: AI-enabled disinformation as a multi-level public policy challenge. Journal of cyber policy, 5 (2), 199–217. [Taylor & Francis Online], [Google Scholar]

Woolley, S.C., and Howard, P.N., 2018. Computational propaganda: political parties, politicians, and political manipulation on social media. New York: Oxford University Press. [Crossref], [Google Scholar]

Work, B. 2016. Remarks by Deputy Secretary work on third offset strategy. U.S. Department of Defense. [Crossref], [Google Scholar]

York, J.C., 2021. Silicon values: the future of free speech under surveillance capitalism. London: Verso. [Google Scholar]

Zhang, D., et al., 2022. The AI index 2022 annual report. Stanford, CA: Stanford Institute for Human-Centered AI. [Google Scholar]

Zielonka, J., 1998. Explaining euro-paralysis: why Europe is unable to act in international politics. Basingstone: Macmillan. [Crossref], [Google Scholar]

Zuboff, S., 2019. The age of surveillance capitalism : the fight for a human future at the new frontier of power. London: Profile Books. [Google Scholar]

Chapter 14: Towards Democratic Intelligence Oversight: Limits, Practices, Struggles. Ronja Kniep, Lina Ewert, Bernardino Léon Reyes, Félix Tréguer, Emma Mc Cluskey and Claudia Aradau

*Suggested citation: Kniep, Ronja, Lina Ewert, Bernardino Léon Reyes, Félix Tréguer, Emma Mc Cluskey, and Claudia Aradau. 'Towards Democratic Intelligence Oversight: Limits, Practices, Struggles'. Review of International Studies, March 2023, 1–21. https: //doi.org/10.1017/S0260210523000013.**Authors have been listed according to their inverse order of seniority in academia, a choice intended to promote the visibility of early career scholars.

1 Interview with civil society actor, UK, 2019/09/25.

2 David E. Sanger, 'New N.S.A. Chief Calls Damage From Snowden Leaks Manageable', The New York Times (2014).

3 Hugh Bochel, Andrew Defty, and Jane Kirkpatrick, Watching the Watchers: Parliament and the Intelligence Services (London: Palgrave, 2014), p. 200.

4 Clare Birchall, 'Radical Transparency?', Cultural Studies - Critical Methodologies, 14:1 (2014), pp.77–88.

5 Hager Ben Jaffel, Alvina Hoffmann, Oliver Kearns, and Sebastian Larsson, 'Toward Critical Approaches to Intelligence as a Social Phenomenon', International Political Sociology, 14:3 (2020), pp. 323–44; Peter Gill and Mark Phythian, Intelligence in an Insecure World (Cambridge: Polity, 2018).

6 Ben Jaffel et al. (2020).

7 Since the 1980s, theorists of 'agonistic democracy' have formulated a series of theoretical objections to liberal promoters of 'deliberative democracy' like Jürgen Habermas or John Rawls, the latter setting as a normative horizon the generalisation of democratic procedures based on the rational exchange of arguments between participants deemed equal. The Belgian philosopher Chantal Mouffe is one of those who best embodies this 'agonistic' current. Instead of seeing conflict as a degeneration of political participation and deliberation, Mouffe makes it the constitutive element of democracy.

According to her, political struggles are an unavoidable reality of pluralist societies. They are not only the result of localised differences of opinion – differences which could be overcome through deliberation – but question the very nature of the political order, the issues that should be debated and how they should be debated, as well as people who are legitimate to take part in the debate. Chantal Mouffe (ed.), Dimensions of Radical Democracy: Pluralism, Citizenship, Community (London: Verso, 1992).

8   A special issue of Millennium was dedicated to revisiting relations between democracy and IR in 2009 ('Democracy in International Relations', vol 37(3)). IR scholars have challenged conceptions of liberal democracy from a variety of constructivist, poststructuralist, postcolonial and feminist perspectives.

9   Hager Ben Jaffel and Sebastian Larsson. 'Introduction: What's the Problem with Intelligence Studies? Outlining a New Research Agenda on Contemporary Intelligence' in Hager Ben Jaffel and Sebastian Larsson (eds) Problematising Intelligence Studies: Towards a New Research Agenda (London: Routledge, 2022): pp. 3-29.

10   Arthur S. Hulnick 'Home time: A new paradigm for domestic intelligence', International Journal of Intelligence and counterintelligence 22:4 (2009): 569-585.

11   Loch K. Johnson, 'The Church Committee Investigation of 1975 and the Evolution of Modern Intelligence Accountability', Intelligence and National Security, 23:2 (2008), pp. 198–225.

12   Félix Tréguer, 'Can State Surveillance Be Contained? A Sociogenesis of Intelligence Oversight in the United States (1960-1975)' (Paris: CERI Sciences Po, 2022).

13   Kathryn S. Olmsted, Challenging the Secret Government: The Post-Watergate Investigations of the CIA and FBI (Chapel Hill: University of North Carolina Press, 1996); Tréguer (2022).

14   For instance, a 2017 report on oversight of government surveillance regimes in 24 countries found that oversight arrangements in the US, UK and Germany were ineffective. Korff, Douwe, Ben Wagner, Julia Powles, Renate Avila, and Ulf Buermeyer, 'Boundaries of Law: Exploring Transparency, Accountability, and Oversight of Government Surveillance Regimes', 2018, available at https://www.statewatch.org/media/documents/news/2017/jan/boundaries-of-law.pdf.

15   Rubinstein et al (2013), pp. 19-20.

16   In selecting the literature on intelligence oversight for this paper, we followed a twofold inductive method: on the one hand, revising the most referenced publications (n=100) about 'intelligence oversight', 'intelligence accountability' and 'intelligence control' in both Google Scholar and SCOPUS and, on the

other hand, gathering the profiles of the authors with more publications in SCOPUS.

17 Elspeth Guild, 'Data Rights. Claiming Privacy Rights through International Institutions', in Didier Bigo, Engin Isin, and Evelyn Ruppert (eds), Data politics. Worlds, subjects, rights (Routledge, 2019), pp. 267–84.

18 Asaf Lubin, "We Only Spy on Foreigners': The Myth of a Universal Right to Privacy and the Practice of Foreign Mass Surveillance', Chicago Journal of International Law, 18:2 (2018).

19 Peter Gill, 'Evaluating Intelligence Oversight Committees: The UK Intelligence and Security Committee and the "War on Terror"', Intelligence and National Security, 22:1 (2007), pp. 14–37; Jon Moran and Clive Walker, 'Intelligence Powers and Accountability in the UK', in Zachary K. Goldman and Samuel J. Rascoff (eds), Global Intelligence Oversight: Governing Security in the Twenty-First Century (Oxford: Oxford University Press, 2016).

20 Hans Born and Ian D. Leigh, 'Making Intelligence Accountable: Legal standards and best practice for oversight of intelligence agencies', (Oslo: Publishing House of the Parliament of Norway, 2005), p. 13; Aidan Wills, 'Democratic and effective oversight of national security services. Issue Paper', (Council of Europe, 2015), p. 17.

21 Marina Caparini, 'Controlling and Overseeing Intelligence Services in Democratic States', in Marina Caparini and Hans Born (eds), Democratic Control of Intelligence Services. Containing Rogue Elephants (Farnham: Ashgate, 2007), p. 12; Claudia Hillebrand, 'The Role of News Media in Intelligence Oversight', Intelligence and National Security 27:5 (2012), pp. 689–706; 'With or without you? The UK and information and intelligence sharing in the EU', Journal of Intelligence History 16:2 (2017), p. 692.

22 Florina Cristiana Matei, 'The Media's Role in Intelligence Democratization', International Journal of Intelligence and CounterIntelligence, 27:1 (2014), p. 76.

23 Karen Barnes and Peter Albrecht, 'Civil Society Oversight of the Security Sector and Gender', in M. Bastick and K. Valasek (eds), Gender & security sector reform toolkit (Geneva: DCAF, 2008), p. 2; Megan Bastick, Integrating gender into oversight of the security sector by ombuds institutions & national human rights institutions (DCAF, The Geneva Centre for the Democratic Control of Armed Forces, OSCE, 2014), p. 6.

24 Hillebrand (2012), p. 693; Charles D. Raab, 'Security, Privacy and Oversight', in Andrew W. Neal (ed.), Security in a Small Nation: Scotland, Democracy, Politics (Open Book Publishers, 2017), p. 82.

25 Caparini (2007), p. 12.

26 Barnes and Albrecht (2008), p. 2; Eden Cole, Kerstin Eppert, and Katrin Kinzelbach, Public Oversight of the Security Sector: A Handbook for Civil

Society Organizations (Valeur, Slovak Republic: United Nations Development Programme, 2008), p. 16.

27 Hanna Fenichel Pitkin, The Concept of Representation (Los Angeles: University of California Press, 1972).

28 Born and Leigh (2005), p. 13; Hans Born, Ian Leigh, and Aidan Wills, 'Making International Intelligence Cooperation Accountable' (Norwegian Parliamentary Oversight Committee and DCAF, 2015), p. 7; Wills (2015), p. 9; Amy B. Zegart, 'The Domestic Politics of Irrational Intelligence Oversight', Political Science Quarterly, 126:1 (2011), p. 4.

29 Moran and Walker (2016), p. 300.

30 Richard J. Aldrich and Philip H. J. Davies, 'Introduction: The Future of UK Intelligence and Special Operations', Review of International Studies, 35:4 (2009), p. 887; Ian Leigh, 'Changing the Rules of the Game: Some necessary legal reforms to United Kingdom intelligence', Review of International Studies, 35:4 (2009), p. 955.

31 Richard J. Aldrich, 'Beyond the vigilant state: globalisation and intelligence', Review of International Studies, 35:4 (2009), p. 892.

32 Peter Gill, 'Obstacles to the Oversight of the UK Intelligence Community', EInternational Relations, (2013); see also the notion of 'ambient accountability' in Richard J. Aldrich and Daniela Richterova, 'Ambient Accountability: Intelligence Services in Europe and the Decline of State Secrecy', West European Politics, 41:4 (2018), pp. 1003–24; Hans Born, 'Towards Effective Democratic Oversight of Intelligence Services: Lessons Learned from Comparing National Practices', Connections, 3:4 (2004), pp. 1–12.

33 Steven J. Balla and Christopher J. Deering, 'Police Patrols and Fire Alarms: An Empirical Examination of the Legislative Preference for Oversight', Congress & the Presidency, 40:1 (2013), pp. 27–40; Mathew D. McCubbins and Thomas Schwartz, 'Congressional Oversight Overlooked: Police Patrols versus Fire Alarms', American Journal of Political Science, 28:1 (1984), pp. 165–79.

34 Zachary K. Goldman and Samuel James Rascoff (eds), Global Intelligence Oversight: Governing Security in the Twenty-First Century (New York, NY: Oxford University Press, 2016), pp. xxiii–xxv.

35 Lisa Hahn and Myriam von Fromberg, 'Klagekollektive "Watchdogs"', Zeitschrift für Politikwissenschaft, (2020), pp. 1–23.

36 BVerfG 2020, p. 33.

37 Ibid p. 47.

38 Josef Hufelschulte, 'Lauscher ohne Ohren', Focus (2020).

39 DPA, 'Ex-BND-Chef Schindler warnt Karlsruhe: Sicherheit nicht gefährden', Zeit Online, (2019); August Hanning, 'BND-Debatte: Gastbeitrag – Absurdistan in Karlsruhe!', Bild.de, (2020).

40   Ronja

41   Necessary & Proportionate, 'International Principles on the Application of Human Rights to Communications Surveillance', available at: {https:// necessaryandproportionate.org/images/np-logo-og.png}   accessed   9 September 2021.

42   Luc Boltanski and Laurent Thévenot, 'The Sociology of Critical Capacity', European Journal of Social Theory, 2:3 (1999), p. 359.

43   POTUS, 'Presidential Policy Directive. Signals Intelligence Activities', (Washington, DC: White House, 2014). 44Guild (2019).

45   Deutscher Bundestag, 'Stenografisches Protokoll der 5. Sitzung. 1. Untersuchungsausschuss', (2014), p. 6f.

46   BVerfG (2020), p. 91.

47   Ibid., p. 86.

48   Ibid., p. 165.

49   Ibid., p. 269.

50   Ben Jaffel et al. (2020), p. 17.

51   Michael M. Andregg and Peter Gill, 'Comparing the Democratization of Intelligence', Intelligence and National Security, 29:4 (2014), p. 490; Barnes and Albrecht (2008), p. 2; Born et al. (2015), p. 7; Caparini (2007), p. 7; Cole et al. (2008), p. 16; Raab (2017), p.82; Reginald Whitaker and Anthony Stuart Farson, 'Accountability in and for National Security', IRPP Choices, 15:9 (2009), p. 8; Wills (2015), p. 25.

52   See especially Owen D. Thomas, 'Security in the Balance: How Britain tried to keep its Iraq War secrets', Security Dialogue 51:1 (2020), pp. 77-95.

53   William Walters, 'Secrecy, publicity and the Milieu of Security', Dialogues in human geography 5:3 (2015), pp. 287-290; WilliamWalters, State Secrecy and Security. Refiguring the Covert Imaginary (London: Routledge, 2021).

54   Didier Bigo, 'Shared Secrecy in a Digital age and a Transnational World', Intelligence and National Security, 34:3 (2019), pp. 379-394.

55   Tom Lundborg, 'Secrecy and Subjectivity: Double Agents and the Dark Underside of the International System', International Political Sociology, 15:4 (2021), pp. 443-459.

56   Claudia Aradau, 'Assembling (Non) Knowledge: Security, law, and surveillance in a digital world', International Political Sociology, 11:4 (2017), pp. 327-342.

57   Marieke De Goede, Esmé Bosma, and Polly Pallister-Wilkins, (eds), Secrecy and Methods in Security Research: A guide to qualitative fieldwork (Abingdon: Routledge, 2019). More sociological accounts of leaking, disclosure and whitewashing have also gained traction in recent years. Most notably, see

Rahul Sagar, Secrets and leaks (Princeton, NJ: Princeton University Press, 2016).

58 Marieke De Goede and Mara Wesseling, 'Secrecy and Security in Transatlantic Terrorism Finance Tracking.' Journal of European Integration, 39:3 (2017), pp. 253-269.

59 Walters (2021), p. 91.

60 Hannah Gurman and Kaeten Mistry, 'The Paradox of National Security Whistleblowing: Locating and Framing a History of the Phenomenon', in Kaeten Mistry and Hannah Gurman (eds), Whistleblowing Nation: The History of National Security Disclosures and the Cult of State Secrecy (Columbia University Press, 2020), p. 22.

61 Peter Gill, 'The Intelligence and Security Committee and the challenge of security networks', Review of International Studies, 35:4 (2009), p. 932.

62 Loch K. Johnson, 'The Church Committee Investigation of 1975 and the Evolution of Modern Intelligence Accountability', Intelligence and National Security, 23:2 (2008), pp.198–225.

63 Porter Goss, 'Loose Lips Sink Spies', The New York Times (10 February 2006).

64 Jack Shafer, 'Edward Snowden and the selective targeting of leaks', Reuters (11 June 2013).

65 Mark Phythian, 'An INS Special Forum: The US Senate Select Committee Report on the CIA's Detention and Interrogation Program', Intelligence and National Security, 31:1 (2016), p. 17.

66 Melina J. Dobson, 'The last forum of accountability? State secrecy, intelligence and freedom of information in the United Kingdom', The British Journal of Politics and International Relations, 21:2 (2019), p. 323.

67 Loch K. Johnson, Spy Watching: Intelligence Accountability in the United States (Oxford University Press, 2018), p. 438.

68 Ibid., p. 463.

69 Damien Van Puyvelde, 'Intelligence Accountability and the Role of Public Interest Groups in the United States', Intelligence and National Security, 28:2 (2013), p. 150.

70 Hillebrand (2012), p. 703.

71 Aldrich (2009), p. 56. Similarly, Van Buuren warns of the lack of democratic mandate of whistleblowers in relation to public/private assemblages in Jelle van Buuren, 'From Oversight to Undersight: the Internationalization of Intelligence', Security and Human Rights, 24:3–4 (2014), pp. 239–52.

72 See, e.g., Johnson (2018), p. 460.

73 Andregg and Gill (2014), p. 489.

74 Fredrik Sejersted, 'Intelligence and Accountability in a State without Enemies: The Case of Norway', in Hans Born, Loch K. Johnson, and Ian Leigh (eds), Who's Watching the Spies? Establishing Intelligence Service Accountability (2005), p. 130.

75 Loch K. Johnson, 'Lawmakers and Spies: congressional Oversight of Intelligence in the United States', in Wolbert K. Smidt (ed.), Geheimhaltung und Transparenz: demokratische Kontrolle der Geheimdienste im internationalen Vergleich (LIT Verlag Münster, 2007), p. 192.

76 Theodore H. Winkler and Leif Mevik, 'Foreword', in Hans Born, Loch K. Johnson, and Ian Leigh (eds), Who's Watching the Spies?: Establishing Intelligence Service Accountability (Dulles, VA: Potomac Books, 2005), pp. ix–x.

77 Goss (2006)

78 David Brooks, 'The Solitary Leaker', The New York Times, (10 June 2013).

79 'Richard Cohen: NSA is doing what Google does', Washington Post, (1 November 2013); Alex Lyda, 'Edward Snowden is more narcissist than patriot', The Chicago Tribune (24 December 2014); Ratnesar Romesh, 'The Unbearable Narcissism of Edward Snowden', Bloomberg.com, (1 November 2013); Jeffrey Toobin, 'Edward Snowden Is No Hero', The New Yorker (10 June 2013).

80 Jenna McLaughlin, 'Watergate-Era Church Committee Staffers Urge Leniency for Snowden', The Intercept (29 November 2016).

81 Interview, Loch K. Johnson, 2021/11/05.

82 William Scheuerman has refuted many of these criticisms of Snowden and their 'paltry' evidence in developing a sustained account of his whistleblowing as a practice of 'civil disobedience'. William Scheuerman, 'Whistleblowing as civil disobedience: The case of Edward Snowden', Philosophy & Social Criticism, 40(7) 2014: 609-628.

83 Edward Snowden, Permanent Record (New York: Metropolitan Books, 2019), chapter 21.

84 New York Times Co. v. United States, 403 U.S., 714–20.

85 ECHR, Bucur and Toma v. Romania, 2013/01/08.

86 Open Justice Initiative, 'Understanding the Tshwane Principles', available at: https: //www.justiceinitiative.org/publications/understanding-tshwane-principles, accessed 15 December 2021.

87 Parliamentary Assembly of the Council of Europe, 'Resolution 1954 (2013) - National security and access to information', available at: {https://assembly.coe.int/nw/xml/XRef/Xref-XML2HTMLen.   asp?fileid=20190&lang=en} accessed 15 December 2021.

88   Tom King, A King Among Ministers: Fifty years in parliament recalled (London: Unicorn, 2020).

89   See for example Marvin C. Ott, 'Partisanship and the Decline of Intelligence Oversight', International Journal of Intelligence and CounterIntelligence, 16:1 (2003), p. 79; Hillebrand (2012), p. 698; Jennifer Kibbe, 'Congressional Oversight of Intelligence: Is the Solution Part of the Problem?', Intelligence and National Security, 25:1 (2010), p. 42.

90   Anne Karalekas, History of the Central Intelligence Agency (Walnut Creek CA: Aegean Park Press, 1983), p. 27.

91   Anthony Glees and Philip H.J. Davies, 'Intelligence, Iraq and the limits of legislative accountability during political crisis', Intelligence and National Security, 21:5 (2006), p. 854.

92   Fred Schreier, 'The need for efficient and legitimate intelligence', in Marina Caparini and Hans Born (eds), Democratic Control of Intelligence Services (Routledge, 2016), p. 41.

93   Johnson (2008).

94   Ott (2003); Gill (2007); Kibbe (2010), p. 41.

95   Gill (2007), p. 15.

96   Kibbe (2010), p. 46.

97   Ian Leigh, 'More closely watching the spies: Three decades of experiences', in Loch K. Johnson, Hans Born, and Ian D. Leigh (eds), Who's Watching the Spies? Establishing Intelligence Service Accountability (Dulles, VA: Potomac Books, 2005), p. 8.

98   Hillebrand (2012), p. 698.

99   Aldrich (2009), p. 901.

100 'Don't Spy on Us', available at: {https://www.dontspyonus.org.uk/} accessed 10 December 2021.

101 Claudia Aradau and Emma Mc Cluskey, 'Making Digital Surveillance Unacceptable? Security, Democracy, and the Political Sociology of Disputes', International Political Sociology, (2021), pp. 1-19.

102 nterview with civil society actor, 2020/10/04.

103 David Anderson, 'Report of the Bulk Powers Review' (Independent Reviewer of Terrorism Legislation, 2016), p. 204.

104 Ibid. p. 61.

105 Interview with civil society actor, 2020/11/09.

106 Interview with civil society actor, 2020/10/21.

107 Interview 2020/09/25.

108 'Don't Spy on Us'.

109 Interview with civil society actor, 2020/11/08.

110 David Omand, 'Privacy and Security Inquiry. Public Evidence Session 8. Uncorrected Transcript of Evidence' (Intelligence and Security Committee of Parliament, 2014).

111 'House of Commons - Counter-terrorism - Home Affairs Committee', available at: {https://www.publications.parliament.uk/pa/cm201314/cmselect/cmhaff/231/23110.htm} accessed 5 May 2017.

112 Interview with independent expert, 2021/4/1.

113 Interview 2020/10/27.

114 Mouffe (1992).

115 Etienne Balibar, 'Democracy and Liberty in Times of Violence', The Hrant Dink Memorial Lecture 2018, Boğaziçi University, Istanbul.

Chapter 15; Between a Rock and a Hard Place: The Precarious State of a Double Agent during the Cold War. Eleni Braat & Ben de Jong

1   James M. Olson, To Catch a Spy: The Art of Counterintelligence (Washington, DC: Georgetown University Press, 2019), p. 87. In other words, Aldrich Ames and Robert Hanssen were Russian agents inside the Central Intelligence Agency (CIA) and the Federal Bureau of Investigation (FBI), respectively; they were not double agents.

2   A classic work on double agentry like the one by J.C. Masterman on the Double-Cross System of World War II fame, is indeed largely written from the perspective of the service that ran them. This is not surprising given the fact that Masterman for most of the war was the chairman of the XX Committee that ran the operation. J.C. Masterman, The Double-Cross System 1939–1945 (London: Pimlico, 1995). The Double-Cross System or XX System was an elaborate system of dozens of double agents who had been recruited or turned by the British against the German military intelligence service, the Abwehr. Its most impressive achievement was the successful deception of the German High Command regarding the location of the Allied landings in France in the spring of 1944.

3   He was originally recruited and run by one of the internal departments of the MfS and later handed over to the Hauptverwaltung [Chief Directorate] A (HV A), the foreign intelligence branch of the MfS.

4   For most of the past century and also during the Cold War, the world of intelligence was a very male-dominated one, especially when it came to agents and case officers in the field. Women working at an intelligence or security service were primarily employed in secretarial positions and agents were rarely women. Eleni Braat, "The Construction of Secret Intelligence as a Masculine Profession," International Journal of Intelligence and CounterIntelligence,

Advance Online Publication. DOI: 10.1080/08850607.2022.2055429. This article therefore refers to an agent or double agent when talking in the abstract as "he."

5   John Barron, Operation Solo: The FBI's Man in the Kremlin (Washington, DC: Regnery Publishing, 1996), pp. 4, 109–110, 156–157, 243–244, and passim.

6   This is the notorious case of Nicholas Shadrin, real name Nikolai Artamonov. He was a Soviet naval officer who had defected to the United States in 1959 and was allegedly killed by the KGB by accident. Oleg Kalugin, The First Directorate: My 32 Years in Intelligence and Espionage Against the West (New York: St. Martin's Press, 1994), pp. 152–157 and Boris Volodarsky, The KGB's Poison Factory: From Lenin to Litvinenko (Barnsley: Frontline Books, 2009), pp. 123–134.

7   See, for instance, Nigel West and Madoc Roberts, SNOW: The Double Life of a World War II Spy (London: Biteback Publishing 2011), pp. 34–38, 85–90, and passim; Masterman, Double-Cross, pp. 39–40. The British double agent Eddie Chapman was treated with suspicion by the Abwehr and interrogated harshly several times during a stay of more than a year in German-occupied Europe in 1943–1944 when he was often in fear of his life. (The money he received from the Germans over this period was spent freely by him and not handed over to the British once he came back.) When he came back to England in June 1944, the British on their turn were for some time also suspicious of him. Nicholas Booth, ZIGZAG: The Incredible Wartime Exploits of Double Agent Eddie Chapman (London: Portrait 2007), passim. For another example, see GARBO: The Spy Who Saved D-Day. Introduction by Mark Seaman (Kew, Richmond, Surrey: The National Archives 2004), pp. 284–288. GARBO is often seen as the most important agent of the Double-Cross System.

8   The Dutch BVD, for instance, sometimes felt it had to inform the partner of an agent to reassure her and explain that her husband was regularly gone for several hours, not to meet a secret lover but to be debriefed by his case officer. Ben de Jong, Op de bres voor de rechtsstaat in het Verzet en bij de BVD. Ad de Jonge 1919–2002 [In Defense of Democracy in the Resistance and with the BVD. Ad de Jonge 1919–2002] (Amsterdam: Panchaud 2020), pp. 333–334. In the case of the FBI double agent Morris Childs, his wife was not only in the know about his activities: she even accompanied him on most of his missions to the USSR and to the benefit of the FBI cultivated her own relationships with the wives of Soviet leaders. Barron, Operation Solo, pp. 105–107 and passim. The wife of the FBI double agent Joe Cassidy knew about his activities, but she was the only person he could confide in apart from his FBI handlers. His children and friends had to be kept out of the loop. David Wise, Cassidy's Run: The Secret Spy War over Nerve Gas (New York: Random House, 2000), pp. 75, 129. GARBO's wife also knew about his spying activities from the outset. GARBO, pp. 10.

9   As a former high Dutch security official put it when discussing the relationship between an agent and his handler, "For an agent it was incredibly important that he could always turn to his case officer if there was a problem. There could be a wide variety of issues having to do with his job, his marriage, or even the homework of his children. In the case of marriage problems, we sometimes tried to find a solution by offering some extra money and friendly words. Such actions were always taken after internal deliberation within the service." De Jong, Op de bres, p. 334.

10 Jerrold L. Schecter and Peter S. Deriabin, The Spy Who Saved the World: How a Soviet Colonel Changed the Course of the Cold War (New York: Maxwell Macmillan International, 1992), pp. 217–218. A successful double operation against the Polish intelligence service that the Dutch BVD ran for many years, from the late 1950s through 1991, offers another example. After the operation had been terminated, the head of the service paid a personal visit to the double agent to express his gratitude for services rendered. Dick Engelen, Frontdienst. De BVD in de Koude Oorlog [Service at the Front. The BVD in the Cold War] (Amsterdam: Boom, 2007), pp. 253–256.

11 This is often not just done by way of a humane gesture, but in the worst case, it also serves to prevent a dissatisfied former agent who was not taken care of properly from opening up to the media, for instance, about his past spying career. Within the Dutch service during the Cold War, there was apparently no proper script to take care of agents after an operation was over. Decisions in this regard were taken on a case-by-case basis. In the case of the double agent against the Polish service, regular meetings with his handler were still taking place after the end of the operation. In most cases, such meetings would take place with decreasing frequency over time, but even after several years, contact with an agent could sometimes be reestablished. Engelen, Frontdienst, p. 254.

12 For the money taken from American double agents and the case of Cassidy, see Olson, To Catch a Spy, p. 97 and Wise, Cassidy's Run, pp. 54–55. For BVD double agents and their money see Engelen, Frontdienst, pp. 266, 273; De Jong, Op de bres, p. 256.

13 The sums given to the double agent by the opposing service can sometimes be substantial. According to one FBI official, over a period of 20 years, from 1959 to 1979, the GRU paid Cassidy $200,000 in total. Wise, Cassidy's Run, p. 202. In a BVD double agent operation against the GRU that ran from the early 1960s through 1982, the agent received almost 50,000 Dutch guilders in total, also a substantial sum by the standards of those days. The BVD took this money, but paid the double agent considerably less over the same period, namely 30,000 Dutch guilders. In other words, this particular operation was a very profitable one for the Dutch service. According to Dick Engelen, who for many years served with the BVD himself, in most cases the Dutch service paid its double agents roughly the amount they received from the adversary

service, not less, unless the double agent was not interested in a financial reward. Engelen, Frontdienst, pp. 266, 273.

14 Georg Simmel, "The Sociology of Secrecy and of Secret Societies," American Journal of Sociology, Vol. 11, No. 4 (1906), pp. 441–498; Eva Horn, "Logics of Political Secrecy," Theory, Culture & Society, Vol. 28, No. 7–8 (2011), pp. 103–122; Eleni Braat, "Recurring Tensions between Secrecy and Democracy: Arguments about the Security Service in the Dutch Parliament, 1975–1995," Intelligence and National Security, Vol. 31, No. 4 (2016), pp. 532–555.

15 "Risk" is defined as the potential to invest in a relationship (or exchange) with someone else without getting something valued or expected in return. Linda Molm, David Schaefer, and Jessica Collett, "Fragile and Resilient Trust: Risk and Uncertainty in Negotiated and Reciprocal Exchange," Sociological Theory, Vol. 27, No. 1 (2009), p. 5.

16 Edward J. Lawler and Jeongkoo Yoon build on the uncertainty-reduction hypothesis in the establishment of relationships. Edward J. Lawler and Jeongkoo Yoon, "Commitment in Exchange Relations: Test of a Theory of Relational Cohesion," American Sociological Review, Vol. 61, No. 1 (1996), pp. 89–108.

17 Mario Mikulincer and Philipp Shaver, "Adult Attachment and Happiness: Individual Differences in the Experience and Consequences of Positive Emotions," in Oxford Handbook of Happiness, edited by Susan David, Ilona Boniwell, and Amanda Conley (Oxford, UK: Oxford University Press, 2012), pp. 834–846.

18 On differences between reciprocal and negotiated exchange, and the role of risk and uncertainty in the development of reciprocal exchange, see Molm, Schaefer, and Collett, "Fragile and Resilient Trust," pp. 1–32.

19 Gratitude is understood as an emotion one feels after receiving a gift that one did not expect or is out of the ordinary. Feelings of gratitude entail expressions of recognition for the other's effort, profoundly influencing interpersonal relationships. Robert A. Emmons and Cheryl A. Crumpler, "Gratitude as a Human Strength: Appraising the Evidence," Journal of Social and Clinical Psychology, Vol. 19, No. 1 (2000), pp. 56–69.

20 Following attachment theory in the field of social psychology, individuals have an innate behavior to attract and maintain proximity to "attachment figures."

21 David Richards and Aaron Schat, "Attachment at (Not to) Work: Applying Attachment Theory to Explain Individual Behaviour in Organizations," Journal of Applied Psychology, Vol. 96, No. 1 (2011), pp. 169–182; Mikulincer and Shaver, Oxford Handbook, pp. 834–846.

22 Attachment theory has been applied primarily to attachment mechanisms of infants toward caregivers (e.g., M. D. S. Ainsworth and J. Bowlby, "An

Ethological Approach to Personality Development," *American Psychologist*, Vol. 46, pp. 331–341), and to a lesser degree to attachment mechanisms between adults, where the main emphasis lies on romantic relationships (e.g., Mikulincer and Shaver, Oxford Handbook, pp. 834–846). Adult attachment in the workplace is limited to organizational contexts (Richards and Schat, "Attachment at (Not to) Work," pp. 169–182).

23 Interview, 8 August 2019.

24 The authors of this article agreed M. himself would remain anonymous, and they would not mention his employers, other than the main services he worked for and against. They also agreed that the transcribed, anonymized interviews will be archived in the Dutch national center of expertise and repository for research data. Finally, they agreed that M. would be given the opportunity to correct factual inaccuracies in this article, while they would bear the final responsibility for the contents. The Ethical Committee of the Faculty of Humanities of Utrecht University approved of these agreements.

25 Both M. and the authors of this article had little interest in an operational reconstruction of his espionage activities, even if operational aspects cannot be completely separated from agent–handler relationships. For instance, the informal and cordial way in which East German handlers met M. in several locations in Eastern Europe, how they lionized him materially and verbally, could be considered part of the East German modus operandi to deal with him as an agent. The gratitude, or lack thereof, services expressed for M.'s efforts was a principal ingredient of their relationship with him.

26 For a general introduction on the research possibilities of oral history methods, see Lynn Abrams, Oral History Theory (London: Routledge, 2010). For a general introduction on the practice of oral history, see Paul Thompson with Joanna Bornat, The Voice of the Past: Oral History (Oxford, UK: Oxfrd University Press, 2017).

27 For instance, at first during the interviews M. was surprisingly reticent on his experience in East Berlin with a mock arrest by the HV A in the 1980s. In the last interview, the authors of this article shared this observation with him, encouraging him to explain why he had trouble delving into this particular aspect of his espionage past. His subsequent explanation resulted in one of the most probing parts of the interviews with him.

28 The BVD transitioned into the General Intelligence and Security Service (AIVD) in 2002.

29 For the case of Aldrich Ames, see Sandra Grimes and Jeanne Vertefeuille, Circle of Treason: A CIA Account of Traitor Aldrich Ames and the Men he Betrayed (Annapolis, MD: Naval Institute Press, 2012); David Wise, Nightmover: How Aldrich Ames Sold the CIA to the KGB for $4.6 Million (New York: HarperCollins Publishers, 1995); Pete Earley, Confessions of a Spy: The Real Story of Aldrich Ames (New York: Putnam, 1997).

30 Ames may have had access to M.'s files at the CIA and, as a result, he may have betrayed him to the KGB as a double agent who operated against the HV A. If so, it is plausible the KGB informed the HV A, as the two services collaborated closely. M. mentioned a telling example of the close cooperation between the HV A and the KGB. On several occasions, at a prearranged brief meeting to exchange information and instructions with one of his East German contacts in a Third World country, he unexpectedly met a Russian contact instead. Interview, 7 August 2019. For the close cooperation between the MfS and the KGB during the Cold War, see, for instance, John O. Koehler, Stasi: The Untold Story of the East German Secret Police (Boulder, CO: Westview Press, 1999), pp. 73-106; JürgenBorchert, Die Zusammenarbeit des Ministeriums für Staatssicherheit (MfS) und dem sowjetischen KGB in den 70er und 80er Jahren. Ein Kapitel aus der Geschichte der SED-Herrschaft [The Cooperation between the Ministry of State Security (MfS) and the Soviet KGB in the 1970s and 1980s. A Chapter in the History of SED Rule.] (Berlin: Lit Verlag, 2006).

31 The authors of this article have interviewed former intelligence officers extensively about their careers. Several of them, who had spoken to hardly anybody about their careers after their retirements, expressed their pleasure at finally sharing their memories with an "outsider." For rare oral history publications based on interviews with former BVD officers see Eleni Braat, Van oude jongens, de dingen die voorbijgaan... Een sociale geschiedenis van de Binnenlandse Veiligheidsdienst 1945-1998 [Of Old Boys, Things that Pass... A Social History of the Domestic Security Service 1945-1998] (Zoetermeer: AIVD, 2012); Eleni Braat, "Self-Reinforcing Secrecy: Cultures of Secrecy Within Intelligence Agencies," in Transparency and Secrecy in European Democracies: Contested Trade-Offs, edited by D. Mokrosinksa (New York: Routledge, 2021), pp. 118-134; De Jong, Op de bres. The endless flow of memoirs by former CIA personnel exemplifies this need to share memories of a career in secrecy with a broader public. Intelligence and security services sometimes respond with legal action to an attempt by former personnel to publish their memoirs, as happened in the well-known case of Peter Wright's Spycatcher in 1987. The CIA formally allows its ex-officers to write memoirs (and even facilitates in the writing of some), provided they submit their manuscript to the Publications Review Board (PRB). As such, while (reluctantly) acknowledging their personnel's need to share their experiences with a broader public, the PRB functions as a means to control the contents of memoirs even though the process can often be cumbersome and there are regularly accusations of double standards. Christopher Moran, Company Confessions. Revealing CIA Secrets (London: Biteback Publishing, 2015).

32 From Der Bundesbeauftragte für die Unterlagen des Staatssicherheitsdienstes der ehemaligen Deutschen Demokratischen Republik [The Federal Authority for the Records of the State Security Service of the Former German Democratic Republic] (BStU) to M., "Verwendung personen bezogener Unterlagen

THE US LEAKED FILES, AND DEMOCRATIC INTELLIGENCE OVERSIGHT IN EUROPE

des Staatssicherheitsdienstes der ehemaligen Deutschen Demokratischen Republik," 17 December 2015. Personal archive M.

33 Interview, 4 September 2019.

34 Ibid.

35 E-mail from M. to Eleni Braat and Ben de Jong, 11 September 2020.

36 Interview, 14 October 2019.

37 According to M. there were different moments, ranging from 1966 to 1968, when he was contacted by the MfS. Interview, 8 April 2019; 4 September 2019. A publication on MfS documents mentions that operation JANSEN (according to M. his operational name at the MfS) started in 1968. Helmut Müller-Enbergs, Hauptverwaltung A (HV A). Aufgaben-Strukturen-Quellen. MfS Handbuch [Chief Directorate A. Tasking-Structures-Sources. MfS Handbook] (Berlin: BStU, 2011), p. 158. The MfS records agency also confirms that M. was codenamed JANSEN. Letter from the BStU to M., 17 December 2015. Personal archive M.

38 Hauptabteilung II was responsible for offensive counterespionage, which also entailed operations in West Germany, among others. Operations against Western secret services, the Bundeswehr, the police, and mass media, all mainly in West Germany, were part of its remit. https://www.bstu.de/mfs-lexikon/detail/hauptabteilung-ii-spionageabwehrha-ii/ (accessed 30 November 2020).

39 In 1989, shortly before the end of the MfS, Erhard Schierhorn was the head of HA II/2. Hanna Labrenz-Weiß, Die Hauptabteilung II: Spionageabwehr (Handbuch) [Chief Department II: Counterintelligence (Handbook)] (Berlin: BStU, 1998), pp. 10, 15, 16. http://www.nbn-resolving.org/urn:nbn:de:0292-97839421300593 (accessed 30 November 2020).

40 At the time, this transfer happened without his knowledge. He only found out about it upon inspecting his MfS files in 2015. Interview, 8 July 2019.

41 Interview, 8 April 2019; Schütt headed HV A IX from 1977 to 1989. Roland Wiedmann, Die Diensteinheiten des MfS 1950-1989. Eine organisatorische Übersicht [The Service Units of the MfS 1950–1989. An Organizational Overview] (Berlin: BStU, 2012), p. 379; Müller-Enbergs, Hauptverwaltung A, p. 260.

42 Among its objects of interest were the Organization of Ukrainian Nationalists and the well-known American-financed radio station Radio Free Europe/Radio Liberty. The administrative designation of the subunit was HV A IX/A/3. Koch was at some point succeeded as its head by Nötzelmann. Müller-Enbergs, Hauptverwaltung A, p. 157.

43 From an East German perspective, an allegedly successful American recruitment of M. would allow the MfS to set up a double agent operation

against the Americans and thereby get information about the targets and modus operandi of the agency. Then again, from an American perspective, a "recruitment" of M. by the MfS as a double agent against the CIA would offer the Americans insights into what type of information on the CIA the East Germans were seeking. In such a complex, many-layered game, M. would continue to operate as a double agent for the CIA, as he already had done for a few years, while simultaneously lifting his relationship with the East Germans to a new level by pretending to them that he allowed himself to be recruited by the Americans as a double agent on behalf of the MfS against the CIA.

44 Couriers could be diplomats whom M. had met before, or they could be unknown individuals, at times even Russians, whom he would identify by the passwords or other recognition signals they would use. Sometimes at a particular location in Asia or Africa, a hotel lobby for instance, instead of meeting an East German contact M. would unexpectedly be approached by a Russian. After the prearranged recognition signals the exchange of information and money would then take place. Such an unexpected rendezvous with Soviet intelligence personnel illustrates the close collaboration between the KGB and the HV A that existed during the Cold War. When living in the Netherlands M. used public holidays to travel with his wife, for instance, to West Berlin, leaving her there, and crossing over to East Berlin to meet his handlers. Traveling with his wife to Berlin would raise less suspicion than traveling on his own. Interview, 8 July 2019.

45 This was a one-way voice link of the HV A, where M. deciphered messages spoken by a female voice with the help of one-time pads. Often on Wednesday evenings around midnight he would be listening to his short-wave radio to receive possible assignments from the MfS on a specific wavelength. Interview, 8 April 2019; 8 July 2019.

46 The double operation with M. ran from 1968 to 1990. Sometimes double agent operations run for a surprisingly long time. The FBI double agent operations against the Russians mentioned earlier, with Morris Childs and Joe Cassidy, respectively, each lasted about twenty years. Both were terminated in the late 1970s. Barron, Operation Solo, pp. 57, 308; Wise, Cassidy's Run, pp. 19, 177.

47 In order to be convincing to the adversary service as an agent, the double agent has to hand over real intelligence. Indeed, this is one of the reasons "[a]n ideal [double] agent should have good access but not spectacular access." If the double agent has very good access, he has to hand over many important secrets to remain convincing in the eyes of the adversary service and for obvious reasons such a situation is to be avoided. Olson, To Catch a Spy, pp. 105–106.

48 Some assignments the HV A gave him were of Soviet rather than East German interest. For instance, the MfS was interested in the Urenco ultracentrifuge project in Almelo, in one of the eastern provinces of the Netherlands, especially its founder, the physicist Jacob Kistemaker, and other specialists.

As a student of mechanical engineering in the 1970s, M. could rather easily find opportunities to approach these people. Interview, 4 September 2019.

49 Anticommunist organizations and Russian émigré groups such as Narodno-Trudovoy Soyuz [Popular Labor Union], better known as NTS, in Frankfurt am Main were an important target, as was a fascist paramilitary rightwing organization such as Jeune Europe [Young Europe]. Interview, 8 April 2019; 8 July 2019; 4 September 2019 and 14 October 2019. Jeune Europe had a branch in the Netherlands that M. managed to contact easily. The BVD was, of course, also interested in these organizations, especially if it was felt there was a potential for political violence, as was the case with Jeune Europe. On the postwar ties between the CIA and the NTS and their efforts to roll back communism, see also David C. S. Albanese, "'It Takes a Russian to Beat a Russian': The National Union of Labor Solidarists, Nationalism, and Human Intelligence Operations in the Cold War," Intelligence and National Security, Vol. 32, No. 6 (2017), pp. 782–796.

50 M. approached these individuals, for instance by interviewing people in proximity to these targeted individuals while pretending to conduct marketing research or population studies.

51 Interview, 8 April 2019; 4 September 2019.

52 Interview, 8 April 2019; 14 October 2019. Since his year at an American high school made him the odd man out and could raise suspicions, M. emphasized to the East Germans that his American episode had opened his eyes to the unjust and deplorable situation of the black population in the United States and had made him critical toward American capitalism. Adding his own working-class background to this critical stance vis-à-vis this racial and class division, M.'s American experience presumably was an asset in the eyes of his handlers (Interview, 8 April 2019; 14 October 2019). As another means to strengthen his credibility, M. also made sure that the amount and type of information he passed on to his handlers corresponded to what they considered realistic for him to obtain. Interview, 4 September 2019.

53 Such new contacts would include diplomats who would be acting as MfS co-optees. The MfS sometimes made use of diplomats for operational purposes. They would be tasked with transmitting messages to agents, for instance, or handing over money. The KGB regularly made use of Soviet diplomats in the same way.

54 Interview, 8 July 2019; additions via e-mail 30 September 2020 and 6 October 2020.

55 Interview, 8 April 2019 and addition via e-mail 30 September 2020. Ursula Kuczynski (1907–2000) was a famous illegal of the Soviet military intelligence service GRU in the 1930s and 1940s. She operated in China, Switzerland, and Great Britain, among other places. SONYA was one of the codenames she used and one of the agents she ran was the atomic spy Klaus Fuchs. For a

recent biography, see Ben Macintyre, Agent Sonya: Lover, Mother, Soldier, Spy (New York: Viking, 2020).

56 Interview, 4 September 2019; 14 October 2019.

57 Interview, 8 July 2019; 8 April 2019. Understandably, M.'s Dutch handlers noticed his enthusiasm and appreciation for his East German handlers, in particular for their comradeship. Interview, 14 October 2019. From a perspective of counterespionage, they arguably wondered whether M. was not sympathizing too much with the other side.

58 Interview, 8 July 2019; 4 September 2019. His East German handlers obviously knew M. only "to a certain degree" because they were not aware of the fact that his real loyalty was with the BVD and the CIA. It was only at the end, as we shall see, that they started to doubt his loyalty to their cause.

59 In the years he worked for the HV A, M. knew his handlers only by their first names for security reasons. This is a common practice among intelligence and security services in their relations with agents. M. only found out the real surnames of "Heinz" and "Wolfgang" by doing his own research in the voluminous literature on the MfS that was published in the decades after the end of the Cold War.

60 Interview, 14 October 2019; 8 July 2019.

61 Interview, 14 October 2019.

62 Interview, 8 April 2019.

63 E-mail from M. to the authors, 30 September 2020.

64 Interview, 8 April 2019.

65 Ibid.

66 Interview, 8 April 2019. Toward his social environment, M. explained his possession of such items with a reference to his frequent travels to countries from where these items originated.

67 Interview, 8 April 2019; 8 July 2019. The Golden Distinguished Service Medal of the National People's Army came in "a beautiful scarlet red box" with a certificate that mentioned his name and nationality. While he was allowed to take home the medal, he was only permitted to view the certificate. "I secretly copied the text that same evening," M. recollects. "Obviously, this was rather risky." Interview, 4 September 2019.

68 Interview, 14 October 2019. It was not unusual for Markus Wolf, who was chief of the HV A from 1952 to 1986, to meet personally with agents. He had several personal meetings, for instance, with Gabriele Gast, a Federal Intelligence Service (BND) officer since 1973 who was an agent of the HV A from 1968 to 1990. Their meetings took place in the GDR or in countries such as Yugoslavia. Wolf and Gast discuss these meetings in their respective memoirs. Gabriele Gast, Kundschafterin des Friedens. 17 Jahre Topspionin

der DDR beim BND [Spying for Peace. 17 Years as a Spy for the GDR at the BND] (Berlin: Aufbau Taschenbuch Verlag, 2000), pp. 186–213; Markus Wolf, Spionagechef im geheimen Krieg. Erinnerungen [Spy Chief in the Secret War. Memoir] (München: List Verlag, 1997), pp. 468–473. Also present at M.'s meeting with Wolf were two colonels, Schütt and a Russian. Interview, 14 October 2019.

69 Interview, 14 October 2019.

70 Ibid.

71 Ibid.

72 For the MfS, "Kundschafter" (literally: "explorer") was roughly synonymous with the English "secret agent," but it had a very positive connotation. The term was only applied to their own agents abroad (in most cases foreigners) or MfS intelligence officers who operated in the West under deep cover. These would often be called "Kundschafter des Friedens" (literally: "peace explorers"). The term "Kundschafter" was never used by the MfS for agents or employees of Western services.

73 Interview, 4 September 2019; 14 October 2019.

74 Interview, 8 July 2019.

75 Ibid.

76 Ibid.

77 Interview, 8 April 2019. Regarding the postwar educational level within the BVD and the experience of the postwar generation in wartime resistance groups, see Braat, Van oude jongens, pp. 42–47, 55.

78 Braat, Van oude jongens, pp. 53–55.

79 Interview, 8 April 2019.

80 Ibid.

81 Ibid.

82 M. showed the authors of this article his double-entry bookkeeping. To the right were the expenses that resulted from East German assignments, which M. could claim with his East German handlers and that amounted to about 90 to 95% of the total amount of operational expenses. To the left of his bookkeeping are the expenses that he made for the BVD, amounting to a tiny proportion of total expenses and relating to, for instance, travel costs to meet his Dutch handlers.

83 Fl. 40,- (guilders) in 1975 is the rough equivalent of €57,- in 2020.

84 Interview, 14 October 2019.

85 Interview, 8 April 2019; 8 July 2019.

86 Interview, 4 September 2019.

87 M. is not entirely consistent in his recollection of the number of BVD and CIA representatives. The numbers range from "a couple" and five BVD representatives and two to three CIA representatives.

88 M. referred to this signed agreement in all our interviews.

89 Interview, 8 April 2019; 8 July 2019.

90 Interview, 8 April 2019; 14 October 2019. It is standard operating procedure for the CIA to regularly polygraph their agents, especially if they are in regular contact with an adversary service on foreign territory. Observation by Dan Mulvenna, 25 February 2021.

91 The FBI codenamed the operation BUCKLURE and the CIA called it RACKETEER. The CIA and FBI used up to one million dollars of hard cash for each approach, and the amount increased over the years. Grimes and Vertefeuille, Circle of Treason, p. 108; David Wise, Spy: The Inside Story of How the FBI's Robert Hanssen Betrayed America (Toronto: Random House, 2012), pp. 199–204; Gus Russo and Eric Dezenhall, Best of Enemies: The Last Great Spy Story of the Cold War (New York: Twelve, 2018), p. 174.

92 Several of those agents had been recruited by the FBI in the United States. These losses were mainly due to the betrayal by Aldrich Ames of the CIA and Robert Hanssen of the FBI who offered their services to the KGB in 1985. Milt Bearden and James Risen, The Main Enemy: The Inside Story of the CIA's Final Showdown with the KGB (New York: Ballantine Books, 2003), pp. 145–161 and passim. Ames's betrayal alone is said to have led to the execution of ten Russians. Wise, Nightmover, pp. 254–271, 331–332.

93 John Marks, The Search for the "Manchurian Candidate": The CIA and Mind Control. The Secret History of the Behavioral Sciences (New York: W.W. Norton & Company, 1991), 175-93

94 "Traits to look for." Personal archive M., undated.

95 Interview, 8 July 2019.

96 It could be argued that the fact that his CIA handlers invited M. to their homes, to have dinner even with their families in some cases, was extremely poor tradecraft. The same could be said about the fact that M. knew some of his CIA handlers by their real names. Observation by Dan Mulvenna, 25 February 2021.

97 Interview, 8 April 2019.

98 "Otherwise, she could think I was having an affair, because I went on regular trips with the Americans," M. explains. Interview, 8 July 2019.

99 Interview, 8 April 2019. Wives of CIA intelligence officers often got involved in operations in support of their husbands or their agents, as they did in MI6. Bearden and Risen, The Main Enemy, p. 19; Ben Macintyre, The Spy and the

Traitor: The Greatest Espionage Story of the Cold War (New York: Viking, 2018), pp. 241–242.

100 Interview, 14 October 2019.

101 M., "Psychologie van een dubbelagent" [Psychology of a double agent]. Personal archive M., undated.

102 Interview, 8 April 2019.

103 Interview, 8 July 2019.

104 M., "Psychologie van een dubbelagent."

105 Interview, 8 July 2019.

106 Ibid.

107 Ibid.

Chapter: 16: Enemy image? A comparative analysis of the Russian federation's role and position in the leading national security documents of Estonia and the Czech Republic. Monika Gabriela Bartoszewicz & Michaela Prucková.

1.   Along with the National Defence Strategy, National Defence Development Plan, and Military Defence Action Plan, all of which derive from the Concept.

2.   We include all the derivatives into our analysis, i.e. 'Russia', 'Russia's', 'Russian'.

Ahuvia, A. 2001. "Traditional, Interpretive, and Reception Based Content Analyses: Improving the Ability of Content Analysis to Address Issues of Pragmatic and Theoretical Concern." Social Indicators Research 54 (2): 139–172. https://doi.org/10.1023/A:1011087813505. [Crossref], [Web of Science ®], [Google Scholar]

Bachleitner, K. 2021.Ontological Security as Temporal Security? The Role of 'Significant Historical others' in World Politics. International Relations. Epub ahead of print 9 September 2021. https://doi.org/10.1177/00471178211045624. [Crossref], [Google Scholar]

Bahador, B. 2015. "The Media and Deconstruction of the Enemy Image." In Communication and Peace, edited by J. Hoffman and V. Hawkins, 120–132. New York: Routledge. [Crossref], [Google Scholar]

Baret, D. 2014. "Tajná služba varuje před agenty Ruska a Číny, vláda a prezident ale velebí tyto dvě země." Reflex. 29 October. Accessed April 5, 2021. https://www.reflex.cz/clanek/komentare/59945/tajna-sluzba-varuje-pred-agenty-ruska-a-ciny-vlada-a-prezident-ale-velebi-tyto-dve-zeme.html. [Google Scholar]

Bartoszewicz, M. G. 2014. "European Identity: Europe as Its Own "Other"." Horyzonty Polityki 5 (10): 31–49. [Google Scholar]

Bartoszewicz, M. G. 2021. Intermarium: A Bid for Polycentric Europe. Geopolitics. Epub ahead of print 9 September 2021. https://doi.org/10.1080/146500 45.2021.1973439. [Google Scholar]

Bezpečnostní informační služba. 2016. Výroční zpráva Bezpečnostní informační služby za rok 2015. Prague. Accessed 20 April, 2021. https://www.bis.cz/ vyrocni-zpravy/vyrocni-zprava-bezpecnostni-informacni-sluzby-za-rok-2015-0032e412.html. [Google Scholar]

Bezpečnostní informační služba. 2017. Výroční zpráva Bezpečnostní informační služby za rok 2016. Prague. Accessed April 20, 2021): https://www.bis.cz/ vyrocni-zpravy/vyrocni-zprava-bezpecnostni-informacni-sluzby-za-rok-2016-d30334e2.html. [Google Scholar]

Bezpečnostní informační služba. 2018. Výroční zpráva Bezpečnostní informační služby za rok 2017. Prague. Accessed April 20, 2021. https://www.bis.cz/ vyrocni-zpravy/vyrocni-zprava-bezpecnostni-informacni-sluzby-za-rok-2017-d85907e6.html. [Google Scholar]

Bezpečnostní informační služba. 2019. Výroční zpráva Bezpečnostní informační služby za rok 2018. Prague. Accessed April 20, 2021. https://www.bis.cz/ vyrocni-zpravy/vyrocni-zprava-bezpecnostni-informacni-sluzby-za-rok-2018-ddd066bb.html. [Google Scholar]

Bezpečnostní informační služba. 2020. Výroční zpráva Bezpečnostní informační služby za rok 2019. Prague. Accessed April 20, 2021): https://www.bis.cz/ vyrocni-zpravy/vyrocni-zprava-bezpecnostni-informacni-sluzby-za-rok-2019-c665e2a7.html. [Google Scholar]

Brüggemann, K., and A. Kasekamp. 2008. "The Politics of History and the 'War of monuments' in Estonia." Nationalities Papers 36 (3): 425–448. https:// doi.org/10.1080/00905990802080646. [Taylor & Francis Online], [Google Scholar]

Burke, W. 2017. Images of Occupation in Dutch Film: Memory, Myth and the Cultural Legacy of War. Amsterdam: Amsterdam University Press. https:// doi.org/10.1017/9789048527090. [Google Scholar]

Cottam, M. 2000. "Enemy Image." In Encyclopedia of Psychology, edited by A. Kazdin, Vol. 3, 204–206. Washington DC: American Psychological Association. https://doi.org/10.1037/10518-076. [Crossref], [Google Scholar]

ČT24. 2019. "Zákon o statusu veterána pro okupační vojáky podporují v ruské dumě hlavně komunisté a nacionalisté. Jednou už neprošel." ČT24, 5 June. Accessed April 2, 2021. https://ct24.ceskatelevize.cz/domaci/2834540-za-kon-o-statusu-veterana-pro-okupacni-vojaky-podporuji-v-ruske-dume-hlavne-komuniste. [Google Scholar]

Diez, T. 2004. "Europe's Others and the Return of Geopolitics." Cambridge Review of International Affairs 17 (2): 319–335. https://doi.org/10.1080/095575704 2000245924. [Taylor & Francis Online], [Google Scholar]

Dodge, T. 2012. "Enemy Images, Coercive Socio-Engineering and Civil War in Iraq." International Peacekeeping 19 (4): 461–477. https://doi.org/10.10 80/13533312.2012.709756. [Taylor & Francis Online], [Web of Science ®], [Google Scholar]

Dong, Y. 2019. "The Jus Ad Bellum in Cyberspace: Where are We Now and What Next?" New Zealand Journal of Public and International Law 17 (1): 41–66. [Google Scholar]

Eckhardt, W. 1991. "Making and Breaking Enemy Images." Bulletin of Peace Proposals 22 (1): 87–95. https://doi.org/10.1177/096701069102200110. [Crossref], [Google Scholar]

Estonian Foreign Intelligence Service. 2021. International Security and Estonia 2021. Tallinn. Accessed April 23, 2021. https://www.valisluureamet.ee/pdf/raport/2021-ENG.pdf. [Google Scholar]

Estonian Internal Security Service. 2016. "Annual Review 2016." Tallinn. Accessed April 23, 2021. https://kapo.ee/en/content/annual-reviews/. [Google Scholar]

Estonian Internal Security Service. 2017. "Annual Review 2017." Tallinn. Accessed April23, 2021. https://kapo.ee/en/content/annual-reviews/. [Google Scholar]

Estonian Internal Security Service. 2018. Annual Review 2018. Tallinn. Accessed April 23, 2021. https://kapo.ee/en/content/annual-reviews/. [Google Scholar]

Estonian Internal Security Service. 2020. Annual Review 2019-2020. Tallinn. Accessed April 23, 2021. https://kapo.ee/en/content/annual-reviews/. [Google Scholar]

Finlay, D. J., O. Holsti, and R. Fagan. 1967. Enemies in Politics. Chicago: Rand McNally and Co. [Google Scholar]

Frank, J. D., and A. Y. Melville. 1988. "The Image of the Enemy and the Process of Change." In Breakthrough: Emerging New Thinking: Soviet and Western Scholars Issue a Challenge to Build a World Beyond War, edited by A. Gromyko and M. Hellman, 198–207. New York: Walker and Company. [Google Scholar]

Fromm, E. 1955. The Sane Society. New York: Rinehart & Company, Inc. [Google Scholar]

Gerő, M., P. P. Płucienniczak, A. Kluknavska, J. Navrátil, and K. Kanellopoulos. 2017. "Understanding Enemy Images in Central and Eastern European Politics: Towards an Interdisciplinary Approach." Intersections East European Journal of Society and Politics 3 (3): 14–40. https://doi.org/10.17356/ieejsp.v3i3.365. [Web of Science ®], [Google Scholar]

Ginger, C. 2006. "Interpretive Content Analysis." In Interpretation and Method: Empirical Research Methods and the Interpretive Turn, M.E, edited by D. Yanov and P. Schwartz-Shea, 331–348. Armonk, NY: Sharpe. [Google Scholar]

Government of the Republic of Estonia. 2017. National Security Concept 2017. Tallinn. Accessed April 23, 2021. https://kaitseministeerium.ee/sites/default/files/elfinder/article_files/national_security_concept_2017_0.pdf. [Google Scholar]

Hakauf, M. 2011, 20. "výročí odchodu sovětských vojsk a ukončení vojenské okupace Československa." Informační centrum vlády, 21 June. Accessed April 26, 2021. https://icv.—ada.cz/cz/tema/20–vyroci-odchodu-sovetskych-vojsk-a-ukonceni-vojenske-oku—ce-ceskoslovenska–85082/tmplid-560/. [Google Scholar]

Herrmann, R. K., and M. P. Fischerkeller. 1995. "Beyond the Enemy Image and Spiral Model: Cognitive–Strategic Research After the Cold War." International Organization 49 (3): 415–450. [Crossref], [Web of Science °], [Google Scholar]

Holt, R. R. 1989. "College Students' Definitions and Images of Enemies." Journal of Social Issues 45 (2): 33–50. https://doi.org/10.1111/j.1540-4560.1989.tb01541.x. [Crossref], [Web of Science °], [Google Scholar]

Holzer, J., and M. Mareš, ed. 2019. Czech Security Dilemma: Russia as a Friend or Enemy?. Bern, Switzerland: Palgrave Mcmillan. https://doi.org/10.1007/978-3-030-20546-1. [Google Scholar]

iROZHLAS.cz. 2021. "Akt státního terorismu, označil Vystrčil aktivitu ruských agentů v Česku. Vyzval k tvrdé reakci." iROZHLAS.cz, 18 April. Accessed April26, 2021. https://www.irozhlas.cz/zpravy-domov/senat-milos-vystrcil-vybuch-ve-vrbeticich-rusko-agenti_2104181129_tzr. [Google Scholar]

Jung, K., S. H. Ang, S. M. Leong, S. J. Tan, C. Pornpitakpan, and A. K. Kau. 2002. "A Typology of Animosity and Its Cross-National Validation." Journal of Cross-Cultural Psychology 33 (6): 525–539. https://doi.org/10.1177/0022022102238267. [Crossref], [Web of Science °], [Google Scholar]

Kazharski, A., and A. Makarychev. 2021. "From the Bronze Soldier to the "Bloody Marshal": Monument Wars and Russia's Aesthetic Vulnerability in Estonia and the Czech Republic." East European Politics and Societies 36 (4): 1151–1176. Epub ahead of print 16 September. https://doi.org/10.1177/08883254211043856. [Crossref], [Web of Science °], [Google Scholar]

Keen, S. 1991. Faces of the Enemy: Reflections of the Hostile Imagination. USA: Harper San Francisco. [Google Scholar]

Kopecký, J. 2018. "Babiš oznámil vyhoštění tří Rusů z ambasády v Česku kvůli útoku v Británii." iDNES.cz, 26 March. Accessed April 15, 2021. https://www.idnes.cz/zpravy/domaci/babis-stropnicky-mimoradna-tiskovka-rusove-diplomate-skripal.A180326_142148_domaci_kop. [Google Scholar]

Kryvda, N., and S. Storozhuk. 2020. "Image of an "Enemy" as a Factor of Constructing the Ukrainian National Identity." Ideas Philosophical Journal Special Scientific Issues, (1 (15)–2 (16)): 57–66. https://doi.org/10.34017/1313-9703-2020-1(15)-2(16)-57-66. [Google Scholar]

Landman, T. 2002. Issues and Methods in Comparative Politics: An Introduction. London: Routledge. [Crossref], [Google Scholar]

Luostarinen, H. 1989. "Finnish Russophobia: The Story of an Enemy Image." Journal of Peace Research 26 (2): 123–137. https://doi.org/10.1177/00223433890 26002002. [Crossref], [Web of Science ®], [Google Scholar]

Mandelzis, L. 2003. "The Changing Image of the Enemy in the News Discourse of Israeli Newspapers, 1993-1994." Conflict & Communication 2 (1): Accessed April 3, 2021. https://regener-online.de/journalcco/2003_1/pdf_2003_1/mandelzis.pdf. [Google Scholar]

Ministry of Foreign Affairs of the Czech Republic. 2015. Bezpečnostní strategie České republiky 2015. Prague. Accessed March 24, 2021. https://www.mocr.army.cz/images/id_ 40001_50000/46088/ Bezpecnostni_ strategie_2015.pdf. [Google Scholar]

Ministry of Foreign Affairs of the Czech Republic. 2020. "Prohlášení MZV k vyjádřením Ruské federace." Embassy of the Czech Republic in Moscow, 10 April. Accessed March 30, 2021. https://www.mzv.cz/moscow/cz/vzajemne_vztahy/prohlaseni_mzv_k_vyjadrenim_ruske.html. [Google Scholar]

Mouffe, C. 1993. The Return of the Geopolitical. New York, UK: Verso. [Google Scholar]

Muižnieks, N., ed. 2008. "Manufacturing Enemy Images." In Russian Media Portrayal of Latvia. Riga, Latvia: Academic Press of the University of Latvia. [Google Scholar]

Neumann, I. B. 1996. "Self and Other in International Relations." European Journal of International Relations 2 (2): 139–174. https://doi.org/10.1177/13540 66196002002001. [Crossref], [Google Scholar]

Oppenheimer, L. 2006. "The Development of Enemy Images: A Theoretical Contribution." Peace and Conflict 12 (3): 269–292. https://doi.org/10.1207/s15327949pac1203_4. [Taylor & Francis Online], [Google Scholar]

Osipian, A. 2015. "Historical Myths, Enemy Images, and Regional Identity in the Donbass Insurgency (Spring 2014)." Journal of Soviet and Post-Soviet Politics and Society 1 (1): 109–140. [Google Scholar]

Ottosen, R. 1995. "Enemy Images and the Journalistic Process." Journal of Peace Research 32 (1): 97–112. https://doi.org/10.1177/0022343395032001008. [Crossref], [Web of Science ®], [Google Scholar]

Petersson, B. O. 2009. "Hot Conflict and Everyday Banality: Enemy Images, Scapegoats and Stereotypes." Development 52 (4): 460–465. https://doi.org/10.1057/dev.2009.59. [Crossref], [Google Scholar]

Pezard, S., A. Radin, T. S. Szayna, and F. S. Larrabee. 2018. European Relations with Russia: Threat Perceptions, Responses and Strategies in the Wake of the Ukrainian Crisis. Santa Monica, USA: RAND Corporation. https://doi.org/10.7249/RR1579. [Google Scholar]

Piotrowski, S. 2018. "Security Policy of the Baltic States and Its Determining Factors." Security and Defence Quarterly 22 (5): 46–70. https://doi.org/10.5604/01.3001.0012.7586. [Crossref], [Google Scholar]

Prozorov, S. 2011. "The Other as Past and Present: Beyond the Logic of 'Temporal Othering'in IR Theory." Review of International Studies 37 (3): 1273–1293. https://doi.org/10.1017/S0260210510000586. [Crossref], [Web of Science ®], [Google Scholar]

Runnel, P., P. Pruulmann-Vengerfeldt, and K. Reinsalu. 2009. "The Estonian Tiger Leap from Post-Communism to the Information Society: From Policy to Practice." Journal of Baltic Studies 40 (1): 29–51. https://doi.org/10.1080/01629770902722245. [Taylor & Francis Online], [Web of Science ®], [Google Scholar]

Sande, G. N., G. R. Goethals, L. Ferrari, and L. T. Worth. 1989. "Value-Guided Attributions: Maintaining the Moral Self-Image and the Diabolical Enemy-Image." Journal of Social Issues 45 (2): 91–118. https://doi.org/10.1111/j.1540-4560.1989.tb01544.x. [Crossref], [Web of Science ®], [Google Scholar]

Schindler, J. R. 2017. "Putin's Central European Spy Base." Observer, 18 May. Accessed April 15, 2021. https://observer.com/2017/05/vladimir-putin-prague-czech-republic-spy-base/. [Google Scholar]

Schmitt, C. 2008. The Concept of the Political. Expanded Edition ed. Chicago: University of Chicago Press. [Google Scholar]

Sierzputowski, B. 2019. "The Data Embassy Under Public International Law." International and Comparative Law Quarterly 68 (1): 225–242. https://doi.org/10.1017/S0020589318000428. [Crossref], [Web of Science ®], [Google Scholar]

Silverstein, B. 1989. "Enemy Images: The Psychology of US Attitudes and Cognitions Regarding the Soviet Union." American Psychologist 44 (6): 903–913. https://doi.org/10.1037/0003-066X.44.6.903. [Crossref], [Web of Science ®], [Google Scholar]

Skocpol, T. 1979. States and Social Revolutions: A Comparative Analysis of France, Russia and China. Cambridge, UK: Cambridge University Press. [Crossref], [Google Scholar]

Sodaro, M. J., and D. W. Collinwood. 2004. Comparative Politics: A Global Introduction. Boston: McGraw-Hill. [Google Scholar]

Stoneman, A. J. 2015. "Socialism with a Human Face: The Leadership and Legacy of the Prague Spring." The History Teacher 49 (1): 103–125. [Google Scholar]

Szalay, L. B., and E. Mir-Djahali. 1991. "Image of the Enemy: Critical Parametres, Cultural Variantions." In The Psychology of War and Peace: The Image of the Enemy, edited by R. Rieber, 213–250. Boston: Springer. https://doi.org/10.1007/978-1-4899-0747-9_9. [Crossref], [Google Scholar]

Wæver, O. 1993. Securitization and Desecuritization. Copenhagen, Denmark: Centre for Peace and Conflict Research. [Google Scholar]

Yarhi-Milo, K. 2014. "Knowing the Adversary." In Knowing the Adversary. Princeton University Press. [Crossref], [Google Scholar]

Zheltukhina, M. K., N. A. Krasavsky, and E. B. Ponomarenko. 2016. "Political Facebook Posts Using Ideological Symbols for Media Image Designing of Russia as Enemy." International Journal of Environmental & Science Education 11 (18): 12005–12013. [Google Scholar]

Index

A

AeroScope drone detection software 87

Agent-handler relationship 295

AI in a Digital Age 263

Al Jazeera 52, 68, 339, 340

al-Qaeda 19

Anti-satellite 84

Arms Control 63, 91, 343, 344

Artificial Intelligence vi, 47, 49, 56, 245, 255, 256, 257, 259, 291, 338, 401, 405, 407, 411, 412, 416, 419

Artificial Intelligence Strategy 56, 255

Asia-Pacific Economic Cooperation 253

B

Black Sea 3, 63

Brexit 18, 23, 30, 57, 66, 67, 336

C

Center for Responsive Politics 108, 351

Central Intelligence Agency 101, 115, 135, 174, 294, 375, 376, 377, 378, 379, 427, 428

Centre for International Governance Innovation 27, 336

China's Ministry of State Security 68, 192, 211

Cold War vi, 1, 4, 48, 67, 77, 78, 79, 87, 117, 119, 134, 135, 147, 148, 160, 173, 191, 192, 194, 195, 201, 208, 210, 211, 226, 294, 296, 301, 311, 313, 315, 319, 322, 353, 354, 360, 375, 389, 390, 398, 399, 401, 428, 430, 433, 435, 436, 437, 439, 440, 443

Communications Security Establishment 27

Counter-Disinformation Unit 48

Counter Terrorism 24, 130

Creating an Environment for Nuclear Disarmament 93

Criminal Code of the Russian Federation 14

Critical infrastructure protection 235

Cyber operations 76, 82, 215, 216, 217, 218, 219, 220, 228, 229, 230, 241, 243

D

Daesh 25

Danish intelligence report 7, 341

Deep fakes 83

Department for Culture, Media and

Sport (DCMS) 31, 48

Double agent 202, 294, 295, 296, 297, 301, 302, 303, 309, 312, 313, 428, 429, 430, 432, 434, 435, 440

Draft Communications Data Bill 2012 286

Dutch Security Service 134, 136, 142, 294, 375, 377, 378

E

Emerging Technologies v, 1, 74, 77, 81, 95, 262, 341, 342

EU Digital Sovereignty 245, 246, 248, 249, 250, 251, 258, 261

EU Joint Research Centre 260

European Court of Human Rights 34, 164, 282, 383, 384

European Union v, 1, 2, 6, 7, 9, 14, 18, 21, 22, 25, 28, 33, 37, 39, 54, 55, 57, 58, 59, 60, 72, 115, 246, 249, 250, 252, 258, 324, 327, 336, 339, 340, 356, 364, 368, 412, 414, 415, 417, 418, 419

European Union Agency for Fundamental Rights 28, 336

F

Facial Recognition Technologies 69, 72

Federal Intelligence Service 73, 437

Federal Security Service 16, 38, 55

Finnish codebreakers 123

Foreign Intelligence Inspectorate 159, 161, 162, 387

Foreign interference and information

manipulation 5

G

General Data Protection Regulation 249

Grey Zones 218

H

Human Intelligence 48, 70, 115, 396, 436

Hypersonics 82

I

Informationized warfare 1

INF Treaty 93

Intelligence Community Whistleblower Protection Act 278

Intelligence oversight in Sweden 159

Intelligence, surveillance, and reconnaissance 83

International intelligence cooperation 28, 34, 114, 115, 116, 117, 119, 120, 121, 122, 125, 131, 132, 171, 213, 356

Islamic State of Iraq and Syria (ISIS) 69, 249

Israeli-U.S. operations 54

J

Jihadism 67

K

Kosovo 4

L

Lobbying Disclosure Act of 1995 108

M

Martyrdom Operatives Battalion.
    See Katibat al-Istishadiin

Masculine professional standards 142

Ministry for State Security 119

N

National Cyber Security Centre
    (NCSC) 23

National Defence Radio Establishment
    159, 160, 387

National Geospatial-Intelligence
    Agency 178

National Intelligence Estimate 178

NATO 2, 7, 9, 11, 13, 15, 16, 20, 21,
    23, 40, 56, 71, 76, 85, 86, 124,
    125, 236, 237, 316, 318, 320,
    324, 325, 327, 329, 335, 341,
    361, 364, 374, 400

Neo-Nazi infiltration 88

Neo-Nazi junta 9

Nord Stream 8, 9, 10, 22, 334

Normative Power Europe 252, 417

O

Open Source Intelligence 48, 350

Operation CHAOS 175

Operation COINTELPRO 175

Operation MINARET 175

Operation SHAMROCK 175

Organisation for Economic Co-opera-
    tion and Development 253

P

Politicization of United States domes-
    tic intelligence 98

R

Regulation of Investigatory Power Act-
    2000 41

Russian Military intelligence 13

Russian oligarchs 21

Russia's Federal security Service (FSB)
    192

S

Signals Intelligence 44, 48, 115, 123,
    128, 160, 161, 162, 163, 164,
    165, 166, 167, 190, 203, 204,
    294, 295, 371, 382, 385, 387,
    394, 398, 399, 424

Snooper Charter Surveillance 69

Snowden 17, 19, 20, 27, 28, 31, 33, 34,
    41, 43, 45, 46, 68, 72, 151, 167,
    169, 177, 199, 202, 203, 227,
    232, 236, 246, 249, 268, 271,
    272, 275, 280, 281, 282, 285,
    286, 287, 337, 379, 388, 420,
    425, 426

South China Sea 1

SpaceX 88, 89, 90, 92, 93

Spy Power vi, 172, 173, 174, 177, 186

Swedish Armed Forces Intelligence
    and Security Agency 159

Swedish National Audit Office 164

T

Think Tank Influences 103

Types of Politicization 101, 102

U

United Nations 123, 238, 290, 365,
    416, 419, 423

Unmanned Aerial Vehicles 83, 84, 172

USAUK intelligence 19, 62

V

Vietnam War 175

W

Wagner Private Military Company 10,
    13

War in Ukraine v, 1, 10, 13, 74, 81, 95,
    334, 341, 342, 344, 345, 409

WMD proliferation 233

World War I 98, 136

World War II 104, 105, 106, 123, 296,
    308, 428, 429

About the Author

Musa Khan Jalalzai is a journalist and research scholar. He has written extensively on Afghanistan, terrorism, nuclear and biological terrorism, human trafficking, drug trafficking, and intelligence research and analysis. He was an Executive Editor of the Daily Outlook Afghanistan from 2005-2011, and a permanent contributor in Pakistan's daily *The Post*, *Daily Times*, and *The Nation*, *Weekly the Nation*, (London). However, in 2004, US Library of Congress in its report for South Asia mentioned him as the biggest and prolific writer. He received Masters in English literature, Diploma in Geospatial Intelligence, University of Maryland, Washington DC, certificate in Surveillance Law from the University of Stanford, USA, and diploma in Counter terrorism from Pennsylvania State University, California, the United States.